W9-CZU-556

WITHDRAWN

# PROCESSES

## OF AGING

VOLUME II

Edited by Richard H. Williams,
Clark Tibbitts, Wilma Donahue

*In collaboration with James E. Birren,
Alan T. Welford, Ewald W. Busse,
Marian Radke Yarrow,
Jean-René Tréanton,
Robert J. Havighurst, Martin Roth,
Henning Friis,
and Seymour L. Wolfbein*

# PROCESSES

## OF AGING

*Social and
Psychological
Perspectives*

### VOLUME II

CARL A. RUDISILL LIBRARY
LENOIR RHYNE COLLEGE

ATHERTON PRESS
70 Fifth Avenue, New York 10011

301.435
W67p

V.2

56910
Jan. 1967

PROCESSES OF AGING, VOL. II
Social and Psychological Perspectives
*Richard H. Williams, Clark Tibbitts, and Wilma Donahue, editors*

Copyright © 1963 by Atherton Press

Copyright under International, Pan American,
and Universal Copyright Conventions

All rights reserved. No part of this book may be
reproduced in any form, except for brief quotation
in a review, without written permission from the
publisher. All inquiries should be addressed to

*Atherton Press*
*70 Fifth Avenue*
*New York 10011*

Library of Congress Catalog Card Number 63-13841
Printed in the United States of America
Second Printing, March 1966

# PREFACE

*Processes of Aging: Social and Psychological Perspectives* is based on studies prepared for an international seminar on the psychological and social aspects of aging in relation to mental health. The seminar was convened to give scientists from North America, Western Europe, and other countries an opportunity to explore together the concepts, methodological problems, and conclusions of their researches in the rapidly growing field of gerontology. Much editorial work has been done in an attempt to present this material in sequential and systematic fashion. Original work of sixty-six research workers from twelve countries is represented in these volumes. They are an inventory of the principal fields of gerontological research, except in the purely biological and medical areas, in the countries where most of the work is currently being done.

Human aging, in its many ramifications, is becoming one of the major areas of research interest among an increasing number of students in the biological, behavioral, and social sciences. Although the phenomena of aging were largely overlooked as subject matter for research during the early stages in the development of all the basic sciences, it was inevitable that students would eventually become curious about the final processes of maturation. What are the causes of decline in the organism? What are the characteristics of psychological capacities, personality, and social adjustment over the life span? What influences do older people exert in creating social norms and expectations? What societal adjustments are being adapted to the increasing number of old people?

Events of recent years have hastened the need for social action on behalf of older people and, consequently, the need for scientific knowledge about their characteristics, circumstances, and requirements. The first half of the century witnessed a great increase in the number and proportion of older people in all highly developed societies of the world and in almost all other countries. Simultaneously, economic changes, stemming largely from the exponential growth in the use of inanimate energy and machines in the production of commodities and services, and changes in culture patterns have altered the status and roles of older people and created many new personal and social problems.

Thus, over the past twenty or more years, all Western nations have shown increased concern over the changes in the age structure of their populations and in the dislocations, problems, and accommodations associated therewith. All affected countries have developed or are developing programs of income maintenance, medical facilities and services, institutional care and housing, and social services designed to enable older people to live as healthy, secure, and satisfied members of society. At the same time, knowledge about the processes of aging, about older people and their needs, and about the impact of older people on social institutions and practices has become a necessity. Research has, in fact, been initiated in virtually every country of the Western world and in the more developed countries elsewhere. The scientific literature on aging has grown enormously, particularly over the past ten to fifteen years. There is increasing evidence of the willingness of public agencies to support research and teaching in gerontology in order to increase understanding of the processes of aging and to provide a firm basis for social planning. It was against this background that the seminar and the two meetings that preceded it took place.

The seminar was a joint undertaking of the Social Research Committee of the International Association of Gerontology, represented by Drs. E.W. Burgess and Clark Tibbitts; of the Professional Services Branch of the National Institute of Mental Health, represented by Dr. Richard H. Williams; and of the Division of Gerontology of The University of Michigan, represented by Dr. Wilma Donahue. The seminar had its origin in a meeting of social and psychological scientists held in Sheffield, England, under the auspices of the Nuffield Foundation, just prior to the Third International Congress of Gerontology (1954). The Foundation's guess that researchers would have common interests was borne out in the enthusiastic response to the conference and in the subsequent establishment of the Social Research Committee with European and American branches in the framework of the International Association of Gerontology. The first seminar organized by the committee took place in Merano, Italy, in 1957.

The first two seminars produced positive results in the form of international acquaintances which led to discussion of mutual research interests, international visits and exchanges, and development of parallel or cross-national studies. The seminar for which the materials in the present volumes were prepared was an extension of the enthusiasm engendered at the first two meetings. The National Institute of Mental Health became involved because it had been cooperating in and supporting several important American studies in some of the areas proposed for consideration in the third seminar. The Professional Services Branch of the National Institute of Mental Health collaborated with the Division of Gerontology at The University of Michigan because of the Division's long experience in organizing conferences, symposia, and seminars on aging and because of its chairman's knowledge of research and research personnel in Europe as well as in her own country.

The National Institute of Mental Health financial support (Grant MHO1962-02) made it possible to bring four Europeans to the United States almost a year before the seminar in order to plan with the American branch of the Social Research Committee. From Europe came Henning Friis of Denmark, Martin Roth and Alan T. Welford of England, and Jean-René Tréanton of France; from the United States the planners were E. Everett Ashley, III, Walter M. Beattie, Jr., James E. Birren, Leonard Z. Breen, Ernest W. Burgess, Ewald W. Busse, Wilbur J. Cohen, Wilma Donahue, Margaret S. Gordon, Robert J.Havighurst, Robert W. Kleemeier, Bernice L. Neugarten, Harold L. Orbach, Klaus F. Riegel, Leo W. Simmons, Alexander Simon, Clark

Tibbitts, Richard H. Williams, Seymour L. Wolfbein, and Marian
Radke Yarrow. Maria Pfister attended as a representative of the World
Health Organization.

The planning group selected four general topics for the discussions and appointed leaders for each one, as follows: psychological
capacities, Alan T. Welford and James E. Birren; personality, life
styles, and social roles, Jean-René Tréanton and Robert J. Havighurst;
mental health and rehabilitation, Martin Roth and Wilma Donahue;
and income, employment, and retirement, Henning Friis and Seymour
L. Wolfbein. The seminar was held in Berkeley, California, over a
five-day period during August, 1960. The National Institute of Mental
Health support, along with National Institute of Health travel grants
for the Congress itself, made it possible to defray the travel and subsistence costs of the Europeans. These, with sixty-three American and
Canadian contributors and discussants, brought the number of participants to ninety.

Invited papers were prepared in advance of the seminar and
made available to all participants. Seminar sessions were conducted as
four simultaneous roundtables on specific research problems in each of
the areas mentioned above. A final general session gave rise to repeated
expressions of the continuing need for interdisciplinary conferences of
an international character.

Alan T. Welford, James E. Birren, Marian Radke Yarrow,
and Harold L. Orbach participated in the early phases of the editorial
work. Final editorial responsibility was taken by Richard H. Williams
for Volume I, Parts I and II, and Volume II, Part V; by Wilma
Donahue for Volume I, Part III, and Volume II, Part VI; and by Clark
Tibbitts for Volume II, Part VII. In Volume I, the focus is largely on
individual aging processes. Volume II is concerned largely with social
factors and influences on the individual and with the effects of aging
on family and social relationships and the larger institutions and norms
of society.

*Processes of Aging: Social and Psychological Perspectives*
will be of interest to research workers, teachers, and advanced students
concerned with the psychological, psychiatric, psychosocial, and socioeconomic aspects of aging. Many of the theoretical and analytical discussions and the specific studies offer guidance for top-level planners
and administrators in public agencies and voluntary organizations.

—*Richard H. Williams*
—*Clark Tibbitts*
—*Wilma Donahue*

# CONTENTS

*Volume II*

# CONTRIBUTORS

*Volume II*

Brian Abel-Smith, lecturer, The London School of Economics and Political Science, University of London, England

Leonard Z. Breen, associate professor and co-ordinator of research in gerontology, Department of Sociology, Purdue University, Lafayette, Indiana

Ernest W. Burgess, professor emeritus of sociology, The University of Chicago, Illinois

Ewan Clague, commissioner, Bureau of Labor Statistics, Department of Labor, Washington, D.C.

Wilbur J. Cohen, assistant secretary, Department of Health, Education, and Welfare, Washington, D.C.; professor of public administration, The University of Michigan, Ann Arbor

Wilma Donahue, chairman, Division of Gerontology, Institute for Human Adjustment, and lecturer in psychology, The University of Michigan, Ann Arbor

Robert H. Dovenmuehle, M.D., research co-ordinator, Center for the Study of Aging, Duke University Medical Center, Durham, North Carolina

Sven P.M. Forssman, M.D., professor; president, Division of Occupational Health, Swedish Employers' Association, Stockholm

Eli Ginzberg, professor of economics and director, Conservation of Human Resources Project, Columbia University, New York

Margaret S. Gordon, associate director, Institute of Industrial Relations, University of California, Berkeley

Sven Hydén, director, International Social Security Association; assistant director, Swedish Employers' Association, Stockholm

Robert W. Kleemeier, research professor of psychology, Washington University, St. Louis, Missouri

Gerrit A. Kooy, professor of rural sociology, College of Agriculture, Wageningen, Netherlands

Helen H. Lamale, chief, Branch of Consumption Studies, Bureau of Labor Statistics, Department of Labor, Washington, D.C.

Marjorie Fiske Lowenthal, co-investigator, Geriatric Research Project, Langley Porter Neuropsychiatric Institute, San Francisco, California

Poul Milhøj, The Danish National Institute of Social Research, Copenhagen

Harold L. Orbach, assistant director, Social Gerontology Project, Division of Gerontology, Institute for Human Adjustment, The University of Michigan, Ann Arbor

Angelo Pagani, director, Sociological Section, Operations Research Center, Bocconi University, Milan

Paul Paillat, research associate, National Institute of Demographic Studies, Paris

Ian M. Richardson, M.D., senior lecturer, Department of Public Health and Social Medicine, University of Aberdeen, Scotland

Irving Rosow, associate professor of sociology, School of Applied Social Sciences, Western Reserve University, Cleveland, Ohio

Peter Sainsbury, Medical Research Council, Clinical Psychiatry Research Unit, Graylingwell Hospital, Chichester, England

Ethel Shanas, associate professor, Department of Sociology, and research associate, Committee on Human Development, The University of Chicago, Illinois

Barbara E. Shenfield, lecturer, Department of Economics and Social Studies, Bedford College, University of London, England

Walt R. Simmons, statistical advisor, U.S. National Health Survey, Public Health Service, Department of Health, Education, and Welfare, Washington, D.C.

Gordon F. Streib, professor of sociology, Cornell University, Ithaca, New York

Erik Strömgren, M.D., department of psychiatry, Aarhus University, Risskov, Denmark

Rudolf Tartler, Faculty of Law and Social Sciences, University of Münster, Germany

Clark Tibbitts, deputy director, Special Staff on Aging, Department of Health, Education, and Welfare, Washington, D.C.

Peter Townsend, lecturer in social administration, The London School of Economics and Political Science, University of London, England

Richard H. Williams, chief, Professional Services Branch, National Institute of Mental Health, Bethesda, Maryland

Seymour L. Wolfbein, deputy assistant secretary, Department of Labor, Washington, D.C.

P.M. Yap, M.D., psychiatrist, The Mental Hospital, University of Hong Kong, B.C.C.

# PROCESSES

# OF AGING

VOLUME II

# PART FIVE

*Relations with
Family and Society*

# INTRODUCTION

Why are people becoming concerned about aging and the aged? In what sense, if at all, is aging a major social problem? Is it a meaningful and proper focus for sociological research?

It is clear that people in all Western nations are showing a growing interest in aging and its problems. Volunteer associations are spending much time on them; Congressional committees devote attention to them; Congress earmarks funds for research on them; on federal, state, and local levels, committees, councils, and commissions have been established to study them.

There is also no doubt that the amount of research on the social and sociopsychological aspects of aging has increased significantly in the past eight years, especially in the past four. For example, research and training grants from the National Institutes of Health

3

relating primarily and secondarily to aging have increased more than sixfold in the past four years.

Social theory, especially the theory of action, can do much to explain why aging has become a problem, can give important perspective to programs intended to cope with the issue, and can indicate ways in which scientific study of social and sociopsychological aspects of the processes of growing old can contribute to an understanding of general human behavior. The study of child development has long been considered a fruitful field of scientific endeavor. An equally good case can be made for studies of social processes during other phases of the life cycle, and perhaps an especially good case can be made for its last phase.

Macroscopic sociological theory is useful in broad comparative studies of institutional patterns, cultures, and whole societies. If aging becomes increasingly important as it becomes a more problematical issue and if it is less likely to be viewed as a self-evident aspect of life, these facts are themselves important data about the social system and can be systematically related to other characteristics of the society in question. One should first look, however, at the conditions of social behavior to see whether they account for the marked shift in the way aging is regarded.

A cursory look at conditions in modern Western society suggests that they do not explain the matter adequately, if they explain at all. There are, to be sure, more elderly people. So what? This fact could be viewed as merely a triumph of modern medicine. The combined effects of our technological system (action-oriented toward adapting to conditions by efficient use of tools) and our economic system (action-oriented toward maximum realization of ends at minimum cost) are such that we are capable of supporting the entire population, including its older members, at the highest standard of living known to man. Some older people are put at a disadvantage by technological change, and some have serious difficulties in maintaining their incomes in their later years, but these problems come from economic institutions which are a part of the social structure, rather than from the technological and economic systems themselves.

If, by contrast, one examines the general institutional pattern of Western society, particularly its value system and general norms of conduct, it is possible to learn why aging has become a social problem. The pattern is undergoing significant changes. The classic pattern of economic individualism is shifting toward a pattern which emphasizes such values as security, the right to a job, social responsibility, organized social control, and recognition of group interests. This pattern, however, is not yet fully institutionalized, and there is much ambivalence about many of its values, particularly security. Older people have not only experienced this transition and, perhaps, been somewhat bewildered by it, but they have also been put into an ambiguous social position. Being old does not in itself have very much prestige, and the moral value of old-age security, if not directly achieved by the individual, is unclear and provokes ambivalent attitudes. Thus the problem of aging may be representative of some of the tensions in this transition for society as a whole.

Kooy (Chapter 30) presents a particularly interesting study of part of a society, Achterhoek in the Netherlands, which maintained a virtually unchanged, isolated, and traditional social structure from the Middle Ages to the end of the nineteenth century. Then, the isolation was broken and significant changes occurred in family structure. Separate nuclear units deprived the elderly people of many traditional duties and activities. Their role in preserving the economic integrity of the extended family diminished or was lost, their social status was lowered, and they exercised much less authority in the economic and moral spheres. Kooy also shows that the development of the modern nuclear family in the Netherlands and throughout Western culture has had a profound effect on the social position of older people.

In Chapter 31, Tartler presents a similar picture with somewhat more emphasis on a functional analysis. He uses sociological theory, as do many European sociologists, to question widespread notions of what older people want and what should be done for them. He calls special attention to a point sometimes overlooked in programs for the elderly—that leisure and its activities have functional significance in contrast to work, which is the major stabilizing factor giving a limited and manageable system of action in this complex world. When a person no longer has an occupational role, leisure is taken in earnest. Tartler makes a plea for the development of meaningful social systems for older people, rather than palliative, piecemeal approaches. Kleemeier (Chapter 34) points to another important aspect in developing meaningful social environments for the aged—the degree to which older people live, or want to live, in special settings. He delineates the dimensions of special settings, each dimension being a continuum. Not much research has been done on this problem, as Kleemeier points out. Burgess (Chapter 32), in his comments on the chapters by Tartler and Kooy, takes a definite stand on this issue, for he believes it is possible to develop special social environments for the aging that are not retreats but opportunities. This question of the type of social setting and psychological environment which is most appropriate for the aging should become the focus of a major research effort. Shanas (Chapter 28) and Streib (Chapter 29) describe methods which would supply much of the necessary data.

Tartler stresses a point that is often ignored: older people of the present generation lived through a period of rapid social change before they became old. This is generally true, but, as Tartler would undoubtedly admit, the exposure to social change would probably vary widely. This point suggests an important variable for further research. In Chapter 33 Pagani does give some data from the metropolitan area of Milan and its hinterlands, on attitudes toward social change. His study indicates that older people look with particular favor on changes which have occurred in economic and working conditions, but have much less favorable attitudes toward changes in social relations. The stand of older people on social change, as well as their relation to the existing social structure, is an important issue.

In modern Western societies, there may be structural and functional aspects that make aging a more critical transition than it is in most other societies, that give ambiguous status to age, and that create special problems for older people. To understand these problems adequately, we need more microscopic studies of older people, their personalities, their styles of life, their immediate social systems, and the degrees of success with which they face the problems of being old in their society—matters which are analyzed in Volume I.

# SECTION I

*Methodological
Considerations*

# CHAPTER 28

*National Studies of*
*Older People in*
*the United States*

ETHEL SHANAS

Survey methods for the study of older populations have been used extensively in the past two decades. Although certain basic information about older people is available in the censuses of various countries, more detailed information about the life of older people has usually been secured through surveys of this special population. Many of the problems associated with aging populations are common to the urbanized western countries in Europe and in North America. Recognizing the need for world-wide comparable information about the aged, considerable attention has been given to the possibility of cross-national surveys of the aging (International Association of Gerontology, 1958), and a pilot study for a future cross-national survey has been made in England (Townsend & Rees, 1959).

9

In the United States, surveys of older people, usually defined as people sixty-five or more years of age, have become almost commonplace. Such surveys vary in their purposes, techniques, and methods. In general, surveys of the aged may be divided into two groups: descriptive surveys whose primary concern is over-all fact-gathering and problem-oriented surveys. In the first instance, information is collected on certain characteristics of some segment of the older population in order to fill a gap in available factual knowledge. Examples of this type of descriptive survey are the state surveys done in preparation for the 1961 White House conference on aging. The second type of survey, the problem-oriented, gathers selected information which will enable the organization using the survey data to formulate an answer to a particular problem or set of problems. An example of this is the survey of the Kips Bay-Yorkville area, made by the New York City Department of Health to aid in determining the types of services which it could offer older people (Kutner, Fanshel, Togo, & Langner, 1956).

Although it is relatively simple to divide surveys into those that are primarily fact-oriented (descriptive) and those that are primarily problem-oriented, it is almost impossible to classify American surveys of the aged by their techniques and methods. The populations surveyed vary from those with a common geographic base, such as all older people in a state, a city, or even a parish (Bower, 1957), to those in specific economic or political groups of older people, such as old-age assistance recipients (Bond, Baber, Vieg, Perry, Scaff, & Lee, 1954; Shanas, 1950) or members of the California Institute of Social Welfare (Pinner, Jacobs, & Selznick, 1959). The samples of older people range from probability samples of an older population to some or all members of groups readily available to the investigator, such as members of golden age clubs, residents of a housing project, residents of a home for the aged, and so on. The American Institute of Public Opinion interviewed four hundred and two members of a selected group ninety-five years old and older, building up their sample with "the help of newspaper files, clergymen and old-age homes" (Gallup & Hill, 1960, p. 35). The techniques used in American surveys include face-to-face interviews, mail questionnaires, and schedules completed by the respondent. As might be expected, therefore, the quality of surveys of the aged made in the United States varies greatly, and so findings from these surveys must be evaluated against a background of study design, investigation methods, and analysis techniques.

## NATIONAL SURVEYS

There have been many surveys of selected groups of older people in the United States, but national surveys of the aged are very few. Survey information about all older people in the United States is secured routinely by the United States Bureau of the Census in its decennial census and current population survey. The National Health Survey, which has been in progress since 1957, also gathers material about the older groups. In addition, most national surveys made by nongovernmental agencies usually include age among the variables used in their analyses.

Both the census and National Health Survey data are secured in household interviews. In collecting census data, any adult can answer for all other household members, and, despite the efforts made in the National Health Survey to have each adult household member report for himself, it is also possible to have one adult report about the others in his household in this survey.

Information about older people based on interviews with other members of their households differs from information collected in interviews with older people themselves. Since many investigators recognize the desirability of interviewing older people about themselves, a number of such interview studies of limited older populations have been made in the United States.

In only two interview studies, however, are most older people in the United States represented in the sample. These national surveys are the study of the economics of the aged made by the Institute of Industrial Relations, University of California, and reported in Steiner and Dorfman (1957) and the study of older people's health needs as seen by themselves and their responsible family members, made by the National Opinion Research Center, University of Chicago (Health Information Foundation, 1959a; Health Information Foundation, 1959b; Shanas, 1959a; Shanas, 1959b; Shanas, 1959c; Shanas, 1960a; Shanas, 1960b). In addition to these two nationwide surveys, the Bureau of Old-Age and Survivors Insurance, Social Security Administration, made national surveys of its beneficiaries in 1951 and in 1957. Since the bureau surveys cover only older people receiving old-age and survivors insurance benefits, they represent only 45.4 per cent of the people sixty-five years or older in 1956, the sample year of the latest survey (U. S. Department of Health, Education, & Welfare, 1960, p. 74).

The two major reasons why more nationwide interview studies of older people have not been made are that such studies are expensive and that the difficulties of locating and interviewing older people are believed to be different from the difficulties associated with nationwide interviewing of all adults.

There is no doubt that nationwide interview studies of older people are expensive.[1] There is no evidence, however, that these studies are any more expensive than nationwide interview studies of any other selected adult groups. Further, the special problems associated with locating and interviewing older people are not insurmountable. As the following review of national surveys will show, there is no evidence that the difficulties associated with interviewing older people are greater than the difficulties encountered in interviewing other adult populations.

The present review of national surveys of the aged in the United States will focus on the California and National Opinion Research Center surveys, although appropriate mention of the beneficiary surveys will be made. An analysis will be made of the study design and investigation methods in these surveys. The topics to be considered will be the purposes of the surveys, the problems of sampling, the content of the interviews, and the type of interviewers used. Any special survey problems associated with the age of respondents will be mentioned. Following the analyses of study design and investigation methods, some consideration will be given to a general evaluation of the use of national surveys in the study of older people in the United States.

### Purposes

The two national surveys of the aged which have been made in the United States differ in their purposes. These differences in ultimate goals influenced both the design and analytical methods of each study. The purpose of the California survey was to pinpoint and analyze the economic status of older people in the United States "in order to provide some of the facts requisite for intelligent discussion of the problem of the aged and for formulation of a constructive social policy" (Steiner & Dorfman, 1957, p. 4). The purpose of the National Opinion Research Center study was to determine the health needs of older people as perceived by older people themselves, and

[1] The Rockefeller Foundation supported the study of the aged conducted by the Institute of Industrial Relations, University of California; the Health Information Foundation financed the National Opinion Research Center survey.

people other than the spouse to whom older people would turn in a crisis affecting their health. Since the National Opinion Research Center study was designed to yield information on the demographic characteristics, family situation, and points of view of older people and to relate these facts to the health status of the respondents, it was expected that the study would provide facts useful for the formulation of social policy.

The beneficiary survey of 1957, like the earlier 1951 beneficiary survey, was designed to secure information on the resources of beneficiaries of Old-Age and Survivors Insurance. The beneficiary surveys were made by an official agency of the United States government. As such, their findings must be considered as a direct aid to public-policy formulation. The rationale behind the beneficiary surveys is the desirability of relating government action to survey findings.

The California study involved interviews only with older people; the beneficiary study interviewed a sample of beneficiaries most of whom were sixty-five and older; the National Opinion Research Center study involved an interview with an older person and, for each older person, a second interview with an adult child or other responsible relative or individual.[2]

## Problems of Sampling

The findings of a survey can be no better than its original data. The original data reflect the sample design, the schedule, and the skill of the interviewers. No amount of sophisticated analysis can compensate for inadequacies in original data. In this section, attention will be given to the design and execution of samples used in the national surveys of the aged.

*Sample Design.* The California and the National Opinion Research Center surveys collected data from persons sixty-five and over living in households in the general population. Both surveys used multi-stage area probability sampling, a sampling method developed by the Bureau of the Census, which ensures every older person in the noninstitutionalized population an equal chance of being located (Hansen, Hurwitz, & Madow, 1953; Hansen, Hurwitz, Nisselson, & Steinberg, 1955).

[2] The National Opinion Research Center interviewed two separate samples of older people, one sample composed of people from sixty through sixty-four and another of people sixty-five and over. Responsible children or relatives were interviewed for both samples. The present review will give data only from the survey of people sixty-five and older.

Both surveys excluded the older population living in such institutions as mental hospitals or homes for the aged. The proportion of the older population in institutions is estimated at between 3 and 5 per cent of this age group in the United States. The exclusion of the institutional population from household surveys is the usual practice in the United States and is not unique to surveys of the aged.

The California survey screened 15,000 households in sixty-eight sample areas in the United States. From this screening 3,000 households which contained one or more people over sixty-five were located. "These households, containing a total of 3,600 aged individuals were included in the . . . survey" (Steiner & Dorfman, 1957, p. 156). The National Opinion Research Center study screened a probability sample of 7,528 households in sixty-eight sample areas and located 2,090 persons sixty-five and older.[3] In both these surveys, when more than one older person was found in a household, each person was interviewed. In the National Opinion Research Center study there were complete, separate interviews with husband and wife; in the California study only partial interviews were held with women over sixty-five whose husbands were also in the sample (Steiner & Dorfman, 1957, pp. 164-167).

Like the other two surveys, the 1957 beneficiary study was a survey of a probability sample. The survey was made in seventy selected areas in the United States. In this study there was no need to screen households to locate beneficiaries. Once a selection of sampling areas was made, the names and addresses of respondents were secured from government records (U.S. Bureau of Old-Age and Survivors Insurance, Division of Program Analysis, 1958, pp. 22-23).

*No Response.* Once older people have been located in the general population by probability methods, the next hurdle which confronts the investigator is ensuring response. If enough people fail to complete the interview, the sample may turn out to be no better than a convenient slice of the population. As Deming (1950) has said, "A good sample design is lost if not carried out according to plans. . . . Neither an incompleted 'complete count' nor an incompleted sample is a sample but rather a form of *chunk*" (p. 8).

The data used in the Steiner and Dorfman report were

[3] James S. Coleman, now at The Johns Hopkins University and formerly of the Department of Sociology at the University of Chicago and the National Opinion Research Center, was responsible for the sample design in this study. Jacob J. Feldman of the National Opinion Research Center succeeded Dr. Coleman as the sampling consultant on this study.

gathered by the Bureau of the Census. From the reports of the California survey, it is difficult to determine either the number of older people in the Census Bureau household screening who could not be interviewed or the number of older people on whom data was secured by interviewing some other household member. Although Steiner and Dorfman give considerable attention to the reliability of their income data, there is no evaluation of the characteristics of the total sample of older people as originally located by the Census Bureau (Steiner & Dorfman, 1957, Appendix A).

The National Opinion Research Center materials make possible an evaluation of the problems involved in securing a probability sample of people sixty-five and older in the United States (Shanas, 1959c). In this survey, 2,090 persons in the desired age group were located. For various reasons about 17 per cent of them were not interviewed. To begin with, 8 per cent refused to be interviewed. This figure is undoubtedly higher than the refusal rate for this age group in surveys under government auspices. An additional 9 per cent of the older population could not be interviewed. Half of these people were "too sick"; this group included some people in general hospitals at the time of interviewing. The other half could not be interviewed because they were too hard of hearing, spoke no English, or could not be located after repeated visits. Eighty-three per cent of all the older people located (1,734 people) were interviewed in the National Opinion Research Center survey. If those who were too sick to be interviewed are excluded from the total located, the response rate rises to 87 per cent. This proportion is comparable to the response rate in nongovernmental nationwide studies based on a cross-section of all adults. In surveys of the general population, however, it would seem likely that a smaller proportion of the sample would be unable to complete the interview because they were "too sick," too hard of hearing, or unable to speak English. On the other hand, since older people are more likely to be at home, a larger proportion of a general population sample would be lost because they could not be located.

*Sample Evaluation.* In planning a national survey of older people in the United States, whether as part of a larger cross-national survey or as an independent study, the most desirable sample design would seem to be a multi-stage area probability sample of the noninstitutionalized population. Such a design would guarantee that all older persons in the United States would be located in their true proportions of the general population.

It has been demonstrated that such a sample can be successfully used in studying the aged. Both the California survey and the National Opinion Research Center survey have compared certain demographic characteristics of the older populations they interviewed with the estimates of these characteristics for all older people as reported by the Census Bureau (Shanas, 1959c, p. 14; Steiner & Dorfman, 1957). In both samples agreement with the Census Bureau estimates is good. Despite this agreement in demographic characteristics, however, any national survey of the noninstitutionalized aged in the United States must expect, as the detailed analysis of the National Opinion Research Center's sample has shown to underrepresent the very sick in their own homes and to lose certain cases because they are too hard of hearing, or because they speak no English and foreign-language interviewers may not be available.[4]

*The Institutional Population.* Thus far, no one has attempted to make a study of a probability sample of the institutionalized aged in the United States. Such a study may not be feasible because of the difficulties in locating institutions with aged residents, as well as the difficulties in interviewing old people who may be senile or confused. Instead, it might be desirable to study the residents of selected institutions for the aged by a variety of such techniques as interviewing residents in homes for the healthy aged and record-search and evaluation in nursing homes and mental hospitals. Some start has already been made in this direction (Poland, Lembcke, & Shain, 1959).

### The Interview

*Length.* There has been considerable discussion about the length of the interview to be used in studies of older persons. All investigators seem to feel that brevity is desirable. In the national interview studies of older people in the United States, only the schedule used in the California study appears to be brief. The average interview in the 1957 beneficiary survey has been informally reported to be one and one-fourth hours. The average interview in the National Opinion Research Center study was one and one-half hours, although about 8 per cent of the interviews were completed in less than an hour and 17 per cent took two or more hours. It may be suggested that, although brevity is desirable in an interview, an interview of an hour or longer

---

4 In the National Opinion Research Center study, the demographic characteristics of those who were too sick to be interviewed were secured from the people who were taking care of them. These characteristics were then compared with the characteristics of the very sick who had been interviewed. The two groups appear to be similar.

can be conducted successfully when older people are asked about things that interest them.

*Content.* The content of the interviews used in national surveys reflects the primary purposes of the investigators. The interviews used in the California and beneficiary surveys focused on income and asset data; the interview in the National Opinion Research Center study focused on health and family relationships.

The schedule used in the California survey of the economics of the aged dealt briefly with several factual items. The schedule covered work experiences of the respondent, sources and amounts of income, savings and assets, sources of support, and some brief questions on living arrangements, medical expenses, and condition of the dwelling unit (Steiner & Dorfman, 1957, pp. 164-167). The beneficiary survey schedule covered most of these items, but was much more comprehensive.[5] This schedule included detailed questions on sources and amounts of income, assets and liabilities, employment during the survey year, health status at the time of interview, health insurance coverage, and medical-care costs and the means of meeting these costs (U.S. Bureau of Old-Age and Survivors Insurance, Division of Program Analysis, 1958, p. 23).

The National Opinion Research Center schedule covered the health and the family relationships of older people in great detail and gave much less attention to income and asset data than did the beneficiary study. Specifically, the National Opinion Research Center schedule included detailed questions on health status and complaints, the use of physicians and nursing care, disability, special living arrangements necessitated by health conditions, the use of appliances, health insurance coverage, opinions on government health insurance, medical-care costs and ways in which high medical-care costs may be met, attitudes toward health, whom the respondent would consult in a health crisis, sources of income, living arrangements, relationships with children and attitudes toward family life, employment and attitudes toward work, and religious affiliation and attitudes toward religion.

As may be seen, the two national surveys of older people and the beneficiary study covered some of the same areas; where question format was not too different, it is possible to make comparisons among

[5] Through the cooperation of the Beneficiary Studies Section, Division of Program Analysis, Bureau of Old-Age and Survivors Insurance, Social Security Administration, the writer has had an opportunity to review the schedules used in the 1957 and 1951 surveys.

these surveys and to use findings from each survey to reaffirm or modify the findings of the others.

*Design.* Should schedules designed for interviewing older people differ in format from those designed for younger adults? There is some feeling that perhaps interviewers should be free to rephrase questions if they are not too clear to the older adult.

The experience of the National Opinion Research Center may be of value. In designing the schedule for their study and in developing instructions for interviewers, no deviations from the agency's usual policies were made because of the advanced age of the respondents.

The National Opinion Research Center schedule included closed questions in which the respondent is given a choice of answers and free-answer questions which the respondent answers as he chooses; his answer is recorded verbatim. A closed question is, "Would you say your health is better or worse than the health of other people your age? Just your opinion!"; a free-answer question asks, "Are there any things you especially need that you've had to do without because you don't have enough money? What kinds of things?"

In addition to the usual closed and free-answer questions, the respondents in the National Opinion Research Center survey were read several hypothetical cases, each of which dealt with a special aspect of the relationships between an older parent and his adult child. After each case had been read, the respondent was asked to comment. An example of a narrative question follows:

> Tom and Mary Jenkins have four children. They live in a new section in a small three-bedroom house, and it gets pretty crowded. Mary's mother, Mrs. Stevens, is a widow with a very small pension, and her health is poor. The doctor doesn't think Mrs. Stevens should live alone. He says that she doesn't need any special nursing care, just someone to keep an eye on her. What do you think Mary should do?

The narrative questions in the National Opinion Research Center survey were designed to elicit certain information about older parents and their adult children which might not be readily forthcoming in direct question-and-answer interviewing. Narrative questions with other subject matters have been successfully used in the study of other populations.

As in all National Opinion Research Center studies, interviewers were instructed to ask questions precisely as worded in the same sequence in which they appear on the questionnaire. Only in this way can the investigator be sure that differences among respondents are not the result of the interviewers' changes in question wording or order.

*Respondents' Reactions.* Some critics have felt that survey interviewing is distressing to the older person. Data from the National Opinion Research Center study yield information on the reactions of older people to that interview.

The center's interviewers were asked to evaluate respondents' attitudes and behavior during the interview in order to assist the analysts in their consideration of the interview data. In answer to a question on respondent cooperation, the interviewers described 93 per cent of the respondents as cooperative. This reply might be expected, since interviewers pride themselves on securing interviews. Interviewers also were asked about the respondent's over-all reaction to the interview and whether specific areas of it seemed to bring signs of anxiety, distress, or discomfort to the older person. In terms of over-all reaction, 50 per cent of the respondents were reported as having enjoyed the interview, 37 per cent were reported as interested but not particularly concerned, 7 per cent were reported as bored but not concerned, and only 4 per cent were reported as being disturbed by the interview.[6] In the analysis of specific areas of the interview, 55 per cent of the respondents were reported as having shown no evidence of anxiety or distress during any part of the interview. In only two sections of the interview did as many as 10 per cent of the respondents exhibit any signs of distress; these sections were those dealing with finances and the narrative questions about parent-child relationships.

In general, the National Opinion Research Center interviewers found 93 per cent of the older respondents cooperative, 91 per cent alert, and 89 per cent able to concentrate during the lengthy interview. Only 4 per cent of the respondents were reported as upset or concerned at the conclusion of the interview.

*Interviewers.* In the two national surveys and the beneficiary survey, the recruitment, training, and survey experiences of the interviewers presented no problems unique to studies of the aged. Regular Census Bureau interviewers were used in the California survey; members of the district office staffs of the Bureau of Old-Age and Survivors Insurance were used as interviewers in the beneficiary survey (U.S. Bureau of Old-Age and Survivors Insurance, Division of Program Analysis, 1958, pp. 22-23). The National Opinion Research Center employed its usual interviewing staff on this study.

6 This question was not answered for 2 per cent of the respondents.

Shanas and Monsky (1957) reported the composition of the National Opinion Research Center field staff and their attitudes toward studying the aged. Ninety-one per cent of the interviewers were women; 83 per cent were married; 74 per cent had had some college training, but only 47 per cent were college graduates. Thirty-six per cent of the interviewers were forty-five or older, 37 per cent were between the ages of thirty-five and forty-five, and 27 per cent were less than thirty-five years old. With the exception of former social workers (eleven on an interviewing staff of 197), the field staff reported only limited previous experience with older people outside their own families.

After the interviewing was completed, the members of the National Opinion Research Center interviewing staff who had had previous experience on comparable studies of other subjects were asked a number of questions about the survey, two of which are reported here.

The first question was, "Generally speaking, did you find this an easier or a harder assignment than most special surveys you have worked on? Why?" Twenty-five per cent of the interviewers said this study was easier than other studies, and an additional 31 per cent said that they could notice no real difference in the difficulty of the interviewing assignment. Only 44 per cent of the interviewers rated this study harder. Since the actual design of the study was exceedingly complex—older people were located, interviewed, and asked to name the person (who was subsequently interviewed) to whom they would turn in a health crisis—one would have expected a higher proportion of interviewers with comparable experience to rate this study as harder.

Interviewers were also asked, "Taking everything into consideration, would you say you enjoyed this survey more or less than most studies you have worked on?" The answers to this question were divided equally among the three possible responses: one-third of the interviewers said that they had enjoyed this survey more, one-third said that they had liked this survey less, and one-third said that they could see no difference between their reactions to this and other surveys.

The National Opinion Research Center interviewing staff apparently accepted the survey of older people as another assignment in a series of such assignments; Shanas and Monsky state, however, that the interviewers' experience with older people tended to make a significant number of them more sympathetic to the aged.

### EVALUATION

Only a few national surveys of people sixty-five and older have been made in the United States. From the experience gained in these surveys, it is apparent that the difficulties of locating and interviewing older people are no greater than or different from the difficulties of interviewing cross-sections of other adults. The sample design, interview format, and the interviewers used in national surveys of other populations may be successfully employed in the study of the aged.

The contributions made by national surveys to the knowledge about older people in the United States are already substantial, for they yield information which is not otherwise available. The California survey and the beneficiary survey give detailed presentations of the income, assets, and resources of the aged; for the first time in this country, the National Opinion Research Center survey reports on the health status of older people and its relation to living arrangements and family situations.

Second, national surveys delineate the dimensions of a problem. To illustrate, in the United States there has been much discussion about making changes in the patterns of retirement. Some advocates of these changes have argued that large numbers of older people who wish to work are unable to do so only because of age restrictions. The California survey, however, indicated that only about 7 per cent of the retired men were able to work and interested in working (Steiner & Dorfman, 1957, p. 39). As a further illustration, there has been a need for an estimate of the extent of illness among the older population. The National Opinion Research Center survey, through an index of illness, estimates that the very sick in the older population comprise between 10 and 14 per cent of all people sixty-five and older in the noninstitutionalized population. "The general picture which emerges from interviews . . . is of an older population with many complaints but with relatively few complaints which the respondent considers serious enough to require medical care" (Shanas, 1960b, p. 106).

Finally, since the groups whose needs are greatest—the indigent, the sick, the mentally disturbed, the socially isolated—are those who come to public and professional attention, much of American thinking about older people is based on these special categories of the aged. National surveys help to correct this thinking by reporting that members of these categories are not representative of all the older people in the United States.

There are also limitations in national surveys. Such surveys give no information about social processes. From a survey of a group of older people at any one time, not much can be determined about the factors responsible for the present situation of the group, nor can predictions about its future development be made. For studies of social processes and the changing situation of the aged, longitudinal studies are greatly needed. In recognition of this need, the beneficiary study section of the Bureau of Old-Age and Survivors Insurance has proposed a thirteen-year panel study of a probability sample of older beneficiaries.

The findings of national surveys are related to a given point in time, and certain factual findings may be quickly outdated. In 1957 the National Opinion Research Center survey reported that 39 per cent of the population sixty-five and older had some kind of health insurance coverage; by 1960 the proportion of the older population with health insurance had risen well above this figure. Legislation on health insurance would accelerate these changes and quickly render present estimates obsolete. Attitude data, rather than factual data, may well be the most stable information secured by national surveys. The attitudes of older people toward their health, physicians' services, living arrangements, and religion are far less likely to change in a short time than are such objective items as income, health insurance coverage, or the utilization of hospitals.

National surveys of the aged in the United States can be undertaken with techniques now available. The data from such surveys provide a broad picture of the older population which can serve as a framework for the study of special aged groups. Such data also furnish a reference point from which one can measure changes in the characteristics of the aged population.

### REFERENCES

Bond, F.A., Baber, R.E., Vieg, J.A., Perry, L.B., Scaff, A.H., & Lee, L.J., Jr. *Our needy aged: A California study of a national problem.* New York: Henry Holt and Co., 1954.

Bower, Janet. *Older people of St. Boniface parish, "the fruit belt."* Buffalo: Catholic Charities of Buffalo, 1957.

Deming, W.E. *Some theories of sampling.* New York: John Wiley & Sons, 1950.

Gallup, G., & Hill, E. *The secrets of long life.* New York: Bernard Geis Associates, 1960.

Hansen, M.H., Hurwitz, H.N., & Madow, W.G. *Sample survey methods and theory.* New York: John Wiley & Sons, 1953.

Hansen, M.H., Hurwitz, H.N., Nisselson, H., & Steinberg, J. The redesign of the current population survey. *J. Amer. Statist. Ass.*, 1955, **50,** 701-719.

Health Information Foundation. Voluntary health insurance among the aged. *Progr. in Hlth Serv.*, 1959, **8** (1). (a)

Health Information Foundation. Use of health services by the aged. *Progr. in Hlth Serv.*, 1959, **8** (2). (b)

International Association of Gerontology, Social Science Research Committee. *The need for cross-national surveys of old age: Report of a conference at Copenhagen, October 19-23, 1956.* Ann Arbor: University of Michigan, Division of Gerontology, 1958.

Kutner, B., Fanshel, D., Togo, Alice M., & Langner, T.S. *Five hundred over sixty: A community survey on aging.* New York: Russell Sage Foundation, 1956.

Pinner, F.A., Jacobs, J., & Selznick, P. *Old age and political behavior: A case study.* Berkeley and Los Angeles: University of California Press, 1959.

Poland, Eleanor, Lembcke, P.A., & Shain, M. Kansas nursing homes: A study of nursing homes, boarding homes, and homes for the aged and their patients or residents. Kansas City, Missouri: Community Studies, 1959.

Shanas, Ethel. The personal adjustment of recipients of old age assistance. *J. Geront.*, 1950, **5,** 249-253.

Shanas, Ethel. Some sociological research findings about older people pertinent to social work. In *Toward better understanding of the aged.* Vol. I. New York: Council on Social Work Education, 1959. Pp. 49-58. (a)

Shanas, Ethel. Some findings from a national study of the health needs of older people. In *Proceedings of the first national conference, joint council to improve the health care of the aged.* Chicago: The Joint Council, 1959. Pp. 81-85. (b)

Shanas, Ethel. *Financial resources of the aged: Reported resources available to those aged 65 and over in meeting medical costs up to $500.* New York: Health Information Foundation, 1959. (c)

Shanas, Ethel. How sick are older people? *J. Amer. med. Ass.*, 1960, **172,** 169-170. (a)

Shanas, Ethel. Reported illness and the utilization of medical care. *Publ. Welf.*, 1960, **18,** 103-105. (b)

Shanas, Ethel, & Monsky, Selma F. Interviewers' attitudes in a nation-wide study of older people. Paper presented at the annual meeting of the Gerontological Society, Cleveland, 1957.

Steiner, P.O., & Dorfman, R. *The economic status of the aged.* Berkeley: University of California Press, 1957.

Townsend, P., & Rees, B. *The personal, family and social circumstances of old people: Report of an investigation carried out in England in 1959 to pilot a future cross-national survey of old age.* London: London University, London School of Economics, 1959.

U.S. Bureau of Old-Age and Survivors Insurance, Division of Program Analysis. Income of old-age and survivors insurance beneficiaries: Highlights from preliminary data, 1957 survey. *Soc. Security Bull.,* August 1958, **21,** 17-23.

U.S. Department of Health, Education, and Welfare. *Health, education, and welfare trends.* Washington, D.C.: U.S. Government Printing Office, 1960.

# CHAPTER 29

## Longitudinal Studies in Social Gerontology

GORDON F. STREIB

It has become almost a cliché in discussions of research in social gerontology to state the importance and need for longitudinal studies. There have, however, been very few papers which have examined some of the problems of translating the idea of a longitudinal study into operating research. Probably the most useful and informative sources are those by Jones (1958b), Birren (1959, pp. 20-23), and Goldfarb (1960, esp. pp. 11-100). To the writer's knowledge there have been very few longitudinal studies in social gerontology; the standard bibliographies report very few items. However, there are several studies underway or planned, and where information is available on these works, it is mentioned below. Many of the examples which follow are based on experience in "The Cornell Study of Occupational Retirement" (Streib, Thompson, & Suchman, 1958). Since many of the problems involved in conducting longitudinal studies are not unique to social gerontological research, it seemed appropriate and useful to include research in other substantive fields and on younger age groups.

## DESIGN AND TYPES

Longitudinal studies differ fundamentally from cross-sectional studies in that the investigator obtains information by interviewing or other means from the same group of people on two or more occasions. The longitudinal design is most useful for studying changes in behavior and attitudes because one does not have to rely on retrospective questions or observations. In essence, the longitudinal study is an attempt to approximate some of the rigor of the before and after design of the experiment except for two important differences—in the longitudinal study one does not use matched groups, and one does not have control over the independent variable. A relatively uncomplicated longitudinal study would be one in which the investigator obtains a measure of the criterion variable—for example, attitudes towards national health insurance for the aged—on the first interview. Let us assume that between the first and second interviews an information or propaganda campaign employing the mass media is conducted. In the second interview the investigators would determine which members of the study population were exposed to the information campaign, the nature of the contact, and whether exposure or lack of exposure had any effect on the criterion variable, attitudes toward national health insurance for the aged. In contrast, in a controlled experimental design the investigator would designate which people were or were not exposed to the stimulus variable—in this instance, the information campaign. This example obviously oversimplifies the kind of longitudinal studies in which many social gerontologists will be involved, for this hypothetical case involves only one causal (stimulus) factor and one effect variable. Most longitudinal studies in social gerontology will probably be broader in scope, involving such complicated social situations as the relationship between family structure and disengagement processes among the aged, the impact of the change in status from worker to retired worker on a person's social adjustment, and so on.

It may be useful, therefore, to think of longitudinal studies as being of two broad types which may vary in three important characteristics: the nature of the external stimulus, the criterion or effect variables, and the time interval between contacts. In Table I the two types are shown.

## TABLE 1
## TWO TYPES OF LONGITUDINAL STUDIES

| *External Stimulus* | *Type I: specific* | *Type II: diffuse* |
|---|---|---|
| Criterion-effect variables | Restricted | Broad |
| Time interval | Short | Longer duration |

Type I studies have been used to study a variety of subjects, most notably political attitudes and behavior patterns. Lazarsfeld and others have called this a "panel study." The first of these panel voting studies conducted by Lazarsfeld and his associates (Lazarsfeld, Berelson, & Gaudet, 1944) took place in Erie County, Ohio. A sample of 600 people were interviewed in May, 1940, and then once a month for six additional months from June until after the presidential election in November. The panel study is particularly suited for the study of short-term attitudinal and behavioral changes, for the "changers" can be more easily and reliably identified than they can be in cross-sectional surveys, and differential changes in the subgroups can be determined.

Undoubtedly some students of social gerontology will use Type I, or panel studies; it seems, however, that there is more interest and potentially richer findings in the long-term studies of Type II. An example of a Type II study, presently on the frontier of social gerontology, is the well-known study of 1,500 gifted children carried out by Terman and his associates (Terman & Oden, 1959). It is suggested that this research is on the frontier of social gerontology because the subjects are now, for the most part, in their early forties. In fact, it is planned that the research will continue as the subjects grow older, for, as Robert Sears has said, "On actuarial grounds, there is considerable likelihood that the last of Terman's Gifted Children will not have yielded his last report to the files before the year 2010!" (Terman & Oden, 1959, p. IX). The study by Terman and his associates has probably had the greatest time span of any longitudinal study in the social sciences, for it started in 1921-1922 when the author was in his forties and has continued after his death.[1] Here is a study

[1] Three longitudinal studies carried out for more than twenty-five years at the University of California, Berkeley, should also be mentioned. For a very brief summary of the studies and a bibliography see Jones (1958a).

which Sears well describes as "a study of man that will encompass the span of the *subjects'* lives, not just those of the researchers" (Terman & Oden, 1959, p. IX). In very broad terms, Terman conceived of the research as obtaining basic facts concerning the physical, mental, and personality traits of intellectually superior children and the type of adults they become. To date the study has involved three major field follow-ups: the first was in 1927-1928, about six years after the start of the study, the second in 1939-1940 when the subjects were about eighteen years old, and the third in 1950-1952, approximately thirty years after the start of the study, when the subjects were around forty years old. There was a supplementary mail questionnaire in 1955.

These two general types of longitudinal studies obviously do not exhaust the possibilities. One type not included here is illustrated by the studies of economic behavior conducted by the Survey Research Center at The University of Michigan and the continuous labor-force panel conducted by the United States Bureau of Labor Statistics. These studies tend to be primarily concerned with getting factual information on a limited subject, but they are set up to run for an indefinite time. There are also commercial studies, usually unpublished, on consumer behavior in which weekly or monthly reports are obtained from the participants. In communication research there are also many commercial market surveys of reading, listening, and viewing behavior in which a panel of participants is interviewed a number of times. Indeed, some of these so-called panel or longitudinal studies are actually cross-sectional studies. They are set up as longitudinal studies, however, to save money by using the same sample for more than one survey. Thus the word longitudinal can encompass a variety of research designs, methods, and subject matters.

## SAMPLING

If one employs the criteria of the natural sciences, sampling theory and practice are probably the most rigorous aspects of contemporary social science research. As Birren and others have pointed out, however, the term "sampling" usually has a restricted meaning because it refers to the sampling of respondents (Birren, 1959, p. 28). Sampling methods can and should be used in the selection of time periods, social processes, and social settings like institutions, groups, communities.

Perhaps this is the appropriate place to ask why we do sample. Some researchers feel that too much emphasis may be placed on rigorous sampling of respondents to the neglect of other aspects of research such as concept formation, index construction, and so on. Moreover, the rigor in sampling theory and the sophistication of its application in sampling practice have, perhaps, tended to obscure the fact that valuable, useful research can be carried out without adhering to the most rigorous canons of sampling.

The major purpose of sampling is to ensure that the selected population is representative. Jerome has summarized the aim very clearly: we sample "to secure a sample population that will be judged sufficiently unbiased to provide a basis for generalization or, on the other hand, that is sufficiently restricted to permit conclusions concerning a specific segment of the population in which interest happens to be concentrated" (Jerome, 1959, p. 660). Many gerontologists are interested in the internal analysis of variables and the ways in which the variables are related in subgroups of the population under study; this kind of analysis can be carried out without precise knowledge of the parameters of the universe. Moreover, much current research in social gerontology attempts to determine whether relationships exist between such variables as age, occupation, health, economic level, and the like. In other words, the investigator is interested in knowing whether the variables tend to go together or are independent.[2] This kind of exploratory research usually does not involve the systematic testing of hypotheses. Thus, if the investigator is not concerned with descriptive statistical statements or does not plan to extrapolate his findings to a specified population, it may not be essential to obtain a random sample.

In longitudinal research there is the important problem of whether significant subgroups are included in numbers sufficient to be comparatively analyzed. And there is a greater possibility, that significant subgroups may be inadequately represented in quota or selective sampling in research on older groups than in research on younger groups. If one is interested, for example, in studying the senile, the chronically ill, the socially isolated, or the psychologically alienated, it is important to have adequate numbers of these types.

These remarks should not be interpreted as a suggestion that

---

[2] But, as Festinger has pointed out, the discovery and demonstration of the relationships of variables is not a process of blindly trying to determine whether all are related. The investigator must have some hunches, ideas, and insights to guide him in the search for relationships. "If his idea is a 'correct' one, he may discover something. If his idea is not valid, his research may be wasted unless some lucky accident occurs" (Festinger, 1959, p. 360).

sampling should be neglected or rejected. It is recommended that, wherever it is feasible, rigorous, precise methods be used in selecting respondents and other research subjects. It seems likely, however, that there are some types of longitudinal studies in which particular types may be required, in which the demands on the participants may be great, or in which the subject matter may be of an intimate nature, so that it might be more practical to use volunteers, a quota sample, or some less rigorous method of selecting the study population. John Anderson (1958) has made the excellent suggestion that one untapped source of longitudinal data is the follow-up of adult populations who were participants in studies conducted ten, fifteen, or more years ago. The follow-up of these people may make it difficult to adhere to precise probability standards, but the net gain in longitudinal knowledge may be great. In such cases, the researcher will have to decide whether the possibility of rich longitudinal data outweighs the disadvantage of a biased sample.

One specific problem of longitudinal research is how large an original sample is necessary to ensure an adequate number of cases at the end of the study. A longitudinal study of almost any duration is almost certain to have some "true mortality" because of death and "research mortality" because of refusal to cooperate, inaccessibility, or unavailability. Within certain limits true mortality is a predictable loss, but research mortality is much more difficult to forecast because experience in this area is limited. Campbell and Katona state that in nationwide cross-section surveys one can expect a loss of 25 per cent or more after one year (Campbell & Katona, 1953, p. 29). In a Type I study of political behavior conducted in Elmira, New York, over about five months, it was necessary to draw a random sample of 1,267 people of voting age to ensure having at least 1,000 cases for analysis at the end of the fourth wave of interviewing (Berelson, Lazarsfeld, & McPhee, 1954).

In Type II studies with older people, there is no reported experience with probability samples, but one can cite studies underway or being planned. The twenty-year longitudinal study being planned by the Danish National Institute of Social Research contemplates drawing a national sample of approximately 2,000 sixty-three-year-olds to have about 700 cases available for analysis at the end of the data-gathering. It is expected that almost all the loss will be the result of death, for only a small research mortality is anticipated. The small size of Denmark, the relative social immobility of the older population, and a system of national registration are all factors which will probably minimize research mortality. These factors are not operative in most parts of the United States, and so the researcher must anticipate a larger research mortality. The nationwide study of OASI beneficiaries to be conducted by the Bureau of Old Age and Survivors Insurance will have a sample of approximately 4,500 aged beneficiaries for a twelve-year national study in order to have sufficient cases for statistical analysis.

One factor assumed to contribute to research mortality among older people is that respondents move, particularly at retirement. Our experience in the Cornell study, and experience reported in several other nonprobability studies suggest that many older people do move after they retire, but the overwhelming percentage moves only a short distance, staying within the general area of the former residence. Even people who move only a short distance, however, create problems in record-keeping and follow-up.

## NUMBER OF CONTACTS

One of the researcher's basic decisions in a longitudinal study is how many times he will contact the respondents. Time and money are usually restricting factors, but there are two other important research elements which need consideration, respondent co-operation and the possibility of bias when re-interviewing the participants. Unfortunately experience is so limited on longitudinal studies that it is impossible to state with any certainty how long respondents remain cooperative and how many contacts may be made before biases are so significant that the information becomes distorted.

In the Cornell study we contacted our respondents five different times over a period of almost seven years. The degree of cooperation remained high, particularly since the follow-ups were made by mail. The percentage of people who were still alive and returned questionnaires was approximately 80 per cent in the first follow-up and about 90 per cent in the second and third follow-ups (Streib, Thompson, & Suchman, 1958).

The work of Terman and his associates is somewhat similar, although with a different age group. They have been fortunate to receive an amazing cooperation from the nearly 1,500 members of the original group of gifted children. Nearly 95 per cent of those who were alive were active research subjects thirty-five years after the research had begun. During this research, three major field studies, several mail follow-ups, and a testing of a large proportion of the subjects' children were carried out. It must be emphasized, however, that Terman's subjects were far above average in mental abilities; moreover, the overwhelming majority demonstrated their superiority in adulthood. Thus it seems that sustained interest and cooperation is more likely with a group of above average intelligence than with a group of average intelligence.

Turning to studies which have been started or are being planned, we learn that the researchers of the Bureau of Old Age and Survivors Insurance will contact the participants annually in their twelve-year study. On the other hand, the Danish researchers are planning to contact the respondents six times during the nineteen years in which data will be gathered. It seems probable that the problem of boredom or annoyance will be less in the long-range study than in such panel studies as the voting researches which have been conducted during election campaigns. In the Elmira panel study of voting, for example, it was found that older people were more likely to be refusals than younger people, who were more likely to be unavailable. In this study the two types of losses tended to cancel each other in terms of biasing the study population. It should be noted, however, that this was a study of relatively short duration, involving only four interviews with each respondent in a period of five months.

Information on the bias from re-interviewing is also limited. Glock's (1950) study is one of the few studies on the subject. There is evidence from the voting study in Sandusky, Ohio, that re-interviewing may have an effect on the panel. It was found that repeated interviews had a tendency to increase the respondents' interest in political affairs. Until more studies have been conducted, however, it is difficult to state the effects of re-interviewing on kinds and forms of questions. A measure of control on the possible bias from re-interviewing can be obtained through a control group which is not repeatedly interviewed during the study. This procedure was followed in the Sandusky voting study. It seems unlikely, however, that budgetary and practical research considerations would permit this procedure in longitudinal studies conducted over five, ten, or more years.

### Maintaining Participation

The number of contacts in a study is closely related to motivating the participants. Unlike anthropological research with key informants, practically all contemporary sociological and social psychological research outside the laboratory does not involve paying respondents in any way. Occasionally a study will involve medical or psychological examinations, but the investigator should make the difference between research and the therapeutic aspects of the examinations clear to the participants. He may not always succeed in his explanation, but it is an essential step in initiating the research. A small subgroup in the Cornell retirement study was given a free medical examination. In the cases in which the examination was available, it was mentioned to the respondent in the hope that it might increase his long-term interest and cooperation in the study.

Usually the researchers appeal to feelings of pride or prestige, pointing out the importance of the scientific undertaking. In the case of Terman's thirty-five–year research, we are told that his study "grew into a very close personal relationship between him and the members of his group" (Terman & Oden, 1959, p. XI). In one of the letters accompanying a questionnaire Terman said, "Although the published reports will be largely statistical, I want you to know that each of you is to me a real person and not just another statistic" (Terman & Oden, 1959, p. XI). However, the maintenance of close personal ties with 1,500 subjects for thirty-five years is an accomplishment which few social scientists can hope to achieve. Sometimes appeals to social responsibility or community usefulness are employed. In some cases it has been possible to create interest and maintain cooperation by pointing out how important accurate information about a particular situation, problem, or category of persons is to policy-makers. In a longitudinal study of British education, one incentive was telling the participating university students that through the study questionnaires they could state their grievances against the schools, their teachers, and the administrators. It seems likely, however, that such incentives may boomerang in a negative way if used on a cross-section of the general population. In general, it does not seem difficult to obtain initial cooperation in field research; it is continued participation that raises problems, particularly with older persons. Experience is limited, but it seems essential that the researcher be as explicit as possible concerning the nature of the study and its duration. In the Cornell study we gave all respondents a printed brochure which stated that the study was longitudinal and would involve periodic contact with the research staff. Despite the original and later statements regarding follow-up contacts, however, there was a small group of participants who apparently were surprised to be contacted each time. This misunderstanding did not affect the generally high degree of cooperation, and it may have been mere forgetfulness, which is more likely with older participants. A further complication which may arise in longitudinal studies is that the researchers may have to secure the continued cooperation of people other than the primary participant; this is more likely in the case of older people, especially those whose closest relatives, for whatever reasons, may attempt to place a protective screen around the participant.

The whole subject of the participants' motives is virtually unknown terrain. One notes with surprise, for example, that in a detailed, sensitive study of the family as a group in which family members were interviewed for about twenty hours, the investigator states: "The motives for participating in the study were not explicitly or systematically explored" (Hess & Handel, 1959, p. 291). This observation is more surprising when one notes that 43 per cent of the fifty-eight families who were selected to participate declined to do so. With an increasing number of longitudinal studies planned or underway in social gerontology and other fields, it may be necessary to obtain more precise information about respondent motivation and about various incentives and their effect on the research information to be obtained. One suspects that a fair proportion of the participants in current social science research participate because they do not know how to escape the investigator's net.

## Mail Studies

It is appropriate to review some of the advantages and disadvantages of mail for research purposes, for there have been several longitudinal studies which have employed mail questionnaires, and it is likely that future investigators may also consider using them. The major advantages of mail are practical: initial and follow-up costs are considerably less than in an interview study, and the investigator can have wider geographical coverage than is feasible in a field study. Respondents who reside in isolated areas may be included more easily than they could be in interview studies.

There are, however, some limitations which need to be considered, particularly in longitudinal research. It is well-known, for example, that mail questionnaires always elicit a greater percentage of response from people with high educational attainments and prestigeful occupations.[3] It has also been pointed out that the investiga-

[3] For a discussion of some aspects of this problem in social gerontology, see Havighurst (1950, esp. pp. 165-166). Lenski and Leggett (1960) have shown how deference norms influence low-status respondents questioned by middle-class interviewers. Moreover, they assert that "even on the self-administered questionnaire there is good reason for predicting acquiescent responses from subjects of low status" (p. 467).

tor has limited control over the interval between interviews in longitudinal studies using the mail. This may be a drawback when the longitudinal study is a short-range one, but if the study is concerned with long-term changes, a variation of a few weeks, or even a month or two, may not be of great importance. Moreover, in actual practice the interval between waves in a mail study may not be greater than in an interview study. The field work in the follow-ups of Terman's study took approximately a year to complete. Macpherson (1958) reports that, in his longitudinal study of 1,200 Scottish school children, replacing interviewers for the successive waves resulted in a considerable lag in obtaining information. In one follow-up the interval between the dispatch and return of the schedules was stretched out to almost a year by some of the interviewers. This was probably because the interviewers were teachers who volunteered to do the work. Macpherson points out, however, that a time lag is not necessarily a disadvantage if the data are utilized as continuous data and taken up each time where the previous contact left off. In the Cornell study it was found that about 75 per cent of the mail questionnaires, which were twenty pages long, were returned within a month. This experience is similar to that of other investigators in that additional mailings and solicitation of responses do increase the number of final returns, although the bulk of responses comes in rather quickly.

A more fundamental limitation—and one over which the researcher has little control—is that the answers to mail questionnaires may be discussed with other people. Indeed, it is possible—although it probably occurs very rarely—that the questionnaire may be filled out by someone other than the respondent. If the questionnaire is intended to obtain the personal attitudes, behavior, and values of a particular person, the information may be distorted if someone else supplements or fills out the questionnaire. However, if the investigator designs a study in which the desired information does not necessarily have one person as a referent, it would be appropriate to have collaboration in answering the questions. In most surveys employing mail questionnaires and in the majority of interview studies it is presumed that one person will be the primary source of information for each questionnaire or interview. This notion, as we said above, may be violated in mail studies; the more interesting point, however, is that collaboration also occurs, perhaps to a greater degree than is thought, in interview studies. In reading research notes and appendixes, one finds that many investigators are aware of the possible bias introduced by the "intrusive third party" (Goode, 1956, p. 349). It seems to be

extremely rare, however, for investigators to offer facts on the extent
to which privacy was violated in the interview, the status and roles of
the people violating the privacy, the disposition of those cases in
which this kind of bias occurred, and the possible differences in response between private and nonprivate interviews. Taietz (1960)
is one of the few researchers who have systematically analyzed the
problem. He found that there are marked differences in the responses
given by older people on attitudinal questions in private and nonprivate interviews, and, therefore, the two kinds of interview data
are not strictly comparable. He found, for example, that older people
respond differently to a question about living with their children
when the children are present at the interview than when the children
are not present.

## ANALYSIS

The final area which warrants discussion is that of analysis.
We have pointed out earlier that through longitudinal studies the
researcher has the advantage of studying changes in attitudes and
behavior more directly than is possible when he must rely only on
retrospective information. The problems associated with the analysis
of Type II longitudinal data require considerable systematic attention;
there is a rich source of ideas in the methodological and substantive
work done on Type I studies however. The work of Lazarsfeld and
his associates has probably been the most productive source of in-
triguing suggestions for longitudinal analysis (Glock, 1955; Kendall,
1954; Lazarsfeld, 1959; Lazarsfeld & Merton, 1954).

Lazarsfeld (1959) has pointed out some kinds of changes or
sequences which may be analyzed longitudinally. Three of these sequences are changes over time for each variable, correlations between
variables and their changes over time, and conditional relations (particularly differences) between subgroups which initially differ according to a specific variable, the qualifier.[4] Data from "The Cornell Study
of Occupational Retirement" can be used to illustrate these types of
changes (Thompson & Streib, 1958).

Examples of the first type are changes which take place on
single variables like occupational status, health, self-image, adjustment,
attitudes toward retirement, and the like. One might be interested in

4 Lazarsfeld also suggests a fourth type of sequence, concurrent changes of two
or more variables, but the Cornell data which have been analyzed cannot be used
to illustrate this type of sequence.

determining whether the proportion of people who were working, retired, or had returned to work after retirement had changed at two different times. This type of change is probably the kind which is currently of most interest to policy-makers and the administrators of applied programs.

The second type is illustrated by the correlation between two variables, such as occupational status and economic deprivation or between economic deprivation and adjustment to retirement. The findings show, for example, that a shift in occupational status leads to a higher incidence of economic deprivation, as one would predict; economic deprivation is significantly related to indexes of adjustment. Here one is interested in the relationship of the two variables and not in the incidence of a particular characteristic.

Finally, there are those kinds of changes which are called conditional relations. This type of change is illustrated by an examination of the relationship between economic deprivation and adjustment to retirement among subgroups who differ in preretirement attitude. The latter variable was determined before retirement at the first contact with the participants. The findings show that during the initial year of retirement this conditional variable—preretirement attitude toward retirement—affects the frequency of changes in the direction of deprivation. If a person has a negative preretirement attitude toward retirement, he is more likely to have difficulty in reorienting himself to a lower income. In the second year of retirement, however, a somewhat different picture emerges. Here, people in each category of retiree are more likely to become economically deprived than those who are gainfully employed. However, the differences among the categories of retirees show a distinction between those who were retired administratively (by the employer) and the voluntary retirees, rather than between those who were willing and those who were reluctant to retire.

Lazarsfeld has also pointed out that panel materials on attitudes and behavior can be studied in a manner similar to that which economists have employed in time series studies to analyze business cycles and economic growth. Economists have been able to derive formal equations for analyzing time series materials because economic theories have been more rigorously conceptualized and because economic data are more amenable to mathematical manipulation. Social gerontology, however, is not so highly developed as economics in either theory or application of mathematical techniques. Even so, it is possible to use more rigorous descriptive techniques than we do at the present time, and it is hoped that more rigorous methods may be employed as technical knowledge in the field advances.

## REFERENCES

Anderson, J.E. Psychological aspects of aging. In Wilma Donahue, W.W. Hunter, Dorothy Coons, & Helen K. Maurice (Eds.), *Free time— challenge to later maturity*. Ann Arbor: University of Michigan Press, 1958. Pp. 29-44.

Birren, J.E. Cross-sectional and longitudinal studies. In J.E. Birren (Ed.), *Handbook of aging and the individual: Psychological and bio- logical aspects*. Chicago: The University of Chicago Press, 1959. Pp. 3-42.

Berelson, B., Lazarsfeld, P.F., & McPhee, W.N. *Voting*. Chicago: The Uni- versity of Chicago Press, 1954.

Campbell, A.A., & Katona, G. The sample survey: A technique for social science research. In L. Festinger & D. Katz (Eds.), *Research methods in the behavioral sciences*. New York: The Dryden Press, 1953. Pp. 15-55.

Festinger, L. Sampling and related problems in research methodology. *Amer. J. ment. Defic.*, 1959, **64,** 358-369.

Glock, C.Y. Participation bias and re-interview effect in panel studies. Un- published doctoral dissertation, Columbia University, 1950.

Glock, C.Y. Some applications of the panel method to the study of change. In P.F. Lazarsfeld & M. Rosenberg (Eds.), *The language of social research*. Glencoe, Ill.: The Free Press, 1955. Pp. 242-250.

Goldfarb, N. *Longitudinal statistical analysis*. Glencoe, Ill.: The Free Press, 1960.

Goode, W.J. *After divorce*. Glencoe, Ill.: The Free Press, 1956.

Havighurst, R.J. Problems of sampling and interviewing in studies of old people. *J. Geront.*, 1950, **5,** 158-167.

Hess, R.D., & Handel, G. *Family worlds: A psychosocial approach to family life*. Chicago: The University of Chicago Press, 1959.

Jerome, E.A. Age and learning—experimental studies. In J.E. Birren (Ed.), *Handbook of aging and the individual: Psychological and bio- logical aspects*. Chicago: The University of Chicago Press, 1959. Pp. 655-699.

Jones, H.E. Consistency and change in early maturity. *Vita humana*, 1958, **1,** 43-51. (a)

Jones, H.E. Problems of method in longitudinal research. *Vita humana*, 1958, **1,** 93-99. (b)

Kendall, Patricia. *Conflict and mood: Factors affecting stability of response*. Glencoe, Ill.: The Free Press, 1954.

Lazarsfeld, P.F. Problems in methodology. In R.K. Merton, L. Broom, & L.S. Cottrell, Jr. (Eds.), *Sociology today*. New York: Basic Books, 1959. Pp. 39-78.

Lazarsfeld, P.F., Berelson, B., & Gaudet, Hazel. *The people's choice*. New York: Duell, Sloan and Pearce, 1944.

Lazarsfeld, P.F., & Merton, R.K. Friendship as a social process: A substantive and methodological analysis. In M. Berger, T. Abel, & C.H. Page (Eds.), *Freedom and control in modern society*. New York: D. Van Nostrand, 1954. Pp. 18-66.

Lenski, G.E., & Leggett, J.C. Caste, class, and deference in the research interview. *Amer. J. Sociol.,* 1960, **65,** 463-467.

Macpherson, J.S. *Eleven-year-olds grow up.* London: University of London Press, 1958.

Streib, G.F., Thompson, W.E., & Suchman, E.A. The Cornell study of occupational retirement. *J. soc. Issues,* 1958, **14** (2), 3-17.

Taietz, P. Role relationships and the modification of the expression of attitudes in the interview. Unpublished paper, Department of Rural Sociology, Cornell University, 1960.

Terman, L.M., & Oden, Melita H. *The gifted group at mid-life.* Stanford: Stanford University Press, 1959.

Thompson, W.E., & Streib, G.F. Situational determinants: Health and economic deprivation in retirement. *J. soc. Issues,* 1958, **14** (2), 18-34.

# SECTION II

*Substantive Studies*

# CHAPTER 30

*Social System and*
*the Problem of Aging*

GERRIT A. KOOY

      A major contribution of general sociology to the study of the processes of aging is to place them in the perspective of the total social system and its culture. Research in general sociology results in knowledge—on a high level of abstraction—about principles and trends of general validity in human society. At the same time, sociologists also contribute, without having to abandon their objectivity, to solutions of cultural and social problems. These two approaches present a dilemma, because the development of abstract principles does not necessarily contribute to the solution of practical problems.

      This dilemma is particularly prominent in attempting to extend our insight into the status and role of aged people in modern Western society. The aged millions in Western society are by no means a culturally homogeneous group. The sociologist can be asked, therefore, whether, given this diversity, it is of any practical value to analyze their status and role in relation to the basic structure and dynamics of modern Western society. In our judgment the answer to this question should be affirmative. This answer was the starting point for this paper in which I try to realize the sociologist's twofold aim—bringing empirical knowledge to a high level of abstraction and attempting to explain problems and issues. Furthermore, we believe that the understanding of contemporary social systems requires historical comparison. The past plays a part in every contemporary social and cultural pattern. Even when it is almost forgotten, the past acts as a guide for all we do. For this reason I shall consider the traditional as well as the contemporary status and role of aged people.

Material in this chapter is closely related to an intensive program of sociological research on marriage and family life. This research resulted in two publications, *Het veranderend Gezin in Nederland* ("The Changing Nuclear Family in the Netherlands," Kooy, 1957) and *De oude Samenwoning op het Nieuwe Platteland* ("The Traditional Household in the Modern Countryside," Kooy, 1959), both of which throw light on the changing status and role of the Dutch aged during the past seventy-five years.

## THE TRADITIONAL HOUSEHOLD
## IN THE MODERN COUNTRYSIDE

This study deals with the agrarian population of Achterhoek, one of the sandy districts of eastern Holland. It is part of the province of Gelderland, situated east of the Yssel River, which had been a barrier to contact with the western coastal districts. The German border lies to the south and east. Achterhoek makes up an area of roughly 1,740 square kilometers; its present population is about 295,000. During the twentieth century, industry has expanded rapidly in this district, and the population of a number of towns increased within a short period. In 1875, Doetinchem and Winterswijk, for instance, had 6,500 and 7,500 inhabitants respectively; both towns now have populations of more than 25,000, indicating the dynamic social character of modern Achterhoek. From market centers without any urban outlook, Doetinchem and Winterswijk grew to towns similar to other vital small towns in the Netherlands. As could be expected, urban life has radiated to the rural surroundings. Three-quarters of a century ago Achterhoek was an isolated borderland, but today it interacts significantly with the larger society.

Population centers with more than 10,000 people are still exceptions in Achterhoek. The majority of their population is rural, and for these rural residents agriculture is the main source of income. The agricultural enterprises, as in other districts of Holland, vary in size. Besides poultry farms of one or two hectares, there are also farms of fifty (approximately one hundred acres) or more hectares. However, the large majority of farms are small, according to European standards, and labor is provided entirely by the farmer and his immediate family or relatives. The average size is about eight hectares, and, because of their size as well as their mixed character (field crops and/or cattle-breeding), they require much human power. All capable members of the household usually participate in the work, and even labor requiring a great deal of physical strength is done by women.

The composition of the farm household differs greatly from that in the Dutch coastal provinces. In several towns there are "extended-family" households on more than 50 per cent of the farms. Such a household comprises not only the nuclear family—the married couple and their unmarried children—but also a group of relatives. Sometimes the household includes a brother or sister of the husband or his wife; in this case it is a two-generation extended family. Sometimes a young nuclear family lives and works with either the parents of the farmer or his wife or with one of their parents, making a three-generation household. Four-generation households can also be found, but they are in the minority (2 per cent).

The excessive isolation of Achterhoek lasted until the end of the nineteenth century. Contacts with surrounding areas were few and of little importance. Practical possibilities of breaking this regional isolation were highly restricted, and the internal social structure reinforced it. It remained a district with its own social character and a way of life which was markedly different from that of Holland's coastal districts and somewhat different from that in adjacent Dutch and German areas.

There was not only regional insulation, but also local isolation. Interaction and communication between local units were far more restricted than in other districts of Holland. The individual had little identification with the regional society; he felt himself to be a member of a local group, and the world he trusted ended at its boundaries. The district was comprised of scores of "neighborhoods," sociogeographical units of a very special character that have never been known in northern and western Holland. This general form of social organization is not unique to Achterhoek and has been known in other parts of the Netherlands and in areas of western Germany. In Achterhoek, however, it retained its extremely isolated character until the end of the nineteeth century.

### Development of the Neighborhood

The general character of the old Achterhoek neighborhood is best understood in terms of its historic development. It represents a very old pattern of community life which closely resembles the march (German, *Mark*), the origins of which are still obscure. Clearly the march existed before the reign of Charlemagne (768-814). It was a small community of free colonists, sharing rights and rules related to the management and use of a walled-in territory. It maintained communal landed property in addition to the individual landed property of the march's members. The size of each march differed, but it usually covered an area of ten to fifteen square kilometers. A wall indicated the border, so those who approached it were aware of the barrier separating it from the outside world. The land within the march's borders was only partially cultivated. Very often the virgin forest was not cut down, nor was the moor cleared in the border areas. All full members of the march had a claim to the uncultivated territory. According to the rules and personal needs, anyone could chop wood, dig turf, or tend flocks there. The cultivated area usually comprised one or more closed blocks of fields, occupied by various members of the march. The farms were situated on poor land around these blocks, with shabby dwellings for men and animals.

The development of feudalism in the early Middle Ages curtailed the independence of these originally sovereign communities, but even when a march came under the domination of a lord it kept its closed character. After 1795, when the French arrived in the Netherlands, the seignoral rights were revoked, and the marches recovered their special charters. From 1830 to 1850, the central government distributed the communal property, although not fully in accord with the wishes of the marches. Although the system of communal property was thus destroyed, there was no essential change in the life of these small communities, and the march system persisted. The march—now a neighborhood—remained a strongly insular community ruled by its own traditional standards.

It is evident that at least until 1870 Achterhoek was a traditional, static, and isolated society. In addition, the material dependence of the community on poor soil necessitated long workdays and prevented economic stratification which might have served as a foundation for social and cultural change. There was no internal impulse for change, and ideas, conduct, and pattern of social relations remained the same from one generation to the next.

The average inhabitant of Achterhoek was born in or near the neighborhood, grew up there, married (if possible), tried to gain some economic independence, and died after a life of hard labor and simple living. The traditional order in this small world was supported by material dependence on the neighborhood group and relatives, the limited intellectual development of the individual, the homogeneity of the community, the intensive social control, and the probability, intensified by insulation, of rules' hardening into inviolable standards. Even today, three institutions—church, family, and neighborhood— vitally influence the life of the individual in Achterhoek.

In the social life of the neighborhood the church plays and has played an important part, extending its influence beyond the purely religious sphere. For example, the parson or verger conveys useful information for the economic welfare of the agrarian population. He might announce that farmer Sikkink has a sow with piglets for sale or that farmer Vorkink wants to sell a colt. Formerly, young and old gathered to tell each other the latest news before or after the service, and for some attending church was the only occasion to go out. Going to and coming from services, the young people wandered in quiet hidden spots where they could make love.

Although the church was an important institution in neighborhood society, it does not mean that the moral standards were determined primarily by it. It is doubtful that churchgoing in the neighborhood stemmed from deep personal religious needs. Open infidelity was considered a serious deviation from normal social behavior, but the individual's Christian feelings were never really put to the test. Thus, regular participation in church activities did not necessarily indicate complete acceptance of Biblical Christian morality.

Even today, relatives and neighbors have more influence on individual behavior than the church does. The family had—and, to some extent, still has—rights of decision concerning marriage, and even the choice of a partner was not considered the exclusive responsibility or right of an unmarried man or woman. In this type of communal situation, each marriage has a tremendous influence on every member of both families of an engaged couple, causing significant changes in the personal relations of many relatives who customarily cooperate economically and socially. A marriage could harm or benefit all these relatives. There were no serious objections to sexual liberties among youth, but marriage could not be based on mutual attraction or romantic love. A marriage was primarily a labor contract, the terms of which were reinforced by the fact that the young couple did not often settle independently. They tended to live with one of the families, usually the husband's.

The traditionally unromantic marriage, coupled with the lack of personal ambition and sober life in Achterhoek, produced children regularly. Because the parents had to spend most of their time working in the farmyard or fields, the responsibility for raising the children fell to the grandparents. They transmitted the skills of the farmer and housekeeper. The extended family with its variety of generations and relatives, not the parent-children unit, controlled the education and dominated the behavior of the family.

The neighborhood also controlled the family unit, inhibiting its independence of action. Its importance was only slightly less than that of the extended family. It was not founded on neighborliness in the narrow sense; historically, neighbors were people who accepted certain mutual duties pertaining to common law. Thus, although neighborliness was terminable in principle, great care was taken not to break the bonds by quarreling. There was no fixed rule for choosing the number of households in the neighbor group. Four or five and fourteen or fifteen represented the upper and lower limits. Interaction and communication within this group was very intensive, but these relations were not based primarily on friendship. Personal compatability was not needed to meet such requirements of neighborliness as assisting at births, weddings, or funerals in a neighbor's household; helping in difficult situations; or visiting and receiving neighbors in winter. If the need arose, neighbors would not hesitate to discipline the child of someone else within the group.

### The Changing Neighborhood

The traditional neighborhood still existed in Achterhoek until around 1875, when a new era started. The isolation was broken, bringing in the influence of the outside world. Integration into the life of the larger community was necessary, but the old local standards did not immediately collapse from intensive contact with a more dynamic society, alien to Achterhoek.

Profound changes in the conditions of life occurred which made the traditional social standards somewhat dysfunctional. However, loyalty to the neighborhood remained strong, the extended-family household was not questioned in principle, and the bonds of neighborliness were not broken. The neighborhood's role in setting standards gradually decreased, but the process was only partially apparent.

Since the last quarter of the nineteenth century the position of this district of the Netherlands has altered considerably. Achterhoek, once known as the "backward corner" because of its insulation and immobility, now has a different viewpoint. The contributing factors are many: improved and extended roads, accelerated private and communal transportation, increased educational facilities, mass communication, and new agricultural methods. It is hard to say which of these factors is of greatest importance, for each one seems to be a precondition of the others. Achterhoek's own creativity has also played an important role. The accomplishments of Achterhoek's population during the past seventy-five years are rooted in new outlooks on life, both individual and group.

In 1875, concrete roads connected only places of importance. The total length of concrete roads in the district was fewer than 600 kilometers; today it is more than 3,200 kilometers. The old sandy roads, dusty in summer and muddy in winter, have been paved, and hundreds of kilometers of good cycling paths have been laid. At the beginning of the twentieth century the population's horizons were expanded when horses were substituted for oxen. Then came the bicycle, which proved to be an excellent means of transportation for Achterhoek. After World War II, the autobicycle came into use among the less prosperous people. Today, some farmers own cars, although they are in the minority. Around 1880, transportation was facilitated by an extension of the railways and the advent of the tramway. Railroad service has been extended further, and tramways replaced by buses. Today Achterhoek has efficient and frequent bus service. Most people in the neighborhoods live close to bus stops, and they can reach distant places in a short time.

Many secondary and vocational schools have been established since 1875. The neighborhood is informed of daily events by newspapers, radio, and sometimes even television. Each family receives one or more newspapers, magazines, and technical journals; at least the neighborhood inn has television. In 1875 no newspapers were read in many neighborhoods.

The introduction of fertilizers about 1900 broke the vicious circle of low soil fertility. Thus a poor farm that had meager possibilities for animal-breeding is today a relatively prosperous enterprise for cattle-breeding or poultry-farming. In 1875 the small farm seldom produced a surplus for market, but today production surpasses by many times the needs of a farmer's household. The present value of mixed farming in Achterhoek is equivalent to that of the long prosperous enterprises in the animal-breeding districts. Today the average Achterhoek cow annually yields more than 4,000 liters of milk with a fat content of 3.6 per cent or more.

Achterhoek eagerly accepted the invitation from the world beyond its borders. The stability of the neighborhood, formerly the controlling force in community life, was shaken by its intercourse with the modern world of material benefits and technical improvements. Despite these changes, however, there was a desire to maintain the traditions and standards of the neighborhood. Compared to the coastal areas, Achterhoek is still old-fashioned. On the coast, the nuclear family acts independently in determining how much of contemporary civilization it wants. Cooperation among neighbors is rare. In Achterhoek, however, the tradition of the neighborhood persists although group loyalty is weakening. Neighbors have developed individual interests, and professional service is beginning to replace community cooperation for arranging a wedding or ploughing a field. The younger neighbors especially look on communal duties as a burden. Accustomed to selecting their own friends and entertainment, they prefer something more intimate than a traditional wedding feast attended by 300 neighbors and would rather spend their money on improving their homes and farms.

### The Position of the Aged

The status and role of the aged in the neighborhood have changed considerably since Achterhoek has been caught in the stream of modern Western development. In the traditional neighborhood, most older people were dependent because of their increasing disability, but the social position of the elders was still very influential. The elders held a high rank in the closed community, and they were treated with profound respect, born of sincere affection. Their will held like an unwritten law for the younger generation. In family affairs, in the neighborhood, in the church, and in the community as a whole, the views of the oldest generation—although not formally ordained— were conclusive.

In the traditional neighborhood, the high rank of the elders was reinforced by the community's desire to preserve its customs, a collectivist mentality, the Christian command to respect age, and the proprietary rights of the older generation. Almost every person in the community was economically dependent on his parents during the parents' lifetimes. It was exceptional for a farmer to furnish his son or daughter with the means to start his own farm during the farmer's life. If the children did not work with some other family, they worked at their parents' farm in exchange for board and lodging. In principle they could free themselves from this dependence, and unusually ambitious children sometimes gained their freedom. But they gained it at a considerable price, for those who left their parents' homes were disinherited and seldom gained true independence.

Despite the elders' respected age and position, they lived comfortably with members of the younger generations. Normally they had family obligations to all the members of the younger generations. Strong affections grew up between the oldest and the youngest generations, for grandparents usually spent more time with the children—and, of course, indulged them more—than the parents did. Outside the household, little happened in which the elders did not participate. They were always invited to weddings, visits, community evenings, and other neighborhood celebrations.

Thus in the neighborhood of the past the elders were restricted only by limitations imposed by time. Advanced age did not reduce the number of institutional roles played by a person. Indeed, the character of the Achterhoek community created a dominant role for the aged. (Recent grandparents, for instance, often accepted their new position without giving up their important parental status and role.) Old age meant higher rank in the community. Many people gained their complete independence only after the death of their parents.

In the contemporary neighborhood almost all older people live with their relatives under one roof.[1] As in the past, their influence is still very strong within the household, and the attitude of the younger people toward them still indicates affection and esteem. Outside the household, many members of the oldest generation still play important parts in the community. It might, therefore, appear that the traditional position of the elderly has not significantly changed

[1] In 1956 we investigated the composition of all households on farms of three or more hectares in twenty-three Achterhoek municipalities (10,024 households). It appeared that 4,658 (46.5 per cent) of these households were organized as extended families. These were most frequent in northeastern Achterhoek. In Ruurlo, 61.9 per cent (301 of the 486 households) included a nuclear family unit plus one or more relatives.

within the neighborhood society despite enormous changes in community life since the last quarter of the nineteenth century. This conclusion, however, conflicts with the actual situation.

In the neighborhood of the past, the family was incorporated with the more powerful extended family, which, in turn, was closely integrated with the neighborhood and the church. This arrangement was not considered injurious to the integrity of the nuclear family. On the contrary, the situation was normally considered beneficial. Institutionalized relations were reinforced by moderate individual aspirations. Subordination to or cooperation with others, as long as they accepted the traditional values of the community, were seldom resisted. Since World War II, which played its part in this matter, the nuclear family's resentment toward the other relatives, especially toward the aged, has been increasing. The family has taken on a new value. We interviewed many farmers and countrywomen between the ages of twenty-five and forty-five. From their remarks (below), it is obvious that they oppose extended-family households, especially those with older people in them:

I do not support living with the extended family members.

Father does not trust anything beyond his hands, and the other generation never gets a chance. Such a life does not have any advantage.

Marriage can be fully enjoyed only when husband and wife are together.

Those who have experienced the disadvantages of living with their extended family cannot help speaking differently about this matter from people who never had any such experience.

Living with relatives is entirely wrong because a young woman feels like a maidservant. Previously she accepted this, but the younger generation does not.

In the households I know the atmosphere shows that these people should not live together. The person who has married into this extended family suffers the most. The older people do not give up their authority. The younger ones are [treated] no better than servants.

The elders do not wish to see children punished. A great deal of trouble is often raised about chickens and children. The same with clothes and shoes.

After receiving your invitation for this evening's group interview, I did not dare to show it to my mother-in-law.

A woman taken into an extended family loses her personality. Very often she cannot lead her own life because of the domination of her in-laws, especially her mother-in-law. The loss of personality is common.

You have to become a grandfather in order to be permitted to bring up children.

In my opinion only a mother and father should have authority over their children.

These statements express very well the feelings of the majority of married people of the middle generation who have lived or are still living within an extended family of the older generation.

The same frustration can be seen in recent building patterns; farmhouses are being remodeled for two households. Although still under one roof, the younger and the older generations now lead lives of their own. Almost without exception, the initiation for the rebuilding is taken by the younger generation. Many of them hesitate a long time before daring to propose separate households. The proposal is usually accepted, but seldom wholeheartedly. It comes like a slap in the face to the older people. To the question, "Don't parents ever think of the welfare of their children?" the parents answer, "Why this ingratitude for all the things we have always done for you?"

The frustration of the middle generation and the remodeled farmhouses have significant effects on the rank held by older people. They indicate the elders' loss of authority. The breakdown of neighborhood society resulted in the discovery of the value of the nuclear family and in the subsequent weakening of the traditional power of the older generation in the extended family. Considering that the traditional authority of the elders outside the extended family always rested on their power within the family, it is not surprising that older people are also losing authority in the neighborhood. Even if they can keep their disproportionate representation on the boards of various modern associations, this authority will gradually decrease.

The older people in the traditional neighborhood society participated in all the recreational activities of the community. As isolation diminished, however, their participation gradually lessened. As long as the neighborhoods were isolated, entertainment for young and old was found in the community. Now the younger generation (those from fifteen to fifty) seeks its entertainment outside the local society, attending meetings, football matches, horse shows, movies, and the like in the growing towns. In the neighborhood itself, football clubs, theater companies, choruses, and other societies are springing up, supported almost exclusively by younger people.

The broadening of neighborhood society gives opportunities for interaction and communication to all ages, but considerably fewer to older people. As a result, personal isolation for the elders replaces the community isolation. In general, the older people are restricted to their own age group.

For generations, the problem of old age was primarily biological; today it is often social and cultural. Growing old means losing rank and becoming an outsider in the small society with which the individual has always identified himself. Achterhoek, despite all its changes, is still an agricultural community. The contemporary problem of aging, therefore, is not peculiar to an industrial community.

## THE CHANGING NUCLEAR FAMILY

This study attempts to show all the relevant sociological and psychological changes that have affected Dutch family life in the past fifty years. Far-reaching changes have taken place in marriage and family life. The conclusions of this study rest on data collected from varied sources: personal experience, the Dutch Central Bureau of Statistics, regional sociological investigations, and fiction in which the Dutch family plays an important part. A composite picture of the changing Dutch family was created from these sources.

It is important to realize the extent to which relations between the nuclear family and its surrounding social environment have changed. During the past half century, the Dutch family has become increasingly individualized. This trend started slowly in Achterhoek after World War II, although it was under way much earlier and more intensely in other districts. In the first half of the twentieth century, the family began to liberate itself from the communal bonds which, although previously important, were now considered obstructions to the family's own needs and wishes. The individualized emancipated Dutch family, however, does not live entirely apart from its social surroundings. Individual families often have strong ties to relatives, neighbors, and the church, but not with all relatives and all neighbors, for ties are now based on personal feelings. Today the words "relative" and "neighbor" have new connotations. Once the prevailing concept for family and neighborhood relations was *Du und ich in wir* ("you and I in we"), whereas now it is more nearly *ich in Dir und Du in mir* ("I in you and you in me"). The contemporary family interests itself in this relative or in that neighbor, but it might also turn away from them. Individualized families are not necessarily isolated families, although this individualism tends toward emotional introversion. As far as the relation between the individual family and the church is concerned, the family accepts church discipline on the basis of free choice and inner conviction, although the situation is often such that a person cannot help conforming to church standards.

The ever growing individuality of families in the Netherlands has been encouraged by many factors: increasing individualism, sometimes in the form of social Darwinism; romantic love; economic stratification; greater purchasing power; more extensive internal migration; larger cities; "massification" (the inability of people to realize traditional goals and maintain moral standards because of conflicting social opportunities); social mobility; better educational facilities; changing social controls; and declining church attendance.

The individualism is self-confident and frequently aggressive, rising from opposition to a society in which the individual has to conform to "natural" bonds. It is a state of mind which denies all compulsions except those of the individual's conscience and emotions. This individualism appeared as early as the eighteenth century, but only in certain so-called enlightened intellectual circles. In the nineteenth century, it came forth and continued to do so in the twentieth century despite the rise of collectivism. Individualism is the ideological foundation of the bourgeoisie, that, contrary to Marxist predictions, is still growing. Tinged with social Darwinism, this individualism is a radical doctrine, taking the individual as a measure for all things. This kind of individualism makes it difficult for a person to subordinate himself to traditional group discipline. Romantic love—glorified, although extramarital, by the medieval nobility—flourished in the twentieth century as a basis for and condition of marriage. Today, marriage is a matter of emotion (*Neigugsehe*), making uninvited intervention in matters of marriage and family relations intolerable.

Economic stratification increased considerably in the Netherlands in the twentieth century. In 1899, 33 per cent of the workingmen were employed in agriculture; today the number has dropped to 12 or 13 per cent. Meanwhile occupational opportunities are increasing; the common occupational interest of the family and the neighborhood, like the traditional economic interdependence of the extended family, is diminishing. When family purchasing power expands, economic dependence decreases. Goods and services can be bought for money rather than borrowed from neighbors. Inland migration generally decreased; in 1900-1904 there were sixty migrants for every 1,000 people in the population, whereas in 1954 there were forty-three. Migration over longer distances, however, kept increasing. The growth of industrial and mining centers caused many workers to move to districts of a totally different character from those of their birth. The famous Philips factories, for instance, have drawn non-Roman Catholic workers to the Roman Catholic district of East Brabant. Mobility of labor reinforces individualism of families. The geographical distances become too great to keep alive neighborhood loyalties and traditions. In the new neighborhood, the extended family, if it is accepted at all, meets with much reserve.

The Netherlands has undergone significant urbanization in the twentieth century. The individualism of the family is reinforced by many factors in the towns. Some of the older cities are growing less rapidly than the total population, but smaller places, even the villages, are expanding. Eindhoven, for instance, had a population of 20,000 in 1899; today it has more than 150,000. Brunssum had 1,200 in 1899 but now has 25,000. In 1899, 35 per cent of the Dutch people lived in municipalities of fewer than 5,000; in 1958, only 12 per cent lived in such municipalities. Thus the over-all proportion of the population living in relatively undifferentiated social environments has decreased considerably in the twentieth century.

"Massification" is the inability of people to realize traditional goals and maintain moral standards because of continuous confrontation with conflicting social and cultural possibilities. The massified individual is an opportunist. He accepts the daily changes that are most in keeping with his subjective needs. Fashion is a good illustration of massification. This tendency has been marked in the twentieth century, and the foundations of the traditional hierarchy of relations, like the subordination of the family to other institutions, are being shaken by it.

Social mobility has also increased substantially in the Netherlands. A large number of lower class children rise above the positions of their parents, especially through education. Extended educational facilities have not only augmented the chances for social mobility, but have also contributed to self-confidence and independence. The tendency for occupations to be hereditary has declined, again diminishing the dependence on family and neighborhood. General compulsory elementary education was introduced in 1900. Still more important was the growth of secondary schools. As a result of all these changes, children today differ in conduct from their parents and grandparents; they are more self-confident, less conservative, and increasingly aware of new opportunities.

As formal social control increases and face-to-face control decreases, the individual tends to suit his standards and behavior to influences beyond his horizon. Formal social control has increased considerably in the twentieth century. Newspapers, books, films, radio, and television are ever more eagerly used, and their themes by no means stimulate maintenance of local traditional ties. Mass communications are considered a threat to the existing bonds of the church, and churches have attempted to meet this threat by establishing denominational radio corporations, film censorship, and newspapers (Roman Catholic and Protestant). Abandoning the church reduces family participation in church activities and weakens the sacred aspects of family and neighborhood life. By 1899, 115,179 people (2.2 per cent of the population) had abandoned the church; by 1947, this number had grown to 1,641,214 (17 per cent of the population).

The factors influencing individualism within the family differ in strength from one community to the next, depending on specific social environment. The strongest individualism is found among urban middle-class families, whose behavior and aims become, in turn, models for the general population. Apart from the hereditary and financial aristocracies whose families have been individualized only to a small extent especially in relation to extended-family ties, the level of individualization is in proportion to the social status of the family. The situation is vaguer in rural districts. Farmers and farm workers usually show less individualism than the rest of the rural population, but in these two groups striking differences are noticeable. For example, Achterhoek farmers still accept, at least for the sake of appearance, living with extended-family relatives and maintaining the duties of neighborliness. This is also true of the majority of the rural population in other eastern sandy districts. The farmers' families in the coastal districts, however, are not usually less individualized than the middle-class families of the larger cities.

The individualization of families in the Netherlands is accompanied by growing governmental intervention in family life. Respecting the newly won freedom of the family, the government endeavors to protect the family and improve the family's welfare. The original intent of this support was not to aid the nuclear family as a specific structure; the government is concerned almost exclusively with financial care for the individual, not the family. Nevertheless, the authorities are convinced of the value of the nuclear family. As direct financial aid increases, so does nonfinancial aid. Social aid for the family is becoming one of the most important aspects of social work. Perhaps the Dutch division into denominational groups is the most important reason that private religious organizations take major responsibility for this work. They perform it, however, in close cooperation with and with strong financial support from the government. The government's concern for the family emphasizes the importance of the individual family, indicates the enlarged role of the government, and records acceptance of new standards in a new situation. The government acts as a guardian of family interests, but a guardian who, unlike the traditional extended family, neighborhood, and church, lets the family determine its own interests.

The increasing individualism of the family has a degrading effect on the older people in the extended family. The command of the older generation in extended-family matters or with particular members has decreased as rapidly as the individualism of the family has grown. The aged find fewer possibilities for interaction and communication. There is a parallel change in status as well as in role, making old age a burden to many people for whom it was a privilege a few generations ago.

At the beginning of the twentieth century, it went without saying that out of love and esteem the nearest relatives would provide medical care for the aged. Even today the aged expect support and care if it is needed. Their relatives, however, feel burdened by the presence of the aged and their insistence on making their influence felt; standards differ, and this leads to problems. A family taking care of the husband's or wife's parents finds it necessary to lay down the rules of the house to which the older people must resign themselves. Older people think things ought to be changed back to the way they were because everything was so much better when they were young. But the older generation also has ambivalent feelings. Out of respect for their age, the elders expect certain traditionally defined rights, but they also seem willing to accept the right of the younger generation to lead its own life. In some instances, the members of the younger generation emphasize their desire for complete independence, but they often feel guilty about their aging relatives, especially their parents. These ambivalences make the present status of aged people in the Netherlands still more problematical.

The declining importance of the neighborhood has also lowered the position and role of the aging. What are the status and role of the aged in today's church life? A majority of the older generation complains that the officials of the church pay too little attention to the needs of the aging. Radio broadcasts of religious services do not compensate for the almost total lack of personal contact with ministers. This alienation, of course, is certainly not attributable only to the trend away from extended toward individual family life. Many older people who avoided contact with church officials in their younger years develop, as they grow older, expectations with respect to the churches. The social structure of church life has definitely changed, however.

## CONCLUSIONS

Should our conclusion be that in the Netherlands of the twentieth century the aging incur an increasing isolation and loss of status? Although this conclusion seems right, further research of a different kind would be necessary in order to ensure accuracy.[2] For purposes of this chapter, it is far more important to consider whether the research which has been done can contribute to the enlargement of the sociologist's view of the social and cultural aspects of aging in modern Western society. The developments in Achterhoek need not be typical of the Netherlands, and the developments in the Netherlands as a whole need not be typical for Western society in general, but they are both subject to factors which influence all Western societies. It seems reasonable, therefore, to advance the following hypotheses about the status and role of the aging in contemporary Western society:

1. Where the local society loses the character of a closed society, the status and role of the aged will decrease. The number of institutional roles played by aged people increases in the absolute sense, but decreases relatively. Lowered status and decreased role, though not always perceived as such by the aged themselves, cause frustration among older people.

2. As the individual grows older, he attaches a higher value to prestige and harmonious interaction and communication in his extended-family group, but breakdown of the local community reduces the importance of the extended family and increases the importance of the nuclear family. Thus, the elders lose their main point of support not only for their needs of self-maintenance, but also for self-development.

3. Older people's feelings of frustration and uncertainty will grow stronger as communities become more modern because of the factors discussed above.

[2] Our aim was to develop hypotheses, based on field work in one of the Western countries, about the status and role of the aged in Western society in general. Behind his desk the sociologist can easily invent hypotheses, but to hypothesize without a realistic approach leads to field work the results of which are not at all in accordance with the costs. Also, the more hypotheses, the greater the chance that testing them all at the same time will be impossible.

These hypotheses are suitable for testing, perhaps along lines now being followed within the International Union of Family Organizations. A working group is trying to gain a better insight into the values and living conditions of rural Western families by investigating, in several European countries, numerous rural communities with varying degrees of isolation and individualism. Such an investigation certainly will be profitable, both theoretically and practically. As far as the Netherlands is concerned, our impression is that measures have been taken to serve aging people, but the government is insufficiently informed about their needs. We do not mean to reproach the government. Social gerontology, a branch of applied science, needs to be more rapidly developed, however, if it is to benefit the aging. For this reason, testing the hypotheses suggested above would be particularly useful.

### REFERENCES

Kooy, G.A. *Het veranderend gezin in Nederland* ("The changing nuclear family in the Netherlands"). Assen: Van Gorcum, 1957.
Kooy, G.A. *De oude samenwoning op het nieuwe platteland* ("The traditional household in the modern countryside"). Assen: Van Gorcum, 1959.

# CHAPTER 31

*The Older Person in
Family, Community, and
Society*

RUDOLF TARTLER

Although old age and the aging processes have
been objects of scientific research for a long time, sociology entered
this field rather late and is still encountering the question of whether
old age is a legitimate sociological problem. This question can be
answered affirmatively with the following arguments.

Modern sociology seems to be the science of crisis; its themes
are furnished by social ruptures and changes which make the patterns
of social life instable. At the moment when the "unreflected self-
evidentness," as it has been called, of the behavioral regulatives of
social life do not function correctly any more—which is the only reason
that the social aspect is liberated for scientific analysis—the human
need for orientation turns to new sources of knowledge. This is the
well-known process of scientization in modern society.

Sociology was relatively late in subjecting sections of human life to sociological analysis because these were exactly the sections which had been especially secure, safe from reflection of any kind. It is hardly surprising, therefore, that the sociological aspect of old age suggests itself as a subject of research at the very moment that old age is becoming a social problem in our society. A special place in this analysis is occupied by the concept of the "nature" of man, the biological conditions of life which have until recently been, and even today are partially, classified as constituents of the biological-natural endowments of man. It is to modern anthropology in America—above all to Malinowski, Mead, and Benedict—and Germany—to Scheler, Plessner, Gehlen, Portmann, and others—that we owe the knowledge of man's extreme variability, which is distinguishable by different forms and always marked by significant social factors. After the "plasticity of man," as Gehlen called it, was known, the way was paved for discovering the social determinants of human life.

The aim of sociology in studying the social aspects of old age is to show the social factors which, with other factors, determine the situation of the old person in the present social structure. By empirical research it is necessary to correct the still widespread conviction that old age depends exclusively on biological and somatic processes and, at the same time—what is possibly even more difficult today—to delineate the accepted social images and models to show that they are oriented to a completely different set of social circumstances.

In this chapter, I shall try to indicate the social determinants of the present situation of old age in three spheres of life—family, work, and leisure.

## OLD AGE AND FAMILY

Over and over again, especially in Europe, the complaint is heard that old age is constantly being separated from the family. This complaint is a reproach directed almost exclusively against the younger generation, which is said to shrink from its moral duty of offering the aged a peaceful evening of life within the family. What is usually ignored in this connection is that the far-reaching changes in our social structure during the last decades have been accompanied by equally radical changes in the family structure, so that it is really questionable whether keeping the aged in the family is the optimal situation.

In the preindustrial society of agrarian and craft occupations, the family was a structure made up of three to four generations; the old members were either grandparents or elderly unmarried members of the family. In this family setting it was possible for the generations to live together without any particular strain, since the family structure was a productive unit, a form of which we find only suggestions in the farmstead or small workshop of today. In such a family setting, based on productive functions, the old people had their more-or-less well-defined roles and economic and social functions which were necessary for the existence of the whole family. Work and occupation, as well as leisure and social life, took place almost exclusively in the sphere of the family. At the same time, the family was, with few exceptions, the sole bearer of social security, protection, and welfare, all of which have long since been transferred to the state's bureaucratic institutions.

In this preindustrial family system, old people were not only sustained, protected, and cared for, but, according to their individual capabilities, they also contributed to the subsistence and care of the family. Added to the social-economic functions of the old people was the role of the testator, a role whose importance cannot be overestimated. Psychological categories are inadequate in grasping the significance of the testator. It was the institutionalized principle of "function preserving heritage" (Schelsky, 1960, p. 322) that rendered the security of the old unquestionable and made their place within the family a matter of course. At that time it was the family, not the individual, that was the bearer of functions, rights, and duties in most of the spheres of human life; these were handed down from generation to generation.

The enormous spread and popularization of psychology in bourgeois society and the trend to psychologize all domains of life make it difficult to avoid the mistake today of seeing the preindustrial relation of old age and family and the relations of the individual family members as an emotional, social, and moral idyl—which it never was. Unlike the family relations of modern times, the connections and intercourse within the family were primarily determined by common property and social status, according to productive, functional patterns. Such emotional factors as sympathy, love, and affection, which seem to us to be the basis of family life, were of little importance compared to the family solidarity that was conditioned by function and thus was life-sustaining. Selecting a marriage partner and marriage based exclusively on love are very recent developments and, as new research seems to show, only a passing attitude of the late bourgeoisie. Furthermore, the valid norms of the relation of the generations as forcible social expectations have stabilized, if only externally, the intercourse of the generations.

Finally we must conceive the social role of old age as a gradual social retirement and a loss of rights and duties which was at best compensated by general social and moral prestige. By reading historical sources in fiction and law cases pertaining to the reservations made by the parents (*Altenteil*), it is not difficult to show that aging within the family could be full of tensions and complications.

The essential differences between the modern family system and the preindustrial family, whose structure has only been sketched here, are obvious. One of the most decisive facts, and actually the starting point of the processes which changed the old family pattern, is working away from the home, which is becoming a matter of course for an increasing part of the population. Working in purely productive or administrative units—a situation created by industrial production and bureaucratization of the administration and economy—was accompanied by the separation of the home (the private sector) from work (the public sector). In this way, functions that were formerly attached to the family are now transferred to institutions external to the family, so that they become neutral or even hostile to the family unit. In short, the steadily increasing loss of familial functions can be comprehended as a decisive development in the modern family. Disintegration of productive functions is followed by the loss of other functions; tasks formerly carried out at home have been taken over by industry and trade. In European metropolitan areas, for example, only 25 to 28 per cent of the laundry is done at home, and no laundry facilities are installed in modern, newly built housing blocks. Since the introduction of compulsory school attendance, education, which was formerly obtained at home, is increasingly delegated to public institutions. Recreation, amusement, celebrations, and feasts almost all take place in business enterprises catering to these needs. Above all, as the services of social welfare increase, the former benefits of familial solidarity and social security have been taken over by officially organized institutions or large bureaucratic organizations. Hospitals, old-age homes, and social welfare and charitable organizations care for and treat sick and old people.

This development is, by the way, accelerated by the progress of the sciences—that is, by increased efficiency—a fact that is often not noticed. Because of the precision of modern medicine, therapeutic measures can be successfully applied only by experts in special institutions equipped with the necessary apparatus. People now expect to take full advantage of these modern facilities. Thus it is no longer a matter of course for the aged to expect optimal care and therapeutic treatment at home in the family; they go to the hospitals. In short, and in a somewhat exaggerated way, one could say that birth and death, the most decisive phenomena of human existence, are excluded from family life. (In Germany only 28 per cent of the births in 1958 took place at home, and these were among the rural population.) The result of these and other processes is that the functions which originally supported the aged in the family are being lost.

Because of the modern employment situation, the family is reduced to a unit of two, or even one and one-half, generations. What is left is the personal community of the parents and the minor children, the so-called small family, which is always concerned with keeping down the number of family members in relation to their economic situation since every member who does not contribute to the existence of the family by outside employment must become an economic burden to the family. The economic dependency of children is indisputable, but the unemployment of the aged, who are out of the labor market, is felt as an economic burden, and the family is no longer willing to bear, and, in many cases, no longer capable of bearing, the burden. This small family, which, after the children have found employment, sometimes is reduced to the husband and wife, is no longer considered incomplete, but is considered the typical family (von Friedeburg & Weltz, 1958).

At this point it must be stressed that many studies have shown that the aged suffer from material dependence on the family if they are not able to offer some material compensation. Where, on the other hand, the income from pensions or other revenue enables the old to offer some compensation, individual life patterns and expectations have, in many cases, generated the desire of the old to be materially independent of their children.

As the care of the old must by necessity be delegated to large organizations which are independent of the family and free of crisis and private and social emergencies, the function of the aged as testator for the family is becoming increasingly unimportant because old-age pensions are not inheritable. Because of the collective security systems, old age assumes an individually and familially indifferent status in its economic and material existence.

There are, however, certain countervailing tendencies in this structural development. In some of the monographs from the study carried on by The Institute of Economic and Social Science of the University of Munster, it was evident that the people who receive old-age pensions can sometimes barely defend themselves against the covetous demands of their children's families. In such cases, old people are again important, because of the pension by which they can contribute to the family income, thus taking over the doubtful role of a testator for life. A family arrangement of this kind, however, by no means contributes to the relief of intergeneration tensions.

Thus the tendency to separate the aged from the family is not exclusively or primarily generated by the younger generation; it also comes from the old themselves and their desire for independence and self-sufficiency. This is a desire, however, which allows for no major conclusions about the relations between the old and the succeeding generations. Ernest W. Burgess (Chapter 32, *infra*) has also pointed out that, from the standpoint of the parents as well as of their children, separate housing for each generation is considered the most satisfactory. Official statistics also show the growing tendency toward separate households for young and old.

Against these developments in our society, it is constantly claimed that, precisely because of the situation of the modern family as it has just been depicted, the reintegration of the old into the family should be furthered for various reasons. The aged person is assigned the social functions of educating, fostering tradition, and consciously cultivating human relations. Reuben Hill (1957) is of the opinion that the modern family, because it is no longer a productive unit, must seek new functions in the cultivation of personality and human relations. Von Bracken (unpublished) and Groth (1954) express the conviction that for the family, as well as the whole society, old people must foster education and tradition. The importance of the grandparents' educational functions is supported mostly by the fact that the parents, although competent to educate their children, do not have the time necessary to fulfill this task because of the exacting requirements of modern occupational life.

This conviction is gaining momentum because of the steadily increasing number of working mothers and the numerous incomplete families from which the father was lost during the war. Awaiting old people is a task which had been fulfilled by them in the larger family unit of the preindustrial era and which they could also fulfill in our times. The analogy of the present educational situation with that of the past is, for more than one reason, incorrect. What is ignored is that educational functions were not confined to the grandparents or the parents in the former family corporation, but were performed by many other members of the family. In modern times it is only the parents who are concerned with the education of their children. More decisive than the reduction of multiple educational influences, however, is the fact that the aged—leaving the peasant family aside—have lost all the well-defined independent functions and competence they possessed in the old family system; these functions did not encompass the education of the grandchildren.

The complete loss of economic and familial functions and the consequent desire of the old to assume new tasks within the family are the reasons that grandparents today are devoting themselves to the education of their grandchildren much more intensively and consciously than ever before. Thus, the education of the grandchildren becomes a consciously reflected and directed performance on the part of the grandparents; this was certainly not the case with the educational contribution of the older generation in former times. Although grandfathers or grandmothers met their grandchildren in different and well-defined roles and functions in former times—of which only a few were oriented toward the grandchildren (grandmother as story-teller, grandfather as toy-maker)—the relation between grandparents and grandchildren is now that of a consciously or unconsciously isolated pedagogic role.

This situation almost always brings about tensions between grandparents and parents because the educational goals and standards of the parents as well as, and sometimes even to a higher degree than, those of the grandparents, have lost their traditional security and indisputability and are replaced by scientific or pseudoscientific education. It is possible, however, that the convictions and recommendations of psychologists and teachers do not often agree with those of the grandparents, apart from the fact that psychology and pedagogy are in a state of continuous experimentation and progress. This leads to a situation in which, as Stern (1955) says, the younger generation often complains about the unappreciativeness of their old parents, their demands, and their tyranny which makes them interfere with everything—the education of the children, the behavior of the marriage partner, the life style, the management of the household, and so on.

It seems to me that the fundamental difference in the educational situation between the dynamic society of the present and the static society of the preindustrial era is the fact that, with increasing mobility, the educational goals and, therefore, the principles of education are constantly changing. In a static society where the patterns of the whole society and, therefore, the roles of the adults change only gradually, from generation to generation, the parents, as Riesman (1956) says, "train the child to succeed them" (p. 56). Against this background, Riesman quite rightly describes the present social conditions as being in such a state of continuous, enduring, and swift change that it is impossible to know, during the education of the child, under what social conditions he will have to behave and stand the test of life as an adult.

From this situation emerge two other tendencies which are important in the attitude of the parents toward education by the grandparents. The parents are losing that authority over their children which is based on tradition and recognition of traditional values, and so they fear, rightly or wrongly, that the grandparents might gain more authority than they have over the children. This is the reason that, in many cases, parents consciously or unconsciously, but mostly in a way that the children notice, undermine the authority of the grandparents. This deprivation of authority on the part of the parents, however, can be traced to another motive, the conviction that the old people might compel the children to accept behavioral patterns and attitudes which might prevent the children from successfully adjusting to the contemporary expectations of society. Riesman even says that grandparents today serve as examples of how little of real importance one can learn from them. Certainly this attitude is also significant in the problematic relationship between the generations which appears to be fostered by the necessity for adjustment after immigration, a problem which is possibly more acute in America than in Europe where such convictions are also present, but do not provoke acute conflict between the generations.

Even in families where the grandmother is in charge of the whole household and education of the child and the daughter or daughter-in-law is employed (in Germany there is a large number of war widows who must support the family), the situation of the family and the functional integration of the grandmothers cannot be compared with the role of the grandmother in the family of the preindustrial era. Modern employment creates a situation in which the separation of mother and child is much longer than it was under the working conditions of the preindustrial era. It follows that the child is almost completely in the custody of the grandparents and subject to their educational influences. This situation carries the risk that the grandparents might not be able to prepare the children for the realities of contemporary life because of their own outmoded convictions and attitudes. Greater and more frequent, however, is the danger that a rivalry springs up between the mother and grandmother since the child is naturally more attached to his grandmother because of his enduring and almost exclusive social contact with her.

This situation is further aggravated by the impact of popularized psychological and pedagogic discussions in the mass media about the problem of working mothers. Since this gives evidence of what the child might suffer when his mother leaves the house to go to work, these mothers cannot help having a permanent bad conscience. The result is that they try to compensate for this lack in the short periods when they are with the child. In this way the child is often subjected not only to differing, but sometimes to conflicting, educational influences. Thus we can say that the chances of the grandparents making a positive contribution to the education of the grandchildren are relatively small, except possibly when they visit or function in an exceptional situation.

Closely related to the educational functions of the aged in the family is the question of whether the aged could possibly become the preservers of tradition for the family and the whole society at the same time. It is not possible to treat the problem of tradition in any detail here. In spite of this, it should be evident that in our highly mobile society the aged can hardly become representatives of traditional behavioral and attitudinal patterns. The generations who are now old were forced to adjust their behavior to new situations created by the transformations which have probably been more intensively experienced in Germany than in the United States. The conviction, which is still widespread, that the role of the traditionalist is usually found among the old, whereas the role of the young is that of the revolutionist, might be true given static social conditions, but it is certainly not true of the modern situation, which is characterized by its eruptive and multilinear structural transformations. The older generation might be much more likely to readjust and adapt their behavior to new situations than the young.

Furthermore, the modern mass media present a much better and more complete source of historical information than individual experience. The press, movies, radio, and audiovisual documentation promise to deliver much more reliable and objective information than human memory, which is necessarily overloaded with impressions and experience and limited to a relatively small section of the reality in which it had the opportunity to participate.

Finally, it must be asked again whether and how far the transmission of traditional behavior within the family is a real accomplishment for a person in the setting of our mobile society.

These hints must suffice to illustrate the place of old age in the family. I should like to characterize the structural development as follows: the separation of the generations which we are observing in our society must be seen as the result of the loss of familial functions of the old. This leads to an overly close emotional involvement which, because of its permanence, severely impedes family life. Functional neutrality is the prerequisite for cultivating human relations and for satisfying the emotional needs within the family. Emotional strain will result when the individual is given no social role and function by which intimacy and cordiality are regulated and standardized in the intimate group. It is not the separation of old people from the family which deprives the old of their functions; rather, the development runs in the opposite direction. The separation between the generations occurred as a result of the loss of functions of old people within the family. And it must not be overlooked that by this separation the maintenance of positive familial relations is reached, a process that could be described by the motto, "intimacy through remoteness."

The desire of the old for independence and self-sufficiency must be conceived not only as the emancipation of the old from the family, but also as the emancipation of the aged from a typical old-age situation in which the older person is inevitably a member of the family who has, to some degree, lost his functions in this group.

## OLD AGE AND OCCUPATION

Although work does not encompass the whole of man's life in our society, the meaning of work for the life of modern man can hardly be overestimated. The social functions and stabilizing role of work for human existence are perhaps never more evident than in the situation of enforced unemployment. Work still satisfies a number of fundamental social needs which have become more important today than they were in former times. Modern society has, therefore, rightly been characterized as an occupational society in which the enormous importance of work is emphasized. Friedmann and Havighurst (1954) have drawn a very good picture in calling work the axis of life today.

The main function of work for modern man seems to me to be the primary guarantee of social and material security. It is hardly surpassed by any other accomplishment in determining social prestige and the possibilities of climbing the social ladder. (This might be less true in America than in Germany.) To a great extent, professional qualifications have already become an important means of production which are decisive for the economic status of the individual. Furthermore, work is the principal source of social contacts on which even private social activities frequently depend. Finally, a man finds in his work a primary, if not the only, reliable interpretative medium in a world that is steadily becoming more complicated and anonymous, and it is even relatively unimportant whether the outlook on life thus gained is correct.

### Work: A Stabilizing Force

Work has the social function of coordinating and confining the uncontrollable and intricate possible human activities to a more-or-less limited system of actions, and work thus plays an important role in helping the individual master life, even if it is felt to be a burden. In this way work functions as a relief because it helps a man establish himself in his environment through continuity of action in an occupational structure which is circumscribed by relatively constant means and goals. Thus the environment is stabilized, and the worker himself is stabilized in it.

The importance of a stable environment is that the "external hold" thus built up reacts internally in the individual. This relief is effected because, as Bürger-Prinz (1951) says, "The outside world is, as long as it is stabilized, conditioning the stability of the inside self. If I destroy the environment, the individual does not emerge the real person he is, but the personality is to a higher or lower degree also destroyed" (p. 229).

Although work is not the only means of attaining stability and relief, the individual's chances of satisfying these needs through his work are certainly optimal, especially as another important factor, necessity, is associated with it. At first, and most impressively, the necessity of working is earning a living. This primary necessity of human activity must have an unreflective character, since inactivity would threaten existence. The moral elevation of and emphasis on the value of work in modern societies is comprehensible only because of necessity. Work is consolidated into a general value, for direct success or failure is lost because of different occupational performances and social conditions. With every division of labor, the necessity of work is increasingly concealed and must be replaced by other sanctions of necessity. Thus every specialization—and this means constitution and specialization of vocations—will always be accompanied by the creation of socially supported sanctions of success and definitions of necessity. Professional ethos and morale then indirectly take over these sanctioning functions. Whether work is then, by religious transformation, ascribed a positive or negative role or whether it is regarded a curse or a blessing is relatively unimportant compared to its necessity.

Now, if the category "necessity" really constitutes a vital principle in relieving human existence, it is not probable that it can simply be loosened or renounced. It is presumed that it will be transferred from work to other spheres, namely to exactly those for which work is also evaluated as a pure means.

Realizing on one hand the importance of occupational activity for stabilizing the individual's environment and inner self and, on the other hand, the fact that retiring is the social act which today marks the beginning of the social status "aged," the problem is clear: today old age, in its social sense, means, for the majority of the working population, foregoing one of the most significant means of stabilizing environment and personality. In this connection, it must not be overlooked that most of the aged do not retire because they are old and incapable, but because social regulations relegate them to the status of old age.

Abrupt and complete retirement destroys important habits and institutional supports, interrupting the continuity of the individual's daily life and confronting him with a new situation which he has to tackle by altering his accustomed patterns of behavior. Instead of gradually entering a new phase of life, the aging person in our society is compelled to change his habits abruptly in order to stabilize himself in his new social environment.

In view of these facts—and setting technological, administrative, and economic considerations aside—why is this awkward situation not only generally tolerated, but also seemingly welcomed, by our society?

### The Security of Old Age

The image which encourages the idea of retirement is that of a socially secure person whose income is safeguarded by the state and who is free from constraint and want. A secure old age is one of the few functioning Utopias in our society. It is taken into account early in life and plays an important role in the decisions pertaining to occupation and the plan of life. In their study of old age, old-age insurance, and the worker, von Friedeburg and Weltz (1958) were able to show not only the high degree to which the desire for security influences the image of old age, but also how far life and occupation are oriented toward this security long before this stage of life is reached.

The idea of a secure old age is nourished by various sources. First, there is the still influential model of the bourgeois *rentier* with his secure existence. This is a bourgeois standard, yet it involves socialization. It is also a potent standard, so much so that the structural implications of socialization are likely to be overlooked. The bourgeois *rentier* was not able to lead his ideal life because he lived on his capital, but because he had, at the same time, social obligations and because he devoted himself to voluntary jobs or cultural interests—the activities dictated by his social rank. Furthermore, the secure life without work occupied the top of the social scale at that time, thus the *rentier's* old age did not constitute a break in continuity from his former way of life; to some extent it was a continuation, perhaps a more intensive enjoyment of a life with numerous obligations and functions. This picture of the *rentier* has been widely idealized in the imagination, but this evening of life, in the shade of the welfare oak (Benn, 1952, p. 46) is, of course, only part of the *rentier's* life. Furthermore the idyllic light in which the lower-middle classes especially see the security of old age has become a real mass restorative in our times.

This ideal, which is indiscriminately demanded by all political parties, has two decisive functions to fulfill in our increasingly bureaucratic and administrative apparatus in modern society: first, it serves as a symbol of secure aging, and, second, in so doing, it lends a legend to the collective measures of old-age insurance. Secure aging constitutes, moreover, one of the few effective social Utopias in our insecure and unstable modern society, and consequently instability and insecurity are obscured. The promise of security and stability in contemporary society is, however, either naïve or deceiving, most likely naïve.

### Old Age and Leisure

The incongruity between the ideal *rentier* and the social reality becomes evident when the ambivalent and endless discussions about leisure and old age are considered. Next to material security in old age, the inactivity of old age after retirement has attracted so much attention that the general problem of leisure seems increasingly superseded by the problem of leisure in old age. Obviously this discussion is based on the conviction that the *rentier's* way of life was essentially determined by leisure. Since, however, the modern concept of leisure, as well as the arrangments for leisure activities, has, as Schelsky (1957) says, "been produced by the separation of the sphere of work from the sphere of the home and the family, which is a constituent of industrial society" (p. 326), leisure complements work, pertaining to the time when the individual is not regulated by the necessities of work. This means that there cannot be any normal leisure time for the retired person and consequently no problem of leisure.

Rather, the retired old person has to tackle the task of finding a way of life without work. This means that his free time is in earnest because it must carry the total living of every day. Because of the complete loss of functions in other domains of life, all leisure activities are stressed; they are no longer playful, purposeless activity or recreation. Under these circumstances many leisure activities and hobbies very soon become meaningless, for they are continuous activities, no longer interrupted by the requirements of an occupation. Work might thus be a positive frustration, keeping alive the image of an ideal retirement as long as retirement does not occur.

Today the helplessness of the old is frequently observed when they face the task of filling their free time with a sense of vitality. As in many other instances, modern organizations are prepared to help the individual master this situation. The tendency to help through collective measures is common to the state, community, church, educational institutions, or business organizations. Today planned activity with the claim and promise of meaningful organization of free time is offered not only to the young and middle aged, but also to the old. Planned happiness for the aged is the goal; where it is to be found and how it is to be realized have been clearly expressed by Jerome Kaplan (155): "Diversion and entertainment as planned social life is a relatively new field insofar as the old are concerned. The possibilities offered are infinite" (p. 20).

Against this, warnings are heard about an excessively organized old age. Two conflicting views are juxtaposed: on one hand, there is the offer to enrich the life of the old by organized measures; on the other, there is the appeal to the freedom of the individual, who should fill his life with meaning and master it privately. Both intentions are objectionable when pronounced as absolute demands and generalizations. It is not probable that every old person is willing and in a position to realize the problems of life as such, nor is it to be expected that organized assistance will be desirable and elevating for all old people. It seems questionable to me whether the relatively small group of old people who depend on organized measures should serve as the only model for the assistance rendered to old age.

## PLANNING LIFE AND
## DAILY PERFORMANCES

What conclusions can be drawn from this analysis of old age, leisure, and modern sociopolitical measures to organize meaningful leisure activities for the old?

First we conclude that the meaning of life, which must also be imparted to the aged by social roles, is to be found in the unquestionable necessity of life. The surest way to impart this meaning is through the self-evident requirements of daily living. If meaning is to be accomplished by diversion from boredom, amusement, escape from isolation, or cultural stimulation even for a person who has not given much thought to it, then we must reckon with the fact that in this way the meaning of life becomes questionable—if it is not completely lost. Every policy and kind of assistance for old people must, therefore, aim at maintaining the meaning of life through continuity. Wisdom is not a proper goal for social planning, but can be achieved only by individual experience. It is, therefore, important to create for the old, social conditions which allow them to continue, as much as possible, the plan and order of their daily lives. To accomplish this, all efforts must be directed toward maintaining continuity with the complementary relation of work and leisure which existed before the beginning of old age. In old age a person is constantly confronted with unavoidable discontinuities which modern society imposes by isolation from the family and complete occupational separation through retirement. Thus attempts to organize the life of the aged must be aimed at preserving continuity in the other spheres of life, linking the enforced "new" life—the life without children and work—with the habits and security of life. Above all, is it feasible to make the continuity of work and leisure, perhaps in altered form, available to the old as a social role? The attempt simply to replace the occupational role with the leisure role by organizing play, education, and entertainment as the main activities and central meaning of life will certainly end in a dilemma.

Furthermore, it is not probable that simply entertaining himself will give the old person the psychological and social security which he needs if he is to find his place in, and feel that he belongs to, society. Therefore, all social roles must be regarded as more advantageous for the old if these roles keep him in touch with social processes and the members of other age groups and prevent the formation of an isolated world to which he may retreat. The world of the old—which is perhaps nowhere more evident than in an old people's home—is experienced as a forecast of death, since the old person's transfer to a useless group cannot give a feeling of necessity to the psychological and social meanings of his age. Thus the problem of meaning in old age becomes most evident when we analyze the relation of old age and leisure, and this problem should induce a critical review of the models which form the base of our social policy and well-meant measures for the aged.

In a society where age has only statistical value, age becomes an individual state. This is the reason that the attempt to restore age to its former social status must have a negative effect in our society. It handicaps the older person. Disintegration in old age will, therefore, most certainly occur when the social and sociopolitical measures for old people are built on a structure conceived under totally different social conditions and when they foster roles which have become illusions in our society.

## REFERENCES

Benn, G. *Die stimme hinter dem vorhang.* Wiesbaden: Limes-Verlag, 1952.
Bracken, H. von. Der alte mensch im familienleben. Rundfunkvortrag, in der Sendereihe "Der alte mensch in seinem lebensraum."
Bürger-Prinz, H. Psychiatrie und probleme der umwelt. *Studium generale,* 1951, **4.**
Friedeburg, L. von, & Weltz, F. *Altersbild und altersvorsorge der arbeiter und angestellten.* Frankfurt/Main: Europäische Verlagsanstalt, 1958.
Friedmann, E.A., & Havighurst, R.J. (Eds.), *The meaning of work and retirement.* Chicago: The University of Chicago Press, 1954.
Groth, S. *Das alter im aufbruch des daseins.* Frankfurt/Main: Neue Druck- und Verlagsgesellschaft, 1954.
Hill, R. Are we expecting too much of families? *Soc. Casework,* 1951, **32,** 153-155.
Kaplan, J. *Das alter als soziales problem.* Zurich: Rascher, 1955.
Riesman, D. *The lonely crowd.* New York: Doubleday and Company, 1956.
Schelsky, H. Die paradoxien des alters in der modernen gesellschaft. In *Festgabe für Friedrich Bülow.* Berlin: Duncker and Humblot, 1960.
Stern, E. *Der mensch in der zweiten lebenshälfte.* Zurich: Rascher, 1955.

# CHAPTER 32

*The Transition from*
*Extended Families to*
*Nuclear Families*

ERNEST W. BURGESS

The two preceding chapters, by Dr. Kooy and Dr. Tartler, are of particular interest to American sociologists. In my judgment, each represents a new facet of older people's intergeneration family relations in Western societies. The chapters are widely different in focus and research methods. Kooy is concerned mainly with objective changes taking place in intergeneration family relations, first in a selected closed neighborhood where the centuries-old, three-generation family household is only now breaking up and, second, in an analysis of the changes now taking place in the role of the aged in the extended-family grouping in Dutch society. Tartler directs his attention to a social psychological description of the relations among the three generations.

A closed neighborhood is a self-contained residential and

industrial community with intensive social relations within its boundaries and few social relations outside them. The district of Achterhoek, which Kooy studied because of its excessive isolation, remained, like an archeological layer, an insulated community, unchanged in its economic and social characteristics until 1875. Since then, intergeneration relations in these isolated neighborhoods have changed very slowly. In 1956, nearly half (46.5 per cent) of the investigated households were still of the extended-family type.

With the opening of the closed neighborhoods to outside influences, the nuclear family begins to free itself from the domination of the aged couple and to form an independent unit with changes in the social relations between the generations. Significantly Kooy notes that, with the emergence of the nuclear family, the older generation loses rank and becomes more or less an outsider toward the small society with which the individual had been identifying himself.

Certain questions, however, seem to me to be unanswered by this study. First, Kooy believes that in the past the members of the nuclear family did not resist incorporation in the extended family. Undoubtedly this is correct as far as overt behavior or open feeling was manifested, but was not this social system often frustrating to the son who had to delay marriage and management of the farm until his father's old age or death, to the sons and daughters who were forced to remain unmarried at least until middle age, and to the daughter-in-law under the rigid supervision of her mother-in-law?

Second, what changes, if any, have taken place in farming as a result of the independence by the nuclear family? Do these changes precede or follow the breakup of the extended family? Third, how many nuclear families reside in the three- or four-generation household? Fourth, what is the composition by members of the extended family living in one household?

The second part of Kooy's chapter, on the changes in the Dutch nuclear family during the past fifty years, gains much from comparison with the older system of the extended-family household that was widespread in rural areas of the Netherlands. Kooy analyzes the factors—growing individualism, romantic love, economic differentiation, rising purchasing power, increasing migration over long distances, the growth of cities, the increase of "massification," increasing vertical mobility, the extension of educational facilities, the changes in social control, and the mass abandonment of churches—which have been leading to the individualized Dutch nuclear family of today.

The abandonment of churches in the Netherlands is striking,

from 2 per cent in 1899 to 17 per cent in 1947. Compared to Scandinavia and other countries, this change seems to represent a small drop in church attendance, but the hold of the Dutch church still seems exceptionally strong to an American. It is of interest to know how effective the influence of the church and religion is in family relations.

In my survey of Europe, reported in *Aging in Western Societies* (Burgess, 1960), I was struck by the similarity of the gross changes in family relationships in all countries, according to their stages of industrialization and urbanization. In Europe, Great Britain and Sweden seem to be farthest along this course, with the United States the most advanced in the world.

As described by Kooy, the relations of the older and the younger generations appear ambivalent. The old parents still derive certain traditional rights from their age, but they also seem willing to accept the idea that the younger generation has a right to a life of its own. In the most advanced circles, however, the younger generation emphasizes its desire for complete freedom although the adult children feel guilty, particularly toward their parents.

Until very recently, this ambivalent attitude was also characteristic of intergeneration relations in the United States. It is now being superseded by the growing number of members of both generations who desire to lead independent lives.

The first two hypotheses stated by Kooy seem valid to me. First, where the local society loses the character of a closed society, the status of aged people will be lower, and their roles will decrease. Second, because the integration of the local society into a larger one reduces the importance of the extended family, the aged lose points— in fact, their main point—of support for their needs of self-maintenance and self-development.

The third hypothesis, that the frustration and uncertainty of the aged will grow stronger in the unlocked, dynamic community, appears more questionable. The increasing force of the individualizing factors Kooy enumerates may indeed increase the frustration of older people, but at a certain point the aged will tend to respond positively rather than negatively to the new social system. In the United States older people are already developing social roles and a style of life that are relatively independent of their children's.

In Great Britain as well as in the United States, society is much concerned with taking social action to meet the needs of the aging. In the Netherlands, partly under the sponsorship of the churches, about one thousand social clubs for the aging, with a membership of 11 per cent of the population sixty-five and over, have been established (Havighurst, 1960). We should also call attention to Kooy's conclusion that social gerontology needs to be developed rapidly to get more adequate care for the aged.

Tartler (Chapter 31, *supra*) explodes the myth that an idyllic relation between old age and the family existed in preindustrial society. This relation was not ideal, but the old family system was satisfying to the older generation, although oppressive to the younger one.

Tartler analyzes the factors—such as the separation of family life and work and the transfer of family functions to institutions—which undermined the extended family and led to the development of the modern family. The functions which the family surrendered—production, education of the young, and religion—formerly provided the activities of older people. He also points out how the care of older people in industrial society has by necessity been delegated to large organizations independent of and outside the family.

In a penetrating analysis, Tartler takes up the claim that grandparents, with their free time, would be competent for the education of children, especially since many mothers work outside the home. As bearers of tradition, grandparents should be the ones to transmit it. Having survived the crisis of unsettled existence, they should be able to steer the young.

Both Kooy and Tartler present a gloomy picture of the parents' and grandparents' role in rearing the child. The working mother has little time for the child and tends to overemotionalize the relationship. The father—if he is alive—spends even less time with the child and is often indifferent to him. The grandparents are functionless in their relation with grandchildren. Accordingly, the child's education is relegated to mass communication and its portrayal of violence, shooting, and patterns of heterogeneous conduct.

From my standpoint, this situation is probably all for the good, but Kooy and Tartler give an incomplete analysis. The desideratum in child development is the formation in children of a basic personality structure which corresponds to contemporary life. Obviously this cannot be imparted by parents, grandparents, or school teachers, at least not consciously or culturally. It has to be impressed upon the child by his reactions to his experience.

What is the situation to which the child will need to respond as an adult? It is a world of uncertainty, recurring crisis, patterns of heterogeneous behavior, brutality, possibly violence, leading from the cold war to World War III. It is a world of mechanization, increasing travel in space. It is a world of large organizations with scant consideration for the rugged individualist. This is the world which is forming the basic personality structure of modern children, at least those in the United States.

What are some of the conditions in the situations of children today which are molding their basic personality structure? First, there are the uncertainty and insecurity of the parents. In the past parents knew that their methods of child-rearing were right. Now they are plagued by questions: "It this the right thing to do?" "What would the book say?" Thus the child faces an uncertain environment in his relation with his parents.

There is also contradiction between what parents and others say and what they do. The child reacts to attitudes and behavior rather than to ideology. If children accept the ideas of their parents, the ideas do not enter into the formation of the basic personality structure, but are a rather superficial cultural overlay. These acquired ideas are something to be mouthed rather than practiced.

The influence of mass communication has already been commented on.

The influence of a mechanized world can be seen in the toys of boys, which now are far different from those of my childhood. Boys play with shotguns and engage in gang battles. Children, even some not yet two years old, know the different makes of automobiles.

Finally there is the influence of peer group. The games played by boys introduce them to adult life. Baseball requires team play but permits individual action. Football, however, is preparation for becoming an organization man, a necessary cog in today's industrial machine. Thus, the basic personality structure of today's children is being oriented to uncertainty, to violence, and to organized behavior.

The objection may be raised that Tartler's chapter and the second part of Kooy's chapter are not scientific; at best, they are "soft" rather than "hard" science. It is true that they give no statistics and present little or no data. Kooy frankly admits that his analysis was partially based on novels and personal observations of modern social life. If an inquiry promotes understanding and shows discernment and reflection, however, I am not troubled by the objection that it is not scientific. Social science, as I view it, is different from biology and physics, the research methods of which many social sciences like to take for their models of investigation. It is significant that the social sciences lie between biology and the humanities. The social sciences must, therefore, seek understanding as well as exact knowledge. Even more, they must have an understanding of their own phenomena before they can expect to gain significant knowledge by the application of rigorous methods to their data.

The essential contribution of the chapters by Kooy and Tartler is that they do give us an understanding of intergeneration relations as they are in the process of change. Now it will be possible, in the light of this new understanding, to make significant, rather than trivial, inquiries. Understanding thus paves the way for studies that are not only rigorously designed, but which also advance knowledge.

Kooy asks that social gerontologists, from their research, give guidance to society. What can be done for the welfare of the old? Tartler opposes all that is presently being done for the old and implies that, the less society does for the aging, the better.

Certainly great caution needs to be exercised in social action. I do not share Tartler's pessimism about a social world for the aging. It is not a retreat, but an opportunity. The aged are left out of groups at present. They need to participate in mixed-age groups, but even more in their own age group. In the organization of their peers they can obtain an identification, role, and status that may be difficult, if not impossible, to obtain in groups dominated by young and middle-aged members.

### REFERENCES

Burgess, E.W. (Ed.) *Aging in western societies.* Chicago: The University of Chicago Press, 1960.

Havighurst, R.J. Beyond "the family and work." In E.W. Burgess (Ed.), *Aging in western societies.* Chicago: The University of Chicago Press, 1960. Pp. 299-352.

# CHAPTER 33

*The Impact of Age on
Attitudes toward
Social Change*

ANGELO PAGANI

In 1960, I was charged with the direction of some field research sponsored by the public administration of Milan. It was carried out by the Centro Ricerche Economiche e Sociali (CENTRES). A first report of this research, with a complete analysis of one-thousand interviews in Milan and a general view of another one-thousand interviews in the rural area surrounding Milan, was included in the official Italian contribution to the International Congress on Technological Progress and the Italian Society held in Milan in June, 1960.

This is the most important research carried out in Italy in the field of social stratification. The survey probed attitudes toward work, social change, education, and social classes. In attitudes toward social change, particular attention was paid to changes in the conditions of life, work, qualities required to rise socially, the chances of social mobility, and the propensity to take risks. The main concern of the research was the opinions that lead to acceptance of the social change produced by technological progress in an industrialized area. The age, birthplace, occupational stratum, and level of education of the respondents were used as independent variables. This research also provides some important data for social gerontology and contains valuable suggestions for the study of the impact of age on attitudes toward social change.

Some methodological considerations, based on my personal research experience, have persuaded me that monographs about an aged population or some section of it could contribute little to understanding the social status of elderly people. Such studies lack a general context and tend to be purely descriptive, even in the best-designed research projects. It is preferable, therefore, to include the special problems of elderly people in a more general research project. This procedure combines the advantages of an intensive inquiry with those of general information permitted by a broader sample.

This chapter focuses on items from the more general study that were shown, in a preliminary inquiry, to be significantly influenced by age. Important items have to do with attitudes that reflect a sense of time, particularly a comparison with the time of the respondent's father.

TABLE 1
AGE DISTRIBUTION OF THE SAMPLE

| Age groups | Men | | Women | | Total | |
|---|---|---|---|---|---|---|
| | Number | Percent | Number | Percent | Number | Percent |
| Under 40 | 164 | 33.6 | 23 | 12.2 | 187 | 26.7 |
| 40 to 60 | 227 | 46.6 | 88 | 46.8 | 315 | 46.6 |
| Over 60 | 90 | 18.4 | 74 | 39.4 | 164 | 25.2 |
| No reply | 7 | 1.4 | 3 | 1.6 | 10 | 1.5 |
| Total | 488 | 100.0 | 188 | 100.0 | 676 | 100.0 |

The sample was drawn from the official register of the population and contained three main groups—the male heads of households, married women living with their husbands, and single women acting as heads of households. For present purposes, married women living with their husbands have been eliminated in order to give greater homogeneity to the analysis. Thus we are concerned with one male and one female group—whether single, widowed, living alone, or living with children—each member of which acts as the head of a household. The age distribution of the sample is given in Table 1.

A general question was introduced in the questionnaire: "Do you believe that today the conditions of life and work are the same or different from those effective in the times of your father?" This question was qualified in two ways. First, the comparison with the father's generation was related to an occupation that the respondent knew personally (the occupation of men and women in the labor force, husband's former occupation for widows, and father's occupation for women without work experience). Second, the general judgment about conditions was divided into housing, working conditions, economic conditions, chances for promotion, social relations, and education of children. The respondents were then asked to judge whether conditions in each of these categories were better or worse in comparison to their fathers' time.

The general results, as indicated in Table 2, suggest a predominantly optimistic view about the present. With the sole exception of "education of children," the highest percentage of replies falls in the category "better," that is, the respondents saw a distinct improvement.

### TABLE 2
### OVER-ALL DISTRIBUTION OF THE RESULTS

| Category | Better | Worse | Equal | No reply |
|---|---|---|---|---|
| Housing | 64.8 | 13.6 | 13.5 | 8.1 |
| Working conditions | 60.2 | 14.2 | 12.8 | 12.8 |
| Economic conditions | 51.0 | 24.6 | 16.1 | 8.3 |
| Chances of promotion | 44.1 | 22.9 | 17.5 | 15.5 |
| Social relations | 39.8 | 27.0 | 21.8 | 11.4 |
| Education of child | 12.0 | 50.3 | 11.7 | 26.0 |

If all replies for the six categories are grouped, 45.5 per cent recognize an improvement in the present situation. If we disregard the "no-reply" and the probably less reliable "about-equal" responses, the percentage which judges changes favorably rises to 54.1 against 35.9 with a negative view. Thus it appears that for about two-thirds of the respondents present conditions are certainly no worse than those of their fathers' times and that for most of them present conditions appear better. No relation was found between sex or birthplace and favorable replies. The higher occupational strata tend to have more favorable replies than the lower.

The interpretation of the results of this study raises a methodological problem. When we are faced with the interpretation of a set of opinions expressed by various groups of respondents, we can assume some correspondence between the opinions and experienced reality—that is, we can assume that the rate of positive evaluation of change increases with the rate of personal satisfaction experienced by the subjects. This simple interpretation, however, has to be further considered in relation not only to the reality experienced by the subjects, but also to their value systems. As Gunnar Myrdal (1962) expressed it, opinions are based on beliefs and valuations, not only on ideas about how reality is or was, but also on ideas about how reality ought to be or has been. It is extremely difficult to differentiate between the impact of beliefs and values in matters of this kind. We also have to consider the more refined interpretation proposed by Robert K. Merton (1949) in terms of expectancies. The positive or negative meaning attributed to experienced changes must then be interpreted according to the degree of correspondence with the respondent's main expectations. People can appraise a change that goes in a positive direction as negative if the magnitude or speed of change is less than their expectation. We recognize, of course, that this kind of interpretation requires a set of objective data that have not generally been available in field research and were not available in this research. In the present analysis, we have limited the interpretation to two elements, the objective situation experienced by the various groups and the general elements of their social outlook.

If, for example, we wish to explain the impact of occupational level on the rates of positive evaluation in housing, we can follow two lines of argument. First, we can assume that improvement of the objective situation in housing has been greater than it was in the times of the respondents' fathers, primarily among the upper and middle occupational strata, professional and urban middle classes, and even in the higher section of the working classes. Second, the impact of housing considered as a cultural value or consumption pattern has been greater in the lower-middle classes, which in the former generation were still obliged to live in insufficiently equipped and badly placed houses. Combining these two observations—the verified, objective change and the diffusion of a new cultural value—we begin to under-

TABLE 3
HOUSING

Do you think that present housing conditions are better than, worse than, or equal to those of the time of your father?

| Age groups | Present conditions are | | | | | | | | | |
|---|---|---|---|---|---|---|---|---|---|---|
| | Better | | Worse | | Equal | | No reply | | Total | |
| | Number | Percent | Number | Percent | Number | Percent | Number | Percent | Number | Percent |
| Under 40 | 122 | 65.2 | 30 | 16.0 | 25 | 13.4 | 10 | 5.4 | 187 | 27.7 |
| 40 to 60 | 205 | 65.1 | 40 | 12.7 | 41 | 13.0 | 29 | 9.2 | 315 | 46.6 |
| Over 60 | 105 | 64.0 | 21 | 12.8 | 24 | 14.6 | 14 | 8.6 | 164 | 24.2 |
| No reply | 6 | | 1 | | 1 | | 2 | | 10 | 1.5 |
| Total | 438 | 64.8 | 92 | 13.6 | 91 | 13.5 | 55 | 8.1 | 676 | 100.0 |

stand the different rates of positive replies. The situation of the lowest occupational stratum can also be evaluated in light of the fact that the objective changes in housing for manual workers have been less important and less general and that the diffusion of new consumption habits has not yet reached the bulk of the working class. There are no significant differences in rates of positive reply in housing according to age (Table 3).

The question on working conditions referred to the total work situation, with special attention to working hours, the physical environment, stress and fatigue on the job, and social relations in the plant. Sixty and two-tenths per cent of the respondents indicated that social changes have substantially improved working conditions. The lowest occupational stratum seems to be somewhat less favorably impressed by these changes. At first glance, this result seems somewhat curious in relation to actual objective changes that have occurred in working conditions. We would expect to find a higher rate of positive attitudes among the occupational strata where the working conditions have been improved with greater speed and to a greater extent, that is, the industrial workers. The results are contrary to this and show that the highest rate of positive responses are found among such groups as clerical and commercial workers whose conditions, even if improved, have changed in a relatively negligible way.

This lack of correspondence between the factual situation and attitudes can, perhaps, be explained by two considerations. First, we can assume that the question, even though it was specified in a personal way, suggested a more general response and evaluation of social change in this field. Such a consideration might explain the expression of a positive attitude for the groups which have not experienced any very effective changes. Second, the groups who have in fact experienced the highest rate of positive changes tend to have the most critical attitudes toward industrial society, a mark distinguishing the lower working class, at least in Italy. Such a consideration accounts for the relatively low rate of positive answers in this group.

In terms of age, respondents over sixty and respondents under forty tend to have higher rates of positive response (63.4 and 65.8 per cent, respectively), whereas the forty-to-sixty group has somewhat lower rates of positive response (55.6 per cent), as indicated in Table 4.

This finding suggests that the span of time to which the comparison is applied is not always relevant in understanding the

## TABLE 4
### WORKING CONDITIONS

Do you think that present working conditions are better than, worse than, or equal to those of the time of your father?

|  | *Present conditions are* | | | | | | | | | |
|  | Better | | Worse | | Equal | | No reply | | Total | |
| *Age groups* | Number | Percent | Number | Percent | Number | Percent | Number | Percent | Number | Percent |
| Under 40 | 123 | 65.8 | 24 | 12.8 | 21 | 11.2 | 19 | 10.2 | 187 | 27.7 |
| 40 to 60 | 175 | 55.6 | 51 | 16.2 | 47 | 14.9 | 42 | 13.3 | 315 | 46.6 |
| Over 60 | 104 | 63.4 | 21 | 12.8 | 16 | 9.8 | 23 | 14.0 | 164 | 24.2 |
| No reply | 5 |  |  |  | 2 |  | 3 |  | 10 | 1.5 |
| Total | 407 | 60.2 | 96 | 14.2 | 86 | 12.8 | 87 | 12.8 | 676 | 100.0 |

attitudes expressed. Indeed, assuming that any differences are accounted for by the period of time that divides the respondent from his father would be the simplest way of coping with the relation of age distribution to attitudes. The respondent might be stimulated to call objective transformations changes when the span of time he has to consider is extended, as it is with elderly people. The above results, however, tend to throw doubt on such an interpretation. Other considerations can be introduced to explain the difference between the middle groups and the older ones, but these considerations can be more clearly presented in relation to economic conditions.

Again, more than half the respondents considered changes in the economic field (standards of living, level of wages, rates of economic development, and so on) positive. Occupation, birthplace, and education appear to bear no relation to the distribution of responses. On the other hand, the age distribution does show some differences. As indicated in Table 5, respondents over the age of sixty tend to think that present economic conditions are better than the younger groups do (59.1 per cent of those over sixty in contrast to 47.6 per cent of those under forty). Similarly, the older people are less likely to say that conditions are worse (15.2 per cent over sixty contrasted with 28.4 per cent under forty. These results contrast sharply with the traditional idea that the elderly are culturally bound to the past, adverse to change, and inclined to judge the present as generally worse than the past. Of course, these results are not sufficiently extensive or well-tested to be accepted as definitive proof in this regard; they are, however, valuable in suggesting a new line of interpretation.

In the past, elderly people certainly had a more hostile attitude toward change. There are important differences between the idealized aged man of the humanistic tradition and the typical elderly person today. An attitude of hostility toward social change can be an active position shared by the majority of older people only when the pace of social progress is kept within certain limits. When change affects the entire society and tends to be assumed as a major cultural value of the whole population, the attitudes of older groups undergo substantial modification. Elderly people do not become alienated from society. Of course, their rate of acceptance can vary according to the times and specific patterns of social integration, but, in the long run, elderly people appear to succeed in participating in the main societal values. However, we still have to explain why it is the elderly

TABLE 5
ECONOMIC CONDITIONS

Do you think that the present economic conditions are better than, worse than, or equal to
those of the time of your father?

*Present conditions are*

| Age groups | Better | | Worse | | Equal | | No reply | | Total | |
|---|---|---|---|---|---|---|---|---|---|---|
| | Number | Percent | Number | Percent | Number | Percent | Number | Percent | Number | Percent |
| Under 40 | 89 | 47.6 | 53 | 28.4 | 33 | 17.6 | 12 | 6.4 | 187 | 27.7 |
| 40 to 60 | 154 | 48.9 | 86 | 27.3 | 49 | 15.6 | 26 | 8.2 | 315 | 46.6 |
| Over 60 | 97 | 59.1 | 25 | 15.2 | 26 | 15.9 | 16 | 9.8 | 164 | 24.2 |
| No reply | 5 | | 2 | | 1 | | 2 | | 10 | 1.5 |
| Total | 345 | 51.0 | 166 | 24.6 | 109 | 16.1 | 56 | 8.3 | 676 | 100.0 |

group which appears to have the most favorable attitude toward the economic changes of the past generation.

In an earlier piece of research, using a sample of residents of an old-age institution, I was surprised by the insistence with which the respondents made reference to the times of their youth and emphasized the positive changes in working and economic conditions which had come about since then. This attitude was shared by nearly all the respondents and was expressed even when the interviewer did not ask questions of this kind. At that time, I tended to disregard the finding, considering it related to the special status of these people in an institution. It appeared that the residents tried to justify their position by claiming to have lived in times more difficult than the present. The motivation, it seemed, was their desire to divest themselves of any responsibility for their relative failure in occupation. The results of the present inquiry suggest that the tendency to devalue conditions during the time of their first working experience is indeed connected with an attitude of self-esteem. It is not simply a matter of covering up for professional failure, but of calling attention to the greater amount of hard work and incentive which was required of them in comparison with the requirements today.

As far as chances for job promotions are concerned, less than half of the respondents (44.1 per cent) think the changes in this respect have been favorable. We might expect to find the same situation in relation to age that we found in economic conditions, but such is not the case. One aspect of the method used in gathering the data may throw some light on the situation. There were two rather similar questions, one relating to career and one relating to occupational mobility. The intent was to get at a more direct personal or "internal" view of mobility and to get a more general judgment about the "external" mobility of the social system. The wording of the first question may not have been sufficiently clear to bring out this distinction. The uncertainty of the answers is indicated by the high rate of "no reply" (Table 6).

When we look at views about changes in social relations, we find that positive attitudes are still lower, with 39.8 per cent of the respondents seeing the changes as favorable. By occupational level, the highest and lowest levels evaluate the changes more positively; the middle levels take a less favorable view of them.

Older people are less likely to say that present conditions are better than are younger people, with only 31.7 per cent of those over

### TABLE 6
### CHANCES OF JOB PROMOTION

Do you think that the present chances for job promotion are better than, worse than, or equal to those of the time of your father?

*Present conditions are*

| Age groups | Better | | Worse | | Equal | | No reply | | Total | |
|---|---|---|---|---|---|---|---|---|---|---|
| | Number | Percent | Number | Percent | Number | Percent | Number | Percent | Number | Percent |
| Under 40 | 85 | 45.4 | 49 | 26.2 | 31 | 16.6 | 22 | 11.8 | 187 | 27.7 |
| 40 to 60 | 132 | 41.9 | 80 | 25.4 | 53 | 16.8 | 50 | 15.9 | 315 | 46.6 |
| Over 60 | 76 | 46.4 | 24 | 14.6 | 32 | 19.5 | 32 | 19.5 | 164 | 24.2 |
| No reply | 5 | | 2 | | 2 | | 1 | | 10 | 1.5 |
| Total | 298 | 44.1 | 155 | 22.9 | 118 | 17.5 | 105 | 15.5 | 676 | 100.0 |

## TABLE 7
## SOCIAL RELATIONS

Do you think that contemporary social relations are better than, worse than, or equal to those of the time of your father?

*Present conditions are*

| Age groups | Better | | Worse | | Equal | | No reply | | Total | |
|---|---|---|---|---|---|---|---|---|---|---|
| | Number | Percent | Number | Percent | Number | Percent | Number | Percent | Number | Percent |
| Under 40 | 95 | 50.8 | 45 | 24.1 | 31 | 16.6 | 16 | 8.5 | 187 | 27.7 |
| 40 to 60 | 121 | 38.4 | 89 | 28.3 | 72 | 22.8 | 33 | 10.5 | 315 | 46.6 |
| Over 60 | 52 | 31.7 | 48 | 29.3 | 43 | 26.2 | 21 | 12.8 | 164 | 24.2 |
| No reply | 1 | | 1 | | 1 | | 7 | | 10 | 1.5 |
| Total | 269 | 39.8 | 183 | 27.0 | 147 | 21.8 | 77 | 11.4 | 676 | 100.0 |

### TABLE 8
### EDUCATION OF CHILDREN

Do you think that the education of today's children is better than, worse than, or equal to that of the time of your father?

*Present conditions are*

| Age groups | Better | | Worse | | Equal | | No reply | | Total | |
|---|---|---|---|---|---|---|---|---|---|---|
| | Number | Percent | Number | Percent | Number | Percent | Number | Percent | Number | Percent |
| Under 40 | 29 | 15.5 | 94 | 50.3 | 17 | 9.1 | 47 | 25.1 | 187 | 27.7 |
| 40 to 60 | 28 | 8.9 | 171 | 54.3 | 43 | 13.6 | 73 | 23.2 | 315 | 46.6 |
| Over 60 | 31 | 18.9 | 72 | 43.9 | 25 | 15.2 | 36 | 22.0 | 164 | 24.2 |
| No reply | – | | 3 | | 1 | | 6 | | 10 | 1.5 |
| Total | 88 | 13.0 | 340 | 50.3 | 86 | 12.7 | 162 | 24.0 | 676 | 100.0 |

sixty giving "better" answers, contrasted to 50.8 per cent of those under 40 (Table 7).

Older people are somewhat more likely to say conditions are worse, although the differences in this resepect are not pronounced, since older people also have a somewhat greater tendency to say conditions are about equal or to give no reply in this field. Actual changes in this field have certainly made striking modifications on the whole social context of life. Elderly people experienced these changes at a time when their social personalities were already formed, and it is therefore not surprising that they would tend to resent the new patterns more than other groups do. From a cultural point of view, elderly people, who met these changes later in their lives, have been less likely to assimilate the cultural values inspiring the changes.

The last area explored related to the care and education of children. This is the field in which the rate of positive attitudes reached its lowest level, 13 per cent. Respondents in the age group from forty to sixty are most likely to think the changes have been for the worse, and those over sixty are the least likely to think so, although the differences are not large (Table 8).

One can imagine that in the middle-aged group are found those for whom there has been the greatest amount of difficulty in rearing children and giving them an education. Elderly people are less involved in educational problems. Thus they are not so fully engaged because of the psychological distance which they have from the questions in this field.

Table 9 sums up the results by rates of positive attitudes, eliminating the "no-reply" responses.

Although the differences are not large, the favorable rates of elderly people exceed the general average in all the categories except housing and social relations. In work, economic conditions, chances of job promotion, and the education of children, the elderly group shows the highest rate of positive answers.

If we assume that age is a determinant of attitudes toward change, we would expect to find a more coherent trend, an increasing or decreasing course correlated with age. That is the situation for only two of the fields studied, economic conditions and social relations. For the first of these, the rate of positive attitudes increases with age, and for the second it decreases. The internal coherence of the data is disturbed by the groups in the middle-aged bracket. For three categories (working conditions, chances of job promotion, and education of children), the rates for the middle-aged group are the lowest. In only one category, housing, is their rate the highest. These facts suggest that we should not look for a unitary interpretation relating changes of attitudes to ages of respondents. We must dismiss this ambitious attempt and limit our efforts to more monographic considerations.

TABLE 9
SUMMARY OF DISTRIBUTION OF RESULTS BY AGE

| Categories | Age groups | | | |
|---|---|---|---|---|
| | Under 40 | 40 to 60 | Over 60 | All ages |
| Housing | 68.9 | 71.6 | 70.0 | 70.5 |
| Working conditions | 73.2 | 64.1 | 73.7 | 69.1 |
| Economic conditions | 50.8 | 53.2 | 65.5 | 55.7 |
| Chances of job promotion | 51.5 | 49.8 | 57.5 | 52.1 |
| Social relations | 55.6 | 42.9 | 36.4 | 44.9 |
| Education of children | 20.7 | 11.6 | 24.2 | 17.1 |

We can make no important suggestive interpretations in the categories of housing and education of children. In the former the differences are so low that they are insignificant, and in the latter elderly people are too far from the immediate problems of education. The difficulties in adjusting to new patterns of social relations which occurred after these elderly people had become social beings readily account for the relatively negative attitudes in that respect. The relatively higher rate of favorable attitudes toward economic and working conditions cannot be explained by the more extended span of time to which the comparisons apply, because the replies of the older group are fairly similar to the replies of the youngest one and differ markedly only from the middle-aged group. We have emphasized that older people's hostility to social change ceases to be active when the elderly are integrated in a society that assumes change is essential. It has to be interpreted as an effort to assign a new value to their occupational and social achievements. They emphasize the difficulties they had to face in acquiring an education and skills, getting a job, and making a living, and at the same time they recognize that the situation with which young people are now confronted is better. Hence, the elderly aim to underline the differences of the two social backgrounds. Much of this emphasis is clearly the desire for higher esteem and a favorable judgment of what the elderly person has been able to achieve.

Recent studies in the field of social stratification have indicated the utility of combining field research on empirically measured objective trends of social mobility with analyses of opinions about mobility. Some indication can be gained about the correspondence of social consciousness to different rates of social mobility. The problem of verifying the degree of cultural consciousness about change compared to measurable rates of change has special importance for societies in transition.

For these reasons, the present research questioned opinion about chances of social mobility ("Generally speaking, do you believe it is less difficult or more difficult for a capable person to rise in the social scale today in comparison with the time of your father?"). The focus is on intragenerational mobility, the movement in the social scale that people can achieve within their lives. In general the results show a prevalence of positive answers, as indicated in Table 10. Sixty-one and two-tenths per cent of the women and 54.3 per cent of the men recognized that the chances of social mobility are now greater than they were at the time of their fathers.

In terms of age, the elderly group had the most favorable attitudes, followed by the youngest and middle-aged groups, in that order. Again, if it were a matter of objective experience, we would expect a direct relation between age and favorable response, but the situation of the middle-aged group goes against such an interpretation. If, on the other hand, we assume that it is largely a matter of accepting the cultural value of change, we would expect an inverse relation between favorable response and age. Thus, we come back to the same explanation that we had in the results of the economic question. The elderly again express a need for defense and desire for social esteem, and, in so doing, they underplay the chances of social mobility during their youth.

Thus, it is clear that our interpretations do not all derive from one general principle. The results do not suggest any general correlation which would relate rates of positive attitudes in a direct or an inverse direction. There is no simple relation between age and attitudes toward social change. We are again confronted with the

TABLE 10

CHANCES OF SOCIAL MOBILITY

Generally speaking, do you believe that it is less or more difficult for a capable person to rise in the social scale today, compared with the time of your father?

| Age groups | Present chances are | | | | | | | | | |
| | Higher | | Lower | | Equal | | No reply | | Total | |
| | Number | Percent | Number | Percent | Number | Percent | Number | Percent | Number | Percent |
| Under 40 | 107 | 57.2 | 65 | 34.8 | 9 | 4.8 | 6 | 3.2 | 187 | 27.7 |
| 40 to 60 | 166 | 52.7 | 123 | 39.1 | 12 | 3.8 | 14 | 4.4 | 315 | 46.6 |
| Over 60 | 103 | 62.8 | 47 | 28.7 | 5 | 3.0 | 9 | 5.5 | 164 | 24.2 |
| No reply | 3 | | 2 | | 1 | | 4 | | 10 | 1.5 |
| Total | 379 | 56.1 | 237 | 35.1 | 27 | 4.0 | 33 | 4.8 | 676 | 100.0 |

necessity of elaborating different interpretations for different relations to various aspects of change. There is a strong suggestion that we need to revise the traditional idea that elderly people are culturally removed from the present and hostile to change.

## REFERENCES

Merton, R.K. *Social theory and social structure*. Glencoe, Ill.: The Free Press, 1949.
Myrdal, G. *An American dilemma: The negro problem and modern democracy*. New York: Harper and Row, 1962.

# CHAPTER 34

*Attitudes toward Special*
*Settings for the Aged*

ROBERT W. KLEEMEIER

In this chapter, we focus on attitudes toward special settings for the aged.[1] There are many reasons that this area is important, and the following five seem sufficient to justify interest in this topic. First, public attitudes toward such special settings as retirement communities, homes for the aged, hospitals, nursing homes, and other group settings influence public acceptance and support of these living arrangements for older people. Second, attitudes have significant influence on the demands made for such facilities by old people themselves. Third, a study of such attitudes will forward understanding of the need for these accommodations and the services they provide. This

[1] Based in part on material presented by the author in Chapter 10 of *Aging and Leisure* (Kleemeier, 1961).

101

CARL A. RUDISILL LIBRARY
LENOIR RHYNE COLLEGE

understanding is necessary in order to construct proper settings which offer needed assistance in a way most conducive to acceptance by the older person and the public.

A fourth reason for our interest is that knowledge of representative current attitudes toward special settings will better enable us to predict present and future demands for various facilities for the aged. Since these attitudes are very important in determining the facilities and services, it is good to understand that attitudes may change. Thus a fifth reason for this study is to keep abreast of opinion about these facilities as conditions change and the possible use of such settings in modern form becomes more generally known.

In order to facilitate understanding the attitudes toward special settings, some explanation of the type of facilities included under this general term is necessary. It will be noted that the term "institution" has been avoided. This has been deliberate, although at times awkward, because the referent for this term is ill-defined and because at best it focuses attention on only a very limited aspect of the spectrum of special living arrangements and services available for older people.

## SPECIAL SETTINGS

Broadly conceived, the term "special settings" includes a wide variety of living arrangements, perhaps more than can be conveniently handled in a discussion such as this. It is possible, however, to arrange these settings into four classifications, each with its own distinguishing characteristics, and thereby confine the significant variables in manageable limits.

Not all institutional or special settings in which aged people are found will be considered; major attention will be given only to those established specifically to serve older people or those in which a large number of people are old even though the institution's primary objective may not be to serve the aged. Examples of this latter type would include nursing homes, chronic hospitals, and certain mental hospitals.

### Specialized Housing and Communities

There are many housing projects and communities that are especially suited to the older person's living needs after retirement. Here the older person ostensibly remains a free agent. The essential feature of such settings is simply the provision of housing. Although some program aimed at fulfilling health and activity needs may be available, this program is always subordinate to providing shelter. The individual remains his own responsibility, at least as far as his daily activities are concerned. Although economic and other assistance may be forthcoming from the community, there is no agent on whom the older person may depend besides his friends, family, and himself. Included in these settings are public housing units for the aged, boardinghouses, rooming houses, trailer parks, hotels, various retirement communities, and real-estate developments. In addition, we are not necessarily dealing with the single-dwelling unit, but with clusters of dwellings, apartments, and neighborhoods of a city, even with towns of respectable size in which the majority of residents are at least middle-aged. Beyond this there are cities like Saint Petersburg, Florida, in which the elderly person, although not in the majority, so characterizes the population that the city physically and socially accommodates itself to his presence (Harlan, 1954).

Such dwelling units, serving a uniformly middle-aged or elderly population, must have some significant bearing on both the attitudes and activities of their residents. What these influences may be is imperfectly known. Certainly the attitudes toward these settings will vary, depending on the type and quality of community they represent. For example, an expensive retirement community such as Port Charlotte, Florida, where retirement homes costing $7,425 may be found among larger, more expensive residences, may evoke a positive attitude in a person who would flatly reject a trailer court or an apartment in a building reserved for elderly people.

### Residential Homes for the Aged

Attempts to define residential homes for the aged with precision have not met with unqualified success, but many have been made in conjunction with the establishment of licensing for these accommodations in various states of the United States. The decision to license must be based on criteria as tangible and objective as possible, and such criteria are less obvious than one first supposes. What is generally understood to be a home for the aged is fairly unequivocal: it is a residence for old people, most of whom are reasonably well both physically and mentally although they require certain services or some support in their daily living.

Crucial to the distinction between the home for the aged and the nursing home or chronic hospital is the health of the people it serves. This is no idle distinction, yet it is difficult to maintain. Residents of homes for the aged are free from chronic illness and disability. Even those residential homes requiring incoming residents to be in good health upon entry find these standards difficult to maintain. One such home, for example, found that over half (55 per cent) of eighty consecutive admissions exhibited some obvious physical disability when entering the institution (Kleemeier, 1953). Although it is impossible to interpret this figure in terms of the general population of similar aged people, some suggestion of its probable significance is the fact that 14.3 per cent of old-age assistance recipients during this period in 1953 required considerable care from others because of either physical (12.2 per cent) or mental disabilities (2.1 per cent) (U. S. Social Security Administration, 1955). Even when an additional 3.5 per cent of this population which is classified "bedridden," is added to the latter percentages, one is left with the distinct impression that the health of residents of homes for the aged is considerably below that of their peers in the general population.

As a matter of policy, some old-age homes attempt to screen their applicants in a way that favors the entry of the definitely disabled, preferring that those better able to care for themselves be maintained in their own homes. To the extent that this policy is followed, it would seem that such homes become nursing homes or hospitals. In one sense, this thinking tends to deny the legitimacy of the purely residential function of the home for the aged. Although justification for this policy may be found in the desire to utilize these scarce accommodations for those exhibiting the most imperative needs, an equally pressing need exists for residential care for healthy aged people who require only minimal support and supervision in their daily living. It may be well to add that the distinction between the residential home and the hospital is still commonly accepted, even though every home for the aged must solve the difficult problem of providing care for the residents who become chronically incapacitated. Many set up well-staffed infirmaries, thus accepting a dual function; others insist that such patients be transferred to more suitable settings. A good example of the latter policy is the extensive system of public old-age homes in Sweden (Kleemeier, 1960). Here, in order to preserve residential atmosphere, as well as provide good medical care, the state insists that chronically ill residents be transferred to appropriate hospitals.

### Settings for the Ill Aged

There are also institutions established to take care of the ill or disabled older person. Usually such institutions cannot be considered exclusively old-age settings, for their primary purpose is to serve the infirm regardless of age. Nevertheless, the predominant number of old people in nursing homes and mental and chronic hospitals marks these settings. Here again these settings have difficulty in maintaining the identity of the particular service they are most suited to offer. Just as the home for the aged may be embarrassed by the necessity for providing care for its physically and mentally ill resident, these medical settings face the problem of continuing care for patients who no longer require medical or custodial services, but must be kept because there is nowhere else for them to go. This is particularly the case of mental hospitals, which, in addition to their primary function, too frequently serve as both geriatric hospitals and old-age homes (Kleemeier, 1960).

Obviously the distinctions drawn here are not always maintained in practice. Equally obvious is the fact that attempts are made to fit the type of service to a particular incapacity. Residential care, which is here conceived to be primarily nonmedical, is often considered a type of nursing-home service. Such, for example, was clearly the intent of the 1958 "National conference on nursing homes and homes for the aged," which, following U.S. Public Health Service definitions, classified old-age residences as skilled nursing homes, personal care homes (either with or without skilled nursing), and sheltered homes. The last ". . . provides 'shelter' with its associated minimum services to aged residents who essentially manage their own care and affairs," whereas the first offers its patients the advantages of technical nursing skills beyond those which can be administered by an untrained person (U.S. Public Health Service, 1958, p. 3).

Confounding the functions of the home for the aged, the nursing home, and the chronic hospital results from the justifiable reluctance of both the patients and administrators to move a patient to a different setting if he undergoes changes in health. Indeed, limited facilities and high cost most frequently combine to preclude a move. Reaction against the restricted view of the special setting's function has led to a broader interpretation of the scope of service which may be offered by a single institution. Such thinking has encouraged new and imaginative developments in the care of the aged. Thus in some instances individuals become members of a home for the aged while they still reside in the community. Membership entitles them to recreational, medical, and other services of the home even though they maintain independent living arrangements. Although illness or incapacity may bring them into the home or its medical unit, the transition is made with minimum trauma because it occurs in a familiar psychological and physical milieu. Unfortunately such arrangements are exceedingly rare, but they provide valuable experience and examples.

It is obvious from this discussion that attitudes become most significant in effecting a change of living arrangements, even within the setting itself. Thus, the resident of a cottage may resist entry to the hospital section of the same institution, even though it is obvious to him that better care can be more easily given to him there. The reasons for these attitudes and their prevalence is interesting and important to the administration of the institution and, if investigated in properly selected samples, may permit the social scientist to derive valuable generalizations.

### Part-Time Settings

Limited settings include varied settings designed to provide care or services for older people during part of the day. They do not offer residential services or, under ordinary circumstances, beds for nursing care. They may be health-oriented, as the day hospital is, or may simply furnish recreational facilities. The latter are undoubtedly more common. The recreation may range from uncomplicated social gatherings to elaborate programs of arts, crafts, and adult education. Day hospitals, on the other hand, may carry out therapeutic and rehabilitative procedures with older patients who come one or more days a week for all or part of the day. Apart from recreational and social advantages, one of the purposes of these limited settings is maintaining the elderly person in the community without resorting to full-time institutional care. Although the latter purpose may apply more directly to the day hospital, it is felt that recreation and other similar centers serve some preventive functions in physical and mental health and, at least, to this extent reduce the necessity for full-time care.

Thus in our study, we should include attitudes toward these limited settings in the hope that this would lead to a better understanding of their usefulness and place among other services for the older person.

## THE PLACE OF SPECIAL SETTINGS

In society's status scales, special settings for the aged rank very low. Why this should be so is obvious and presents a problem worthy of detailed study. This observation is readily verifiable. In the

United States and many West European countries, mental hospitals complain that they are being used as geriatric hospitals and old-age homes (Kleemeier, 1960). Homes for the aged, because of the great need, become chronic hospitals with consequent confusion about how best to fill their ambiguous functions. The national conference alluded to earlier expressed concern over ". . . prevalent negative attitudes toward nursing homes and homes for the aged on the part of professional groups and the public at large. It was felt that these facilities would have better opportunities to improve if more positive cooperative attitudes prevailed among these sources" (U.S. Public Health Service, 1958, p. 32).

Some measure of the need for these various settings can be obtained from the census and other data, but this picture can be misleading, for only the actual numbers of patients and residents are given without the number of people who, under more favorable circumstances, might have called upon these facilities for service. According to the 1950 United States census, 5.7 per cent of the United States population sixty-five and over were living in quasi-households (3.1 per cent in institutions, and 2.6 percent in other quasi-households). Of the 385,419 persons over sixty-five living in institutions, 217,536 were residents of public and private homes for the aged and dependent, with an additional 141,346 in mental hospitals, and the remaining 26,537 in chronic disease hospitals, correctional institutions, and other such settings. As age advances beyond sixty-five, the proportion of the population living in institutions increases. Thus, in 1950 7.9 per cent of the population seventy-five and over lived in quasi-households (5.3 per cent in institutions, and 2.6 per cent in other quasi-households) (U.S. Bureau of Census, 1953).

More recent figures would indicate growth in these numbers. Thus it is estimated that the 25,000 nursing homes in the United States contain about 450,000 beds and serve a population with an average age of eighty, more than half of whom cannot walk without assistance. In addition, one-third are incontinent, and more than half have periods of disorientation (Solon, Roberts, Krueger, & Baney, 1957).

From this it is clear that the major portion of the facilities in nursing homes and similar settings is devoted to the care of markedly debilitated aged persons. Undoubtedly this also applies to most homes for the aged. This in turn suggests the reason for the generally negative attitudes held toward these settings. They are associated with disability, limited activity, and chronic and terminal illness. These are by no means positive associations and unquestionably foster the rather dismal prevailing attitudes about these settings. It would appear that the attitudes toward all settings for older people, whether for the ill or healthy, become associated with this negative outlook.

The above figures also suggest the probability that the urgent need to care for the physically dependent person has encroached on the available facilities for residential services to the abler person. To what extent such additional services might be used in the United States is suggested by the Swedish adoption of the ratio of one bed for the healthy aged in a residential home to every ten people over seventy in the population. If a similar ratio were adopted in the United States, using the age of seventy-five instead of seventy, over 500,000 beds would have been necessary in 1958 with a projected need for 250,000 additional beds by 1975. In New York state recent estimates indicate that 26 per cent of the population over sixty-five, although ambulatory, are capable of only limited activity. The provision of housing with special community resources for supplemental and medical care for those in this group who have inadequate incomes will require over 100,000 housing units in New York alone (Steinle & associates, 1958, p. 40). Clearly places in residential settings do not exist in such quantity, and the suggestion remains that present capacities for this service are minimal, if that.

Before this situation can be properly evaluated, however, it seems apparent that sound research and planning are called for. Any research and development program directed toward this problem must, of course, include a substantial investigation of attitudes toward the special settings in order to determine the role of such attitudes in the acceptance of various types of living facilities for older persons.

### DESCRIPTIVE DIMENSIONS

It is apparent from the above that the names applied to the different types of special settings for older people are at best inaccurate indicators of the function they serve. For convenience, four types of settings have been distinguished in the foregoing discussion: (1) specialized housing and communities, (2) residential homes, (3) settings for the ill aged, and (4) part-time settings. Other classifications are possible and have actually been adopted for various purposes (U.S. Public Health Service, 1958). Such classifications, however, are not dimensional in types of administration or services offered and, therefore, do not adequately describe the nature of the setting and its influence on resident life and activities. Three somewhat different dimensions have, however, been suggested, and they permit a more accurate description of the impact of the setting on the way of life of the residents (Kleemeier, 1956). These dimensions are the segregate-nonsegregate continuum, the institutional-noninstitutional continuum, and the congregate-noncongregate continuum.

### Segregate Dimension

The segregate dimension refers at one end to the condition under which older people live exclusively among their age group, having little contact with other age groups; at the other end are living arrangements which constantly keep older people with people of all ages. Thus, living arrangements may be distributed along the segregate-nonsegregate continuum by the opportunity they provide for interaction with all age groups in the community.

### Institutional Dimension

The institutional-noninstitutional dimension may, in other terms, be referred to as the control dimension. Specifically it is applied to the degrees to which the individual must adjust his life to imposed rules, discipline, and means of social control utilized by the administrators, medical staff, personnel, residents, and patients themselves in order to bring about desired behavior patterns. Although this dimension is more commonly thought to apply to large group settings, it is largely independent of the size and constitution of the group.

### Congregate Dimension

The congregate-noncongregate dimension refers to the group aspects of the setting, not only to the size of the group, but also to the intimacy and privacy it is possible to attain in the setting.

Although refinements of these dimensions are possible and for research purposes, desirable, these dimensions are valuable in assisting the analysis of attitudes toward special settings for the aged. Thus, by considering these dimensions separately, it may be possible to obtain information concerning the contribution of each to the total attitude toward the setting. As long as we consider the setting only by name, type of service, or some other general category, the attitudes are likely to be obscured. In the following discussion some attempt at learning the attitudes will be made with the limited amount of applicable material which is available in the research literature.

## ATTITUDES TOWARD SPECIAL SETTINGS

People enter special living settings because these arrangements allow them to satisfy basic needs more economically and efficiently than is otherwise possible. The setting is presumed to offer them the services and tools for living at less cost in energy and with greater satisfaction than was possible in their own homes, even if they were assisted by friends and relatives. Such a step represents an effort to conserve energy in the face of real or anticipated impairments and decrements in physical energy. In addition, it represents a break with past concepts of self and forces upon the person, often for the first time, the recognition of the severe limitations of old age. In whatever setting, this move represents withdrawal (or disengagement) at least to some degree. Withdrawal and conservation are obviously associated with residential and medical settings for the elderly, but these differ from special housing and retirement settings only in degree. Even such part-time settings as the recreation center for older people, however skillfully disguised, force some degree of recognition of the fact that old age has arrived because of their segregated character. This itself is personally significant, because, with the identification of the self with the image of age, some reconciliation must take place between the image and personal patterns of activity.

Thus entry into special settings represents a turning point in life and is commonly a decision thrust upon a person by unfavorable circumstance. This is clearly shown in the attitudes of people in homes for the dependent aged. Even when the institutional setting approaches the ideal, residents often feel called upon to explain to friends or acquaintances the circumstances necessitating their entry into the home. Thus it seems that negative valences tend to predominate the decision to enter a special setting. This arises not only because a person faces the unwelcome fact of an age change in himself, but also because of the generally negative public attitudes toward congregate, segregate, and institutional settings for the aged.

### The Setting and the Person

As indicated above, special settings for the aged may be described in three independent dimensions—congregate, segregate, and institutional. The senile ward in a mental hospital would be high in all three characteristics, whereas a ward in a general hospital serving all age groups would be highly congregate, highly institutional, but low in age segregation. The frail or ill aged person who lives with his family but receives various home medical and nursing service is in an institutional setting which is neither congregate nor segregate. On the other hand, a residential hotel patronized exclusively by older people could be characterized as highly segregate and congregate but not institutional. It is our contention that these characteristics have predictable effects on the attitudes and behavior of their inhabitants and that these effects depend on a person's rate of energy expenditure and total behavior repertory. It is the purpose of the following to explore these relations and offer hypotheses on which predictions concerning probable attitudinal effects may be based.

## Acceptance

From the assessment of the reasons for entering special settings, we derive this hypothesis: The more congregate, segregate, and institutional any special setting for the aged is, the greater the healthy older person's resistance to it will be.

Since people do enter special settings, it is apparent that the resistance is not complete and that personal factors modify its force. Thus, the degree of resistance is a function not only of setting characteristics, but also of personal characteristics. It is hypothesized, therefore, that two related attitudinal factors strongly influence the decision to enter a special setting: (1) the need felt for assistance and (2) the self-concept. The need for assistance may be rooted in economic or physical disability, desire for companionship, or greater opportunity for self-expression. The greater the feeling of need, the less resistance generated if the special setting is seen as the proper source of help. In large measure, this depends on the self-concept. If a person believes that he is old, is willing to admit it, and is ready to withdraw from much of the activity of his prime, the old-age setting will appear more appropriate to him. In addition, these two factors partially determine the type of setting selected where selection is possible. Thus a need primarily for companionship would indicate a retirement community with minimal institutional characteristics, whereas a need for personal services coupled with the self-concept of old age would make the home for the aged acceptable.

## Influence of the Setting

Although at present there has been no systematic attack on the problem of attitudes, data gathered from several surveys can be analyzed to suggest relevant answers. Two studies are particularly useful in this respect. One is a survey carried out in the town of Hamilton, Scotland, (Scottish Housing Advisory Committee, 1952), the other is a questionnaire circulated in Florida (Sahle, 1952). The Hamilton study was carried out in September, 1950, and in it 868 people of sixty and over were interviewed. In the Florida study, questionnaires were mailed to 861 people who had corresponded with the Florida Improvement Commission and to 900 annuitants of a large New York company.

TABLE 1

OLDER PEOPLE'S PREFERENCES FOR NEW

ACCOMMODATIONS (HOUSEHOLDS WANTING TO MOVE)

|  | Willing | Unwilling | Undecided |
|---|---|---|---|
|  | per cent | per cent | per cent |
| Bungalow | 79 | 13 | 8 |
| Flat on its own in a two-or three-story block | 42 | 45 | 13 |
| Flat on its own in a block of flats with an elevator | 32 | 53 | 15 |
| Bungalow in a group of bunga- lows looked after by a warden | 45 | 37 | 18 |
| Flat looked after by a warden | 24 | 58 | 18 |
| Lodgings | 2 | 86 | 12 |
| Private hotel | 2 | 86 | 12 |
| Bed-sittingroom in a hostel | 13 | 76 | 11 |
| Bedroom only in a hostel | 4 | 84 | 12 |
| Shared bedroom in a hostel | 1 | 87 | 12 |

Source —Scottish Housing Advisory Committee (1952, Table 12, p. 69). Reprinted with permission of the Controller of Her Britannic Majesty's Stationery Office.

## Congregate and Institutional
## Dimensions

If we look at the list of living accommodations in tables 1 and 2, it is apparent that they are arranged in order along the congregate dimension. Although this may not be the only factor involved in this ordering, it is the most prominent one. This is particularly truc of Table 1, in which ten distinctly different types of living arrangements have been identified and for which preferences are given.

It is clearly evident that the "bungalow" in Table 1 and the "separate dwelling" in Table 2 represent the limiting class of independent living accommodations. As we go down the list in Table 1, the congregate aspects of the living arrangements increase. Thus a "flat on its own in a two- or three-story block" is likely to be one of a smaller group of flats that houses fewer people than a "flat in a large building served by an elevator."

TABLE 2
PREFERENCE FOR TYPE OF RETIREMENT LIVING
ACCOMMODATION (FLORIDA SURVEY)

|  | *Corporation group N=84* | *Improvement commission group N=208* |
|---|---|---|
|  | per cent | per cent |
| Separate dwelling | 64.2 | 75.5 |
| Two-family dwelling | 7.2 | 3.8 |
| Apartment | 20.2 | 12.0 |
| Other | 1.2 | 0.5 |
| No answer | 7.2 | 8.2 |
|  | 100.0 | 100.0 |

Source—Sahle (1952, Fig. 8, p. 20).

The introduction of a supervisor or warden not only affects the degree of congregate character, but adds another confounding dimension. It would appear that the presence of a warden implies some degree of institutionalization or control which must be considered as an influence apart from the influence of the congregate aspects of the accommodation. Certainly from the specified duties of the warden the degree of control or supervision would be minimal. These duties ". . . include a visit to each house daily to make sure that the older people are well; he (the warden) will be able to assist them with minor repairs, receive complaints, collect rents and generally make himself useful in any small ways which are required" (Scottish Housing Advisory Committee, 1952, p. 15).

The warden would call the doctor and help get domestic help, cooked meals, and shopping provisions. The congregate character of the living arrangement increases to the extent that daily visits from a warden are considered to reduce privacy; the degree of institutionalization increases to the extent that the warden exercises control or supervision.

Hostels represent a relatively high degree of congregate character. They are of two types. The first is intended for people who require small self-contained dwellings with minimum services; usually a common room and warden are provided. The second is intended for single people, either young people working away from home or elderly employed people, who do not need separate self-contained dwellings. Thus, hostels are not intended for people who require care.

Table 1 shows the preferences expressed by the elderly people (households) who were dissatisfied with their present accommodations and desired to move. This group represents 20 per cent of the total sample. Let us look at these results in terms of the congregate and institutional dimensions.

Clearly the bungalow is looked upon as the most desirable accommodation. Even though the bungalow may be in a group of bungalows looked after by a warden, it still maintains second place, although the percentage drop is considerable. The same drop in preference occurs in the three types of flats listed in Table 1. A flat in the large building is apparently less desirable than a flat in a smaller building, but both are preferred to a flat looked after by a warden.

In both the bungalow and the flat, the addition of the warden apparently decreases desirability. It would seem as though the presence of the warden is viewed as an unnecessary intrusion into the individual's privacy or a compromise of his independence. Here the self-image of the person is undoubtedly important. If he does not consider himself aged or dependent, it is likely that he will be unwilling to accept such helpful services. It is interesting to note in Table 1 that the rank order of the percentage of respondents willing to accept the various accommodations (Column 2) complements that of the percentage unwilling to accept them (Column 3).

In view of these considerations, the results in Table 1 must be atributed to the influence of both institutional and congregate factors. The factor of age segregation does not, however, enter into these preferences, because all the accommodations are presumably open to all age groups.

Table 2 gives the same picture. Here, however, the list of available accommodations is not nearly so complete as in the Scottish survey. Since there was clearly no implication of any institutional or control characteristics in the questions on this survey and since it was clearly understood that the accommodations would be in a retirement community, only the congregate dimension enters into the preference. Here again the separate dwelling was most popular.

The reason for preferring an apartment over a two-family dwelling cannot be readily given on the basis of available information; however, it is easy to present possible explanations. For example, the two-family dwelling does not give the independence of a detached house, but at the same time it usually requires the same obligations to maintain the premises. This shared obligation may actually be less independent (or more congregate) than the rather impersonal attitude one can have toward neighbors in a larger apartment building.

## TABLE 3
## THE KIND OF NEIGHBORS PREFERRED

### (In percentages)

| | *All ages* | *Up to 69* | *70 and over* |
|---|---|---|---|
| Unwilling to have younger people without children | 4 | 5 | 2 |
| Unwilling to have people with children | 20 | 22 | 14 |
| Preferences<br>Persons of own age | 24 | 30 | 10 |
| Younger people without children | 9 | 10 | 6 |
| "Don't mind either" | 67 | 60 | 84 |
| Sample of older people wishing to move | 168 | 116 | 52 |

Source—Scottish Housing Advisory Committee (1952, Table 14, p. 69). Reprinted with permission of the Controller of Her Britannic Majesty's Stationery Office.

### *The Segregate Dimension*

Table 3 gives some interesting information about the segregate dimension. In the Scottish sample of older people wishing to move, about one-quarter preferred to be with people their own age, and about two-thirds did not care. Only 4 per cent were unwilling to have younger people as neighbors, but 20 per cent were unwilling to have people with children as neighbors. The curious thing about this preference is the tendency for people over seventy to be more tolerant of younger persons and children as neighbors than those from sixty to sixty-nine. This shift, however, cannot be interpreted as an increase in preference for younger persons or children; apparently it represents a decreased interest in the entire issue. Thus while only 60 per cent of those from sixty to sixty-nine said that the age of their neighbors made no difference to them, 84 per cent of those over seventy expressed this point of view. The unwillingness to express such a preference may be another illustration of the increasing tendency toward disengagement with advancing age, although other explanations may present themselves. Although I have suggested elsewhere ". . . that the older respondents, in their diminishing strength, [may have] felt greater security in the nearness of younger people" (Kleemeier, 1959, p. 442), this explanation is not warranted here because of the large percentage of the older age group refusing to express a preference.

TABLE 4
RESPONSES TO FLORIDA SURVEY QUESTION

"Would you like to live in a village made up largely of retired people?" (In percentages)

|  | Corporation group N=137 | Improvement commission group N=334 |
|---|---|---|
| Yes | 73.0 | 72.7 |
| No | 15.3 | 10.2 |
| Undecided | 8.8 | 14.4 |
| No answer | 2.9 | 2.7 |
|  | 100.0 | 100.0 |

Source—Sahle (1952, Fig. 5, p. 17).

In Table 4 some additional information on the relation between age segregation and attitude is given from the Florida survey. Almost three-quarters of both groups surveyed indicated that they would like to live in a village with a majority of retired people. Of course, this survey reports findings on a highly select group from a population whose characteristics are generally unknown. Nevertheless, it offers the suggestion that, among older people, an unknown proportion prefers to live among its age group.

There is other less systematic information on this point. Hoyt (1954), in a study of retired people living in a trailer park, determined that one of the great appeals this kind of living held was what he called "mutuality." By mutuality he meant being among one's contemporaries, not feeling out of place, enjoying the same status and interests as one's neighbor, and being in a situation in which mutual aid was possible. Although age was not the major component of mutuality, it appears to be one of the basic characteristics on which mutuality depends.

These fragmentary findings can do no more than suggest that the special settings dimensions set forth here are potentially useful in the study of attitudes toward special settings for the aged. Perhaps, their use will give a more complete, meaningful picture of the environmental influences which shape the attitudes toward the living arrangements available to older people.

### Personal Characteristics and
### Attitudes

As indicated, a person's attitude toward a special setting will be partially determined by the need he feels for the services and conveniences offered by the settings and by his self-concept. The importance of the self-concept as a determinant of attitude toward settings for the aged cannot be underestimated. Part of its origins is in the past attitudes of the individual and his present needs and circumstance. The extent to which the past history of his attitudes has significant bearing on his acceptance of special settings may be estimated by and reflected in general public attitudes toward these special settings.

If the popular conception of the old-age setting is the chronic hospital, the county poor farm, or the alms house, it will not be surprising if the older person exhibits a generally negative feeling toward all special settings for the aged, even though his current, urgent needs may be met most satisfactorily by some appropriate living facility.

The attitudes currently held by contemporary older people may have been formed with reference to special settings which differ markedly from those now available. The current interest in and emphasis on improved care and attractive living arrangements for the aged may be creating a demand which will not be fully felt for a generation or more. If this is so, there is a need to continue attitudinal studies and studies covering the entire age range rather than just older people.

In addition to the history of a person's attitudes, certain other individual circumstances and characteristics play a part in the attitudinal structure related to old-age settings. One of these factors is illustrated in Table 5, which is derived from the same set of data presented in Table 1. The preference expressed by the Scottish sample depended very much on the size of the household. The most marked shift occurred in the percentage of people preferring a bungalow. This type of accommodation is not the most popular for a one-person household, but with larger households it is almost universally acceptable. For the single person smaller accommodations are preferable, and resistance to a hostel or a warden decreases markedly.

An additional illustration of this fact has already been presented and discussed in Table 3, in which it was shown that willingness to live in a neighborhood of people of all ages changed in the age subgroups over sixty. Thus an interesting hypothesis begins to emerge, namely, that the attitudes of older people toward special settings are likely to change in the senium and with household constitution. Once more we see evidence to support the warning not to consider older people as a homogeneous group.

The foregoing suggests not only that studies of personal characteristics, personal history, and interview data may prove valuable in helping us to understand reasons for variations in attitudes toward special settings, but also that such studies may prove useful in making predictions about these attitudes. For example, Hoyt (1954) showed that the pattern of reasons for preferring life in a retirement trailer community was dependent on the occupational group (self-employed versus not self-employed) of the respondent. This study suggests that the analysis of personal data of residents in special settings for the aged might yield valuable clues for understanding the attitudes behind their decision to enter the special setting. For example, in a study of personal history and interview data of eighty consecutive admissions to a home for aged dependent people, the author found evidence to suggest that those admitted to the home tended to have joined the organization for whose members this facility was provided at a somewhat older age than the average member, that a large percentage of the men had never married (32.8 per cent versus 8.4 per cent for the total United States population seventy-five and over), that most of them lived alone before coming to the home (52 per cent), and that almost

TABLE 5

NEW ACCOMMODATIONS PREFERRED BY "MOVING" HOUSEHOLDS OF DIFFERENT SIZES

(In percentages)

| | One person | | | Two people | | | Three or more people | | |
|---|---|---|---|---|---|---|---|---|---|
| | Willing | Unwilling | Undecided | Willing | Unwilling | Undecided | Willing | Unwilling | Undecided |
| Bungalow | 50 | 36 | 14 | 96 | 1 | 3 | 90 | 2 | 8 |
| Flat on its own in a two- or three-story block | 58 | 26 | 16 | 34 | 62 | 4 | 34 | 46 | 20 |
| Flat on its own in a block of flats with an elevator | 44 | 40 | 16 | 31 | 63 | 6 | 22 | 56 | 22 |
| Bungalow in a group of bungalows looked after by a warden | 41 | 41 | 18 | 50 | 35 | 15 | 46 | 34 | 20 |
| Flat looked after by a warden | 36 | 43 | 21 | 16 | 73 | 11 | 20 | 57 | 23 |
| Lodgings | 5 | 84 | 11 | - | 94 | 6 | 2 | 82 | 16 |
| Private hotel | 5 | 79 | 16 | - | 94 | 6 | 2 | 84 | 14 |
| Bed-sittingroom in a hostel | 30 | 61 | 9 | 7 | 87 | 6 | 4 | 82 | 14 |
| Bedroom only in a hostel | 14 | 72 | 14 | - | 94 | 6 | - | 86 | 14 |
| Shared bedroom in a hostel | 2 | 84 | 14 | - | 94 | 6 | - | 86 | 14 |

Source—Scottish Housing Advisory Committee (1952, Table 13, p. 69). Reprinted with permission of the Controller of Her Britannic Majesty's Stationery Office.

two-thirds of them had already received some financial assistance from the organization which was now caring for them (Kleemeier, 1953). Such personal history data collected in conjunction with attitudinal studies on populations residing in special settings for the aged are likely to be useful not only for the immediate practical purposes of administrators of the settings, but should also contribute to general knowledge concerning factors which influence decisions to enter special settings.

It must be emphasized once more, however, that factual studies on attitudes toward special settings for the aged are extremely rare. This is remarkable in view of the tremendous increase in the number of retirement communities, homes for the aged, and other facilities designed specifically for the care of older people. Studies of this sort should be carried out at local as well as regional and national levels. In addition, such studies lend themselves to international cooperative effort.

Events have proven that homes and other special settings for the aged can be built without either intensive or extensive attitude studies, but these events have not demonstrated that in following this course the needs of the aged were necessarily better served. Unquestionably such studies could help community planners, governments, builders, and the many other organizations concerned with living accommodations and settings for older people.

*REFERENCES*

Harlan, W.H. Community adaptations to the presence of aged persons: Saint Petersburg, Florida. *Amer. J. Sociol.*, 1954, **59,** 332-339.
Hoyt, G.C. The life of the retired in a trailer park. *Amer. J. Sociol.*, 1954, **59,** 361-370.
Kleemeier, R.W. A study of 80 consecutive admissions to Moosehaven. In Fourth annual report of the director of the Moosehaven Research Laboratory. Orange Park, Florida: The Laboratory, 1953. Pp. 49-61.
Kleemeier, R.W. An analysis of patterns for group living for older people. In I.L. Webber (Ed.), *Aging, a current appraisal.* Gainesville: University of Florida Press, 1956. Pp. 167-179.
Kleemeier, R.W. Behavior and the organization of the bodily and the external environment. In J.E. Birren (Ed.), *Handbook of aging and the individual: Psychological and biological aspects.* Chicago: The University of Chicago Press, 1959. Pp. 400-451.
Kleemeier, R.W. The mental health of the aged. In E.W. Burgess (Ed.), *Aging in western societies.* Chicago: The University of Chicago Press, 1960. Pp. 203-270.

Kleemeier, R.W. Use and meaning of time in special settings. In R.W. Kleemeier (Ed.), *Aging and leisure: A research perspective into the
meaningful use of time*. New York: Oxford University Press, 1961.
Pp. 273-307.

Sahle, R.S. *Retirement village planning for Florida*. Tallahassee: Florida State
Improvement Commission, 1952.

Scottish Housing Advisory Committee. *Housing of special groups*. Edinburgh:
H.M. Stationery Office, 1952.

Solon, J., Roberts, E.W., Krueger, D.E., & Baney, A.M. Nursing homes, their
patients and their care. *Publ. Hlth Serv. Publication,* 1957, No.
503. (Washington, D.C.: U.S. Government Printing Office)

Steinle, J.E., & associates. *Home care and housing needs of the aged*. New
York: New York State Division of Housing, 1958.

U.S. Bureau of the Census. *Special reports,* part 2, chapter c: Institutional
population. Vol. 4. *U.S. census of population: 1950*. Washington,
D.C.: U.S. Government Printing Office, 1953.

U.S. Public Health Service. National conference on nursing homes and homes
for the aged. *Publ. Hlth Serv. Publication,* 1958, No. 625.

U.S. Social Security Administration. Recipients of old age assistance in early
1953, part I—state data. *Publ. Assistance Report,* 1955, No. 26.

# PART SIX

*Social Factors in*
*Psychiatric Disorders*

# INTRODUCTION

WILMA DONAHUE

The general concept of aging usually includes recognition of the fact that the good health of earlier years will suffer some impairment in the later years of life. This is not a welcome prospect, but it has become so familiar in our thinking that probably most of us are prepared to accept increasing ill health with a fair degree of equanimity. But mental illness is a different matter. The idea that mental illness may come to be accepted as the norm—just as "excellent for your age" may reassure one whose physical health is faltering—has not yet successfully challenged the laymen's notion that mental health and mental illness are discrete states. We have not yet learned to think of mental change as a process of becoming which can be modified by developments, especially by well-directed intervention, in either direction.

125

When mental illness is recognized to involve a developing process (Rosow, Chapter 38) not necessarily associated with frank psychosis or implying an irreversible change, we will be ready to take full advantage of the methods—not yet fully utilized—for the prevention, amelioration, and possible cure of aspects of mental illness. Simultaneously, the fear of mental illness on the part of older people, their families, and their friends will no longer encourage neglect of opportunities for early treatment and may stimulate more general demand for adequate provision of therapeutic measures which may contribute to the rehabilitation of disturbed people.

## DIMENSIONS OF THE PROBLEM

Discussions of diagnosis and classification (Volume I) have already revealed that studies of mental illness seldom achieve the criteria of exact definition and verifiable conclusions which are demanded in exact science. Some of the contributors to this volume have selected problems which are more susceptible to that kind of treatment. Discussions of suicide in England and Wales (Sainsbury, Chapter 36) and in Hong Kong (Yap, Chapter 37) show significant points of agreement in respect to some epidemiological data and also provide bases for clearer understanding of the causes of differences in other respects. Similarities are revealed in frequency distributions by sex and age, but certain differences appear to be derived from cultural patterns. Analyses of these statistical data suggest that some social circumstances may foster liability to suicide. Some of these situations may prove to be of almost universal significance whereas others may be peculiar to special cultures or special events in time. The cogency of these two reports on varying incidence of suicide is well supported by information from the World Health Organization which indicates that concordant data have been reported from twenty-two of the twenty-five countries which have reported relevant statistics.

Strömgren's report (Chapter 35) concerning epidemiological aspects of mental illness in Sweden and Denmark is a similarly decisive study of a less specific problem. Recognition that homogeneity of the population contributes much to the practicability of such a study does not limit its value. The indicated conclusions are also supported by an Asian study.[1] A cautious but suggestive paragraph from the Sixth

[1] World Health Organization. Mental health problems of aging and the aged: Sixth report of the expert committee on mental health. *Technical Report Series,* 1959, No. 171. (World Health Organization, Geneva)

Report of the Expert Committee on Mental Health of the World Health Organization refers to the significance of these studies in stating, first, "It is uncertain whether there has been a real increase in the incidence of mental disorder in old age," and concluding, ". . . so that it is unlikely that in the trends for admission rates of old people in highly-industrialized countries we are witnessing the effects of 'medicated survival' of individuals of poor constitutional stability who formerly succumbed to physical or mental illness in earlier life" (pp. 9-10). This raises the question, already suggested in Volume I, concerning the contribution that changing social attitudes may be making to the recognition of mental illness.

Epidemiological reports which represent limited but impeccable studies can do much to counteract misconceptions regarding the increasing number of admissions, especially among older groups, to mental hospitals. Such information, valuable in itself, is not legitimately extended to signify anything more than what is reported—that an increasing number of older people are sharing in the available public facilities for the care of the mentally ill. No legitimate inferences can be drawn from such data in respect to expectancy of mental illness in geriatric populations nor any other age group. The dimensions of the problem cannot be discovered by merely compounding data concerning the number and age distributions of those being admitted to mental hospitals. Reliable studies which reveal unmet needs (Lowenthal, Chapter 39) are essential if we are to discover facts about the incidence of mental illness and substitute these facts for impressions derived chiefly from current use of mental hospitals and their frequently expanding facilities. Capacity appears to be a significant factor in determining the age distribution of those accepted for inpatient care; limited facilities inevitably call for the adoption of admission policies which then bias any conclusions about the frequency of mental illness in different age groups.

We must continue to explore the dimensions of the problem of mental illness in the older population. Misconceptions derived from misleading statistics and obsolete notions signify the importance of recasting our estimates of the relative importance of items of data (Rosow, Chapter 38). The number of older admissions to mental hospitals tells us only that the problem is significant in terms of facilities and their adequacy in meeting the needs of those who seek help by appealing to public health services. Such data give no reliable clues as to the number who might benefit by temporary care of that kind or of the number of those whose prodromal symptoms may have long preceded the age of sixty-five or over. Then first admission to a public hospital may represent a concatenation of unfortunate circumstances in a developing process rather than a significant change in the state of the patient's mental health.

## SOCIAL CONSIDERATIONS

Withdrawal from social activities may denote appropriate adaptation to the requisite conservation of the declining energies of the aged, but it is not yet clear where we should draw the line between normal, healthful disengagement and symptomatic withdrawal. "Is there such a kind of omnibus withdrawal," Lowenthal (Chapter 39) asks, "and, if so, is it a prodromal symptom to the development of psychiatric disturbance?" In his study of suicide, Sainsbury (Chapter 36) emphasizes the disproportionate frequency with which suicide, attempted suicide, or admission to mental hospitals is associated with social isolation. Besides indicating the apparent importance of preventing such isolation among those who remain in the community group, these observations suggest the desirability of assessing the effects of institutional care on such tendencies. Some of the observations of Lieberman and Lakin (Volume I, Chapter 22, *supra*) and Lowenthal's query suggest that a kind of withdrawal may be fostered in such situations.

An unknown number of mentally ill are currently being maintained in their own households. And, as pointed out in several papers in this section, the social policies now being recommended place even more responsibility on families and communities to keep the mentally ill, especially the aged, out of the mental hospital. Although some social advantages no doubt will accrue, it must also be recognized that such procedures will lead to furthering the incidence and prevalence of mental disease. Planning for mental-health services for organizing preventive measures, identifying problems, and carrying out the research needed to determine causes and treatment in old age will be made even more difficult. Dovenmuehle's (Chapter 40) statistics and the community sample being studied under the comprehensive research program at the Langley Porter Institute support this observation with respect to the United States, and it has already been recognized in Denmark (Strömgren, Chapter 35) and encouraged in England and Wales (Townsend, Chapter 41). In any case, such observations would follow from awareness that admission to a mental hospital usually signifies a change in a developing situation rather than a first manifestation of difficulty. One project of the Langley

Porter study is to discover significant points of difference between those who are being maintained in the community and those who are admitted to public institutions.

If further investigation supports the suggestion that a large proportion of the mentally ill may be effectively cared for as outpatients, we need sound bases for judging the measure of independence which such patients can successfully support. Townsend's (Chapter 41) study of their capacities for self-care indicates that reliable estimates cannot be derived from observing what residents actually do in an institutional situation. What they can do or what they say they can do must be judged by other measures.

Approaches to aspects of rehabilitation also indicate that ability to approximate acceptably normal behavior in situations less protected than an institution cannot be judged by diagnosis of classification of disability or by behavior in a situation which offers little scope for demonstrating capabilities. Potentialities for improvement in attitude and self-dependence can be discovered by such empirical studies as Townsend reports.

Social situations, particularly social isolation and severe physical illness or disability, are already identified as conducive to admission to mental hospitals. Would good physical health, normal family life, and community activity support the maintenance of mental health? Is normal (nonspecialized) community life possible and socially desirable for those who have been judged mentally ill and for members of the family or community who are asked to receive them?

Experience in England, especially the long-term results of outpatient care in Maudsley Hospital (Sainsbury, Chapter 36) suggests that outpatient care combined with community living may have significant advantages for the patient and also for social recognition of the true dimensions of the problem of mental illness. Scandinavian experience also seems to indicate advantages from this solution. It is encouraging that there is further research on the effects of inpatient care or outpatient care on other members of the household. In the United States adequate outpatient care is seldom available for the older people who must depend on public financing of the care they need. No widespread change in this situation can be anticipated until more extensive and unbiased research provides bases for sound decisions concerning the best means of conserving individual and social values. There is a need for full investigation of the possible gains to be achieved through public support of well-designed programs of outpatient care comparable to the programs of inpatient care, which now attract most attention.

# SECTION I

*Epidemiology
and Ecology*

# CHAPTER 35

*Epidemiology of Old-Age*
*Psychiatric Disorders*

ERIK STRÖMGREN

One of the most impressive facts concerning the study of old age is the rapid increase of problems in this field, certainly in old-age psychiatry. But *what* is really increasing? It is obvious that there is a swift rise in the cases needing treatment and care. This, however, may mainly be a consequence of the changed social structure and the increasing urbanization which make the care of disabled old people difficult in their own homes. We cannot conclude that the increasing number of old people seeking care exceeds what would be expected as a consequence of population growth. And even if such augmentation were proved, a great part of it would easily be explained by the change of the age distribution of the population. An additional reason for increased psychiatric problems is probably the fact that the high mortality rate of disabled old people has decreased considerably

133

in recent years. Until the relative importance of these factors has been settled exactly, it will be impossible to state that an increase in the incidence or expectancy of the morbid processes really does exist. Very few epidemiological studies concerning the psychiatric disorders of old age have taken into full consideration all the factors which have an impact on the prevalence of these disorders.

Which figures are most relevant? That naturally depends on the problem with which we are concerned. In some cases the focus is mainly on the frequency of true old-age disorders caused by involutional processes seen only in old people. In other connections it may be more important to determine the number of all cases of disorders occurring in old people, regardless of whether such disturbances may also occur among younger people. Finally the point may be to determine the number of all the sick old people, including diseases which developed before old age.

In other contexts, viewpoints other than the biological (etiological-pathogenetic) may be of importance. In such cases it may be of interest to count not only the number of diseased people in the population group, but also to determine which fraction of the group needs medical or social assistance. Or it may simply be a question of determining the rate of hospitalization of such cases.

The available statistical studies concerning old-age mental disorders are, of course, colored by the nature of the problem under scrutiny. Some investigations are further tainted by the fact that, in general, figures which were easily available have been used. It is obvious that the results of such technically diverse research procedures cannot be easily compared.

For epidemiological investigations lucidly defined concepts and terms are of vital importance. Three concepts are of fundamental significance: (1) disease expectancy, (2) incidence, and (3) prevalence of disorder.

Disease expectancy means the probability of person's developing the disease concerned at one or another time during his life on the assumption that he will live through the whole "danger zone," (the age range during which there is the possibility of the disease's starting). Disease expectancy is also termed "life expectancy" or "morbid risk" (in German *Krankheitserwartung* or *Erkrankungswahrscheinlichkeit*). Determinations of disease expectancy have been of special interest in genetic research. In an investigation of the expectancy of a particular disease among the relatives of sick probands, the significance of expectancies can be evaluated only by a comparison with the expectancy of the general population. It is for this reason that geneticists have been intensely interested in determining the average expectancy for a great many diseases and abnormalities.

In certain instances, morbidity and disease expectancy are closely related, as in a chronic disease for which the time of onset is reasonably definite, such as Huntington's chorea or *diabetes mellitus*. By and large, schizophrenia also falls into this category; it seems reasonable to date this disease from the time when the first symptoms appear regardless of whether there are subsequent remissions and relapses—presuming, in other words, that the disease has a definite time of onset and has been continuously present since then. Such diseases as manic-depressive psychosis and multiple sclerosis can be regarded in the same way even though in these diseases there may be intervals of complete freedom from symptoms. The essential point is that one wants to record just when the decisive etiological factor first manifests itself as illness. The recording of individual attacks may, of course, be of interest for other purposes, but it is always important to distinguish between the disease's true onset and recurrences or between first admission to a hospital and readmissions.

The incidence (morbidity) of a disease is identical with the proportion of the population stricken by the disease during a certain, usually short, period of time or during a succession of such periods. Cases of recurrence as well as first attacks may be included.

Prevalence is the fraction of the total population in a particular area which consists, at one particular time, of sick or abnormal persons. Ascertaining prevalence is of special significance for chronic diseases and has little meaning in diseases of short duration. Measurements of prevalence have varied purposes—investigating what proportion of the population needs treatment for a particular disease, establishing the need for hospital beds and other treatment facilities for patients suffering from a particular disease, determining the importance of the disease from the point of view of welfare measures. The prevalence of a disease depends, moreover, on its morbidity and especially on its duration and rate of mortality—the latter insofar as it differs from the average rate for the age group concerned.

### DISEASE EXPECTANCY

The determination of disease expectancy is especially difficult in geriatric disorders. The abnormalities under consideration very often have no clear-cut borderlines. In many cases the onset is so insidious that it is impossible to state the time at which a person is passing from the "healthy" group to the "ill" group. In addition, the nosological entities in many cases are not sharply defined, with the result that frequently it may, in principle, be impossible to say definitely whether the case under consideration should be included in the group.

## Organic Psychoses

Senile dementia clearly illustrates the difficulties. The fact that the biological basis of the disease is an organic brain damage would seem to give possibilities for an accurate demarcation based on anatomical examination. Unfortunately this is not the case. It is true that in cases with gross clinical symptoms we will always find definitely morbid changes of the brain structure. But it is just as true that the correlation between the degrees of clinical symptoms and anatomical alterations, respectively, is extremely low and that neither qualitatively nor quantitatively is there a sharp line between the anatomical changes found in mentally normal old people and those found in old people with clear-cut senile dementia. It might be possible to agree on some arbitrary quantitative criteria in the form of a certain number of senile plaques in certain areas of the brain, for example. In this way it might be possible to establish a statistically significant difference between old people with and without senile dementia, respectively. Such samples must, however, be very large, and in the individual case the criteria would, nevertheless, be useless.

Similiar difficulties would arise if psychological tests were used. No doubt there is a relation among anatomical changes, clinical symptoms, and results of testings, but the correlation is rather low. Often we meet patients who clinically are definitely deteriorated but who, nevertheless, get amazingly good scores in test situations. Thus it cannot be doubted that the most reliable—but, unfortunately, not *very* reliable—way of delimiting senile dementia is by clinical criteria, including the history and present social adjustment.

With regard to the anamnestic data, the speed with which the symptoms have developed is of especial importance for the differential diagnosis between senile dementia and normal senile involution. If a person of sixty-five develops a deep deterioration in the course of just one year and if the symptoms and the pathology accord with the picture of a senile dementia, we would have no objection to making this diagnosis, but the situation would be quite different if similar symptoms had developed in a ninety-year-old person and then progressed at a low rate. It is probable that the anatomical and pathophysiological foundations are the same in both cases, but nevertheless we would, in the first case, prefer to speak of a morbid process, whereas we would hesitate to do so in the second case.

Here it is obviously not a matter of sharp definition. The practical distinction may be easy in extreme cases, but it is certainly not in many of the cases which lie between the extremes.

Accordingly, attempts to establish with accuracy the disease expectancy for senile dementia are meaningless. Claims that the disease is more frequent in one population than in another must, therefore, be critically evaluated. Only when conspicuous differences are found by one investigator who has examined different population groups can such figures be taken seriously. In this connection we are referring especially to differences of such magnitude as those between disease expectancies in the general population and among the relatives of sick propositi. It is possible that determinations of disease expectancy for senile dementia can be valuable as a tool in genetic investigations, but these procedures will not usually be sufficiently accurate for the comparison of health conditions in different social strata, in different countries, or in the same population at different times.

In the calculation of disease expectancy, there are special problems with diseases which do not have a circumscribed "risk zone." In the case of senile dementia there is certainly no upper limit for the risk period; on the contrary, the risk must be assumed to increase with age, and theoretically the risk must be 100 per cent if the individual lives for a sufficiently long period. In these cases the risk up to a certain age must be calculated, or the risk must be separately determined for each age group. In the Larsson and Sjögren (1954) comprehensive investigation of a rural Swedish population of 25,000 people, the upper limit was fixed at eighty years, and the disease expectancy for senile dementia was thus found to be 0.6 per cent for males and 0.8 per cent for females. For obvious reasons these figures cannot be assumed to be generally valid, but they are, nevertheless, the best-founded figures which we have at the present time.

In most respects the points previously advanced are also relevant to the second most frequent disorder of old age, cerebral arteriosclerosis. This process usually starts decades before senescence. Post-mortem we may also find definite arteriosclerotic affections in the brain in cases which did not display any mental symptoms. When trying to determine expectancy, we are usually obliged to use clinical criteria, and we know that what we are delimiting in this way does not correspond to any pathoanatomical entity. In addition, even if senile involution of the brain and arteriosclerotic encephalopathy do not have anything in common with regard to etiology, it is not uncommon to find traces of both affections in the same brain, sometimes to the extent that even after an autopsy it is impossible to decide whether the mental symptoms in a particular case have been caused predominantly by senile dementia or by arteriosclerotic encephalopathy.

Taking these sources of error into consideration, it is amazing that it has been possible to ascertain certain reasonably significant differences in disease expectancy, especially between sexes. There is no doubt that in many populations cerebral arteriosclerosis is relatively more frequent in males than in females, whereas the reverse is true with senile dementia. Even with due regard to the selective action of social factors on these figures, there cannot be any doubt that a real sex difference exists in this respect. This could possibly throw some light on the pathogenetic problems connected with these two disorders.

Some of the mental disorders of old age are clinically and anatomically more sharply delimited; most of them, however, are so rare that they are of no great practical significance in gerontopsychiatry. Intensive research in recent years, especially by Sjögren, Sjögren, and Lindgren (1952) has, on the other hand, shown that at least Pick's and Alzheimer's diseases are so frequent that they constitute a significant part of the cases in this area. It should be possible to make a reasonably accurate determination of the disease expectancy for these two diseases. The Swedish investigators have made the interesting statement that the expectancies for the two diseases show great variations geographically, even in a relatively homogeneous population like that of Sweden. They found that about 10 per cent of all presenile and senile psychoses in Sweden belong to this group and that the combined expectancy for the two disorders is about 0.1 per cent. This would mean that the incidence of new cases in Sweden is about seventy-five each year and that the number of living patients with these disorders should be about five hundred (in a population of approximately seven million). In the eastern part of Sweden Pick's disease was more frequent than Alzheimer's disease, whereas the opposite was the case in the western parts.

### Functional Psychoses

If we turn to the so-called functional psychoses, the problems are in some directions more, in other directions less, complex. The clinical delimitation of manic-depressive psychosis and schizophrenia is somewhat easier than the corresponding delimitation of senile dementia and cerebral arteriosclerosis. On the other hand, the occurrence of functional disorders in the aged is a field of great controversy.

Until a few decades ago, it was generally accepted that the onset of a manic-depressive psychosis almost always took place during maturity. The geneticists usually considered the risk zone to last from the fifteenth to the fiftieth or sixtieth year. Some later investigations, especially those of Slater (1938) and Fremming (1951), have, however, made it quite clear that a considerable fraction of these cases start in old age, especially among males. A manic or depressive condition occurring in a person of seventy who has never before had similar emotional psychoses may very well be of a manic-depressive nature. In earlier times it was customary to regard depressions, especially those that developed late, as involutional psychoses. In these cases it was thought that there was an organic brain process which produced mainly melancholic symptoms in the beginning, but later developed more definite organic symptoms. Stenstedt (1959) has, however, shown that the majority of these depressive reactions in the aged belong to the manic-depressive groups. The results of his genetic investigations confirm this; in fact the majority of the depressions in the aged disappear without leaving any trace of organic disorder.

On the other hand, there is no doubt that, if a depression occurs in a person suffering from an organic brain disorder (usually of an arteriosclerotic nature), the presence of this process will usually tend to protract the course of the depression. This observation corresponds to the fact that in the case of younger manic-depressives the presence of organic brain damage also seems to protract the course of the psychotic periods. If, as we believe, the majority of the depressive syndromes in the aged should be considered manic-depressive, the disease expectancy for this disorder must be considerably higher than previously assumed. In the Scandinavian countries it seems to be at least 1 per cent, whereas earlier German studies suggested a figure of about 0.2 to 0.4 per cent. It is likely that the expectancy for this disorder varies in different populations and different social strata much more than the expectancy for schizophrenia. More attempts at accurate determinations of the expectancy in different populations would be of interest, and the instigation of such investigations must be recommended. Because there is still some doubt in many circles about the nosological grouping of the old-age depressions, it may be advisable to calculate the expectancy of these cases separately.

Apart from these epidemiological considerations, it should be stressed not only to psychiatrists, but also to general practitioners and all others who have responsibility for old patients, that benign emotional disorders constitute a large portion of psychoses in old age. These cases demand active treatment, which often leads to excellent results.

One of the main problems for the gerontologist is whether the paraphrenias should be included in schizophrenia. The term "paraphrenia," which had practically gone out of use for a long time, has been reintroduced in recent years, mainly by English psychiatrists. The patients display a very characteristic delusional-hallucinatory picture which shares many features of schizophrenia; the patients are, however, usually emotionally well-preserved, and they do not show typical schizophrenic autism. It is, therefore, not surprising that there is some hesitation about simply grouping the paraphrenias with the schizophrenias. On the other hand, this deviation from the typical schizophrenic picture may be explained by the fact that the disease process started at an age when the personality of the patient has completely matured and resists the personality-dissolving processes which, at an earlier age, may cause the typical schizophrenic picture. Genetics should be in a position to throw some light on the nosological grouping of the paraphrenias. Schulz (1930), Knoll (1952), Bleuler (1943), and Kay and Roth [1] have made important contributions in this direction. Results seem to indicate that the majority of the paraphrenias are closely related to schizophrenia. This is especially true of the cases which are dominated by hallucinations. The more purely delusionary syndromes will, in many cases, belong to other groups, especially to the psychogenic psychoses or to the atypical manic-depressive conditions. The paraphrenics should, of course, not be confused with paranoid-hallucinatory syndromes in the initial stages of Alzheimer's disease; in these cases typical organic symptoms will invariably occur later.

### INCIDENCE

Incidence investigations aim at determining the rate of new cases during a given period in a given population. Such determinations are easy to establish in cases of acute disorders with conspicuous symptoms, especially if the condition necessitates immediate hospital

[1] See D.W.K. Kay & M. Roth, "Schizophrenias of Old Age" (Volume I, Chapter 20, *supra*).

admission in all cases, for instance because of the danger of contagion. These conditions are never present in psychiatry, and a true incidence determination is imposible in disorders like senile dementia which have an insidious onset. In this case, as in a number of other cases, one has to acquiesce to the evidence which the incidence itself gives in the form of first admission to the hospital. The correlation between admission figures and true incidence is very low and subject to wide variations, depending on the inclination to hospitalization in the population at the given moment. That the number of first admissions for senile dementia has been rising rapidly in many populations during recent years is therefore no proof of real changes in the incidence. Nevertheless the figures can be of great social and administrative significance.

When investigating statistics on the first admissions of old psychiatric patients, it is tempting to try to avoid all difficulties of diagnosis. This can be done most easily by simply ascertaining the admission rates of different age groups regardless of diagnosis. In many countries statistics have shown a considerable increase in the percentage of admissions of old patients to psychiatric wards. These statistics have caused a widespread belief that admissions of old patients constitute a rapidly increasing percentage of admissions to all psychiatric hospitals. This, however, is not the case. In many hospitals the increase in admissions of old patients is absolute, not relative. In the Psychiatric Hospital in Risskov, Denmark, a study (Rafaelsen & Strömgren, 1956) was conducted on the age distribution of admissions in the period 1910-1954. It turned out that patients of sixty and over constituted 10-12 per cent of all admissions during the period. This is a regional hospital which receives all the psychiatric admissions from a certain district of rural areas as well as small and medium-sized cities. In metropolitan populations, for instance, that of Copenhagen, it seems to be a rule that old patients constitute a constantly rising percentage of admissions to psychiatric wards.

Sjögren and Larsson (1959) have studied first admissions to all psychiatric hospitals in Sweden. They were especially interested in the changes during the period 1930-1950. They found that in the period 1931-1935 the men patients of sixty or over constituted 8.7 per cent of all first admissions, in 1941-1945, 15.5 per cent; for women patients the corresponding figures were 10.4 per cent and 18.3 per cent. The incidence figures (the number of admissions for each 100,000 people in the corresponding age group) were, however, practically unchanged in the corresponding period for the sixty–sixty-nine age group whereas for the seventy–seventy-nine group they had increased from 65 to 109 (men) and 69 to 106 (women). These figures seem to indicate that the society's increasing inability to tolerate old psychiatric patients is of significance only for patients over seventy.

## PREVALENCE

The prevalence figures have, of course, a still lower correlation with the disease expectancy than the incidence figures have. The prevalence investigations have mainly practical social or therapeutic purposes. In principle, it is possible to use prevalence figures, for example, those acquired in census investigations, as a basis for calculating expectancy figures. This can, however, only be done if we also have accurate knowledge of the duration of the disease and the mortality rates in both the sound and sick populations. In very few cases is this necessary information available.

Determinations of prevalence have the obvious advantage of being easy to carry out in theory. The methodology is not very intricate —it is just a question of gathering information, if possible through personal examination, concerning all members of a given population who were alive at a certain moment. One drawback of these investigations is that they are time-consuming; only if they are very comprehensive is it possible to collect sufficient material for statistical evaluation. Comparisons between prevalence figures from different populations are, of course, only meaningful if the age distribution and mortality rates are identical in both populations or if it is possible to make corrections for differences in these respects. If only hospitalized cases are counted, there are still more serious difficulties because the nosocomial factors have to be taken into consideration.

Prevalence figures for hospitalized cases are of great practical importance. It is especially interesting to follow the movements of the prevalence figures since they may serve as a basis for attempted predictions about the need for hospital facilities for the different kinds of patients. We know that the age distribution and diagnoses of psychiatric disorders among hospitalized cases have changed considerably in recent decades. Since the structure and function of hospitals depend very much on the nature of patients treated there, it is obviously essential in planning hospital buildings to have an estimate of the future distribution of patients in these respects.

Such predictions will always be liable to grave error. Theoretically it is possible to attempt to determine which factors influence the prevalence figures, to estimate the probable development of each factor in years to come, and to integrate them. But factors of disease expectancy, disease duration, age distribution of population, mortality in the general population and among sick people, the willingness of the population to seek admission to hospitals, and the number of available hospital beds cannot be determined with certainty, and, if attempts are made to combine all these factors in one mathematical formula, the result will be so uncertain that it is questionable whether the procedure would be worthwhile.

It seems reasonable to use other approaches. The simplest will probably prove to be the most reliable—to proceed empirically, making a series of consecutive determinations of prevalence from statistics reported for preceding decades and making extrapolations for the decades to come if a definite trend is shown.

## A Representative Study

An investigation of some of the criteria in question has recently been conducted in Denmark (Arentsen & Strömgren, 1959). All patients resident in the state hospitals (which comprise all psychiatric hospitals with the exception of one which serves Copenhagen) were included in the study. Analysis included the census materials for 1942, 1947, 1952, and 1957; distribution of the hospitalized patients according to age and sex; and comparison of subgroups with distributions in the total population. The results are shown in Table 1 and in figs. 1 and 2.

In Fig. 1 all the material is presented—all patients fifteen or over. The ordinate gives the rate for each 100,000 for males (black columns), females (hatched columns), and both sexes (white columns). The rate was very constant from 1942 to 1957, being close to 300 for each 100,000. Supposing that the number of available psychiatric hospital beds in coming years will grow at the same speed as the population figures, the rate should remain constant, as shown on the diagram where the extrapolations for 1960, 1965, and 1970 have been made.

When the material was distributed into age groups (Fig. 2), it became clear that the tendencies in the different groups varied. In the youngest age group (fifteen to twenty-four) the changes since 1942 have not been impressive, and we have no reason to predict significant changes in the years to come. In the twenty-five–thirty-four group, it is probable that there will be a slight decrease in the rate. The thirty-five–forty-four group will decrease considerably during the period from

TABLE 1
AGE DISTRIBUTION OF PATIENTS IN
DANISH STATE PSYCHIATRIC HOSPITALS
IN 1942, 1947, 1952, AND 1957*

(Rates for each 100,000)

| Age | 1942 | 1947 | 1952 | 1957 |
|---|---|---|---|---|
| -14 | 0.3 | 0.6 | 0.8 | 0.5 |
| 15-19 | 22 | 21 | 28 | 34 |
| 20-24 | 73 | 60 | 61 | 60 |
| 25-29 | 137 | 107 | 86 | 105 |
| 30-34 | 196 | 171 | 147 | 144 |
| 35-39 | 303 | 233 | 226 | 181 |
| 40-44 | 395 | 321 | 273 | 241 |
| 45-49 | 462 | 416 | 345 | 317 |
| 50-54 | 478 | 458 | 468 | 368 |
| 55-59 | 472 | 462 | 508 | 464 |
| 60-64 | 453 | 480 | 531 | 525 |
| 65-69 | 390 | 441 | 516 | 530 |
| 70-74 | 383 | 432 | 526 | 581 |
| 75-79 | 395 | 450 | 549 | 670 |
| 80- | 312 | 395 | 606 | 733 |
| All ages | 206 | 196 | 203 | 199 |

*Reports as of January 1, 1942, 1947, and 1952; and September 26, 1957.

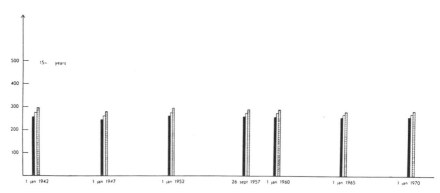

FIG. 1. Distribution of all patients fifteen years of age and over in Danish psychiatric hospitals for the years 1942, 1947, 1952 and 1957 with extrapolations for 1960, 1965, and 1970. The ordinates give the rate for each 100,000 for males (black columns), females (hatched columns), and both sexes (white columns).

## TABLE 2
### DIAGNOSTIC DISTRIBUTION AMONG PATIENTS
### IN DANISH PSYCHIATRIC HOSPITALS ON SEPTEMBER 26, 1957

(In percentages)

| Diagnoses | Males | Females | Males and females |
|---|---|---|---|
| Schizophrenia | 62.2 | 57.1 | 59.5 |
| Manic-depressive psychosis | 6.6 | 9.6 | 8.2 |
| Organic disorders: | | | |
|   Presenile and senile psychoses | 5.6 | 9.0 | 7.4 |
|   Cerebrovascular disease | 3.3 | 2.0 | 2.6 |
|   Neurosyphilis | 3.4 | 1.3 | 2.2 |
|   Epilepsy | 1.4 | 0.8 | 1.1 |
|   Other organic disorders | 2.8 | 1.5 | 2.1 |
| Reactive conditions:* | | | |
|   Psychogenic psychoses† | 3.3 | 4.9 | 4.2 |
|   Neuroses | 1.9 | 4.1 | 3.1 |
|   Psychopathy | 2.4 | 3.7 | 3.1 |
|   Mental deficiency | 1.4 | 1.4 | 1.4 |
|   Alcoholism | 2.5 | 0.3 | 1.3 |
|   Drug addiction | 0.5 | 0.5 | 0.5 |
| Other conditions: | | | |
|   Unclassifiable psychoses | 2.0 | 3.1 | 2.6 |
|   Other diagnoses | 0.6 | 0.6 | 0.6 |

*The "reactive conditions" consist partly of cases which represent clearly situational reactions (psychogenic psychoses and neuroses), partly of relatively static conditions which are not themselves the immediate cause of admission and lead to admission only under certain external circumstances to which these vulnerable individuals "react."
†The "psychogenic psychoses" are psychoses which arise in immediate connection with a mental stress.

1957 to 1970, the rate dropping from 211 to 111 for each 100,000; in 1957 this group comprised 14.3 per cent of all resident patients, and the percentage will probably drop to about 6 in 1970. In the forty-five–fifty-four group there will be a similar decrease, the rate falling from 341 to 221 and the percentage from 21.3 to 12.9. After this age the tendency is likely to reverse itself; for the fifty-five–sixty-four group a considerable rise will take place, more for the males than for the females. The most striking increase will be found in the group sixty-five and over. Here the rate is calculated to increase from 601 to 776, which means that the percentage among the resident patients will rise from 29 to 42.4 per cent (38 per cent for males and 46.5 per cent for females). More than 50 per cent of the patients will be sixty or more years of age.

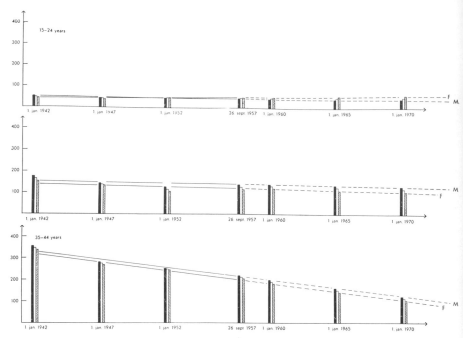

FIG. 2. Distribution by age group of patients in Danish psychiatric hospitals for the years 1942, 1947, 1952, and 1957 with extrapolations for 1960, 1965, and 1970. The ordinates give the rate for each 100,000 for males (black columns), females (hatched columns), and both sexes (white columns).

### Extrapolation

What right do we have to make such extrapolations and to attribute predictive importance to them? In the pure mathematical sense the extrapolations are quite sound, being of a simple linear nature. Probably the main objection is that one important factor—the rate at which hospital beds become available—is supposed to remain constant although there is a definite possibility that it may change. Any considerable change in this rate will have a tendency to influence the age distribution; if the rate decreases, the older age groups will become relatively more dominant. If, on the other hand, the number of available beds increases more quickly than the population, the patients in the younger age groups will have better chances, and the patients who presently do not receive needed hospital treatment will have a chance to receive it.

Up to the present the development seems to show that old patients are more successful than young patients in the competition

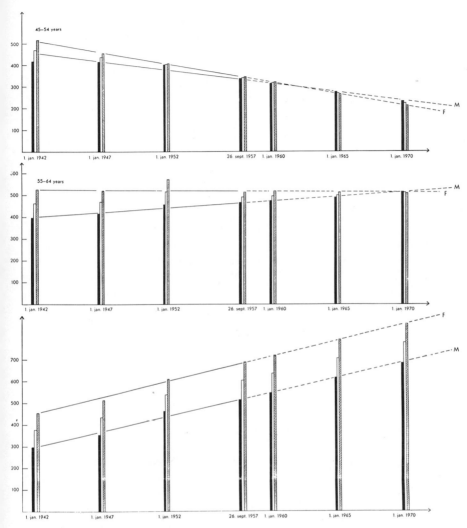

for hospital beds; otherwise it is difficult to explain the fact that the rate for each 100,000 has decreased for the younger groups. It is, of course, possible that more efficient treatment has contributed to this decrease, but it is improbable that the whole decrease can be explained that way. Is it really true that when an old and a young patient compete for a chance to go to a hospital the older one will be preferred? One might believe that the opposite would be the case, and, in fact, this is probably true most of the time, but the reason that the

## TABLE 3
### DIAGNOSTIC DISTRIBUTION OF PATIENTS IN DANISH PSYCHIATRIC HOSPITALS ON SEPTEMBER 26, 1957

(In percentages)

| Age | Schizophrenia | | Manic-depressive psychosis | | Organic disorders | | Reactive conditions | | Other conditions | | Total | |
|---|---|---|---|---|---|---|---|---|---|---|---|---|
| | M | F | M | F | M | F | M | F | M | F | M | F |
| -14 | 100.0 | 0.0 | 0.0 | 0.0 | 0.0 | 0.0 | 0.0 | 66.7 | 0.0 | 33.3 | 100.0 | 100.0 |
| 15-19 | 32.1 | 14.5 | 7.5 | 5.5 | 13.2 | 5.5 | 39.6 | 61.8 | 7.5 | 12.7 | 99.9 | 100.0 |
| 20-24 | 47.0 | 25.7 | 6.0 | 8.3 | 3.6 | 3.7 | 34.9 | 55.0 | 8.4 | 7.3 | 99.9 | 100.0 |
| 25-29 | 62.6 | 37.6 | 2.7 | 8.5 | 4.4 | 6.4 | 24.3 | 43.3 | 5.9 | 4.3 | 99.9 | 100.1 |
| 30-34 | 62.2 | 43.5 | 4.6 | 6.7 | 5.8 | 3.6 | 23.6 | 40.8 | 3.9 | 5.4 | 100.1 | 100.0 |
| 35-39 | 69.0 | 57.5 | 4.5 | 7.3 | 8.7 | 3.6 | 15.1 | 26.2 | 2.7 | 5.5 | 100.0 | 100.1 |
| 40-44 | 73.6 | 63.2 | 3.4 | 5.1 | 6.3 | 4.6 | 14.2 | 24.4 | 2.4 | 2.7 | 99.9 | 100.0 |
| 45-49 | 70.8 | 61.9 | 7.1 | 9.6 | 7.3 | 5.1 | 13.0 | 20.3 | 1.8 | 3.1 | 100.0 | 100.0 |
| 50-54 | 68.1 | 66.6 | 7.2 | 8.3 | 9.6 | 6.2 | 12.4 | 15.6 | 2.8 | 3.3 | 100.1 | 100.0 |
| 55-59 | 68.6 | 66.9 | 8.3 | 9.1 | 11.4 | 8.3 | 9.0 | 10.8 | 2.8 | 4.9 | 100.1 | 100.0 |
| 60-64 | 65.4 | 66.3 | 6.9 | 10.9 | 15.9 | 9.1 | 9.6 | 8.9 | 2.2 | 4.7 | 100.0 | 99.9 |
| 65-69 | 63.2 | 64.7 | 7.5 | 13.9 | 19.1 | 11.1 | 8.3 | 7.0 | 1.9 | 3.3 | 100.0 | 100.0 |
| 70-74 | 50.7 | 54.8 | 9.2 | 13.3 | 32.3 | 25.8 | 5.0 | 4.4 | 2.8 | 1.7 | 100.0 | 100.0 |
| 75-79 | 44.4 | 43.9 | 7.2 | 9.4 | 40.8 | 40.4 | 5.8 | 3.4 | 1.8 | 2.8 | 100.0 | 99.9 |
| 80- | 24.0 | 33.4 | 6.8 | 8.2 | 65.0 | 55.0 | 3.2 | 2.1 | 0.9 | 1.3 | 99.9 | 100.0 |
| All ages | 62.2 | 57.1 | 6.7 | 9.6 | 16.4 | 14.7 | 12.1 | 14.9 | 2.6 | 3.7 | 100.0 | 100.0 |

hospitals are increasingly dominated by old patients is not that the old patients prevail among the admissions; the main reason is that those who were admitted at a younger age now stay in the hospital for a much longer time than they used to, and gradually they are advancing to the higher age groups. This fact is explained by the decreasing mortality rate of psychotic patients and especially of schizophrenics. In the 1957 hospital census investigation, which included all Danish patients in psychiatric hospitals, patients were grouped according to age, sex, and diagnoses (tables 2 and 3). The older groups were not dominated by senile and arteriosclerotic patients, but schizophrenics. Only after seventy-five did the true involutional disorders begin to outnumber the schizophrenics.

### *Hospital Planning*

On the basis of these prevalence studies it must be concluded that in planning hospital buildings, due respect must be paid to the fact that in the years to come the hospitals will be dominated by old patients. At the same time, however, it must be stressed that the problem cannot be solved by establishing new wards or nursing homes for the senile or, alternatively, psychiatric wards in homes for the aged, as the majority of the old patients in psychiatric hospitals are not suffering from involutional diseases, but are old schizophrenics who do not belong in distinct geriatric institutions. Many of these old schizophrenics are in such a condition that most of the time they need facilities which are found only in regular psychiatric wards; this applies to therapeutic as well as nursing needs, physical treatment, and occupational and recreational therapy.

It has been mentioned several times that in Denmark, as in most other countries, there is an increasing inclination to hospitalize disabled old persons. Can we take it for granted that this tendency will continue in the future? Can no measures to counteract this tendency be conceived? A recent experience in Denmark gives a hint that some possibilities do exist. In the country there are a great number of small nursing homes for the aged and disabled. Both these institutions and the public old-age homes have been overcrowded because of the decreasing ability of the population to keep their old relatives in their homes. In 1956, the government decided that there should be a considerable increase in invalid and old-age pensions. Since then there has been a definite tendency to leave these institutions. The explanation is, no doubt, the fact that the old people now have more money so that, despite the costs their disabilities cause, they can manage very well outside institutions. Even their relatives have displayed an unexpected willingness to take them into their homes. The prestige and self-esteem of the old people have increased, and their helplessness has decreased correspondingly. Older people have left nursing and old-age homes in great numbers, but have left the psychiatric hospitals only to a small degree. The reason for this difference is that Denmark has relatively few psychiatric hospital beds, with the consequence that only patients who cannot possibly live anywhere else are in the hospitals.

Although the expectancies of mental disorders in Denmark probably do not differ from those in Sweden, England, or the United States, the number of hospitalized psychiatric patients is only about 60 per cent of that in the other countries mentioned. The Danish hospitals would, therefore, be able to house very few patients who would be motivated to leave by an increase in income. In other countries which have more hospital beds available, a greater number of such patients might be in a hospital, and an increase in the old-age pension might then cause a decrease of hospitalized patients.

## SUMMARY

Epidemiological studies may aim at determining disease expectancies, incidence figures, or prevalence figures. The expectancy figures are of the greatest biological revelance; incidence figures may also be of biological significance, but all of these figures, especially the prevalence figures, are greatly influenced by social factors. The determination of the different figures serves different purposes. Only expectancy figures are quite reliable for the purpose of comparing different populations, whereas incidence and prevalence figures are of great practical importance in problems within a population. Unfortunately, very few reliable determinations of expectancies for psychiatric disorders of old age have been carried out, and here is a broad area for further investigation. On the other hand, many useful investigations have already been performed on incidence and prevalence figures.

## REFERENCES

Arentsen, K., & Strömgren, E. *Patients in Danish psychiatric hospitals. Results of a census in 1957.* Aarhus: University of Aarhus Press, 1959.

Bleuler, M. Die spätschizophrenen krankheitsbilder. *Fortschr. Neurol. Psychiat.,* 1943, **15,** 259-297.

Fremming, K.H. *The expectation of mental infirmity in a sample of the Danish population.* London: Cassell, 1951.

Knoll, H. Wahnbildende psychosen der zeit des klimakteriums und der involution in klinischer und genealogischer betrachtung. *Arch. Psychiat. Nervenkr.,* 1952, **189,** 59-92.

Larsson, T., & Sjögren, T. *A methodological, psychiatric and statistical study of a large Swedish rural population.* Copenhagen: Munksgaard, 1954.

Rafaelsen, O.J., & Strömgren, E. Ten years' geriatrics in a Danish psychiatric hospital. In *Report on the eleventh congress of Scandinavian psychiatrists in Oslo, Norway, 1955.* Copenhagen: Munksgaard, 1956. Pp. 103-110.

Schulz, B. Über die hereditären beziehungen paranoid gefärbter alterspsychosen. *Z. ges. Neurol. Psychiat.,* 1930, **129,** 147-190.

Sjögren, T., & Larsson, T. The changing age-structure in Sweden and its impact on mental illness. *Bull. World Hlth Organ.,* 1959, **21,** 569-582.

Sjögren, T., Sjögren, H., & Lindgren, Å., *Morbus Alzheimer and morbus Pick.* Copenhagen: Munksgaard, 1952.

Slater, E. Zur erbpathologie des manisch-depressiven irreseins. Die eltern und kinder von manisch-depressiven. *Z. ges. Neurol. Psychiat.,* 1938, **163,** 1-47.

Stenstedt, Å. *Involutional melancholia.* Copenhagen: Munksgaard, 1959.

# CHAPTER 36

## Social and Epidemiological Aspects of Suicide with Special Reference to the Aged

PETER SAINSBURY

The value of statistical and epidemiological studies in psychiatry has been limited by difficulties of definition and classification. There is not only a lack of agreement in defining a "case" of mental illness, but there is disagreement among psychiatrists about the diagnostic classification and description of patients, and this problem is aggravated when statistical comparisons are made between cultures or between one time and another.

Suicide is the one abnormality of behavior in which the problem of definition and case-finding is largely avoided. When death has been self-inflicted, it is usually obvious. Where there is doubt, the diagnosis is safeguarded by various medicolegal procedures so that a decision is made whether the death should be registered as a suicide. Suicide has another diagnostic advantage to the epidemiologists—it has been mandatory for many decades in many countries to record *all* suicides. Consequently, the incidence of suicide in different nations and in different periods may be compared. Because of these peculiarities, the epidemiology and statistics of suicide have a special position in psychiatry and therefore in the psychiatry of old age. Besides providing a fund of information such as we have about no other behavioral disturbance, the data on suicide are particularly suited to test general propositions about the interaction among abnormal human behavior and social or cultural variables and among abnormal behavior and physical or psychological factors. The notions, for example, that "civilization" has increased mental disturbances, that psychoses vary with the social and cultural characteristics of a community, or that social isolation fosters mental illness in the aged still require objective confirmation. The likelihood that sociocultural considerations of this sort are important determinants of behavior can often be more easily explored, in the first place, by finding whether they apply to suicide; if they do, then the more difficult methodological problem of comparing the incidence of mental illness in different cultures, say, can be more confidently faced.

The reliability of suicide rates is not, of course, beyond reproach; such rates are clearly unsatisfactory in a number of respects. But one must beware of discarding such a comparatively valuable source of information altogether because of its imperfections, as some writers are inclined to do (Zilboorg, 1936). There are regularities and consistencies in rates of suicide which can have emerged only because the trends they reflect are grosser than the imperfections of our epidemiological data; these will be discussed later.

My intention is to discuss how the epidemiology of suicide, particularly of suicide in the aged, may be applied to various facets of the suicide problem—first, how by this means the size of the problem may be clearly defined; second, how its causes may be explored and, if not discovered, promising paths discerned; third, how its clinical forms may be distinguished; and, last, how epidemiological methods can serve to guide its prevention and treatment.

## EXTENT OF THE PROBLEM
## OF SUICIDE

Only incidence and prevalence studies of suicide are able to describe the boundaries of the problem, put it into proportion, and locate the vulnerable vital (age, sex, civil status, and so on), social, and other groups.

In the occupational mortality tables of the registrar-general
of England and Wales (1958a), the sixty most important and frequent
causes of death during 1949-1953 are listed by age. Suicide in males
appears as the fifth most common cause in the age groups twenty to
thirty-four; at fifty-five to sixty-four it is the twelfth most common;
but at sixty-five and over it ranks only twentieth. Therefore, although
the suicide rate increases sharply with age so that it reaches a numer-
ically formidable level in later life, it is, in fact, a relatively more
prominent cause of death in youth. In Japan in 1955, it was the
principal cause of death from ages eighteen to twenty-four in both
sexes.

In both males and females, suicide increases with age. There
is a sharp increase in early middle age and a further increase in the
old-age group, the latter trend being more consistent and more pronounced in males than in females. In England and Wales, the suicide
rate for men aged forty to fifty-nine is about three times their rate
below the age of forty, and in those over sixty it is about five times
higher. For females, the increase in middle life is proportionately as
great, or even greater, than for males, but thereafter the rise is com-
parativly slow. Age and sex curves such as these have been reported
for the past fifty years in England (Fig. 1).

The rise in suicide with age just described for Englishmen is

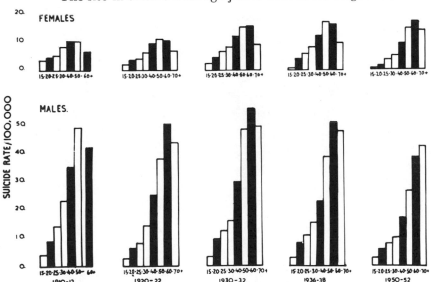

Fig. 1. Mortality from suicide per 100,000 by sex and age at various periods
in England and Wales (World Health Organization, 1956).

## TABLE 1
### CHANGES IN SUICIDE RATES BY SEX IN SELECTED COUNTRIES
(Suicides per 100,000 population aged fifteen and over)

| Country | Male | | | | | Female | | | | |
|---|---|---|---|---|---|---|---|---|---|---|
| | 1901–1903 | 1910–1912 | 1920–1922 | 1952–1954 | Direction of change | 1901–1903 | 1910–1912 | 1920–1922 | 1952–1954 | Direction of change |
| South Africa | | 25 | | 24 | – | | 3 | | 7 | + |
| Canada | | | 16 | 16 | 0 | | | 5 | 5 | 0 |
| United States—total | | | 27 | 23 | – | | | 8 | 6 | – |
| United States—nonwhite | | | 10 | 10 | 0 | | | 3 | 2 | – |
| Australia | | 29 | | 21 | – | | 7 | | 7 | 0 |
| New Zealand | | 28 | | 20 | – | 5 | | | 7 | + |
| England and Wales | 23 | | | 18 | – | 7 | | | 10 | + |
| Scotland | 14 | | | 11 | – | 4 | | | 5 | + |
| North Ireland | | | 12* | 7 | – | | | 4* | 2 | – |
| France | 56 | | 40* | 30 | – | | | 12* | 9 | – |
| Switzerland | | 16 | | 50 | – | 11 | | | 14 | + |
| Netherlands | | 16 | | 12 | – | | 5 | | 6 | + |
| Denmark† | 36 | | | 32 | – | | | 11 | 21 | + |
| Finland | | | 29 | 44 | + | | | 7 | 10 | + |
| Norway | 15 | | | 15 | 0 | 3 | | | 5 | + |
| Sweden | 35 | | | 35 | 0 | 7 | | | 10 | + |
| Ireland | | | 7* | 5 | – | | | 2* | 1 | – |
| Italy | 15 | | | 13 | – | 4 | | | 5 | + |
| Belgium | 31 | | | 26 | – | 6 | | | 9 | + |

| | | | | | | | | | |
|---|---|---|---|---|---|---|---|---|---|
| Spain | 34 | 20 | 10 | 12 | + | 21 | 3 | | 4 | + |
| Portugal | | | 8 | 22‡ | + | | 8 | | 6‡ | − |
| Chile | | | | 11 | + | | | 2 | 3 | + |
| Japan | | | | 39 | + | | | | 25 | + |

Between 1902 and 1953, male suicides have:

　Increased in one country
　Decreased in six countries
　Not changed in two countries

Between earliest decade for which figures are available and 1953, male suicides have:

　Increased in five countries
　Decreased in fourteen countries
　Not changed in four countries

Between 1902 and 1953, female suicides have:

　Increased in nine countries
　Decreased in no countries
　Not changed in no countries.

Between earliest decade for which figures are available and 1953, female suicides have:

　Increased in fifteen countries
　Decreased in six countries
　Not changed in two countries

Source—World Health Organization (1956).
*Based on period 1925–1927.
†From Dreyer (1959).
‡Based on period 1947–1949.

broadly the pattern found in twenty-two of the twenty-five nations whose rates of suicide by age and sex in various periods are listed in the World Health Organization report (1956) on morbidity from suicide. Of the three exceptions, Northern Ireland and Finland have their peak rate at ages fifty to fifty-nine, but in South Africa it is at ages forty to forty-nine. Ceylon, Chile, and especially Japan, have a distinctive and important subsidiary peak at twenty to thirty in both sexes. This is a postwar phenomenon in Japan and is associated with a marked rise in serious crime. Both changes have been ascribed to the dissolution of traditional social institutions and customs which followed the war (Tatai, 1958).

In seventeen of twenty-three nations, the rates of female suicides in the three broad age groups are similar to those found in Englishwomen, but in Northern Ireland, South Africa, and Finland the peak was in middle life, as was found in males. Denmark, Norway, and Sweden also have the female peak at this age.

### An Increasing Problem

The World Health Organization report (1956) also tabulates the incidence of suicide and its evolution since the beginning of the century at various periods by age groups for twenty-five nations. From this and other sources (Dreyer, 1959), it is clear that male suicide rates have decreased in the majority of nations. In Table 1, the rates of twenty-three countries in 1952-1954 are compared with those in the decade nearest the beginning of the century for which figures are available. In only five nations (Japan, Chile, Portugal, Spain, and Finland) has there been an increase; in fourteen countries there was a decrease, and in four there was no change. The opposite obtains for females, among whom suicide has increased in fifteen nations, decreased in six, and did not change in two. If female rates in 1953 are compared with those in 1901, they are found to have increased in all nine nations for which statistics are available (Table 1). There has, therefore, been a decrease in male suicides and an increase in female suicides greater than can be attributed to chance ($\chi^2 = 6.42$, $p < .02 >$ .01) in those nations which are sufficiently organized to record mortality rates and so politically organized as to publish them.

Such are the total suicide trends of the nations by sex. When the trends are further analyzed by age groups, it becomes clear that there are also consistent and important changes, especially as regards suicide in old age. Swinscow (1951) calculated the standardized mean age of suicides in England and Wales from 1861 to 1948. He found that the mean age of male suicides had steadily risen from 57.7 in

1861-1871 to 61.1 in 1946-1949; the rise in females was from 53.0 in 1861-1871 to 57.1 in 1946-1949. He concluded that, for both sexes, suicide has increasingly become a disorder of elderly people; this author also calculated the standardized numbers of suicides in men and women above and below the age of fifty-five in the years 1934-1948. He found that there has been a steady increase in the number of both men and women over fifty-five who commit suicide. The proportion of male suicides over fifty-five as compared to those under fifty-five increased by 5.5 per cent during this fourteen-year period; similarly, female suicides increased by 12.8 per cent. These increases raise the question whether this trend in suicide in the aged is general and, if there is not an absolute increase in the incidence of suicide in the elderly, whether there is still a relative increase as compared to other age groups.

When the suicide rates of the nations in the age group sixty and over are compared in the two periods 1920-1922 and 1952-1954 (it has sometimes been necessary to take the period nearest those figures for which data are available), the male suicide rate is now found to have increased in nine of the nations, decreased in twelve, and remained unchanged in one. The female rate increased in sixteen and decreased in five.

The rise in suicides in the elderly, therefore, contrasts unfavorably with the over-all suicide trends. Furthermore, suicide in males sixty and over has increased proportionately to the other age groups in twelve of the countries and, in females, in fifteen of them.

Table 2 is adapted from the data published by the World Health Organization in 1956. It compares the change in incidence of suicide in males and females over sixty with that for two other age groups during the period 1920-1922 and 1952-1954.

What may we conclude about the extent of the suicide problem? There is a tendency for male suicides to decrease in the majority of Western nations, but this decrease in rate is not shared to the same extent by the elderly males who are now providing a greater proportion of the suicides in the majority of nations. Female suicide rates, on the other hand, are increasing, and this is due to an absolute and proportionate increase in suicide in the older age groups during the past three decades.

### Factors Relating to the Increase

Since suicide is increasingly becoming a problem of old age, we are required to find the underlying reasons for it. First, are the rates related to the increase in the proportion of the population age sixty-

TABLE 2
## CHANGES IN INCIDENCE OF SUICIDE IN SELECTED COUNTRIES
## BETWEEN 1921-1923 AND 1952-1954* BY AGE GROUPS

(Percentage change—mortality around 1921 - 1923 = 100)

| Country | Males | | | Females | | |
|---|---|---|---|---|---|---|
|  | 20-39 | 40-49 | 60+ | 20-39 | 40-49 | 60+ |
| South Africa | - 9 | - 15 | - 20 | + 14 | + 69 | +12 |
| Canada | -18 | - 1 | + 13 | - 20 | 0 | +25 |
| United States | -32 | - 28 | - 15 | - 40 | - 21 | -19 |
| Australia | -22 | - 33 | - 15 | - 12 | + 46 | +56 |
| New Zealand | -46 | - 43 | - 12 | - 46 | + 10 | +43 |
| England and Wales | - 8 | - 31 | - 20 | - 22 | + 9 | +62 |
| Scotland | -43 | - 29 | + 3 | - 4 | - 9 | +33 |
| North Ireland | -67 | - 34 | - 54 | - 54 | - 39 | -24 |
| France | -43 | - 10 | - 27 | - 49 | - 18 | -19 |
| Finland | +21 | + 61 | + 92 | 0 | +114 | +56 |
| Denmark | +31 | + 58 | - 2 | +122 | + 86 | +50 |
| Norway | - 9 | + 21 | + 22 | + 11 | + 89 | + 9 |
| Sweden | - 7 | - 8 | 0 | + 23 | + 16 | - 1 |
| Switzerland | - 2 | - 25 | - 18 | - 12 | - 13 | - 8 |
| Netherlands | -36 | - 34 | - 21 | - 21 | + 17 | +55 |
| Spain | -17 | + 19 | + 9 | +. 14 | + 18 | +46 |
| Ireland | -38 | - 41 | - 28 | - 43 | - 59 | +24 |
| Portugal* | +11 | +107 | +106 | + 2 | + 50 | +61 |
| Italy | -49 | + 3 | + 12 | - 43 | + 26 | +42 |
| Belgium | -50 | - 18 | + 17 | - 54 | - 3 | +35 |
| Chile | +14 | +124 | + 54 | 0 | + 22 | - |
| Japan | +25 | - 29 | - 15 | + 6 | - 5 | +13 |
| Number which increased | 5 | 7 | 9 | 7 | 13 | 16 |
| Number which decreased | 17 | 15 | 12 | 13 | 8 | 5 |
| Number which did not change | 0 | 0 | 1 | 2 | 1 | 0 |
| Number of times age group had: | | | | | | |
| Highest increase | 1 | 4 | 5 | 2 | 4 | 12 |
| Highest decrease | 11 | 6 | 2 | 10 | 4 | 1 |

Source—Adapted from World Health Organization (1956).
*Nearest available year for Portugal was 1948.

five and over, and, second, is mortality greatest where the social and economic problems of old age are most conspicuous?

In order to examine the first of these propositions, fifteen nations were ranked in order of the percentage increase in their populations aged sixty-five and over between 1910 and 1950. These rankings were then compared with those of the suicide rates of both males and females in 1952-1954. Since no significant correlations were found (male $r_s = -.021$; female $r_s = +.074$), the countries' rank orders in percentage increase of their aged population and percentage increase of their suicide in old age (Table 2) were compared. For males, the correlation was $-0.027$; but for females it was $+0.38$ (to reach significance at the 5 per-cent level, $r_s$ would have to be 0.43).

To test the second hypothesis—that suicide in the elderly is related to their economic hardship—the suicide rates at sixty and over in the period before old-age pension schemes were introduced in ten countries were compared to their rates in the period immediately following. The incidence of suicide in both sexes rose in the latter period in the majority of countries. Furthermore, the rise was independent of the type of provision for old age; it occurred in countries with the more comprehensive old-age pension schemes as well as in those with the least. Any beneficial effect of such schemes, therefore, appears to be overshadowed by more potent social factors.

If financial stress were a major factor in suicide of old age, then suicide in the lower classes and economic groups could be expected to show a greater rise than in the upper after age sixty-five, as the former are unlikely to have private savings and superannuation benefits but must live on subsistence-level state pensions. Predictions were made in thirteen socioeconomic groups concerning those in which suicide would increase after sixty-five and those in which it would decrease (Table 3). The registrar-general's tables (1938b) were consulted for occupational mortality in England and Wales from which the proportionate mortality ratios (PMR) for suicide in males can be obtained.

The predictions were as expected in ten of the thirteen groups, and in one group there was no change in the PMR (this was counted as a wrong prediction). The changes occurred in the predicted direction more often than is likely to have been accounted for by chance ($\chi^2 = 5.40$, P $<.05$).

Suicide therefore tends to decrease after sixty-five in the higher social classes and increase in the lower ones. The former retire to more secure economic circumstances than the latter. This may not

TABLE 3
### CHANGES BETWEEN THE PROPORTIONS OF DEATHS IN MALES DUE TO SUICIDE IN VARIOUS SOCIOECONOMIC GROUPS BY AGE

(Proportionate mortality ratios)

| Socioeconomic group | 20-64 | 65 and over | change in PMR on retirement at | |
|---|---|---|---|---|
| | | | *Predicted* | *Observed* |
| Farmers | 179 | 86 | − | − |
| Agricultural workers | 153 | 87 | + | − |
| High administration | 144 | 98 | − | − |
| Other administration | 112 | 81 | − | − |
| Shopkeepers | 129 | 104 | − | − |
| Clerical workers | 101 | 95 | − | − |
| Shop assistants | 116 | 94 | + | − |
| Personal service | 109 | 109 | + | 0 |
| Foremen | 70 | 74 | + | + |
| Skilled workers | 91 | 105 | + | + |
| Semiskilled workers | 79 | 84 | + | + |
| Unskilled workers | 91 | 120 | + | + |
| Armed forces | 106 | 146 | + | + |

Source—Registrar-General (1938b).

be the crucial factor, however; the higher social classes also have a greater tendency both to retire from more responsible positions which are known to have high suicide rates and to retire to opportunities for more varied interests.

It is not possible to draw definite conclusions from these scanty data. There is some evidence that economic hardship in old age may be adversely affecting their rate of suicide, as the customary inverse relation between suicide and class status is less evident in those over the age of sixty-five. More detailed inquiries than these are required.

## EPIDEMIOLOGY AND THE CAUSES OF SUICIDE

How are these varied observations on the incidence of suicide in later life, on its changes with time and with relation to nationality and social group membership, to be interpreted? The epidemiological approach can contribute in a number of ways to the search for causes or at least by providing facts can serve as a fruitful source of hypotheses about them.

The suicide rate of large, heterogeneous populations is made up of the separate rates of many component groups. If these are identified, and if any that contribute disproportionately to the over-all suicide rate are recognized, their ecological, social, or other likely characteristics may be studied. I will attempt to illustrate this procedure of breaking a total rate into smaller components with identifiable features by considering suicide in relation to districts.

In most European states the rural suicide rate is less than the urban one (Dublin & Bunzel, 1933). For example, the standardized rate in London as a percentage of that for all England and Wales is 115, for the country towns it is 106, for other urban districts 97, and for rural districts 88 (Registrar-General, 1938a). Holland is an interesting exception, and the reasons for its high rural suicide rate have been investigated. It was found to be due to the larger number of rural aged who felt themselves a burden on the community and who lacked a socially useful role (Gargas, 1932). The implications of this conclusion are discussed below.

That there are features of urban life which engender suicide is apparent if the analysis is taken one step further. For example, it has been found in the United States that the suicide rate increases with the size of the city (Dublin & Bunzel, 1933). When, next, the districts within a city such as Chicago (Cavan, 1928) or London (Sainsbury, 1955) are examined, the relatively high over-all suicide rates of these cities is found to be the effect of certain districts which have a consistently high rate. In London, for example, the West End boroughs of Holborn, Kensington, and Westminster had rates over twice as high as the working-class boroughs of Poplar and Deptford. If measures are then obtained of the social characteristics which are likely to determine suicide and which also differentiate the populations of these smaller, more homogeneous, areas, these may profitably be related to the suicide rates of the districts.

In London, for example, indexes of economic status and of social isolation were obtained for each borough. A significant negative correlation between the suicide rates and the measures of economic status and a positive correlation to isolation were found. It was not possible, however, to be sure whether such statistical associations were an effect of some third variable or whether they were causal, as originally predicted. The next step, therefore, was to examine the coroners' records of successive cases of suicide to find whether they were, in fact, of higher social status and leading lonelier and more isolated lives than the general population. The case studies confirmed the original correlations. Suicides in London were more isolated and of higher social status than the other inhabitants of the boroughs in which they lived.

A recent re-examination of the case material shows that 39 per cent of suicides aged sixty and over were living alone, a significantly higher proportion than for the middle-aged (23 per cent) or young (16 per cent) suicides. The proportion of aged living alone in the population at risk was significantly less. An urban area was subdivided into smaller districts with identifiable social characteristics; it was then possible to show that the prevalence of suicide related to these characteristics in a predictable manner. It was concluded by this means, for instance, that social isolation is a probable factor engendering suicide in the elderly. Such conclusions may be put to the test by seeing whether the same hypothesis can (a) reasonably account for other patterns in the incidence of suicide and (b) successfully predict differences in mortality. If any hypothesis, such as the one relating to social isolation, can be shown to explain and predict in this way, then it is likely to be valid. These approaches will now be considered.

The abundance of data on the incidence of suicide in vital and social groups, by districts and at different periods in time, reveals regularities in the material from which reasonable notions as to cause may be derived. Durkheim (1930) first observed that the suicide rate of any nation held a remarkably constant position in relation to the rates of other nations. From this constancy he inferred an order of causes distinct from those that determined suicide in the individual; it suggested a tendency to suicide inherent in the social structure. Using Durkheim's method, the suicide rates of both men and women aged sixty and over of twenty-four nations were rank-correlated for the periods 1920-1922 and 1952-1954. The male suicides in this age group correlated 0.89 for the two periods, and the female, 0.92. It seems likely, therefore, that the social and cultural structure of the nations determine the incidence of suicide among the aged as well as the over-all rate. Similarly, when the suicide rates of the London boroughs were correlated over three decades, each borough retained its characteristic position. Again, a social explanation is the one most readily invoked for such regularities. That social factors determine suicide rates becomes even more probable when other recurrent themes in suicide rates are identified. Reverting once more to the World Health Organization report (1956) on suicide mortality, it is evident that two

TABLE 4
EFFECT OF WAR ON SUICIDE RATES BY SEX
IN SELECTED BELLIGERENT AND NEUTRAL COUNTRIES

(Suicides per 100,000 population aged fifteen and over)

| Country | Male | | | Female | | |
|---|---|---|---|---|---|---|
| | 1938 | 1944 | Percentage difference | 1938 | 1944 | Percentage difference |
| **Belligerent countries** | | | | | | |
| Union of South Africa | 15.5 | 10.7 | -31 | 5.0 | 3.4 | -32 |
| Canada | 13.1 | 8.9 | -32 | 3.7 | 3.2 | -14 |
| United States | 23.5 | 14.9 | -37 | 6.9 | 5.4 | -22 |
| Ceylon | 10.1 | 8.2 | -19 | 3.9 | 4.1 | + 5 |
| Austria* | 60.7 | 28.1 | -54 | 28.6 | 13.8 | -52 |
| France | 31.0 | 18.2 | -41 | 8.9 | 6.1 | -32 |
| Italy | 11.0 | 6.0 | -46 | 3.6 | 2.0 | -44 |
| England and Wales | 18.0 | 13.5 | -25 | 8.2 | 5.8 | -30 |
| Scotland | 12.3 | 9.1 | -26 | 6.3 | 4.5 | -29 |
| North Ireland | 6.9 | 5.6 | -19 | 6.9 | 5.6 | -19 |
| Australia | 16.4 | 9.9 | -40 | 5.0 | 4.9 | - 2 |
| New Zealand | 19.5 | 14.6 | -25 | 5.1 | 5.7 | +12 |
| Belgium | 27.6 | 18.1 | -34 | 8.6 | 6.5 | -24 |
| Denmark | 28.9 | 24.0 | -17 | 12.9 | 20.5 | +59 |
| Finland | 32.8 | 27.7 | -16 | 7.3 | 5.3 | -27 |
| Norway | 10.7 | 8.2 | -23 | 5.3 | 9.8 | +85 |
| Netherlands | 11.6 | 7.4 | -36 | 5.4 | 5.6 | + 4 |
| Japan†‡ | 21.0 | 18.7 | -11 | 12.9 | 12.9 | 0 |
| **Neutral countries** | | | | | | |
| Chile | 6.8 | 6.5 | - 4 | 2.5 | 2.3 | - 8 |
| Ireland | 4.7 | 4.6 | - 2 | 1.8 | 0.6 | -67 |
| Portugal | 16.6 | 13.9 | -16 | 5.0 | 4.8 | - 4 |
| Sweden | 25.0 | 20.6 | -18 | 6.8 | 5.7 | -16 |
| Switzerland | 38.4 | 37.2 | - 3 | 11.6 | 14.7 | +27 |
| Spain§ | 6.9 | 8.8 | +28 | 2.3 | 2.6 | +13 |

Source—World Health Organization (1956).
*Nearest figures available for Austria were for 1946.
†Nearest figures available for Japan were for 1947.
‡Japan was also at war in 1938.
§Civil war in Spain in 1938.

social cataclysms—the war of 1939-1945 and the economic depression of 1929-1932—markedly affected rates of suicide.

## War

Table 4 shows that the male suicide rate decreased by between about 20 and 50 per cent in all the nations which were at war in 1944, when compared with 1938. Male suicides even decreased in the neutral countries during this time. Spain, as might be expected, was exceptional in that the suicide rate was lower in 1938 than in 1940-1945; the former period was one of civil war, and during the latter Spain was neutral. The same trends, with a few exceptions, were apparent for women (Table 4).

The *Statistical Review of England and Wales, 1940-45* (Registrar-General, 1949) enables us to discover the age group contributing most to the decrease in suicide in England during the war. This gives the suicide rates by age group per million population in 1938 and 1944. Suicide decreased most in the age group forty-five to sixty-four. Male suicides in the age group forty-five to sixty-four decreased by 42 per cent, female, by 37 per cent. At sixty-five and over, males decreased by 30 per cent and females by 19 per cent; at twenty-five to forty-four, males decreased by 21 per cent and females by 27 per cent.

## Economic Depression

The converse picture, however, was found when the nations' suicide rates in 1930-1932, the period of world-wide economic depression, were compared with those of 1921. The World Health Organization report (1956) gives national suicide rates by age groups for these two periods. The comparative effect of the depression on suicide in different age groups in twenty nations was thereby determined.

It is clear, as Table 5 shows, that the economic depression had significantly differing effects on the three large age groups. Suicide increased most in middle age and increased a little more in the elderly than in the young.

Again, it is the regularity with which these effects occur which compels one to consider social and cultural factors as a major influence on the prevalence of suicide.

## Unemployment and Poverty

In wartime, most males are usefully occupied, and this is particularly true of the middle-aged, who are more vulnerable to the effects of unemployment; during an economic depression, the converse obtains. The changes in suicide by age during economic depression and during wartime, the positive correlations reported between

TABLE 5
CHANGES IN THE INCIDENCE OF SUICIDE BY SEX AND AGE
IN SELECTED COUNTRIES BETWEEN 1921-1922 AND 1931-1932
(ECONOMIC DEPRESSION)

(Percentage change—mortality around 1921-1923 = 100)

| Country | Males | | | Females | | |
|---|---|---|---|---|---|---|
| | 20-39 | 40-49 | 60+ | 20-39 | 40-49 | 60+ |
| South Africa | + 10 | - 4 | +17 | + 63 | +104 | +35 |
| Canada | + 29 | + 48 | +33 | + 32 | + 15 | +23 |
| Chile | + 96 | +150 | +41 | + 90 | +200 | - |
| United States | + 6 | + 28 | +36 | + 19 | + 21 | +20 |
| Germany | - 3 | + 17 | + 1 | + 13 | + 28 | +15 |
| Belgium | + 29 | + 19 | +19 | - 6 | + 18 | + 2 |
| Denmark | + 13 | + 22 | - 9 | + 88 | + 6 | + 5 |
| Spain | - 5 | + 36 | +23 | + 14 | + 26 | +33 |
| Finland | +108 | + 58 | +68 | + 39 | + 42 | +13 |
| France | + 8 | + 3 | 0 | - 5 | + 5 | - 5 |
| Italy | + 5 | + 76 | +55 | - 4 | + 47 | +52 |
| Norway | + 22 | + 35 | +49 | + 63 | + 18 | -24 |
| Netherlands | - 14 | + 11 | - 1 | + 15 | + 54 | +38 |
| Portugal | + 14 | + 61 | +54 | - 10 | + 5 | +46 |
| England and Wales | + 41 | + 20 | +16 | + 42 | + 32 | +45 |
| Scotland | + 56 | + 77 | +76 | +128 | + 91 | +68 |
| Sweden | - 9 | + 8 | - 2 | + 3 | - 2 | -15 |
| Switzerland | + 13 | + 5 | + 5 | - 4 | + 13 | - 9 |
| Australia | + 25 | + 10 | 0 | 0 | + 17 | - 7 |
| New Zealand | - 10 | + 26 | +19 | - 15 | + 28 | +47 |
| | | | | | | |
| Number which increased | 15 | 19 | 15 | 13 | 19 | 14 |
| Number which decreased | 5 | 1 | 3 | 6 | 1 | 5 |
| Number which did not change | 0 | 0 | 2 | 1 | 0 | 0 |
| Number of times age group had: | | | | | | |
| Greatest increase | 6 | 11 | 3 | 5 | 10 | 5 |
| Greatest decrease | 5 | 1 | 1 | 4 | 0 | 4 |

Source—Adapted from World Health Organization (1956).

unemployment and suicide rates (Dublin & Bunzel, 1933; Swinscow, 1951), and case studies in which a high incidence of unemployment is found among suicides (Sainsbury, 1955; Stearns, 1921) all suggest that being gainfully occupied is an important factor protecting the individual from suicide. The rise in male rates around the time of their retirement; the much less conspicuous increase at this time in women, the character and mode of whose working life did not, until recent decades, entail the same abrupt change; and the smaller effects of war on female rates, all indicate that lack of occupation is a factor predisposing to suicide, and especially to suicide in the elderly male. In a consecutive sample of 409 suicides in London, for example, lack of occupational interest was recorded as a factor in the suicide of 20 per cent of males over the age of sixty-five (Sainsbury, 1955).

Occupation must also be considered in its wider social aspect. To the individual, being occupied means that he has a purpose in his activities, but also that he is fulfilling a valued social function and that he is a useful member of his community; to be unoccupied is to become isolated from society. However, the inverse relation between class status and suicide indicates that occupation considered simply as a shield against poverty is not a sufficient explanation of its association with suicide. That poverty per se is less important than

### TABLE 6
### EFFECT OF ECONOMIC DEPRESSION AND THE
### INCIDENCE OF SUICIDE IN SOCIAL CLASSES

(All males aged 20-64)

| Social class | Standardized mortality ratio | | |
|---|---|---|---|
| | 1921-1923 Prosperity | 1930-1932 Economic depression | 1949-1953 Welfare state |
| I. Professional | 113 | 120 | 140 |
| II. Intermediate between I and III | 125 | 137 | 113 |
| III. Skilled workers | 89 | 95 | 89 |
| IV. Intermediate between III and V | 87 | 87 | 92 |
| V. Unskilled workers | 96 | 87 | 117 |

Source—Registrar-General (1938b; 1958a).

the loss of membership and of a role in society may be inferred from a comparison of the registrar-general's figures (1938b, 1958a) for suicide by social class during a period of prosperity, 1920-1923, and one of economic depression, 1930-1932. The greatest rise in suicide occurred in the latter period in classes 1 and 2 (professional and intermediate groups); but in Class 5 (unskilled workers) suicide actually decreased (Table 6).

A paper was referred to earlier in which the standardized number of suicides above and below the age of fifty-five for the years 1934-1948 were compared (Swinscow, 1951). The trend was for suicides above fifty-five to increase proportionately to those below. Two predictions were made, based on the hypothesis that suicide in later life is inversely related to the opportunity society provides its elderly members to perform a socially useful and purposive role. First, male suicides over fifty-five would *decrease* proportionately during the war years because the demand for labor would lead to the employment of more elderly males, including many who had retired; the elderly would therefore be fulfilling a socially valued role. This prediction was confirmed. The previously observed trend for suicide to increase in males over fifty-five was reversed in wartime to the extent of 2 per cent (see Table 7).

TABLE 7
EFFECT OF WAR AND ECONOMIC DEPRESSION AND
INCIDENCE OF MALE SUICIDES
UNDER AND OVER AGE FIFTY-FIVE

| *Periods compared* | *Per cent male suicides in age group* | |
|---|---|---|
| | Under ·55 | Over 55 |
| Prewar and war | | |
| 1934-1938 (Prewar) | 53.9 | 46.1 |
| 1939-1945 (war) | 54.9 | 45.1 |
| Depression and prosperity | | |
| 1934 (depression) | 54.9 | 45.1 |
| 1938 (prosperity) | 52.6 | 47.4 |
| Difference in suicide rates | | |
| Wartime | +1 | -1 |
| Depression | +2.3 | -2.3 |

Source—Adapted from Swinscow (1951).

Second, during the economic depression (1934), suicides below the age of fifty-five would be proportionately higher than in 1938. A major effect of any economic depression is to introduce unemployment in that age group which previously, as wage earners, considered themselves needed and useful citizens. They suddenly become superfluous. Economic depression, then, would tend to have a greater impact on males who would normally be occupied. This hypothesis was also confirmed as the proportion of suicides changed by 4.6 per cent in the predicted direction (Table 7). However, this difference is also in the direction of the general trend for these age groups.

It would seem that poverty becomes an important factor in suicide according to its context. The indigenous poor, to whom poverty is an accepted feature of their position in a static hierarchical society, tolerate it with equanimity. This attitude does not foster suicide. A change from comparative affluence to poverty, or loss of employment is, however, more disruptive, since the person affected often fails to adjust himself to his altered circumstances (Sainsbury, 1955, pp. 21-22).

This conclusion is supported by the incidence of suicide by class in the last United Kingdom census (1951). It seems true to say that, since the war, class mobility has increased in the United Kingdom. Suicide is now found to be proportionately higher in Class 5 than at the two previous censuses (Table 6).

### Social Isolation

The relation between suicide and occupation has been considered from the point of view of social participation or isolation; much of the other epidemiological data on suicide, both in old age and in general, may be similarly understood.

When the incidence of suicide in various isolated groups is compared, those in the more socially isolated are found to have a higher rate. Suicide, as has already been mentioned, had a higher incidence in the districts of London which foster isolation. Similarly, its incidence increases in relation to marital status (with age held constant) as follows: the married, the widowed, the single, the divorced. Moreover, among the married, suicide decreases as each child is added to the family—up to five, anyway. In fact, you are least likely to commit suicide if you are one of a family and working in the country or if you live in an overcrowded city working-class neighborhood. You are most likely to commit suicide if you live alone or if you are the wealthy proprietor of a hotel in a superior but mobile and anonymous city district.

### THE PHYSICAL FACTOR IN SUICIDE

Another epidemiological approach to the problem of suicide is by the study of successive, unselected cases, either from coroners' records or by surveys in which the relatives and associates of the deceased are interviewed.

An important contribution of this kind was one in which the endometriums of twenty-three women of child-bearing age who committed suicide were examined post-mortem (MacKinnon & Mac-Kinnon, 1956). Twenty-four successive cases of accidental death and disease which also came to the coroner's notice were similarly examined. Only two deaths were found to have occurred in the follicular phase of the menstrual cycle, one of which was a suicide. Deaths from suicide were more numerous in the middle than in either the early or late luteal phase. This is convincing evidence that a physiological factor, in this instance endocrine, may predispose to suicide.

The high incidence of physical illness in 409 successive suicides coming to the coroner was surprising. From the post-mortem reports and coroners' records, illness was judged to have been a primary cause in 18 per cent and a contributing one in 29 per cent of the cases. In suicides aged sixty and over, physical illness was estimated to have contributed in 35 per cent of cases, as compared with 10 per cent in the age group fifteen to twenty-nine and 27 per cent in the middle-aged. Physical illness as a determinant of suicide in the elderly might be further examined epidemiologically by comparing its incidence in suicides with that in accidental deaths.

### OTHER SITUATIONS PRECIPITATING SUICIDE

Other factors precipitating suicide in old age might be similarly investigated either by comparing the incidence of critical situations preceding suicide in the various age groups or by comparing their incidence in the elderly suicides to that in the elderly population at risk. Are bereavement or financial hardship, for example, found preceding suicide more often in the elderly than in the young? Is loneliness, retirement to unfamiliar surroundings, or a lack of social and occupational interests more conspicuous in suicides than in a suitably matched sample of old people dying from other causes? Surveys planned to contact the relatives soon after death, such as that carried out in St. Louis (Robins, Murphy, Wilkinson, Gassner, & Kayes, 1959), but with special regard to the elderly, would be required to answer these questions adequately. Similarly, there is a special need for studies on the incidence of depressive illness preceding suicide attempts in old age. In two valuable contributions of this kind, its incidence has been found fairly high (Batchelor & Napier, 1953; O'Neal, Robins, & Schmidt, 1956). This brings up another aspect of suicide to which epidemiological studies can contribute.

## IDENTIFICATION OF CLINICAL SYNDROMES

Among the uses of epidemiology which Morris (1957) discusses in his book is the "identification of syndromes." The kind of question to which this application of epidemiology can contribute is that of the relation of suicide to the common clinical categories of depression. Comparing the incidence of suicide to that of depressive illness in various social and vital groups provides a way of finding out whether those who die from suicide and patients with depressive illnesses are distinct or similar populations. For example, if the suicide rates for the months of the year are examined, they show a characteristic increase in early summer; but so also do the first admission rates for depressive psychoses. This similarity could be because suicides and depressives are both drawn from the same population. The first admission rates for manic-depressive psychoses by age groups also resemble those for suicide by age. However, the suicide and depressive populations clearly differ as regards their incidence by sex and social class (Registrar-General, 1958b; Roth, 1959). There are, therefore, both resemblances and differences between the two when these very broad comparisons are made. It may well be that, if more detailed comparisons of this kind were undertaken, but limited to suicide and depressive illness in the age group sixty and over or middle age, the two populations would then be found to resemble one another more closely, since there are clinical grounds for supposing that depressive psychoses occur more frequently in suicides in these age groups.

Another example of the way in which incidence studies might contribute to the clinical problem of suicide is in differentiating the population which commits suicide from that which attempts it.

Stengel has compared the incidence of attempted suicide with that of suicide by age, sex, marital status, and in a number of other respects (Stengel & Cook, 1958). His sample of attempted suicides was consecutive cases taken from various sources—general hospital, mental hospital, and observation ward. Together they might therefore be expected to broadly represent the characteristics of the attempted-suicide population of London. If, using his tables, we compare this population with those who achieved suicide, we find that the two populations differ significantly as regards age distribution, though there is no difference between age distributions of the various attempted-suicide samples. The incidence of suicide attempts is less in the elderly than in the younger age groups. It has been observed that the seriousness of the intention to die is especially marked in the elderly who attempt suicide (O'Neal et al., 1956) and also in those in whom physical illness (which so frequently accompanies suicide in later life) prompts the attempt (Hendin, 1950; Metropolitan Life Insurance, 1927).

Stengel's suicides and attempted suicides also differ significantly in sex distribution; the degree to which they were alone; the categories of mental disorder from which they suffered; and in the incidence of psychoses, reactive depression, and psychopathy. Clearly, the populations must overlap, but Stengel's detailed clinical and descriptive account of the differences between them is supported by the epidemiological evidence that the two populations are distinct and are, therefore, in two separate clinical categories—those who attempt and those who achieve suicide.

When the suicide rates of the resident population of mental hospitals in England are examined, it is apparent that they did not change appreciably between 1920 and 1947 (Stengel & Cook, 1958). The advent of ECT in the 1940's appeared to have no effect on suicide in hospital. The rates for 1920-1922 were 48.0 per 100,000 residents, and for 1945-1947 they were 51.5. Two recent publications (Registrar-General, 1958b; Registrar-General, 1960) made it possible to compute the suicide rates for 1953 and 1954-1956. In the former period, the rate was 27.3, and, in the latter, 37.7. A significant decrease in suicide therefore occurred in a period when our mental hospitals adopted a more liberal policy, including that of "open doors." This reduction has occurred in spite of an increased admission rate for depressive psychoses and in spite of a higher average age of people who might be expected to be more suicide-prone. Criticism of the open-door policy on the grounds of the risk of suicide is not supported by these figures, though, of course, they require a more critical analysis.

Important, though unfortunately unspecific, indications regarding the prevention of suicide emerge from these epidemiological inquiries. Social circumstances, for example war, can reduce suicide in a country by about one-third. Manifestly, mortality from suicide is highly susceptible to social influences. The social welfare of the aged —particularly, I believe, in the sense of society providing them with a satisfactory role as valued members—is a goal to pursue, but one more easily described than achieved.

## SUMMARY

The use of epidemiological methods to further understanding of suicide in the aged has been described and various studies relating the incidence of suicide to the social and vital characteristics of the community have been applied to the problem as it affects the aged.

The extent of the problem was examined and found to be increasing among the elderly, more so in women than in men. By relating suicide in large age groups to such social factors as district, class, occupational status, and economic status and to such changes in social conditions as war and economic depression, certain patterns in incidence and regularities in their trends were discerned.

Hypotheses to account for these consistencies, such as social isolation and social role, were developed, and predictions were made from them of the incidence or fluctuations in suicide to be expected. Some etiological notions were then explored in this way. The differentiation of aged suicides from suicides in other age groups on clinical, psychological, situational, and physical criteria were considered.

Suggestions for further research into, and on the prevention of, suicide were made. The implications of the epidemiology of suicide for the wider field of social psychiatry were discussed.

*REFERENCES*

Batchelor, I.R.C., & Napier, M.B. Attempted suicide in old age. *Brit. med. J.*, 1953, **2**, 1186-1190.
Cavan, Ruth S. *Suicide*. Chicago: The University of Chicago Press, 1928.
Dreyer, K. Comparative suicide statistics. *Danish med. Bull.*, 1959, **6**, 65-82.
Dublin, L.I., & Bunzel, B.C. *To be or not to be; a study of suicide*. New York: Smith and Haas, 1933.
Durkheim, É. *Le suicide*. (nouv. éd.) Paris: Librairie Félix Alcan, 1930.
Gargas, S. Suicide in the Netherlands. *Amer. J. Sociol.*, 1932, **37**, 697-713.
Hendin, H. Attempted suicide; a psychiatric and statistical study. *Psychiat. Quart.*, 1950, **24**, 39-46.
MacKinnon, P.C.B., & MacKinnon, I. L. Hazards of the menstrual cycle. *Brit. med. J.*, 1956, **1**, 555.
Metropolitan Life Insurance Company. Diseases associated with suicide. *Statist. Bull. Metrop. Life Insur. Company*, 1927, **8** (4), 4-5.

Morris, J.N. *Uses of epidemiology.* Edinburgh: E. & S. Livingstone, 1957.

O'Neal, P., Robins, E., & Schmidt, E.H. A psychiatric study of attempted suicide in persons over sixty years of age. *Arch. Neurol. Psychiat.,* 1956, **75,** 275-284.

Registrar-General for England and Wales. *Statistical review of England and Wales for the year 1935.* London: H.M. Stationery Office, 1938. (a)

Registrar-General for England and Wales. *Decennial supplement, England and Wales, 1931.* Part IIa. London: H.M. Stationery Office, 1938. (b)

Registrar-General for England and Wales. *Statistical review of England and Wales, 1940-45.* Vol. 1. London: H.M. Stationery Office, 1949.

Registrar-General for England and Wales. *Decennial supplement, England and Wales, 1951.* Part II, Vol. 2. London: H.M. Stationery Office, 1958. (a)

Registrar-General for England and Wales. *Statistical review of England and Wales for the two years 1952-53.* Supplement on mental health. London: H.M. Stationery Office, 1958. (b)

Registrar-General for England and Wales. *Statistical review of England and Wales for the three years 1954-56.* Supplement on mental health. London: H.M. Stationery Office, 1960.

Robins, E., Murphy, G.E., Wilkinson, R.H., Gassner, S., & Kayes, J. Some clinical considerations in the prevention of suicide based on a study of 134 successful suicides. *Amer. J. Publ. Hlth,* 1959, **49,** 888-899.

Roth, M. The phenomenology of depressive states. *Canad. Psych. Ass. J.,* Special Supplement, 1959, **4,** 32-54.

Sainsbury, P. Suicide in London. *Maudsley Monographs,* 1955, No. 1. (Institute of Psychiatry, London)

Stearns, A.W. Suicide in Massachusetts. *Ment. Hyg., Concord,* 1921, **5,** 752-777.

Stengel, E., & Cook, M.G. Attempted suicide. *Maudsley Monographs,* 1958, No. 4. (Institute of Psychiatry, London)

Swinscow, D. Some suicide statistics. *Brit. med. J.,* 1951, **1,** 1417-1423.

Tatai, K. A further study of suicides in Japan. *Bull. Inst. Publ. Hlth,* 1958, **7,** 52-58.

World Health Organization. Mortality from suicide. *Epidem. Vital Statist. Rep.,* 1956, **9,** 243-287.

Zilboorg, G. Differential diagnostic types of suicide. *Arch. Neurol. Psychiat.,* 1936, **35,** 270-291.

# CHAPTER 37

*Aging and Mental Health
in Hong Kong*

P. M. YAP

The latest estimate of Hong Kong's population (Maunder & Szczepanik, 1957) was 2,407,000. Those aged sixty and above number 34,000 men and 46,000 women, together making up only 3.3 per cent of the total. People under age fifteen come to 38.2 per cent of the total, indicating that as a population it is rather younger than those of highly industrialized Western countries. In these countries, the percentage of those aged sixty and over is at least double that for Hong Kong. Not a single country in Asia, Africa, or Latin America has a population aged to this degree, although the situation is rapidly changing in Japan.

If the Hong Kong population is projected to 1977, the proportion of persons aged sixty and over will then be 8.7 per cent (Maunder & Szczepanik, 1957). A survey of crude mortality rates gives clear evidence of aging. The mortality of so-called degenerative diseases associated with age has been rising, while mortality from such infectious diseases as tuberculosis, syphilis, gastroenteritis; from infections of the new-born; and from malaria—all of which shorten the expectation of life—has been falling. Thus, between 1950 and 1959, deaths per 100,000 from neoplasms increased from 29.0 to 66.3; from vascular diseases of the central nervous system from 15.2 to 40.0; from arteriosclerosis and degenerative heart diseases from 22.2 to 25.9; from hypertension with or without heart disease from 4.6 to 13.3; and from senility from 5.0 to 15.3 (Wylie, 1960). The suicide rate has also been increasing (Yap, 1958a; Yap, 1958b), and suicide concerns mostly the aged.

TABLE 1
PATIENTS IN HONG KONG MENTAL
AND CASTLE PEAK HOSPITALS*
ON MARCH 31, 1960, BY AGE AND SEX

(Percentage distribution)

| Age in years | Male | Female | Total (N=937) |
|---|---|---|---|
| 10–19 | 6.1 | 4.5 | 5.4 |
| 20–29 | 37.3 | 26.4 | 32.3 |
| 30–39 | 32.9 | 33.5 | 33.2 |
| 40–49 | 15.2 | 23.0 | 18.9 |
| 50–59 | 6.3 | 7.8 | 7.0 |
| 60–69 | 1.6 | 4.0 | 2.7 |
| 70–79 | 0.6 | 0.8 | 0.5 |
| 80 and over | - | - | - |
| Total | 100.0 | 100.0 | 100.0 |

*Oligophrenics are not admitted to these hospitals.

## SOME INDEXES OF MENTAL HEALTH
## IN THE AGED

### Age Distribution

Inpatient psychiatric practice is concerned with only a comparatively small proportion of the aged (Table 1). Whereas the percentage of those aged sixty and over in the Hong Kong Mental

Hospital was only 3.2 per cent, the percentage for a similar population in Sweden between 1946 and 1950 was 17.9 (Sjögren & Larsson, 1959). On the other hand, Mayer-Gross, Cross, Harrington, and Sreenivasan (1958) have shown that the population structure of an Indian mental hospital is similar to that found in Hong Kong. They also noted that aged females outnumbered the males. This may be due to the larger female population at risk, to increased pressure for the admission of females, to their special vulnerability, or to a combination of these factors.

TABLE 2
ANNUAL RATES PER 100,000 OF FIRST ADMISSIONS,
HONG KONG MENTAL HOSPITAL

(Based on figures for 1956-1958)*

| Age in years | Male | Female | Total (N=2220) |
|---|---|---|---|
| 0-9 | .9 | 1.9 | 1.3 |
| 10-19 | 16.0 | 17.4 | 16.7 |
| 20-29 | 69.8 | 53.4 | 61.9 |
| 30-39 | 57.4 | 48.8 | 53.3 |
| 40-49 | 51.0 | 41.0 | 46.2 |
| 50-59 | 34.3 | 28.3 | 31.6 |
| 60-69 | 28.5 | 33.3 | 31.3 |
| 70-79 | 16.1 | 33.3 | 26.7 |
| 80 and over | - | - | - |
| 60 and over | 25.5 ±8.8 | 32.5 ±8.3 | 29.5 |

*All non-Chinese excluded.

### First-Admission Rate

Table 2 gives the annual rate of first admissions for various age groups to the Hong Kong Mental Hospital, which handles all psychiatric cases from the territory. The rates are calculated on the basis of 2,220 first admissions between 1956 and 1958, inclusive.

These rates are lower for all age groups than in the United States. The highest rate occurs between ages twenty and twenty-nine, quite unlike the case in the United States, where the highest rate is in old age. For those aged sixty and over, the rate is some six or seven times lower in Hong Kong. The World Health Organization report (1959) on mental-health problems of the aged gives the following rates per 100,000 for the United States: 0 to 15 years, 2.3; twenty-five to thirty-four years, 76.3; thirty-five to fifty-four years, 93.0; and sixty-five years and over, 236.1. In Japan, it has been reported (Shinfuku, 1955) that the highest rate occurs between ages fifty and fifty-five; after that it declines, the rate between ages sixty and sixty-five being half that between fifty and fifty-five. Comparable findings are reported by Kato (1960) in his ecological study of mental patients from Ichikawa. It should be noted that the same kind of pattern was also found in England, Wales, Sweden, Norway, and Switzerland before the late 1940's (Kolb, 1956).

Whereas the Hong Kong male admission rate gradually declines in middle and old age, the decline in the female rate is arrested in the sixth decade, and a higher rate is then maintained. After age fifty-nine, the female rate is higher than the male. However, although the trends in the male and female rates with aging appear definite, and the rates after age fifty-nine for each sex are reliable, the difference between the male and the female rates after fifty-nine (25.5 ± 8.8 and 32.5 ± 8.3, respectively) does not exceed the 5 per-cent level of confidence. The possible significance of these findings will be discussed later.

### Effect of Age

Failing a census survey, the number of cases of combined in- and outpatients referred for treatment for the first time provides the most accurate indication of the extent of mental disease in a community. The rates of referral, calculated on this basis, show that the incidence of mental illness falls with advancing age (Table 3), and there can be no question here of bias being introduced by factors affecting the decision to admit or not admit. This is not to say, of course, that the process of referral can be altogether free from selective influences.

The rate of in- and outpatient referral of females aged sixty and over again exceeds that for the males, and, although each rate is reliable (52.0 + 10.6 and 38.2 ± 10.6, respectively), the difference between them is not significant at the 5 per-cent level of probability. However, it is improbable that the difference is without meaning. Table 4 shows that, for males, females, and the two sexes together, the numbers observed in different age groups differ significantly on calculating $\chi^2$ from the numbers to be expected from their propor-

TABLE 3
ANNUAL RATES PER 100,000 OF FIRST REFERRALS OF
IN- AND OUTPATIENTS COMBINED,
HONG KONG MENTAL HOSPITAL

(Based on figures for 1956-1958)*

| Age in years | Male | Female | Total (N=3447) |
|---|---|---|---|
| 0-19 | 13.2 | 11.3 | 12.3 |
| 20-39 | 100.8 | 70.9 | 86.5 |
| 40-59 | 67.8 | 53.7 | 61.0 |
| 60 and over | 38.2 | 52.0 | 46.1 |
| 60 and over | 38.2 ±10.6 | 52.0 ±10.6 | 46.1 |

*All non-Chinese excluded.

tions in the general population, assuming that age had no influence on the rate of referral (P < 0.001). For men aged sixty and over, the number in our series is less than expected, but for women it is greater than expected. For both sexes together, the number is almost as many as to be expected. The differences found are not large, but they suggest that, taking each sex by itself, age has a differential effect on the susceptibility to mental illness.

Even if there is a real difference between the rate of referral of men and women in old age, it does not necessarily mean that women are more vulnerable, but simply that they may be more readily hospitalized by their families or more readily referred to the outpatient clinic with a view to admission. Whether this is so is a subject for further investigation.

The rates of referral that we have discussed above are a measure of incidence rather than prevalence of mental illness, for it can be assumed that most referrals will be in their first attack. Our finding is that, among the Chinese, the incidence of mental illness falls with old age—in contrast to Western populations (Rose & Stub, 1955). In Taiwan, Lin (1953; 1960) found that the prevalence of mental illness also fell with advancing age. His study was based on a census survey which took into account both active and inactive cases, the latter being cases who had been ill at an earlier age. Prevalence studies

TABLE 4
OBSERVED AND EXPECTED DISTRIBUTION OF
FIRST REFERRALS OF IN- AND OUTPATIENTS COMBINED,
HONG KONG MENTAL HOSPITAL
(BASED ON FIGURES FOR 1956-1958)*

(2,220 inpatients and 1,227 outpatients)

| Age in years | Observed* | | | Expected | | |
|---|---|---|---|---|---|---|
| | Male | Female | Total | Male | Female | Total |
| 0-19 | 218 | 171 | 389 | 894.2 | 620.9 | 1513.2 |
| 20-39 | 1282 | 830 | 2112 | 687.8 | 478.4 | 1165.1 |
| 40-59 | 484 | 351 | 835 | 386.4 | 267.7 | 651.5 |
| 60 and over | 39 | 72 | 111 | 54.6 | 57.0 | 117.2 |
| Total | 2023 | 1424 | 3447 | 2023.0 | 1424.0 | 3447.0 |

$\chi^2 = 1053.4$    627.3    1657.0    Df = 3
P = <.001    <.001    <.001

*All non-Chinese excluded from the figures for numbers observed.

might be expected to show the maximum amount of illness at some-what older ages than incidence studies, and Lin's highest rate was found among the group aged fifty to fifty-nine, whereas the maximum incidence in Hong Kong was between ages twenty and thirty-nine. However, Lin's finding of a declining prevalence in old age can be compared legitimately with the Hong Kong finding of a declining incidence, since it is known that the major "functional" psychoses, as well as the psychoneuroses, do not in the majority of cases arise *de novo* in the senium, and general paresis and epilepsy also show no predilection for the aged. It is true that some early cases may die after the first attack so that they will not contribute to the prevalence of disease in later ages, but it is common knowledge that mental illness is not, in the great majority of cases, fatal. Therefore, if the over-all prevalence rate falls, it can be assumed that the over-all incidence rate also falls (or at least does not rise). As a matter of fact, Lin's data also revealed that the prevalence rates for each of the individual diseases fell in old age. Confidence that the Taiwan findings fit in with our demonstration in Hong Kong that the rates for first referrals of in- and outpatients fall with old age is strengthened by the fact that, even if we added readmissions and referrals of outpatients to the first referrals, the rates still fall with advancing age (Table 5).

TABLE 5
ANNUAL RATES PER 100,000 OF FIRST AND
SUBSEQUENT REFERRALS* OF IN-
AND OUTPATIENTS COMBINED,
HONG KONG MENTAL HOSPITAL

(Based on figures for 1956-1958)†

| Age in years | Male | Female | Total |
|---|---|---|---|
| 0-19 | 16.8 | 14.3 | 15.6 |
| 20-39 | 139.8 | 107.4 | 124.3 |
| 40-59 | 88.6 | 79.8 | 84.4 |
| 60 and over | 46.2 | 60.6 | 54.5 |

*Each patient enumerated once only within the period.
†All non-Chinese excluded.

One of Lin's interesting discoveries was that the incidence for senile psychoses (senile dementia and arteriosclerotic psychosis) in the aged was high enough to be comparable with what has been found for such Western populations as those of Thuringia and Bavaria. Although the crude rate was low,[1] owing to the relative youth of the general population, for the population over sixty the rate for senile psychosis was as high as 5.4 per 1,000. Lin also quotes from an investigation in Tokyo which similarly revealed a high rate of senile psychosis.

At first glance, there would appear to be a strange divergence between the high rate for organic senile disease among Chinese and their low over-all rate for mental diseases in old age. But, as far as incidence is concerned, the rate appears lower than it really is only by comparison with the high and rising rates in the West. For prevalence, Lin's data show that the group aged sixty to sixty-nine had the second highest rate, next only to those aged fifty to fifty-nine, which had the highest rate. It is also necessary to take into account the definition of senile psychosis used. Lin himself admits that the category of senile dementia may be arbitrary, and he defines the condition

[1] Lin also notes that, between 1947 and 1949, cases of senile dementia and arteriosclerotic psychosis in his outpatient clinic came to only 0.5 per cent of the total.

broadly in terms of old people who are unable to adjust themselves because of intellectual deterioration and who are a burden on their families. Recent work has revealed how often it is that reversible functional conditions can masquerade as organic senile dementia.

All we can conclude from Lin's data and ours is that, although organic senile diseases may not be as infrequent among Chinese as previously thought, the incidence of mental disorder as a whole in aged Chinese is nevertheless low compared to the incidence among Westerners, and the incidence moreover declines with increasing old age. However, as we shall see in connection with suicide, it would be wrong to conclude from this that aged Chinese have few problems of mental adjustment.

Authoritative opinion, although by no means unanimous, is inclined to view the steep rise in first admissions for the aged in the West as the result, to a greater or less extent, of increasing confidence in mental hospitals, increased pressure on public facilities for the general care of the aged sick and infirm, inability on the part of mental hospitals to resist this pressure, and in some cases the failure to provide for the economic welfare of the old (Kolb, 1956; Mayer-Gross, Slater, & Roth, 1960). That there is a real rise in mental disease of the senium may therefore be doubted (World Health Organization, 1959). Still, even if much of the increased admission rate can be ascribed to sociological factors influencing admission, these factors are inevitably associated with others that have the effect of lowering the sense of worth and security of the old, so that whatever tends to raise the admission rate is also likely to provoke mental distress in the aged.

## OLD AGE AND SUICIDE
## IN HONG KONG

We have so far been unable to adduce any evidence that old age especially predisposes Chinese to mental disorder. A study of suicide rates, however, indicates that the aged cannot be in so happy a position as it seems. There is an important difference between mental illness and suicide. Many cases of suicide do not give grounds for believing that mental illness is involved, but, on the contrary, in the light of the subject's own circumstances, the suicide provides a rational solution to an inescapable problem; and this is especially common among helpless, aged people. It is of course stultifying to regard suicide as abnormal per se. In Hong Kong, it has been found (Yap, 1958a; Yap, 1958b) that only 7.8 per cent of cases gave a history suggesting mental disease, although if cases exhibiting depression—largely reactive to real difficulties—are included, this figure rises to 20 per cent. Many mental patients, moreover, have no inclination toward suicide. And, finally, although there is some evidence that the monthly distribution of suicide may be correlated with the distribution of mental hospital admissions (Dahlgren, 1945), this has not been found true for Hong Kong.

Nevertheless, suicide is an extreme form of behavior, often the culmination of grave and psychologically understandable stress. If it could be understood by merely invoking abstruse psychodynamic mechanisms involving childhood experiences or by resorting to explanations built on biological constitution, only then would it be logical to incriminate specific mental diseases. Since this is not commonly so, the suicide rate can be taken as a highly sensitive index of psychological and social maladjustment and, in a wider sense, of mental ill health. Within a given culture, it can be usefully employed as a measure of the amount of psychological breakdown from stress as between one group and another or from one time to another. However, it must be remembered that, even within a single culture, there may be a difference in the attitude toward suicide between males and females.

### Age and Sex Differentials

Fig. 1 gives the suicide and attempted-suicide curves for Hong Kong, by age and sex, based on a total of 263 and 894 cases, respectively. The male suicide curve rises with age, especially old age, and this is also true of Western populations. The female suicide curve, however, differs from the common Western finding in that it starts to rise rapidly after fifty-five, instead of decreasing, remaining steady, or slowly rising, as it does in many other countries. Since it is important to be certain that the rates for the higher ages differ significantly from zero, it should be stated that this is so for males except in the case of persons aged seventy-six and over ($133.5 \pm 94.3$). But, if we put together all cases aged seventy-one and over, the rate for this age group then becomes reliable ($111.3 \pm 49.5$), so that we can be confident that the rise at the older age levels is real. In the case of females, the rates for the group seventy-one to seventy-five and for those seventy-six and over are not reliable (respectively, $73.4 \pm 52.0$ and $220.3 \pm 126.5$). However, the rate calculated for all women aged seventy-one and over is reliable ($122.4 \pm 54.6$), so that again we may regard the rise in the female suicide curve in old age as real. It should be noted, moreover, that, taking the rates in the later ages as a whole, the trends that we have identified are consistent.

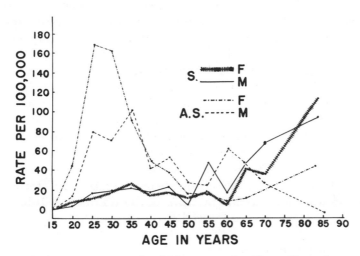

FIG. 1. Suicide and attempted suicide curves for Hong Kong in rates per 100,000 by age and sex. Age groups are indicated by the upper limits for each five-year range.

Rates for attempted suicide are likely to be less trustworthy than those for suicide, because not all such cases will be discovered or reported. Nevertheless, there is no reason to suppose that age plays a significant part in bringing cases to notice, so that the shape of the curve is still of interest. We find that the female curve rises in old age to overtake the male one, which apparently falls in old age. There were no male cases aged seventy-six or over. The male rate is $33.4 \pm 12.6$ for those between sixty-one and seventy-five, and the female rate is $51.4 \pm 9.8$ for those aged sixty-six and over, both of these being reliable.

A further point is that the observed distribution of suicide and attempted-suicide cases in different age groups significantly differs from the distribution expected from the proportions of these age groups in the general population, assuming that age had no influence on proclivity to suicide (Yap, 1958a; Yap, 1958b). There is good reason for believing that, taking both suicide and attempted suicide together, old age predisposes females to suicidal behavior rather more markedly than males; for, while both the suicide and attempted-suicide rates rise in aged females, only the suicide rate does so in the case of males.

The rise in the suicide rate for the older ages in women is also marked in Japan and Ceylon, although this is not the rule in Western countries (World Health Organization, 1956). In Ceylon (1952-1954) and Japan (variously, 1902-1954), the rates for women (as well as men) at least double when we go from the sixth decade to the seventh and beyond. The rate for females aged seventy and over is very high in Japan and high in Ceylon. In Western countries, with the sole exception of Portugal, the increase is never so steep, and in many the rates even drop in these later decades of life. It is important to bear in mind that, in Hong Kong, Ceylon, and Japan, the crude suicide rate for women is more than half that for men, whereas in Western countries the female rate is usually one-third that of the male. There may be a traditional proneness to suicide among females in certain Asian cultures, and this is certainly true where Chinese are concerned. However, we must still explain the rapid rise of suicide in old age in women (as well as in men), and to do this it will be advantageous to view the problem in its historical setting.

### *Effects of Modernization*

Data on suicide in Chinese are scanty, but an important study was made by two American sociologists in Peking in 1917 (Gamble & Burgess, 1921). If their figures are converted into age-specific rates, we find that, quite unlike the pattern in contemporary Hong Kong or in the West, the highest rate for women was between twenty-one and thirty, after which the curve fell to reach its lowest in those aged sixty-one and over; for males, the peak was reached in those aged thirty-one to forty, after which the curve fell to its lowest between forty-one and fifty, after that showing only a slight rise (Fig. 2). There is thus a striking difference in proneness to suicide for different ages, comparing the classically patriarchal society of Peking forty-three years ago, untouched by modern commerce and industry, and the busily industrializing seaport of Hong Kong today (whose population is 99 per cent Chinese).

Undoubtedly, the old culture gave much prestige and support to the aged of both sexes. It seems that, with its dissolution, with urbanization, industrialization, increase in social mobility, and the weakening of the sentiment of filial piety, the aged are placed in a less happy and secure position. There is no clear evidence that Western countries undergoing industrialization and modernization in the middle of the last century showed a steep rise in suicide among the

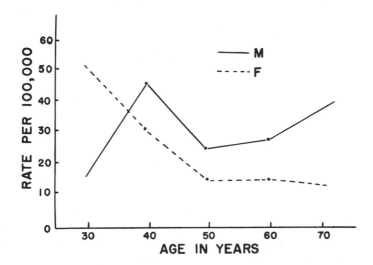

Fig. 2. Suicide rates per 100,000 in Peking in 1917. Age groups are indicated by the upper limits or each ten year range (from Gamble & Burgess, 1921).

old. A glance at the tables given by Durkheim (1951) for France, Italy, and Saxony at that time demonstrate this. Thus, there is an apparent difference from Japan early in this century and from Ceylon and Hong Kong in recent years—these Asian countries at the respective times undergoing processes of urbanization and developing individualistic attitudes characteristic of modern urban communities. Comparisons of this kind are, of course, very broad, but they suggest that we are not warranted in expecting that industrialization and urbanization must have identical effects on Asian and Western populations, with their differing traditions. That there are similarities there can be no doubt; but there are differences, too, as shown by the rapid increase of suicide in aged women no less than in aged men. It is possible that the difference is related to the fast pace with which the underlying social and economic processes have been taking place in the East.

We may now return to an examination of the position of Chinese women of advanced age, whose mental health at present appears so vulnerable to breakdown. It has been demonstrated (Yap, 1958a; Yap, 1958b) that, in aged Chinese of both sexes, suicide is closely associated with poverty, physical handicap, chronic illness (especially tuberculosis), social isolation, and often "social desolation" (to use the phrase coined by Townsend, 1957) following deprivation. The factors of poverty and chronic illness operate with greater weight in countries where social-welfare provisions are not well developed on a universal basis and where kinship ties and the security related to them are weakening or have weakened.

Women are likely to suffer more than men for a number of reasons. Many more women than men of these ages are widows, and widowhood is known to be associated with mental ill health, in Hong Kong as elsewhere. Many aged women are illiterate, and this allows them few interests outside the home, reduces their mobility, and seriously impairs their ability to cope with the broader society outside the family, which itself is contracting in size and becoming less stable. They have fallen status and as a result are bound to encounter difficulty with their children-in-law, especially the daughter-in-law, whom, according to past experience, it was her privilege to dominate. There are not uncommon instances of old women attempting suicide after acute quarrels with their sons- or daughters-in-law. This kind of suicidal behavior is usually carried out in a state of hypereridism or morbid hostility (Lindemann, 1950; Yap, 1958a; Yap, 1958c) which disorganizes the individual psychologically and thereby often renders unsuccessful the attempt at suicide. A significant part of the rise in the attempted suicide rate in old women is due to hypereridic states. Chinese women of all classes have in the past been brought up with the notion that suicide is not dishonorable either as a protest or as a way to remove shame when placed in an intolerable situation. Such a reaction is, not surprisingly, reactivated in old age when a woman is relegated to a helpless status. The above analysis applies only to cases under pressure of a personal kind. It does not exclude the possibility that aged women in poverty and sickness may also in many cases commit suicide from altruistic motives.

It is conceivable that in the future the high suicide rates of older women will fall with stabilization of the rapid socioeconomic changes that have occurred, an increase in the national income, a multiplication of the economic roles open to women, sex equality, more education, and the development of a new attitude towards suicide. In Americanized Chinese there is no increase in suicide in women of advanced age (Yap, 1958a; Yap, 1958b). Yet a low suicide rate for old women is not universal in industrially advanced countries of the West, and industrial Japan, as we have pointed out, still shows the old pattern of suicide. It is a moot point whether traditional attitudes toward suicide can change easily, and in this matter we must also consider the probable fate of certain indigenous, non-kin, social institutions that have long provided support for the aged.

## SUMMARY

The relevant facts may be briefly restated. (1) There are few aged patients in Chinese mental hospitals, and among them women outnumber men. (2) The first admission rates for both sexes in the older age groups are quite low. For men there is a gradual decline, but for women the decline is arrested, and there is a slight rise in the sixth decade which is maintained in old age, although the rate does not approach the peak attained in earlier ages. (3) The rate of first referral of in- and outpatients combined falls in old age for both sexes, the fall being apparently less marked in women than in men. (4) The same relation of age to the rate of referral is found when all in- and outpatients referred for the first or subsequent times are taken together. (5) In women, old age is associated with an increased number of them being referred for in- or outpatient treatment, more than might be expected from their numbers in the population; but in men, old age shows the opposite effect. (6) On Taiwan, outpatient cases of senile dementia and arteriosclerotic psychosis come to less than 1 per cent of the total. (7) On Taiwan, census techniques reveal that the prevalence rate for all mental diseases together falls in old age for both sexes combined, although for senile dementia and arteriosclerotic psychosis together the age-specific rate is not low. (8) The rates for suicidal acts (that is, suicide and attempted suicide combined) rises sharply for women in old age, but less so for men.

We are forced to the conclusion that, whereas mental disease is not frequent among aged Chinese compared to those of younger ages, this by itself cannot give an adequate indication of the degree of mental health enjoyed by them. The high suicide rate in this group shows that they encounter more difficulty in psychological adjustment than those of younger ages, and there is evidence to suggest that old Chinese women are in an especially unenviable position, compared with their contemporaries in the West. To a limited extent, the dissociation of mental disease incidence (and prevalence), on the one hand, and suicide, on the other, is understandable; where suicide is traditionally regarded as a rational mode of reaction to environmental pressures, this reaction might occur more readily than a forced pathological distortion of the psyche ending in mental illness. However, the reciprocal relationship between illness and suicide is not a simple one in the case of aged women, for, as we have noted, the rate of first admissions also appears to rise slightly in the senium, though the rate still remains below the peak reached in the fourth decade. A possible explanation for this could be that Chinese women (old as well as young) have ambivalent attitudes toward the expression of aggressiveness, so that they are prone to hypereridism which can end in suicidal behavior, in explosive and aggressive behavior (acute psychopathic reaction), in hysteria, or in depressive conditions, either nonstructured or structured depending on the time relationships involved. Another explanation could be that there is more pressure to admit old women than men, so that the sex difference in admission rates is not real, but this is improbable as far as can be judged from experience in Hong Kong.

The low incidence and prevalence of mental disorder in the aged as a whole is not incompatible with a relatively high rate for organic senile diseases. In our material, rather more than half of the in- and outpatients referred were organic cases (including subdelirious states), as opposed to schizophrenic and affective. If there is any discrepancy discerned, this depends on certain preconceptions about the effect of mental stress on the aging process. Only if psychological hardships aggravate organic aging would we expect the functional and the organic diseases of the senium to increase in parallel. We are faced with the general problem of the nature of aging and the environmental influences that regulate it.

### REFERENCES

Dahlgren, K.G. *On suicide and attempted suicide: A psychiatrical and statistical investigation.* Lund: Lindstedts Univ. Bokhandel, 1945.

Durkheim, É. *Suicide.* Glencoe, Ill.: The Free Press, 1951.

Gamble, S.A., & Burgess, J.S. *Peking: A social survey,* New York: George H. Donan, 1921.

Kato, M. Ecological study of mental disorders in a small city. *Chiba ment. Health,* 1960, **3,** 19-30.

Kolb, L. The mental hospitalization of the aged: Is it being overdone? *Amer. J. Psychiat.,* 1956, **112,** 627-636.

Lin, T.Y. A study of the incidence of mental disorder in Chinese and other cultures. *Psychiatry,* 1953, **16,** 313-316.

Lin, T.Y. *Reality and vision.* Manila: Bureau of Printing, 1960.

Lindemann, E. *Epidemiology of mental disorder.* New York: Millbank Memorial Fund, 1950.

Maunder, W.F., & Szczepanik, E.F. Hong Kong housing survey, 1957. Hong Kong: University of Hong Kong, 1957.

Mayer-Gross, W., Cross, K.W., Harrington, J.A., & Sreenivasan, U. The chronic mental patient in India and England. *Lancet,* 1958, **1,** 1265-1267.

Mayer-Gross, W., Slater, E., & Roth, M. *Clinical psychiatry.* London: Cassell, 1960.

Rose, A.M., & Stub, H.R. Summary of studies on the incidence of mental disorders. In A.M. Rose (Ed.), *Mental health and mental disorder.* New York: W.W. Norton and Company, 1955. Pp. 87-116.

Shinfuku, N. Quoted by K. M. Bowman, Review of psychiatric progress, 1955. *Amer. J. Psychiat.,* 1955, **112,** 537-541.

Sjögren, T., & Larsson, T. The changing age-structure in Sweden and its impact on mental illness. *Bull. World Hlth Organ.,* 1959, **21,** 569-582.

Townsend, P. *The family life of old people.* London: Routledge and Kegan Paul, 1957.

World Health Organization. Mortality from suicide. *Epidem. vital Statist. Rep.,* 1956, **9,** 243-287.

World Health Organization. *Mental health problems of aging and the aged.* Geneva: Author, 1959.

Wylie, H.W. Unpublished manuscript, 1960.

Yap, P.M. *Suicide in Hong Kong.* Hong Kong: University of Hong Kong Press, 1958. (a)

Yap, P.M. Suicide in Hong Kong. *J. ment. Sci.,* 1958, **104,** 266-301. (b)

Yap, P.M. Hypereridism and attempted suicide in Hong Kong. *J. nerv. ment. Dis.,* 1958, **127,** 34-41. (c)

# SECTION II

*Social Processes
and Variables*

# CHAPTER 38

*Adjustment of the Normal Aged:*
*Concept and Measurement*

IRVING ROSOW

Interest in social adjustment dates from the earliest period of modern gerontology and has remained of focal concern since that time (Cavan, Burgess, Havighurst, & Goldhamer, 1949; Folsom & Morgan, 1937; Pollak, 1948). The effort to untangle the web of correlates and causes of "good adjustment" in old age reflects not only scientific interests, but the pressures of a compelling social problem. Accordingly, our ideological values and commitments have lent a sense of urgency to research. But this has also obscured some vital issues in the concept of adjustment and confused thinking in the area. This paper will consider several of the major problems and propose an alternative, sociological approach to them.[1]

[1] The work on which this paper is based is supported by a grant from The Ford Foundation, whose aid is gratefully acknowledged.

195

The adjustment concept is related to various welfare and action programs for "social-problem" cases in the older population. This allows a ready classification of people according to their "good" or "bad" adjustment into social-problem categories. Such an approach has some precedent, notably in dealing with other personal and social pathologies—crime, juvenile delinquency, mental illness and psychopathology, unemployment, broken homes, and the like. In each instance, the problem case shows a florid clinical pathology or a clear violation of social norms. Both epitomize the opposite of the "normal," for which there are gross but clear criteria—in our examples, the law-abiding, the juvenile not in trouble, the adequately functioning personality, the gainfully employed, the intact family, etc. These essentially clinical judgmentus of adjustments are most apparent in social work and other applied fields, but their assumptions also appear in technically sophisticated research on the aged.

This presents a fundamental problem: although clinical experience and cultural expectations provide a basis for classifying adjustment in some areas, there are no comparable norms of adequate adjustment to the social roles of old people in our society. Kuhlen (1959) correctly warns that the lack of objective criteria paves the way for charges of value judgments against adjustment ratings. Indeed, the absence of clear social roles and expectations of the aged exposes the core of the "adjustment" dilemma (Cavan et al., 1949; Donahue, Orbach, & Pollak, 1960; Orbach & Shaw, 1957). Without commonly accepted criteria, arbitrary assumptions about desirable attributes of the aged become the basis of adjustment ratings. The adequacy of the concept thereby hangs on the validity of these assumptions as criteria of social adjustment.

Three general approaches have been used to evaluate adjustment: (1) sociological, (2) psychological, and (3) social-psychological. The sociological has identified life patterns, relationships, activities, or social roles in objective data, and has related these to various correlates (Albrecht, 1951; Bell, 1957; Burgess, 1954; Havighurst, 1957; Havighurst & Albrecht, 1953; Williams, 1956). The psychological approach has classified people's adjustment according to various kinds of subjective data—personality factors, psychological states, self-images or -evalautions, and other attitudes (Beckman, Williams, & Fisher, 1958; Havighurst, 1951; Kleemeier, 1951; Kuhlen, 1958; Kutner, Fanshel, Togo, & Langner, 1956; Lebo, 1953; Mason, 1954; Morrison & Kristijanson, 1958; Peck, 1956; Phillips, 1957; Pollak, 1948; Reichard, 1959; Rose, 1955; Schmidt, 1951; Srole, 1956; Streib, 1956). These classifi-

cations have not always been clinical, although some have, and attitudinal data have typically been handled as objectively as in
communications or political research. But the adjustment standards
have invariably involved arbitrary premises about healthy or desirable
subjective states and attitudes. Some of these will be considered below.
The third approach, the social-psychological, which includes many of
the studies already cited, has typically combined objective and subjective variables—patterns of relationships and activities with various
attitudes and psychological resources (Havighurst & Albrecht, 1953;
Landis, 1942; Riesman, 1954). In the absence of clear role expectations
for the aged, especially for the retired and widowed, psychological
data can supplement the objective patterns, although this has been
used systematically in very few studies (Streib, 1956; Thompson, 1958;
Thompson & Streib, 1958). To the extent that role expectations remain
broad and open, with a minimum of prescription and a maximum of
individual choice, the blending of subjective and objective data may
well continue.

## EQUILIBRIUM THEORY

Regardless of the sources of data, most conceptions of adjustment rest implicitly on assumptions of equilibrium. Indeed, adjustment often becomes tantamount to equilibrium, as exemplified in a
recent unpublished manuscript (Sussman, 1959) on chronic illness and
disability.

> The basic assumption of this [equilibrium] theory is that the human
> organism seeks constantly both internal and external equilibrium,
> namely adjustment within the internal and external environment. There
> is a consistent strain towards balance or harmony within both systems.
> In other words, the human being seeks physical and emotional balance
> within its own body system and social adjustment within the environ-
> ment where it has its interactions with other individuals. Adjustment
> may be one of the basic processes of equilibrium theory.

This formulation is conceptually related to the notion of
tension-reduction which has a substantial foundation in personality
theory. But the difficulty of the equilibrium concept lies in the criteria
for "balance" or "harmony" in judging individuals and in discrimi-
nating differences between them. How and in what terms can we judge
consistently the forces in a person's life to be in balance or his internal
state to be harmoniously attuned to the external forces around him?

## IDEOLOGICAL BIASES

In judgments of harmonious adjustment, two criteria have dominated gerontological thought—(1) personal happiness and (2) activity and participation.

### *Personal Happiness*

Because of our culture's emphasis on the value of personal happiness, several investigators have explicitly used happiness or life satisfaction as an adjustment index (Kuhlen, 1948; Lebo, 1953; Pollak, 1948; Rose, 1955), and this approach has colored virtually all other research. As a feeling about an objective life situation, happiness is similar to measures of personal morale (to be discussed below), except that it is content-free and simply indicates an over-all attitude at any given time.

The basic difficulty lies in the confusion between happiness as a value and its usefulness as a scientific concept. As a value, happiness can simply be asserted as a social philosophy or as a personal premise in life. But our personal preferences have no scientific stature in analyzing aging problems. Scientific utility must rest on other grounds. For example, happiness might be an over-all adjustment index if it were highly correlated with important sociological variables which in turn were meaningfully related to various happiness levels. Such variables might include such social class correlates (Kutner et al., 1956), as differential life chances, prestige, rewards, and similar aspects of differential advantage in the social order. Although such relationships are certainly possible, the present evidence is spotty and irregular, quite apart from the quality of the available data (Inkeles, 1960; Inkeles & Bauer, 1959). Their great variation indicates that happiness is far from a unitary dimension, however crude, which makes the meaning of group comparisons, and certainly of individual judgments, extremely uncertain. But, even if this were not the case, happiness is at best only an index of something else of greater analytic importance.

What are the major weaknesses of happiness as a scientific concept? First, it is excessively culture-bound. It varies in content and importance from one society to another, even among Western nations or between subgroups within them, as a brief comparison of American experience with recent European research shows (Townsend, 1957; Wylie, 1957). Certainly, we cannot readily distinguish in expressions of happiness genuine satisfaction levels from distortions imposed by cultural imperatives, and such discrepancies can be marked (Inkeles, 1960). Consequently, happiness affords no stable, objective referrent, and this seriously limits the useful comparisons which can be made.

Furthermore, although happiness may be a general social value, it cannot be ensured or built into a system in the way that such institutions as universal education or socialized medicine can be built in. As the product of complex social forces and personal life histories, it cannot be either a normative statistic or a moral imperative. Differential life chances may carry differential happiness probabilities on an actuarial basis. But, on the moral level, there can be no meaningful dilemmas of choice between happiness and unhappiness or between happiness and the heavier sanctions of obligation and responsibility. Social roles and their attendant problems are built into social systems on statistical and moral lines, and these become the crucial questions to study.

This indicates, then, that happiness is not a strategic analytic variable in the study of social problems and systems. Although we may accept it as an empirical datum, happiness does not explain anything, much less any of its own determining characteristics.

At the grossest level, happiness may reflect a secure, respected status or smooth institutional functioning. Or it may roughly indicate the extent to which people share the values of a social order, enjoy its rewards, be committed to it, or be motivated to full role performance. But such attitudes and the integration they imply cannot be inferred directly from expressions of happiness, and they must be measured independently. It is not surprising, then, to find that old people's roles and adjustment may vary widely from one society to another regardless of the variation in their personal happiness (Simmons, 1945). Consequently, those factors which govern their social position are more significant than those which only superficially affect their happiness.

On the other hand, widespread unhappiness may indicate an insecure or inferior status, extreme disaffection, *anomie,* social strain, or ineffective institutions. By this token, unhappiness may be a signal of impending social change (for example, the New Deal or the Forand bill) or of tightening of social controls (for example, the Russians in Budapest or the whites in South Africa). But strain and its associated personal unhappiness is important in the study of individuals primarily when they have choices open to them in behavior. This means decisions or options on the basis of which they can act, where different choices lead to different consequences. But such behavioral choices are primarily available to people other than the old—political figures, prospective employers, family members, and the like. It is mainly in the narrowest spheres that old people can still make decisions, and these of limited importance. The dominant conditions and influences of their lives usually lie beyond their effective control.[2]

Societies may be ordered and thrive without the value of happiness. Indeed, one dilemma of modern democracies is that social systems can function, and do function quite effectively, in pursuit of massive social goals which basically discount or subordinate considerations of personal happiness—regardless of whether happiness may be a by-product of the social process. Thus, though they may do so, happiness ratings do not necessarily tell us much about the social processes which they presumably reflect. To this extent, they may be insensitive indexes of life patterns and therefore of little analytic value.

But our ideological commitments bind our thought to happiness criteria of adjustment and divert us from more penetrating questions. The critical problem in old people's lives is not simply the facts and correlates of their happiness (nominal end products), but the values and processes which shape their lives (nominal causes). Yet our concern with happiness tends to deflect serious analysis from these basic forces.

### Activity and Participation

A second pervasive assumption of gerontologists is that, the more active old people are, the happier and better adjusted they will be. In terms of the equilibrium premises above, they are interacting freely with their environment. This assumption is not without foundation, for many studies report strong correlations between various measures of adjustment and extent of activity or social participation (Albrecht, 1951; Albrecht, 1956; Burgess, 1954; Havighurst, 1951; Havighurst, 1957; Havighurst & Albrecht, 1953; Kleemeier, 1951; Morrison & Kristijanson, 1958; Snyder, 1955). Presumably, the more active a person is, the better adjusted he is according to these studies.

However, the deviant cases are not simply statistical anomalies, but call the meaning and generality of the findings into question on several grounds. First, extensive sociological data show major class differences in social participation, even among the aged

---

[2] Clearly, the failure of old people to exercise options available to them would be a significant area of study.

(Bell & Force, 1956). White-collar and middle-class groups show much higher rates of organizational membership and similar formal activities than working-class groups. Consequently, any adjustment index based on activity scores contains a built-in class bias which penalizes the working class and favors the middle class. With this basis in middle-class norms, manual groups will have lower and white-collar groups higher adjustment ratings. The very least that one can expect of an adjustment measure is that it give each group an equal chance to score well according to its own class norms. But, in the face of class differences in participation, the middle-class conception of the good, active life penalizes manual groups arbitrarily.

Second, the relation between activity and "good" adjustment applies under conditions which are typically ignored. Kutner and his associates (1956) and Barron (1956) are virtually the only ones to point out that only activity which is meaningful to the individual can contribute significantly to his morale.

But, beyond this important qualification, many inactive, sedentary people have otherwise "good" adjustment when judged clinically or by measures other than activity. In recent intensive clinical research, Reichard (1959) outlined three distinctive types of "well-adjusted" older people which she designated the mature, the well-defended, and the passive-dependent. The passive-dependent is clinically well-adjusted, but markedly inactive. Ironically, she also found a group of hyperactive people (who would score extremely high on any participation inventory) whose activity was a form of defense against anxiety, but presumably they lacked the emotional balance and satisfaction of the clinically "mature" group. The well-adjusted but inactive people caused Havighurst (1949) to acknowledge the graceful "rocking-chair" pattern as consistent with "good" adjustment. However, this anomaly is difficult to reconcile with adjustment measures which depend on activity scores. Moreover, aside from Reichard's work (1959), no conceptual scheme of aging has satisfactorily accounted for this pattern. Her psychodynamic thought, based implicitly on complementary personality fits between dependent-dominant spouses, departs sharply from the prevailing notions about the tonicity of participation.

Both happiness and activity, then, represent ideological biases based on middle-class values which limit our thinking about what adjustment involves and the framework within which we should analyze it. Such orientations are common enough, possibly even inevitable, in early work in social-problem areas. But this does not mean that they should become insurmountable obstacles, for they help to crystallize issues which demand conceptual development and clarification.

## ADJUSTMENT MEASURES

What are the major measures of adjustment appearing in the literature and in contemporary research? We can review here only the principal, albeit typical, techniques in use. But these will reveal the terms in which the concept has been viewed and how it has been operationalized.

### The Chicago School

Undoubtedly the most prevalent measure is the Cavan adjustment rating scale, developed from the early work at The University of Chicago (Cavan et al., 1949). This has been clearly formulated in Havighurst and Albrecht's *Older People* (1953), which has been used extensively by Havighurst's colleagues and students and still figures in various gerontological studies.

The adjustment rating is derived from an activity score on three subscales (primary-group contacts, secondary-group contacts, and nongroup activities) and an attitude score on three other subscales (feelings of emotional security, status, and happiness). These are used to give a "master rating." The master rating represents

> . . . a flexible summary of the six more specific scales. On the basis of the six scales, the rater arrives at a decision about the general degree of personal adjustment, but he takes into account *other things that he knows* about the individual and he weighs the separate scales in accordance with *what seems to him their importance* in the individual case. The master rating is the score that is used in our study as the Adjustment Rating (p. 407; italics inserted).

In other words, the master rating of personal adjustment is an over-all rating which is guided by the activity and attitude scores. But it is modified to bring the score into agreement with general impressions about the person's over-all, qualitative adjustment. To this extent, its advantage over a simple impressionistic adjustment rating is dubious, except as the reminder of activity and attitude scores may check gross error in the rater's impressions. Insofar as the activity and attitude scores are almost incorporated into the adjustment rating, their uniformly high correlations with adjustment reported in all of Havighurst's work are simply tautological. It could not be otherwise. Such correlations are a direct artifact of the scoring techniques, and they might show little relationship to adjustment if this were independently measured. This possibility is strengthened by the fact that there is a low correlation between measured attitude scores and adjustment as separately rated by community judges—people who know the respondent and independently rate his over-all personal adjustment (Havighurst, 1951). Yet Havighurst is content to disregard this important discrepancy.

The basic data on attitudes consist of respondents' agreement or disagreement with statements about health, work, friends, finances, and the like. These are simple and straightforward. But, as a basis of rating adjustment peculiar to older people, such material may be deceptive. For example, in a recent unrelated study on attitudes toward growing older, Neugarten and Garron (1959) found forty-year-olds in Kansas City just as concerned with the prospect of increased dependency and loss of income and health as people in the sixties. Therefore, if attitudes in old age may simply persist intact from an earlier period, any attitudinal data which ignore this possibility may be suspect in classifying adjustment of the aged.

The data on activities, however, have been used for the analysis of older people's social roles in the family (parent, homemaker), in group and individual relationships (club, friendship, church activities), and in the community (civic and business). These data are then used to rate the competence or success of people in each role, from which a composite rating can be derived. In the absence of clear norms for aged roles, there are, again, several objections to this procedure. First, it assumes such norms, as if there were uniform expectations of all older people. Obviously, a person who withdraws from some roles will score lower in competence than someone who does not. Second, it places a heavy premium on activity and involvement, since the rating criteria reward these. We have discussed the assumption about activity above. In general, then, although we do not have proper standards for role performance among older people, this role analysis proceeds as though we do.

The Havighurst data suggest that various roles have differing importance for older people, although their relative significance has not been quantified through a system of weighting. Clearly, this would be extremely valuable for documenting the crucial roles in old age. Further, the relative significance of various roles does not change uniformly through time. But activity in some roles changes more than in others, notably those of parent, spouse, and user of leisure time which are related to shifting familial and occupational status. One would expect this from objective life changes alone. But a recent study (Sussman, 1960) has disclosed that such role shifts are greater for middle-class than for working-class groups.

In general, the analysis of role content and change is the most significant potential focus of these materials, yet it is, curiously, the one which has received the least systematic attention from those working with the Cavan adjustment ratings.

### Morale Measures

The second most common type of adjustment index is found in measures of morale, best exemplified in the work of Kutner and his associates (1956). Others have used the same or modified morale indexes of this type (Morrison & Kristijanson, 1958). Kutner defines morale as

> . . . a continuum of responses to life and living problems that reflect the presence or absence of satisfaction, optimism, and expanding life perspectives. It should be clear from this definition that morale and adjustment are part of the same phenomenon. Morale refers to a mental state or a set of dispositions, while adjustment refers to the behaviors that stem from these dispositions. Hence, we may assume that an attitude or evaluation scale of morale measures life adjustment (p. 48).

On this basis, morale is measured by a Guttman scale of responses to the following seven items:

1. How often do you feel there's just no point in living?
2. Things just keep getting worse and worse for me as I get older.
3. How much do you regret the chances you missed during your life to do a better job of living?
4. All in all, how much unhappiness would you say you find in life today?
5. On the whole, how satisfied would you say you are with your way of life today?
6. How much do you plan ahead the things you will be doing next week or the week after—would you say you make many plans, a few plans, or almost none?
7. As you get older, would you say things seem to be better or worse than you thought they would be?

These items resemble those of Srole's "anomia scale" of alienation (1956), except that Srole taps more general and Kutner more specific attitudes. Both are basically optimism, or satisfaction, scales. Kutner's respondents fall into approximately equal thirds of high, medium, and low morale scores.

One might seriously question the inferred correspondence between verbal data ("morale") and actual behavior ("adjustment"), especially in charged areas where considerable denial takes place. Also, in many respects, the sheer face-validity of these items may be questioned. It is possible, especially with certain respondents, that they are not tapping attitudes so much as objective conditions. For many people, then, this might constitute a reality scale of objective perception rather than attitudes. Further, is planning ahead (Item 6)— a middle-class more than a working-class perspective—intrinsic to high morale? Or is the correspondence between expectations about aging and subsequent experience (Item 7) a morale index, even though there may be a relation between them (Streib, 1958; Thompson, 1958)?

There was one direct attempt to test the validity of the Kutner and Srole items (Cumming, Dean, & Newell, 1958a; Cumming et al., 1958b). Cumming et al. found that, however related to morale these items might be, they did not measure morale itself. In intensive, qualitative interviews, serious discrepancies appeared in which manifestly depressed, demoralized people scored high on morale and ebullient respondents of high spirits and a sense of well-being scored low. Further work showed that the Kutner-Srole items actually elicited ideological responses which proved to be a function of the respondent's social class and the frequency of his interaction with others.

Once these reservations about the validity of the Kutner morale scale had been confirmed, the Cumming group attempted to develop a more valid measure through independent approaches to morale criteria, both in quantitative and intensive qualitative work. The results showed extremely high correlations between the independent investigations, serving as a check on the validity of the criteria developed for morale judgments. These criteria proved free of ideological content or bias, but at the same time they were psychological in nature and could as easily be viewed as an index of mental health. The criteria were the following: (1) sheer vitality, which Cumming et al. saw as a temperamental quality; (2) ability to relate to others; (3) motility, or the flexibility of adaptive means and goals in the face of problems or new situations; (4) fortitude, or the acceptance of responsibility for one's own behavior; and (5) goals appropriate to achievement ability. The relative importance of these respective criteria for morale has not yet been established. However, they are all fundamentally personality dimensions, some of them seen as enduring elements of the basic personality structure. Cumming et al. use as a point of departure Durkheim's (1951) concept of morale, according to which morale is related to an integration-alienation dimension and is conceived as "the intervening variable between the social nexus and the individual act of suicide . . . a logical correlate of what we meant by success in aging" (Cumming et al., 1958a, pp. 4-5).

Independently of the validity problem or the relative merits of alternative psychological indexes of adjustment, these typically present two difficulties, and the Cumming group's proposal is no exception: (1) reliability of ratings, which assuredly can be minimized by explicitness of criteria, and (2) the uniqueness of an observed state of morale to the later years, as opposed to the persistence of a previous endemic state. If we measure in the seventies conditions which also typified the thirties, we are learning little about old age. The danger is that we might do this unwittingly and, in the process, delude ourselves as well.

### Other Adjustment Indexes

The Cavan, the morale, and various personality ratings are the most frequently used types. But several other approaches may be briefly noted.

*Fantasy.* Phillips (1956, 1957) uses a measure of fantasy, or the degree of withdrawal from reality. His index is a Guttman scale based on frequency of thoughts about death, absent-mindedness, and daydreaming about the past. Adjustment is equated with the ability to accept and come to terms with reality, as opposed to withdrawal from its duress and pain. Although different in content, this index is conceptually allied to morale measures, and, because it is nonideological, its validity may suffer less.

Its major errors may appear in misclassifying various deviant types: the culturally withdrawn, such as the intensely religious with a strong otherworldly orientation; people otherwise poorly adjusted (by whatever measure) whose psychological defenses do *not* take the form of withdrawal, who may think concretely, and be unimaginative and present-oriented; and the otherwise well-adjusted, with a rich imagination and fantasy life. Such respondents may get short shrift in this scale. In addition, the items concerning thoughts about death used in the Cornell studies do not tap only morbid self-concern, but also the realistic adaptation to prospective death, as in planning for survivors or providing for the transmission of property. Further, the studies of the Cumming group indicate a general life constriction and withdrawal of affect from the environment with increasing age, and it is uncertain how this general process would affect a fantasy scale (Cassetta, Newell, & Parlagreco, 1960; Cumming, Dean, Newell, & McCaffrey, 1960; Cumming & McCaffrey, 1960).

Aside from his particular measure, however, Phillips found that major role changes have a vital effect on adjustment, and this is of major importance.

*Self-Images.* Several investigators have also used self-images as an index. They have shown a strong relationship between younger self-conceptions and "good" adjustment and between older self-images and deteriorating adjustment (Blau, 1956; Deutsch & Solomon, 1959; Mason, 1954; Phillips, 1957; Tuckman & Lorge, 1954; Tuckman, Lorge, & Spooner, 1953).

Shifts in subjective age are notably related to significant status changes, as suggested by Phillips. And, the clutch on youthful self-images in America is more impervious to the definitions of significant others than are any other self-conceptions (Blau, 1956; Deutsch & Solomon, 1959). The old accept others' favorable evaluations which correspond with their wishes, but reject the unfavorable ones until massive declines in health or independence make further denials untenable.

Under these conditions, the acceptance of an older self-image may be tantamount to the acceptance of (or resignation to) the fact of an old status. This is consistent with adult socialization experience in all role transitions (Goode, 1956). There simply is no role transition without the emergence of new self-images. To this extent, self-conceptions represent a critical variable in research. But this does not presuppose the quality or kind of adjustment to be found with stable or changing self-images. Indeed, the evidence poses a distinctive theoretical issue. Normally, new self-images are associated with "good" adjustment and effective functioning in new roles, whereas the gerontological data pose the reverse relationship. New (that is, older) self-conceptions are related to poor adjustment, and the failure to develop new self-images is related to effective performance and good adjustment. This is telling evidence against the appeal of aged roles.

### Retirement Responses

Other adjustment indexes are used in special studies. For example, in the Cornell studies of occupational retirement, adjustment is seen in terms of goal-centeredness, current life satisfaction, and responses to stress (Streib, 1956) or of length of time required to get accustomed to retirement, difficulty in keeping busy, and dissatisfaction with retirement (Thompson, 1958). Clearly, these measures, though adapted to special problems, are related to others discussed in this section. They combine objective and social-psychological data in the dependent variable of adjustment so as to analyze the determinate independent variables.

The basic unsolved problem in virtually all the approaches reviewed here is that of adjustment norms. This conceals a major dilemma: How do we know that these people were any different before?

## ADJUSTMENT NORMS

Cultural or scientific norms are typically based on any of three notions of "normality"—(1) ideal standards, (2) statistical norms, or (3) clinical normalcy.

Ideal standards, often implicit, epitomize the models of what behavior ideally ought to be. However, they vary in their moral compulsion so that some ideal standards are more binding and correspond more closely to real behavioral expectations than others. In contrast, many ideals express model values, but have less compelling force. The critical factor, however, is that ideal standards are reducible to statements of what behavior should be, and their realization ultimately depends on fairly clear cultural imperatives and consensus about them.

In contrast, statistical norms represent actual behavior in force, essentially what *is*, regardless of its approximation to ideal standards. They are immediate, direct reflections of empirical modes. Thus, statistically normal behavior is basically what people do under any given set of conditions and depends on prevailing conditions and cultural practices.

Clinical notions of normality represent acceptable personality organization, psychodynamic functioning, and mental health according to standards of psychiatry and clinical psychology. These standards have been criticized both for a pathological bias in application and for an inherent lack of clarity and objectivity which perhaps accounts for the high levels of disagreement that are common in clinical diagnosis and practice. If clinical work in the field of personality is as much an art as it is a science, then as much depends on the intuition and virtuosity of the clinician as on the common acceptance and application of a firm body of theory and knowledge.

### Evaluation

All three sets of standards—the ideal, the statistical, and the clinical—have been invoked in the judgment of adjustment in old age. What are their major strengths and weaknesses?

The clinical norms may be suitable for the investigation of problems of personality, especially as they constitute the clinician's established frame of reference. But they seem unsuited to the study of wide variations of social adjustment within the clinically normal range. Although clinicians may show consensus about psychosis and extreme pathological conditions, these are not our major concern. Their disagreements may be much greater in the "normal" ranges of adjustment where our problem centers. If this is the case, then the variability of clinical standards is a major weakness in their use as adjustment norms. Furthermore, although we may be handicapped at present, we must ultimately analyze social adjustment in terms of social variables and a social frame of reference, rather than in concepts of personality.

The ideal norms are valuable less as programmatic goals than as a means of clarifying the conditions under which they may be approximated.

But ideal norms are also weak, on two grounds. First, they are commonly the norms of the researcher rather than of the culture. Then they are most likely to be arbitrary, divorced from both cultural sanction and empirical reality. For example, assumptions that X represents "successful" adjustment and Y "unsuccessful" or that old people should have youthful self-images are ideal norms arbitrarily imposed by the investigator's personal sense of fitness..

Second, ideal cultural norms about old age lack clarity, force, and general applicability. Although young and old may agree about "appropriate" behavior for old people in specific situations, this consensus typically has extremely narrow, limited referents (Havighurst & Albrecht, 1953). Aside from such focal guides, the ideal standards of the culture fail to provide reasonably clear, widely applicable role models, behavioral expectations, or prescriptions to guide adjustment. Norms for the aged are generally quite flexible and permit a broad range of acceptable behavior, especially when other people are not affected by its consequences. Loose norms maximize the scope of individual choice rather than impose the clear obligations and rights typical of earlier life stages. Alternatively, they stress such values as independence which become objectively impossible for large numbers of the aged because of their limited income or poor health. Such unrealistic norms and role ambiguity invariably impede adjustment (Cottrell, 1942).

Ideal norms also have limited applicability because of the unrealistic role models they invoke. The present movement in applied gerontology is distinguished by a pollyannish outlook of almost cloying optimism, playing on such themes as "the golden years," "adding years to life," "the best is yet to be," and similar assertions of a personal renascence in senility. The emphasis is uniformly on goals of personal creativity and the cultivation of heretofore undeveloped personal abilities. (This, incidentally, is the implicit basis of the education and arts-and-crafts movements in programs for the aged.) Marshaled as evidence that old age can be productive and creative are such inspiring exemplars as Einstein, Toscanini, Schweitzer, Titian, Baruch, Verdi, and others. These models are commonly buttressed by more prosaic, anonymous figures who belatedly discover and develop previously unsuspected talents—a rural pastor who builds organs, an eighty-seven–year–old widow who has uncovered a flair for ceramics, or the archetype of them all, Grandma Moses.

As heartening and encouraging as such ideal models may be, their relevance for the common run of humanity is dubious. Fried (1949) has indicated that the working classes, which include the bulk of the present-day aged, have relatively few nonwork interests to engage and sustain them. Implicitly, their creative personal resources are limited. Further incidental evidence appears in a study in Grand Rapids by Hunter and Maurice (1953). Although most of their older sample were able to fill out their time, boredom seemed a significant problem, for almost 40 per cent expressed a desire for new activities. Of those who wanted new experience and whose health allowed it, fully three-fourths did not know why they did not undertake new activities. In other words, the lack of personal resources, creative talent, interests or self-starting qualities seriously limit the inspirational value of ideal role models for the general older population. This would also have implications for Riesman's ideal patterns of aging (1954). He posits three types: the autonomous, the adjusted, and the anomic. Autonomous people have both personal resources and cultural supports for their expression. The adjusted have no significant internal creativity, but function adequately because role demands structure behavioral expectations, opportunities, and guides. The anomic have neither personal resources nor cultural supports. If the Grand Rapids data can be generalized, this implies that relatively few older people may be in the autonomous category; that a substantial number would be of the adjusted type until retirement or serious declines appeared in income, health, and domestic obligations; and that thereafter increasing numbers might fall into the anomic category. This possibility simply underscores the irrelevance of roseate role models for the life conditions of large masses, if not the majority, of older people.

The statistical norms of adjustment pose a different problem. Their major shortcoming is that there are not enough of them. Not enough social research has been done to establish many modal tendencies, although this will be corrected with further research. But more data will only deepen another dilemma: to what extent can normative adjustment standards be inferred from modal distributions? How can more data give these guides? Although this is a generic problem in the use of any statistics, it becomes especially pressing in gerontology. Specifically, can any meaning be given to deviant patterns, and how can they be interpreted? For example, consider the problem of the use of leisure time. Although current activity check lists may give way to more sophisticated research techniques, we will still face judgments about nonmodal or alternative leisure patterns, about the "adjustment" of sedentary as opposed to active retirees (or perhaps vice versa if the mode becomes the norm). This is like the problem of inferring the "adjustment" of Republican voters from a Democratic election victory. The type and meaning of deviance from the mode do not inhere in sheer distributions of attributes. Nor do additional statistical data solve the problem if the data grow while the culture fails to generate preferences for one pattern over another. The same dilemma applies if norms from various subgroups, membership groups, or reference groups remain weak.

Thus, the inadequacy of cultural norms—whether ideal, statistical, or clinical—and role definitions for the aged remain the crucial problem in the adjustment arena. They are less our present data that are at fault than our interpretation of them and our standards of judgment.

### THE PROBLEM AND A PROPOSAL

The root of the problem is in regarding adjustment as a state or condition at a point in time. The researcher assesses this in various ways that seem inadequate.

### Adjustment as Process

But adjustment is also a process, and its dynamic, rather than static, aspect affords some purchase on the problem. In a study of Polish immigrants' adjustment in Britain, Zubrzycki (1956) argues that their "solutions are not static but dynamic; they serve to describe not the *state* of interaction . . . but rather the *tendency* in this process" (p. 75). Aging similarly involves trends and a process of change, although gerontologists have not taken a sufficiently hard look at this process. Nonetheless, the writer and others (Breen, 1960) are convinced that this is far more important than the single point in time currently studied. What gerontologists have called adjustment is actually the result or the product of the aging process. Yet the process itself or some equivalent time perspective is vital in evaluating the conditions observed in old age.

Gerontology concerns that which is distinctive or peculiar to the later stages of life, the new attributes or changes which distinguish old age from earlier periods. Stable elements which persist in later years are also important, but largely as context for the interpretation of change. Thus, it follows that the only way to evaluate conditions in later life is to compare them to some earlier patterns. These are value-free criteria, the best available objective standards for interpreting stability and change. It also follows that, in the absence of significant cultural or group norms, the individual himself must be taken as the source of standards. We thereby avoid wishful thinking and arbitrary values or premises about the "good life" which no reputable social scientist ever imposes on the study of any younger age groups. With other problems, we analyze the forces which generate and support them and the consequences which flow from them. By the same token, this derivation of scientific knowledge is distinct from its practical application in social action, and confusion between them can only compromise both.

Recognition of the individual as the source of norms can also avoid many judgmental traps, especially of deviant and apparently maladaptive patterns which may characterize broad periods of a person's adult life. In current gerontology, many of these patterns are routinely stigmatized as poor adjustment simply because they persist into old age and happen to be studied at that time. Our assumption should rather be that any stable life pattern which persists is not peculiar to this period and, therefore, should not be deemed poor adjustment of later life.

To illustrate the proposition, let us consider a recent instance, reported in the Cleveland press, of the death of an old recluse.

### HELP HE REFUSED CAME
### TOO LATE, RECLUSE DIES

[A man], 79, had lived as a recluse for many years.

In a rooming house at . . . St., he had only a tattered blanket to cover him at night.

During the ten years he lived there, almost everyone in the neighborhood came to know the silent, elderly man.

He always turned away offers of help. He didn't bother anybody. He just wanted to be left alone.

[He] died in . . . Hospital shortly before midnight last night, apparently the victim of starvation. . . .

Although his room was grimy and littered, [a cleaning woman] said, he threatened to call the police if she entered it. On Friday, she saw him leave his room and walk down the street. Although he was staggering, she said, he refused to let a passer-by help him.

On Saturday, she sent her nephew to his room with a bowl of soup. . . . [She] came yesterday with more soup and found him lying on the floor.

She summoned a police ambulance twice, but he refused to go to the hospital. Finally, when his sister . . . was called, she persuaded him to go to the hospital. He died a few hours after he got there.

"We were a big family—eight brothers and sisters," [she] said. "But [he] always kept to himself."

. . . He never married.

"We always thought he was wealthy," the sister said. "But a few years ago I found he was living on Social Security and had only $100 in the bank.

"He was just a quiet man who wanted to be left alone. I guess he died the way he lived."

Here is an extreme case, not only of an aged isolate, but one who rejected help and continued to live in seclusion with minimal contact with others, including his own family. By any current standards, this man personifies a case of extreme poor adjustment. To be sure, he might even have been misanthropic, but in this he did not change in old age. And, aside from his income and possibly his health, his old age was presumably fundamentally no different from his middle age. So there is little that was changed or distinctive in his later life. The critical factor is not that he was a maladjusted isolate, but that he remained an isolate; his adjustment was unchanged.

Note that, in our view of adjustment, "poor" adjustment will not necessarily correspond to cases of need as a social worker would identify them. Rather, this approach aims to put our knowledge of old age on a firmer scientific footing. We are not studying adjustment or life patterns in the general population, but only among older people; hence the importance of identifying their distinctive characteristics and changes. Thus, we propose as the key to the concept of adjustment the relationship between earlier life patterns and those of old age.

Gerontologists have not been oblivious to the implications of this view, but few have acted on them. Peck (1956) notes the importance of the life history for later adjustment. Busse, Barnes, Silverman, Thaler, and Frost (1955) emphasize that adjustment in old age is basically an extension of earlier patterns of childhood and youth. Data from a study of Rockford, Illinois (Cavan, 1947), indicate that current satisfactions and dissatisfactions with life conditions are largely a function of earlier standards which serve as the individual's frame of reference. Cavan says that some old people who have never had a high standard of living are content and happy; but for others, who are reduced in circumstances, the change has brought bitterness and resentment. This is a succinct indictment of the futility of absolute, static adjustment standards. Dennis (1956) argues strongly and persuasively for the use of longitudinal and life-history data in evaluating patterns of old age, yet he doubts that any exhortation will be effective: "But let me say that I am dubious that this suggestion, even if repeated many times, will have much effect" (pp. 191f).

To be sure, not all gerontologists have completely neglected the time perspective. Havighurst and his colleagues have attempted to examine some role shifts and changes from middle to later life in the Kansas City studies. These have employed samples of people aged forty to seventy, and the analysis has largely controlled for age as a technique for bringing out trends. This is common practice, and more of it is necessary. But it has one major disadvantage in comparison with true longitudinal studies of the same group of people through time. In 1970, for example, the Kansas City samples or their equivalent would contain people born between 1900 and 1930. Differences between the older and younger segments would reflect, not only changes due to aging, but social changes due to sheer generational differences. These are pure differences between successive cohorts, generations who grew up and lived somewhat differently. And this contaminates the picture of differences attributable to sheer aging. Such contamination can be avoided if the same group of people is studied through an extended period so that differences between ages sixty and seventy clearly result from the aging process itself, rather than from other social changes.

The social scientist who has most seriously attempted to study the aging process itself and to develop a systematic theory of aging in research has been Elaine Cumming and her associates in the five-year Kansas City panel study of adult life (Cassetta et al., 1960; Cumming & McCaffrey, 1960; Cumming et al., 1960). Preliminary reports are only beginning to appear, and these are most promising in their trenchant, penetrating analysis. Further monographs should be even more valuable. The primary research interests were only incidentally concerned with adjustment. Although Cumming earlier criticized the validity and assumptions of the morale measures of Kutner and Srole (Cumming et al., 1958a; Cumming et al., 1958b), the immediate needs of analysis obliged her to fall back on a morale index based on their items which was adequate for her work. In this sense, she has not materially advanced on the central problem of this paper. But Cumming's approach is one of the best applications of theory to gerontological research. Her general time perspectives are similar to those advocated here, and they are eminently adaptable to adjustment measures based on the personal life history.

As desirable as true longitudinal studies may be, their duration and expense will probably limit the number undertaken. Therefore, it is necessary to approximate their data from the individual life history on an economical research basis. This will require retrospective data whose disadvantages can be accepted because of the substantial gains they offer.

### The Criterion Period

If the individual is used as the source of norms for his own adjustment, then his old-age patterns must be compared to those of some earlier period. Ideally, this base, or criterion, period should be after a person has raised, and discharged the bulk of responsibility to, his children, leaving him freer to exercise choices and make decisions about himself. If we allow for a transitional adjustment to the new childlessness, the age at which this post parental period ensues will vary somewhat from one person to another, but for most people will be during their early or middle fifties (Sheldon, 1958). At this time, their adult lives are at a peculiar point of balance. Their major familial obligations are discharged, they are virtually at their peak incomes, the big decrements of age and senility are still at bay, and they are probably as free to live at their maximum potential as at any other time in their adult lives. Thus, objective restraints are at a minimum and opportunities at a maximum. Under these conditions, the person can perhaps most closely approximate and realize his picture of the good life. To the extent, then, that this is an optimal period in the vestibule to old age, it offers a criterion for later adjustment.

Contrary to the gerontologists' cherished mythology about the Golden Years, there is ample evidence that old age is not eagerly anticipated in our society. Havighurst (1949) contends that America neither honors nor rejects the aged, but simply ignores them. Certainly it is not an honored period, but in many respects one of institutionalized rejection, as exemplified in compulsory retirement—the alienation from a major status-position. Inasmuch as ours is a youth-oriented society and old age is attended by a deterioration in prestige, power, prerogatives, rewards, resources, and the role clarity of earlier life, there is no particular reason why age should be impatiently awaited. Actually, older people's tenacious clutch on youthful self-images, which virtually all studies disclose, is certainly a defensive denial and rejection of the implications of a devalued status. Clearly, then, people in America do not want to grow old. Thus, they implicitly share the assumptions underlying our selection of a criterion period. By inference, their basic premise in viewing old age is that the best life is the life that changes least. Heuristically, this is our supposition as well.

### Continuity and Discontinuity, Deprivation and Gain

In deriving individual criteria of adjustment, we employ two sets of variables—continuity and discontinuity, and relative deprivation and gain. These cover the two assumptions which together define our sociological concept of adjustment in comparing the criterion period with later stages.

First, "good" adjustment is represented by maximum continuity and minimum discontinuity of life pattern between the two periods. Insofar as they resemble one another and life has few major changes, the over-all pattern is stable and has high continuity. If, however, there are major changes, instabilities, and shifts, then the over-all pattern has high discontinuity, which we regard operationally as a "poor" adjustment state.[3] Thus, extent of objective change becomes a primary index of adjustment.

Second, this is further qualified by the subjective meaning or impact of the change or lack of change observed. Thus, our first assumption is subject to this proviso: changes which eliminate previous negative aspects of life (frustrations, onerous burdens, and the like) or add new positive features (satisfactions, sought opportunities, etc.) shall be regarded as contributing to "good" adjustment. For our purposes, these changes represent net gains to the person. Conversely, stable patterns which intensify persistent frustrations or introduce new dissatisfactions contribute to "poor" adjustment. Therefore, the second index of adjustment becomes the person's deprivation or gain in old age relative to his own earlier patterns.

We schematize this paradigm of adjustment, with illustrations of various employment-retirement patterns, in Table 1.

TABLE 1
ADJUSTMENT TYPOLOGIES: THE OCCUPATIONAL ROLE

| | Objective change | |
|---|---|---|
| *Subjective impact* | Continuity | Discontinuity |
| Positive | Voluntary employment | Voluntary retirement |
| Negative | Involuntary employment | Involuntary retirement |

Although the empirical patterns may vary, we expect continuities to be strongly associated with positive attitudes and discontinuities with negative attitudes. But the analysis of deviant patterns is specifically provided for in our model.

Henry and Cumming (1959) have considered the equivalent of our first adjustment variable—extent of change—in these terms:

Our conceptions predispose us to use the middle-age status as a model of desirable social and personal development, and hence to see

[3] It would obviously be better to discard the term "adjustment" entirely and deal strictly with the process, the data, and analytic problems. However, disciplines seldom develop by fiat. Until such time as gerontologists and social scientists can relinquish the adjustment concept, it will remain in use. So our present concern is to modify its content and the manner of its use.

any deviation from this model as negative and undesirable. This may perhaps result in a failure to conceive old age as a potential developmental stage in its own right, having features qualitatively different from middle age (p. 383).

This criticism of any assumption about limited potentials in old age refers to personality changes, rather than to social adjustment. For our part, we do expect social role and adjustment changes to be primarily decremental. But this is purely prediction or a statement of probability, not of necessarily inherent limitations. The manifestation of growth, whatever its frequency or expression, is amply accommodated by our second adjustment variable—relative deprivation and gain—which we expect to result from changes of role, personal relationships, situational factors, or other life conditions more often than from personality change.

Several points should be borne in mind. First, we make no assumption that change will not occur in old age. Quite the contrary. We expect change, even though we know little of its rate, and we are trying to systematize its description and analysis. This approach can focus sorely needed studies on the nature, causes, and effects of the changes themselves, on their statistical distribution—so that statistical norms may be developed—and on the rates at which changes occur. Second, we make no assumptions about how a person is meeting and adapting to his new problems or opportunities, either those resulting from stabilities or from changes in life pattern. However, without studying the adaptive process directly, its effects are largely assimilated in the subjective-impact variable. Third, this approach affords a functional basis of age-grading, in preference to the chronological age definitions so distressing to gerontologists. Such functional classifications are feasible on the basis of typologies of change which can, at least initially, be built around major role changes. Once the strategic change variables are identified, functional classifications will be possible with easily managed, relatively inexpensive survey data. Fourth, we do not assume that this proposal is a final solution to the conceptualization and measurement of adjustment. It is simply an interim, value-free alternative which should reduce the serious margin of error which present biases allow.

### Strategic Variables

The principal remaining problem is to identify the most strategic variables for the comparison of the criterion period with later patterns. We can specify perhaps a dozen or so here which should prove theoretically important. These focus on social roles, group memberships, and social-psychological factors. We can begin with several possible role changes outlined by Phillips (1957): (1) occupational status, including women's domestic role; (2) marital status; (3) health status; (4) income and (5) social class position, including such correlates as (6) selected residential neighborhood factors. These should be supplemented by: (7) relations with significant others—children, kin, friends, and other important associates; (8) institutional connections and participation; (9) relations with other major reference and membership groups, whether formal or informal; and (10) role conflicts. Further, analysis should be made of the patterns and correlates of (11) constricting life space, (12) changing norms, and (13) changing affective involvements and identification. Certain social-psychological dimensions should also be examined, including: (14) subjective social class identification and (15) self-image, since a shift in subjective age probably signals the crystallization and acceptance of a stable new older role. This might ultimately even be conducive to older people's mental health under conditions yet to be specified. Finally, the social-psychological variables of (16) happiness, morale, or life satisfaction are useful, provided that they are anchored in norms from the person's previous life. This relative standard gives them a meaning which they otherwise lack.

Obviously, the important variables will differ for different problems, particularly as they become specialized. Those listed here pertain to over-all adjustment. However, they are at best only provisional. Much exploratory work is necessary to test their importance, to revise them, and to abstract the small number which most effectively measure stability and change within the limitations of retrospective data. This small set must ultimately be refined, simplified, weighted, and adapted for easy use in survey interviews. Thus, with normal scaling techniques and the construction of indexes and typologies, a limited amount of sensitive data can, it is hoped, tell us a great deal about older people.

## CONCLUSION

What general results might be expected from such an approach to adjustment? With our present biases, the situation of older people is not sufficiently seen as a natural product of our society and its institutional functioning. By focusing on the dynamic processes affecting older people, we can clarify the basic determinants of their position and the levers and conditions of programmatic social change. If life styles and problems are seen as products of changing life conditions, we can shift present research from its concentration on a static inventory of attributes (health, income, housing, and the like) to a clarification of the major axes of old people's alienation from, and integration into, the larger social order.

## REFERENCES

Albrecht, Ruth. The social roles of older people. *J. Geront.*, 1951, **6**, 138-145.
Albrecht, Ruth. Personal adjustment in the later years. In I.L. Webber (Ed.), *Aging: A current appraisal.* Gainesville: University of Florida Press, 1956. Pp. 76-92.
Barron, M.L. The dynamics of occupational roles and health in old age. In J.E. Anderson (Ed.), *Psychological aspects of aging,* Washington, D.C.: American Psychological Association, 1956. Pp. 236-239.
Beckman, R., Williams, C., & Fisher, G. An index of adjustment to life in later maturity. *Geriatrics,* 1958, **13**, 662-667.
Bell, W. Anomie, social isolation, and the class structure. *Sociometry,* 1957, **20**, 105-116.
Bell, W., & Force, Maryanne. Urban neighborhood types and participation in formal associations. *Amer. sociol. Rev.,* 1956, **21**, 25-34.
Blau, Zena S. Changes in status and age identification. *Amer. sociol. Rev.,* 1956, **21**, 198-203.
Breen, L.Z. The aging individual. In C. Tibbitts (Ed.), *Handbook of social gerontology.* Chicago: The University of Chicago Press, 1960. Pp. 145-162.
Burgess, E.W. Social relations, activities, and personal adjustment. *Amer. J. Sociol.,* 1954, **54**, 352-360.
Busse, E.W., Barnes, R., Silverman, A., Thaler, Margaret, & Frost, L. Studies of the process of aging, X. Strengths and weaknesses of psychic functioning in the aged. *Amer. J. Psychiat.,* 1955, **111**, 896-901.
Cassetta, Rhondda, Newell, D.S., & Parlagreco, Mary. Morale changes in women during aging. Paper read at annual meeting of the Midwest Sociological Society, St. Louis, 1960.
Cavan, Ruth. Old age in a city of 100,000. *Ill. Acad. sci. Trans.,* 1947, **40**, 156-159.
Cavan, Ruth, Burgess, E.W., Havighurst, R.J., & Goldhamer, H. *Personal adjustment in old age.* Chicago: Science Research Associates, 1949.
Cottrell, L.S., Jr. The adjustment of the individual to his age and sex roles. *Amer. sociol. Rev.,* 1942, **7**, 617-620.
Cumming, Elaine, Dean, Lois, & Newell, D.S. Measuring successful aging—a validity problem. In *Proc. Ninth Annual Sympos.,* The University of Chicago, Committee on Human Development, 1958, 1-11. (a)
Cumming, Elaine, Dean, Lois, & Newell, D.S. What is morale? A case history of a validity problem. *Hum. Organiz.,* 1958, **17** (2), 3-80. (b)

Cumming, Elaine, Dean, Lois, Newell, D.S., & McCaffrey, Isabel. Disengagement—a tentative theory of aging. *Sociometry*, 1960, **23**, 23-25.

Cumming, Elaine, & McCaffrey, Isabel. Some conditions associated with morale among the aging. Paper read at annual meeting of the American Psychopathological Association, New York, 1960.

Dennis, W. The use of biographical materials in psychological research on aging. In J.E. Anderson (Ed.), *Psychological aspects of aging*. Washington, D.C.: American Psychological Association, 1956. Pp. 191-194.

Deutsch, M., & Solomon, L. Reactions to evaluations by others as influenced by self-evaluations. *Sociometry*, 1959, **22**, 93-112.

Donahue, Wilma, Orbach, H.L., & Pollak, O. Retirement: The emerging social pattern. In C. Tibbitts (Ed.), *Handbook of social gerontology*. Chicago: The University of Chicago Press, 1960. Pp. 330-406.

Durkheim, É. *Suicide*. Glencoe, Ill.: The Free Press, 1951.

Folsom, J.K., & Morgan, Christine. The social adjustment of 381 recipients of old age allowances. *Amer. sociol. Rev.*, 1937, **2**, 223-229.

Fried, Edrita. Attitudes of the older population groups toward activity and inactivity. *J. Geront.*, 1949, **4**, 141-151.

Goode, W. J. *After divorce*. Glencoe, Ill.: The Free Press, 1956.

Havighurst, R.J. Old age—an American problem. *J. Geront.*, 1949, **4**, 298-304.

Havighurst, R.J. Validity of the Chicago attitude inventory as a measure of personal adjustment in old age. *J. abnorm. soc. Psychol.*, 1951, **46**, 24-29.

Havighurst, R.J. The social competence of middle-aged people. *Genet. Psychol. Monogr.*, 1957, **56**, 297-375.

Havighurst, R.J., & Albrecht, Ruth. *Older people*. New York: Longmans Green, 1953.

Henry, W.E., & Cumming, Elaine. Personality development in adulthood and old age. *J. proj. Tech.*, 1959, **23**, 383-390.

Hunter, W.W., & Maurice, Helen. *Older people tell their story*. Ann Arbor: The University of Michigan, Division of Gerontology, 1953.

Inkeles, A. Industrial man: The relation of status to experience, perception, and value. *Amer. J. Sociol.*, 1960, **66**, 1-31.

Inkeles, A., & Bauer, R. *The soviet citizen*. Cambridge: Harvard University Press, 1959.

Kleemeier, R.W. The effect of a work program on adjustment attitudes in an aged population. *J. Geront.*, 1951, **6**, 372-379.

Kuhlen, R.G. Age trends in adjustment during the adult years as reflected in happiness ratings. *Amer. J. Psychol.*, 1948, **3**, 307. (Abstract)

Kuhlen, R.G. Aging and life adjustment. In J.E. Birren (Ed.), *Handbook of aging and the individual: Psychological and biological aspects*. Chicago: The University of Chicago Press, 1959. Pp. 852-897.

Kutner, B., Fanshel, D., Togo, Alice M., & Langner, T.S. *Five hundred over sixty*. New York: Russell Sage Foundation, 1956.

Landis, J.T. Social-psychological factors of aging. *Soc. Forces*, 1942, **20**, 468-470.

Lebo, D. Some factors said to make for happiness in old age. *J. clin. Psychol.*, 1953, **9**, 385-390.

Mason, Evelyn. Some correlates of self-judgments of the aged. *J. Geront.*, 1954, **9**, 324-337.

Morrison, D.E., & Kristijanson, G.A. Personal adjustment among older persons. *Agric. Exper. Sta. Tech. Bull.*, 1958, No. 21. (South Dakota State College of Agriculture and Mechanical Arts, Brookings, S.D.)

Neugarten, Bernice L., & Garron, D. The attitudes of middle-aged persons toward growing older. *Geriatrics*, 1959, **14**, 21-24.

Orbach, H.L., & Shaw, D.M. Social participation and the role of the aging. *Geriatrics*, 1957, **12**, 241-246.

Peck, R. Psychological developments in the second half of life. In J.E. Anderson (Ed.), *Psychological aspects of aging.* Washington, D.C.: American Psychological Association, 1956. Pp. 42-53.

Phillips, B.S. A role theory approach to predicting adjustment of the aged in two communities. Unpublished Ph.D. thesis, Cornell University, 1956.

Phillips, B.S. A role theory approach to adjustment in old age. *Amer. sociol. Rev.*, 1957, **22**, 212-217.

Pollak, O. *Social adjustment in old age.* New York: Social Science Research Council, 1948.

Reichard, Suzanne. Personality and aging. *Newsletter (Geront. Soc.)*, 1959, **6** (2), 15-16.

Riesman, D. Some clinical and cultural aspects of aging. *Amer. J. Sociol.*, 1954, **59**, 379-383.

Rose, A.M. Factors associated with life satisfaction of middle-class, middle-aged persons. *Marriage fam. Liv.*, 1955, **17**, 15-19.

Schmidt, J.F. Patterns of poor adjustment in old age. *Amer. J. Sociol.*, 1951, **57**, 33-42.

Sheldon, H.D. *The older population of the United States.* New York: John Wiley & Sons, 1958.

Simmons, L.W. *The role of the aged in primitive society.* New Haven: Yale University Press, 1945.

Snyder, Ruth. *Community activities for the aging.* (Publ. No. 107). Chicago: Research Council for Economic Security, 1955.

Srole, L. Social integration and certain corollaries. *Amer. sociol. Rev.*, 1956, **21**, 709-716.

Streib, G.F. Morale of the retired. *Soc. Probl.*, 1956, **3**, 270-276.

Streib, G.F. Cornell longitudinal study of occupational retirement. *Publ. Hlth Rep.*, 1958, **73**, 1119-1120.

Sussman, M.B. Unpublished manuscript, 1959.

Sussman, M.B. Intergenerational family relationships and social role changes in middle age. *J. Geront.*, 1960, **15**, 71-75.

Thompson, W.E. Pre-retirement anticipation and adjustment in retirement. *J. soc. Issues*, 1958, **14** (2), 35-45.

Thompson, W.E., & Streib, G.F. Situational determinants: Health and economic deprivation in retirement. *J. soc. Issues*, 1958, **14** (2), 18-34.

Townsend, P. *The family life of old people.* London: Routledge and Kegan Paul, 1957.

Tuckman, J., & Lorge, I. Classification of self as young, middle-aged, or old. *Geriatrics*, 1954, **9**, 534-546.

Tuckman, J., Lorge, I., & Spooner, G.A. The effect of family environment on attitudes toward old people and the older worker. *J. soc. Psychol.*, 1953, **38**, 207-218.

Williams, R.H. The adult's social life space and successful aging: Some suggestions for a conceptual framework. Paper presented to the annual meeting of the Gerontological Society, Chicago, 1956.

Wylie, L. *Village in the Vaucluse*. Cambridge: Harvard University Press, 1957.

Zubrzycki, J. *Polish immigrants in Britain: A study of adjustment*. The Hague: Martinus Nijhoff, 1956.

# CHAPTER 39

*Some Social Dimensions of*
*Psychiatric Disorders in Old Age*

MARJORIE FISKE LOWENTHAL

This paper presents some preliminary findings of a long-range interdisciplinary research program on geriatric mental illness conducted at the Langley Porter Institute under grants from the National Institute of Mental Health and the State of California Department of Mental Hygiene.[1] The general objectives of the first phase

[1] Members of the staff are Dr. Alexander Simon, director; Mrs. Marjorie Fiske Lowenthal, social scientist and coordinator; Dr. Miron C. Neal, research psychiatrist; Dr. Guy Hamilton Crook, research psychologist; Dr. Lawrence Katz, associate research psychologist; Dr. Helen Jambor, associate research social psychologist; Mrs. Karen Many, assistant research sociologist; Mrs. Patricia Gumrukcu, assistant research sociologist; and Mr. Joseph Spaeth, associate research sociologist. The staff of the follow-up study, which began in February, 1960, consists of Dr. John Langton, internist and surgeon; Dr. David Zappella, psychiatrist; Dr. Margaret Clark, anthropologist; Dr. D. Jay Nichols, psychiatrist; and Mr. David Ross, psychologist.

The project is a collaborative undertaking; preliminary reports on other aspects

of the program are (1) to assess the comparative importance of the medical and social factors involved in the admission of older persons to psychiatric wards and state mental hospitals and (2) to locate those diagnostic, psychological, and social problems which are sufficiently critical or common to warrant further detailed study.

To accomplish the project's objectives, it is necessary to assess the major respects in which older persons who have been arriving in psychiatric wards in increasing proportions differ from those who remain in the community. Assuming that the major difference will be that the hospitalized are mainly psychiatrically ill and that the non-hospitalized for the most part are not, are there also physical, social, economic, or psychological differences between them, suggesting correlates of psychiatrically disturbed aging? If there are some older persons in the community at large who suffer from psychiatric problems, are those problems different in kind or in degree from those of persons arriving in the screening wards? And, if older people with serious psychiatric disturbances do live in the community at large, how are they maintained there?

Only with answers to questions of this order, however preliminary, will it be possible to formulate hypotheses about age-linked psychiatric disturbances. Only by close and continuing analysis of populations which include hospitalized and nonhospitalized can we hope to contribute to the development of a conceptual framework broader than a dichotomy of normal and abnormal.

With the cooperation of the hospital staff, arrangements were made with San Francisco General Hospital for the project research staff to examine, test, and interview older people arriving in the psychiatric screening wards. The sample consists of 534 such persons admitted during the calendar year 1959 and 600 older persons in the city of San Francisco, interviewed between October, 1959, and April, 1960. The hospital group comprises a universe of consecutive admissions of all persons aged sixty and older, except for 232 persons,

of this material have been prepared by several staff members (see footnotes below). In the preparation of this paper, the research assistance of Mrs. Many and Mrs. Gumrukcu, the editorial assistance of Mrs. Bernice Engle, and the editorial and secretarial assistance of Mrs. Helen Hosmer were indispensable.

In matters of research design, the staff is particularly indebted to the suggestions of Prof. David Blackwell, chairman, Department of Statistics, University of California (Berkeley); Professors Charles Y. Glock and Hanan Selvin, Department of Sociology, University of California (Berkeley); and Dr. Herta Herzog, vice-president in charge of research, McCann Erickson, Inc. The writer is also indebted to Professor Selvin for several helpful suggestions in the presentation of the material.

excluded for the following reasons: (1) failure to meet the one-year residence requirement of the psychiatric wards, excluded because of the possibility that they would be transferred to another state or to a distant part of California (25 per cent); (2) a history of psychiatric admissions (62 per cent) or criminal arrests (3 per cent) prior to age sixty, excluded in order to maximize the location of age-linked disorders; (3) persons still on state hospital rolls who had violated parole, escaped, or become disturbed while on visit status (10 per cent).

In planning the community sampling procedure, one of the main problems was how, within a limited budget, to locate older persons of both sexes who represent a wide range of age and socioeconomic groups. The plan finally evolved was to draw the sample from the eighteen census tracts having the highest proportion of persons sixty and over; these tracts, according to available census data, include a broad range of socioeconomic strata, as well as areas of high and low psychiatric-ward admission rates in the older age group.

A rapid survey based on interviews in every third residential unit in every other block yielded information about approximately 2,500 older people in these tracts. These survey data included such items as age, sex, marital status, living arrangements, and answers to a few questions bearing on physical and psychological health. On the basis of this survey, a probability sample of 600, stratified by age, sex, and whether living alone or with others was then drawn.[2] These stratifying variables were selected after a preliminary analysis of the first 150 hospital cases had suggested that certain patterns of psychiatric disorder may be more common to one age and sex group than to another and after it was found that the absence of another person in the household may be an important factor in the older person's admission to the psychiatric ward.

This first, or extensive, phase of the project, then, was planned to collect physical, psychiatric, social, and psychological information about older hospitalized and nonhospitalized persons; to gain insight into the range of aging patterns in healthy and ill populations; and to provide a basis for detecting key patterns and problems associated with psychiatric receiving-ward admission and state hospitalization. An equally important function of this extensive phase of the project

[2] The methodological and technical advantages and disadvantages of the sampling and interviewing procedures are to be reviewed in detail in a paper by Prof. Charles Y. Glock, director, and Miss Ursula Beghard, field supervisor, of the Survey Research Center, University of California (Berkeley), the institution to which the community field work was subcontracted.

was to provide psychiatric, physical, and socioeconomic information about a sufficiently large pool of persons to allow for the drawing of subsamples for more intensive study of the patterns and problems thus isolated.

Provision was also made for additional quantitative analysis of large segments of the initial sample. Well over half the initial community sample was drawn on a random basis, and this probability subsample will eventually be compared with the locating survey sample of 2,500, and that in turn with 1960 census reports for the older population of San Francisco as a whole. Comparisons may then also be made between the probability subsample in the community and those persons in the hospital group who come from these eighteen tracts and between hospitalized and nonhospitalized from high and low admission-rate areas within the eighteen tracts. In addition, the project staff is currently engaged in the development of an index of degree of psychiatric impairment. It is now expected that four or five "degree-of-impairment" subgroups, matched for age and sex, can be drawn from the two samples; these subgroups, in turn, will provide the basis for a more detailed exploration of the findings presented here.

A team of psychologists, psychiatrists, and social interviewers (sociologists and social workers) examined, tested, and interviewed the patient group; social interviewers also interviewed one or more collaterals—relatives, friends, landlords, and the like—of about 90 per cent of the patients. For the remaining 10 per cent, either no collateral could be identified or located, or, if they were found, they evaded or refused the interview.

The interviewers for the community group were graduate students in the social sciences or well-educated housewives with previous interviewing experience, all of whom received thorough training in the pretest phase of the field work.

The community questionnaire covered much material comparable to that collected from patients, including some abbreviated mental status tests, but the community people were not examined by physicians. One hundred persons were given a more complete battery of psychological tests by a clinical psychologist.[3] Collaterals of another one hundred persons in the community sample were also interviewed in order to provide a basis for comparing attitudes and to assess the consistency of reporting on factual questions.

This paper is limited to the material gathered by social

3 Psychological data are reported on separately in Crook and Katz (1962).

interviewers from both groups. A companion paper, devoted to a more detailed analysis of the hospital sample, utilizes material based on physical, neurologic, and psychiatric examinations by physicians as well (Simon & Neal, Chapter 21, *supra*). The field work for this phase of the project was completed only about two months before this paper was written. It is therefore necessary to limit this report to an analysis of simple counts on selected questions; cross-tabulations were available only for age and sex variables. The analytical methods used to meet these exigencies are limited to a thematically ordered review of the major similarities and differences between hospitalized and nonhospitalized [4] and individual case analysis of small groups. This review is meant to provide a descriptive backdrop and suggest problems warranting detailed study within carefully selected subgroups.

## SOCIAL DIFFERENCES BETWEEN HOSPITALIZED AND NONHOSPITALIZED

The extent to which older people with psychiatric disturbances are being maintained in the community has never been conclusively established. The psychiatric symptoms reported from the community, thus far only tentatively reviewed, indicate the obvious— that the community sample has far fewer symptoms than the hospitalized,[5] but that they are by no means symptom-free. A great many report increasing forgetfulness and irritability, and there are at least a few who report psychiatric symptoms generally considered serious.

Preliminary analysis of the hospitalized leaves no room for doubt that the great majority are, or were at the time of hospitalization, not only mentally but physically ill. This suggests that one possible explanation for the maintenance of some mentally disturbed older people in the community is that their psychiatric problems are not compounded by physical disability. A detailed analysis of this question is at present under way; for the time being, a look at fourteen cases in the community sample for whom serious mental or emotional symptoms were reported may provide some preliminary insight. This small subsample will be drawn on in various contexts throughout this

---

[4] I am indebted to Professors Hanan Selvin and Paul Lazarsfeld for suggesting this method of examining large arrays of data in a preliminary fashion.

[5] "Hospitalized" refers to persons interviewed in a psychiatric screening ward; from there, some went to state hospitals, others to other medical facilities, and still others were discharged. Analyses of differences among these subgroups is now under way.

paper; here it is examined only to determine the extent to which its members are free of physical health problems.

These fourteen persons reported a variety of symptoms that may be linked to mental disorder: feeling seriously depressed, getting lost, being unable to handle money, or having visited a doctor or clinic for psychiatric reasons. Nine had two such symptoms, and, of these, one person had three. In addition, each reported at least one condition which could result either from physical or psychological deficiency, but in any case is ordinarily considered to require supervision by a responsible person—failure to take care of their own health needs (visits to the doctor, medication, special diets); indoor or outdoor safety problems; incontinence; or inability to leave their homes without assistance. All but one of the fourteen reported at least two such deficiencies; eight had three or more.

As to physical condition, no fewer than eleven also reported serious illnesses or disabilities, often with more than one ailment—most frequently heart, kidney and gall-bladder diseases, and serious fractures. For example:

> A widow of three months, sixty-seven–year–old Mrs. B (C/162), who lives alone, is subject to "blackouts," has poor vision and hearing, has periods in which she feels life is not worth living, is incontinent, unable to leave home alone, and needs help in meeting her health needs. She also has a heart condition, for which she takes digitalis; high blood pressure; and a kidney ailment.

> Mr. W (C/213), who is seventy-six, single, and lives alone, is depressed, has been to a physician for "nerves" and has safety and locomotion problems. He had two serious heart attacks, in connection with which one leg was amputated to the hip about seven years ago, kidney disease, "multiple neuritis," and poor hearing and vision.

Thus, for these psychiatrically disturbed people at least, it is not simply a higher level of physical health that has enabled them to remain in the community. When we return to this subsample later, we shall see that there are, indeed, some decisive differences between them and their age counterparts among the hospitalized, but they are in the socioeconomic rather than the physical-health sphere, and they are, in fact, often the very differences in which the sharpest distinctions between the community and hospital samples in general are found.

Turning now to the 600 community and 534 hospitalized people, we find that one of the most striking differences between them lies on a time dimension: The hospitalized are almost invariably characterized by change—in economic role and status, in family or

other social relationships, in place of residence, or in individual activities and pastimes. The nature of these changes would have to be
interpreted as negative by any social norms.

The obvious question is whether negative social changes
are not such natural consequences of psychiatric disturbance that they
are scarcely worth exploring. There are at least three sets of findings
which suggest that these changes are not always the expected ones and
that they are not necessarily the consequences of illness. First, there are
some unexpected similarities, as well as differences, between the two
groups which neither research on the social concomitants of mental
disturbance in other age groups nor accepted social axioms would
have led us to expect. Second, the social and economic changes which
characterize the hospitalized often took place in the distant past.
Finally, the differences between the two samples in regard to negative
changes narrow with advancing age, suggesting that different rates as
well as different patterns of abnormal aging may characterize successive
age groups.

### Change in Economic Condition

Judged by their main gainful occupation, the patients'
standards of living have always been lower than those of the community group, but the differences are by no means as dramatic as one
might expect in view of the fact that they were hospitalized in a
public institution. There are more professional and managerial people
in the community sample and, at the other end of the scale, more
blue-collar workers among the hospitalized. The difference between
the two groups is far greater, however, in regard to *change* in standard
of living, with many more of the hospitalized reporting that they are
on the economic downgrade. Nearly two-thirds of them, as compared
to only one-third of the community people, report a decrease in
standard of living since age fifty, and many more of the hospitalized
report that their living standard has become "much worse." (Unless
otherwise noted, the differences between the two samples hold for
each sex at all age levels.)

Certainly they were much poorer at the time of hospitalization than were their counterparts in the community: more than half,
compared to about one-fourth in the community, reported annual
cash incomes of under $1,500. And, along with this low income, more
of them live in low-rent homes and are on public welfare rolls. The
difference in the proportion receiving Social Security pensions is not

great, but this is more likely to be the main source of income for the hospitalized.

A few people in both groups relied on savings withdrawals as a main source of income. A spot check, however, suggests that, for the hospitalized, such withdrawals frequently exhausted all financial resources.

> Miss W (541), for example, a sixty-three–year–old trained nurse of excellent professional reputation who had been unable to work at all for nearly two years and only part-time for several years before that, because of a serious skin condition, eventually used up her savings. She was then supported for a few months by a charitable religious group which withdrew help when it was discovered that she had been drinking and not eating adequately.
>
> Seventy-six–year–old Mr. D (688), a retired house-painter who lives with his wife, had developed prostate and gall-bladder trouble two years before admission and had exhausted his savings in paying for an operation. "I'll get out [of debt] though, if I can get back on my feet. I'd work again if I could." In answer to the interviewer's question about current problems, his reply was, "Nothing but money, sweetheart. And I'd like to get out of here."

Though having held well-paying positions, neither Miss W nor Mr. D had any form of health insurance when they were admitted, and they are not unique: only about one-fifth of the persons in the hospital sample had health insurance, compared to over half in a community subsample (for reasons of economy, some questions were asked of only one-third of the community respondents).

These differences in economic conditions are not reflected, however, in the reported reactions to them. In both samples, the majority said they had no unmet needs. But, among those who did report unmet needs, the community people were more likely to emphasize recreation, particularly travel, whereas such essentials as food, clothing, and medical care were mentioned somewhat more often by the hospitalized. The two groups differ more in their reports of inconveniences in their dwellings, but not in the expected direction; the hospitalized are, paradoxically, more likely to say that they have none.

Since most people in a psychiatric screening ward want to go home rather than to a state hospital, the hospitalized could be expected to minimize problems related to their circumstances. These questions were therefore also asked of relatives or others likely to be informed. Not only did more collaterals report deficiencies, but they emphasized different ones, particularly lack of adequate medical or dental care and the need for someone to help out with household tasks or to assist or supervise the patient. To be sure, some of these informants, for their part, could be expected to exaggerate unmet needs and inconveniences in the patients' daily lives to justify having taken the patient to the psychiatric ward. But a preliminary inspection of the open-ended interviews conducted with both collaterals and patients suggests that, for the most part, although more pessimistic than the patients, they, too, tended to minimize, by middle-class standards at least, the patients' external difficulties.

### Change in Economic and Social Roles

The two samples differ dramatically in proportion of retired persons. Excluding women who have been housewives most of their adult lives, constituting about one-fourth of each sample, almost all (94 per cent) of the hospitalized were retired or unemployed in the period just prior to hospitalization, compared to three-fifths in the community group who did not have a job at the time of the interview. Even among people under sixty-five in the hospital group, less than one-fifth were holding a job just prior to admission, compared to nearly two-thirds among the nonhospitalized. (These younger hospitalized people were nearly as likely to report that they were unemployed as that they were retired, but a check of their records indicates that most of them had not sought work for several years.) [6]

### Social Relationships and Activities

The family roles and living arrangements of the two groups are remarkably similar: the proportions of single persons and the proportions of childless married persons are almost identical. Even the proportions having just one child are similar. Nor are hospitalized persons who have children any more likely to be further removed from them geographically than parents among the nonhospitalized. About as many in each group live with one of their children, and they are comparatively few: about one-eighth of both live with a child, including a few who live with spouse and children. No comparable information for all older San Franciscans is available, but 1950 census data reveal that about one-fourth of all Americans who are sixty-five or older live with their children (Steiner & Dorfman, 1957).

Details bearing on the role of grandparent will have to await further analysis. Certainly, the presence or absence of a grandchild

[6] This important area of differences in work status is analyzed in detail in Jambor (1962).

in the household does not distinguish the two groups. In fact, remarkably few (10 per cent or less) in either group live in three-generation families. The only comparable data available at this writing come from Peter Townsend's (1957) study of the working-class district of Bethnal Green in London, where 10 per cent of the older people in his sample were living with grandchildren.

There are, however, notable differences between the two groups in regard to family social contacts in general. Nearly two-thirds of the hospitalized report a decrease in such contacts since the age of fifty, compared to less than one-third of the nonhospitalized. Few in either group report an increase. The existence and whereabouts of other members of the family, particularly siblings, is to be explored in future analyses. At this point, the open-ended interviews with the hospitalized and their collaterals and the marginal notes on the community schedules indicate that, except for a few sister relationships, sibling contacts are rare among both groups.

As to contacts with friends and acquaintances, several community people, compared to almost none of the hospitalized, report that they have more than they had at fifty. Conversely, three-fourths of the hospitalized, compared to somewhat more than one-third in the community, report a decrease in informal social life. The extent to which these are voluntary or forced withdrawals and whether, in line with the disengagement hypothesis developed in the Kansas City studies (Cumming, Dean, Newell, & McCaffrey, 1960), these discrepancies indicate a more rapid pace of aging among the hospitalized, will be explored briefly in the section on age levels.

In regard to the kinds of social identifications and activities which are reflected in formal affiliations, the hospitalized again seem to have had similar prime-of-life roles followed by considerably more withdrawal from religious affiliation and activity, but this pattern is not so clear in affiliations with other organized groups. Although the hospitalized are, if anything, more likely than the community people to identify with a religious group, they are considerably less likely to attend religious services. About half the community people report that they attend services at least several times a year, compared to little more than one-fourth among the hospitalized; but nearly half the hospitalized report a change in religious participation since age fifty, almost invariably a decrease. Among persons in the community, on the other hand, about half as many report an increase as a decrease in formal religious activity.

Proportionately, about twice as many of the community

people report that they currently belong to at least one civic, fraternal, professional, or occupational organization, and many more of them are active participants. Unlike familial and other informal social contacts and religious participation, however, where a decline in participation is far more likely to be found among the hospitalized, a sizable proportion of the community sample also reports a decline in organizational activity since age fifty. An inspection of the protocols of the hospital group, however, indicates that this seeming similarity may be a misleading one, for the hospitalized may have been less active in their prime. (If this is borne out in the forthcoming analysis of subgroups selected on the basis of degree of disability, it will lend support to the hypothesis that, the fewer the social resources at middle age, the greater the difficulties in aging. Why this should be more true of organizational roles than of other social relationships will also be an important question to explore.)

### *Leisure*

The hospitalized evidently did not compensate for their withdrawal from economic and social activities by pursuing the traditional pastimes of leisure; in fact, some of the greatest disparities between the two groups occur in reading and watching television. Almost all (96 per cent) in the community report that they do some reading every day, compared to slightly more than half of those who came to the psychiatric wards, and the discrepancies are almost as great in regard to watching television and listening to the radio. Again, the disparity reflects a change in the habits of the hospitalized: well over half now read less, and nearly half watch television and listen to the radio less, than they did at fifty. In sharp contrast, persons in the community were more likely to report that they now read, listen to the radio, and watch television more than formerly. Although more persons among the hospitalized suffer from impaired hearing or eyesight, such disabilities are not frequent enough to account for their notably less frequent use of these media.

The hospitalized have, in short, contracted their activities in all spheres. Although such a withdrawal could well be related to the psychiatric condition which resulted in hospitalization, there are many instances where the withdrawal preceded the disturbance by some years, that is, where there is no apparent reason why the individual should not have engaged in such activities. For them, more general questions may be pertinent. Is there such a kind of omnibus withdrawal, and, if so, is it a prodromal symptom to the development of psychiatric disturbance? Is it simultaneous in all areas, or does constriction in one conduce to constriction in others by some such process as creeping lethargy? That this may be so is suggested by mass media studies with healthy populations which have shown that, at a given point in time, people little exposed to one medium tend also to be little exposed to others and that minimal readers and viewers are also likely to be persons who are less active socially, civically, and in pursuit of their own interests and hobbies (Lazarsfeld, 1953). To be sure, these studies are cross-sectional and lack a time dimension, but this does not preclude the possibility that, for some, the still picture may reflect a stage in a process. In any case, an attempt will be made in subsequent analyses of this material to determine which changes came first and how they were triggered and to trace the course of the subsequent withdrawal.

Reports of the hospitalized about the things they find pleasurable in life do not shed much light on how they spent their time before admission. Indeed, offering some support to an omnibus withdrawal hypothesis is the fact that nearly one-fifth, compared to very few in the community (2 per cent), said they had no pleasures at all. Those who did report some pleasures reported fewer, and their interests tended to be of a less social nature than those of persons in the community.

A few persons in both samples, particularly the very old, enjoy a rather vegetative variety of pleasures, such as "just sitting," looking out the window, or sitting on a park bench. Sociologist Erving Goffman has observed, in a personal communication, that the jockeying of position for a place to "just sit" in the ward can take several hours of a geriatric patient's day every day. His observation is confirmed in the follow-up reports on the eighty- and ninety-year-old seniles who seem likely to live out their days in a mental hospital. They sit with their faces "pointed at" television, but, so far as the project psychiatrists and interviewers are able to observe, they neither actually see nor hear it. The attraction seems, in short, to be more mechanical than substantive, rather like that of a moving light for an infant.

Such observations, together with the "I-just-like-to-rest" reports from the oldest segment of the community group and the frequent "vegetating-in-the-sun" scenes of old persons in both classical and modern fiction, in rural China or in Saint Augustine, Florida, suggest that much remains to be learned about the nature and significance of apparent passivity among both sick and well. Popular stereotype has it that these sitters are reminiscing, reliving their lives. Certainly, the content of their open-ended interviews indicates that this is indeed the case for many. It suggests that, just as the very young child requires several years to incorporate the notion of time into his conception of the universe, so at the other end of life time may for some—perhaps mercifully—no longer exist as a working concept. Still another quality is apparent in this seeming inactivity, one which may be variously described as wondering, watching, perhaps waiting. As one hospitalized woman put it, "When you're older, you begin to think what the future is all about." These states of mind appear to be characterized by contentment, regardless of the degree of disorientation of the patient, and they present a sharp contrast to the moods of agitation, anger, and anxiety often found in others. There are, of course, patients who fluctuate between seeming contentment and agitation. But an examination of a few cases showing considerable consistency in either direction suggests differences in long-standing personality and value patterns. The agitated patients are more likely to be described as having been fun-loving and irresponsible in their prime, whereas the serene patients more frequently have histories of active and productive lives. In exploring further the possibility that the satisfactions and problems of old age may be related as much to the past as to the present life, it should prove fruitful to take into account not only the concepts of social science— particularly those bearing on the relationship between prevailing value systems and individual adjustment—but the insights of the philosopher and the poet into the aging process and the passage of time.

### Isolation and Mobility

It is apparent that two phenomena—social isolation and physical mobility—rather commonly assumed to be symptomatic of social disintegration and therefore to have some bearing on individual adjustment need some reassessment in relation to the problems of aging. The relationship between the objective state of isolation and the subjective feeling of loneliness, for example, seems to change at successive age levels; and geographic mobility does not appear to be so closely related to maladjustment as it has been reported to be among younger persons.

With 45 per cent of the hospital sample and 50 per cent of the community sample (which, it will be recalled, was preselected on this item) living alone, neither group differs much from the picture presented by the 2,500 older San Franciscans in the eighteen-tract locating survey, in which nearly half were living alone. The proportion living alone in all three groups is only slightly lower than that reported from the Kips Bay-Yorkville study in New York City (Kutner, Fanshel, Togo, & Langner, 1956). In short, isolation in living arrangements does not appear to be a factor distinguishing the hospitalized from the nonhospitalized. But, as we have seen, the hospitalized do offer a profile of notably fewer social contacts beyond the living arrangement sphere. Many fewer of them had recently attended formal or informal social gatherings, many more had only casual contacts or none at all, and many fewer, particularly among the very old, had a person with whom they can discuss their problems.

Isolation does not inevitably result in loneliness, however, nor do social contacts necessarily prevent it. An inspection of the protocols of the forty community people who live alone and who report only casual contacts and of seventeen who have only the contacts needed for self-maintenance showed that few regretted their comparative isolation. Only two of the forty having only casual contacts and none of the seventeen having only self-maintenance contacts complained about lack of companionship. On the other hand, of the people reporting loneliness as a major problem, only two have *not* had recent visits with friends or relatives, and, among the fifty-one persons who live alone and complain of absence of companionship in their living arrangements, all but three do have social contacts with friends and relatives.

Assistance from friends and relatives in the event of a health crisis of some length is certainly not taken for granted by the community people who are in contact with friends and relatives. Less than one-fifth would turn to a friend or relative for help, and one-fourth said that they would not know where to go if they needed care for an extended period of time. Whether this hesitancy reflects independence, prejudices about two- and three-generation families in one home, or an assumption that their friends or relatives would be unwilling or unable to help can only be conjectured, pending further analysis.

The hospitalized, for their part, are not only much more isolated, in the sense of having only casual contacts or those required for self-maintenance, but they also, it will be recalled, are far more likely to report a reduction in social contacts since age fifty than are the community people. Yet the hospitalized person is scarcely more inclined to report loneliness as a major problem than is his counterpart in the community. These data indicate, as Townsend (1957) has suggested, that the extent and nature of the social relationships of old people are not necessarily related to their feelings of well-being.

## Mobility

Insofar as admission to a psychiatric ward can be taken as evidence, this material lends little support to the assumption that geographic mobility is often associated with poor adjustment; about one-fourth of the persons in each sample were born in California; about one-seventh of each were born in San Francisco. Well over two-thirds of each have lived in San Francisco for twenty years or more, and very few of either group have lived there less than five years. To be sure, if those persons screened out of the hospital sample because they had not lived in San Francisco for a year had been included, recent geographic mobility would have shown up more clearly among the hospitalized: of the total of 832 older first admissions in 1959, fifty-nine (7 per cent), compared to six (1 per cent) in the community sample, had moved to the city in the past year. These mobile people admitted to the psychiatric ward tend to be younger males, often having a prior history of mental hospitalization for alcoholism.

But even if persons who moved to the city within the past year had been included in the sample, the fact would remain that recent moves *within* San Francisco are found far more often among the hospitalized than are moves from outside it: nearly one-third of them, in contrast to less than 10 per cent in the community sample, had moved within the past year. Closer inspection shows that thirty-six of the hospitalized, compared to two in the community, had moved at least three times. In other words, for a number of patients, the psychiatric ward was the latest in a series of recent shifts in living arrangements. This in turn raises the question, to be explored in future analyses of this material, of the extent to which residential moves are symptoms, consequences, or, as a few cases suggest, precipitants of psychiatric disturbance in old age.

## Time of Change

As was anticipated, more of the hospitalized have undergone social and economic transitions than have members of the community group. But that these events (except for changes in residence) were not likely to be recent came as a surprise. Most of those among the hospitalized who are widowed or divorced became so some time ago. In fact, the hospitalized look surprisingly like the community people:

for two-thirds of each, the marital change took place at least ten years ago. Similarly, changes in work status were no more recent among the hospitalized: relatively few of them (10 per cent), in fact fewer than in the community group, had retired in the past year. That there are more older people among the hospitalized does not appreciably influence these findings: at each age level, remote rather than recent changes in marital and work status predominate.

Reports from two subsamples of the hospitalized tend to strengthen the possibility that, if the basic life changes—mainly losses —that come with age have any bearing on hospitalization for psychiatric reasons, they frequently take several years to produce this adverse effect. A review of the first 150 hospitalized cases revealed that the death of a relative (only half of them spouses) or a friend was related to the present condition of about one-sixth of the patients. (The connection between the death and the hospitalization was made either by the individual himself or by someone who knew him at the time of the bereavement.) All but three of these significant deaths had taken place more than a year before the patient's admission, and more than half had occurred three or more years before. (The important question—whether these changes are related to the date of the onset of illness which ultimately resulted in hospitalization—is now being explored.)

Similarly, a search of the nature and duration of health problems reported among the first 100 hospitalized cases revealed that about one-third had serious physical illness (mainly strokes, heart attacks, and cancer, in that order) or serious locomotor or sensory handicaps; most of these illnesses were believed by the informant to be related to the mental disturbances resulting in admission. Only five of these thirty-odd people reported that these illnesses had been discovered within the year, and several dated them back ten years or more. The time-lag manifest here tends to support a hypothesis growing out of a series of disaster, migration, and industrial retirement studies and postulated by Tyhurst (1957): the time immediately following a shock or major loss is the most favorable period for reorientation; changes made, or not made, at that point have serious consequences for the future adjustment of the individual. Applied to the transitions of aging, the questions to be explored in future analyses of these data are: (1) Is there any evidence that the hospitalized did not reorient themselves or adopted another form of reorientation during and immediately after the period of crisis? (2) What kinds of maladjustment result from lack of reorientation during periods of stress? (3) Do such maladjustments in fact evolve, or do they become manifest slowly?

As a corollary to these questions, it will be highly pertinent to inquire, during the follow-up study of patients, into modes of adjustment to the stress of having been in the psychiatric screening ward or in a state mental hospital for the first time at age sixty or over, the early or delayed consequences of various modes, and the extent to which the various patterns of readjustment are linked with morale.

### Satisfaction with Life

It may eventually be possible to develop a typology bearing on mood, morale, or satisfaction with life and to compare position on such a dimension with position in typologies (or scales or indexes) of psychiatric and physical health and certain socioeconomic situations. Meanwhile, a direct question on the subject of mood had the obvious result that considerably more of the hospitalized reported that they had been in "low spirits lately": about one-third, compared to one-tenth in the community. In view of the sometimes vast differences in psychiatric and physical condition of the two samples, it is, if anything, surprising that, on this and other topics bearing on morale (not having any current pleasures, being worried, afraid, or lonely), the gap between the two groups is not greater than it is, that, for example, two-thirds of the hospitalized were not in low spirits. Perhaps we encounter here again the possibilities that the hospitalized deny such problems because of a wish to avoid commitment or that they are simply less able to assess themselves and their circumstances realistically. In any case, their self-appraisals of mood were considerably more optimistic than were the observations of their collaterals: about half again as many collaterals as patients reported that they (the patients) had recently been "blue," or depressed. Not only were collateral reports from the community more consistent with those of the subjects, but the differences that did appear were in the other direction: the subjects were more likely to report themselves despondent than were collaterals.

Why low spirits tend to decrease with age cannot be properly appraised without considerably more detailed analysis. At this point, the evidence from the hospital sample suggests two tendencies, both of which may be at work to produce this result. First, possibly because they are more likely to have organic brain disorders, older persons seem to have less insight into their true condition; second, morale in the eighties may well be related to quite different factors than it is for the seventies and sixties. As to the first point, hospitalized persons in their eighties are, for example, much more likely to blame others for their admission, whereas younger persons tend to acknowledge that something is wrong with them. As to the second, there is some evidence that the hospitalization of persons in their eighties is less closely associated with poor physical health or physical handicap than it is among persons in their seventies. Furthermore, their economic circumstances are less likely to be desperate than those of persons in their sixties. In short, perhaps for quite objective reasons, the older patients really are in better spirits.

### AGE PATTERNS

Whatever chronological stages may be hinted at here result from comparing persons in different age groups at the same point in time. At this writing, in other words, the study is a cross-sectional and not a developmental one. We therefore deal not only with persons of different ages, but with persons born into a different world. Until panel data from the follow-up studies become available, to any generalizations about age levels must be attached the reservation that differences in behavior may result from variations in environmental stress at earlier periods of life, as well as from the phenomenon of aging itself. Persons now in their eighties, for example, grew to maturity before the shocks of World War I, its aftermath, and the Depression; persons in their early sixties were in a highly impressionable stage of life at the outbreak of World War I and may have been just at the peak of their financial responsibilities during the Depression. Reservation about the meaning of age level differences in a cross-sectional study does not, however, reduce the significance of any differences that may be found between or among two or more groups within one age level.

Two age-level patterns are suggested by this material, and there is at least a hint of a third. First, the differences among successive age groups are often sharper in the community group than they are among the hospitalized (at least insofar as social factors are concerned, and preliminary analysis suggests that this may also hold for physical factors). Second, the successive age groups in the hospital sample tend to form a continuum with those in the community, with the youngest hospitalized continuing a downward trend from the oldest in the community. Third, persons in their seventies sometimes deviate from this trend in respects which may have some bearing on survival factors within a given age cohort.

The first two patterns appear in both economic and social spheres. For example, as is to be expected, the proportion of retired and unemployed moves steadily upward with age in the community sample. The sixty–to–sixty-four-year-olds in the hospital sample, however, have more retired among them than do the oldest in the community. The difference between youngest and oldest in the hospital group is also considerably less than it is between oldest and youngest in the community sample.

Not surprisingly, a similar trend is apparent if one looks at the proportion having very low income. There is in this case, however, a sharper drop between the seventy- and the eighty-year-olds among the hospitalized than is seen in the employment picture. Probably not unrelated to retirement and low income, possession of health insurance also shows a downward trend with age in both samples, and, again, the continuum moves from oldest nonhospitalized to youngest hospitalized and on downward to oldest hospitalized. Thus, over two-thirds of the youngest in the community have health insurance, compared to less than 10 per cent of the oldest hospitalized.

In the social sphere, organization memberships reported by the community sample decline with age at a rather even pace, and, conversely, reports of withdrawal from social activity increase: one-fourth of the youngest (sixty to sixty-nine) report less social contact than at age fifty, compared to three-fourths of the oldest (eighty or older). The youngest among the hospitalized do not differ greatly from the oldest in the community, and again the difference between youngest and oldest among the hospitalized is comparatively slight. These trends combine to make the oldest hospitalized patients resemble their age peers in the community to a far greater extent than patients in the sixties resemble theirs.

At least one deviation from the chronological pattern suggested here is found among people in their seventies in both samples. People from seventy to seventy-nine in the community and those from seventy to seventy-four among the hospitalized are less likely to report a decrease in living standards than are persons in other age groups. Among the hospitalized, more seventy-year-olds belong to organizations and have confidants. At the same time, feelings of loneliness are more likely to characterize seventy-year-olds than persons in the sixties or eighties. Since they are considerably more likely to have social contacts than are younger or older persons, it appears that, for reasons still to be sought, seventy-year-olds are the ones most apt to be suffering from a loneliness not linked to social isolation. The opposite is true of eighty-year-olds, particularly of women in this age group. Half of the hospitalized women eighty or over (twenty-four of the forty-eight who were sufficiently well-oriented to be asked this question) reported that they have no confidant, yet very few reported loneliness as a problem.

All this suggests that, possibly because of selective factors involved in survival at successive age levels, the problems and supports respectively conducing to or deterring hospitalization for psychiatric reasons may vary with advancing age. (The extent to which the factors conducing to or deterring hospitalization are also related to the development of psychiatric symptoms, hospitalization or no, will be explored through the previously mentioned "degree-of-psychiatric-disability" subgroups.)

### Age Patterns Suggested in Small Subsamples

Among the hospitalized subsample of 100, at least four patterns of stress associated with psychiatric disturbance can be detected. All but one of these tend to be more characteristic of one age level than another.

1. Men in their sixties and some women whose psychiatric symptoms are for the most part functional (alcoholics or depressives, for example) and who attribute their deterioration to such social stresses as retirement or the death of a close person, usually in the fairly distant past.

2. Seventy-year-olds of both sexes who have had strokes or who have handicaps (other than serious illness)—such as near or total blindness, extreme deafness, or limb impairments—which make them at least potentially dependent on others.

3. Women eighty or older who have gradually slowed down and deteriorated over a period of several years with no marked social or economic concomitants and no more (possibly fewer) signs of serious physical illness than are found among the younger people.

4. Persons of all ages having serious physical illnesses which have persisted for some years.

Although fourteen cases can scarcely support sweeping assertions, the subsample of psychiatrically ill in the community does fall readily into patterns of both stress and disorder very similar to those exhibited by their age counterparts in the hospital. But, at the same time, the extent to which they have the very external supports that the hospitalized most lack is striking.

The two psychiatrically disturbed sixty-year-olds in the community subsample (one man and one woman) are retired. The man is sixty years old and has blackouts, a drinking problem, and has been seeing a doctor for "nerves" for more than ten years. The woman, who is sixty-seven, is very depressed, worried, irritable, has memory loss, and frequently loses her belongings. Both had been married three times. (To be sure, multiple marriages are found most frequently in the sixty-year bracket in general, but more of the hospitalized sixty-year-olds have had multiple marriages than have those in the community group.) On the other hand, neither of these disturbed people remaining in the community is socially isolated, and, though they have money problems, they do not live at the bare subsistence level so conspicuously reported by sixty-year-olds in the hospital. Both had been white-collar workers; the woman had retired four years ago; the man, two years ago, both because of illness. Both had above-average education for the community sample, whereas sixty-years-olds among the hospitalized were, if anything, less well-educated than the older groups in the hospital sample.

Three of the four seventy-year-olds in the subsample of community people who reported psychiatric symptoms also have locomotion problems. One is an amputee, one has not been able to walk alone since breaking a leg six years ago, and one suffered a hip fracture about a year before the interview and was still confined to bed or chair. Three of them also have severe sensory impairments, and two reported serious physical illness (heart). In these respects, as well as in a comparative freedom from economic problems, they tend to resemble the hospitalized who are in their seventies. Unlike some seventy-year-olds in the hospital sample, however, none say they are lonely (one is socially isolated, but he reports that he always has been, and happily so). Two continue an active social life. They are not only visited by friends and relatives, but manage to procure the help necessary to make visits themselves.

The eight community people with psychiatric symptoms who are eighty years or older resemble the hospitalized of this age group in that the majority are women, that they are about as likely to be in good as in poor physical health, and that half have no social life beyond relatives and do not seem to miss it. The happy ninety-nine-year-old widow (C/915) who lives well, if not luxuriously, with her maid-companion is both wealthier and more euphoric than the others, but she epitomizes the half of this group that quite literally enjoys physical good health. Her companion handles the details of everyday life and waits on her as she whiles away her days with telephone, correspondence, magazines, and television, sitting tailor-fashion, elegantly negligeed and groomed, on her bed. "Why get up if I have nothing special to do and it's so nice in bed?" was her rhetorical query to the interviewer. She is escorted to luncheons, Town Hall lectures, and concerts and apparently enjoys these events, though she gaily (and truly) quipped that she could not recall what she or anyone else had said, whether yesterday or two minutes ago. Her pleasures may be the limited ones of old age—physical comforts and food, mainly, but they seem unmitigated. "I'm happy all the time, I have nothing to make me unhappy—enough money, enough of everything. I'm able to eat anything I like. . . . I'll bet you haven't seen many people 100 years old that are so healthy."

As the story of this fortunate woman suggests, however, both the living arrangements and the socioeconomic level of these psychiatrically impaired eighty-year-olds in the community differ markedly from those of their age peers in the hospital sample. In addition to the ninety-nine-year-old living with maid-companion, four live with their children and two with a spouse—leaving only one who lives alone. All but two (or their spouses) have held white-collar, professional, or managerial positions. Four require and have constant care or supervision from family or nurse; two require less help, but have it when they need it. This leaves two who appear to need (and say they need) more assistance than they are getting, and they will be watched with interest in the course of the follow-up study.

The small subsample of psychiatrically disturbed people who have not been hospitalized for their disorders, then, often show patterns of disability similar to those revealed by their respective age peers among the hospitalized. At the same time, and to a notable extent, they can also claim the very supports the hospitalized most lack. The obvious analytical task, and one on which we are now embarked, is to determine the extent to which this finding holds true if we compare all psychiatrically disturbed persons in the community sample with their age and degree-of-disability peers in the hospital group. In so doing, we hope to elaborate further on the inducements and deterrents to mental hospitalization at work at the various older age levels. Simultaneously, our attention will be focused on the more fundamental and challenging question: Can correlates to the development of psychiatric symptoms and other mental disabilities among older persons—regardless of whether these symptoms lead to hospitalization in a psychiatric ward—also be pinpointed?

## REFERENCES

Crook, G.H., & Katz, L. The intellectual functioning of aged patients and non-patients. In C. Tibbitts & Wilma Donahue (Eds.), *Aging around the world*. Vol. I. *Social and psychological aspects of aging*. New York: Columbia University Press, 1962. Pp. 555-567.

Cumming, Elaine, Dean, Lois R., Newell, D.S., & McCaffrey, Isabel. Disengagement—a tentative theory of aging. *Sociometry*, 1960, **23**, 23-35.

Jambor, Helen. A comparative analysis of employment patterns of older psychiatric male patients and men in the community. In C. Tibbitts & Wilma Donahue (Eds.), *Aging around the world*. Vol. I. *Social and psychological aspects of aging*. New York: Columbia University Press, 1962. Pp. 537-546.

Kutner, B., Fanshel, D., Togo, Alice M., & Langner, T.S. *Five hundred over sixty: A community survey on aging*. New York: Russell Sage Foundation, 1956.

Lazarsfeld, P.F. Audience research. In B. Berelson & M. Janowitz (Eds.), *Reader in public opinion and communication*. Glencoe, Ill.: The Free Press, 1953. Pp. 337-346.

Steiner, P.O., & Dorfman, R. *The economic status of the aged*. Berkeley: University of California Press, 1957.

Townsend, P. *The family life of old people*. Glencoe, Ill.: The Free Press, 1957.

Tyhurst, J.H. The role of transition states—including disasters—in mental illness. In *Symposium on preventive and social psychiatry*. Washington, D.C.: U.S. Government Printing Office, 1957. Pp. 149-172.

# CHAPTER 40

*Hospitalization of the*
*Elderly Psychiatrically Ill*

ROBERT H. DOVENMUEHLE

One of the most important practical problems confronting our society is the increase in admission of elderly persons to psychiatric hospitals. Mental illness is now the third-ranked cause of chronic illness in this country (U.S. Department of Health, Education, and Welfare, 1960). Malzberg (1959) states that the evidence appears conclusive that there has been a genuine increase in the rate of first admissions, and it may be inferred that there has been a corresponding increase in the incidence of mental disease. With specific reference to psychosis with cerebral arteriosclerosis, his statistics indicate that the rate of increase of this condition has been five times that for mental disease in general after corrections for age and sex of population. The rate of admission for senile psychosis increased at a lesser rate.

Rates for mental illness are at a maximum in the upper age

groups, and Malzberg suggests that one explanation is that there is currently less selection of people living to middle age and beyond (because of reduced incidence of disease in early years) and that this allows more people to develop degenerative diseases with accompanying psychiatric disorders. As would be expected, Malzberg also found that the rates of discharge were low for the organic psychoses, in fact that these had the poorest rates of discharge for all groups of mental illnesses.

According to the report on patients over sixty-five in public mental hospitals prepared by the American Psychiatric Association (1959), 30.5 per cent of state hospital residents are presently over sixty-five. Twenty-seven per cent of all first admissions are in this age group. Acute and chronic brain syndromes, including senile and cerebral arteriosclerotic brain syndromes, predominate. In other diagnostic categories, the percentage of resident patients over sixty-five is larger than for first admissions, since such patients have grown old in the hospital and are rarely admitted after sixty-five. It was also noted that Southern states are below the U.S. average for both residents and first admissions over sixty-five. This, however, may be partly a reflection of the generally lower percentages of older citizens in Southern states (U.S. Department of Health, Education, and Welfare, 1960).

A number of states have initiated nursing homes, foster homes, and home care plans for elderly psychiatric patients, and from 1 to 36 per cent of people over sixty-five "on the books" of state institutions are living outside. The modal occurrence is 8 per cent (American Psychiatric Association, 1959).

These facts have given rise to lively discussion, both within the psychiatric profession and in the community, of the measure of responsibility that communities should take for the care of the senile elderly. There is clear agreement that many cultural factors in our modern society contribute to the increasing hospitalization of the elderly person. There is not clear agreement as how to best handle those concerned.

There are essentially two factors involved in determining appropriateness of hospitalization for a particular person. The primary factor, of course, is whether there are quantitative and qualitative medical problems that require hospital management. The second is dependency.

The fact is that many elderly people are dependent on others for financial resources and for varying degrees of supervision of daily activity and of provision of basic needs of life (many of which can be subsumed under "nursing care"). Many of these aspects of dependency are viewed as the responsibility of relatives or of the community when the individual does not have the personal resources.

Medical criteria, on the other hand, are oriented to alleviating disease factors. When remaining disability results in dependency of the individual involved, the nature of the disease itself often determines the manner in which such dependency is handled. In the case of physical injury and disease acquired during wartime service, for example, the veteran is provided financial resources which allow him to meet these needs in his community. Psychotic individuals often become the subjects of institutional care. One of the prominent factors in determining psychosis seems to be the degree of difference between the behavior of the individual and the "normal" person as defined by the local community. These cultural factors bear heavily on the attitude of the medical practitioner when such processes as commitment to a psychiatric institution are considered. Thus, certain kinds of problems demanding dependent care are of medical concern.

It is the purpose of this presentation [1] to discuss in detail the psychiatric and medical "differences" between a group of elderly individuals hospitalized for psychiatric reasons and a group of normally functioning volunteers from a Southern urban area as a basis for establishing criteria for care.

### SUBJECTS

Table 1 indicates the total number of subjects examined in the community and gives a rough indication of the sources from which they were drawn. Table 2 shows the age distribution. All the community subjects were volunteers. In addition, seventy-eight hospitalized subjects were examined.

The extensive research examinations required some two

[1] The data reported come from a study directed by Ewald W. Busse and supported by Public Health Service Research grants H-3582, M-2109, and M-900 from the National Institutes of Health, Public Health Service. The author expresses special indebtedness to his colleagues who collaborated closely in this series of studies: Gustave Newman, Carl Eisdorfer, and Walter Obrist. The gracious cooperation of the staff of the John Umstead Hospital, North Carolina, made possible the collection of data on hospitalized subjects.

TABLE 1
DISTRIBUTION OF SUBJECTS IN COMMUNITY GROUP

| Socioeconomic group* | Males | | Females | |
|---|---|---|---|---|
| | White | Negro | White | Negro |
| Lower | 44 | 31 | 47 | 34 |
| Higher | 42 | 9 | 42 | 11 |

*The lower socioeconomic group was made up of Golden Age Club members
and others; the higher group included top-level business and professional
people.

TABLE 2
AGE GROUPING OF SUBJECTS IN COMMUNITY GROUP

| Age Range | 60-64 | 65-69 | 70-74 | 75-79 | 80+ |
|---|---|---|---|---|---|
| Number of subjects | 47 | 72 | 69 | 38 | 33 |

and one-half days of the subject's time.[2] The complete series of examinations required a high degree of social interaction and active collaboration on the part of the subject. This fact alone accounts for a
high degree of selection of hospitalized subjects. Because of technical
problems, it was impossible to obtain the detailed ophthalmologic and
auditory examinations on the hospitalized subjects.

Most of the hospitalized subjects were studied from December, 1954, through November, 1955. The project sample was
compared to all other admissions over the age of sixty for that year
in order to specify the exact bias of the sample. The populations
appeared similiar in most respects.

---

[2] The research examination consisted of medical, psychiatric, and social histories; mental status; physical examination; E.E.G., EKG, B.C.G., chest X ray,
urinalysis, complete blood count, blood N.P.N., and blood sugar; neurological
examination with special sensory examinations for olfaction and somesthesis; complete ophthalmologic examination and tests of visual function (color vision, depth
perception, and perimetry); complete auditory examination, including pure tone
and speech perception; complete dermatologic examination; psychological examination with WAIS, Rorschach, Wechsler memory scale, and reaction time test; microscopic examination of the bulbar conjunctival vasculature and retinal photography.

In comparison to the project group, the nonproject patients tended to have a higher rate of first admissions, and these were on an involuntary basis. Once admitted, they tended to have a longer period of hospitalization. They also had a higher death rate. In regard to diagnostic category, chronic brain syndrome as opposed to functional psychoses was more prevalent. In general, the data indicate a greater degree of sickness, both mental and physical, in the nonproject group.

The hospital subject group was matched with the group of community subjects by age, sex, and socioeconomic condition as far as possible. (All were of the white race.) In previous studies with our community subjects, it was found that education and occupation rankings correlated quite significantly with socioeconomic rankings (p < .001). It was possible to match the hospital and community groups on educational level, but impossible to match them completely according to occupational ranking because more farmers were included in the hospital group and more clerks and salespeople in the community group. Even so, it was apparent that the majority of the hospitalized subjects corresponded most closely to the lower socioeconomic group in the community.

### Psychiatric Symptom Categories

Over-all diagnosis according to the "Diagnostic and Statistical Manual of Mental Disorders" of the American Psychiatric Association was not used as a basis for this study. It was considered more efficient to classify all subjects into groups on the basis of the symptoms recorded during a mental-status examination of a standard type (Noyes & Kolb, 1953). These are the data from which global diagnostic classification is made, and they offer a more discrete and specific basis for comparison of groups of subjects. Appendix A indicates the breakdown used. Psychiatric symptoms occurring rarely were not used. Memory defect was so common as to be unusable as a differentiating factor.

On the basis of this classification the hospital and community groups broke into the categories indicated in Fig. 1. As can be seen, two of the hospitalized subjects had recovered during the brief period between admission and the time they were seen for research examination (average time: two weeks). One of the subjects was an elderly woman who has been treated for her suicidal depression in another hospital and, for financial reasons, was transferred to the state hospital for convalescence. The other case was an elderly man who became agitated and paranoid as a reaction to being left alone and whose

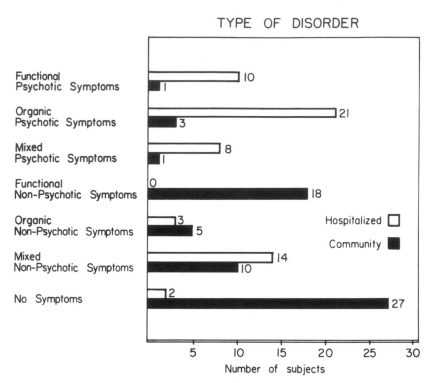

FIG. 1. Frequencies of diagnostic classifications in hospitalized
and community groups.

symptoms invariably decreased markedly whenever he had supervised
care. There were only five of the matched community group who were
considered psychotic, and twenty-seven were normal. These are the
same percentages of psychiatric problems found in the total community
group of 260 subjects, and the distribution of symptoms among nonpsychotic, functional, organic, and mixed groups was very nearly the
same as in the total community group.

The hospitalized group has, of course, more psychosis
(p < .01). There were not enough subjects in the psychotic community
group to test the level of probability in the area of psychosis, but in
nonpsychotic symptomatology the hospitalized subjects had significantly more organic and mixed organic and functional symptoms
than did the community group (p < .001).

A descriptive examination of the specific symptoms occurring in each of the categories indicates that a few of the symptoms have very high incidence in each category. Unfortunately, here, again, we have very few cases of psychotic community people and no cases of purely functional nonpsychotic symptomatology in the hospitalized group. Except where applicable, therefore, only the larger groups are considered. No tests for statistical probability could be applied, since many of the variables were not independent; therefore, descriptive examination only is used throughout this section.

Functional psychotic symptoms did not often include somatic delusions in the hospital group, occurring only once in ten subjects. Instead, other delusional activities and persecutory trends dominate the picture.

With organic psychotic symptoms, confusion and defective intellectual function (below the borderline level) were frequently responsible for classification of subjects in this group. Of the hospitalized patients with organic symptoms, twelve were described as confused and fifteen as having defective intellectual function. Illusions and disturbance of speech production occurred relatively infrequently. All three of the community subjects classified in the organic-psychotic-symptom group suffered confusion, but none of the three was rated defective in clinical evidence of intellectual functioning.

In considering subjects with mixed symptoms, of whom there were eight, three were said to show confusion and five were said to show defective intellectual function, but there were several subjects with multiple symptoms. The single community subject had neither perceptual disturbance nor deterioration of intellectual functioning. Again it is noted that somatic delusions play an infrequent role in the psychoses represented, whereas persecutory feelings and delusions dominate the picture.

Of the nonpsychotic functional symptoms, only the community group could be examined. Of the eighteen subjects in this group, twelve were reported to show affective change (again, classifications were not exclusive). Currently depressed affect was responsible for eleven of these cases, and one subject was elated. Anxiety, chronic mood disturbance, obsessions, and compulsions did not appear to afflict the group to any great degree. Hypochondriasis occurred in six of this group, which is the percentage (33) found for the entire community group (Busse & Dovenmuehle, 1958). It is interesting to note that self-condemnation and expansive trends were absent from this group. None of the subjects examined showed either of these phenomena. These were also an infrequent occurrence in the entire community group.

The number of subjects with organic nonpsychotic symptoms was few. Disturbance in motor activity was noted in only one of the five community subjects so classified and in none of the three hospital subjects. One hospital subject and two community subjects suffered speech impairments. Speed of reaction showed no change, and responses were appropriate from all but two community subjects. Two of the hospitalized subjects had impairment of insight and judgment, and one of the community group had impaired insight but intact judgment.

The differences between the two groups on mixed functional and organic nonpsychotic symptoms were recorded for the ten community subjects and the fourteen hospital subjects. Changes in speed of reaction were more prominent in community subjects, although the number of cases was small. Poor judgment in general activities and concerning future plans appeared to be more frequent in hospitalized subjects. Current or prolonged depression is responsible for much of the discomfort of both groups. Anxiety is less important in both groups. Obsessions and compulsions appear in both groups, but are more frequent in the hospitalized group. Again, hypochondriasis occurs with greater frequency in the community than in the hospital group.

In work done with Eisdorfer (Eisdorfer, Busse, & Cohen, 1959), it was found that the I.Q. differences between the groups of matched hospital and community subjects were significantly different. The verbal, performance, and full-scale I.Q. were significantly lower for hospital subjects than for the matched community group, owing to inability of many of these subjects to complete this part of the research examination.

There are several fairly clear points of difference between subjects hospitalized for psychiatric illness and those functioning in the community. The high incidence of bodily overconcern in the community group and an accompanying low incidence of the same symptom in hospitalized subjects has been consistently noted in all reports from this project (Busse & Dovenmuehle, 1958). Bodily overconcern was found to relate inversely to age and may indicate an adjustment reaction to the early years of old age or may be related to a negative survival factor. However, it also relates quite closely to depression and anxiety and may be part of a milder depressive syndrome than that seen in hospitalized subjects. It is also interesting to note that bodily overconcern can be part of a pattern of dealing with other people (Busse, 1954).

Inspection of the groups with psychotic symptoms appears to indicate that preservation of intellectual function in spite of some degree of confusion helps the person cope with the organic deficiency in a manner consistent with continued community functioning. Considering that defective intellectual function must inevitably affect judgment in dealing with current situations, it is not surprising that this occurs frequently in people committed to the hospital. In the few subjects with organic nonpsychotic symptoms, the impact of deficiencies on judgment is also noted. This is also indicated as a marked difference in those with mixed symptoms.

The relatively high occurrence of depressed mood and affect as a cause for discomfort in both hospitalized and community groups is being investigated separately. There appear to be important differences in the nature of the depressive syndromes that occur in these two groups, with the depressive syndromes of hospitalized subjects conforming much more to the usual textbook picture of psychotic depression than do subjects in the community (Dovenmuehle, Reckless, & Newman, 1960).

In the psychotic hospitalized person, delusions of various kinds and persecutory feelings dominate the picture. Both delusional activity and persecutory feelings tend to precipitate behavior that is seen as odd by others in most communities.

The relative superiority of verbal I.Q. performance to the performance I.Q. noted in the hospitalized and community subjects has not been fully explained (Eisdorfer et al., 1959). This has been a consistent finding in all our subject groups and represents, perhaps, a difference in populations drawn from an area of the United States other than that on which the WAIS was standardized. The importance of the intellectual deterioration in hospitalized subjects is quite apparent, however. This tends to reinforce the clinically noted psychiatric findings.

### Physical Factors

The relationships between physical functioning and age have been clearly defined in our community group and in the hospital group (Dovenmuehle, Newman, & Busse, 1960). It is also important to consider physical functioning in relation to hospitalization for psychiatric illness per se. During the collection of data, there was strong clinical impression that these subjects exhibited more physical illness than did community subjects. The predominant occurrence of "organic" symptomatology in the hospital group also makes it imperative to examine physical factors.

In the course of the study, a method was developed for rating the functional physical status of each subject. Although it would have been desirable to base this rating on direct measures of functional capacity, such tests are either not standardized or are too cumbersome for general diagnostic purposes. From the diagnostic physical examination, however, it was possible to make use of the pathology orientation of the usual medical approach.

By using a scale modified and adapted from those of the United States Army and Veterans Administration for rating disability, it was possible to rate limitations on physical functioning as follows:

0—No pathology or disability
1—Disease diagnosis; no limitation
        of social or industrial function
2—20 per cent or less limitation
3—20 to 50 per cent limitation
4—50 to 80 per cent limitation
5—80 to 100 per cent limitation

For our purpose, social limitation is defined as any restriction on activity or communication involved in social activities usually possible for the particular subject. This is sometimes a hypothetically "normal" situation, but is often reinforced by specific information on the subject's daily activity. For example, arthritic limitations severe enough to prevent the subject from pursuing usual interests in church and civic clubs because of the immobility factor but still permitting enjoyment from social intercourse with visiting friends would be rated 30 to 50 per-cent social incapacity. On the other hand, limitation of vision and hearing to the point where understandable social relationships are for all practical purposes terminated would call for a complete incapacitation rating.

Where industrial incapacity is concerned, we considered useful occupations, whether or not done for pay, since most of our subjects were retired. For example, an individual with arthritic limitation who cannot possibly get to a place of work or part-time hobby activity if located outside the home is seriously disabled. If, in spite of this limitation, the individual is able to actively engage in productive work around the home, this would not be considered complete disability.

It must be noted that psychiatric limitations on ability to perform were not considered in conjunction with this rating. Only the physical aspects of the individual's social and industrial capacity were considered (Dovenmuehle, Newman, & Busse, 1960).

A comparison of the matched hospitalized and community groups indicates significantly more physical disability in the hospitalized group (p < .01). Only seventeen of the hospitalized group had no pathology or pathology without disability. Thirty-two of this group had some disability accompanying physical problems. As against this, thirty-five of the community group had no disease or disability from any disease, and thirty had some degree of disability.

In a previous study of the physical functional capacity of the community group, it was found that physical disability increased directly with age and was significantly related inversely to socioeconomic condition. There was no relationship to race or sex (Dovenmuehle, Busse, & Newman, 1961).

The entire community group suffered principally from visual and hearing loss, arteriosclerosis, high blood pressure, pulmonary disease, arthritis, and joint limitation. There were no significant dif-

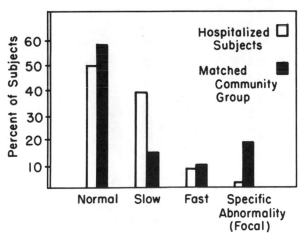

Fig. 2. Differences in E.E.G. patterns between hospitalized and community groups.

ferences in the patterns of disease among socioeconomic, age, or other groups, but only in terms of frequency and severity of disease.

When hospitalized subjects are compared to their matched community group, however, there are distinct differences in disease patterns. It must be noted here, however, that many of these conditions (for example, diminished olfactory sensation) would not enter into physical functional rating in any direct fashion.

One of the prominent differences is in the E.E.G. pattern. In Fig. 2 is seen a significant difference in the amount of generalized abnormal slow records in the hospitalized subjects and a significantly higher number of specific abnormalities in the community subjects. The latter finding is explained largely by the frequency of temporal focuses in community people. This has been reported extensively by Silverman, Busse, and Barnes (1955) and by Obrist and Henry (1958).

Further confirmation of the trend toward E.E.G. slowing in the hospitalized subjects can be seen from Fig. 3, concerning dominant alpha frequency. Only two of the matched community group have records whose dominant frequency is below 8 per second, whereas thirty-three of the hospital group have records between 6.9 and 7.9 dominant frequency.

Because of the clear differences in E.E.G. pattern, special

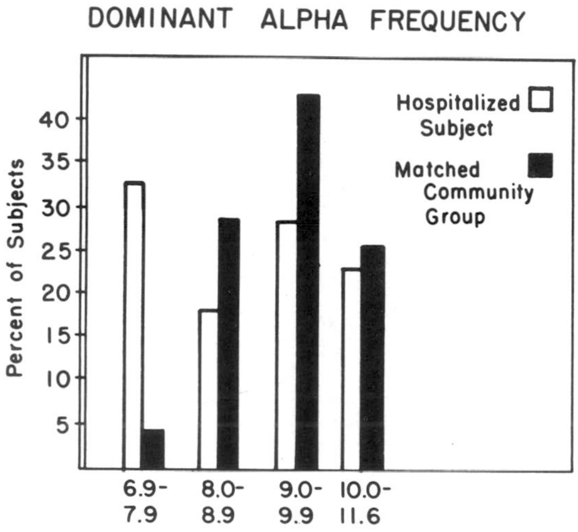

FIG. 3. Distributions of alpha frequencies in hospitalized and community groups.

attention was given to neurological findings in the two groups. Unfortunately, our program of complete auditory and visual examinations was focused on the community group, and the examination equipment was not available for the hospitalized subjects; thus, the two groups cannot be compared in this respect. Only diminution of vibratory sense and diminished olfactory sensation reached statistical significance. A clinical estimate of the origin of any neurological signs was made, and all abnormal signs thought to have their origin in cortex, cerebellum, brain stem, or basal ganglia were rated as possible brain disease. Reduction in vibratory sensation was invariably confined to the lower extremities. Diminution of olfactory sensation was judged by presence and/or correctness of response to four distinct odors. Tonus and strength of muscles were estimated in relation to age. Abnormal involuntary movements were various types of neurologic tremors.

Some of the other significant differences between hospitalized and community subjects will not be emphasized here. One of the prominent abnormalities in the community group was elevation of both systolic and diastolic blood pressure. (Hospitalized subjects consistently manifested a higher incidence of more normal pressures.)

Differences existed in general nutritional status, with 23 per cent of the hospitalized subjects being classified as poorly nourished and more of the community subjects tending toward obesity. Arthritis and joint limitations were significantly higher in the community group, with peripheral venous disease and pulmonary disease more frequent. No essential differences were found in the cardiovascular diseases of any type, in history of or presence of cardiac failure, or in the presence of peripheral arterial disease.

Subjects hospitalized for psychiatric illness do evidence more physical disability, as indicated by ratings. Although the rating does not differentiate between acute and chronic physical disability, it is probable that the more severe degrees of disability include many persons with serious acute physical problems. The mortality rate of all hospitalized persons would indicate that this is generally more marked than appears in our selected subject group.

It is also apparent that neurological conditions are important factors in the hospitalized elderly. Of most definite statistical significance are those conditions indicating diminution in sensory function. Unfortunately, our comparative examination had to be limited to vibratory sensation and olfactory function because of technical problems, but, in view of current research on the disorganizing effects of sensory deprivation, further control studies of differences in seeing, hearing, and touch would be most important.

Obrist and Henry (1958) established that more normal blood pressure in hospitalized subjects is more apt to be accompanied by E.E.G. slowing. It is possible that the higher incidence of E.E.G. slowing may in turn account for some of the increase in organic psychiatric symptoms in this group.

The finding of more subjects with poor nutritional status in the hospital group may be a result of psychiatric illness or an accompaniment of chronic physical disease.

### Interrelations

In considering physical functional rating, the thirty-two psychotic hospitalized subjects were examined according to symptom category (Table 3). Although a much larger proportion of subjects with organic symptoms exhibited physical disability, this did not reach statistical significance. (Student's $t$-test was used throughout this section.) This was partially because of the small number of subjects involved. No significant differences in physical disability were determinable in comparing the subjects with psychotic symptom occurrence and the subjects without psychotic symptom occurrence.

TABLE 3
PHYSICAL FUNCTIONAL RATING IN
THIRTY-TWO PSYCHOTIC HOSPITALIZED SUBJECTS

| Symptoms | No disability | Disability |
|---|---|---|
| Functional | 4 | 5 |
| Organic | 4 | 13 |
| Mixed | 5 | 1 |

Of the twelve subjects with mixed nonpsychotic symptomatology in the hospital group, nine had disability.

A combined rating of cardiovascular disease was made from the number of items on the medical history and the physical examination. If a subject had a history of, or presence of, cardiac failure; was diagnosed as having moderate to severe arteriosclerosis and/or obliterative peripheral arterial disease; or had any type of cardiac disease diagnosis or any type of cardiac symptom, he was rated as having cardiovascular disorder. When the psychiatric illness categories for the hospitalized group were examined in relation to this rating, it was found that the organic-psychotic-symptom group had more subjects with such disease than without. The reverse was true for those with functional symptoms. This difference approached statistical significance (p < .10 > .05). In the nonpsychotic group, only organic and mixed cases were available in the hospitalized group. Two of three organic cases exhibited cardiovascular disorder, and six of thirteen mixed cases did so.

In the community group, only the nonpsychotic symptomatic group was sufficiently large to gain useful statistical information. In every case, more subjects with cardiovascular disease than without were present. There were no significant differences between these groups. The presence of cardiac failure was examined separately, but very few subjects were found to exhibit either a history or presence of such condition. All three of the subjects in the hospitalized group who had this condition were also rated as having organic psychotic symptoms.

Of twenty-one subjects with organic psychotic symptoms, fourteen had evidence of E.E.G. slowing whereas three of nine subjects with functional symptoms showed such slowing and none of the mixed group did. (These data approached statistical significance.) No case of E.E.G. slowing was noted in the community subjects with psychotic symptoms.

There were only nine subjects in the community group who exhibited E.E.G. slowing, and five of these were without psychiatric symptoms. Two of them had mixed nonpsychotic symptoms, and two had functional nonpsychotic symptoms.

In the nonpsychotic symptomatic hospitalized group, only one of the three subjects with organic symptomatology had brain-wave disturbance, and four of thirteen of the mixed group showed a similar disturbance.

Also investigated was the incidence of dominant alpha frequency above and below eight cycles per second in the hospital group. Although there are more cases of low frequency in the group with organic symptomatology, this does not reach statistical significance. Only two subjects in the hospitalized group with nonpsychotic symptomatology had alpha frequencies below eight cycles per second. There was a significant difference between the groups with psychotic symptomatology and those with nonpsychotic symptomatology (p < .02).

The differences in both systolic and diastolic blood pressures were evenly distributed throughout all symptomatic groups. There was always, however, a greater number of hospital subjects with blood pressures under 150/90 than community subjects. In all symptom groups, in both hospitalized and community subjects, those subjects with any type of neurological symptom or sign exceeded those without. The hospitalized subjects, as previously noted, had significantly more neurological disease than did the community subjects.

It appears that hospitalized subjects with organic psychotic symptoms tend to suffer specifically from cardiovascular symptoms and to have more E.E.G. abnormality. The low percentage of abnormal E.E.G. slowing in the community group indicates that these subjects are probably part of a "normal" incidence of E.E.G. slowing that one finds in all E.E.G. control samples. Findings of E.E.G. disturbance in organic brain syndromes have been frequently reported.

Generally, however, there is no great differentiation of types of symptom groups according to type of physical illness. Instead, the indications are that the hospital group as a whole, regardless of symptomatic classification, suffers more severely from a variety of physical problems than do the community subjects. This suggests that physical problems are an important contributing factor in psychiatric hospitalization, regardless of the severity of the psychiatric problem.

## CONCLUSIONS

This review of a group of elderly psychiatrically hospitalized subjects as compared with a group of community cohorts would indicate that establishment of criteria for the care of these individuals, whether within the hospital or in the community, will have to be carefully based on principles of appropriate medical and psychiatric treatment.

Frequent occurrence of defective intellectual function, persecutory feelings and delusions, and severe depression would indicate that often not only daily supervision of life activities will be necessary, but also a high degree of skill in dealing with the patient's gross distortions of the environment or of his own personality.

In addition, the occurrence of more severe physical disability, especially with regard to neurological symptomatology, would indicate that ready access to medical supervision of care is necessary.

The present trend is for communities to accept more responsibility for the care of their sick and/or disturbed elderly. Yet, in many cases, the psychiatric hospital does offer the most easily available source of medically supervised care of physical *and* psychiatric problems. It is true that the major emphasis in care in the mental hospital is psychiatric in nature. This series of studies would indicate that an equal emphasis on medical care for the elderly portion of the institutional population needs to be highly developed. The organization of this kind of combined care in the community can probably be worked out in a number of ways with close collaboration between medical and community groups on both a public and private basis.

Comparative studies of the outcome of cases treated by community-based therapy and in-hospital therapy, especially as regards physical and psychiatric problems of patients, will be necessary to properly evaluate various approaches. It would also be desirable to have comparative studies of efficiency, in terms both of financial cost and of "wear and tear" on the environment. The latter may be the most important aspect, since care of the physical and psychiatric problems involved can cause considerable drain of human energy if it is not so well organized as it is in hospitals.

# APPENDIX A

*Psychiatric Symptom
Categories* *

A. Neurotic, nonorganic signs

| | |
|---|---|
| 1. Mood | Calm |
| | ——— |
| | Depressed |
| | Anxious |
| | Confused |
| | Perplexed |
| | Scared |
| 2. Affect | Normally composed |
| | ——— |
| | Wildly elated |
| | Euphoric |
| | Moderately depressed |
| | Deeply depressed |
| 3. Anxiety | Slight situational anxiety |
| | No apparent anxiety |
| | ——— |
| | Panic |
| | Acutely anxious |
| | Chronically anxious |
| | Apathetic |
| 4. Obsessions | None |
| | Mild |
| | ——— |
| | Moderate |
| | Severe |
| 5. Compulsions | None |
| | Mild |
| | ——— |
| | Moderate |
| | Severe |

* Lines indicate cutoff between normal and abnormal.

6. Hypochondriasis

None
Mild
_____
Moderate
Severe

7. Self-condemnatory trends

Absent
_____
Present

8. Expansive trends

Absent
_____
Present

B. Functional psychotic signs

1. Delusions

None
_____
Grandiose beliefs
Nihilistic ideas
Political delusions
Religious delusions
Other

2. Persecutory trends

None
Mild
_____
Actively discriminated against
Severe persecutory feelings,
    unspecific
Severe, circumscribed
Severe, generalized
Severe, systematized

3. Somatic delusions

Absent
_____
Present

C. Organic psychotic signs

1. Illusions

None
_____
Shadows
Voices
Noises
Movements
Odors
Other

    2. Perception                      Hyperalert
                                                Alert

                                                Mildly confused
                                                Grossly confused
                                                Grossly variable

    3. Intellectual function        Very superior
                                                Superior
                                                Normal
                                                Borderline

                                                Mildly defective, spotty
                                                Mildly defective, generalized
                                                Grossly defective
                                                Completely incapacitated

    4. Form of talk                 Neologism
                                                Confabulations
                                                Echolalia

D. Mixed functional and organic
    signs—
    groups B and C combined

E. Probable organic, nonpsychotic
    signs

    1. Motor activity             Normal

                                                Hyperactive
                                              Retarded

    2. Form of talk

                                              Scattered
                                              Circumstantial
                                              Repetition

    3. Speed of reaction       Normal

                                              Increased
                                              Decreased

    4. Appropriate to ideas    Yes

                                              No

5. Insight into defects
   a. physical
   b. mental

Both physical and mental, yes
Yes mental; physical not applicable
Yes physical; mental not applicable

Both physical and mental, no
No mental; physical not applicable
No physical; mental not applicable
Physical; no mental
Mental; no physical

6. Judgment concerning
   a. general activities
   b. future plans

Good on general activities; nothing
   noted on future plans
Good on future plans; general
   activities not noted
Good on both future plans and
   general activities

Poor on general activities; nothing
   noted on future plans
Poor on future plans; nothing
   noted on general activities
Good on general activities but not
   on future plans
Good on future plans but not on
   general activities
Poor on both future plans and
   general activities

F. Mixed neurotic and probable
   organic, nonpsychotic signs—
   groups A and E combined

G. Normal groups—
   none of foregoing abnormal
   signs in groups A through F.

### REFERENCES

American Psychiatric Association. *Report on patients over 65 in public mental hospitals.* Washington, D.C.: Author, 1959.

Busse, E.W. The treatment of hypochondriasis. *Tri-state med. J.,* 1954, **2,** 7-12.

Busse, E.W., & Dovenmuehle, R.H. Patterns of successful aging, Paper read to Gerontological Society, Philadelphia, November, 1958.

Dovenmuehle, R.H., Busse, E.W., & Newman, E.G. Physical problems of older people. *J. Amer. Geriatrics Soc.,* 1961, **9,** 208-217.

Dovenmuehle, R.H., Newman, E.G., & Busse, E.W. Physical problems of psychiatrically hospitalized elderly persons. *J. Amer. Geriatrics Soc.,* 1960, **8,** 838-846.

Dovenmuehle, R.H., Reckless, J.B., & Newman, E.G. Depressive reactions in the elderly. Paper read to Fifth Congress, International Association of Gerontology, San Francisco, August, 1960.

Eisdorfer, C., Busse, E.W., & Cohen, L.D. WAIS performance of an aged sample: The realtionship between verbal and performance IQ's. *J. Geront.,* 1959, **14,** 195-201.

Malzberg, B. Important statistical data about mental illness. In S. Arieta (Ed.), *American handbook of psychiatry.* Vol. I. New York: Basic Books, 1959. Pp. 161-174.

Noyes, A.P., & Kolb, L.D. Examination of the patient. In A.P. Noyes (Ed.), *Modern clinical psychiatry.* Philadelphia: W.B. Saunders, 1953. Pp. 130-169.

Obrist, W.D., & Henry, C.E. Electroencephalographic frequency analysis of aged psychiatric patients. *EEG clin. Neurophysiol.,* 1958, **10,** 621-631.

Silverman, A.J., Busse, E.W., & Barnes, R.H. Studies in the processes of aging: Electroencephalographic findings in 400 elderly subjects. *EEG clin. Neurophysiol.,* 1955, **7,** 67-74.

U.S. Department of Health, Education, and Welfare. *Living longer.* Washington, D.C.: Government Printing Office, 1960.

# CHAPTER 41

## Measuring Incapacity for Self-Care

PETER TOWNSEND

This paper describes a provisional method of measuring an old person's capacity to look after himself unaided in a home of his own.[1] The need for such a method of measurement was felt during the early stages of a national survey of the residential care of the aged in England and Wales, which has now been completed. The survey set out to investigate, among other things, why old people are admitted to institutions and homes provided under

---

[1] This paper owes much to the help and encouragement of my colleagues June Vernon, Ruth Townsend, Robert Pinker, and Brian Rees. With Brian Rees I wrote a pilot study (Townsend & Rees, 1959) which gave an earlier version of our approach to the question of measuring the capacity for self-care, and my debt to him is great.

Part III of the National Assistance Act of 1948.[2] These residential institutions are intended for the infirm and handicapped, rather than the sick. Old people are eligible for admission when, according to the National Assistance Act, they are "in need of care and attention which is not otherwise available to them." This definition is not easy to interpret and apply, for it is rarely possible to rely on the kinds of medical criteria normally used in deciding admissions to hospitals or nursing homes. Account must be taken of both the individual's physical and social condition. The problem for the research worker is to distinguish between these two conditions and investigate each systematically so that he may begin to understand why old people enter nonmedical institutions, why they stay there, whether they need to stay there, and what kind of services should be provided for them.

If a person is in need of "care and attention," he requires certain services to maintain a reasonable standard of health and comfort which he cannot (or should not) perform for himself. Some persons living alone can do everything for themselves except their heavy cleaning and shopping; others require help with every household function and even with their personal toilet. Therefore, it would seem that persons range in their capacity to care for themselves from 0 to 100 per cent. Is it possible to develop an objective method of measuring this general capacity? This question is relevant not only to studies of the institutional care of the aged. In various forms it has arisen in studies of mental patients, of physically handicapped persons living in institutions, and of those living at home who suffer from certain occupational diseases and injuries. It is one of the fundamental questions we have to answer if we are to rationalize our rather muddy concepts of "disability" and "incapacity," decide what role institutional care should play in modern society, and devise fair methods of compensating individuals for injury or disability.

In this paper I shall, first, refer briefly to a number of other studies which have incorporated analogous methods of measurement; then, outline the method adopted in the survey of residential institutions for the aged in England and Wales and illustrate some of the results gained from applying it; and, finally, discuss some of the

[2] The survey was financed by the Nuffield Foundation, and a full report is now being prepared. A summary of a small part of the findings was published in *The Times* of London, May 17 and 18, 1960. A random sample of 173 institutions and homes in England and Wales was visited by a team of five research officers, which interviewed chief welfare officers, matrons, and elderly residents with the aid of prepared questionnaires.

difficulties involved in choosing to develop such a form of measurement.

## PREVIOUS MEASUREMENT METHODS

A number of investigators have attempted to measure "disability" or "incapacity" among, for example, schizophrenics (Baker & Thorpe, 1956), other mental patients (Rawnsley, 1960), spastics (Palmer, 1958), old people living at home (Hobson & Pemberton, 1955), and old people living in hospitals (Cameron, 1959; Katz, Chin, Cordrey, Ford, Grotz, Newberry, Orfirer, Kelly, Mason, Ryder, Bittman, Conley, Hayward, Hofferberth, Mealing, Robins, Sherback, Frew, Priebe, Takacs, & Worrall, 1958).

Two approaches have been followed. One has arisen in response to the limitations of medical assessment and is basically an attempt to infer the extent of disability from medical diagnosis. After surmounting the difficulty of diagnosing a disease, clinicians face the further difficulty of generalizing about its disabling effects. Two men may seem to have an identical pulmonary condition, yet one is scarcely affected in following his normal activities, whereas another is severely limited. Sometimes the explanation of differing effects seems to lie in the presence of other diseases, sometimes in the imprecision of the original diagnosis, and sometimes in differential physical and mental constitution. Few have made much progress in disentangling these complex factors.[3] The difficulty is a practical one because it raises the questions of how far individuals are prevented from following gainful and recreational activities, how much industrial diseases and accidents should be compensated, and what methods of rehabilitation should be practiced in dealing with people suffering from various diseases. Some scientists have begun to differentiate among diseases according to their general disabling effects and sometimes to differentiate between degrees of disease according to observed effects. Such a procedure seems to be particularly important if we are to generalize about the relation between ill health and activity for various sectors of the population.

[3] "Disability" has been defined in the United States Social Security Act, for example, as inability to work in any substantial gainful activity because of any medically determinable physical or mental impairment that can be expected to result in death or to last indefinitely. But, as has been pointed out, this general definition leaves unanswered the specific questions: "What is 'long continued and indefinite duration'? What constitutes 'substantial gainful activity'? What is 'medically determinable'?" (Hess, 1957, p. 14).

In a study of the aged in Sheffield, for example, Hobson and Pemberton (1955) pointed out that multiple pathology was the rule rather than the exception in old age and that ". . . merely to give the incidence of common conditions such as osteoarthritis, angina pectoris, or bronchitis . . . does not tell as much about what may be called the effective health of such a group . . . [as] by trying to summate the effects on activity of the various pathological conditions found" (p. 140). For a sample of old people they therefore (1) listed the diseases and injuries with the highest incidence among the aged; (2) settled on a standardized score for each disease (sometimes adjusted for the degree of the disease suffered) according to its "normal" disabling effects; and (3) assigned a total score to each old person according to the diseases from which he suffered. This was known as the "disability" score. Unfortunately, the technique is little more than a modification of straightforward assessments using medical criteria, and it embodies many of the same disadvantages. Mental impairment and general frailty were not covered. Each disease was scored for its presumed effects rather than for effects which had been systematically observed. Moreover, the technique of modifying the score for degree of disease was not consistently followed. And, finally, the technique did not meet the problem that the presence of a particular disease does not necessarily indicate for any given person the inhibition of activity which naturally results from it.[4]

The second line of approach seems more promising. This is to measure the *consequences* of injury and disease by scoring capacity or behavior without necessarily carrying out at the same time a clinical investigation. Thus, in a study of schizophrenics, the behavior of each patient was rated according to his ability to dress, eat, work, move about, sleep, speak, control his urine, and so on. For example, a patient needing to be fully dressed was given a score of 4; some help in dressing, 3; only slight adjustment, 2; no help, but untidy, 1; no help and tidy, 0 (Baker & Thorpe, 1956; see also Bennett & Robertson, 1955; Lucero & Meyer, 1951; Shatin & Freed, 1955). Another study (Katz et al., 1958) dealt with the problem of measuring the degree of capacity to perform a given task (such as eating, bathing, or dressing) by distinguishing among (1) total absence of functional ability; (2) ability with personal assistance; (3) ability with mechanical assistance (as, for instance, crutches or wheelchair); and (4) complete self-

----

[4] "The mere presence of abnormalities such as hypertension, inguinal hernia, and defective hearing and vision gives little information about physical capacity" (Edwards, McKeown, & Whitfield, 1959, p. 59).

function.[5] Several studies were restricted to the measurment of the capacity to perform single tasks, but a few have tried to rate total ability.[6] Moreover, a number of recent investigations of the health and physical state of the aged, though not employing specialized rating or scoring systems, have classified individuals according to certain general capacities, such as those of managing domestic affairs without help and of full-time employment (Edwards et al., 1959; Lempert, 1958; Richardson, Brodie, & Wilson, 1959; Sheldon, 1948; Thomson, Lowe, & McKeown, 1951). Various social scientists have shown in recent years the need for a measure of the individual's total capacity to lead a normal life. The method now to be described is largely a tentative extension of that work.

### THE METHOD

Table 1 indicates the method of measuring incapacity for self-care finally adopted. We listed those activities which an old person living alone would be obliged to perform and the faculties he would have to employ to maintain life, assuming he received no assistance. As far as possible, we tried to avoid including two activities in the list which demanded the exercise of identical sensory-motor functions. The activities seemed to fall into four groups, as shown in Table 1: I—those which are always or nearly always performed by the individual if he is able to do them; II—those which may be done by others even when the individual is able to do them (but which have to be done by the individual when no help is available); III—the faculties and motor activities used for the purpose of social communication; and IV—those activities or tasks which have to be done only when the individual suffers from some special disabling condition (as, for example, the injections and the preparation of special foods for those with diabetes). We then scored the individual's capacity to perform

[5] The authors showed that classification was not a simple matter. For example, ". . . feeding is with personal assistance if personal supervision is given (as in patients who hold food in mouth and don't swallow) or if attending personnel have to put part of food into patient's mouth. If attending personnel have to put all food into patient's mouth, this indicates patient's complete inability to feed self. Specially constructed devices such as combination utensils are considered as mechanical aids. Cutting meat for patient is not considered as assistance" (p. 333).

[6] For example, Palmer (1958, p. 843): a "capability chart" was drawn up for assessing the abilities of spastics. A score from 0 to 5 was given for the ability to perform each of sixty tasks; e.g., dressing, undressing, buttons, shoes, laces, cleaning teeth, drinking from cup, making a bed, and washing a shirt or blouse.

TABLE 1
A MEASURE OF INCAPACITY FOR SELF-CARE*

| Activities necessary for self-care | Score for old person's capacity to perform activity | | |
|---|---|---|---|
| | Without difficulty or with slight difficulty (restriction) | With moderate difficulty or only in part | Not at all or minimally |
| **I.** | | | |
| 1. Get into and out of bed | 0 | 1 | 2 |
| 2. (a) When bedfast, wash face and hands | 0 | 0 | 2 |
| (b) When not bedfast | | | |
| (i) walk around room | 0 | 1 | 2 |
| (ii) leave building | 0 | 1 | 2 |
| 3. Negotiate stairs | 0 | 1 | 2 |
| 4. Wash | 0 | 1 | 1 |
| 5. Dress | 0 | 1 | 1 |
| 6. Bathe | 0 | 1 | 1 |
| **II.** | | | |
| 7. Prepare meals | 0 | 0 | 1 |
| 8. Clean floors | 0 | 0 | 1 |
| 9. Coordinate mental faculties in performing other personal services | 0 | 1 | 2 |

| | | | |
|---|---|---|---|
| **III.** | | | |
| 10. | See | 0 | 1 | 2 |
| 11. | Hear | 0 | 0 | 1 |
| 12. | Speak | 0 | 1 | 2 |
| 13. | Organize thoughts in lucid speech or other form for purposes of communication | 0 | 1 | 2 |
| **IV.** | | | |
| 14. | Sit or move about without fits, falls, or giddiness | 0 | 1 | 2 |
| 15. | Control passing of urine and feces | 0 | 1 | 2 |
| 16. | Manage other special (named) disabilities without help† | | | |
| | (a).................. | 0 | 1 | 2 |
| | (b).................. | 0 | 1 | 2 |
| | (c).................. | 0 | 1 | 2 |

*This was printed in a somewhat different form in the questionnaire used in the survey, largely to suit the technical requirement of interviewers and those coding and tabulating the results. The questionnaire instructions followed by interviewers can be obtained from the author on request. They will be published in the forthcoming report of the national survey.

†Where they involve restriction or prevention of activities not already listed or the performance of special tasks in caring for oneself (e.g., diabetes and colostomy).

each of the activities, usually with one of the figures 0, 1, or 2 (thereby taking at least some account of degree of incapacity). In theory, the total score could have ranged from 0 to over 20; in practice, we found that it ranged from 0 to 18. An individual scoring 0 was regarded as being fully capable of looking after himself; one scoring from 12 to 18 was regarded as being able to do little or nothing for himself.

The following examples are of people all in their eighties who were interviewed in residential institutions.

Mr. Reave is a well-preserved man of eighty-three, a former carpenter. He went out every day and claimed he could walk twenty miles in one day without trouble. He entered and left the room where he was interviewed with vigorous strides. After a spell in the hospital following a road accident last year, he lost his former lodgings. There was no evidence of any physical or mental infirmity, and none was recorded in his case file. He said that he would have no difficulty in getting meals and cleaning if he lived alone. Total score: 0.

Miss Arthur is a small woman of eighty-two with deep-set eyes and a mass of white hair. She goes out on her own about once a week. She was hospitalized after a bad fall and could not return home. Now, according to her case file, she is "active—needs help bathing—otherwise unaided." She said she would be able to prepare her meals and clean if she lived alone. She complains only of rheumatism and occasional dizziness. Score: help bathing—1; limited in ability to walk outside building—1; climbs stairs with difficulty—1; liable to giddiness and falls—1. Total score: 4.

Mr. Prince is a very thin, moderately deaf man of eighty-four with a slightly deformed leg. He wears a special surgical shoe on one foot. He walks beyond the precincts of the institution without assistance, but only with difficulty, and he makes the effort somewhat less than once a week. He spends most of his time between meals sitting in the garden or lounge reading newspapers. A distant relative running a small hotel had been unable to let him go on living there. He said that his only complaints were constipation; unsteadiness on his legs, and bronchitis, which made him rather breathless at times. Score: limited in outside mobility—1; climbs stairs with difficulty—1; needs help bathing—1; needs help with surgical shoe—1; liable to fall (having fallen two weeks previously)—2; restricted in other activities by bronchial condition—1. Total score: 7.

Miss Church is a round-faced, thickset woman of eighty. After an operation, she finds it difficult to walk and, unaided, can get only from one chair to another in the bedroom or lounge. She usually sits in a wheelchair. "They haven't time to show me how to walk." She is a hemiplegic, and part of her left side, including the arm, is dead. "In the hospital I used to make my bed and wash up with one hand, but not here." Score: unable to leave building without assistance—2; to move freely around room—1; to negotiate stairs—2; to bathe and dress—2; to prepare meals or clean floors—2; and restricted in performing other activities by hemiplegia—2—and mild diabetes—1. Total score: 12.

Mrs. Adams is a widow of eighty. Although I sat with her for some minutes, I could not elicit any information except that her husband had been in the navy and "I was put away by my daughter." She had been seated in a wheelchair and bore signs of heavy bruising around her nose and eyes—from falling out of her bed a week previously. The matron supplied information about her physical condition, and I was able to check most of this by studying the case record and from observation. Although she was said to suffer from "advanced senility," it was difficult to know how far her condition was determined by mental impairment and how far by physical defects, including her deafness. Score: unable to leave bed without assistance—2; to wash face and hands—2; to negotiate stairs—2; to dress, bathe, or wash—3; to prepare meals or clean floors—2; to hear—1; to move without likelihood of falling—2; to control urine or feces—2; and to coordinate mental faculties in performing other personal services—2. Total score: 18.

These examples show how we tried to express in a quantified form each person's capacity to look after himself unaided. They are taken from questionnaires completed during the survey of a sample of residential institutions in England and Wales. Altogether, information was obtained for 530 elderly residents who had been recently admitted to these institutions. Nearly all were interviewed for an average of just over half an hour, and supplementary information about health and previous social circumstances was obtained from case records and from the staff. The measure of capacity applies to the facts found on a particular day (with the qualification that a few people who were temporarily in bed because of a cold or influenza were rated in terms of their capacity immediately before their illness). Table 2 gives a simple summary of the distribution of scores. As many as 31 per cent of the men and 21 per cent of the women were scored as low as from 0 to 2 on our rating. Nearly 52 per cent of the old persons had scores of 5 or less. Women were more incapacitated than men, but this was partly attributable to their greater age.

Without a full analysis of these results showing the relation of the scores to mobility, special handicaps and diseases, mental infirmity, and the actual behavior of the persons concerned, the scores can only be interpreted as follows:

TABLE 2

INCAPACITY FOR SELF-CARE BY AGE AND SEX*

(Percentage distribution)

| Self-care score | Men | | | Women | | |
|---|---|---|---|---|---|---|
| | Under eighty (N=122) | Eighty and over (N=82) | Total (N=204) | Under eighty (N=179) | Eighty and over (N=144) | Total (N=323) |
| 0-2 | 37 | 22 | 31 | 27 | 15 | 21 |
| 3-5 | 34 | 24 | 30 | 27 | 22 | 25 |
| 6-8 | 16 | 28 | 21 | 25 | 21 | 23 |
| 9-11 | 9 | 17 | 12 | 10 | 19 | 14 |
| 12+ | 4 | 9 | 6 | 11 | 24 | 17 |
| Total | 100 | 100 | 100 | 100 | 101† | 100 |

*Unclassifiable: One man, two women
†Total is in excess of 100 because of rounding of percentages.

| Score | Interpretation |
|---|---|
| 0-2 | Very small incapacity—needs little or no help to live alone in own home |
| 3-5 | Small incapacity—needs some help to live alone in own home |
| 6-8 | Moderate incapacity—needs substantial help to live alone in own home |
| 9+ | Severe incapacity—needs substantial and continuous help from others living at home or close at hand |

Why go to elaborate lengths, it may be asked, to build up a system of scoring incapacities when the main object seems to be to produce a simple fourfold classification? Why not get interviewers, doctors, or the institutional staff to rate people in terms of this classification? It is certainly true that it would be technically much easier to follow this course, and, indeed, it is frequently followed in the social sciences. But the difficulties are rarely posed or discussed. Who makes the judgment? What are his criteria? Which criteria weigh most heavily? What effort is made to validate the judgment or to decide which facts are examined and which are not? I was recently shown a behavioral rating scale used by a psychiatrist in a hospital; the scale was made up of twelve items—including intelligence function, mood, orientation, communication, cooperation, and restlessness—each divided into five subcategories. I was told that, with practice, a member of the nursing staff could complete this scale for a new patient in two minutes. This kind of procedure is justifiable only if it is regarded as a first (and very small) step in the exploration of a difficult subject or as a rule of thumb for the convenience of those administering institutions.

A threefold or fourfold classification is just a convenient summary which can too easily disguise a complicated web of unregulated subjective or intuitive judgments based in turn on partial observation and vague definition. The method described here may be regarded as no more than a provisional attempt to spell out the reasoning involved in such a classification. By trying to formulate explicit definitions, by beginning to sort out fact from opinion, it may be possible to gradually develop a form of measurement reproducible by others. I doubt whether the measure can be made entirely objective, but it should be possible to minimize observer variation and validate at least some parts of the procedure. In the belief that some such measure may be useful to other social scientists and in the hope that they may improve on the present formulation, the various difficulties are discussed below in some detail.

## THE QUESTION OF MEASUREMENT

The first problem is that of deciding which tasks are necessary to maintain a normal, independent life. If we think merely of the minimum effort needed to stay alive, then we might lay emphasis only on the ability to find, eat, and digest food; to drink; and to find shelter. The conventions of bathing, dressing, shopping, and cleaning a home would be disregarded. To say this is to draw attention to the fact that any definition of the acts necessary to secure self-care—like definitions, for that matter, of the concepts of "subsistence," "mental health," or "social health"—is one partly prescribed by social convention. Any definition we may produce must inevitably be one which applies to our own society or to similar societies. It could not have universal validity.

To appreciate that a measurement may be appropriate only to our own society, however, is not to solve the problem. Conditions of life vary widely even in Britain. In drawing up the list of items in Table 1, this problem was kept to the forefront, though it cannot have been fully met. The list of items was restricted to those activities minimally necessary to maintain life in present-day society. We tended to ignore those activities which enrich personality and individual participation in social life—such as following certain hobbies and club activities.

The list of activities was determined largely by our experiences in interviewing and observing the old people and was modified by reading of the similar experiences of others. For example, the reader may ask why we included the ability to negotiate stairs. Surely, he will say, there must be many people who live in circumstances where there are no stairs to climb. The answer is twofold: the great majority of the elderly population live (or work) in buildings with stairs. Moreover, to negotiate stairs is to employ locomotor skills which do not have to be used in walking on level ground. The same skills may be used in climbing onto chairs or steps to clean windows and walls, in negotiating uneven ground or a steep hill, and in boarding a bus or train.

Having listed a series of activities, the next problem is to score each of them. There are two separate questions here. How do we take account of variations within, so to speak, the capacity to perform a given activity? Some people can do certain things without difficulty or strain; others, only with a great deal of effort or pain or only in part. In general, we tried to follow the principle of differentiating between the two by assuming that the latter should be treated as if they were semidisabled and scored accordingly. Thus, a person with normal eyesight was scored 0; a partially blind person, 1; and a totally or almost totally blind person, 2. Our method was simply to ask the old person how difficult he found any given activity. A person who could undertake a particular activity with the aid of a mechanical appliance (such as a walking stick, crutches, or a hearing aid) was treated as capable of performing that activity. This may seem to introduce a large subjective element into the assessment, but in practice it took account only of mechanical aids which were being used and did not presume to judge what the old people would have been capable of were they to be given new aids.

Second, and far more important, how should the scoring of various activities be weighted? Note that this difficulty arises essentially only because we wish to add the scores to get a total measure. It should be admitted at once that we proceeded at first on the sort of intuitive reasoning which anyone would apply—"bedfast" being given a higher score than "housebound," "housebound," higher than "unrestricted mobility." In time, following experience gained in the pilot research and even that gained in the initial interviewing in the main survey, we began to evolve a scoring system which seemed to fit the facts better.

There is danger in weighting on the basis of arbitrary value judgments. One means of minimizing the problem would no doubt be to find by time-and-motion study of old people living alone in their own homes which the most necessary activities are and what their relative importance is (in terms of time or energy) in the total process of caring for oneself and then to assign weights accordingly. This is not an arbitrary procedure. It is one, however, which we have not yet been able to adopt. Instead, we have been obliged to try such other means of validating the measure as comparing results to independent information about old people's activities and capacities. One of the main difficulties was that of avoiding double-counting. Suppose, for example, that two individuals have identical incapacities. Neither is able to leave the building, although both can walk fairly freely inside; both are unable to bathe, clean floors, or negotiate stairs, although in other respects they can care for themselves. If one but not the other suffers from rheumatoid arthritis, the research worker may be inclined to allow an additional score for this disability. Yet he would be wrong to do this unless the complaint added appreciably to the tasks which the old person had to undertake in order to care for himself properly.

This reasoning led us to exclude certain items from the list which called into play exactly the same sensory functions or combination of physical and mental processes as others. We deliberately chose to exclude, for example, the ability to wash clothes and to shop. It is difficult to see how anyone already recorded as having unrestricted mobility would not be recorded as being able to shop. It is true that there may be the exception of the mobile person who, because of a heart complaint, cannot carry even a light shopping bag or who, because he is deaf and dumb, cannot state his wants properly to shop-keepers. But we felt that these contingencies were allowed for elsewhere in the scoring—in the first case by the provision for any special disabling condition (No. 16 on the list) and, in the second, by the items covering the ability to communicate socially. The same reasoning applies to washing clothes (already largely covered by Nos. 4 and 6).

It may be argued that partial or total blindness, for example, should not be scored independently, on the grounds that it is covered by the answers to questions on mobility, dressing, and preparing meals. However, a sighted person may be equally restricted in his capacity to walk outside the building, dress, and prepare meals, but still be able to perform other activities which a blind person cannot. The latter is at a disadvantage, not only because he is unable to engage in some of the activities normally undertaken by a sighted person, but because the things he can do take more effort and time and he has to rely more heavily on other faculties.

A special difficulty arises with persons suffering from mental impairment. A mentally handicapped person may have few physical disabilities and yet be able to do little for himself. He may be scored 2 for inability to leave the building without personal assistance, 2 for inability to prepare meals and clean floors (and also perhaps for inability to bathe or dress), 1 or 2 for inability to coordinate mental faculties in performing other personal services, and 1 or 2 for inability to organize his thoughts in lucid speech. The total score could be as low as 7 or 8, which, by comparison with physically handicapped persons with the same score, may not fully represent his relative incapacity to look after himself. Although, in scrutinizing our interview records, we do not consider that this criticism applies to most of those suffering from various forms of mental impairment (largely because mental and physical disabilities are for them largely inseparable), it may apply to the scores given ten to twenty of the persons in the total of 530. The interviewers were instructed to consider the following questions:

> 1. "Is the person mentally capable of organizing personal services for himself *other* than those so far referred to?"—for example, finding his way to the W.C., remembering where articles of clothing can be found; managing gas taps and electric switches; possessing the know-how to get the shopping, to keep food provisions and household goods in order, and to carry through the process of washing clothes—irrespective of physical infirmity. The score should therefore reflect the capacity to organize services *other* than those listed. (No. 9.)
>
> 2. "Is the person capable of organizing his *thoughts* in coherent speech and/or writing, so as to communicate adequately with other members of society, *irrespective of any physical incapacity?*" The score should reflect the capacity for social communication. (No. 13.)

By means of these questions, an attempt was made to take fuller account of the consequences of mental impairment. Further investigation may justify the introduction of such other criteria as behavior actively disturbing other people or "recent memory loss," "apathy," "restlessness," and "depression," which were included in a list of thirty-seven manifestations of mental disorder in old age carefully defined by Gruenberg (1959).

### The Data

I have not so far referred to the question of who decides whether the individual can undertake each activity. The decision on most questions was left to the person interviewed, with one general and important qualification. If we had good reason to believe that the individual was wrong (sometimes because of failure to understand the question), we altered the rating accordingly. Answers were often checked with the matrons of the institutions in which the old people lived (and, in some instances of severely handicapped persons, supplied by them); the case records of 90 per cent of those interviewed in local authority institutions were scrutinized; and, finally, answers could be checked or supplied through personal observation. It was unnecessary to ask the person we were interviewing whether he was deaf and whether he could not speak or organize his thoughts in lucid speech. Nor was it necessary to ask a person who walked into the room whether he could "get out of bed" and "walk around the room." The fitness of many answers could be judged from personal observation. There remains one difficulty against which it will always be necessary to guard in practice. This is the distinction between the actual performance of a task and the capacity to perform it. Some people can negotiate stairs, prepare a meal, or clean floors but do not have to do so in their daily life in an institution. They may say that they can, even if a matron says they cannot. There is no easy way of establishing the truth, except by putting the question to the test. Unless, in such instances of disputed capacity, it appeared that the matron had some special knowledge denied to the old person, the latter's assessment was preferred. In reviewing the sixteen items listed in Table 1, we would place considerable confidence in the accuracy of the data relating to Nos. 1-6 and 10-15 and rather less confidence in Nos. 7-9 and 16.

### VALIDITY

One small inquiry was carried out in which it was possible to investigate the method outlined above. After the main interviewing had been completed, I spent nearly a week living in one institution for forty old persons. During the first two or three days, each person was interviewed and answers gained to questions on the capacity for self-care. During the week, it was possible, through observation, to judge both the accuracy of answers to individual questions and the adequacy of the over-all measure of capacity. Unlike the persons interviewed in the main survey, many had lived in the institution for long periods, sometimes for several years. Some of these had adjusted to the fact and seemed to have dismissed from their minds any possibility of living in their own homes. A few claimed that they were unable to do one or two things which I felt they could. For example, two women said they went shopping and helped others to dress. Both had virtually no incapacity, but neither tried to go far from the institution. They said that they could not get their own meals or clean floors. I doubted this. The fact is that they had not done either of these two tasks for over six years. Another woman who had lived there for three years seemed to overstate her infirmities, and, though she was scored 8 for her capacity for self-care, I felt that, if she had taken a more positive attitude toward her abilities, the score would have been nearer 5. These experiences forcibly remind us that the mental attitude of an old person partly determines any assessment of his capacities. Some questions—on getting meals, cleaning, and shopping—may not be particularly appropriate for long-stay residents, because it is so long since they have done any of these things that they tend to be pessimistic about their capacities.

Another finding was that answers to questions about capacities are sometimes conditioned by the circumstances of the institution, irrespective of length of residence. Two persons said that they could not climb stairs, although, on the basis of observing their activities, I felt that they could. The fact is that they lived and slept on the ground floor and in their daily life were not obliged to climb a single step.

It was also observed that some people seemed to fall between two ratings. For example, one woman said that she could dress herself completely without assistance, but one cold morning while I was there her fingers were stiff and she required help from an attendant to do her buttons. Another said that she could walk around the institution without assistance, but one day after a "dizzy turn" she needed someone to steady her several times. These observations show that particular capacities may vary slightly from week to week, or even from day to day. They suggest that any measure of capacity of self-care, taken on a particular day, may not be fully representative of an individual's capacity over a lengthy period of time, though as a research method, of course, it may be representative of the range of capacity in an institutionalized population at a particular time.

Close observation of people's activities, however, seemed to confirm that over-all scores give a fair representation of the facts. Some of the data could be checked with independent evidence. For example, what the old people said about their capacity to bathe themselves was checked with the attendant who was responsible for supervising all the bathing. She agreed with the assessments of thirty-five of the thirty-six people questioned. Again, fourteen of the residents were listed on a roster for cleaning up during the week in question. The over-all scores for self-care were compared with this list, as shown in Table 3.

### TABLE 3
### RESIDENTS ASSISTING WITH CLEANING UP,
### ACCORDING TO CAPACITY FOR SELF-CARE

| Self-care score | Number cleaning up at least once during week | | Total |
|---|---|---|---|
| | Yes | No | |
| 0-4 | 8 | 1 | 9 |
| 5-8 | 6 | 14 | 20 |
| 9+ | 0 | 7 | 7 |
| Total | 14 | 22 | 36 |

This can only be regarded as a preliminary attempt to explore the validity of the measure. More systematic tests will be attempted in the future.

In the analysis of the main survey it was possible to compare the 530 ratings for self-care with independent information about the activities of those interviewed. As the rating increased, the percentage of those going out, visiting relatives and friends outside the institution, and practicing handicrafts and pastimes *decreased*. Table 4 shows the numbers going out according to their rating of self-care. The results of these checks caused us to place somewhat more confidence in the method that had been adopted.

The question of validating the measure is one to be answered empirically. We must emphasize the tentativeness of our procedure. It is far from giving a scientifically precise measurement of a person's ability to look after himself unaided in a home of his own. But we believe that, although tentative, it may be developed

TABLE 4
RESIDENTS LEAVING THE INSTITUTION WITHOUT ASSISTANCE
ACCORDING TO CAPACITY FOR SELF-CARE*
(Percentage distribution)

| Self-care score | Leaving the institution | | | |
|---|---|---|---|---|
| | Once a week or more | Less than once a week | Not since arrival | Total |
| 0-2 (N=126) | 85.7 | 4.8 | 9.5 | 100 |
| 3-5 (N=128) | 63.3 | 15.6 | 21.1 | 100 |
| 6-8 (N=108) | 25.9 | 18.5 | 55.6 | 100 |
| 9+ (N=131) | 3.1 | 6.9 | 90.1 | 101† |

*Unknown: 34
†Total is in excess of 100 because of rounding.

into a valuable scientific tool. We should welcome, as indicated earlier, a detailed study of the daily activities of old people living alone who depend very little on external help.

We recognize also that the measure might, in the process of use, become much more elaborate. It might also allow for the ability to provide economic self-support. This survey was of institutionalized persons, and the question of earning one's keep seemed largely irrelevant. But, if the measure were applied to other groups, it would be appropriate to allow for this. Individuals could then be scored for their ability to earn a livelihood, irrespective of their desires or opportunities.[7] The danger of developing an elaborate procedure is, however, that it may be cumbersome. The measure we have adopted is a relatively simple one. Its relative simplicity means, of course, that some precision has been sacrificed. We would not for a moment claim that Mrs. X, with a score of 10, is necessarily more incapacitated than Mrs. Y, scoring 9, or Mrs. Z, scoring 8. What we would claim is that all those scoring 10, for example, would tend to be significantly different in their capacity for self-care from those scoring 7 or 8. To put this

[7] Perhaps on the lines already developed by Edwards et al. (1959).

point in a different way, when a given population is divided into four or five groups according to its ratings, we would expect there to be marked and significant differences between each group.

The purposes of this crude measure have already been referred to, but it may be worth elaborating a few of these, if only to indicate why it has been discussed at such length. By using some such measure, future investigators could show the differing degrees of incapacity to be found among institutionalized persons as compared with persons living in private households in the general community. Such evidence is likely to cause administrators and others to look afresh at the purposes and nature of institutional provision. It is also likely to illuminate the all-important question of people's "needs." (Once "needs" are defined and measured, the question of deciding how they are and should be met becomes inescapable.) Other investigators, by using such a measure, might be able to show more precisely the general disabling effects of such diseases as pneumoconiosis, bronchitis, and arteriosclerosis—one result of which could be an improvement in methods of deciding compensation for industrial injuries and diseases. It would be possible to show more clearly how the retired compare with those still at work; how men compare with women in their capacities at various ages; and how those in their nineties compare with those in their sixties, seventies, and eighties—giving further insights into the processes of aging.

## REFERENCES

Baker, A.A., & Thorpe, J.G. Some simple measures of schizophrenic deterioration. *J. ment. Sci.*, 1956, **102**, 838-846.

Bennett, D.H., & Robertson, J.P.S. Habit training and chronic schizophrenic patients. *J. ment. Sci.*, 1955, **101**, 664-672.

Cameron, I. Unpublished communication describing a behavioural rating scale used by the hospital staff at the Geriatric Psychiatric Unit, Crichton Royal, Dumfries, Scotland, 1959.

Edwards, F., McKeown, T., & Whitfield, A.G.W. Contributions and demands of elderly men. *Brit. J. prevent. soc. Med.*, 1959, **13** (2), 59-66.

Gruenberg, E.M. A mental health survey of older people. Syracuse, N.Y.: Mental Health Research Unit, New York State Department of Mental Hygiene, 1959.

Hess, A.E. Old-age, survivors, and disability insurance: Early problems and operation of the disability provisions. *Soc. Sec. Bull.*, 1957, **20**, 11-21.

Hobson, W., & Pemberton, J. *The health of the elderly living at home.* London: Butterworth, 1955.

Katz, S., Chin, A.B., Cordrey, L.J., Ford, A.B., Grotz, R.C., Newberry, W.B., Orfirer, A.P., Kelly, A., Mason, R.E., Ryder, M.B., Bittman, M., Conley, C.C., Hayward, M., Hofferberth, A.O., Mealing, M.L., Robins, L.M., Sherback, M.A., Frew, M., Priebe, J.H., Takacs, S.J., Worrall, R.J. Multidisciplinary study of illness in aged persons: I. Methods and preliminary results. *J. chron. Dis.,* 1958, **7,** 332-345.

Lempert, S.M. *Report on the survey of the aged in Stockport.* Stockport County, England: Borough of Stockport, 1958.

Lucero, R.J., & Meyer, B.T. A behavior rating scale suitable for use in mental hospitals. *J. clin. Psychol.,* 1951, **7,** 250-254.

Palmer, K.W.N. Prested Hall: A residential centre for adult spastics. *Lancet,* 1958, **1,** 842-844.

Rawnsley, K. Unpublished paper describing a rating of patients' social capabilities by the hospital staff of the Pneumoconiosis Research Unit, Llandough Hospital, Penarth, Glamorgan, Wales, 1960.

Richardson, I.M., Brodie, A.S., & Wilson, S. Social and medical needs of old people in Orkney. *Bull. Dept. Hlth, Scotland,* 1959, **17** (4), 75-79.

Shatin, L., & Freed, E.X. A behavioural rating scale for mental patients. *J. ment. Sci.,* 1955, **101,** 644-653.

Sheldon, J.H. *The social medicine of old age.* London: Oxford University Press, 1948.

Thomson, A.P., Lowe, C.R., & McKeown, T. *The care of the aging and chronic sick.* Edinburgh: E. & S. Livingstone, 1951.

Townsend, P., & Rees, B. *The personal, family and social circumstances of old people. Report of an investigation carried out in England in 1959 to pilot a future cross-national survey of old age.* London: London University, London School of Economics, 1959.

# PART SEVEN

*Economics,*
*Health, and*
*Retirement*

# INTRODUCTION

CLARK TIBBITTS

Many of the phenomena and processes of aging are economic in origin, nature, or consequences. Some aspects of aging, such as the number of middle-aged and older people in the work force, derive from the nature of the economy, the methods of production, and the rate at which commodities and services are produced. Thus, in all societies—and strikingly in industrialized societies—production methods and capacity are major factors in determining when an individual is too old for economic employment, and hence they become significant elements in societal definitions of the onset of aging or old age.

Much of the behavior of older people and society toward older people results from the need for security of purchasing power— the ability to buy essential goods and services; thus it is economic or

economically determined. Methods of income support in retirement
and the share of the national wealth and income obtainable by or
assigned to older people are functions of how wealth and income are
produced, of how much are produced, and of the competitive economic
interests among generations, as well as of the number and proportion
of older people in a population. Longer life expectancy and growth
in the size of the older population create a new consumer group which
may have both a positive and a negative influence on the economic
status of younger age groups.

Most industrialized or highly developed societies have devised
social insurance and pension systems to provide income during retirement. Methods of accumulating funds for retirement payments, the
accumulation of huge reserves for pension payments, and policies
governing payments are all raising fundamental questions about their
effects on economies, management policy and control, labor management relations, and the market. The amount of benefits paid in
relation to previous earnings and budgetary requirements is coming to
be seen as an important determinant in whether and when workers
will exercise the option to retire.

Not all the phenomena and processes in this sphere are
so purely economic as the ones cited may appear on the surface. The
determination of whether or when to retire, for example, is also a
function of a person's health, the competition of his other interests,
and the cultural or societal values placed on work versus retirement
or pursuit of noneconomic activities. Similarly, the capacity of an
economy to produce, without the services of older workers, all the
goods and services its population requires may well have broader
implications than those of merely freeing older people from working.
It also creates a large population of retired workers without, or at
least with limited, social roles. And it is now being recognized that
the lack of a defined place in the social system may leave a person
with a negative concept of himself and give rise to one or more psychopathic conditions or psychogenic illness. And, still further, such conditions taken in the aggregate are reported elsewhere in these volumes
to potentially contribute to the ill health of families and entire
societies.

Such economic situations as the ones just identified confront
all industrialized societies in some manner. Common characteristics
are found among societies at similar levels of development, but there
are also significant variations in manifestations, attitudes, and approaches to problem-solution. All of the economies represented in the

seminar report similar patterns of work-force participation among older workers and similar health and motivational factors. All are having problems adjusting their work forces to changing industrial practices and the employment needs of younger workers. There are significant variations among economies, however, in the extent to which older workers are being displaced and, consequently, in management and national policies.

The retirement of large numbers of older people is also characteristic of all industrially developed societies, and retirement is rapidly becoming institutionalized. On the other hand, there are measurable variations among societies in the degree of acceptance of retirement, and this is also reflected in national policies and practices. Part of this variation is further reflected in the nature of superannuation schemes and in the amount of pension payments.

It is precisely these common elements and variations among economies and societies with similar problems and similar value systems that made it seem worthwhile to bring researchers and policy technicians together to share their knowledge and experience.

Against this background, one section of the seminar was to deal with problems primarily in the economic sphere. In the economic section, one of the areas selected for consideration was that of work-force participation patterns and the changes automation made in them. Retirement was another discussion point, with attention given to its growth as an economic and cultural phenomenon and its influence on the development of insurance and pension policies, practices, and payments. Another topic dealt with the budgetary requirements of older people and the evolution and characteristics of superannuation systems.

Attention was not focused per se on such questions as the nature of the economies and their effects on the position of older people in the economy, on the capacity of the economies to support larger numbers of retired older people, or on the implications of pension systems for economies. Nevertheless, such considerations were implicit in many of the papers, and most of the papers and the discussions were relevant to these theoretical and practical concerns.

Although the focus of the section was economics, most of the participants were aware of the interdisciplinary nature of the problems which they would have to handle and of the need to recognize other determinants of individual and societal behavior. They recognized changes in health and psychological capacities as significant factors in continued employment, and they grew increasingly aware that the meanings attached to work and retirement are derived from a complex of economic, sociological, and social-psychological elements. They also became aware that concepts of work and retirement are being greatly altered in the face of current technological, economic, and social changes.

The seminar participants soon recognized that the three topics overlapped, and consequently they had difficulty in restricting their discussions to neat categories. The papers in the first sessions dealt with employment and factors related to it; those in the second group were centrally concerned with retirement. But the reciprocal of employment is *un*employment, and unemployment is, in fact, frequently retirement. Hence, separation of the topics was not only impossible, but also undesirable. Similarly, retirement income plans were discussed as such, but also as factors in employment and retirement and in relation to levels of living.

The relation and interdependence of phenomena and processes again presented itself when it became necessary to organize the material for publication. The papers are grouped according to the topics originally developed by the planning committee, but the reader will have to follow the example of the seminar participants, browsing in several papers to glean all that is said on any particular topic.

## EMPLOYMENT—PATTERNS
## AND HEALTH

Current research is revealing the existence of fairly clear-cut patterns of work-force participation and age-related variations during later life. The well-known decline in participation at advanced ages is the continuation of a trend which actually starts during the years of middle adulthood. More detailed analyses also reveal, more clearly than has been shown before, that withdrawal from employment is not always abrupt; for many it is a gradual process extending over a considerable period of time.

Although age is a useful index to the extent of participation, continued participation in the work force is shown to be a function of many variables, including sex, occupation, motivation, health, and the degree of protection afforded older workers. Health stands out, of course, as one, if not the major, variable. Yet health is a highly subjective matter, its influence often being tempered by psychological and environmental factors and by the nature of the job itself. In addition to identifying these factors, the contributors to this section and the section on retirement report that progress is being made in defining, measuring, and identifying directions for further research. Seymour Wolfbein (Chapter 42), a leading economist in the United States Department of Labor, offers an analysis of the labor-force participation of middle-aged and older workers in terms of age, sex, occupation, and extent of participation. His principal thesis is that the statistical aggregates commonly employed in presenting data on older workers conceal many significant variations. After the age of fifty, the decline in the proportion of both men and women is gradual, then becomes more rapid. This tendency, taken with the age-related increases in part-year and part-time work, suggests that withdrawal is part of the developmental processes characteristic of the later years. Occupationally, both men and women in professions and managerial, agricultural, and personal-service occupations seem to remain employed longer than those in blue-collar occupations and women in clerical work. Women reveal participation and withdrawal patterns similar to those of men, but their participation at all ages below sixty-five has increased to the point that they now constitute one-third of the American labor force.

One of the devices developed in the United States to protect older workers is the seniority provisions in labor-management contracts. In its purest form, this is largely an American practice, according to the analysis developed by England's well-known social economist, Barbara Shenfield (Chapter 43). Presenting data from Great Britain, West Germany, and France, Professor Shenfield notes that straight seniority is seldom practiced in these countries as a method of dealing with either temporary or long-term labor surpluses. Devices more commonly practiced are, however, related to seniority: longer dismissal notices and higher severance pay for those with long work records and more individual treatment, based on the number of dependents, production record, and health. She also notes a tendency in European countries to rely on self-determined management policies and government regulation rather than on the collective bargaining characteristic of the United States. Professor Shenfield concludes with a thoughtful discussion of the advantages and disadvantages of seniority regulations.

Two contributors deal with health: Eli Ginzberg (Chapter 44), economist and long-time student of manpower resources in the United States, and Sven Forssman (Chapter 45), an industrial physician in the Swedish Employers' Confederation in Stockholm. Their research has led to remarkably similar conclusions about the studies they consider important for the future. Like everyone else who has ventured into the field, Ginzberg and Forssman report that the relation between health and employment is not only complex in itself, but that it is also complicated by the presence of other factors. Both identify three factors that condition employment and performance: the strengths and weaknesses of the individual, the requirements of the job, and the stresses and supports of the environment, which includes the activity of the labor market.

The studies of both reveal loss of energy and drive with age and a rising prevalence of long-term physical illness and disability, yet both are able to cite studies which show that many older workers diagnosed as having severe ailments continue to work and do so quite creditably. There is full agreement, however, that advancing age calls for increased attention to suiting the worker to the job or, sometimes, modifying the job to suit the residual assets of the worker. Dr. Forssman makes a number of specific suggestions.

Other factors which are related to employment and employability and which often obscure the significance of health are the availability of jobs, industrialization and mechanization, motivation, employers' attitudes, personnel practices (particularly with regard to medical data), and changing attitudes toward retirement.

Each paper identifies several research problems ranging from studies of individual characteristics and performance to disease and the work environment.

The last paper in Section I is by Walt R. Simmons (Chapter 46), a statistician with the United States Public Health Service. Dr. Simmons gives a history of data-collection on health and employment in the United States and discusses the difficulty of arriving at dependable concepts and assessments. He describes the National Health Survey, which is the most ambitious attempt yet undertaken to obtain continuing reports and evaluations of the health of a total population. Some results of the survey which have particular significance to students of employment are presented.

## RETIREMENT—ATTITUDES, INFLUENCES, AND INCOME

Work does not last forever, even for those who remain healthy and are covered by seniority provisions. Retirement, formerly a prerogative of a select few and the sick and disabled, is now the expectation of most workers in industrialized societies. Much of the basis for retirement was laid earlier, but it is largely a development of the twentieth century. The swiftness of its appearance and the ramifications of its influence open new areas of compelling social concern and raise many questions for investigation and research.

Although the majority of workers over sixty-five or seventy in the United States and in all Western European countries are retired, there is still debate over whether retirement should be encouraged for those who are able to continue at work. Leonard Z. Breen (Chapter 47) makes a compelling case for retirement by enumerating the functions it serves for the worker, employer, labor union, and society. Harold L. Orbach (Chapter 48) portrays the evolution of retirement to the status of a socially accepted right with increasingly uniform rules and provisions for income maintenance.

Breen and Orbach, the American sociologists, also raise the question of personal and social values, pointing out that retirement calls for a complete shift in roles for which there is not an adequate definition in wholly work-oriented cultures. Thus, the attitudes of workers toward retirement and the factors related to their decision-making are principal themes of Section II. Another major problem is the cost of supporting growing numbers of older people for lengthening periods of retirement. Retirement income payments are reflected in business costs and compete with other demands for the available funds. The determination of retirement and pension policies thus becomes a struggle involving retirees, who are seeking higher incomes; employers, who often wish to eliminate superannuated employees at the lowest possible cost; and society, which is ambivalent in its attitudes toward retirement and is always concerned with the apportionment of expenditures.

From his vantage point in the International Labour Organisation, Sven Hydén (Chapter 49) provides a global view of attitudes and trends in retirement and pension policies and practices. Poul Milhøj (Chapter 50) of the National Institute of Social Research in Denmark contributes a thorough discussion of how personal and social values can be reflected in the provisions of pension policies and of the probable effects of pension policies on the decisions of older workers.

Brian Abel-Smith (Chapter 51), intimately involved in pension planning, examines the effects of the United Kingdom's long-term efforts to achieve statutory provisions that will harmonize the interests and needs of the workers, the employers, the economy, and the society. From his analysis, which covers fourteen years, Abel-Smith concludes that small pension increases, increments for work after the age of eligibility for retirement, and limitations on earnings in retirement have little effect on the behavior of workers.

Margaret S. Gordon (Chapter 52) contributes an original cross-national research based on hypotheses similar to those of Milhøj and Abel-Smith. Using data from eighteen countries for the periods around 1950 and 1957, she demonstrates that there is a high inverse relation between the ratio of retirement income to previous earnings and labor-force participation of older men. She also notes that higher pension ratios and lower participation rates seem to be functions of the age of pension systems. These and other significant results of the analysis lead Dr. Gordon to conclude that in the future increasing attention will be given to such matters as adequate income for those forced into retirement by failing health, pension increments to encourage workers to remain in the labor force, and benefit levels that automatically change as wages or purchasing power does.

In another paper on this topic, Ian M. Richardson of Scotland (Chapter 53) returns to the relation between occupation and health, offering a searching discussion of the health factor, its part in the decision to continue work, and how it is affected by occupation and retirement. At once he points out that present data are not adequate to arrive at an accurate assessment of the cause-and-effect relation between health and retirement. With reference to health in retirement, he finds some evidence that the health of retired self-employed workers is similar to that of retired wage earners although the self-employed remained at work longer. Dr. Richardson develops extensive specifications for longitudinal studies to clarify the complex relations in this area. One requisite, he concludes, is that such research must be based on an interdisciplinary or social gerontological approach.

In Chapter 54, Sven Hydén presents data from the International Social Security Association on status and trends in public retirement income systems in thirty-nine countries, with special reference to levels of living. In four-fifths of the countries studied, the pension is designed to bear some relation to previous wages. Generally speaking, national adherents to International Labour Organisation conventions are committed to a policy of providing a pension that is not less than 40 per cent of the standard wage.

The decision to relate pensions to previous wages rather than to established income requirements has meant that little attention is given to systematic estimates of budgetary needs. Dr. Hydén points out that many countries do try to meet minimum requirements through their insurance programs, but they also make provision for added payments through a direct assistance scheme. He forecasts increasing interest in determining such basic needs as food, housing, health care, and maintenance of social participation.

Paul Paillat (Chapter 55) of France, Brian Abel-Smith (Chapter 56) of the United Kingdom, and Wilbur J. Cohen (Chapter 57) of the United States describe the difficulties their countries are having in achieving adequate pension levels in the face of rapidly increasing retirees and rising standards of living. All three note the efforts being made to establish equitable provisions for workers at all income levels. All report assistance allowances to augment insufficient pension payments. Similarly, all report marked growth in private pension programs, which are being partially integrated into the statutory schemes in the United Kingdom.

Cohen points out that the United States system is based more on feasibility of operation and ease of collecting funds than on an underlying theory and scientifically established standard of adequate income. Several contributors consider politics a major factor in determining pension levels and characteristics. Indeed, Abel-Smith's paper is a case study of the struggle between the Conservative and Labour parties to use the pension program to political advantage while trying to retain the highest possible levels for a growing eligible population.

Ewan Clague and Helen Lamale (Chapter 58) go far in developing a basis for establishing budgets for older people. They discuss problems involved in determining valid budgetary concepts, arriving at realistic commodity inventories, and pricing. It is apparent that continued work along these lines will provide the basic data required for evaluating the adequacy of old-age income and pension systems.

# SECTION I

*Employment—*
*Patterns and*
*Health*

# CHAPTER 42

*Work Patterns of*
*Older People*

SEYMOUR L. WOLFBEIN

The prevalence and high incidence of retirement, long-term illness, low income, and other characteristics of older people are well-known. Much of the quantitative data accumulated thus far apply to the total population in what has been defined as the older age group, usually people sixty-five and over. Gross determinations are characteristic of early explorations in new fields. Gerontological research has shown, however, that most aging processes and changes are gradual increments or decrements that come with advancing age. More refined analyses are essential, therefore, if aging is to be adequately understood.

The present analysis deals with the work patterns of men and women at successive ages of late adulthood. The analysis begins at the age of forty-five because it has long been known that certain problems, such as difficulty in finding employment, often begin at this age. It is also recognized that behavior and events of middle age often predetermine those of later years.

## LABOR-MARKET ACTIVITY

One of the major differences among the age groups forty-five and older is their economic activity. Table 1 reveals a spread of more than seventy percentage points in male labor-force-participation rates between the youngest (forty-five–forty-nine) and the oldest (seventy and over) groups in the older adult ages. Although more than 90 per

TABLE 1

LABOR-FORCE-PARTICIPATION RATES IN THE
UNITED STATES BY AGE AND SEX, 1957–1959

(In percentages)

| Age | Males | | | Females | | |
|---|---|---|---|---|---|---|
| | 1957 | 1958 | 1959 | 1957 | 1958 | 1959 |
| All ages | 81.9 | 81.2 | 80.9 | 35.8 | 36.0 | 36.1 |
| 45–49 | 97.1 | 97.1 | 96.9 | 47.5 | 49.1 | 50.0 |
| 50–54 | 95.5 | 95.4 | 94.9 | 45.4 | 46.4 | 47.9 |
| 55–59 | 91.4 | 91.8 | 91.3 | 38.2 | 39.5 | 41.1 |
| 60–64 | 82.9 | 83.2 | 82.8 | 30.3 | 30.4 | 31.4 |
| 65–69 | 52.6 | 50.1 | 48.5 | 17.5 | 17.0 | 16.8 |
| 70 and over | 27.8 | 26.2 | 25.0 | 6.4 | 6.4 | 6.5 |

Source—U.S. Bureau of Labor Statistics, Special labor force reports, 1960, No. 4, Preprint No. 2336. Table B.2.

cent of the men under sixty are workers, the proportion drops to a little over 80 per cent for men from sixty to sixty-four and precipitately thereafter. The table also shows that, whereas participation rates for men under sixty remain steady, there is a downward trend among those over sixty even during the brief three-year period of observation. The range of labor-force-participation rates among women is as great as that among men. By 1959, worker rates among women under fifty-five were almost ten times as high as those among women seventy and over. Unlike the situation with men, however, the participation rates for women either remained steady or increased over the three-year period.

As a result, the sex distribution of workers forty-five and over has changed significantly. In 1950, women accounted for one out of every four workers forty-five and over; in 1960 they accounted for one in every three. Thus, in the relatively brief span of a decade, the answer to the question "Who is the older worker?" has altered enormously, on the basis of this change alone. In turn, this change has generated major differences in the employment and unemployment experience, occupations, and incomes of older workers.

The different labor-force trends among older men and women emphasize another point. As indicated, the downward trend in worker rates among older men continues, perhaps accelerated in part by the recessions of the past few years. The year 1959 was the first in which worker rates for men immediately past sixty-five fell below the 50 per-cent mark for the entire year. In contrast, worker rates have slowly but steadily risen among women under sixty and went above the 50 per-cent mark for the group from forty-five to forty-nine. There is apparently nothing in the immediate future which would reverse these trends.

## Work Experience

In the labor force, there are major variations in work patterns of specific age and sex groups. Recent studies of the pattern of work experience during a calendar year among the sectors of the labor force throw considerable new light on such aspects of working life as the extent to which different groups work primarily full time, part time, and part of the year, or all year (Table 2).

The first observation is that among both men and women increasing age brings not only declining labor-market-participation rates, but also declining proportions of full-time work. For the forty-five–fifty-four group, the experience is much more like that of the younger groups. Almost 95 per cent of the men and 75 per cent of the women in that age group worked primarily full time during 1958. This proportion falls steadily during the decade from fifty-five to sixty-four, taking a sharper drop for men and women in their late sixties and an even steeper decline for those in or over their seventies.

Another indication of the degree of work experience is given by the terms "part-year" and "year-round" worker, the latter being a person who works—whether full or part time—at least fifty weeks during the calendar year. Among the men, the familiar inverse relationship with age is found again: the higher the age, the smaller the proportion of men working year-round. Again, the experience of the

## TABLE 2
## WORK EXPERIENCE OF OLDER MEN AND WOMEN IN THE UNITED STATES
### 1958

(Percentage distribution by amount of time worked)

| Age and sex | Number of people who worked in 1958 000 omitted | Worked primarily full time | | | | | Worked primarily part time | | | | |
|---|---|---|---|---|---|---|---|---|---|---|---|
| | | Total | 1-26 weeks | 27-39 weeks | 40-49 weeks | 50-52 weeks | Total | 1-26 weeks | 27-39 weeks | 40-49 weeks | 50-52 weeks |
| **Men** | | | | | | | | | | | |
| 45-54 | 9,415 | 94.5 | 4.2 | 5.0 | 10.2 | 75.1 | 5.4 | 1.9 | .8 | .7 | 2.0 |
| 55-59 | 3,598 | 92.3 | 4.9 | 5.0 | 9.4 | 73.0 | 7.7 | 2.5 | .8 | .9 | 3.5 |
| 60-64 | 2,898 | 88.5 | 7.1 | 5.4 | 8.9 | 67.0 | 11.4 | 4.2 | 1.7 | 1.3 | 4.2 |
| 65-69 | 1,619 | 73.7 | 13.6 | 5.0 | 6.6 | 48.5 | 26.2 | 10.5 | 2.0 | 1.8 | 11.9 |
| 70+ | 1,312 | 55.0 | 10.9 | 3.2 | 5.4 | 35.5 | 44.9 | 18.0 | 3.3 | 4.3 | 19.3 |
| **Women** | | | | | | | | | | | |
| 45-54 | 5,823 | 72.2 | 10.1 | 7.0 | 8.7 | 46.4 | 27.7 | 9.7 | 2.6 | 3.2 | 12.2 |
| 55-59 | 2,020 | 67.4 | 8.9 | 4.9 | 8.6 | 45.0 | 32.7 | 10.0 | 3.9 | 2.8 | 16.0 |
| 60-64 | 1,445 | 64.3 | 9.2 | 5.3 | 9.0 | 40.8 | 35.8 | 11.0 | 3.4 | 5.0 | 16.4 |
| 65-69 | 686 | 53.4 | 11.3 | 3.6 | 6.1 | 32.4 | 46.5 | 17.2 | 4.1 | 6.5 | 18.7 |
| 70+ | 469 | 42.5 | 9.6 | 3.2 | 4.1 | 25.6 | 57.6 | 17.4 | 4.5 | 5.8 | 29.9 |

Source—U. S. Bureau of Labor Statistics. Monthly report of the labor force. Unpublished data, 1958.

group from forty-five to fifty-four, where the proportion of year-round workers was three in four in 1958, is closer to the experience of men in the younger groups; by the age of seventy or over, this proportion is down to about 55 per cent. Moreover, the proportion of year-round workers who work primarily part time is negligible prior to sixty-five. From sixty-five to sixty-nine, however, it is one-sixth; in the group seventy and over it is one-third.

Among the women, year-round work is much less prevalent, and the gradations by age are not so sharp. Between 50 and 60 per cent of the women forty-five and over were year-round workers in 1958, with the proportion of part-time workers among them significantly rising with age.

Thus not only labor-market participation, but also the degree of that participation, varies significantly by age and sex in the older age group. Among men in their forties, fifties, and even early sixties, the preponderant pattern is for primarily full-time, year-round work. For those past the conventional retirement age, the pattern tends to move toward primarily part-time, part-year work.

Still, these are relative terms. Whether the extent that older labor-market participants work seems high or low may depend on one's a priori expectations. The fact remains that, although the totals are well below those for some of their younger colleagues, three-quarters of the men and more than half the women in their late sixties in the labor force work on their jobs full time; well over half are year-round workers. And for those seventy and over, over half the men and two-fifths of the women workers are on their jobs full time; over half are year-round workers.

### Occupation

One of the factors that most sharply differentiates older workers, both men and women, is occupation (Table 3). Table 3 not only tells a perceptive story about how the older worker fares as he moves into his later years, but it also is an important part of the materials on labor-market activity and work experience already presented.

Among the men, between one-third and two-fifths of the older workers (over forty-five) hold white-collar jobs. There is a remarkable stability in this proportion for each of the five age groups for which data are available. For those who continue to be economically active in their later years, these jobs represent a continuing opportunity. Apparently staying power is strongest among these occu-

## TABLE 3
## OCCUPATIONAL DISTRIBUTION OF OLDER MEN AND WOMEN WORKERS
## BY AGE AND SEX, APRIL 1958

(In percentages)

| Occupation | Men | | | | | Women | | | | |
|---|---|---|---|---|---|---|---|---|---|---|
| | 45-54 | 55-59 | 60-64 | 65-69 | 70+ | 45-54 | 55-59 | 60-64 | 65-69 | 70+ |
| White collar* .......... | 39 | 37 | 35 | 36 | 36 | 52 | 50 | 51 | 30 | 36 |
| Professional and technical ....... | 10 | 8 | 8 | 6 | 9 | 14 | 13 | 14 | 9 | 12 |
| Proprietors, managers, officials ........ | 18 | 18 | 16 | 19 | 17 | 7 | 9 | 9 | 7 | 9 |
| Clerical ........ | 6 | 5 | 6 | 6 | 4 | 23 | 20 | 20 | 15 | 8 |
| Sales ....... | 5 | 6 | 5 | 5 | 6 | 8 | 8 | 8 | 8 | 7 |
| Blue collar ....... | 45 | 43 | 41 | 29 | 22 | 17 | 17 | 12 | 15 | 12 |
| Craftsmen ....... | 21 | 20 | 20 | 14 | 10 | 1 | 1 | 2 | 1 | 1 |
| Operatives ....... | 17 | 16 | 13 | 10 | 6 | 15 | 15 | 10 | 14 | 11 |
| Laborers ....... | 7 | 7 | 8 | 5 | 6 | 1 | 1 | † | † | † |
| Service ....... | 6 | 8 | 10 | 11 | 11 | 26 | 28 | 32 | 37 | 39 |
| Household service ....... | † | † | † | † | † | 11 | 14 | 17 | 20 | 25 |
| Other service ....... | 6 | 8 | 10 | 11 | 11 | 15 | 14 | 15 | 17 | 14 |
| Farm ....... | 10 | 12 | 14 | 24 | 31 | 5 | 5 | 5 | 9 | 13 |

Source—U.S. Bureau of Labor Statistics. Monthly report of the labor force. Unpublished data, 1958.
*Categories and subcategories both add to 100.
†Less than .05 per cent.

pations, particularly in proprietary, managerial, and professional work (Table 3).

For the rest of the men, however, there is a dramatic change in occupation with age. About two-fifths of the men under sixty-five are blue-collar workers, but thereafter the proportion drops sharply to about one-fifth among workers seventy and over. As Table 3 shows, the drop comes particularly in the skilled and semiskilled blue-collar workers; as one goes up the age scale, the proportion working as unskilled laborers remains the same among men forty and over.

Taking the place of blue-collar occupations is the other stronghold of employment for the old worker—the farm. One out of every four men between sixty-five and sixty-nine and almost one out of every three men seventy and over who are still employed are in agriculture—double and triple the corresponding proportions among men under sixty-five.

Thus as a man advances on the age scale in the United States, the white-collar jobs remain a major job opportunity, but industrial blue-collar work diminishes strongly, replaced by correspondingly large proportionate increases in farm employment and personal service (Table 3).

Among the women, white-collar jobs are a particularly important sector of job opportunities in the United States. One out of every two women workers between forty-five and sixty-four is employed in these jobs. After sixty-five, however, the proportion, although still large, drops to between one-third and two-fifths. Practically all of this decline can be traced to the reduction in the proportion of women in clerical occupations. The percentage employed in the professional, managerial, and sales fields show no statistically significant changes in the specific age groups forty-five and over.

Although there is some decrease with advancing age in the proportion of blue-collar workers among employed women, it is in the farm and service sectors that the really big movements occur. The proportion of women workers sixty-five and over employed on the farm is significantly higher than that for their younger counterparts. And the proportion employed in the service occupations rises steadily to the point that these occupations account for almost two-fifths of the employed women seventy and over, in contrast to one in four for the forty-five–fifty-four year age group. Significantly, practically all of this difference is accounted for by the substantial increase in domestic· women workers (household service), which is, incidentally, testimony to the fact that an increasing proportion of workers past sixty-five is nonwhite.

Thus who the so-called older worker is—especially in status, income, skill, and so on—depends on the age group to which we refer.

Among men between the ages of forty-five and fifty-four, 85 per cent are in either the white-collar or blue-collar manual trades, including 20 per cent who are skilled craftsmen and 10 per cent who are professional personnel workers. At seventy and over (there were 1,333,000 male workers in this age group), the picture is dramatically different. More than two-fifths are either on the farm or in personal service.

Among the women from forty-five to fifty-four, 70 per cent are in either white-collar or manual occupations, including almost one in four with a clerical job. At seventy and over (there were about 500,000 in this age group), more than 50 per cent were either on the farm or in personal service. One out of every four works as a domestic.

### Unemployment

One of the most significant aspects of labor-market activity for older people is unemployment. Generally speaking, in the post-World War II period in the United States, the older worker has held his own in this respect, for his unemployment rates have not been significantly different from those of his younger colleagues (Table 4).

As one separates the groups over forty-five, however, significant differences do appear among the individual age groups. There is, in fact, some evidence that the unemployment rate for the male group from sixty-five to sixty-nine is consistently higher than that for the other groups in the over–forty-five category, whereas men seventy and over tend to have the lower unemployment rates. The trend during the 1958 recession was rather sharp in these respects: the unemployment rate for men from sixty-five to sixty-nine rose to a much higher level, and the rate for men over seventy moved in the opposite direction.

It may be that in the age groups immediately after the conventional retirement age are many men who are in the final phases of the transition from work to retirement and who may, therefore, be more vulnerable to unemployment. The sharp change in occupational distribution for these men may attest to this point. For the group over seventy, labor-force activity may be more sporadic, and moving in and out of the labor force as economic activity changes could account for the unemployment trend in this group. Obviously much more re-

TABLE 4
AVERAGE MONTHLY UNEMPLOYMENT RATES BY
SEX AND AGE IN THE UNITED STATES,
1957-1959

| Age | Males | | | Females | | |
|---|---|---|---|---|---|---|
| | 1957 | 1958 | 1959 | 1957 | 1958 | 1959 |
| All ages | 4.1 | 6.8 | 5.3 | 4.7 | 6.8 | 5.9 |
| 45-49 | 3.4 | 5.4 | 4.1 | 3.2 | 5.2 | 4.4 |
| 50-59 | 3.2 | | | | | |
| 50-54 | | 5.2 | 4.2 | 3.1 | 4.7 | 3.8 |
| 55-59 | | 5.4 | 4.3 | 3.0 | 4.5 | 4.4 |
| 60-64 | 3.6 | 5.6 | 4.8 | 3.1 | 4.5 | 3.6 |
| 65-69 | 3.9 | 6.4 | 5.6 | 4.0 | 4.2 | 3.3 |
| 70+ | 3.1 | 3.8 | 3.5 | 2.6 | 3.0 | 1.9 |

Source—U.S. Bureau of Labor Statistics. Monthly report of the labor force. Unpublished data, 1957-1959.

search has to be done before we can get definitive answers to these questions.

### RESEARCH NEEDS

This brief analysis has attempted to highlight in a summary some of the principal data relating to economic activity of older people in the United States. The data raise at least the following five points, which are intended to illustrate, not exhaust, the list.

First, the perception one derives from the "disaggregative" approach is considerable, and it is fair to ask whether further research along this line—not only in employment, but also in the general area of the economics of aging and other fields—would yield fruitful results. This is particularly true of proposed action in our field. What may be relevant for some sectors of the so-called older worker group might be quite inappropriate for another.

Second, these data re-emphasize the importance of the developmental approach toward the problem of aging. Aging, at least in relation to work, does not occur in discrete episodes tied to chronological age, but is typified by enormous individual and group differences.

Third, these data also suggest lines for further research. Again, without intending to present an exhaustive list, this paper highlights at least the great importance of collecting, tabulating, and analyzing data by more specific age and sex groups within the over-all over–forty-five sector. In this connection, we found it particularly important to go beyond the standard "sixty-five–and–over" classification. The great differences, by occupation, for example, within the sixty-five–plus group alone would warrant this conclusion, not to say anything of the differences in labor market participation. The government's recent cessation of tabulating by separate groups some of these important labor-market data within the sixty-five–plus sector is a retrogressive step, but plans are now being developed for restoration.

Further research on the nature of labor-market participation by age would also seem called for. Further examination of the very concept of working, especially at the upper age ranges, seems to be needed. At the very least, assessments of worker activity by age should take account of not only the over-all labor-market-participation rate, but also other such vital factors as part-time against full-time and part-year against year-round work.

Fourth, all these considerations are of obvious importance in international comparisons of the role and status of the older person, and the cross-national research which this seminar is encouraging will have to take them into account.

Fifth, as indicated earlier, these materials raise a number of important questions about who the older workers are. Obviously they are not a homogeneous group, and, just as obviously, they are undergoing extensive changes in size and composition.

What gives all this information added importance is its relevance to research and proposals for action in many other aspects of the economics of aging. To cite one example, in the light of the major change in the sex distribution of older workers in the past decade, it may be necessary to take a new look at our projections for some of the problems of income security. There may be one outlook for the income of a family in which the male who has been the sole provider retires. The situation may be very different when one out of every three older workers is a woman.

# CHAPTER 43

*Seniority Protection for*
*Older Workers*

BARBARA E. SHENFIELD

It is recognized that older workers have more difficulty than younger ones in obtaining employment. On the other hand, many older workers receive much protection from employment policies based on length of service or seniority.[1] These policies include conventions, rules, or regulations relating to such matters as order of dismissal, rates of compensation pay, and rights to rehiring. Policies and practices vary considerably between the United States on one hand and Great Britain, France, and West Germany on the other.

[1] It is not to be assumed that older workers always have lengthy service. An inquiry among forty-six British firms revealed that one-fourth of the men between fifty-five and sixty-four had no more than five years of service with their current employers. The proportion with short periods of service was even higher among women (Shenfield, 1957). Thomas and Osborne (1950) report similar findings from their studies.

## SENIORITY RULES

The operation of seniority rules dealing with surplus labor is a well-established and widespread practice in American industry, where it is claimed to be a valuable protection for the security of older workers. Considerations of seniority are used in European employment policies, but the practice is neither so prevalent nor so strictly applied.

The main procedures provide for work-sharing or, when layoff can no longer be avoided, an agreed order for the reduction of the labor force. Work-sharing includes limiting overtime, reducing the work week, and suspending subcontracting. Reduction of the labor force may be scheduled to begin with probationary and temporary employees, seasonal workers, married women with employed husbands, nonunion members. After that, workers are laid off in order of length of service. Bumping, or downgrading, whereby a junior employee is displaced by one senior to him in length of service is also used. Seniority is carried over to recall procedures, with the last out having the right to be the first back in.

Seniority rules have been negotiated by American labor unions as part of their general agreements on wages and conditions and have been written into contracts of employment. The procedures are formal, detailed, and enforceable. They include special stipulations of "super seniority" for key union representatives, so that the union will retain its leadership while layoff procedures are being carried out.

Not all American contracts state that straight seniority is the only criterion for ordering labor reduction. In more than half the agreements considerations of length of service are modified by taking ability, fitness, and general efficiency into account. Even so, the practice of seniority appears to afford the older worker a considerable degree of employment security. There are 7,600,000 American workers (excluding railroad and airline employees) covered by agreements (U.S. Bureau of Labor Statistics, 1957a; U.S. Bureau of Labor Statistics, 1957b), and one may wonder why this policy has not been more enthusiastically pursued by European trade unions.

In Great Britain straight seniority rules are not widely followed in private industry, except in a very modified form. Calculations of seniority are adjusted with reference to efficiency, suitability for retraining, and preferential treatment in special hardship cases. (For example, a 3 per-cent quota of disabled people is protected by law.)

Key workers may be retained regardless of seniority, whereas women, part-time or shift employees, workers over pensionable age, and sometimes aliens may be dismissed regardless of seniority. In the public sector of industry, on the other hand, "first in, last out" is accepted, with a few exceptions, as a basic principle. Where seniority rules are strictly followed, they tend to be accompanied by a system of downgrading. This is used, for example, in British railways, where some grades receive their old rate of pay for up to three years after downgrading.

In Germany seniority is not the only or first consideration in selecting workers for collective dismissals. Age, family needs, and the income and employment of other members of the family must all be considered. The needs of the business come first, but where the workers involved are of equal value to the employer, the social considerations mentioned above have to be weighed.

In France seniority is an important factor which is always considered, but some agreements or works rules put occupational qualifications and family responsibilities above seniority, and seniority is increased by one year for each dependent child in others. Thus in France and West Germany, straight seniority rules are modified not only by considerations of efficiency, but also by a worker's family responsibilities. In contrast to British practice, recall procedures for re-employment of laid-off workers is provided for in France as it is in the United States.

## DISMISSAL PROCEDURES

Western European countries have dismissal procedures which apply to workers of all ages and are based on law, convention, and collective agreements; many of these procedures embody the concept of seniority. Long service always gives the worker a claim to special consideration, but the seniority procedures are generally less well-defined and less consciously applied as a part of union policy in Europe than in America.

### Great Britain

In Great Britain there is no statutory regulation of dismissal. Arbitrary dismissal is prevented by common law, taking into account the express or implied terms of the contract of service. If employment for a fixed period is terminated by the employer before the period ends, this is a breach of contract entitling the employee to sue for compensation. If there is no stated duration, a reasonable period of notice must be given, reasonable being interpreted by periods of payment (weekly, monthly, and so on), trade customs, status, and remuneration for the job. Higher salaries and more responsible positions carry with them the inference of longer notice for termination of employment.

Dismissal rules are not often found in British collective bargaining, except with reference to the period of notice required. A limited number of layoff agreements have been negotiated in recent years in private industry. All the nationalized industries have clearly defined procedures for labor reduction. In general, however, there has been little union initiative to secure seniority or other rules for labor reduction in advance of a layoff although layoff agreements have nearly always been settled in consultation with union representatives.

A 1958 inquiry into the practices of 2,538 firms in the engineering trades showed that, of the 620 firms that had actually had layoffs in the preceding two years, 463 employing 27,339 workers had no special arrangements,[2] sixty-eight gave extended notice, seventy-seven gave compensatory payments, and twelve gave both. Compensatory payments or severance pay was related to seniority in all cases. It is of interest to note that in 120 of the 157 firms giving these special arrangements the procedure was operated gratuitously by the managements, in thirty-six by agreement with workers and their representatives, and in one case by the works rules.

In 1956 the Trades Union Congress (Trades Union Congress, 1956) took the position that it is the responsibility of the government to require throughout the country the establishment of industrial practices which will ensure every man and woman requiring a job the opportunity of obtaining one. The T.U.C. went on to ask for full consultation in cases of layoff, better compensation for loss of wages, and resettlement. It was further suggested that a fund maintained by contributions from industry and government be created to finance these needs. The emphasis is somewhat different from that in the speech of a fraternal delegate from American labor who, speaking at the congress said, "As a worker, I would rather my union gave me justice on the job, rather than in the Congress of the United States" (Trade Union Congress, 1956, p. 380).

---

[2] These data were privately collected by an organization of employers. The data are not published, but were made available to the author.

Thus, in Great Britain, where layoff agreements have been made, they embody concepts of seniority in ordering dismissal, calculating compensatory payments, and handling pension rights, but none of this is determined by statutory labor codes or, in general, at the initiative of labor unions. With a few exceptions, the layoff agreements are negotiated with individual firms. Exceptions are the cotton industry, where the agreement is industry-wide and government subsidized, and nationalized industry, where national boards and unions have formal agreements. The number of agreements in private industry is not known since they do not have to be reported. Certainly many workers are not covered by any agreements. A 1959 analysis (Personnel Advisory Service, 1960) of 236 firms in the manufacturing industries employing 1,100,000 workers showed that 45 per cent of the companies employing 21 per cent of the workers had no predetermined layoff policies.

The foregoing comments have regard to collective dismissals occasioned by technological change or trade recession. There is no protection for the individual older worker other than the law of contract and any support his union may give him in taking up a grievance over dismissal with his employer. It is not uncommon for unofficial strikes to be called to protest the allegedly unfair dismissal of an individual worker.

### France

In France the labor code lays down general conditions about the termination of employment contracts. There are special provisions which protect a few specified occupations and certain classes of people, such as disabled workers, pregnant women, and workers' representatives. These arrangements cannot be abrogated by private agreements.

Some collective agreements negotiated by French trade unions determine dismissal procedures and are binding except where there are individual contracts which give more advantageous conditions. If there is no collective agreement, all workshops employing more than twenty people must have rules regulating dismissal, and these specify the order in which workers are to be laid off. Collective agreements provide for consultation for work-sharing, seniority in dismissal, recall by seniority, notice, and compensatory payments. In some agreements, for example in the textile industry, the worker's job is suspended, not terminated, during periods of sickness; the length of suspension depends on the length of service.

## West Germany

In West Germany an industrial code details dismissal procedures. In legislation enacted in 1951, the freedom of the employer to terminate employment is hedged with restrictions about what can be deemed "socially unwarranted" dismissals. The trade unions and employers have agreed to this, and workers may appeal to a labor court. A minimum period of notice is stipulated, though collective agreements may improve on this minimum; length of notice is related to length of service. Where collective dismissals involve more than a specified percentage of workers, the employer must consult the works council, and notice cannot be effective for at least one month. The employer has to demonstrate that every effort has been made to avoid redundancy and that only pressing operational needs make reducing the labor force unavoidable. This procedure settles the number to be laid off, not the order of dismissal. When layoff has to be allowed, other social and economic considerations besides straight seniority of service are taken into account in the order of dismissal. For example, a man with short service who was more reliable and productive might be kept over a man with heavier domestic responsibilities and longer service. No older worker with lengthy service, however, would be dismissed before a younger, more productive man with shorter service. This would be deemed an unwarrantable dismissal.

In the case of individual dismissals, justifiable personal reasons—apart from misconduct—would include such matters as persistent sickness, lack of skill, inability to learn the occupation, but not the mere fact of reaching sixty-five years of age. Even though the dismissed employee has received unemployment benefit or has a new job, labor courts have wide powers to oblige employers to pay compensation, on the grounds that the worker has suffered a loss from his unwarranted dismissal. Thus there is considerable legal protection for the job security of German workers.

These three European countries recognize the principle of seniority in laying off workers, but they apply important modifications to it. In addition, all have procedures for giving notice, compensatory payments, and the protection of accumulated rights like holidays or pensions, which are sometimes more extensive than those found in American union contracts. Moreover, some European labor legislation offers more protection against arbitrary dismissal for individual older workers than do American employment practices. Seniority rules are usually part of a package deal and have to be considered with other employment procedures in estimating the degree of employment security.

The protection of employment rights is of six major kinds: (1) seniority rules regulating dismissal and recall, (2) adequate notice of termination of employment, (3) severance pay, (4) preservation of accumulated benefits (pension and the like), (5) aid in securing new employment, and (6) unemployment benefit payments. The first three, being geared to length of service, are more important for older workers. The last three have no particular reference to seniority and are important to all redundant workers.

### NOTICE

Advance notice of layoff to the affected employees, and the union, or both, is a common practice, but the length of time varies widely from country to country. The period of advance notice to American labor unions in about three-quarters of the agreements requiring it is one week or less, with the majority requiring less. The notice to regular employees is also short by British standards; four out of five agreements provide for a week or less, with two-fifths of the workers entitled to only one day or less.

In Great Britain a few firms confine themselves to one week's notice for workers who have worked a certain period (usually three to five years) with the company. Two weeks' notice for five to eight years' employment or four weeks' notice for ten years' employment is a typical arrangement when notice is directly related to employment. Some companies give notice and then pay wages in lieu of notice, freeing the worker to seek other employment and making his remuneration tax-free, since it is treated as compensation, not wages.

Unless there is a special agreement to the contrary, The German Labor Code provides that the industrial worker must have a minimum of two weeks' notice, though this may be raised to four or six weeks by collective bargaining. Salaried workers must have approximately six weeks' notice and after five years' employment, three months' notice.

In France legislation enacted in 1958 provides for one month's notice after six months' employment, except for certain special occupational circumstances, and longer periods for salaried personnel.

## COMPENSATION

Compensation payments, severally called compensation, severance pay, termination allowances, and so on are made to dismissed workers. In 1,693 American agreements (U.S. Bureau of Labor Statistics, 1957b) covering 7,300,000 workers, 16 per cent contained provisions for dismissal pay. Amounts were geared to length of employment, the average tending toward a week's pay for each year. The motives for making these payments are mixed. In part they represent compensation for loss of office, prospects, and seniority, and in part they supplement unemployment benefits [3] to tide a man over until he finds new work. Compensation pay may also be offered as an inducement to a man to stay with his firm until it is convenient for him to leave, rather than seek other employment promptly.

In a study (Personnel Advisory Service, 1960) in Great Britain, an analysis of 236 firms in manufacturing industries, employing 1,100,000 workers, showed that 39 per cent of the companies, employing 60 per cent of the workers, gave separation allowances that were always related to length of employment. A few firms gave a minimum payment to workers near retirement age irrespective of length of employment.

The principle of compensation for dismissals because of layoffs has long been established in public utilities in Great Britain and is also operative for nationalized industries. Three agreements on compensation payments were negotiated in 1959. Following falling demand in the Lancashire cotton trade (118 mills closed in 1958), the government agreed to subsidize the cost of modernizing equipment on the condition that the employers compensate displaced workers. Payments are made in relation to the age [4] of employees in recognition of the fact that the results of reorganization are likely to produce the most unemployment among older men.

The Dock Labor Board introduced in 1959 a more generous pension scheme in order to get older men out of this occupation without undue hardship. More than fifty-five hundred dockers are over sixty-five, and nearly two thousand are seventy, the average age in the industry being just over forty-six years. The offer to men over seventy

[3] In Great Britain weekly compensation to supplement the unemployment benefit is limited to a maximum equal to not more than two-thirds of a worker's basic wage.

[4] This has led to some dissatisfaction since a man of fifty may get only half the compensation available to a man of sixty-five who is eligible for pension.

of a lump sum and a weekly pension in addition to existing state pensions is intended to induce them to leave the industry in the interests of increased efficiency.

Facing reduced trade, the National Coal Board, which has always had a general layoff agreement providing severance pay weighted for length of employment, agreed, in 1959, with the representative unions concerning the compulsory retirement of miners sixty-five and over (about twelve thousand workers). In addition to the state pension and the miner's supplementary pension, the retired miners will receive a lump sum compensation payable according to length of employment.

In France termination allowances are part of collective agreements and to date have been mainly for supervisors or those with some senior status. Arrangements are now spreading for wage earners, in the textile industry for example. Payments are geared to length of employment, but in some cases are weighted for age; for example, there is a 10 per-cent increase if the worker is over fifty, a 30 per-cent increase if over sixty, and so on.

Procedures which preserve accumulated rights (pensions, holidays, and the like) and give aid in securing new employment and income support during unemployment are not, except for pension plans, more important for older workers than for the rest of the labor force. These arrangements are part of the total pattern of available job security, compensation, and rehiring. Countries which do not have so many formal seniority rules as the United States has may have more generous arrangements for income support during unemployment or more positive policies for retraining and rehiring older workers.

### UNION ATTITUDES

In Great Britain the unions have not pressed enthusiastically for seniority rules or, indeed, for layoff agreements of any kind. Their suggestions for dealing with unemployment have tended to be of two kinds: (1) the need for improvements in unemployment insurance benefits,[5] resettlement, and retraining grants; and (2) "taking work to the workers" by industrially developing areas which tend to have a high rate of unemployment. These measures are seen by unions as matters for governmental action.

[5] The British social insurance scheme uses flat rate benefits for unemployment as for other benefits, and payments are not geared to former earnings as in Germany or in America.

The reluctance of British trade unions to actively encourage the negotiation of layoff agreements based on seniority rules may be explained in many ways.

A consistently high level of employment [6] has prevented severe layoff problems, and such dislocation as has taken place has been minimized by the capacity of the economy to reabsorb displaced workers relatively quickly. In these circumstances unions have been mainly preoccupied with wage negotiations.

Layoff agreements have generally been negotiated firm by firm to take account of unique industrial circumstances, and therefore agreements have to be sought at a local level. The centralized structure of British trade unionism does not favor action which further removes authority and decision-making from the central to the local units. It is, perhaps, significant that where unions have been able to negotiate at a national level with one employer—as, for example, the miners with the National Coal Board—layoff agreements exist.

Layoff agreements involving severance pay and other concessions from the employer are still regarded with some mistrust by unionists. Although union representatives have wanted full consultation and have been glad to make the most advantageous arrangements they could secure once unemployment threatened, they have shown no enthusiasm for going out to get layoff benefits. This is also true of the halfhearted way in which they have often approached the provision of pension schemes in private industry. In this field, as in layoff policies, the initiative has come from the employers rather than the unions. Unions would prefer any social benefits to depend on legislation and state social programs rather than on private employers. The trade-union movement feels that, until it has successfully pressed for an adequate basic retirement pension for all workers, it cannot devote too much attention to stimulating private plans of advantage to sectional groups. There are signs that these attitudes to fringe benefits are changing, but only slowly (Trades Union Congress, 1958).

Some unions and employers object to predetermined layoff procedures because they do not wish to be tied to agreements which will operate in circumstances they cannot foresee. Employers are willing to promise to make *ex gratia* payments to mitigate hardship, but do not wish to be committed to a scale of notice and compensation arrangements, which, they feel, might make too severe demands if the

[6] The national unemployment rate was 1.9 per cent in 1958. Some areas have twice this rate, however; the engineering industry is one example.

company was adversely affected by a trade recession. They also believe that provisions for advance warning of layoff are unsettling to the whole labor force and often result in the loss of good workers, who promptly seek other employment.

It is less easy to understand the unions' reluctance to negotiate layoff agreements in advance of a situation requiring them. If negotiation is left until the employer is forced to reduce labor anyway, the unions are in a very weak bargaining position.

Many claims are made by American labor unions for the merits of layoff agreements with clear seniority rules. Seniority rules are said to be the best way of ensuring job security in mass production industries where there is little chance for advancement. They are held to be fair and to avoid favoritism and discrimination in hiring or laying off workers. They use a single standard which is understood by all and easily applied. They underline the responsibility managements ought to have toward men who have given their best years to the service of a company. They protect the older worker not only directly by seniority rules, but also indirectly since the standard of production is not set by the youngest workers. If these claims are accepted, there remains the question of how seniority rules and other forms of job protection should be organized. The four countries referred to here all use collective bargaining in some degree, but to date the European countries have tended to rely more heavily on labor legislation and social benefits to protect dismissed employees. The tendency for European unions to look for state action and legislation reflects their political philosophy and affiliations. American unions also support proposals for improved social benefits, but in placing their emphasis on job security they are following traditional goals of economic independence.

Noted below is evidence to suggest that in some sectors of American industry seniority rules are truly effective in protecting employment for older workers. There are no comparable data available for Great Britain, for the opportunity to compile any has been limited by the fact that there has been little experience in such procedures.

### SUMMARY

Considerations of seniority are not new in employment practices, but to have these formally embodied in legislation or collective agreements is a recent development more widespread in the United States than in Western Europe. Procedures have been described because as yet they are not well-known or studied in most European countries except those directly concerned with their application. Little is known about their impact on job security for older workers.

The advantages claimed for seniority rules are that they protect the employment of older men in a way which is fair, indisputable, and easily applied, thus reducing dissatisfaction when dismissals have to be made. It may be objected that the extent of grievance procedures and arbitration in relation to seniority rules denies that they avoid all disagreements; the incidence of these grievances, however, is limited and would no doubt be very much greater if there were no seniority rules.

Seniority rules, like fixed retirement ages, greatly simplify the problems of management, who would find selective dismissals much more complicated to determine and justify. For example, is the older worker to be judged from the point of view of an accepted level of competence necessary for a job or for his competitive ability compared to younger men? In embodying fairness and recognition of a firm's responsibility to men who have given long service to it, seniority rules can be said to improve general industrial relations.

Seniority procedures give special assistance to the older worker in maintaining his place in the labor market, and this is held reasonable because it is easier for a younger man to retrain or adapt himself to new employment. On the other hand, there is danger that such a policy leaves a firm with a high proportion of older and possibly less efficient workers during a trade recession or technological change, when the firm needs to innovate and become more competitive to survive. A labor force weighted with older men, as in the case of dock labor, is not likely to encourage these objectives.

Seniority rights, like pension rights, may tend to prevent a necessary degree of mobility in a changing pattern of industrial production, since workers will hesitate to surrender established rights. This is an aspect of all fringe benefits which has to be considered. A compensation pool financed by contributions from industry and better unemployment insurance benefits might mitigate the hardships of labor mobility without tying benefits to place of employment. If the firms' contributions varied with the degree of stability of their labor force, it would also encourage a responsible policy toward layoffs.[7]

Dismissal rules in American agreements do not appear to

[7] This policy of basing employer premiums on merit or experience ratings is widely used in American unemployment insurance.

have any concern with family responsibility as do a number of European procedures. It may be argued that it is not fair or socially desirable to dismiss a man of forty with expensive family responsibilities and retain a man of sixty-two who is nearing retirement and whose family responsibilities are confined to himself and his wife.

The effect of seniority rules is to accept the fact that the older worker is unable to take his chance in the labor market on his own merits; seniority rules give him a degree of protection. We are assuming that an older man is less efficient than a younger worker or that discriminatory employment practices erroneously assume this. Either way, it means that the older worker is getting preferential treatment, and there may be the danger of resentment among younger workers if seniority is pushed too far.

Pursuing policies which are narrowly conceived to be in the interest of older age groups is always questionable if the policies create excessive and unreasonable hardships for other groups. No policy for the employment of older workers ought to be considered outside the context of employment policies and prospects for the whole working population. It might be a more constructive approach to explore further the ways of protecting the health of older workers, maximizing their skills, and motivating them to retrain so that they can hold their own more readily in the labor market.

Apart from the consequences for individual older workers, there are the consequences for the economy as a whole from having seniority rules. Clearly they prevent the employer from employing the men who are, in his opinion, the most suitable and presumably the most efficient. They reduce the mobility of older workers and throw a burden of excessive mobility on the younger workers, the majority of whom are likely to have greater family responsibilities than the older men do. The guarantee of the right to a job in a particular plant rather than the right to economic conditions which enable a man who wants work to obtain work interferes with economic freedom; possibly this is not very serious, but probably it is not negligible. If employment is determined by length of service with little regard to individual effort or efficiency, there is the possibility of harmful effects on incentive and of hindrances to reasonable promotion methods. The protection of the old at the expense of the young may even, in a time of severe competition for employment, create serious intergeneration conflicts.

Seniority is not a new concept in employment practices. Traditionally there has been a tendency for older people to move into

TABLE 1
EMPLOYMENT BY AGE AND SEX IN DURABLE-GOODS MANUFACTURING
IN THE UNITED STATES

(In thousands)

| Sex and year | All ages | Age | | | | | | | |
|---|---|---|---|---|---|---|---|---|---|
| | | 14-19 | 20-24 | 25-34 | 35-44 | 45-54 | 55-59 | 60-64 | 65+ |
| **Males** | | | | | | | | | |
| July, 1957 | 8,201 | 291 | 748 | 2,176 | 2,277 | 1,592 | 519 | 398 | 199 |
| July, 1958 | 7,153 | 179 | 585 | 1,800 | 2,002 | 1,463 | 510 | 374 | 159 |
| Change | -1,048 | -112 | -163 | -296 | -275 | -129 | -9 | -24 | -40 |
| Per-cent change | -13 | -39 | -22 | -14 | -12 | -8 | -2 | -6 | -20 |
| **Females** | | | | | | | | | |
| July, 1957 | 1,785 | 132 | 239 | 450 | 506 | 313 | | 146* | |
| July, 1958 | 1,561 | 76 | 187 | 352 | 489 | 307 | | 150 | |
| Change | -224 | -56 | -32 | -98 | -17 | -6 | | +4 | |
| Per-cent change | -13 | -45 | -22 | -22 | -3 | -2 | | +3 | |

Source—U.S. Bureau of Labor Statistics. Monthly report of the labor force. Unpublished data, 1957-1958.
*Age fifty-five and over.

positions, often carrying status and authority, in which they were able to function in accordance with their changed capacities. With the survival of a relatively small proportion of older workers, it was possible for them to be absorbed into suitable occupations, but with a life expectancy which brings a high proportion of the labor force into the older age groups and with industrial changes unfavorable to older workers, it is not so easy to allow older workers to move into employment suitable to their needs, and they are more frequently thrown into direct competition for jobs with younger men.

## Effect of Seniority on Layoffs

The "Monthly Report on the Labor Force" for the period July, 1957, to July, 1958 (U.S. Bureau of the Census, 1957-1958), yields data indicative of the effect of seniority rules on layoffs in an American durable-goods industry.[8] The business cycle moved from peak to trough during this twelve-month period. Employment in durable-goods manufacturing, which has extensive seniority provisions for layoffs, fell by more than 1,250,000, or 13 per cent, between July, 1957, and July, 1958.

The data in Table 1 show a significant age differential in the 1957-1958 employment decline, with younger workers bearing the brunt of the layoff. For men the pattern of unemployment correlates inversely with age until the normal retirement period is approached. For women the correlation continues throughout the age span covered.

Seniority also plays an important role in recall, although this is not revealed by these data. Thus it may be concluded that seniority is an important factor in the pattern of employment and unemployment by age. Expressing a fundamental attitude and philosophy of the trade-union movement in the United States, seniority is likely to continue its protection for older workers in the foreseeable future.

### REFERENCES

Personnel Advisory Service. Redundancy policies in British industry. Examples of redundancy handling in British industry. Unpublished studies, Ministry of Labour and National Service, London, 1960.
Shenfield, Barbara. *Social policies for old age. A review of social provision for old age in Great Britain*. London: Routledge and Kegan Paul, Ltd., 1957.

[8] Excerpted from Seymour L. Wolfbein (Chapter 42, *supra*).

Thomas, G., & Osborne, Barbara. *Older people and their employment. An inquiry made by the social survey in April 1950 for the Ministry of Labour and National Service.* London: Central Office of Information, 1950.

Trades Union Congress. *Report of proceedings of the 88th annual trades union congress.* London: Co-operative Printing Society Limited, 1956.

Trades Union Congress. *Report of proceedings of the 90th annual trades union congress.* London: Co-operative Printing Society Limited, 1958.

U.S. Bureau of the Census. Monthly report of the labor force. *Current population reports: Labor force,* October 1957, **182,** through August 1958, **193,** Series P-57. (Washington, D.C.: U.S. Government Printing Office)

U.S. Bureau of Labor Statistics. Analysis of layoff, recall, and work-sharing procedures. *Bulletin,* 1957, No. 1209. (Washington, D.C.: U.S. Government Printing Office) (a)

U.S. Bureau of Labor Statistics. Collective bargaining clauses: Dismissal pay. *Bulletin,* 1957, No. 1216. (Washington, D.C.: U.S. Government Printing Office) (b)

U.S. Bureau of Labor Statistics. Monthly report of the labor force. Unpublished data, 1957-1958.

# CHAPTER 44

*Reflections on the Health and*
*Employment of Older People*

ELI GINZBERG

This is a modest effort focused on a very large and complex theme. It will not present a new body of data; in fact, it will not present any data at all. Moreover, it will not develop a mathematical or, for that matter, any model to illuminate the manner in which considerations of health influence the employability of older persons. It pretends to nothing more than it is—a series of reflections growing out of my previous research in related areas, organizational experiences, and the findings of manpower theory.

From time to time it becomes important to remind American social scientists that there are many roads to knowledge and wisdom and that neither the computer nor the calculus exhausts the possibilities.

The Bible says that there is a time for everything. This is

particularly applicable to research. With regard to the subject at hand —and this may also be true of the entire field of gerontology—the urgent need is not for adding discrete data or even for refining data that have been collected. Instead, there is a need to develop a framework within which students can identify the major problems and directions for research and policy. We need clarification, and it is hoped that reflection can contribute to it.

## EARLIER RESEARCH

For over twenty years my associates and I have been engaged in research on human resources and manpower, and from this I have derived one overriding impression. Performance in the labor market is never to be explained by a unitary factor, not even by one as basic as health. As we sought to make clear in our study of the ineffective soldier in World War II, performance must be analyzed in terms of the interaction of three sets of determinants: the strengths and weaknesses of individuals, job requirements, and the stresses and supports in the environment (Ginzberg & associates, 1959).

In the present context this means that a person may be both sick and old and still perform effectively. This was strikingly true of Matisse and Freud, to mention only two. It also means that some older individuals who suffer from rather serious disabilities may still be able to meet more-or-less successfully the requirements of a specific job. This was outstandingly exemplified by the late Pope Pius XII. And, finally, whether older people in mediocre or poor health are employed depends in part on society's need for their talents and the supports that are available to them. In recent years some mental hospitals have been successfully experimenting with a plan whereby certain patients leave the hospital daily to go to work and then return at night.

It is easy to say that the foregoing examples are at best moot and at worst irrelevant, for each refers to a man of extraordinary talent, but the world is made up of ordinary people without special aptitudes or attributes. It does not require an intimate knowledge of the labor market, however, to recognize that many undistinguished people in their sixties, even in their seventies, continue to hold jobs despite poor health. Although this observation tells us nothing about the proportions of the sick and crippled who work, it alerts us to the dangers of generalization.

A second finding from our research highlights the importance of health as an explanation for failure in the labor market. In contemporary American culture illness is a respectable explanation for failure to meet existing demands. In our study of the long-term unemployed in New York City in 1940, we learned that many explained their status by poor health (Ginzberg & associates, 1943). But, interestingly, when employment opportunities expanded, these "sick" people were able to surmount their disabilities and return to work. In my earlier study of the Welsh coal miners, I had also been struck by the fact that many of the older men (forty-five to sixty-five) explained their unwillingness to move away from the impoverished mining communities by poor health (Ginzberg, 1943). They used it to buttress their resistance to altering the pattern of their lives even though relocation offered the only prospect of a return to work.

There is not only a one-way, but often a reciprocal, relation between health and employment. In 1949 I had the opportunity to study the hospitals in the state of New York (Ginzberg, 1949b). At that time I noted that during the height of World War II the patient census in the state mental hospitals declined, a unique reversal of the trend up to that point. Inquiry disclosed that a major factor in the reversal was the new employment opportunities, open even to psychotic people, because of the insatiable demands of defense plants for labor. Because of the situation, employers were willing to take risks and to tolerate a low level of performance; consequently many of these sick people were able to keep their jobs and thus stay out of hospitals.

In reviewing the history of federal hospitalization, it became clear to me that fifteen to twenty years after World War I a significant proportion of the men on the books of the veterans' hospitals were more socially than medically ill (Ginzberg, 1949a). With the passage of each year, more and more of those who had failed in their work, marriage, or adjustment to life itself gave up the struggle and entered the hospital, which, thenceforth, was to be their home and haven. Despite this history, the reconstruction of the veterans' hospital system after World War II failed to make adequate allowance for the probable build-up in the census of uprooted men over the years. Current experience suggests that history is repeating itself.

An important dimension of health and employment was illuminated by the National Manpower Council's (1957) recent study, *Womanpower,* where note was taken of the striking change that had occurred in the employment of older women. As recently as World War II, the War Department ruled against sending women over forty overseas on the ground that the menopause would interfere with their performance. Only fifteen years later, the labor force participation rate for women over forty-five was higher than for females in any other age group. Although advances in medicine, particularly in chemo-therapy, have helped to control many of the adverse aspects of the menopause, there may well be more to the story. It seems likely that the first opportunity open to large numbers of middle-aged women to keep busy and useful during the climacteric is as important as—even more important than—the new drugs in contributing to the women's heightened stability.

The paper which I prepared for the Fourth International Gerontological Congress at Merano in 1957 contained a quotation from the Talmud to the effect that if a man stops working he dies (Ginzberg, 1959). Since that time, largely in response to the prompt-ings of my colleagues, Dean Henry David and Mr. Dale Hiestand, I have been forced to rethink my basic approach to the role of work in contemporary American life and have become persuaded that major deviation from the Pharasitic-Puritan tradition no longer necessarily engenders guilt, much less hastens death (Ginzberg, 1958).

If men choose retirement when they can and if many more of them are now offered the choice, then the question of health and its relation to employment among older people should be rephrased as a question of health and its relation to retirement. Since the factors operating to encourage a man to keep working are frequently almost in balance with those supporting his retirement, considerations of health frequently loom large in the final decision. Undoubtedly many men are convinced that they should retire because their health is beginning to fail, whereas others who are being pressed to retire may use their health as the rationale for a decision that they really prefer not to make.

## EXPERIENCE

Long before trade unions came onto the scene, seniority systems, at least loosely defined, had been established in most organ-izations. Power tended to be concentrated among the older members. This being so, the work assignments of older people have long been shaped to their capacities. Older people are not expected to perform the same arduous tasks that are assigned to younger men. By intent and tradition the jobs that older people customarily fill have been shaped and reshaped to accommodate their diminishing powers and health.

Nature has taken care of the matter for women by limiting their period of fertility. Women are best able to cope with the strenuous tasks of childbearing and child-rearing during their younger years. Moreover, the fact that there is a marked diminution in the arduous household tasks of women as they grow older has been interpreted as contributing to their greater longevity. Women are better able than men to establish an effective balance between their reduced strengths and their activities. They are not forced, as their husbands frequently are, to work strenuously for most of their lives only to fall into an abyss of idleness upon retirement.

One important lesson that grew out of the efforts to improve the utilization of military manpower during World War II was the recognition that procedures could be developed to make constructive use of men with physical or educational handicaps, but that it was impractical to try to fit men with multiple handicaps into appropriate assignments. By analogy we can say that the fact that the aging process inevitably brings with it a diminution in physical strength and well-being establishes an unpropitious background for the successful employment of older people, who frequently suffer from disabilities in addition to poor health.

A leading New York surgeon recently commented to me on the marked difference which he noted in the employment experience of his older patients. For the most part, his postoperative private patients shortly returned to their regular work, sometimes on a reduced schedule, whereas many of his ward patients, who had lost their jobs because of the illness or other reasons, were unable to secure another. The ward patients were much more likely to be handicapped by multiple factors hindering their re-employment.

Up to this point, the discussion of health in older people has proceeded primarily in terms of physical considerations, but it may well be that the emotional aspects are the more important. Whether one works depends to a marked degree on whether one wants to or must work. In turn, the intensity of this interest or desire is a function not only of a person's past, but also of his estimate of his future. The older a man is, the less return he will receive for effort expended. A close view of the academic community reveals that only a minority keeps working intensively after forty. The rest, realizing that they will not be able to break through to the top, are willing to make their peace by doing the minimum but little more. Academic communities are not very different from other working environments except that their tenure systems provide maximum protection for older people.

I recently talked with the executive vice-president of one of America's large corporations who had just retired under the optional plan which was in effect in his company. He was a man of sixty and appeared to be in excellent health, yet he remarked that it was very difficult, particularly for older men, to work in a company whose president was a dynamo who was only in his forties. There was little point for him or his peers to constantly attempt to outdo themselves when they realized that they would have to retire within five years or less with no chance of attaining the presidency.

In the early days of World War II when the War Department was being reorganized, it was generally understood around the Pentagon that Henry Stimson would retire once the reorganization had been completed so that a younger man, Judge Patterson, could take the helm. But the retirement was postponed until the war's end despite the fact that Mr. Stimson was not able to work a full day, surely not the extended day which was the prevailing pattern. The urgency of the situation was such, however, that, by reducing his working hours and delegating much responsibility to his excellent civilian and military associates, he was able to make the effort and remain at the helm. This illustration should indicate that it is the exception when older people find themselves in situations where they are stimulated to this degree. They are much more likely to be in positions where they see little point in straining to keep going, especially if they face a tolerable alternative.

## MANPOWER THEORY

Since the employability of older people is determined by the play between their characteristics and the shape and functioning of the labor market, it may be helpful to delineate some of the more important areas of interaction.

Despite the marked reduction in the proportion of jobs in a modern industrial society that demand high orders of physical strength, the total number of such jobs remains high. To the extent that men fail to move up the supervisory ladder or fail to find less demanding work as they grow older, they are likely to be in a vulnerable position, for many of them will experience a marked diminution in physical strength and well-being.

Although many students have exaggerated the proportion of assembly line jobs in the economy, in absolute terms the number is considerable, probably around five million. Older people who have remained on the assembly line and whose health begins to fail are likely to be particularly vulnerable. If there are no easier jobs to which they can be assigned, they must retire, for it is not practical to adjust the work flow to meet their special needs.

The psychologists have sought to prove that the widespread impression that older people are unable to learn new skills is fallacious and that their capacity to absorb the new is not significantly less, if it is less, than that of younger groups. They have presented a considerable body of experimental data to support their conclusion. But there is a wide gap between the laboratory and life. Older people may have the capacity to learn, but the crucial question is whether they have the motivation to do so.

One of the more insidious results of aging is a marked reduction in drive. Older people are less capable or less willing, perhaps both, to put forth the effort required to surmount the difficulties which they face. They are much more likely than younger people to become resigned to circumstances. In an economy characterized by rapid technological changes, the reduction in *élan vital* may add more to the employment difficulties of older people than the increased incidence of chronic disease which characterizes this group (Ginzberg, 1960).

The past decades have seen a vast expansion of so-called scientific personnel practices, the cornerstone of which has been the physical examination as a qualification for employment. World War II should have served as a warning of the dangers in pseudoscientific screening methods. Over three million of the eighteen million young Americans between the ages of eighteen and thirty-seven were rejected for military service on the ground that they were incapable of performing effectively because of a physical disability or could serve only at the risk of aggravating their condition. The director of the Selective Service System has repeatedly called attention to the limitations inherent in a screening which entails subjecting each part of the human body to critical scrutiny, rather than making an over-all assessment of the person's ability to meet the demands of the job. In an effort to keep insurance premiums as low as possible (as well as for other reasons), a great many employers have long pursued a policy of requiring new workers to undergo a rigid physical examination; while others have flatly interdicted hiring men over forty-five. This means that the older person who loses his job and must find another is forced to surmount a special hurdle which other older people, more fortunate because they are still employed though not necessarily in better health, need not face.

## TENTATIVE CONCLUSIONS

It appears that by and large most people reach the conventional age of retirement without health's having played a determining part in their employment history. From many points of view this largely negative finding warrants special emphasis, especially in a presentation to experts in gerontology who are likely to be preoccupied with the "special problems" of older people.

There is no escaping the fact, however, that advancing years are characterized by a decline, sometimes fast and sometimes slow, in physical strength and well-being which may and frequently does represent an important employment hazard. But the job market is so arranged that in the absence of marked disability, most men will usually be able to keep working at their accustomed work, though some may find it necessary to shift to new positions which are less demanding.

A much more serious consideration arises when men in their fifties or early sixties lose their jobs and have to find another. Conventional screening makes it very difficult for them to pass the rigid physical examination which is usually required even when there is no ceiling on age.

It may well be that more older people would be able to find another job despite their physical disabilities if they had greater emotional stamina. It is not easy for a young man to look for work and to be told repeatedly that there is no job for him. It is much more difficult for an older man to cope with repeated rebuffs, especially if the margin between what he can earn and what he will receive in the form of a pension or assistance is narrow.

In this connection it is important to stress again that poor health is an acceptable excuse for being unemployed or retired. It is undoubtedly used by a great many older people whose situation is more nearly a function of their incompetence.

Our society's rapidly changing attitudes toward work and retirement and the equally rapid changes in the structure of income maintenance in old age have also had an impact on the employability of older people. In a society that is not completely the past, men worked until they could no longer stand on their feet. They did so because it was the right thing to do, and they did so because they had few or no options. All this is changing and changing very rapidly. More and more Americans are seeking their major satisfactions in life off, rather than on, the job. They have no reason to be ashamed of retiring early—in fact, early retirement is frequently considered an achievement. Increasingly one hears men say that they stopped working early in order to enjoy their retirement while they were still in good health!

From a policy point of view, this approach suggests that the major gains lie along the following line: improved health throughout life so that fewer people will reach old age in a weakened or debilitated condition. But since the existing and even prospective developments in medicine cannot prevent a marked rise in the incidence of disability among older people, a greater availability of therapeutic and rehabilitative services is indicated.

The reappraisal of employer practices, particularly the rigid physical examination required for employment and a greater flexibility in assignments and reassignments, could contribute to the employment of older people who suffer from defects which are not disabling. In this connection, governmental and voluntary agencies can make a greater contribution by strengthening their guidance and placement services.

There are several implications for research that flow from this analysis. The first is the need to proceed as rapidly as possible with studying the experiences of different groups of older workers in terms of their education and training as well as their occupational distribution and experience. It is not realistic to consider the relation of health to the employability of construction workers and truck drivers in the same terms as that of lawyers and teachers.

The second suggestion points to the desirability of undertaking small studies focused on identifying and evaluating the factors that determine how older people choose among the alternatives that they face: to continue in their present job at a risk to their health or to accept one with less income and prestige; to retire now or to hold on a bit longer; to accept the fact that they will not work again or to move to a new locality where the prospect of their re-employment is much greater.

A third approach would be to explore the subtle relations among physical disability, emotional strain, and motivation as they affect the employment, unemployment, and retirement of older workers.

The fact that such inquiries are difficult to design and even more difficult to carry out does not deny their importance.

The major conclusion of this agnostic piece can be summarized very simply. To the extent that workers are better educated and trained in their youth and to the extent that they continue to acquire skills and competence in their mature years, they are unlikely, even in the presence of moderate physical disabilities, to experience major difficulties in employment in their old age. Lack of competence, not poor health, is the cross of the older worker.

## REFERENCES

Ginzberg, E. *Grass on the slag heaps: The story of the Welsh miners.* New York: Harper and Brothers, 1943.
Ginzberg, E. Federal hospitalization. *Mod. Hosp.,* 1949, **72,** 61-63. (a)
Ginzberg, E. *A pattern for hospital care.* New York: Columbia University Press, 1949. (b)
Ginzberg, E. *Human resources: The wealth of a nation.* New York: Simon & Schuster, 1958.
Ginzberg, E. Strategic factors in the adjustment of older people. In *Proceedings of the fourth congress, international association of gerontology, Merano, Italy.* Vol. 3. Florence, Italy: Tipografia Tito Mattioli [1959]. Pp. 460-467.
Ginzberg, E. Automation and manpower. In *Proceedings of Governor's Conference on Automation.* Albany: New York State Printing Office, 1960.
Ginzberg, E., & associates. *The unemployed.* New York: Harper and Brothers, 1943.
Ginzberg, E., & associates. *The ineffective soldier.* New York: Columbia University Press, 1959.
National Manpower Council, *Womanpower: A statement with chapters by the council staff.* New York: Columbia University Press, 1957.

# CHAPTER 45

*Occupational Health*
*and Old Age*

SVEN FORSSMAN

The World Health Organization has defined health as a "state of complete physical, mental and social well-being and not merely the absence of disease or infirmity" (World Health Organization, 1958, p. 1268). The definition of occupational health, according to a joint ILO/WHO (International Labour Organisation/World Health Organization) expert committee, is as follows:

> Occupational health should aim at: the promotion and maintenance of the highest degree of physical, mental, and social well-being of workers in all occupations; the prevention among workers of departures from health caused by their working conditions; the protection of workers in their employment from risks resulting from factors adverse to health; the placing and maintenance of the worker in an occupational environment adapted to his physiological and psychological equipment and, to summarize: the adaptation of work to man and of each man to his job (World Health Organization, 1953, p. 4).

It is important to note that both mental and social features are included in both definitions. Adjustment to the physical, mental, and social environment at work as well as at home and in society is essential for health. Consequently not only the health and working capacity of men at work should be studied, but also the demand of the work on the man. Complete health will include a balance between the mental and physical capacity of the individual on one side and the specific mental and physical demands of his job on the other. Aging changes these capacities in many ways, for instance, by gradually reducing the maximum physical work capacity and, on the mental side, by reducing the capacity to work constantly at high speed, to combine and memorize new information, and so on. To a certain extent, however, many of these changes in capacity with increasing age may be compensated for through the older worker's experience, which makes it possible for him to adjust his work to his reduced capacity.

The handicaps of the aging population, however, may be caused more by the increasing incidence of disease in higher age groups than from aging as such. Above forty to fifty years of age there is, for instance, a higher incidence of diseases of the heart, blood vessels, lungs, muscles, joints, bones, and central nervous system. Studies of men at work have shown, however, that men with diseases of the heart and blood vessels may be able to do even heavy physical work to a much higher degree than would be expected from the results of medical examinations (Åstrand, 1958). This obviously calls for individual evaluation of the working capacity of old workers. Moreover, great care must be taken not to generalize the findings of the average work capacities of different age groups because the variation of these average values is considerable.

## CHARACTERISTICS OF OLDER WORKERS

Utilizing scientific laboratory studies of aging and physical and mental working capacity (for instance, Welford, 1958) as well as the practical experience of old workers in their places of employment, mostly in manufacturing, one can summarize the positive and negative aspects of old people from the point of view of their work capacities. The principal characteristics of older workers are listed in Table 1. Old workers are, on the whole, absent less often than young

TABLE 1
HEALTH ASPECTS OF OLD PEOPLE AT WORK

| Positive | Negative |
|---|---|
| Capacity to carry out work demanding high degree of accuracy | Reduced capacity to work constantly at high speed |
| Experience, compensating for some negative aspects | Reduced capacity to memorize and combine new information |
| Responsibility | More time for learning new methods |
| Low labor turnover | Reduced near vision and dark adaptation |
| Low short-term absenteeism | Reduced maximum physical working capacity |

workers, but the duration of absence caused by illness increases with age, especially in higher age groups.

A table such as this should be extended on the basis of all available experience concerning the occupational health and working capacities of old people. This would then serve as a useful guide in placing old people at work, preventing unnecessary strain, fatigue, and sometimes disease and at the same time getting the most out of their production.

Indeed many studies have shown that it is possible to keep old workers at work, even in higher age groups, if they are properly placed with reference to their changing health and working capacity. A study demonstrating these possibilities was recently carried out in Sweden (Forssman, 1957a; 1957b). It was shown that in eight industries with good health services the performance of old people was about the same as that of young workers, judging from average income and absenteeism. It is highly significant that 60 per cent of men above sixty had some health handicap, according to the special examination carried out by the industrial physician.

In spite of the increasing morbidity with age, the older workers belong to a select group, since many workers over sixty have already retired because of disability. Information on the incidence of

TABLE 2
MORBIDITY OF OLD MALE WORKERS
IN EIGHT SWEDISH INDUSTRIES

| Age | Employees In Good Health | Employees With Impaired Health | Percentage With Impaired Health |
|---|---|---|---|
| 60-64 years | 226 | 301 | 57 |
| 65-69 " | 104 | 195 | 65 |
| 70-74 " | 10 | 43 | 81 |
| 75-79 " | 0 | 6 | — |
| 80-84 " | 1 | 1 | — |
| No information | 1 | — | — |
| Total | 342 | 546 | 61 |

Source—Forssman (1957).

disability and retirement at higher age groups is to be found in such studies as Richardson (1956), Brown, McKeown, and Whitfield (1958), Le Gros Clark (1959), and Shillito (1959). In order to arrive at methods of preserving health and working capacity in higher age groups, it is important to have more information on retirement and the medical and social reasons for it in age groups above fifty. In the Swedish study mentioned above, the attitude of old workers toward remaining at work after the normal age of retirement is also interesting. Most of them (79 per cent of male workers and 66 per cent of the women) wanted to stay on at the same work, other work, or part-time work after the normal age of retirement. Most of them considered their health and working capacity normal despite the fact that the health examination showed that three-fifths of them had impaired health and reduced working capacity. According to this study, management or foremen also seemed to overestimate the health and working capacity of older workers in a similar way. If, however, the old workers stated that they wanted to leave because of bad health and reduced working capacity, their desire was warranted by the health examination in most cases.

Thus a positive statement by the old worker on his own health and working capacity should be evaluated carefully, although a negative statement may, according to this study, be generally accepted.

TABLE 3

MALE EMPLOYEE'S OPINION OF HIS WORKING CAPACITY IN RELATION
TO HIS HEALTH IN EIGHT SWEDISH INDUSTRIES

| Result of Health examination | Employee's Opinion | | | | | | | |
|---|---|---|---|---|---|---|---|---|
| | Number | | | | Percentage Distribution | | | |
| | Total | Full | Reduced | No information | Total | Full | Reduced | No information |
| Good health | 339 | 330 | 5 | 4 | 100 | 97 | 2 | 1 |
| Impaired health (suggested limitation):* | 577 | 407 | 155 | 15 | 100 | 70 | 27 | 3 |
| Can do present work but should not be transferred without consulting the industrial physician | 532 | 396 | 127 | 9 | 100 | 74 | 24 | 2 |
| Not suitable for his present work but should be transferred to lighter work | 15 | 6 | 9 | — | 100 | 40 | 60 | — |
| Should work only part time | 6 | — | 6 | — | 100 | — | 100 | — |
| Should retire | 24 | 5 | 13 | 6 | 100 | 21 | 54 | 25 |
| No information available | 19 | 14 | 1 | 4 | 100 | 74 | 5 | 21 |
| Total | 935 | 751 | 161 | 23 | 100 | 80 | 17 | 2 |

Source—Forssman (1957).
*The third, fourth, fifth, and sixth lines are the components of the second line.

## GUIDE TO PLACEMENT

A number of general principles based on health and practical experience can be suggested for placing old people at work. Because old people have difficulty adapting themselves to new working conditions, one should always try to keep them on the same work they did before but try to reduce the work load. The work load may be reduced by abolishing overtime, allowing the old worker to adjust his speed of work to fit his own reduced working capacity, transferring him from piece rate to time rate, introducing pauses and intervals (even micropauses may be of value), increasing the lunch break, and suggesting part-time work. Especially after the normal age of retirement, it may sometimes be practical to have two old half-time workers for one full-time job. Extremely heavy physical work should be avoided and the work environment should, as far as possible, be adjusted to changing health and work capacities through lessened speed and more rest periods.

Old workers should not be placed with young workers if the latter will set the speed of work. For psychological reasons, however, it may not always be desirable to segregate older workers. Reports on special workshops for old people have been favorable from some countries, from others they have not. The old worker should be prepared for transfer far enough in advance for him to adjust to the new conditions.

Old people are very sensitive about doing a useful job and playing an important role in the working group. Thus placing them at a job with lower prestige, according to their own opinion or others' attitudes, should be avoided if possible. As far as possible, the experience as well as the responsibility of old workers should be utilized in the new position. If transferring old workers must be combined with retraining, this should be planned early and not delayed until old age. It would be of great practical value if guidance principles for placing old workers could be worked out in more detail than they are here by utilizing current research and practical experience. It could then be stated which jobs would generally be suitable to old people and which jobs should be avoided.

## ECONOMIC AND SOCIAL FACTORS

In spite of experience in many industries showing that properly placed old workers will do good work and that it may be of value to the health of old workers to stay at work as long as they are able to work, there are many practical difficulties and prejudices to overcome.

In all countries the professional distribution of higher age groups shows that the frequency of old workers is high in such professions as agriculture, watchmaker, violin-maker, watchman, and so on and low in such professions as miner, foundryman, docker, construction worker, merchant marine, and so on (Le Gros Clark & Dunne, 1956). Workers retire earlier in some professions than in others. This difference may be because the demands of the work are too high for most old people, but many social and economic factors are also of importance.

In a recent Swedish study (Hydén, Bengtsson, Edgren, & Lundgren, 1960) on age distribution in different professions, it was shown that a high average age, fifty-one years, was found among stone workers. Working in granite-cutting is normally rather heavy physical work. Until recently this industry in Sweden had not been widely mechanized, and to some extent the old workers could adjust the speed of work to their own working capacity. On the other hand, this industry has had difficulty selling its products, and few new employees have entered this profession during the past few decades. The workers already in the profession have tried to stay on, because very few other possibilities for employment are available in the region. Thus not only the physical and mental demands of the job, but also the social and economic factors, influence the age distribution within a profession.

It is often mentioned that old workers have difficulty adjusting themselves to new conditions or new working processes and that it would be difficult and costly to train them. This seems to be one of the most common objections to employing old people. It has been recently shown in a Swedish study that unemployment is much more common among people above forty and that people of higher age groups will stay unemployed for a longer time than younger people will.

Introduction of advanced mechanization and automation will shift the work demands on the human being from the physical to mental side. The work in industry will then be less heavy physical

TABLE 4
UNEMPLOYED MEN AND WOMEN COVERED BY
UNEMPLOYMENT INSURANCE IN SWEDEN*

(In percentages)

| Sex and age | Unemployed | | Unemployed more than two months | |
|---|---|---|---|---|
| | 1958 | 1959 | 1958 | 1959 |
| Men | | | | |
| Under 25 years | 20.2 | 17.7 | 5.0 | 5.8 |
| 25-34 " | 28.5 | 18.6 | 6.7 | 5.9 |
| 35-44 " | 34.1 | 20.2 | 8.3 | 6.5 |
| 45-54 " | 43.8 | 26.6 | 12.9 | 10.2 |
| 55-59 " | 52.4 | 35.2 | 18.8 | 16.1 |
| 60-66 " | 73.3 | 62.4 | 34.5 | 35.0 |
| Above 66 " | 67.2 | 62.2 | 36.3 | 39.2 |
| Total | 38.3 | 26.5 | 12.1 | 11.0 |
| Women | | | | |
| Under 25 years | 7.3 | 8.2 | 2.4 | 3.8 |
| 25-34 " | 12.3 | 14.7 | 5.3 | 7.4 |
| 35-44 " | 17.3 | 18.9 | 8.0 | 10.4 |
| 45-54 " | 22.2 | 25.4 | 10.5 | 14.4 |
| 55-59 " | 28.4 | 32.9 | 14.9 | 19.9 |
| 60-66 " | 40.9 | 49.5 | 22.8 | 31.3 |
| Above 66 " | 44.7 | 49.6 | 24.5 | 33.2 |
| Total | 16.7 | 19.1 | 7.8 | 10.6 |

Source—Hydén et al. (1960).
*Membership is approximately 1,084,000 men and 244,000 women.

work and more complicated mental work, such as receiving information on the instrument panels, memorizing, and making important
decisions at the right moment. Young people will be trained for such
work, and one of the greatest problems of automation, as pointed out
by Heron (1957), will be retraining middle-aged and old workers
whose jobs have been taken over by mechanical or automatic processes.

In the near future one can foresee special difficulties for old people in developing countries which are in a stage of rapid industrialization. This will often include the transfer of large groups of people from agriculture to industries and from rural areas to cities, often splitting family groups traditionally occupied in agriculture in small villages. These social changes, together with the unemployment which is found in most of these developing countries, will make it very difficult for old people, who will not be able to compete on the labor market with younger workers. Industrial health services may prevent some of these difficulties and improve conditions for old people in developing countries (Forssman, 1959).

## PROBLEMS FOR RESEARCH

Some future problems on the occupational health of old age may be briefly summarized. It will be of great importance to start as early as possible to prevent diseases common in old age, such as heart disease, arteriosclerosis, chronic bronchitis, arthritis, and rheumatism. People who retire from work, especially before the normal age of retirement, should be studied in order to find out the incidence of disability in different age groups, learn the medical and social reasons for it, and have a better background for preventing diseases of old age. More knowledge should be gained on what types of work are suitable and unsuitable for old people, and practical guides should be worked out. Better practical methods are needed for evaluating the physical and mental working capacities of older workers. Health education and training for retirement starting long in advance may facilitate the adjustment of old workers to the mental and social problems of retirement and thus prevent the impairment of health. The present knowledge on the influence of aging and related diseases on health and working capacity is mainly based on cross-sectional studies, giving average values of different age groups. More knowledge on longitudinal studies, following the health and working capacity of the same individuals over some time, would be of great value in order to learn more about the change of health and working capacity that occurs with age. The special social problems of old workers in relation to automation and the rapid industrialization in developing countries should be studied, and large-scale preventive measures introduced at an early stage.

348                                                    SVEN FORSSMAN

REFERENCES

Åstrand, I. Clinical and physiological studies of manual workers 50-64 years old at rest and during work. *Acta Med. Scand.,* 1958, **162,** 155-164.

Brown, R.G., McKeown, T., & Whitfield, A.G.W. Observations in the medical condition of men in the seventh decade. *Brit. med. J.,* 1958, **1,** 555-562.

Forssman, S. Health problems of the older worker. A study in Swedish industry. *Trans. Assn. industr. med. Off.,* 1957, **7,** 9-19. (a)

Forssman, S. *Äldre i industrin.* Stockholm: Publikationer från Svenska Arbetsgivareföreningen, 1957. (b)

Forssman, S. Industrial health in industrial and nonindustrial countries. *J. occup. Med.,* 1959, **1,** 15-20.

Heron, A. Psychological research in industry. *Trans Assn. industr. med. Off.,* 1957, **7,** 47-49.

Hydén, S., Bengtsson, S.F., Edgren, G., & Lundgren, I. *Medeländers och äldre arbetskraft.* Stockholm: Bröderna Lagerström Boktryckare, 1960.

Le Gros Clark, F. *Age and the working lives of men.* London: The Nuffield Foundation, 1959.

Le Gros Clark, F., & Dunne, A. *Aging in industry.* New York: The Philosophical Library, 1956.

Richardson, I.M. Retirements. A socio-medical study of 244 men. *Scot. med. J.,* 1956, **1,** 381-391.

Shillito, F.H. Preparation for retirement. *J. occup. Med.,* 1959, **1,** 382-386.

Welford, A.T. *Ageing and human skill.* London: Oxford University Press, 1958.

World Health Organization. Joint ILO/WHO committee on occupational health. Second report. *WHO techn. Report Series,* 1953, No. 66. (Geneva: Author)

World Health Organization. *The first ten years of the World Health Organization.* Geneva: Author, 1958.

# CHAPTER 46

## The Matrix of Health, Manpower, and Age

WALT R. SIMMONS

The action a person initiates to support his well-being in old age, as well as policy and programs societies undertake for the same purpose, should be selected first for human values and second for economic and sociological considerations. In this context, wise decisions can be made only when they are based on facts.

Throughout history a considerable part of the effort expended in religious, philosophical, and scientific endeavor has been the search for truth and for facts. These primary values are not easily determined. Eric Bell (1934) reminds us that Christ did not answer Pilate's question, "What *is* truth?" and that, in the nearly 2,000 years since that question was asked, few of the thousands of replies that have been given are much alike. Lest there be any misunderstanding, it should be immediately stated that the present paper does not pre-

349

sume to engage in analysis of so fundamental a matter. It will be useful, however, to briefly consider a few topics peripheral to the question of what is truth or fact and basic to the point of view I wish to take concerning the matrix of health, manpower, and age. We proceed with much caution, but optimistically recall Aristotle's observation: "The search for truth is in one way hard and in another easy. For it is evident that no one can master it fully nor miss it wholly" (Aristotle, *Metaphysics* ii. 1).

In the study of populations, one idea or concept which has come into being is that of the working population or the labor force. To millions of people the concept "labor force" has meaning. It may be a fact that a survey of the United States estimates that 64,020,000 people are employed and 4,150,000 are unemployed in the week ending nearest January 15, 1960. It may also be a fact that administrative reports show that for this week benefits were paid to 2,200,000 "insured" unemployed people in the country. And it may also be a fact that employers paid Social Security taxes for 51,000,000 employees for the same week. If these are facts, they certainly have some relevance to the size and composition of the labor force in the United States. These numbers, however, do not establish a unique concept of the labor force. This is so for many reasons. First, the concept has a different meaning for demographers, merchants, labor union leaders, military people, Communists, and so on; within each of these groups, the concept differs for each member. It is often different from one objective to another, and certainly it varies from one time to another. Second, although these meanings are not necessarily inconsistent, they are not obviously consistent; they may even appear contradictory. A third aspect of the numerous, sometimes conflicting, meanings for a single concept is the degree of relevance. For example, in a country which insures unemployment of workers only in manufacturing industries when most workers are engaged in agriculture, the number of insured unemployed people has only minor relevance as an indicator of total unemployment.

There is another important link in our chain of effort to realize the truth. This is the relationship between even a rigidly defined concept and its associated facts and the measurement which is made of the factual phenomenon. The word "measurement" is used here in a very broad sense. It is intended to include all rational processes for determining whether the specified phenomenon exists and to what extent or in what amount. It includes such methods as personal speculation, laboratory experiment, and statistical evaluation. Whatever method is used, the measurement process is subject to uncertainty and error, perhaps large, perhaps small. Some processes are clearly superior to others. Some are convincing and widely accepted; others seem less reliable and have little persuasive effect. Many people rate as stronger the methods which are sufficiently controlled to permit at least some evaluation of the resulting measurement.

My purpose in making this excursion into the realm of facts, truth, concepts, and measurement is to emphasize that the determination of facts is a difficult process for a number of reasons, but especially because truth itself has many facets and the recognition or measurement of any one of them is often difficult.

## HEALTH AND THE WORK STATUS
## OF THE AGING

The title of this paper—"The Matrix of Health, Manpower, and Age"—might suggest a mathematically precise functional relation of three social variables. That is not the intention of the title. The relation of these factors is multidimensional and highly complex. It cannot be expressed in a single equation or statistic nor even in a single mode of evaluation. The economist will emphasize one set of features, the sociologist a completely different set; still other aspects will gain the attention of the physician or psychologist.

Every point of view has its own importance. It would serve no purpose to attempt to rate them on relative merit. Rather, it is my immediate purpose to consider the subsequent remarks against a broad, changing background and to seek an interpretation which accepts the idea that truth in this complex topic is many-sided and which stresses that contrasting points of view are not only acceptable, but even necessary, to an understanding of the relation of health, manpower, and age.

### Three Modes of Viewing Health

Another illustration of this thesis is the way information about health can be expressed in separate forms. Consider the matter of days spent in bed as a consequence of illness. The presence of disease and associated bed days is a vital matter to the person with the disease. The first form, then, of the three forms of information is that of the individual case: the medical diagnosis, the treatment, and the social, psychological, and financial impact on the person who is ill and on the people who are close to him. This type of information is unique to each person and condition; it is of paramount importance to the individual, and it cannot be reflected in statistical terms because it is unique. When one seeks to draw conclusions from statistics about health, he should never lose sight of this first form of information, which is critical to the individual.

A second form of information is the global statistic, which attempts to present a summary of the total phenomenon. In the case of our example, a typical measure is the annual number of bed-days owing to illness experienced by people over sixty-five in the United States. An estimate of this number for the year ending June, 1958, is 237,000,000. This, it seems to me, is large in social or economic terms. Converted into the usual 250 working days a year, it represents a direct annual loss by the patients themselves of nearly one million man-years of potential manpower, to say nothing of the additional loss of time contributed by people who cared for the ill. The monetary cost of these days in bed is highly speculative, but certainly it is large—possibly five or ten billion dollars.

An aggregate, however, is usually a number without scale, and thus it is difficult to evaluate for many purposes. A third form of information—some relative measure—is needed. In health statistics the relative number often is expressed in the incidence, prevalence, or experience *per person,* and it is given greater perspective by comparison of the rate for a defined group with corresponding rates for other groups. Thus, for the group over sixty-five, the 1958 rate of days in bed per person has been estimated at 16.3. This compares with a rate of 7.8 days for all people in the United States and with a rate of 5.2 days for males under five living on farms in the United States (U.S. National Health Survey, 1959c).

The choice of descriptive statistic relatives can direct attention to entirely different aspects of a phenomenon. Note what a contrasting picture to the foregoing is obtained when one looks at another rate involving the same bed-day experience of people over sixty-five. From June, 1957, to June, 1958, people over sixty-five spent some 237,000,000 days in bed because of illness; they also lived about five billion days *not* in bed. Thus they spent only about 4 per cent of the year in bed because of illness. This same fact is reflected, though not emphasized, by the annual rate of 16.3 days in bed per person.

Analysis of these and other rates imparts a balance and significance to information which data on aggregates do not tell.

### Definition of Health

Three ways of viewing the fairly specific health phenomenon of days spent in bed because of illness have been noted. Earlier we said that it was not easy to convert the concept "working population" into a unique measurable phenomenon. The corresponding translation for the concept "health" is even more formidable. Health or the absence of health is very difficult to define. The formulation of a procedure for measuring health is difficult. As implied above, this circumstance has resulted in widespread recognition that many measures of health and illness can coexist, each being more appropriate for certain purposes than for others.

Suppose a person is given an extensive medical and physical examination. Such an examination would reveal the presence or absence of certain morbid conditions. Positive findings might lead to a particular diagnosis and to the declaration that the patient was ill. The conditions revealed would depend not only on their existence in some undefined, real sense, but also on the nature of the examination and perhaps on the skill of the doctors, nurses, and technicians administering the examination. The possible outcomes could be elaborated at length. Generally speaking, the judgments of physicians and clinicians are accepted, although the physician's diagnosis or prognosis is usually subject to some uncertainty. It should be made clear that the uncertainty of diagnosis is not merely a function of the state of medicine and of the practice and ability of the physician, but also of the fact that for extremely obscure reasons a given pattern of physical conditions will affect the health of individuals in differing ways.

In quite a different manner, the health of a person can be judged not by the pronouncement of his physician, but by the actions he takes. At any time, a person may or may not go about his usual activities. He may stay in bed; he may consult a physician; he may be absent from his regular job; he may take medication; he may not be able to sleep or eat; he may use a wheel chair, a crutch, or eyeglasses; he may be unable to lift weights; he may be very active and have apparently unlimited energy; he may die. Many of these actions can be considered observable facts and can form the basis of fairly objective measures of physical well-being.

Among the many other possibilities for evaluating the health of a person, let us note one more. This is the "subjective determination." It is vague, sometimes amorphous, but still it is very real. It may be a determination made by a person about himself; it may be rational or irrational. It can range over a wide spectrum from physical or mental helplessness to a man's ingrained belief that he is, has been, and is likely to continue to be in perfect health with almost unlimited stamina. The determination can grow out of an identifiable physical or physiological fact, or it may have a more obscure origin. The subjective determination may also be about another person. In fact, we all make judgments of this sort about others. Again, the judgment may rest on such specific evidence as the other person's statements about his health, our opinions of his appearance and vitality, our assessment of his strength or productivity, or some vaguer, composite impression that he is sickly or in "topnotch" health. Of course, these subjective determinations reflect, or perhaps are induced by, the lack of exact correspondence between a physical condition and the effect of that condition upon a specific person. Any minor hurt will substantially incapacitate some people, yet I have interviewed a fifty-year-old man, completely blind for forty years, who maintained—and, I think, believed—that his activity was in no way limited.

Below I look more closely at some of the current efforts being made in the United States to measure the health of the population. Before doing so, however, it is necessary to consider the types of information available in the past about the relation of health, age, and manpower. This review seeks to recall some of the principal sources of information and is restricted to the United States and major statistical undertakings; thus it omits much that might be pertinent to a full understanding of the relation of health, age, and manpower. Laboratory findings, the mass of unsummarized personal experience, and thousands of smaller studies—usually local—are all omitted.

## The Population and the Work Force

The cornerstone of much demographic work in the United States is the decennial population census. This constitutionally required count has been taken every ten years, beginning in 1790.

In the census of 1790, there was a crude and incomplete classification of people by age. The age breakdown was sponsored by James Madison, who had proposed collection of several other items, including occupation, which was not surveyed. On February 8, 1790, the *Boston Gazette* reported:

> Mr. Livermore apprehended that this plan . . . divided the people into classes too minute to be readily ascertained. For example, many . . . pursued two, three or four occupations, but which was the principal one depended on the season of the year . . . : some followed weaving in

the spring and summer, but the making of shoes was most predominant in the fall and winter; under what class are these people to be thrown, especially if they joined husbandry and carpenter's work with the rest?

By 1820, however, the census was recording the number of people in agriculture, commerce, and manufacturing. Collections in recent decades have shown status in the labor force by class of worker, industry, and occupation for all classes of people by sex, age, residence, and other sociodemographic characteristics.

As early as 1840, the census asked for the number of people in the household who were deaf and dumb or blind. In several subsequent censuses, each person was classified as deaf and dumb, blind, insane, or idiotic. In 1890, the census asked each person whether he was suffering from an acute or chronic disease (plus the name of disease and the length of time afflicted); whether he was defective in mind, sight, hearing, or speech; or whether he was crippled, maimed, or deformed (plus the name of defect).

Analysts are grateful for the census data. These data permit a description of the population in detail which no other procedure has matched. With respect to number of people by age, status in the work force, and occupation, the consensus has been that these figures are useful. Collection of this information continued in the 1960 census. A differing result has obtained for the data on morbidity or health. Here students found the census procedure unsatisfactory, and the census has not been used for that purpose for the past seventy years, except for a 1910 count of the blind or deaf and dumb.

The census is taken at ten-year intervals, but data are needed at more frequent intervals. Furthermore, the decennial census data on labor force are not sufficiently precise for many purposes. Until 1960, they were being collected by crews of relatively untrained temporary enumerators. These enumerators have not always been able to cope with the complex definitions of labor force, unemployment, or occupation.

Although there has been much speculation about the employment status of the general population at intervals between the decennial censuses, prior to 1940 most of these efforts were quite inadequate, judged by present standards. For example, looking for a count of the unemployed in 1937, the Social Security Board was forced to conclude, "Because of a lack of any reliable periodic count for the unemployed, a comparison of a number of different estimates is advisable" and present a range of six to nine million unemployed for August, 1937 (U.S. Social Security Board, 1938, p. 86).

A new era was introduced in 1939 by a group in the Works Progress Administration, especially Howard B. Myers, John N. Webb, M. Starr Northrop, J. Stevens Stock, and Lester R. Frankel. This group instituted frequent, periodic, direct sampling of persons in the population to determine their work-force status. The immediate product of this effort was the "monthly report on unemployment." This direct monthly sampling has continued to the present, the content being modified from time to time and the methodology being refined almost continually. In 1942 the sampling was transferred to the Bureau of the Census, where it remains. Since the summer of 1959, the Labor Department has been responsible for the budget, content, analysis, and publication of what is now called the "Monthly Report on the Labor Force" ("MRLF"). The "MRLF" has striking advantages as a source of information. By taking advantage of modern sampling methods, it secures economy in time, personnel, and cost, and, by using a small force of highly trained interviewers, it is able to produce results of higher quality than is possible in a complete enumeration.

A different measure of employment has its origin in the payroll records of business establishments. Because this source usually omits distinctions by age, we shall treat it briefly, although it does, perhaps, furnish more information on employment, pay, and hours of work than any other system in use. The most prominent use of payroll data is found in the Bureau of Labor Statistics' (BLS) 790 Program. This is a joint endeavor of the federal and state governments. Payroll information is reported monthly by more than one hundred thousand employers for over sixteen million employees. More than thirteen thousand monthly statistical series are maintained by the program, presenting data in extensive geographical and industrial detail on number of people employed, their hours of work, and their earnings (U.S. Bureau of Labor Statistics, 1955-1960).

Important sources of supplementary data on employer payrolls are the industrial and commercial censuses taken by the Bureau of the Census, the tax returns of employers under the Social Security plans, and the reports from pseudopublic utilities to regulatory commissions. Publications of the U.S. Department of Labor give additional illustrations of the use of business records to provide labor-force data (U.S. Bureau of Employment Security, 1950-1960; U.S. Bureau of Employment Security, 1957-1960; U.S. Bureau of Labor Statistics, 1954a; U.S. Bureau of Labor Statistics, 1954b).

Passing over many other useful sources of information on labor-force status, note must be taken of one technique of special significance for the study of work-force status by age. This is the technique of the *Tables of Working Life* (U.S. Bureau of Labor Statistics, 1950). Working-life tables represent the overlay of ordinary life tables by worker rates or ratios of labor force to population at specific ages. They can be constructed for various categories of the population and, aided by such concepts as the probability of retiring at a given age and working-life expectancy, permit an efficiently organized description of the labor force. A desirable addition would be the frequency of illness or physical incapacity as the cause of retirement.

This concludes the review of the leading sources of data on the work force in the population. In human affairs, however, statistical knowledge is never sufficient despite the scope, quality, and detail of information in this area.

### Health Data for the Population

The inventory of sources of health data for the population will be abridged for two reasons. The first is that an excellent concise history of morbidity surveys has been published (Collins, 1951), and it has an extensive bibliography. Listings of principal undertakings since 1951 are also available (U.S. National Health Survey, 1958b). The second reason is the surprisingly limited amount of summarized statistical data on health.

Prior to 1956, principal efforts in the United States in assembling data on morbidity, aside from points already noted, can be summarized under seven headings: (1) illness data in records of insurance companies—limited, of course, to their coverages; (2) military records; (3) mortality data—valuable, but diluted as health statistics by uncertain correlations between cause of death and previous health condition; (4) communicable disease reports; (5) hospital admissions and discharges; (6) panels of physicians and pharmacists; and (7) direct surveys of households, families, and people.

Especially important early work in the latter field has been done by Edgar Sydenstricker (Sydenstricker, 1925; Sydenstricker, Wheeler, & Goldberger, 1918) and by the Committee on Costs of Medical Care in the period 1928-1931 (Collins, 1944). Notable recent contributions are reported for Baltimore (Collins, Phillips, & Oliver, 1951; Commission on Chronic Illness, 1957), San Jose and California (California Department of Public Health, 1954-1955), Kansas City (Peterson, 1958), and Hunterdon County (Commission on Chronic Illness, 1959).

The most prominent landmark in the history of house-to-house canvassing for determining morbidity was the National Health Survey of 1935-1936. This survey was conducted by the U.S. Public Health Service with a grant from the Works Progress Administration. It was a single-visit survey for information on illness and impairments; it covered two million people in eighty-three cities in eighteen states. It sought to distinguish between mild ailments and ailments which were sufficiently severe to cause inability to work or pursue usual activities for seven or more days of the previous year.

### The U.S. National Committee on
### Vital and Health Statistics

In response to a resolution of the World Health Organization, an advisory U.S. National Committee on Vital and Health Statistics was appointed in 1949. From its inception this committee was concerned with formulating specific issues and problems in matters of morbidity and finding better ways of resolving them. By 1951 the committee reached the point at which a Subcommittee on National Morbidity Survey was appointed to define morbidity and to draft a plan for a national morbidity survey. Both the parent committee under the chairmanship of Lowell J. Reed and the subcommittee under the chairmanship of W. Thurber Fales were composed of public-health experts and distinguished statisticians. The subcommittee worked for two years and in 1953 produced its *Proposal for Collection of Data on Illness and Impairments, United States* (U.S. National Committee on Vital and Health Statistics, 1953).

The subcommittee reviewed the uses of morbidity and related data, the types of data needed, and the existing sources of information in the United States and other countries. By 1952, national surveys had been taken in Canada, Denmark, Great Britain, and Japan.

We have observed how difficult it can be to satisfactorily define health or morbidity for the purposes of measurement. The subcommittee was of the same opinion and concluded that no precise, limited definition of the term "morbidity" would be offered. It held that morbidity should remain a general word used to designate both manifest and non-manifest illness, injuries, and impairments. It recommended that an operational definition of morbidity be adopted for any specific objective and that such definitions should vary from one situation to another.

The subcommitee recommended three principal ways to get better information on health and morbidity: (1) A continuing morbidity survey by household sampling of the general population should be undertaken; (2) Data on undiagnosed and non-manifest diseases should be obtained by laboratory tests and physical examinations; and (3) Methodological research should be undertaken to discover improved or auxiliary processes for measuring morbidity.

## THE U.S. NATIONAL HEALTH SURVEY

In 1955 the federal Department of Health, Education, and Welfare drafted—and President Eisenhower submitted to Congress—a plan for collecting data on morbidity for the United States population. This plan closely followed the recommendations of the subcommittee. With bipartisan support in Congress it was enacted in July, 1956 (P.L. 652).

Several provisions of the law deserve special mention for their impact on data relating age and health. The most important of these is that the surgeon general of the Public Health Service is directed to maintain a *continuing* survey to provide statistical information on the amount, distribution, and effects of illness and disability in the United States and the services received for these conditions. The law also recognizes the difficulty of this task and the need for more powerful measuring techniques and, therefore, explicitly directs that methodological research be a part of the program. The legislation is very broad in outlining objectives and needs, but specifically authorizes an analysis of health by age, ability to work or pursue other activities, and occupation; by duration of handicapping illness, injury, or impairment; and by amounts and types of services received for morbid conditions.

In his office the surgeon general established the U.S. National Health Survey (NHS) to seek the goals outlined by Congress.

### Leading Tenets of NHS Policy

In order to understand the NHS program, it is necessary to know a few of the principles which govern the activities of the survey.

It has been emphasized that there is no unique determination of health. This principle is fully accepted by the NHS. The NHS is not a single survey, but a group of projects which are expected to present a useful statistical summary of illness, injuries, impairments, and related health matters of the civilian population of the United States. Although, in the interests of economy in communications, an NHS publication may state, "Heart conditions range from a low rate of 5 per 1,000 persons in the group under twenty-five years of age to a high of 186 per 1,000 for those over seventy-five years of age," a more extended reading of NHS releases will reveal how frequently appears the warning that any health statistic is the product of the procedure which brings it into being and that another procedure emphasizing a different aspect might produce differing results.

Continuity and comparability of estimates for different time periods are desired objectives, but they do not have overriding priority. A substantial part of the resources and energy of the NHS, at least during its early years, is being devoted to studying and evaluating the quality of data input, the efficiency of collection and processing, and the usefulness of output. Guided by active criticism and research efforts, the National Health Survey operates a program which changes as the need for scope, content, method, and specific product changes.

The choice of the phenomena to be measured and the general techniques for attempting the measurement necessarily represent judgment rather than chance. However, a central tenet of the NHS is that it does not advocate any particular health doctrine or policy. The survey is an impartial fact-finding agent. With substantial aid from governmental and public advisory committees which represent many points of view, the survey attempts to present evidence in as unbiased a manner as its ability allows. In particular, social and medical interpretation is left to users. The survey also believes that it is a service unit in the sense that it has a general responsibility to establish and maintain machinery for the collection of health data needed by its users.

A substantial portion of the NHS budget and staff is devoted to maintaining statistical control over collection procedures, evaluating the product, and searching for improved methods. Thus, at any time the survey may be publishing an estimated incidence rate for acute disease, trying to discover how precise the estimate is, and seeking a better way to make future estimates.

Although it is not characteristic of every NHS project, most survey activities measure a defined health condition for the entire civilian population rather than just the sick population. It is believed that analysis is better balanced when it is known, for example, that although one hundred million days per year are spent in bed because of impairments, nearly 90 per cent of the population reports no impairment.

### The Household-Interview Survey

One of the major projects of the NHS is a continuing household-interview survey of the civilian noninstitutional population. This interview survey is the main source of data offered in this paper, partly because the household survey is especially appropriate for the purpose and partly because it is the most advanced project of the National Health Survey. The statistical design, concepts, and definitions of the survey are explained in considerable detail in official publications (U.S. National Health Survey, 1958c; U.S. National Health Survey, 1958d).

There are limitations to the accuracy of diagnostic and other information gathered in household interviews. At best, the diagnostic information the household respondent can give to the interviewer is only the information the physician has given to the family. For conditions that are not medically attended, diagnostic information is often no more than a description of symptoms. However, other facts—such as those concerning the circumstances and consequences of illness or injury and the resulting action taken or sought by the individual—can be obtained more accurately from household members than from any other source, since only the people concerned are in a position to report all of this information. Furthermore, this type of survey greatly facilitates comparison of the sick and well populations and assessment of the impacts of a variety of illnesses and impairments.

The framework of the household survey rests on what, in technical terms, may be called a "stratified multistage probability design" for a continuous sampling of the noninstitutional civilian population of the United States. The first stage of this process consists of selection of 503 of the approximately one thousand nine hundred areas or primary sampling units (PSU) into which the United States has been divided. In a series of steps, a random clustered sample of households is selected in each of the chosen PSU's. The households are in compact geographical areas which contain an average of about six dwelling units. For all people in the sample households, personal interview data are obtained on illness, injuries, impairments; on use of medical, dental, and hospital facilities; and on related health matters.

The interview survey is not only a continuing project, but also has, from the statisticians's viewpoint, the striking characteristic of being *continuous*. The survey is not a one-time tally of the population nor an intermittent activity, but goes on all the time. This is accomplished in the following manner. Each week a sample of about seven hundred households (or twenty-three hundred people) is drawn in such a manner that, despite its small size, it is representative of the national population and is additive with other similarly selected weekly samples. For example, a week's sample may be used alone or combined with thirteen or fifty-two other weekly samples. In a year, the process includes some thirty-eight thousand households and one hundred and twenty thousand people. Thus the design permits both continuous measurement of characteristics of high prevalence or incidence in the population, and, through the larger, consolidated samples, more detailed analysis of less common characteristics and small categories. A week's sample is of little value in studying the problems of older people, for it contains, on the average, only two hundred persons sixty-five or older. But in a twenty-four-month period, interviews are obtained for more than twenty thousand people sixty-five and over.

Under the terms of its enabling and appropriation acts, the National Health Survey plans the content and general formation of the household-interview survey and sets specifications for sampling and interviewing. The Bureau of the Census selects the sample, conducts the interviewing, and carries through a partial processing of the data. Statistical editing and estimation are accomplished on high-speed electronic computers programmed by NHS and maintained by the Bureau of the Census. Analysis and publication of results are duties of the Public Health Service.

Interviews with all people in the sample households are sought. Each person eighteen or older who is available at the time of the interview is interviewed for himself. Proxy respondents are accepted for children and for adults who are not available at the time of the interview provided that the respondent is closely related to the person about whom information is being sought. Interviewers are laymen specially trained to handle the health questionnaires. Aside from statistical advantages, the continuous character of the survey permits use of a much better trained and controlled group of interviewers than an intermittent plan would.

The questionnaire is a structured set of more than one hundred inquiries. The number of questions varies with each respondent. At any time, the questions may be grouped into two categories: one contains questions which are barely changed for several years, the other has questions which change more frequently. Some questions do not apply to everyone. Typically, the questionnaire has about forty items for identification of households and people and sociodemographic description of respondents. This block includes such items as location, population density of the community, nature of the dwelling unit, age, sex, birthplace, marital status, relation to head of household, education, military experience, work-force status, and income. A group of about a dozen illness-recall inquiries follows; the purpose of this group is to reveal any instances of morbidity which the person experienced in the reference period.

For the most part, the remaining questions elicit information about the health conditions identified in the recall part of the interview. The questions seek to discover such facts as whether the condition was medically attended; what the diagnosis is; whether the condition caused restriction of activity, confinement in bed, or work loss; whether it led to other limitations in daily behavior; what use has been made of dentists, physicians, and hospitals.

## The Health-Examination Survey

A second major phase of NHS activity is a health-examination survey. In this continuing project, a probability sample of people from the noninstitutional civilian population is given a limited physical examination. Contrasted with the household-interview survey, in which a third of a million persons have been interviewed, the health-examination survey is just beginning. As currently planned, the examination survey will proceed in stages; the first stage, which included examination of about six thousand people, was completed in the fall of 1962.

The health-examination survey is intensive rather than extensive and is directed at information for which a household interview is not appropriate. The examination secures such physical and physiological measurements as weight, height, blood pressure, visual acuity, a hearing test, several blood analyses, skinfolds, frame measurements. Additional tests are a twelve-lead electrocardiogram, a dental examination, a glucose-tolerance test, a medical history, a limited general physical examination, and X rays of hands, feet, and chest. The primary immediate objectives in the first stage are to obtain distributions of the population—well and unwell—by the measured physical and physiological characteristics and to arrive at estimates of prevalence of certain classes of impairments and chronic conditions, with special emphasis on cardiovascular, arthritic, and rheumatic conditions.

The pattern of the first stage of this project calls for examination of groups of approximately one hundred and fifty persons at some forty general locations in the United States. The procedure involves teams of fifteen, including physicians, nurses, a dentist, laboratory technicians, interviewers, receptionists, administrative aides, and a clerk.

Hopefully, the examination project will yield health data never before available for a general population. It should complement the picture obtained in household interviewing.

### Additional Undertakings

The present account will forego description of purely methodological activities and evaluative projects of the National Health Survey. A partial listing of endeavors under these heads was published in *Proceedings of the Social Statistics Section of the American Statistical Association, 1959* (Simmons, 1959).

Other substantive surveys are likely to be undertaken by the National Health Survey, although it would be premature to say what they will be. Currently three projects are under way. Through a direct sampling of hospital discharge records, one seeks greater precision in diagnosis and associated matters for hospitalized cases. A second deals with morbidity histories of deceased people. (The household-interview survey treats only the living population.) If one is interested in the health, say, in the three months prior to a specified date, interviewing people who were living then may closely approximate the desired result. But for such experiences as hospital days, the deceased may have contributed a substantial share. For this reason, pilot work has begun in sampling death certificates and following hospital morbidity for sample cases. A third area is the health of the civilian institutional population.

### DATA ON AGE, HEALTH, AND WORK STATUS

A look at summary figures on age, health, and the work force will be helpful in fixing the scale of our topic in a few dimensions of possible interest. Rounded numbers are given since the purpose is to focus attention on magnitude rather than on more analytic matters.

There will here be no debate about who should be included in the group "older persons." For convenience, many of the following statistics apply to the group sixty-five or older. In some cases, data are presented for younger groups, and in some the sixty-five–plus group is divided into more than one class. Many topics will be best understood when separate data are presented for the entire population in five-year intervals. Unless otherwise indicated, data presented refer to the United States for the period 1957-1960. No projections are presented, although some of the magnitudes will be altered substantially, even in the next decade.

The United States has a civilian noninstitutional population of roughly 176,000,000, of which something like 9 per cent, or more than 15,000,000, are over sixty-five. About one-third of these are over seventy-five. About 20 per cent of the population, or another 35,000,-000, is in the age range from forty-five to sixty-four. Of the group sixty-five or older, a little over 3,000,000 are classified by the "Monthly Report on the Labor Force" as employed, with another 6,000,000 or 7,000,000 keeping house. The remainder is largely retired or unemployed, including roughly 1,000,000 classified as "unable to work." (U.S. Bureau of Labor Statistics, 1960)

The NHS household-interview survey uses a different method for classifying people by work-force status, placing emphasis on "usual activity" in the twelve months prior to the interview rather than on status in a recent week, as is done in the "MRLF." Under NHS definitions, a little under 3,000,000 of the sixty-five plus group were reported as usually working in the previous year, about 6,000,000 were usually keeping house, and another 6,000,000 fell into the other groups. Well over 5,000,000 of the last block are reported as retired. Better than 2,000,000 of the people sixty-five and over are reported in the NHS as "cannot work at all" and another 3,000,000 as "limited in amount or kind of work" they can perform.

Both the above figures and those which follow exclude the institutional population, partly because concepts suitable for the noninstitutional population often are not appropriate for the institutional population. But, further, summary data on the institutional population are extremely limited. The 1950 census reported 2 per cent of the people sixty-five to sixty-nine and nearly 4 per cent of those seventy and over to be in institutions (Sheldon, 1958).

In Table 1 a selection of rates and percentages which display several features of the relation between age and work force or health has been assembled.

### Data from the Household Interviews

Most health data from the NHS household interviews may be put into one of five classes. In each class, statistics are usually published by sex, age, residence, marital status, usual activity, family

## TABLE 1
### SELECTED RATES AND PERCENTAGES RELATING TO WORK-FORCE STATUS AND DISABILITY DAYS OF UNITED STATES POPULATION BY AGE CLASSES, 1957-1959

| Sex and age | Approximate percentage of corresponding total civilian noninstitutional population | Labor-force-participation percentage* | Percentage in civilian noninstitutional population† | | | Disability days per person per year† | Work-loss days per person per year because of health† |
|---|---|---|---|---|---|---|---|
| | | | Usually working | Keeping house | Others‡ | | |
| **Both sexes** | | | | | | | |
| 25-44 | 27 | 68 | 62 | 34 | 4 | 5.3 | 4.0 |
| 45-54 | 12 | 72 | 66 | 30 | 4 | 6.4 | 5.8 |
| 55-64 | 9 | 62 | 56 | 34 | 10 | 9.3 | 6.5 |
| 65-74 | 6 | } 22 | 24 | 41 | 35 | 11.6 | 3.9 |
| 75 and over | 3 | | 8 | 36 | 56 | 19.4 | 1.7 |
| **Male** | | | | | | | |
| 25-44 | 26 | 98 | 94 | – | 6 | 4.0 | 5.2 |
| 45-54 | 12 | 96 | 93 | – | 7 | 5.3 | 7.9 |
| 55-64 | 9 | 88 | 84 | – | 16 | 8.4 | 9.7 |
| 65-74 | 5 | } 35 | 39 | – | 61 | 11.8 | 6.8 |
| 75 and over | 3 | | 17 | – | 83 | 16.4 | 2.8 |

| Female | | | | | | | |
|---|---|---|---|---|---|---|---|
| 25–44 | 27 | 41 | 32 | 66 | 2 | 6.6 | 2.9 |
| 45–54 | 12 | 50 | 40 | 58 | 2 | 7.5 | 3.7 |
| 55–64 | 9 | 37 | 30 | 66 | 4 | 10.1 | 3.6 |
| 65–74 | 6 | {11 | 10 | 78 | 12 | 11.4 | 1.5 |
| 75 and over | 3 | | 3 | 64 | 33 | 21.7 | 0.8 |

*U.S. Bureau of Labor Statistics (1960). Figures in the table are typical.
†U.S. National Health Survey (1960e).
‡Includes 6,000,000 retired persons.

income, and, occasionally, other factors. The classes are prevalence; incidence; use of medical, dental, and hospital facilities; disability days; and limitation of activity and mobility.

*Prevalence.* Through a series of illness-recall questions, an estimate is made of the proportion of the population which reports, at the time of interview, an injury, impairment, or chronic illness. Through additional inquiries, the conditions become the focal point for other determinations: for example, whether a condition has been medically attended, and what the diagnosis is. For many reasons, reported conditions will differ from those which would be revealed by clinical examinations. To mention two, the respondent may not be aware of the condition or of its diagnosis, or, if aware, he may prefer not to admit to what he may consider a socially threatening condition such as mental illness or hemorrhoids. Detailed evaluation of interview results suggests that correspondence between data from household interviews and records of medical service varies with the degree of inconvenience to the patient and the volume of medical service entailed by the condition (Sagen, Dunham, & Simmons, 1960).

A chronic condition is either one on a check list of thirty-five ailments (for example, heart trouble, tuberculosis, cerebral palsy) or an ailment present sometime in the previous two weeks, but with an onset more than three months before. Other conditions are classified as acute.

About 52 per cent of the people from twenty-five to forty-four report no chronic condition, 40 per cent of the people from forty-five to sixty-four report no chronic condition, and 23 per cent of the people sixty-five or over report no chronic condition. In the older group, then, 77 per cent reports one or more chronic conditions. Almost one-third of the sixty-five–plus group reports the presence of three or more conditions.

For many reasons, the National Health Survey has been unwilling either to rank diagnoses as to relative frequency or to state without rather detailed qualification absolute prevalence figures for specific diagnoses. But once again a few statistics for the group sixty-five or older will suggest the impact of health. More than 1 of every 4, or a total of almost 4,000,000 people, report arthritis or rheumatism. Four million also report high blood pressure or heart disease. Nearly 3,000,000 report hearing impairment.

*Incidence.* Incidence is the number of onsets of illness for some specified time. In the NHS, incidence rates are usually restricted to acute illness and are expressed in the number of conditions per person per year. Incidence statistics compiled from household interviews are influenced by the length of reference or recall period in the interview (Nisselson & Woolsey, 1959). For most items, the NHS uses a two-week recall period. One of the striking characteristics of incidence data on acute conditions classified for age is that the rates for older people are no higher than those for other mature adults and, in some situations, may be lower. The reported incidence rate for persons sixty-five and over is about 1.5 acute conditions per person per year, and, in the first eight quarters of NHS interviewing, it has remained rather stable, the maximum rate (at the peak of the Asian flu epidemic of 1957-1958) being less than twice the minimum rate at any other time in the two-year period. For the remainder of the population, the incidence rate for the Asian flu peak was about three times the observed minimum (U.S. National Health Survey, 1958a; U.S. National Health Survey, 1960e).

*Use of Medical, Dental, and Hospital Facilities.* Use of health facilities is the result of the volume of illness, availability of the facility, and extent of resources of the patient for purchase of service. The NHS seeks to measure use in such terms as number of medical consultations, number of visits to a dentist, and number of hospital discharges per person per year. Statistically these measures are computed like incidence rates, although that term is seldom applied to them. The National Health Survey has published detailed studies for each of the services (U.S. National Health Survey, 1958e; U.S. National Health Survey, 1958k; U.S. National Health Survey, 1960b; U.S. National Health Survey, 1960c). These publications present such facts as: (1) Consultations with a physician gradually increase with age, averaging about five a year for the entire population and about seven a year for people over sixty-five. (2) Visits to a physician are less frequent in rural, non-farm areas than they are in cities, and they are still less frequent in farm areas. (3) The average number of visits to a dentist varies markedly with income, ranging from a little over one visit in two years for families with incomes under $2,000 to 2.5 visits a year for families with annual incomes of $7,000 or more. (4) When maternity cases are excluded, the annual hospital discharge rate per 1,000 people steadily increases with age from fifty-three for children under fifteen to 120 for people between sixty-five and seventy-four and 125 for people over seventy-five. Number of days in hospitals shows a still more striking differential, the annual figure per 1,000 children being 300 and that for people seventy-five and over being 2,000. (5) The discharge rate for people sixty-five or older is higher for white than for non-white people; higher for people with family incomes over $7,000 than for people with smaller incomes; higher for urban areas than for farm areas; about the same for men as for women. (6) For women and men over sixty-five, roughly 40 per cent of hospital discharges have followed stays which included surgery.

These data on hospitals exclude information from institutions in which most patients stay for more than thirty days.

*Disability Days.* In the household-interview survey, one of the most significant measures of morbidity is the estimate of days of disability because of health. The NHS currently uses three such measures. These derive from three inquiries pursued for each condition mentioned in the interview:

1. "Last week or the week before did [this condition] cause you to cut down on your usual activities for as much as a day?" The resulting measure is called "restricted-activity days."

2. "How many of these [days] were you in bed all or most of the day?" This measure is referred to as "bed days."

3. "Last week or the week before would you have been working at a job or business except for [this condition]? If 'yes,' how many days did this condition keep you from work?" This measure is referred to as "work-loss days."

For people six to sixteen, "work-loss days" are called "school-loss days."

The household interview is especially suitable for approaching the matter of disability days since it covers the entire population; since the respondent is in a particularly favorable position to know whether he spent a day in bed; and since this approach permits maximum classification by sociodemographic and economic factors. Table 2 offers summary data on disability days from the interview survey for the period July, 1957, to June, 1959 (see also Table 1).

Note may be taken of a half-dozen facts: (1) People sixty-five or over annually have some 600,000,000 days of restricted activity, 200,000,000 bed days of disability, and about 50,000,000 work-loss days. (2) For the population classified as usually working, the increase with age in bed days and work-loss days per person, is moderate. The surface evidence is that workers who maintain usually-working status through age seventy-four experience only a fractional increase over younger workers in days of disability. (3) The bed days for the retired group and the "other" group (which includes those who are unable to work) is different. With age there is an increase in disability loss,

## TABLE 2
### SUMMARY DATA ON DISABILITY DAYS, 1957-1959

| Sex and age | Annual disability days per year (in millions) | | | Annual bed days per person for people whose usual status is | | | | Annual work loss days per person for people whose usual status is | | | |
|---|---|---|---|---|---|---|---|---|---|---|---|
| | Restricted-activity days | Bed days | Work-loss days | Working | Keeping house | Retirement | Other | Working | Keeping house | Retirement | Other |
| **Both sexes** | | | | | | | | | | | |
| 25-44 | 660 | 244 | 183 | 4.2 | - | - | 13.1 | 5.3 | - | - | 8.6 |
| 45 and over | 1,417 | 475 | 258 | 4.9 | - | 19.7 | 30.8 | 7.8 | - | 2.1 | 15.6 |
| 45-54 | 377 | 128 | 114 | 4.5 | - | 29.8 | 22.0 | 6.9 | - | 14.1 | 17.4 |
| 55-64 | 414 | 139 | 97 | 5.4 | - | 24.6 | 32.2 | 8.7 | - | 7.5 | 19.5 |
| 65-74 | 371 | 112 | 38 | 4.9 | - | 16.1 | 31.7 | 10.0 | - | 1.6 | 13.9 |
| 75 and over | 254 | 96 | 8 | 6.8 | - | 22.4 | 45.4 | 8.8 | - | 0.8 | 5.8 |
| **Male** | | | | | | | | | | | |
| 45-54 | 157 | 51 | 77 | 4.2 | - | 23.2 | 20.0 | 7.2 | - | 17.5 | 18.8 |
| 55-64 | 180 | 60 | 69 | 5.1 | - | 21.1 | 30.2 | 8.4 | - | 7.4 | 24.8 |
| 65-74 | 173 | 53 | 31 | 5.0 | - | 15.0 | 28.9 | 11.6 | - | 1.8 | 21.6 |
| 75 and over | 98 | 35 | 6 | 7.5 | - | 16.7 | 39.5 | 8.9 | - | 0.9 | 16.2 |
| **Female** | | | | | | | | | | | |
| 45-54 | 221 | 77 | 37 | 5.0 | 8.4 | 53.8 | 27.9 | 6.3 | 1.6 | - | 13.5 |
| 55-64 | 234 | 79 | 28 | 6.0 | 10.3 | 41.9 | 38.7 | 9.2 | 1.0 | 8.2 | 3.1 |
| 65-74 | 198 | 59 | 7 | 4.7 | 10.1 | 22.3 | 35.9 | 4.7 | 1.1 | 0.8 | 2.3 |
| 75 and over | 155 | 61 | 2 | 3.7 | 13.0 | 37.1 | 47.7 | 8.5 | 0.4 | 0.4 | 1.8 |

Source—U.S. National Health Survey (1960e).

although people from sixty-five to seventy-four show about the same rate of loss as the next younger group (fifty-five to sixty-four). Again there is a connection between the classification device and the statistic: some of the retired people under sixty-five retire because of ill health and, therefore, tend to experience more bed disability. (4) In the fifty-five–sixty-four group and the sixty-five–seventy-four group, withdrawal from the usually-working status as a person moves from the younger group to the older is certainly partly owing to health as measured by disability days. Only 24 per cent of the older group is classified as usually working, whereas 56 per cent of the fifty-five–sixty-four group is so labeled. The increase in over-all bed disability per person for the older group is only 25 per cent, however. (5) Data in Table 2 and other data from the household-interview survey are subject to sampling error. National Health Survey reports include measures of sampling error from all principal estimates. The sampling errors of statistics in this paper extend over a range from a fraction of 1 per cent to substantial amounts. Any figure is subject to significant sampling error, but the patterns in the tables and groups of numbers are reasonably valid as far as sampling error is concerned. (6) The data are also significantly influenced by non-sampling considerations. They are not immutables, but the product of the interviewing process. Another procedure and another set of questions would undoubtedly produce different statistics.

TABLE 3
AVERAGE ANNUAL NUMBER OF DAYS OF BED DISABILITY
PER PERSON FOR TWO AGE GROUPS AND FOUR CLASSES
OF INCOME, 1957-1959

| Age group | Annual family income | | | |
|-----------|--------|--------|--------|--------|
| | —<br>$1999 | $2000<br>3999 | $4000<br>6999 | $7000<br>and over |
| 45-54 | 11.5 | 7.7 | 5.1 | 4.2 |
| 75 and over | 19.4 | 20.9 | 18.9 | 16.1 |

Source—U.S. National Health Survey (1960e).

Connections among age, disability days, and family income are complex. Data of the type in Table 3 offer evidence on many speculative relationships. For the younger age group, the data suggest that bed disability may have made a distinct contribution to lower income. For the older group this correlation decreases. Perhaps higher family income tends to lessen per capita bed disability. Crosses of this information with data from the survey on such items as number of visits to a doctor per disability day can readily lead to more elaborate hypotheses.

*Limitation of Activity and Mobility.* Another concept of disability is utilized in the NHS attempt to determine the decree to which a person's ailments limit his activity and mobility. For limitation of activity, the person is asked to indicate which of these statements best fits him:

1. Cannot work at all at present.
2. Can work, but limited in amount or kind of work.
3. Can work, but limited in amount or kind of outside activities.
4. Not limited in any of these ways.

For housewives, the words "keep house" are substituted for "work" in these questions. For mobility, the choices, which are not related to the person's major activity, are:

1. Confined to the house all the time, except in emergencies.
2. Can go outside, but need help from another person in getting around.
3. Can go outside alone, but have trouble in getting around freely.
4. Not limited in any of these ways.

For limitation of either activity or mobility, a "yes" answer to Item 1 classifies the person as having a major limitation; "yes" to either 2 or 3, but not 1, classifies the person as partially limited. The over-all distribution of males by degree of limitation and for selected age groups is given in Table 4.

By these criteria, particularly limitation of activity, the gradient increases sharply with age. The proportion of the population with a major limitation rises from 2 per cent for the forty-five–fifty-four group to 30 per cent for those over seventy-five. Even in the sixty-five–seventy-four group the proportion with some limitation is three times that of the forty-five–fifty-four group. One-fourth of all males seventy-five or over show at least partial restriction of mobility.

As one would expect, the distribution among males by degree of limitation differs with status in the work force. For example, in the working group, 77 per cent of the males from sixty-five to seventy-four report no limitation of activity, but in the retired group, 26 per cent report partial limitation, and another 22 per cent report major limitation.

TABLE 4

DISTRIBUTION OF MALES FOR SELECTED AGE GROUPS,
1957-1959

(In percentages)

| Age | Degree of activity limitation | | | Degree of mobility limitation | | |
|-----|------|---------|-------|------|---------|-------|
|     | None | Partial | Major | None | Partial | Major |
| 45-54 | 88 | 10 | 2 | 98 | 1 | 1 |
| 55-64 | 79 | 15 | 6 | 95 | 4 | 1 |
| 65-74 | 61 | 24 | 15 | 89 | 9 | 2 |
| 75 and over | 45 | 25 | 30 | 76 | 18 | 6 |

Source—U.S. National Health Survey (1960e).

For the working group, the proportion of males with some reported limitation of activity rises steadily with age, increasing from 10 per cent for men forty-five to fifty-four to 32 per cent for men seventy-five and over. The correlation of age with limitation of activity is stronger than was the correlation between age and disability days. These facts may reflect an occupational shift into types of work which older people can carry out even with certain physical limitations.

## SUMMARY

Both individuals and societies seek to improve the health of the population. The effectiveness of the effort should be judged first by human values and second by economic and sociological considerations. Efficiency of the effort is likely to be determined by the degree to which plans and actions rest on factual evidence.

Correspondence between evidence and truth in a real world is an elusive and ambiguous relationship, difficult to establish in both philosophical and scientific domains. One should not expect to discover a simple, unique formula which explains interaction of age, health, and manpower. Rather, understanding will be promoted by multiple measurements and descriptions of health and work-force status.

Prominent modes of measurement—certainly not a complete list, however—are the processes to which attention has been called in this review. The United States is fortunate in its variety and extent of data on labor force, including decennial population censuses, quinquennial industrial censuses, annual and quarterly tax returns under Social Security systems, monthly reporting of selected items by employers, monthly sampling of the population through household interviewing, and many more specialized studies by local and national groups, among which are private and public employment offices and universities and nonprofit organizations.

The health of a person or population is a complex phenomenon. The range of measures includes individual clinical, physical, and physiological tests; medical diagnosis; such observed or recorded actions as admission to a hospital, use of a prosthesis, or absence from work; opinions; and an extensive variety of statistical absolutes, averages, relatives, and rates.

Statistical knowledge of the relations of age, health, and work-force status is now being augmented by the continuing projects of the National Health Survey. These activities emphasize the advantages of studying representative samples of all people, well and ill, in a population, thus permitting association of morbidity measures with demographic, sociological, and economic characteristics. The National Health Survey utilizes physical examinations, interviews, and records-sampling.

This paper has attempted little substantive analysis of data on health, work force, and age, but to analysts of many disciplines the challenge of data now available is strikingly exhibited by such contrasting facts as these: (1) In the United States, the noninstitutional civilian population of sixty-five and over annually loses over 200,-000,000 man days through bed disability, and more than three out of every four people in this population block have one or more chronic illnesses or physical impairments. (2) The usual activity of nearly 40 per cent of the males from sixty-five to seventy-four is work, and for this group work loss per person because of health is only two weeks a year, only one-third more than that of males in the next younger ten-year group. Surely this evidence points to the existence of serious problems, but also to reasonable hope for the resolution of those problems.

## REFERENCES

Aristotle. *Metaphysics.*

Bell, E. T. *The search for truth.* New York: Reynal and Hitchcock, 1934.

California Department of Public Health. *California health survey. Health in California.* Berkeley, Calif.: Author, 1954-1955.

Collins, S.D. *The incidence of illness and the volume of medical services among 9,000 canvassed families.* Washington, D.C.: U.S. Public Health Service, 1944.

Collins, S.D. Sickness surveys. In H. Emerson (Ed.), *Administrative medicine.* New York: Thomas Nelson and Sons, 1951. Pp. 511-535.

Collins, S.D., Phillips, F. Ruth, & Oliver, Dorothy S. Age incidence of specific causes of illness found in monthly canvasses of families. Sample of the eastern health district of Baltimore, 1938-1943. *Publ. Hlth Rep.,* 1951, **66**, 1227-1245.

Commission on Chronic Illness. *Chronic illness in the United States.* Vol. IV. *Chronic illness in a large city.* Cambridge: Harvard University Press, 1957.

Commission on Chronic Illness. *Chronic illness in the United States.* Vol. III. *Chronic illness in a rural area.* Cambridge: Harvard University Press, 1959.

Nisselson, H., & Woolsey, T.D. Some problems of the household interview design for the national health survey. *J. Amer. Statist. Ass.,* 1959, **54**, 69-87.

Peterson, W.A. *Metropolitan area health survey—Kansas City rehabilitation experiment.* Kansas City, Mo.: Community Studies, Inc., 1958.

Sagen, O.K., Dunham, Ruth E., & Simmons, W.R. Health statistics from record sources and household interviews compared. In *Proceedings of the social statistics section, 1960.* Washington, D.C.: American Statistical Association, 1960. Pp. 6-14.

Sheldon, H.D. *The older population of the United States.* New York: John Wiley & Son, 1958.

Simmons, W.R. A sample of developments from sampling projects of the U.S. national health survey. In *Proceedings of the social statistics section, 1959.* Washington, D.C.: American Statistical Association, 1959. Pp. 95-100.

Sydenstricker, E. The incidence of illness in a general population group. General results of a morbidity study from Dec. 1, 1921, through Mar. 31, 1924, in Hagerstown, Md. *Publ. Hlth Rep.,* 1925, **40**, 279-291.

Sydenstricker, E., Wheeler, G.A., & Goldberger, J. Disabling sickness among the population of 7 cotton mill villages of South Carolina in relation to family income. *Publ. Hlth Rep.,* 1918, **33**, 2038-2051.

U.S. Bureau of Employment Security. *The labor market and employment security,* 1950-1960. (U.S. Department of Labor, Washington, D.C.)

U.S. Bureau of Employment Security. *The insured unemployed,* 1957-1960. (U.S. Department of Labor, Washington, D.C.)

U.S. Bureau of Labor Statistics. *Tables of working life.* Washington, D.C.: U.S. Department of Labor, 1950.

U.S. Bureau of Labor Statistics. *Mobility of molders and coremakers.* Washington, D.C.: U.S. Department of Labor, 1954. (a)

U.S. Bureau of Labor Statistics. Studies of occupational wages and supplementary benefits. *BLS Bull.*, 1954, No. 1168. (U.S. Department of Labor, Washington, D.C.)

U.S. Bureau of Labor Statistics. *Employment and earnings,* 1955, **1,** through 1960, **6.** (U.S. Department of Labor, Washington, D.C.)

U.S. Bureau of Labor Statistics. *Employment and earnings* (including the "Monthly Report on the Labor Force"), 1960, **6** (10). (U.S. Department of Labor, Washington, D.C.)

U.S. National Committee on Vital and Health Statistics. *Proposal for collection of data on illness and impairments, United States.* Washington, D.C.: U.S. Department of Health, Education, and Welfare, 1953.

U.S. National Health Survey. Current statistics on respiratory diseases. *Provisional Tabulation Report,* 1958, No. 29. (Washington, D.C.: U.S. Government Printing Office) (a)

U.S. National Health Survey. Health statistics from . . . survey: Origin and program of the U.S. national health survey. *Publ. Hlth Serv. Publication 584,* 1958, **A** (1). (Washington, D.C.: U.S. Government Printing Office) (b)

U.S. National Health Survey. Health statistics from . . . survey: The statistical design for the health household-interview survey. *Publ. Hlth Serv. Publication 584,* 1958, **A** (2). (Washington, D.C.: U.S. Government Printing Office) (c)

U.S. National Health Survey. Health statistics from . . . survey: Concepts and definitions in the health household-interview survey. *Publ. Hlth Serv. Publication 584,* 1958, **A** (3). (Washington, D.C.: U.S. Government Printing Office) (d)

U.S. National Health Survey. Health statistics from . . . survey: Preliminary report on volume of physician visits, United States. *Publ. Hlth Serv. Publication 584,* 1958, **B** (1). (Washington, D.C.: U.S. Government Printing Office) (e)

U.S. National Health Survey. Health statistics from . . . survey: Preliminary report on volume of dental care, United States. *Publ. Hlth Serv. Publication 584,* 1958, **B** (2). (Washington, D.C.: U.S. Government Printing Office) (f)

U.S. National Health Survey. Health statistics from . . . survey: Preliminary report on number of persons injured, United States. *Publ. Hlth Serv. Publication 584,* 1958, **B** (3). (Washington, D.C.: U.S. Government Printing Office) (g)

U.S. National Health Survey. Health statistics from . . . survey: Preliminary report on disability, United States. *Publ. Hlth Serv. Publication 584,* 1958, **B** (4). (Washington, D.C.: U.S. Government Printing Office) (h)

U.S. National Health Survey. Health statistics from . . . survey: Selected survey topics, United States. *Publ. Hlth Serv. Publication 584,* 1958, **B** (5). (Washington, D.C.: U.S. Government Printing Office) (i)

U.S. National Health Survey. Health statistics from ... survey: Acute conditions, incidence and associated disability, United States. *Publ. Hlth Serv. Publication 584,* 1958, **B** (6). (Washington, D.C.: U.S. Government Printing Office) (j)

U.S. National Health Survey. Health statistics from ... survey: Hospitalization, patients discharged from short-stay hospitals, United States. *Publ. Hlth Serv. Publication 584,* 1958, **B** (7). (Washington, D.C.: U.S. Government Printing Office) (k)

U.S. National Health Survey. Health statistics from ... survey: Persons injured by class of accident, United States. *Publ. Hlth Serv. Publication 584,* 1959, **B** (8). (Washington, D.C.: U.S. Government Printing Office) (a)

U.S. National Health Survey. Health statistics from . . . survey: Impairments by type, sex, and age, United States. *Publ. Hlth Serv. Publication 584,* 1959, **B** (9). (Washington, D.C.: U.S. Government Printing Office) (b)

U.S. National Health Survey. Health statistics from . . . survey: Disability days, United States. *Publ. Hlth Serv. Publication 584,* 1959, **B** (10). (Washington, D.C.: U.S. Government Printing Office) (c)

U.S. National Health Survey. Health statistics from . . . survey: Limitation of activity and mobility due to chronic conditions, United States. *Publ. Hlth Serv. Publication 584,* 1959, **B** (11). (Washington, D.C.: U.S. Government Printing Office) (d)

U.S. National Health Survey. Health statistics from . . . survey: Chronic respiratory conditions reported in interviews, United States. *Publ. Hlth Serv. Publication 584,* 1959, **B** (12). (Washington, D.C.: U.S. Government Printing Office (e)

U.S. National Health Survey. Health statistics from ... survey: Heart conditions and high blood pressure reported in interviews, United States. *Publ. Hlth Serv. Publication 584,* 1960, **B** (13). (Washington, D.C.: U.S. Government Printing Office) (a)

U.S. National Health Survey. Health statistics from . . . survey: Dental care, interval and frequency of visits, United States. *Publ. Hlth Serv. Publication 584,* 1960, **B** (14). (Washington, D.C.: U.S. Government Printing Office) (b)

U.S. National Health Survey. Health statistics from ... survey: Dental care, volume of visits, United States. *Publ. Hlth Serv. Publication 584,* 1960, **B** (15). (Washington, D.C.: U.S. Government Printing Office) (c)

U.S. National Health Survey. Health statistics from . . . survey: Types of injuries, incidence and associated disability, United States. *Publ. Hlth Serv. Publication 584,* **B** (16). (Washington, D.C.: U.S. Government Printing Office) (d)

U.S. National Health Survey. Health statistics from ... survey: Older persons, selected health characteristics, United States. *Publ. Hlth Serv. Publication 584,* 1960, **C** (4). (Washington, D.C.: U.S. Government Printing Office) (e)

U.S. Social Security Board. Unemployment statistics. *Soc. Security Bull.,* March, 1938, **1** (86).

# SECTION II

*Retirement—*
*Attitudes, Influences,*
*and Income*

# CHAPTER 47

## Retirement—Norms, Behavior, and Functional Aspects of Normative Behavior

LEONARD Z. BREEN

Many people have written of the varying conceptions of the nature of aging and retirement. Some consider aging as an entirely biological phenomenon; others have stressed the psychological component and problem-orientation in attempting to define aging as personal phenomenon as well as a social conception. The position taken on the nature of the aging, its significance, and the ultimate possibility of controlling the process have been considered by many disciplines, and each discipline has argued for the significance of its own point of view. If one were to examine aging as a total conception of personal life change, one would be compelled to conclude that each discipline has a legitimate, albeit narrow, point of view. From the standpoint of the individual or the society in which he ages, the nature of aging is most complex. Certainly, one ages biologically

381

and psychologically; there are also attendant problems of economics, housing, work opportunities, and so on. The conception one has about these phenomena will vary, depending on the person, his discipline, interests, history, and the like, as well as the situation in which he finds himself at the time he expresses his opinion.

As in other periods of life and other aspects of a person's perception of his life and the world about him, the process of aging contains a large component of normative behavior. By normative behavior, we mean behavior in response to the expectations one perceives on the part of those about him. It is not average behavior, but the expected behavior of the group in which the individual operates. The normative aspects of aging and retirement, therefore, are the ways an individual responds to what he believes the expectations of his reference group are. To be sure, any person may have many reference groups and may call on them at various times and places, depending on the situations in which he finds himself. One manages, however, to create a more-or-less consistent behavior in response to his perceptions of the expectations. It is this more-or-less consistent behavior that we focus on in examining the normative aspects of aging.

## LIFE-STAGE CLARITY AND ROLE BEHAVIOR

A person takes cognizance of his reference groups' expectations by noting their conceptions of age as reflected in their practices. For instance, in our society the normative aspects of aging are clearly reflected in retirement practices in industry, in conceptions about the desirability of retirement, in the Social Security laws which are part of the government program, in pension programs as they vary in completeness and coverage, and so on. Because of the way in which aging is approached through retirement, later life is seen as a fairly specific stage to which most people aspire and, barring early death, to which all will come. As one reflects on the nature of the stage and society's expectations about it, one takes on certain characteristics of that stage. Certainly, as a person grows old, the social and personal characteristics of his life stages are reflected in his behavior patterns as they change. The devices by which self-concepts are built into personality are amorphous, yet it is quite clear that the transition from one life stage to another is a critical determinant of the self-concept in any stage. Thus, we note a significant datum: how a person arrives at any stage in life will markedly affect his adjustment to that stage.

To understand the adjustments to various age stages, one must understand the way in which society inducts a person into those stages. The *rites de passage* become the clues which help a person learn to react to the new stages. These rites are devices by which society notifies a person of the expectations for the new period and of what society believes to be true about it. People vary, however, in their ability to comprehend society's expectations and to recognize the points at which life stages shift. Life-stage clarity and social-role behavior, therefore, are critical elements in understanding the way a person will react to changes as he proceeds in life. A person will probably adjust more readily to the stages which are fairly specific and easily identified. For instance, as one ages, the adjustment to later years may be less satisfactory than the adjustment to such an easily identified and clearly determined situation as widowhood. We may have difficulty in agreeing on who is old, but we have no difficulty in agreeing on who is widowed.

### Expectations about Retirement

In the period of life that we identify as retirement, people are expected to conform to society's expectations about retirement. One is supposed to rest, to mow the lawn occasionally, to paint the house from time to time, to garden regularly, to visit once in a while, and to travel now and then.

To recapitulate, we note that aging is seen, first, as a natural process, a change characterized by reaction and adjustment to the physical and social stresses to which all people are subject. Daily living, work, economic pressures, and social intercourse all serve as focuses for the change, inducing variations in personal and social behavior. For the most part such natural processes are seen as physiological in origin if not in emphasis. The physiological stress is identified as one segment of the context in which social behavior occurs. Second, aging is often seen as a pathological condition with a poor prognosis for the individual. It appears to be something that one catches, a disease with behavioral manifestations. Apparently it is a disease that does not respond favorably to known therapies. Finally, aging also may be seen in its normative aspects. One is expected to perform in prescribed ways, and, in response to them, one completes a tautological argument. Yet, expectations generate behavior. As J.M. Barrie says in *Peter Pan,* what counts is "good form," and the person who does not realize that he is in good form is the person most likely to be in good form. In the same sense, the person who has what we would call "good adjustment" is the person who responds to society's expectations with behavior regarded as appropriate for the life stage at which he finds himself. For the older person this is no less true.

### Approaches to Retirement

In an examination of the way in which the norms for retirement are created, one must examine the behavioral expectations of our society. Clark Tibbitts (1954) noted that people derive status from two social functions: (1) perpetuation of the species and (2) maintenance of the economy. For the most part, these two basic and critical functions are concluded before the later years. The question then is, "What norms are evolved to govern behavior in the opportunities which must be created to provide older people with status?" May one derive status from reflection or from being the object rather than the center of activities? Clearly, one derives little status from reflection or being an object for activities.

For a moment, let us examine some of the specific ways in which norms associated with aging are recognized. A group at the University of Chicago has concluded a research project on objective criteria of aging. In this project a group of older workers was compared with a matched group of younger workers. The two groups were asked questions about their own attitudes toward aging and retirement. The younger men wanted to retire early, but men closer to retirement age began to shift the responses, and the men who were eligible for retirement completely reversed the young men's responses. Older people do not wish to retire; younger people do. This datum has been noted in other researches and is fairly well-established. Young people, however, were less realistic about the possibilities of retirement. In the University of Chicago study, many of the younger men said that, on retirement, they were going to start a business of a kind that would clearly require a large amount of capital which they did not have and had no expectation of raising. Their dreams concerning retirement were unrealistic. The men in their later years were more realistic. To be sure, older people also suggested the possibility of "opening a little tavern," or "starting a business." But where this was the case, the schemes were likely to be more modest than were the younger men's.

Of even greater interest in the comparison of- older and younger people in terms of realistic planning for retirement was the finding that retirement was clearly expected by all workers, regardless of age. The forms and concept of retirement have been institutional- ized in our economic system. People do regularly plan for a retire- ment program with standard practices on the part of industry. To be sure, the norms associated with such expressions on industry's part often connote an undesirable meaning for retirement. After a lifetime of service, one is rewarded by a dinner or a gold watch. Other writers have noted the anomaly in this situation—when one no longer needs to be guided by the clock, he is awarded a gold watch.

## FUNCTIONAL ASPECTS OF RETIREMENT

In the literature on retirement, one is struck by the fact that most writers look negatively on retirement norms. There are, however, many functional aspects of retirement; they are not all dis- functional. Certainly there are many disfunctional characteristics, and these have been enumerated at considerable length and with con- siderable ardor. Below I attempt to enumerate four areas in which there are functional aspects of retirement.

### The Individual

For the individual worker, the policy and program of re- tirement in our industrial economy has many functional aspects. First, it provides him with free time which he might otherwise not have and which he has not had in his lifetime of work. This free time may be utilized in many ways and as a person chooses. As far as society is concerned, some ways are productive, and some are not productive. For the individual, this free time itself produces a better view of his own worth. He may see the free time as having been bought with his lifetime of work. No matter how negatively he reacts to it, when it is based on a pension system, the free time has value to him. Second, the growing custom of pension plans and provisions in our society are clearly functional. This is one way in which the individual finds it possible to finance at least some part of the free time which is avail- able to him. With the pension providing financial security for free time, new possibilities arise for the individual. New careers become possible, although, to be sure, most workers are very unrealistic in their view of the opportunities. New careers as presidents of corpora- tions do not come to assistant lathe hands immediately on retirement. With the income—minimal as it is—from pensions, the older person can play a new role, "sage." On reaching retirement age, a person somehow becomes venerable and occasionally venerated. He can speak with the assurance that his job cannot be taken from him if he makes an outrageous statement. Third, when retirement programs become compulsory at given ages, one's planning for retirement and reaction to change must be organized about a specific retirement point. One cannot go on vacillating forever. The time comes when one must leave the job. At this point decisions must be, and are, reached. Finally, because of the prevalent norms concerning the existence and nature of a second childhood, it is possible for a retired person to remove himself from the usual reprovals and censure. A person can truly act as a child again if he so wishes. This permits participation in activities the individual may have thought beyond him at an earlier age.

### The Industrial Organization

From the viewpoint of industry, there are probably more functional aspects of retirement than might be the case for other parts of our economy. To begin, industry requires a mobile labor force. It requires the movement of workers from jobs that are no longer profitable to maintain to jobs which have come into being as a result of changes in industrial production. Industry must provide promotions for younger men in order to retain their interest and productive capacities. Industry must find a way of amortizing the cost of pensions in as specific a way as possible. All of these requirements are satisfied by a program of compulsory and specific retirement. Mobility is increased when one worker is retired; older workers themselves can make moves. In addition, younger men can move into the jobs left by the retirement of older workers. Promotions for younger people become possible when older people retire from their jobs. From an accounting standpoint, the amortization of costs is more easily controlled when one can predict the times when people will leave the job. This, of course, is easy when there is a fixed retirement age.

### Unions

From the standpoint of the unions, the seniority system, which is now institutionalized and built into our economy, must be maintained as an aspect of functional union operation. For the most part, this is supported by the older workers and attacked by the younger workers. If seniority were constantly under attack from the majority of younger workers, it would, no doubt, fail, but through programs of retirement many older people are removed from the seniority scale, thus allowing movement among younger workers. The freedom injected into the system by retirement makes the seniority system workable. It is, in fact, a fluid system only because we have retirement—frequently compulsory retirement. At the present, unions are growing, for the most part by the inclusion of the younger workers. Younger workers are often less well-paid and have been organized in large numbers only recently. They may disagree with the older, higher-paid workers in forming union policy. If the older workers maintain their position in the union, they would comprise a very large part of the voting members; removal by retirement eases this problem. Thus, through retirement, union activity is constantly reorganized in favor of the younger workers.

TABLE 1

SATISFACTION WITH RETIREMENT AS THE RESULT OF
ATTITUDE TOWARD RETIREMENT

| | *Percentage that is satisfied with retirement* | |
| *Approach to retirement* | Favorable preretirement attitude toward retirement | Unfavorable preretirement attitude toward retirement |
|---|---|---|
| Had plans | 86 | 61 |
| Did not have plans | 77 | 58 |
| Self-retired | 83 | 66 |
| Company-retired | 80 | 56 |
| Expected to retire | 82 | 60 |
| Expected to continue working | 68 | 57 |

Source—Streib and Thompson (1957, Table VI, p. 197). Reprinted with permission of University of Michigan Press.

### Society

Society, too, uses compulsory retirement in the framework of the seniority system to retain fluidity in management and policy. There is, in compulsory retirement, a finite end of work to which most people must come. Thus, there is not only a change in personnel, but also in ideas and leadership. This is an important institutionalized scheme for reinforcing the youth orientation of our society. Insofar as our society maintains a fairly positive view toward youth and a fairly negative view toward age, compulsory retirement reinforces these views. As a whole, society shows little inclination to change this system.

## ATTITUDES TOWARD RETIREMENT

Streib and Thompson (1957) have made important contributions to the study of satisfaction with retirement, as a function of attitude toward retirement. Table 1 shows a clear relationship between satisfaction with retirement after retirement and attitude toward retirement prior to retirement. The workers who approached retirement positively were much more likely to have favorable attitudes toward retirement. In this regard the significance of the differences is extremely illuminating.

Attitudes toward aging and retirement clearly reflect the norms of society. People have expectations about retirement and adjust their plans and behavior to these expectations. When the anticipated concepts are positive, the approach to retirement is good; when they are negative, the approach is likely to be bad. These observations are not new or startling, but nevertheless they are fundamental to understanding preparation for retirement in any segment of our economy. Indeed, they are fundamental to the study of aging.

*REFERENCES*

Streib, G.F., & Thompson, W.E. Personal and social adjustment in retirement. In Wilma Donahue & C. Tibbitts (Eds.), *The new frontiers of aging.* Ann Arbor: University of Michigan Press, 1957. Pp. 180-197.
Tibbitts, C. A sociological view of aging. *Proc. Amer. phil. Soc.,* 1954, **98,** 144-148.

# CHAPTER 48

*Social Values and
the Institutionalization
of Retirement*

HAROLD L. ORBACH

Retirement represents the creation in modern society of an economically non-productive role for large numbers of people whose labor is not considered essential to or necessary for the functioning of the economic order. Although departure from a life-long career may serve as the basic operational indicator of retirement, sociologically retirement raises problems of the dynamics of social and institutional roles and relationships of a more basic nature than those associated with a change in occupational role. As a social process, retirement is the prescribed transition from the position of an economically active person to the position of an economically inactive person in accordance with the norms and procedures by which society defines and determines the nature of this change.

From this standpoint, the basic problems of retirement must

389

be approached in terms of the issues involved in the transition from one social role to another, with the consequent implications of the status changes which accompany this role change.[1] On the individual level, this means the problems of varying conceptions and definitions of appropriate individual behavior which problems are derived from the person's self-concepts' growing out of his total social life experience. In the process of role change, the norms for behavior of significant others and of significant reference groups play a crucial part in determining what the nature of one's social role is and ought to be. It is here that the details of a person's retirement role are conceived, refined, and in practice organized into a coherent pattern.

On the societal level, retirement raises the issue of the basic social definition and valuation and brings into focus the value systems underlying the retirement policies and attitudes of society at large and of such major organizations as business and labor, which are directly concerned with the management of retirement systems. It is here that the framework and nature of retirement as a societal phenomenon is built.

In the last analysis, the personal aspects of retirement are the areas to which our interests and inclinations naturally turn. This should not, however, deter us from considering the historic dynamics of retirement as a social phenomenon and from analyzing the character of the basic value systems which have developed on the societal level to deal with this emerging social pattern. It is only through the history of retirement as a social phenomenon and the structural and value questions it poses for modern society that we can develop a systematic understanding of its nature and deal with the individual and social problems it poses.

## THE INSTITUTIONALIZATION OF RETIREMENT

Retirement is a product of modern industrial society. This emerging pattern of social life has no precedence and represents the development of a new and distinct social role that is becoming universally available. Previous socioeconomic systems have had varying numbers of older people, but none has ever had the number or percentage of aged that obtains in the industrialized societies; more im-

---

[1] For a fuller treatment of these issues, see the discussion in Donahue, Orbach, and Pollak (1960), in which more detailed presentation of a number of the arguments presented in this paper may be found.

portant, the older people of previous societies were not retired people. Never before has there been a retirement role, although there were clearly defined roles for older people (Simmons, 1945). Indeed, as Simmons and others have shown, in many primitive societies reaching a state of total productive incapacity implied a loss of the right to live, and appropriate procedures for doing away with non-productive older people were part of the culture.

The development of retirement is a result of complex, related technological, social, political, and demographic changes in modern society. They can be roughly summarized by four developments.

1. *The creation of a technology which is based on the scientific approach* to knowledge and which has shattered, and continues to shatter, conceptions of the potentialities for producing the food and goods necessary for the sustenance and improvement of the conditions of life.

2. *The development and extension of political and social order through powerful national states.* This is a corollary of the growth of rational economic methods inherent in industrialism, which have been able, through modern technology and communication, to exercise an ever increasing purposeful control of man's natural and social environment.

3. *A unique demographic revolution* which has witnessed the growth of human population in the past one hundred years in a measure previously unheard of. As industrial societies have matured, this revolution has ushered in the aging of populations.

4. *The reorganization of man's economic and social life,* as a consequence of the new systems of production and consumption, into a distinctly new set of social roles based on an altered relation between man and the tools he works with and, in consequence, the manner and form in which he reaps the rewards of his labor. The industrial system of production with its rational division of labor, separation of the laborer from control of the instruments of production, and wage system of economic exchange have altered the older systems of social relationships and profoundly changed the structure of the institutional arrangements in man's life.

Each of these has contributed to the economic, social, and political conditions necessary for the institution of retirement. By virtue of its productive capacity, modern society can readily support a non-working segment of its adult population; the political organization of the national state can provide structural apparatus for the operation of universal retirement systems; the demographic revolution has created an aged population, a large number of which will live far beyond their years of maximally potential economic life; and the changing social relationships which have arisen as a consequence of the industrial system have rendered untenable the types of social and economic accommodations which previous societies had created for their older people.

As is usually the case in human affairs, the values and norms of behavior have not kept pace with the changes in the material conditions of life. In order to have retirement, there must be some structural differentiation of the work-life and of the conditions of work so that a period of retirement is defined and the retiring worker can clearly move from the role of an economically active person to the role of an economically inactive person. It is fairly easy to define the time period by chronological limits and, in the case of the wage-earning or salaried employee, to clearly alter the role through a formal retirement procedure. This procedure, however, has not always meant retirement from the world of work so much as it has meant retirement from some specific remunerative employment. But, more important, what of the character of life beyond work? What is the social role of the retired person? We are in the process of slowly adapting to the new conditions which have been thrust upon us. The result is the lack of any clear-cut role for the retired person; there is ambiguity and lack of clarity in the behavioral expectations for the members of this new social position.

Unlike other social role changes throughout the life span which are marked by a series of role transitions and gradations from one more-or-less clearly defined social role to another and which encompass forms of anticipatory socialization for the role through informal preparation, the retirement role lacks socially defined appropriate behavior inasmuch as it also lacks clearly defined position in the social structure. In one sense, retirement is a negation of the traditional values that surround work in Western society, and men are loath to surrender the social identification which a job bestows. Organized preparation for retirement, a notion which has received much attention in recent years, is an attempt to fill the gap in the normative structure of the present by defining, thus readying the individual for, the new social role.

Insofar as one of the most crucial sources of role expectations and behavior is the reference group of position holders of any social role, one of the problems of the retirement role has been the lack of a viable group of people in this category. This feature is, of course, rapidly changing today because of the maturation of the institutional basis of retirement in the United States. As a consequence of Old-Age and Survivors Insurance and the industrial pensions since the end of World War II, we have witnessed, in twenty years, the growth of an institutional economic foundation for retired people as a social category. In other countries, too, similar phenomena have arisen, but only in the past generation have these phenomena achieved the degree of importance to merit attention as the beginning of a new social role.

Although preoccupation with retirement began as a concern for the protection of the wage earner and his family when health and age made it impossible for him to continue working for a living, retirement today involves matters of general social policy, as well as institutional needs and demands. Old-Age and Survivors Insurance was adopted in the United States partly to relieve the pressures of unemployment during the Depression of the 1930's, and it was structured and has been viewed as such almost throughout its history. Similarly, industrial pensions and executive retirement represent calculated policy decisions for the renewal and replacement of labor, skills, and vitality in the market place. Finally, the growth of unionization and its cardinal principle of seniority generated similar pressures for opening up opportunities through the retirement of senior workers holding prized positions.[2]

The development of institutionalized retirement has had more far-reaching consequences than was intended by the mechanisms which brought it about. The continual changes in society, which are accentuated by new demographic characteristics, and automation have served to create further demands for more extensive retirement even as they have raised questions of changes in general work conditions. And yet, we seem unwilling or unable to adjust our work-related values to the acceptance of retirement as a desirable conclusion of the working life. We are faced with seemingly contradictory demands: a demand for freedom to prolong working life and a demand for extension of retirement.

[2] See Breen (Chapter 47, *supra*) for an analysis and discussion of the functional aspects of retirement.

## SOCIETAL VALUES AND RETIREMENT

Part of the problem of retirement can be traced to the basic value orientation which underlies the conception of retirement as a form of social life. By and large, the worker of today still sees retirement in such negative terms as economic deprivation, loss of status and function, and nothing to do with the free time (Donahue et al., 1960; Tuckman & Lorge, 1953). These are issues related to the social and individual definition of the retirement role, based on an entirely realistic appraisal of the status and position of the retired person in today's society. However, the basic societal values which underlie institutionalized retirement systems also are operative. The role of government as an agent ensuring the welfare and well-being of its citizens is a major issue, as is the social nature of retirement and, thus, the nature of pensions or retirement benefits.

On one hand, conceptions of social responsibility have, from the earliest pension systems, been clear in defining retirement pensions as a form of social welfare or assistance which society grants out of charity and self-interest. On the other hand, more recent trends have suggested that retirement pensions are a form of social reward or deferred pay—a form of social justice—which accrues as a matter of right. Shenfield (1957) has put this issue clearly:

> Are pensions to be regarded as a way of discharging community responsibility to those unable to maintain themselves in the same way that support is organized for other disabled persons, or are they a reward for a lifetime of effort, a kind of deferred pay to which everyone should be entitled after a named period of work attendance and contributions? If the latter, then pension schemes should create a right to retirement for all workers on a pension which is adequate to meet their basic needs, while they enjoy their well-earned rest. Those who choose voluntarily to continue to work should gain, either by receiving pension and wages, or by a deferred pension ultimately drawn, in recognition of the surrender of leisure which might otherwise have been enjoyed. The notion of creating a "right" to a pension at a certain age is emphasized by the device of insurance as a method of financing old age (pp. 103-104).

In the United States it would appear that we have institutionalized a system of rights without accepting the values and normative system that it implies. This is undoubtedly a reflection of the continuing ideological struggle that has been waged since the end of the nineteenth century over the nature of the United States political system, directly expressed in the debates about the federal government's powers and functions which dominated the early years of the New Deal. Indeed, the Social Security Act was in the center of this raging controversy, and the federal system of old-age and survivors insurance was not idealogically accepted by the Republican Party until 1944, when its platform advocated "extension of the existing old-age insurance [system] . . . to all employees not already covered." In the realm of rhetoric at least, this issue continues to animate contemporary politics, and the political controversy it arouses has made the development of our Social Security and retirement systems a matter of piecemeal attachments under a restrictive covering justification. In the 1950's, when Old-Age, Survivors, and Disability Insurance benefits were "universalized" or "socialized" by extending them to new categories of workers (including the self-employed and others who do not earn wages) on the basis of equity, not presumed need, the concept of wage-loss offset, which is the official basis of Social Security legislation, was not changed. We still maintain a system of insurance plus welfare assistance, but the insurance system has an underlying orientation of basic subsistence, rather than a reasonable income that ensures a standard of decent living. Retirement systems organized on an insurance basis or involving a notion of social reward should, however, provide such a standard as a matter of consistent policy, and the German and Swedish systems have moved in this direction. Their point of view has been stated by the German Federal Republic: "A pension is no longer a grant-in-aid toward a person's subsistence, but will in future ensure maintenance of the living standard acquired" (Achinger, 1959, p. 26).

Industrial pensions have arisen to fill the gap between subsistence and a decent living standard in the United States, for unions do look on pensions as a right in the form of deferred pay although no similar inclination is currently expressed by employers. Only since the 1949 Supreme Court decision in the Inland Steel case (based on the Taft-Hartley Act, which certainly was not intended as pioneering social legislation) has the right to bargain collectively for pensions been recognized. This decision gave rise to the tremendous growth of union-negotiated industrial retirement systems in the 1950's, just as the development of unions followed similar legislative and legal decisions in the late 1930's.

Clearly, one of the important problems in the further institutionalization of retirement is the need for a consistent expression of social policy on retirement rights in order to clarify the basic social values involved. With the forces inherent in the process of institution-

alization itself, a clarification of values, accompanied by appropriate
social action, will better define and structure the social function and
status of retirement and thus aid the development of the individual's
role conception and attitudes.

Retirement must have a positive meaning and be endowed
with sufficiently rewarding economic, social, and cultural values if it
is to be an acceptable form of social life for the older person and a
successful form of social policy in relation to pressures on the labor
market. Such a course must imply movement toward equality of rights
in retirement since only one-third of the labor force is currently covered by private or public pensions that supplement Social Security
benefits (Holland, 1959), although the basic support for private retirement systems comes from tax exemptions to employers for contributions and, thus, the general public indirectly (Witte, 1951).

## ORGANIZATIONAL ATTITUDES AND
## RETIREMENT SYSTEMS

The differences in attitudes and, consequently, policy positions of labor and management concerning freedom of choice to retire are indicated by the figures in Table 1. The two studies of retirement policies which are compared are of interest because in the
first (Brower, 1955) non-union companies comprised 29 per cent of
the total; the pension plans of the other companies were not necessarily developed by union-management negotiation. In the second,
carried out by the U.S. Bureau of Labor Statistics (Levin, 1959), only
union-negotiated plans were sampled. The striking differences in the
percentage of workers covered by involuntary or compulsory retirement practices represent differing conceptions of the locus of norms
for decisions concerning retirement. At the same time, the union-
negotiated plans with involuntary provisions also have greater flexibility in that only 19 per cent of the employees have conditions of
automatic retirement at a given age without the possibility of continued employment, whereas 65 per cent of those covered by the
other plans are so governed. These differences suggest that the unions'
influence in obtaining pensions as a right is matched, to some degree,
by a demand for greater freedom of choice in exercising this right.

The effects of unions and unionization can be measured in
other ways. For example, a New York State Department of Labor
(1957) study found that 89 per cent of the establishments with 2,500
or more employees had pension plans, but that only 14 per cent of

**TABLE 1**

**TYPES OF RETIREMENT PROVISIONS AND PRACTICES IN PRIVATE PENSION SYSTEMS, 1954 and 1958**

(In percentages)

| Type of provision or practice* | Brower, 1954 | | Bureau of Labor Statistics, 1958 | |
|---|---|---|---|---|
| | Companies (N=327) | Employees (N=4.1 million) | Plans (N=300) | Employees (N=4.9 million) |
| No compulsory fixed-age retirement | 25* | 10* | 40 | 45 |
| Compulsory retirement | 67* | 83* | 60 | 55 |
| Automatic retirement | 48 | 67 | 23 | 19 |
| Non-automatic retirement | 19 | 16 | 37 | 36 |

Source—Adapted from Brower (1955, Table 5) and Levin (1959, Table 2).

*Eight per cent of the companies have a combination of involuntary and voluntary policies for different workers; these policies cover 7 per cent of the employees.

the establishments with fewer than twenty employees had them. The relation to unionization, which is more prevalent in large firms, is apparent. Pension coverage also varies considerably with industry, another feature obviously related to the extent of unionization—compare steel or auto workers with service or domestic workers.

Generally unions have opposed compulsory retirement on the grounds that it is a negation of the seniority rights, thus presenting another area in which the worker's economic security must be protected. This does not imply opposition to compulsory retirement as such, but to the employers' imposition of the conditions of retirement under circumstances which result in involuntary economic deprivation. It is not surprising, therefore, that "as retirement incomes have risen, so has union acceptance of automatic retirement schemes" (Bers, 1957, p. 83). Union attitudes have clearly reinforced the willingness of labor to accept compulsory retirement systems under conditions approved and sanctioned by union members. This means, however, restriction—which management has been reluctant to accept—of management's right to unilateral decisions on the criteria of continued employment for older workers.

An interesting example of the effect of the institutionalization of a retirement system and the provision of more adequate retirement benefits can be obtained by examining changes in the retirement practices of auto workers covered under the Big Three auto companies' pension plans with the United Auto Workers. The UAW has, since its original pension plans were negotiated, obtained improvements in benefits and coverage at each of its bargaining talks with the automobile manufacturers. In addition, the UAW has operated a very active program for retired workers, including preparation-for-retirement courses, drop-in centers for retired workers, and other activities designed to assist UAW members' adjustment to and conditions of retirement. The 1958 contract negotiations saw a number of marked improvements in the pension schemes, especially at Chrysler and Ford.

In the light of this example, it is interesting to observe the changes in the auto workers' retirement patterns since 1953 (Table 2). It is evident from the data that there has been a large decline in the proportion of workers in all three companies who wait for the compulsory retirement age of sixty-eight and an increase in the proportion of those who elect early retirement benefits. In all three companies, too, the proportion electing early retirement with reduced benefits has shown a steady, if slow, increase. The category "special early retirement," which is governed by a mutually satisfactory agreement

## TABLE 2
## NON-DISABILITY RETIREMENTS IN THE BIG THREE AUTO COMPANIES
## UNDER UNITED AUTO WORKERS NEGOTIATED PENSION AGREEMENTS, 1953 AND 1956-1959
(In percentages)

| Year | Early Retirement: 60-64* | | | Normal retirement: 65-67 | Automatic retirement: 68 | Total | Number of Retirements |
|---|---|---|---|---|---|---|---|
| | Regular | Special | Total | | | | |
| **Chrysler** | | | | | | | |
| 1953 | 2 | – | 2 | 50 | 48 | 100 | 508 |
| 1956 | 5 | – | 5 | 64 | 31 | 100 | 1,172 |
| 1957 | 8 | – | 8 | 67 | 26 | 101† | 1,204 |
| 1958 | 10 | – | 10 | 70 | 20 | 100 | 1,462 |
| 1959 | 14 | 10 | 24 | 67 | 9 | 100 | 1,774 |
| **Ford** | | | | | | | |
| 1953 | ‡ | – | ‡ | 57 | 43 | 100 | 1,996 |
| 1956 | 4 | – | 4 | 67 | 29 | 100 | 2,075 |
| 1957 | 5 | – | 5 | 75 | 20 | 100 | 1,926 |
| 1958 | 7 | – | 7 | 81 | 12 | 100 | 2,376 |
| 1959 | 6 | 9 | 15 | 75 | 10 | 100 | 2,160 |
| **General Motors** | | | | | | | |
| 1953 | 3 | 4 | 7 | 39 | 54 | 100 | 2,088 |
| 1956 | 5 | 7 | 12 | 57 | 31 | 100 | 2,824 |
| 1957 | 6 | 8 | 14 | 58 | 28 | 100 | 2,820 |
| 1958 | 6 | 9 | 15 | 62 | 23 | 100 | 2,959 |
| 1959 | 7 | 12 | 19 | 61 | 20 | 100 | 3,085 |

| Big Three Combined | | | | | | |
|---|---|---|---|---|---|---|
| 1953 | 2 | 2 | 4 | 48 | 48 | 100 | 4,592 |
| 1956 | 5 | 3 | 8 | 62 | 30 | 100 | 6,071 |
| 1957 | 6 | 4 | 10 | 65 | 25 | 100 | 5,950 |
| 1958 | 7 | 4 | 11 | 71 | 18 | 100 | 6,797 |
| 1959 | 8 | 11 | 19 | 67 | 14 | 100 | 7,019 |

Source—Communications to the author from the United Auto Workers, Chrysler Corporation, Ford Motor Company, and General Motors Corporation.

*Since 1950, all three of the auto companies have had a system of regular early retirement at age sixty to sixty-four with actuarily decreased benefits. In addition, General Motors has had a special early retirement system with retirement at the option of the company or by mutually satisfactory agreement. The system provides double the normal age-sixty-five retirement pension until the retiree reaches age sixty-five and attains Social Security, at which time the pension is reduced to the normal rate. This system was incorporated in the Ford and Chrysler systems beginning in 1959.

†Differs from 100 because of rounding.

‡Less than 0.5 per cent.

or company option and mainly covers employees in failing health who are not eligible for disability benefits, controls early retirement for health reasons. When these cases are removed, however, there is still a continually increasing proportion of early retirees in all three firms over the eight years, and a complementary decline over the same period in those waiting until the compulsory age. If we view the combined totals for the Big Three as an indicator of the whole auto industry, a clear trend seems to have been emerging since 1953, the year in which automatic retirement at sixty-eight was first accepted by the union as a concession for better pension arrangements and more adequate benefits. To what extent other institutional and idiosyncratic features—the changes in the auto industry because of technology, the age distribution of the work force, and the recurring recessions of the 1950's—are responsible for these patterns and will be responsible for future retirements clearly requires more study.

Nevertheless, this study suggests, as have others (Baker, 1952; Donahue et al., 1960), that increasing the financial rewards of retirement make it more acceptable. More detailed study of the auto industry's pension experience and similar studies of other industries would help establish a more coherent picture of the relative effects of financial incentive, retirement planning, and the general atmosphere of stable institutionalized retirement systems on individual and social values and attitudes.

### REFERENCES

Achinger, H. The economic resources of old age. In *Proceedings of the fourth congress, international association of gerontology, 1957, Merano, Italy.* Vol. 3. Florence: Tipografia Tito Mattioli [1959]. Pp. 17-29.

Baker, Helen. *Retirement procedures under compulsory and flexible retirement policies.* Princeton, N.J.: Princeton University, Department of Economics and Social Institutions, 1952.

Bers, M.K. *Union policy and the older worker.* Berkeley: University of California, Institute of Industrial Relations, 1957.

Brower, F. Beatrice. *Retirement of employees, policies—procedures—practices* ("Studies in Personnel Policy," No. 148). New York: National Industrial Conference Board, 1955.

Donahue, Wilma, Orbach, H.L., & Pollak, O. Retirement: The emerging social pattern. In C. Tibbitts (Ed.), *Handbook of social gerontology.* Chicago: The University of Chicago Press, 1960. Pp. 330-406.

Holland, D.M. What can we expect from pensions? *Harvard Bus. Rev.,* 1959, **37,** 125-140.

Levin, H. Involuntary retirement provisions. *Monthly Labor Rev.,* 1959, **82,** 855-860.

New York State Department of Labor (Division of Research and Statistics).
    Pensions: Larger plans in New York State. *Special Bull.,* 1957,
    No. 232. (Albany: Author)
Shenfield, Barbara. *Social policies for old age: A review of social provisions
    for old age in Great Britain.* London: Routledge and Kegan Paul,
    1957.
Simmons, L.W. *The role of the aged in primitive society.* New Haven: Yale
    University Press, 1945.
Tuckman, J., & Lorge, I. *Retirement and the industrial worker: Prospect and
    reality.* New York: Columbia University, Bureau of Publications,
    Teachers College, 1953.
Witte, E.E. Comments. In Proceedings of a conference on problems of older
    workers. Madison: University of Wisconsin, Industrial Relations
    Center, 1951.

# CHAPTER 49

*Workers' and Employers' Attitudes
toward Retirement Age and Pensions*

SVEN HYDÉN

There have been two schools of thought concerning the age of retirement, one calling for a fixed age for retirement and a pension and the other calling for a flexible pension age which, in principle, coincides with incapacity to work.

The latter attitude, which is losing ground to an increasing extent, regards a pension as a compensation for inability to earn a livelihood by work. The most typical example of such a pension is the sickness annuity provided for workers disabled by accidents at work or occupational diseases. The amount of compensation is generally in direct relation to the nature of the injury and the insured worker's previous income.

Countries which have not yet achieved full economic development can keep costs fairly low by adopting a flexible retirement age policy when they introduce a pension scheme. The number of beneficiaries will be small if the pension age is high, if work must be given up, and if there is a requirement of no private means. Some countries which long ago introduced pension schemes applied these restrictions, but have since modified or abolished them. More recent schemes involve fewer severe restrictions, but have been restricted to workers and salaried employees in industry and commerce and make no provision for self-employed and agricultural workers. Other schemes are even more restrictive, covering only manual workers, as in Chile, or only salaried employees, as in Costa Rica.

There has been, however, a marked tendency in postwar legislation on old-age insurance to prefer compulsory coverage of the entire population or at least of those groups most in need of protection. In cases where the scheme does not cover the entire population, it is often supplemented by forms of voluntary insurance. The insurance coverage is almost always linked to other contingencies such as death of the head of the household or disability.

Restriction of coverage is often accompanied by other legal provisions for support in case of need after retirement. In some countries employers are compelled to support former employees who have given the company long service. This is the case in Finland, where the general old-age pension benefits are low. In other countries, such as the Federal Republic of Germany, local communities are obliged to provide aid for all citizens without means of support, regardless of their age.

## WORKERS' ATTITUDES

The attitude of trade unions toward the problems of security in old age are no doubt influenced by the prevailing legal pension schemes. The unions seem unanimous in preferring a fixed retirement age and a pension based on earlier earnings independent of any means or income test. Thus, a pension is an earned right, based on a person's work and part of the income received. Whether the pension is paid for through contributions from the worker, his employer, or public funds is a matter of method. In the Federal Republic of Germany, the United States, and Sweden, the "earned-right" idea has been accepted, at least in principle, in compulsory legal systems. In other countries it is restricted to special groups. The principle may be modified as a result of stipulations concerning the amount of income, flexible retirement, and means tests during part of the retirement period (a means test to a certain age, then full benefit). In the case of systems which have flexible retirement ages, a certain pension is payable from a stated age, but the beneficiary is entitled to a reduced pension at a younger age or to postponing his right until an older age and receiving a proportionately higher pension then.

There is a strong movement in workers' organizations to lower the retirement age, even in countries where the life expectancy is high. The normal claim is for a retirement age of sixty-five, or, in the case of women, less. In the Scandinavian countries and Iceland the retirement age for manual workers is sixty-seven or more; it is seventy in Norway. In most East European countries the retirement age is sixty or less, at least for women.

In most cases, the claims for a low retirement age are based on the same arguments as the claim for reduced hours of work. The workers want more time for private pursuits, but they also claim that the workers' protection calls for a lower retirement age. Workers who wish to carry on ought to be allowed to decide, they say, but their choice must not depend on whether they get a pension. A variation of this theme is the acceptance of a flexible retirement age with the right to give up work at the lower age and still enjoy a full pension.

Workers generally agree that there should be some flexibility in the retirement age and that a pension—preferably one based on former wages—should be paid following retirement; there is no consensus, however, on the amount of the pension and how the amount should be influenced by other social security benefits. Even though unions generally prefer benefits based on wages, industrial development and economic conditions in various countries have compelled the unions to modify their demands to suit these conditions. In practically all countries, and especially in those which are less developed than the large industrial countries, the demand for pensions must be restricted in favor of other forms of social security. It is for this reason that unions generally start by calling for a fairly low flat rate pension at a high age and withhold demands for better pensions until a more appropriate time.

## EMPLOYERS' ATTITUDES

The employers' organizations seem to have more diverse views on pensions and retirement age. Insofar as general pension schemes introduced by legislation are concerned, the employers are most interested in the cost and the way in which the schemes can be financed. They generally favor such social security measures as old-age and disability pensions and generally oppose fixed retirement and fixed pensions. Employers' organizations are more inclined than are unions to favor traditional approaches to the care of old people and to be satisfied with prevailing private pension schemes.

In some parts of the world—for example, in some Asian countries—employers used to emphasize, at least at international meetings, the psychological value of the family's accepting responsibility for its elder members. As a rule, employers in primarily agricultural countries call for caution in granting pensions. Experience shows that workers and the self-employed in agriculture can continue working longer than workers in industry, because it is easier to adjust agricultural work to the physical capacity of the worker than it is to adjust industrial work.

The employers' organizations have concentrated on the investment of funds, administration problems, and pension policy as an integral part of over-all economic policy. They regard pensions as part of social security insofar as pension schemes cover the basic costs of subsistence in old age, and they are fully in favor of such pensions. Employers have divided opinions about supplementary pensions. In most countries, they prefer private schemes with membership based on a collective agreement or decided through ordinary wage-fixing machinery. In other countries, some employers use pensions as a matter of policy.

Regardless of differing opinions about benefits, retirement age, and administration, employers in most countries have agreed to accept general pension schemes providing incomes greater than the basic costs of subsistence. In most cases, it has been considered suitable to combine the right to a pension with retirement from active work. The employers contend that, if workers who are still fit to earn a living and wish to do so do not receive basic pensions, it will be possible to increase the benefits for those who cannot continue to work. In other countries, the employers have adopted the opposite attitude and have accepted the right of all beneficiaries to receive pensions at a fixed age regardless of means tests and whether they wish to continue remunerative employment.

### Trends

In most countries, increased life expectancy and better health conditions have led both employers' and workers' organizations to favor pension schemes with a later retirement age. In most modern public and private systems, means tests have been abandoned. Beneficiaries who are willing and able to work after retirement age thus receive both a pension and income from work and are thereby encouraged to seek income from work. As far as private pension schemes of the insurance type are concerned, the insured person can postpone his pension benefits and then become entitled to a higher pension rate at a later date. A typical scheme of this kind was recently introduced in Sweden and, according to communications to the International Social Security Association, similar ideas are being discussed in several countries.

At the 1955 International Labor Organization's European Regional Conference in Geneva, the employers' and workers' organizations in Europe agreed on certain principles concerning pensions and age of retirement. In the technical committee which dealt with this subject, the employers' members submitted general observations, drew attention to the diverse problems of the various countries, and emphasized the importance of maintaining adequate flexibility in pension schemes and the age of retirement.

The workers' members submitted a draft resolution setting forth these basic principles:

1. Every worker completing a full working life should have the right to get an adequate pension.
2. Every worker reaching pensionable age should have the right to continue to work if so doing does not injure the interests of other workers.
3. The pensionable age should not exceed sixty for men and fifty-five for women, with lower ages for workers in arduous or unhealthful occupations.
4. Periods of involuntary unemployment and incapacity should be credited as periods of work.
5. Acquired rights should not be modified to the detriment of the workers.
6. Pensions should follow changes in the cost of living.

As a guide to the possible arrangements for retirement, the conference adopted a resolution which embraced the following principles:

1. Legislation should provide an adequate pension for every worker who has completed a full working life so that he can

retire and rest. A full working life includes periods of unemployment and incapacity for work.

2. The minimum pensionable age should be fixed, as a general rule, in the range of sixty to sixty-five, with regard to national differences in the effective earning capacity of the average worker who is sixty or more and in the number of years which he may expect to enjoy his pension. For women this age should be five years lower than that fixed for men.

3. Pensions at a lower age should be provided for arduous and unhealthful occupations. These may be provided under separate schemes or under the national scheme.

4. Many workers who have reached the minimum pensionable age are willing to continue to work and can render effective service. They should be given this opportunity if suitable employment which will not harm the interests of younger workers is available.

5. The pensions payments should correspond to the cost of living.

6. Economic and demographic considerations may justify a variation in the conditions of a pension scheme. Such variations should always take account of the rights acquired or being acquired by insured people. (International Labour Office, 1955, pp. 84-85).

### Areas of Investigation

In some countries, private institutions—that is, institutions that are not affiliated with either labor or management—have carried out or commenced studies of retirement age based on the rising life expectancy. The background of these studies is the general desire among older people to continue working after the statutory retirement age, either at the same work that they had been engaged in or at some easier or part-time work. The restriction linking pension rules to a means test discourages workers from seeking or accepting work, since the increase in income after the deduction of the pension and taxes is considered too low.

It is possible to overcome this difficulty if certain types of income receive priority in calculating the income to be deducted from the pension. Before World War II, some countries had both basic and supplementary pensions, the basic pension being paid without reduction and the supplementary pension being subject to various rules. The rules stipulated that income from work after retirement age was not wholly deducted when fixing supplementary pensions in accordance with means tests. This method has been criticized, however, since it penalizes those who have income from the savings they have accumulated during their active years. The method appears to have been abandoned even though it has been discussed anew during the past decade as a way of encouraging people to work after attaining the stipulated retirement age. As regards ordinary private old-age insurance schemes, the method appears to be unacceptable from the actuarial point of view, and it has not been used.

Finally, some scientists consider that the reduction in working hours justifies higher retirement ages. If the average annual hours of work are 2,200 and the working week is reduced by four hours, the annual average will be 2,000. This means that, spread over the average working period of forty years, the total reduction is 8,000 hours. It would be possible and, in many cases, suitable to use some of the time saved to raise the pension age and thus entitle beneficiaries to a higher pension.

*REFERENCES*

International Labour Office. First European regional conference at the International Labour Organisation. *Official Bull.*, 1955, **38**, 78-92.

# CHAPTER 50

*Income Security,*
*Retirement, and*
*Pension-Deduction Rules*

POUL MILHØJ

This paper discusses the relation between income security and retirement, with special reference to the influence of deduction rules which depend on the recipient's income and reduce benefits payable for disablement, sickness, retirement, and the like.[1] Regulations for reducing benefit payments below established levels are based on (1) the belief that funds available for social purposes are limited and (2) the assumption that there is an aversion to work and saving and that, therefore, payment of benefits equal to loss of income will lessen incentive to earn and save.

[1] The discussion in this paper grows out of Danish experience.

## FACTORS BEHIND PENSION-DEDUCTION RULES

### *Availability of Funds*

If funds for social purposes are limited, it seems unfair to give equal benefits to all, irrespective of income. Deduction rules based on the ends they seek to achieve may therefore be employed. If the "principle of unconditional benefit" governs, benefits paid to those in great need would be smaller because available funds would be shared with the well-to-do whose needs are less. Unconditional benefits are, therefore, socially uneconomic because the needs of those with little or no income are not fully met while individuals with high incomes may be given benefits they do not really need.

Since the distribution of social welfare funds does not stem from natural "rights" but is based on social policy, the "principle of supplementation" seems more equitable. The objective, according to this principle, is to maintain a minimum level of income through benefit payments which will offset loss of income. Thus there will be no benefit payment until income falls below the established minimum.

Somewhat more expensive is the "need-limit principle," [2] according to which benefits are paid in full up to a specified level of the recipient's earned income. If his income exceeds this level, no benefit is paid. Application of this principle may involve a decline in total income (earned income plus benefit) when earned income exceeds the level at which the deduction is 100 per cent. Thus, the supplementation and need-limit principles attempt to distribute social welfare funds where the need is presumed to be greater. A nation's wealth and social policies would determine the minimum income level under the supplementation principle or the need-limit level.

### *Motivation*

The second policy consideration is the effect of benefit payment rules on motivation to work, and earn one's own income. Under the supplementation principle, the individual who has no prospect of earning an income which exceeds the guaranteed minimum will have no economic inducement to work. Furthermore, the advantage of taking a job is limited if it increases income only slightly above the guaranteed level. On the other hand, under the need-limit

---

[2] This assumes that need-limit is fixed at the same level that minimum income would be in the case of the supplementing principle.

principle any income up to the need-limit level goes into the worker's pocket. When earnings exceed this level, however, the loss is greater because the benefit ceases. Total income would be lower than it would have been had earnings remained below the need-limit. Only when a person earns an amount equal to the need-limit plus the benefit will he be as well off as if his own income exactly equaled the need-limit—except that he will have earned the whole income himself, which may be a personal satisfaction.

If we disregard the pleasure that some people take in earning their own incomes, the effect of benefits on income motivation will depend on the minimum income level and need-limit compared to the income distribution of the community. If the limit is much below the community's income, benefits will not, naturally, restrict initiative, but their influence in establishing acceptable social standards will be correspondingly lower. If many wage earners are just above the limit, the benefits will probably have a very discouraging effect on initiative.

At the other extreme, under the principle of unconditional benefit, all problems of motivation are eliminated. Everyone, irrespective of financial situation, is entitled to benefits. Consequently, everyone fully enjoys income gained by his initiative. Of course, no allowance has been made for a suitable distribution of the limited funds available for social benefits.

At this point, the deduction regulations enter the picture as a compromise. If deductions are designed to reduce benefits as income rises and if benefits are reduced less than income rises, the most needy have the greater part of the funds, and motivation will not be undermined. The determining factor in establishing deductions is the balance between the value of benefits—especially for low-income groups—and the fear of discouraging individual motivation for work and self-support.

### Are These Assumptions Correct?

Assuming that benefit payments are not entirely out of proportion to the level of wealth in the community, funds are, in a way, unlimited, since their size depends on the share of the national income that the public is willing to transfer from insurance contributions and tax payments to welfare services. From the point of view of economic balance, welfare benefits paid to high-income groups—in order to avoid discouraging initiative at any level—will probably be saved, thereby withdrawing these amounts from consumer expenditure. In addition, interest in earning an income is stimulated, and thus the national income will be increased.

The problems of administering limited benefit funds are more complex than indicated here, but there may be reason to challenge the widely believed notion that there is an absolute maximum —established without reference to the general economy—available for welfare expenditures. Fixing the limit is a political decision.

So much for the question of limitations. As for the problem of initiative, it is, of course, possible to cite instances of desire to earn an income despite equivalent or superior public benefits. It will, however, no doubt be safer to assume that the opposite is the case. Accordingly, this has been chosen as the basic assumption of all the arguments in this paper.

### DEFINING NEED

The previous considerations do not exhaust the problems of arriving at an equitable deduction formula. The question of personal income versus welfare benefits must, of course, depend on the need the benefit relieves. In a number of cases, need can be defined in apparently objective terms: age, disability, dependence, widowhood, illness, and unemployment. It is assumed that these conditions reduce or destroy the individuals' ability to earn his living. The use of such criteria implies that it is possible to objectively ascertain decline in earning capacity. If age, disability, and the rest could be accurately identified with a measurable decline in earning capacity, benefits could be automatically granted like benefits from ordinary insurance. The problem of motivation disappears, and again we are left with only the problem of the most economical use of funds.

To the extent that a decline in wage-earning capacity could be immediately identified with a corresponding decline in income, the principle of unconditional benefits would avoid conflict with suitable distribution of limited social funds, but this applies to earned incomes only to a limited extent and not at all to incomes from property. If social policy dictates that only an objectively ascertained decline in income merits payment of benefits, distribution of funds presents no difficulties. At the same time, however, stimulating motivation will be neglected if the minimum income guaranteed through welfare benefits is fairly close to that of high-income groups in the community. In this case it must be assumed that personal savings to provide for the future would be reduced and that there will be

less incentive for the individual to overcome the financial consequences of illness or disability by rehabilitation or retraining for
another occupation. This may be considered deplorable on an economic level, but the fact that it also conflicts with the social goals of
rehabilitation is more important.

Instead of trying to trace the history of the compromise
between using scarce funds economically and motivating interest in
earning a living, we can examine social welfare legislation as a consequence of the difficulties of objectively ascertaining the decline in
economic capacity and the impossibility of identifying this decline
with a corresponding decline in income. This could easily lead to
the conclusion that there are no objective criteria for social need
other than absence of income, which, when relieved, discourages initiative and hampers social rehabilitation.

### Full Employment

The difficulty of objectively ascertaining decline in economic
capacity decreases when full employment and an excessive demand
for labor are assumed; unemployment beyond that caused by season
or relocation does not count as need.

If there are jobs for all who are able to work—in some cases
after retraining—loss of income cannot by itself be recognized as a
need. Accordingly, the payment of benefits must be based on an
objectively ascertained decline in or loss of wage-earning capacity;
the wage earner, therefore, must be ill, disabled, dependent, widowed
or the like. If there is no health or other factor which prevents the
wage earner from earning a living, he may be left to find a job. If
an unemployed person receives income during illness (as is the case
for the self-employed and certain types of employees), the illness constitutes need only to the extent of extra medical and nursing expenses.
Thus with full employment the need for deduction rules vanishes,
and it becomes necessary to establish objective criteria for evaluating
need. The problem is passed to physicians, social workers, and the
like, a process consistent with the idea that social authorities interested
in rehabilitation shall take the active role in ascertaining and relieving reduced wage-earning capacity, rather than confine themselves
to passive distribution of money according to given rates.

Thus, the consideration of limited funds no longer requires
that benefits be granted by a supplementing or need-limit principle;
therefore, the principle of unconditional (regarding income from
work) benefits can be used. If a person's wage-earning capacity has

been reduced by 50 per cent, he is granted a benefit which is 50 per cent of the benefit payable for the particular condition, and the recipient can content himself with this benefit or make an effort (objectively, the effort is beyond his capacity) to earn another 50 per cent. In this way rehabilitation will also be taken into account. The objective evaluation of earning capacity does not become easier because there is full employment; it becomes imperative because loss of income cannot be accepted as the sole cause of need.

The situation differs when income is derived from property. If earning capacity is defined by ability to work or possibility of finding work, there will still be a problem of balancing limited funds against motivating people to protect themselves by saving. It seems likely, however, that, in a period of full employment and excess demand for labor, economic policy will motivate saving and not be too concerned with the fact that part of the funds are paid to persons who receive large incomes from property despite reduced earning capacity. This is because of the assumption that welfare benefits added to large incomes will, to a very great extent, be saved or substituted for capital which would otherwise have been spent. Although saving might deepen a depression, it will, assuming an excess demand, be necessary in order to continue economic growth without inflation and prevent deterioration of the foreign-exchange position.

## DEDUCTION RULES AND OLD-AGE PENSIONS

The problems of deductions are naturally most important when the benefit is to be a long-term payment, like an old-age pension, that the recipient can live on. The following discussion refers solely to old-age pensions. As in other cases, deductions for personal income have been introduced as a compromise between using limited funds to pay old-age pensions to people with ample incomes and discouraging interest in achieving income security through one's own work and savings. If the financial status of the individual could be ascertained by an objective measure, there would be no reason, assuming full employment, to consider old age a cause of need. It is in the absence of such objective criteria and with the realization that old age, as a rule, reduces earning ability that the age in itself comes into the picture as a cause of need. The age limit, however, is a substitute for an objective criterion, for which reason it demands deduction rates.

### Three Basic Models

The following analyses of how deduction may influence earning power in connection with calculation of old-age pensions considers three extremely simple pension plans. They have the common feature of recognizing some age limit as a necessary but not always sufficient condition of the right to receive a benefit payment.

By reasoning our way through a few simple pension systems under equally simple assumptions, we should get some knowledge of how the more complicated rules work. By comparing the simple assumptions of the plans with the actual conditions, it should also be possible, in given research situations, to get some guidance in evaluating the effect of actual systems. Finally, and this is of great importance, building simple models provides the best opportunity to set up the hypotheses concerning patterns of reaction which must be examined at the start of a research project.

The three models serve only to examine the influence of the pension rules on the inclination of male employees to retire. Full employment is assumed in all plans. Income from property is disregarded since the right to receive a pension is independent of it, a simplification that corresponds to the actual situation in pension insurance. In order to uncover the basic problems, each of the plans is discussed under gradually changing assumptions. First, it is assumed that the pension is a right, without an obligation to retire, requiring a choice between full pension or full income from work in the original occupation. Second, it is assumed that partial retirement entitles the worker to a partial pension. Here, too, it is assumed that, if work is chosen, it will be in the previous occupation. Third, it is assumed that at the age of retirement there is an unconditional obligation to retire. Finally, although there is a right to seek work in one's previous occupation, the unconditioned assumption that this will be done is modified.

*1. Full Pension at the Previous Income.* The first plan describes a scheme offering full pension at the level of previous income if the worker retires at a given age. In this case, desire and ability to work balanced against the pleasure of retiring will determine retirement time. Typical retirement ages will be established, depending on the demands and/or pleasures of the occupations as well as the possibilities of a rewarding life as a pensioner. If there is a tendency to continue working, such a plan would, under full employment, come close to an objective evaluation of earning capacity. The employer's evaluation of the usefulness of the pensionable employee would then decide how long he could continue to work. The employer's refusal to dismiss a useless pensionable employee for humane reasons would largely disappear if the employee could retire on a pension equal to his former wage. In fields where the the promotion to top jobs is based mainly on seniority, there will be great pressure from the younger employees to induce their older colleagues to retire. In a situation with a low rate of employment, this pressure will be even greater, especially among manual workers. The pressure, of course, will be greatest when dismissals are based on seniority.

The plan may be characterized by 100 per-cent deduction for income from work. On the assumption of minimum motivation to provide for oneself, it will mean that everybody will retire on reaching the age entitling him to do so. To supplement pensions, workers will have to have savings commensurate with their former incomes and desired standards of living.

*2. Pension below the Previous Income.* The second plan describes a scheme offering, after a specified age, the right to receive a pension smaller than the income derived from work. The pension, however, is not below a subsistence level determined by the wealth of the community. In this case, a person's desire to retire must be balanced against the decline in his income. Whereas nothing was gained by continuing to work under the first plan, now there is a difference in incomes. There is still 100 per-cent deduction for income from work.

On the whole, this plan should keep a greater number of people at work than the first would, particularly people with physically taxing work that has no intellectual or other attractions. The actual number will depend not only on the inclination to retire, but also on the difference between wages and pension. Whether the decrease is a certain percentage of income or whether the income is reduced equally for everybody is of particular importance.

The income tax scale and the pattern of consumption are important. If the tax scale is graduated, some of the reduction in income caused by retirement will be counteracted by a reduction in income tax. This means that under the second plan the inclination to retire will be greater if tax scales are graduated rather than proportional. Furthermore, progression in the tax scale will make the loss of income least severe for the highest incomes. Studies of private spending suggest that the proportion of expenditures for housing and food decrease as income rises; higher incomes should, therefore, be able to take a larger cut than lower incomes. Accordingly, retirement should be most frequent among people in higher income groups. On the other hand, high-income jobs may often be more attractive. Actually, however, little is known about what parts, or how large a part, of a budget the individual considers fixed, necessary expenditures—and nothing at all is known about changes in consumption as income fluctuates (in this case, falls). Pressure from below because of seniority rules for promotion and dismissal will, of course, still exist under this plan, but with less strength, since retirement results in lower income.

*3. Pension to Everyone.* The third plan offers a pension to everybody, irrespective of income, at least equaling the subsistence level of the community. Under such unconditional old-age pensions, all deductions are abandoned. Thus a premium is put on older people's work—or on old age as such. Old age is recognized as a cause of need or a reason for reward. This plan will keep the greatest possible number of older people working, partly because they will retain full remuneration and partly because employers will be reluctant to dismiss them.

If the same pension is paid to everybody, irrespective of former income, those in the higher wage and salary groups will be more inclined to continue working than those in the lower groups. If the pension is in proportion to income over the years up to pension age, the choice between living solely on the pension or supplementing it with full income will be more difficult for those in the lowest wage groups. Their work, however, will frequently be physically taxing, which induces retirement.

### Partial Retirement

In each of the three plans, the right to partial retirement with a corresponding income may be introduced, which generally should adjust the balance between desire and ability to work.

Under the first plan, reducing working hours by one-third will not result in a change in total income. Although there is 100 per-cent deduction for income from work, it is likely that the possibility for partial retirement will motivate some employees to go on working. If a shorter working day can reduce the physical strain of a full working day, continued contact with the place of work might be a welcome break in an otherwise boring life of retirement. On the other hand, it is frequently difficult for an employer to fit part-time workers into the production process, especially when the work is primarily physical so that the experience of an older worker will not be an advantage. At the same time, it is exactly this kind of work which is attractive on a part-time basis. The desire to continue working full time will be found especially among the older employees who feel that they have an advantage over their younger colleagues because of their greater experience. Employers' and employees' organizations, however, frequently turn against part-time employment.

Under the second plan the total income in the case of partial retirement will depend on the pension scheme. If the pension is fixed at a certain portion of previous income, for example, one-half—and if the income from work is kroner 18,000 (approximately seven kroner make an American dollar), we will have the following figures:

|  | Income from work | Pension | Total income | Decline in total income |
|---|---|---|---|---|
| Full retirement | — | 9,000 | 9,000 | 9,000 |
| Two-thirds retirement | 6,000 | 6,000 | 12,000 | 6,000 |
| One-third retirement | 12,000 | 3,000 | 15,000 | 3,000 |

It will be seen that the pension is reduced by half the income from work. In contrast to the first version of Plan Two, deductions have now been introduced. The decision to work or retire will now depend on desire to work, loss of income, size of this loss compared with income, and pattern of consumption.

If, under Plan Three, the unconditional pension is combined with the right not only of full, but also of partial, income, employment of older workers will increase.

### Compulsory Retirement

If, on attaining a certain age, everybody must retire with a pension from his previous occupation, any income from work must be earned in a new occupation. Under Plan One there will be little inclination to seek new work after retirement. Under Plan Two the likelihood of a labor demand for retired workers will be greater than under Plan One, assuming full employment and a production schedule with possibilities of independent work, such as running a small shop. Moreover, it assumes that labor organizations do not oppose such a demand. If these assumptions hold, the scheme of deduction rates and tax scales will play a decisive part. Taking a new job after retirement is often likely to yield a relatively modest income. The demand .for retired workers, therefore, will increase if a good wage is offered and the pension is not reduced because of this additional income.

Whether or not this is done, a progressively rising deduction scale will have a discouraging effect, particularly on earning high incomes after retirement. If, moreover, the pension is in proportion to previous income, people with higher pensions will probably refrain from extra work on a large scale. Recruiting retired people for the labor market will therefore consist chiefly of former low-income workers. On the other hand, if pensions are uniform or at least less than proportional to previous income, people with previously higher incomes will probably experience difficulties in living on a reduced income, and therefore they will seek this special labor market to a greater extent. Since old people seek work to which they are accustomed, the labor demand for retired people will come close to being a miniature picture of the ordinary labor market. The very existence of deduction rates, however, implies that small invisible incomes or incomes in kind will generally be favored at the expense of ordinary incomes. Irrespective of the deduction rates, the possibility of such incomes will probably be a dominant aspect of the special labor demand for retired persons.

Under Plan Three an obligatory retirement age will lead to the maximum demand for retired persons. Since there are no deduction rates in this plan, there will be no inclination toward jobs with small invisible incomes.

### Continuing Previous Work or
### Taking a Retirement Job

The above testing of the three pension plans was based, first, on an assumption that, if people were entitled to pensions without the obligation to retire, they would balance pension against full- or part-time work in their previous occupation. Next, it was assumed that retirement was compulsory so that work, if desired, would have to be sought by changing occupation.

In the first testing, the picture becomes more complicated if the assumption that people will always retain the work to which they are accustomed is abandoned. It is doubtful whether many older people would seek new work, but it might happen if the older person had a particularly difficult time coping with his previous job or if the possibility of establishing oneself as an independent worker is particularly great and, perhaps, attractive by tradition.[3]

[3] If this is the case, it may act as a pressure for reducing the pension age.

Under Plan One, in order for a person to seek a new job after reaching the pension age, there must be a desire to work at a new job adapted to age or interest. Pressure from employers and from younger colleagues to retire an older person may contribute to this. Under Plan Two, there is financial gain attached to working. Working in a previous or new occupation will depend on the advantages and/or disadvantages of the two occupations. People may leave physically taxing occupations. In addition to this, the deduction rates will, in this case, also lead to small jobs with invisible incomes. Under Plan Three, the choice between the previous job or a new job will depend solely on the advantages and disadvantages of these jobs.

## CONCLUSIONS

It has not been my intention to express preference for one of these pension plans. If full employment is still assumed, however, there may be reason to ask whether it is desirable that age in itself should confer or, in many cases, force a pension. Objective criteria esablishing loss of, or decline in, working capacity as the basis of the right to an ample pension would solve many sociopolitical problems involved in the relation between retirement and income security in old age. If such criteria are considered Utopian, the right to retire without any obligation to do so seems the best solution. Which of the three pension plans is preferable will depend on workers' personal opinions of retirement versus employers' and unions' opinions of the usefulness and desirability of older employees. If the desire to retire seems great, Plan Two or Three must be chosen. If the efficiency of older people is low, Plan One must be chosen. Establishment of Plan One or Three—the two extremes—depends on the relation of inclination to retire and usefulness of older employees. Thus, the solution cannot be general because there are differences from occupation to occupation. Some people will pay for being allowed to work, others will feel it a burden. In some occupations old people are automatically inefficient. If employers favor an early retirement age, it must be presumed that wages are high. For this reason, Plan Three is probably not necessary, although it will, of course, stimulate occupational mobility for those who have to retire.

### *Suggestions for Research*

Proceeding from this simplified analysis, one may suggest that the most promising lines of research lie in studies of older people's capacity and desire to work and of their opportunities for work. Studies carried out by asking employees, employers, and unions hypothetical questions would have little or no value. Useful conclusions can be expected only when precise conditions can be stated and behavior traced in relation to them. The more nearly the conditions correspond to those given in the models presented above, the more adequately the hypotheses stated will be verified.

The clear-cut case of a full pension equivalent to earnings (Plan One) occurs so rarely that there seems to be no point in studying it at the present time. Pensions lower than wages, paid as a right without the obligation to retire (Plan Two), are available to Danish civil servants from their sixty-seventh year until compulsory retirement at seventy. Here there is reason to examine the behavior patterns in various occupations. Studies of tax regulations, consumption in various age and income groups, and, ideally, longitudinal consumption studies on the most frequent retirement ages will also be of great importance, as will studies of typical income reductions after retirement. It must be established, moreover, how widespread promotion and/or dismissal based on seniority are, as these determine the pressure from below.

Plans Two and Three—absolutely compulsory retirement—come closest to reality. Plan Two corresponds to compulsory retirement and general pensioning with deduction rates; Plan Three corresponds to the situation of many civil servants and salaried employees with unconditional pensions. Here there is the obvious and fairly easy task of trying to get a clear picture of the job opportunities for retired people in various income and age groups and the like. Retiring in order to seek new work although it is possible to remain in the old position can be studied in the age groups in which there are many people who are entitled, but not forced, to retire. Reactions of employees with very large life annuities (or large lottery prizes, inheritances, gifts, and the like) which have not been reduced by inflation could give an idea of the extent to which people in differing jobs will work in order to retain their incomes from work.

# CHAPTER 51

## State Pensions and
## Retirement Age

BRIAN ABEL-SMITH

In Britain since the war, there has been a variety of changes in provisions for pensions. The level of benefits has been increased fairly often. Rules on deductions for earnings have been amended more than once. And the increments which can be earned by postponing retirement have been increased. In this paper, an attempt is made to learn whether any of these changes have affected retirement habits.

### RETIREMENT AGE

Retirement pensions are normally awarded immediately on retirement when this occurs within five years after reaching pensionable age—sixty-five for men and sixty for women. Thus, it would

423

seem possible to use statistics of age at which pension was awarded as an indication of the age of retirement in the community. It is not possible, however, to reconstruct these statistics over a period of sixteen years, partly because it was several years before a wholly reliable series of statistics was developed and partly because rights to pension have varied at different periods.

The situation has been complicated by special provisions for people who were not insured under the old scheme or became insured late in life. Those who became insured before September 30, 1946, and who were within five years of pensionable age were treated as retired and awarded pensions exactly five years after they became insured. Those who became insured on or after that date and who were within ten years of pensionable age were treated as retired ten years after becoming insured. Thus, the statistics of persons becoming entitled to pensions before September, 1951, include those who did not necessarily retire at the time they were given pensions. The number of these cases was a very small proportion of the total, but it varied somewhat from quarter to quarter. Thus, the series of figures up to autumn, 1951, are not strictly comparable.

The figures between October, 1951, and October, 1956, do cover a broadly similar group of persons, but are not comparable to the earlier series because no late-age entrants were becoming entitled to pensions during that period. More late-age entrants became entitled to pensions between October, 1956, and July, 1958; the great majority of these became entitled in July, 1958. After this month, a reliable series should be available covering virtually the whole population.

Thus, it is not possible to show long-term trends of the age of retirement in Britain from these statistics. It does, however, seem possible to study shorter-term changes if one bears in mind the qualifications mentioned.

There have been a number of studies of the ages at which cohorts of prospective pensioners took their pensions. The results of these studies are quoted in the text of this paper. The main series of statistics has, however, been based not on cohorts of persons reaching particular ages but on the proportion of awards made to people of various ages in a quarter or a year. Such statistics give a less reliable picture of retirement trends, but the only continuous series are in this form. The figures are shown in tables 1 and 2 in the form to which the statistics were changed in 1953.

TABLE 1
PERCENTAGE OF AWARDS OF RETIREMENT PENSIONS
IN GREAT BRITAIN TO MEN ATTAINING CERTAIN AGES
IN EACH QUARTER BETWEEN APRIL, 1949,
AND DECEMBER, 1954

| Quarter ending | Age | | |
|---|---|---|---|
| | 65 | 65-67 3/4 | 65-69 3/4 |
| June 1949 | 47 | 71 | 80 |
| September 1949 | 47 | 69 | 79 |
| December 1949 | 43 | 70 | 80 |
| March 1950 | 42 | 68 | 78 |
| June 1950 | 44 | 70 | 80 |
| September 1950 | 46 | 70 | 78 |
| December 1950 | 45 | 72 | 81 |
| March 1951 | 44 | 69 | 79 |
| June 1951 | 47 | 71 | 79 |
| September 1951 | 44 | 68 | 77 |
| December 1951 | 38 | 68 | 79 |
| March 1952 | 37 | 67 | 78 |
| June 1952 | 40 | 68 | 79 |
| September 1952 | 40 | 65 | 76 |
| December 1952 | 34 | 67 | 78 |
| March 1953 | 38 | 69 | 80 |
| June 1953 | 38 | 67 | 79 |
| September 1953 | 41 | 70 | 81 |
| December 1953 | 37 | 66 | 79 |
| March 1954 | 41 | 67 | 79 |
| June 1954 | 40 | 66 | 77 |
| September 1954 | 40 | 66 | 77 |

Sources—Ministry of Pensions and National Insurance (1953, p. 29); Ministry of Pensions and National Insurance (1954, p. 23).

These two tables suggest that there was remarkably little change in retirement behavior between 1949 and 1958. During this period, there were many changes in the level of pension and in the conditions on which pensions were granted.

TABLE 2
PERCENTAGE OF AWARDS OF RETIREMENT PENSION AT
PENSIONABLE AGE AND LATER IN GREAT BRITAIN FOR
YEARS ENDING JUNE 30, 1954-1958

| Year ending June 30 | Retirement at or within four weeks of mini- mum pen- sionable age | Retirement deferred over four weeks and less than six half-years | Retirement deferred 6-9 half- years | Retirement deferred ten half- years |
|---|---|---|---|---|
| **Men** | | | | |
| 1954 | 42.4 | 26.1 | 11.5 | 19.9 |
| 1955 | 41.7 | 25.8 | 11.2 | 21.3 |
| 1956 | 41.5 | 25.5 | 11.4 | 21.5 |
| 1957 | 41.4 | 27.0 | 11.2 | 20.4 |
| 1958 | 40.2 | 29.0 | 13.1 | 17.6 |
| **Women** | | | | |
| 1954 | 65.0 | 17.5 | 5.4 | 12.0 |
| 1955 | 63.3 | 18.8 | 5.2 | 12.8 |
| 1956 | 62.8 | 18.7 | 6.0 | 12.4 |
| 1957 | 63.6 | 16.8 | 5.7 | 13.9 |
| 1958 | 64.4 | 17.3 | 5.8 | 12.3 |

Sources—Ministry of Pensions and National Insurance (1954; 1955; 1956; 1957; 1958).

Before 1946, there was a threefold system of pensions:
1. Contributory pensions of 10s. per week given to men at sixty-five and women at sixty without any income test and irrespective of whether they were working. This pension was limited in practice to those who had been employed.
2. Noncontributory pensions of 10s. or less at the age of seventy subject to an income test.
3. Supplementary pensions confined to persons receiving Nos. 1 or 2, above, subject to an income test differing from that applied in the case of No. 2.

In October, 1946, the level of contributory pensions was raised to 26s. for a single person and 42s. for a married couple subject to an earnings rule for men between the ages of sixty-five and seventy and for women between the ages of sixty and sixty-five. One pound could be earned without loss of pension. Any earnings above this were wholly deducted from the pension which would otherwise be available.[1] Above the ages of seventy for men and sixty-five for women, the pension was available without an income test of any kind.

From a small sample of men and women reaching pensionable age in 1946, 1947, and 1948, it was estimated that, when the higher pension of 26s. conditional on retirement first became payable, a slightly larger proportion of persons retired on reaching pensionable age than in the next two years.

> Only 60 per cent of men continued in employment as compared with a figure of 65 per cent for 1947 and 1948. After allowing for sampling errors, the difference is not of any great significance. It may be that the immediate effect of raising pensions was to increase the number of those retiring. It is more likely, however, that the slightly higher figures of retirement for 1946 should be explained as the continuance of the flow from industry of elderly workers who had worked on to advanced ages to meet war-time needs. The general inference to be drawn so far is that the granting of a bigger pension conditional upon retirement from October 1946 onwards has no appreciable effect on retirements, neither stimulating them nor checking them. (Ministry of National Insurance, 1951, p. 17).

There was little change between 1947 and 1951 in the proportion of men and women who carried on employment to the ages of seventy (men) and sixty-five (women), whether they had reached pensionable age well before 1946 or during 1946, when the pension was increased (*loc. cit.*).

There were modest increases in the pension in 1951 and 1952, but the next large increase came in April, 1955, when the rate was raised from 32s.6d. to 40s. for a single person, with corresponding increases for a married couple. There was "no marked change in the incidence of retirement" (Ministry of Pensions and National Insurance, 1957, p. 26). The next increase was in 1958, when the rates were increased from 40s. to 50s. Again, there was no noticeable tendency toward earlier retirement. These changes were largely to meet changes in prices. An index of prices appropriate to retirement pensions has never been constructed, but it was not until 1958 that it could be claimed that the pension rates provided any higher living standard than in 1946.

---

[1] Beveridge (1942, p. 97) suggested that £3 should be earned without any deduction and that one-half to two-thirds of any excess of £3 be deducted.

The fact that these changes in pension rates did not seem to affect retirement behavior does not prove that much larger increases would have no effect. Indeed, there is some basis for thinking that much larger pensions could cause earlier retirement. An inquiry was conducted in 1953 into reasons for retirement (Ministry of Pensions and National Insurance, 1954a). The inquiry covered 10,000 men and 9,000 women. Over half the retirements were stated to be for reasons of health—chronic illness, ill health, or heaviness or strain of work. A further quarter of retirements were stated to be caused by employers' action. In the case of men aged sixty-five, the retirements which were not accounted for by these reasons were: 6.9 per cent, wish for rest or leisure; 2.2 per cent, family reasons; 5.6 per cent, other reasons; and 2.7 per cent, reasons not known. Thus, few retirements were voluntary.

Persons staying at work beyond the minimum pensionable age were asked the reason for dong so. Out of men at age sixty-five, 54 per cent gave financial need as their most important reason, 15 per cent said that they felt fit enough, and 21 per cent said that they preferred to work. At the level of pension which was available, nearly everyone who could be at work was at work. At a higher level of pension, some of those who said they were staying at work for financial reasons might have retired.

When asked what kind of thing they would consider most likely to make them leave work, only 6.2 per cent of men aged sixty-five said sudden financial gain on sufficient means, and 0.8 per cent said increased rate of retirement pension. The answers to this question were, however, completely overshadowed by the fact that 72.3 per cent answered ill health. Moreover, one doubts whether any reliable indication of behavior in hypothetical circumstances can be gained from a straight questionnaire survey. The first reaction to improved financial circumstances might well be to contemplate retirement. But the attractiveness of the prospect may not grow with longer and deeper contemplation.

## INCREMENTS FOR POSTPONED RETIREMENT

Beveridge hoped to encourage later retirement by granting increments to those who postponed their pensions. "The conditions governing pension should be such as to encourage every person who can go on working after reaching pensionable age, to go on working and to postpone retirement and the claiming of pension" (Beveridge,

1942, p. 98). Accordingly, he recommended an increment of pension of 2s. per week for a married couple and 1s. per week for a single person for each year that the pension was postponed. These increases in pension were "designed to give to the individual some, though not all, of the saving in pension expenditure resulting through his postponement" (*ibid.*, p. 97).

The system of increments for postponed pensions did not come into operation until July 5, 1948. An increment to pension of 1s. per week could be earned by every twenty-five weekly contributions that were paid. Despite this inducement to stay at work, the percentage of men remaining employed within one month of attaining pensionable age fell from 65 per cent in April, 1947, and April, 1948, to 60 per cent in midsummer, 1949. In the case of women, the percentage fell from 50 to 45 per cent between the same periods (Ministry of National Insurance, 1951, p. 18). The ministry was not overly dismayed.

> It is too early to say with any assurance whether these new provisions have in fact induced older workers to stay on at work beyond 60/65 to a greater extent than they would have done otherwise. [It did, however, seem to be true that they had stayed on *less* than before.] Until the new arrangements have had at least a full five years' run, it will not be possible to trace precisely what is happening. . . . It will take time for workers and employers to adjust themselves to the new attitudes towards old age and retirement on which the new provisions are based: it is not by any means clear that the full significance of the provisions is yet appreciated (*ibid.*, p. 17).

In 1951, the financial attractions of postponing retirement were increased. The increments were raised from 1s. to 1s.6d. for every twenty-five weekly contributions paid. At the same time, the amount which could be earned by the retired without reduction of pension was increased from £1 per week to £2 per week. These changes went into effect on July 18, 1951. There was no marked change in the proportion of awards made to men of different ages between the second and third quarters of 1951 (see Table 1). From other statistics, the ministry reported that the proportion of men remaining employed within one month of reaching minimum pensionable age was 60 per cent at the end of 1951. This was the same figure as at the end of 1950 and as in midsummer, 1949.

> These figures do not indicate any appreciable change in retirement trends which could be associated with the changes made by the Act of 1951. It should be remembered, however, that the figures . . . for end

of 1951 . . . relate to a period when the rate of increments to pension for those who defer retirement had only recently been increased. The attitude of individuals to retirement is, however, subject to a variety of factors, and inevitably changes only slowly (Ministry of National Insurance, 1952, p. 24).

Hope was not abandoned.

Two years later, there was still no sign of the later retirement which it was hoped that the increments would induce. The inquiry conducted in 1953 into the reason for retirement or staying at work (Ministry of Pensions and National Insurance, 1954a) showed that more than 93 per cent of men were aware of the system of increments. Nevertheless, only seven in 1,000 gave this as their reason for staying at work. Only five in 1,000 gave it as the most important reason for staying on at work. In 14 per cent of the report forms, several reasons were given as the main one. In such cases, more definite reasons—such as the desire to earn increments—were given precedence over less definite reasons when the results were tabulated. Thus, this figure of five per 1,000 is in this sense an overstatement of the results of the inquiry. When asked specifically about the increments, on the other hand, one in four men said that knowledge of the increments had influenced them in making their decisions.

Commenting on these results a year later, the Phillips Committee (The Treasury, 1954, p. 53) said that it was clear from the evidence that increments had little effect on the incentive to remain at work. There were good reasons for not having a system of increments at all, but the committee did not go so far as to recommend their abolition.

> They may have little effect as an incentive to postpone retirement but they are a well-known feature of the National Insurance Scheme and if they were removed or materially reduced we should expect the public reaction to this change to be seriously unfavorable to the success of the steps now being taken to facilitate and promote voluntary postponement of retirement (*loc. cit.*).

The most frequent reasons given for staying at work in the inquiry mentioned above were "financial need," "feel fit enough," and "prefer to work." Would there really have been any serious effect on retirement if increments had been withdrawn?

Although a new dogma had been promulgated about the negative effects of increments, at least the argument about a positive inducement had been abandoned. It was, moreover, interesting to note that, when increments were further increased by the 1959 act, the minister of pensions did not mention encouragement to stay at work as a reason for the change (House of Commons, 1959, Cols. 889-892). He saw it as a way of providing higher pensions for the more robust group of pensioners.

### THE EARNINGS RULE

The retirement condition and earnings deduction which were introduced in 1946 were intended primarily to keep down the cost of pensions. Beveridge (1942) wrote:

> [T]o give a full subsistence income to every citizen on his or her reaching the age of 65 or 60 would impose an unjustifiable and harmful burden on all citizens below that age. . . . The object of encouraging continuance of work in later life will not be attained by granting pensions without a retirement condition. If the pensions are adequate for subsistence, they will obviously encourage retirement. Even inadequate unconditional pensions will encourage early retirement in many cases (p. 96).

The amount that could be earned without loss of pension had been increased in 1951 from £1 to £2 without any noticeable effect on retirement behavior. Any earnings above £2 were wholly deducted from the pension. There was pressure for liberalization of the rule. The question was considered by the National Insurance Advisory Committee, which reported in 1956. The committee recommended that the limit of earnings be raised to £2.10s.0d. and that, on the next pound of earnings, only 6d. be deducted from the pension for each 1s. of earnings. Any earnings above that level should be wholly deducted from the pension. In addition, a person who had retired should be allowed an option to return to work and start earning increments.

These recommendations were adopted and the new rules came into effect on July 31, 1956. There was little change in retirement behavior. In the year July, 1955, to June, 1956, 41.5 per cent of men and 62.8 per cent of women retired within four weeks of minimum pensionable age. In the year 1956-1957, the figures were 41.4 and 63.6 per cent, respectively (see Table 2).

Although statistics are not yet available to assess the effects of later changes in the earnings rule, it may nevertheless be of interest to bring up to date the history of the rule in Britain. In January, 1959, the minister of pensions proposed a further increase of the amount which could be earned without deduction of earnings from

£2.10s.0d. to £3. The National Insurance Advisory Committee supported this increase, since it was justified by increases in earnings since 1956, but stated that there was no case for raising the earnings limit "any higher than the level proposed" (Ministry of Pensions and National Insurance, 1959).

In the manifesto for the election of October, 1959, the government announced that, if returned, it would raise the earnings limit by another 10s.[2] Accordingly, the National Insurance Advisory Committee was asked to approve another 10s. in November, 1959. Despite its statement only nine months earlier, the committee reluctantly approved another 10s.

> We take it . . . that it is the Government's deliberate intention to make the earnings rules more generous than they are at present. . . . How far the earnings rules can be relaxed without jeopardizing the retirement principle is, of course, a matter of judgment; there is no exact point at which it can be said that the limit has been reached. . . . While the proposed increase of 10s. in the level of free earnings goes rather beyond our previous recommendation, we do not think it is possible to say categorically that it will, of itself, imperil the retirement principle (Ministry of Pensions and National Insurance, 1960, pp. 3-4).

After this qualified approval, the earnings limit was raised again.

Between 1948 and 1960, the earnings rule has been greatly relaxed. The limit of earnings without deduction has been raised from £1 to £3.10s.0d., and a range of earnings where the deduction is at the rate of 50 per cent has been introduced. There is as yet no evidence of any effect on retirement behavior.

What evidence is there to support Beveridge's sweeping assertion quoted earlier: "Even inadequate unconditional pensions will encourage earlier retirement in many cases"? There is certainly no evidence to support him in the inquiry into reasons for retirement. Men and women staying at work were asked, "What kind of thing would be most likely to make you leave work?" The report on the inquiry does not mention the abolition of the retirement condition and the earnings rule as having been given as an answer. Much depends, however, on how this question was interpreted by the respondents. Did it imply "leave all work" or "leave present work"?

---

[2] This decision so soon after the earlier increase seems rather odd. There is a rumor which attempts to account for it. It is said that the election manifesto was in draft form in 1958. When the election was announced in the summer of 1959, this part of the draft was retained because those responsible had failed to notice that the 10s. increase in the earnings limit had already been implemented.

Similarly, men and women retiring were asked, "What kind of thing would have been most likely to persuade you to continue working?" Nearly 50 per cent of the men did not give an answer to this question. Indeed, the question was not asked of those suffering from chronic sickness. A further 10 per cent answered, "Nothing." It is of interest, however, that, of those men retiring at age sixty-five who did give a specific reply, 2.5 per cent specified, "the payment of retirement pension with wages."

Let us look at Beveridge's argument in practical terms. The average earnings for men are now about £13 per week, and the pension for a man and his wife is £4 per week. With an earnings rule, there is a choice between £13 and up to £7.10s.0d., if we take the maximum which can be earned without any deduction of pension. If there were no earnings rule, there would be a choice between £17 (pension plus earnings) and any lower sum which could be had by reduction of work. It is assumed that reductions in work would be made in these circumstances more than in the earlier ones.

The argument assumes that there is no loss of status for the elderly worker in abandoning his old job or working less at it, that being different in this way involves no loss of self-esteem. It also assumes that opportunities for reduced work are available in his old job or that a change of occupation or employer, involving a change of work companions, is available and acceptable to the elderly worker. These assumptions are questionable, however desirable such flexibility might seem for the welfare of elderly workers.

Even if opportunities were available to do less work and even if there were no psychological barriers to accepting it, is the extra income likely to be thought worth the extra work? The elderly worker sees himself faced with the prospect of retirement sooner or later, which in most cases means a considerable drop in living standards. About three-quarters of men see ill health as the most likely cause of retirement, and this could happen at any time. Surely this is the stage when the incentive to save is powerful. It may well be true that, in heavy occupations, the unpleasantness of extra work increases with age, but it may also be true that the attraction of earning extra income is very high at advanced ages. Thus, both the man with an income of £13 and the one with an income of £17 would be trying to earn as much as he could. Put more formally, it is possible that the marginal utility of income is greater than the marginal disutility of work. This would seem to be true for the 21 per cent of men who said that the most important reason for staying at work was because they preferred to work.

Are elderly workers with the prospect of inadequate pensions anxious for overtime? How large are savings during the last few years of work? If information were available to answer these two questions, more light might be thrown on this question.

## CONCLUSION

We can conclude, therefore, that changes in the level of pension, in increments, and in the earnings rule do not seem to have affected the age of retirement. Nor is this conclusion surprising in view of the fact—demonstrated by the inquiry mentioned earlier—that nearly everyone who can stay at work does so. What is surprising, if I may be wise after the event, is that it was ever assumed that minor adjustments in pension arrangement would affect the age of retirement. Thinking on all these questions seems to have been dominated by oversimple assumptions about economic motivation and by the use of an unreal economic model with excessive flexibility in institutional arrangements.

The real reasons for retirement are extremely complex. Little has been learned about them or can be learned about them from a simple questionnaire such as was used in the 1953 inquiry.

Previous pension and retirement provisions indicate little relation between the level of benefits and the age of retirement in Britain since the war. I have suggested that a much higher benefit level might cause earlier retirement. Would sensitivity to offers of increment or to changes in earnings limits be greater at a higher benefit level? If the pension for men were doubled, would changes in earnings and increment rules be more important?

In Britain the average man earns about twice what is earned by the average woman. Thus, with a standard rate for both men and women, the pension represents a much higher proportion of women's than of men's earnings. It is, of course, wrong in any circumstances to assume that men behave in the same way as women. And, in the particular circumstances of this inquiry, women at work are a diverse group including a high proportion of married women who are not solely dependent on their earnings. It is nevertheless interesting to note that the retirement behavior of women has changed no more than that of men, despite the changes in the conditions on which the pension is granted.

## REFERENCES

Beveridge, W. *Social insurance and allied services.* London: H.M. Stationery Office, 1942.

House of Commons. *Parliamentary debates, January 27, 1959.* London: H.M. Stationery Office, 1959.

Ministry of National Insurance. *Second report of the Ministry of National Insurance.* London: H.M. Stationery Office, 1951.

Ministry of National Insurance. *Third report of the Ministry of National Insurance.* London: H.M. Stationery Office, 1952.

Ministry of Pensions and National Insurance. *Reasons given for retiring or continuing at work.* London: H.M. Stationery Office, 1954. (a)

Ministry of Pensions and National Insurance. *Report of the Ministry of Pensions and National Insurance for the year 1953.* London: H.M. Stationery Office, 1954. (b)

Ministry of Pensions and National Insurance. *Report of the Ministry of Pensions and National Insurance for the year 1954.* London: H.M. Stationery Office, 1955.

Ministry of Pensions and National Insurance. *Report of the Ministry of Pensions and National Insurance for the year 1955.* London: H.M. Stationery Office, 1956.

Ministry of Pensions and National Insurance. *Report of the Ministry of Pensions and National Insurance for the year 1956.* London: H.M. Stationery Office, 1957.

Ministry of Pensions and National Insurance. *Report of the Ministry of Pensions and National Insurance for the year 1957.* London: II.M. Stationery Office, 1958.

Ministry of Pensions and National Insurance. *Draft of the national insurance (earnings) regulations.* London: H.M. Stationery Office, 1959.

Ministry of Pensions and National Insurance. *Draft of the national insurance (earnings) regulations.* London: H.M. Stationery Office, 1960.

The Treasury. *Report of the committee on economic and financial problems of the provision for old age.* London: H.M. Stationery Office, 1954.

# CHAPTER 52

*Income Security Programs and*
*the Propensity to Retire*

MARGARET S. GORDON

Throughout the world, and particularly in the more industrialized nations, the proportion of men aged sixty-five and over in the labor force has been declining for many decades.[1] The trend has been interrupted or reversed in time of war and has been accelerated in periods of comparatively severe unemployment. Yet, despite these short-term fluctuations, the dominant pattern has been one of almost steady decline in every country for which relevant statistics are available over a considerable period.

[1] I wish to express my gratitude for the able assistance of Malcolm Gutter, formerly a member of the research staff of the Institute of Industrial Relations, University of California, Berkeley, in the preparation of data for the present paper. I am also indebted to Robert J. Myers, chief actuary of the U.S. Social Security Administration, and to my colleague, Lloyd Ulman, for helpful critical comments.

The decline has been attributable in part to shifts in the occupational and industrial structure of the economy (Bancroft, 1958; Durand, 1948; Long, 1958). It is clear, also, that rising income levels and the development of income security programs for the aged have played a role. But we still have a far from adequate understanding of the way in which income levels per se or income security programs influence decisions to retire. Indeed, relatively few studies have been designed specifically to analyze these relationships.

One of the difficulties is that income exerts its influence in conjunction with other factors. The most important of these factors are probably age, health, occupation, industry, and the labor market. Even after all these influences have been taken into account, there are undoubtedly individual variations in attitudes toward retirement that are related to deep-seated personality differences. But it is probable that most of the variation is explained by the social and economic factors mentioned.

As a result of research conducted in the 1950's, we have a far better understanding than formerly of the role of ill health in bringing on retirement. Large-scale studies conducted on both sides of the Atlantic indicated that, when retired persons were asked about their reasons for retirement, a large proportion replied that they had retired voluntarily because of ill health (Great Britain: Ministry of Pensions and National Insurance, 1954; Stecker, 1955; Steiner & Dorfman, 1957). Only a relatively small minority indicated that they had retired because of compulsory retirement systems or other types of forced separation from their jobs. Furthermore, a significant fraction of those elderly people who were forced to leave their jobs involuntarily—either because of compulsory retirement systems or for other reasons—later returned to work, usually in some type of part-time employment, whereas those who retired because of ill health were less likely to return to work. Thus, the retired population reflects the net effects of a sifting process which tends to leave those who are suffering from some type of physical or mental disability in the permanently retired group.

Yet it is clear that the "ill health" that brings on retirement embraces a wide variety of conditions. In some cases, the decision to retire may be precipitated by a single, catastrophic event, such as a stroke or a severe heart attack. Far more frequent, in all probability, are the cases in which ill health takes the form of debilitation.

It seems reasonable to assume that, in a substantial proportion of cases in which ill health is the ultimate reason for retirement, prospective retirement income will have an important influence on the timing of the decision to retire. There is scattered evidence—to be discussed more fully later—suggesting that significant numbers of elderly workers keep postponing the decision to retire, despite slow physical deterioration, at least partly because of the prospect of seriously inadequate retirement income.

Furthermore, as Long (1958) has pointed out, there is no reason to suppose that the long-run decline in the proportion of elderly men in the labor force has been associated with any long-run deterioration in the health status of elderly men. On the contrary, a gradual increase in life expectancy, even for those persons who have already reached sixty-five, suggests that the health of the aged has improved over the decades.

These considerations suggest that we need more careful studies of the relation of income to retirement. It might be useful to express the complex relationships involved in mathematical terms. Thus, the propensity to retire might be expressed as a function of age, health, income, occupation, and the other factors identified above. But how should the income factor in such an equation be expressed? Are attitudes toward retirement related to the incomes of employed workers while they are still working? Or is prospective retirement income the decisive variable? Or should we focus our attention on the ratio of expected retirement income to income before retirement? Or, finally, does it make relatively little difference which of these income measures is used, since all three are highly correlated? This paper will attempt to give tentative answers to at least some of these questions.

## RECENT RESEARCH

One of the few empirical investigations that has shed a good deal of light on the influence of income on attitudes toward retirement is the Cornell retirement study. Designed as a longitudinal investigation, the study was based primarily on responses to questionnaires distributed to a large sample of urban males at approximately two-year intervals from 1952 to 1956. When initially contacted, the men included in the study were all employed and were approaching sixty-five, the conventional retirement age. For the 1,625 respondents to the initial questionnaire, favorable attitudes toward retirement were positively correlated with anticipated retirement income (Thompson, 1956; Thompson & Streib, 1958). It was also found that favorable attitudes toward retirement were correlated with current weekly income, but there was a tendency for those with higher weekly incomes to anticipate a higher income in retirement. When respondents were cross-classified by current income and anticipated retirement income, it was found that current income did not have a significant influence on attitudes toward retirement.

Of course, men employed at higher occupational levels tended to have higher current income and to anticipate higher income in retirement. Furthermore, occupation as such did not appear to influence attitudes toward retirement, except in the case of professional workers. A sizable majority of the professional workers had an unfavorable attitude toward retirement, but, in other occupation groups, the higher the occupational level, the larger the percentage in favor of retirement. This relationship was found to reflect, in turn, differences in expected retirement income.

Anticipation of a comparatively low retirement income tends not only to be associated with an unfavorable attitude toward retirement but also to delay retirement on the part of those who *are* favorably disposed toward retirement and who are not forced—through involuntary retirement policies—to retire at sixty-five. This was indicated in the responses to the second questionnaire distributed in the Cornell retirement study in 1954, by which time a sizable proportion of the respondents had retired (Thompson, 1956, p. 80).

That financial need plays an important role in decisions of elderly persons to continue at work was clearly indicated in the British retirement study which was previously mentioned (Ministry of Pensions and National Insurance, 1954). Of men continuing at work beyond the minimum pensionable age of sixty-five, 44.7 per cent mentioned financial need first as the reason for deciding to continue at work, whereas 54.4 per cent said financial need was their most *important* reason for staying at work. Similar results were obtained for women who stayed at work beyond the minimum pensionable age of sixty.

A particularly interesting finding was that only an insignificant fraction (0.7 per cent of the men and 1.2 per cent of the women) who stayed at work beyond the minimum pensionable age said that they had done so in order to qualify for a larger national insurance retirement pension. They were clearly more impressed by the sharp drop in income they would typically experience on retirement than by the fact that through postponing retirement they would be eligible for a somewhat higher pension. This is not surprising if one considers the amounts involved. In 1953, average weekly earnings of male workers in Great Britain were approximately 189s. (International Labour Office, 1955). A single man retiring at sixty-five would qualify for the uniform weekly national insurance pension of 32s.6d. a week, whereas a married couple would qualify for 54s. (if the wife were not eligible for a retired worker's benefit on the basis of her own earnings). By postponing retirement to seventy, the single man could increase his pension to, at most, 47s.6d., whereas the married man could increase the amount for himself and his spouse to 79s.[2]

Data are not available on the extent to which persons with deteriorating health delay retiring because of the prospect of an inadequate retirement income. However, in a study of employer retirement policies in the San Francisco area based on lengthy interviews with representatives of sixty-five firms, a number of management representatives in firms that did not have private pension plans made references in the course of the interviews to elderly employees with failing health who would probably have retired if a private pension were available to supplement the limited benefits they could expect from the Social Security program (Gordon, 1960).

It can be argued that, for those who are subject to compulsory retirement policies, neither income while employed nor prospective retirement income has any bearing on the decision to retire. However, this is true only in a qualified sense, if retirement is defined to mean final withdrawal from the labor force. For, among persons who are forced to retire under the provisions of formal retirement systems, a good many return to work. Steiner and Dorfman (1957) found that, of men sixty-five and over in the United States in 1952, 12 per cent of those who had retired under compulsory systems had returned to work, whereas an additional 11 per cent considered themselves well enough to work and were interested in returning to work. They did not, however, investigate the relationship between retirement income and the decision to return to work. But a study conducted by the Life Extension Foundation indicated that, of 1,500 retired persons who responded to a mailed questionnaire, 32 per cent of those with incomes under $5,000 indicated that they would like to return to their old jobs, as compared to only 8 per cent of those whose retirement incomes were $5,000 or more (Johnson, 1956).

---

[2] These amounts have since been increased, and, under 1959 amendments, a new system of graduated benefits is to be superimposed on the flat-benefit system.

## INTERNATIONAL COMPARISONS

Few, if any, studies have utilized the ratio of expected retirement income to income before retirement in analyzing the influence of income on the propensity to retire. Such a ratio could readily be used in studies of retirees of individual firms. It would also seem to lend itself particularly well to international comparison.

The evidence discussed thus far suggests that international variations in the proportion of elderly men in the labor force may be related to differences in prospective retirement income, or in the ratio of prospective retirement income to earnings before retirement, in various countries. Even though there are differences in the proportions of workers affected by compulsory retirement policies from country to country, these variations may not seriously interfere with such a relationship if those who retire under compulsory retirement systems are particularly likely to return to work in countries where average retirement income is low.

In one of the most comprehensive studies of labor-force participation ever attempted, Clarence Long (1958) analyzed, among other things, the influence of income differences on variations in labor-force participation from country to country. He found that there was a significant inverse correlation between real income per worker (or per capita) and the labor-force-participation rate of the adult population as a whole. He did not, however, find a significant correlation between real per-capita income and the proportion of men sixty-five and over in the labor force. Evidently, differences in income levels per se do not explain national differences in the propensity to retire.

Long did not, however, investigate the relationship of retirement income to international variations in the labor-force participation of elderly men. Indeed, comparisons of retirement income as such would be difficult because of the problem of developing comparable measures of the cost of living of elderly people in order to compare their real incomes.

As previously suggested, however, the ratio of expected retirement income to income before retirement would seem to lend itself particularly well to international comparison. Although it is difficult to obtain data on income before retirement, we may assume that average earnings of elderly men approaching retirement are highly correlated with average earnings of all workers. Thus, average-earnings data may be utilized in the analysis. Furthermore, there is a good deal of evidence suggesting that, in countries with a reasonably mature national old-age insurance or pension scheme, the average level of retirement benefits under that scheme is by far the most important determinant of the level of retirement income for many of the country's aged.

Thus, we propose to investigate the hypothesis that there is an inverse relationship, from country to country, between the labor-force-participation rate of elderly men and the average level of old-age benefits under the country's general old-age income security scheme *when average benefits are expressed as a percentage of average annual earnings in the country.*

Since labor-force data by age and sex are available for most countries only from general population censuses, the analysis will be focused on differences in the proportion of elderly men in the labor force in censuses conducted around 1950. For some countries, the nearest census date is as early as 1947, and in a few other countries it is as late as 1954; but, since labor-force-participation rates tend to change rather slowly, this should not constitute a serious difficulty. For those countries in which the census was conducted in the first half of the year, we have attempted to obtain old-age-benefit and average-earnings data for the preceding year. Where the census was conducted in the second half of the year, we have, in general, used social security and earnings data for the same year.[3]

The investigation was confined to countries in which less than half of the labor force was engaged in agriculture. Since labor-force-participation rates of elderly men tend to be higher in rural than in urban areas—though this difference seems to be gradually disappearing in some industrialized countries—inclusion of countries in which most of the labor force was engaged in agriculture would probably mean that variations in the proportion of elderly men in the labor force would be explained largely by differences in the proportion of agricultural workers in the population. This was apparent merely from inspection of the data, whereas this particular relationship did not show up clearly in the more industrialized countries. Furthermore, it is only in the industrialized countries that agricultural workers tend to be included in old-age income-security programs.

Once the predominantly agricultural countries were elimi-

---

[3] Countries in which the census was conducted in the first half of the year were Austria, France, the United Kingdom, Australia, New Zealand, Canada, and the United States. This point should be kept in mind in comparing the benefit ratios in tables 1 and 2.

nated, it was necessary to restrict the list of countries still further, since not all the necessary statistics were available for all countries. In general, reliance was placed on data published by the International Labour Office in its annual *Yearbook of Labour Statistics,* supplemented where necessary by data obtained from government agencies of individual countries.

Average old-age benefits were computed by dividing total expenditures on old-age benefits by the total number of beneficiaries in each country. However, a further difficulty arose out of the fact that the ILO does not publish data on expenditures for old-age benefits alone, but lumps them with expenditures for invalidity and survivor benefits. This problem did not turn out to be nearly so serious as anticipated. Wherever possible, data were obtained on average old-age benefits from reports issued by individual governments. When these were compared with average old-age, invalidity, and survivor benefits for the same country and year, it was found that in most countries there was little difference between the two average amounts. There are several reasons for this. In the first place, old-age beneficiaries tend to be considerably more numerous than either invalidity or survivor beneficiaries in most countries, so that average benefits paid to old-age recipients tend to dominate the composite average. Second, amounts paid to invalidity and survivor beneficiaries tend to be closely related to old-age benefits.

One additional point needs to be mentioned. In those countries in which, at the time to which the data refer, both old-age insurance and old-age-assistance programs were playing major roles in providing income for elderly people (for example, the United States and France), we computed a combined average for the two programs, on the ground that what we were seeking to measure was the average income available to elderly persons through broad public income-maintenance programs. For similar reasons, Canada's old-age-assistance program, which was the only large public income-maintenance program for elderly persons in Canada in the relevant year (1950), was included in the analysis, as were the old-age-pension programs of such countries as Australia and Denmark, which made benefits conditional on an income test.

### Benefit Ratios and Labor-Force
### Participation of Elderly Men

In order to test our central hypothesis, two correlation coefficients were computed between what we shall call the "benefit ratio" (the ratio of average benefits to average annual earnings) and the proportion of men sixty-five and over in the labor force. In the first computation, which included fourteen countries, average benefit amounts were based on data for old-age, survivors, and invalidity benefit programs.[4] In the second, which included nine countries, the benefit data related to old-age benefits alone.

The resulting correlation coefficients were −.83 and −.78, respectively. The first was significant at the 1 per-cent level; the second, at the 2 per-cent level. Evidently a substantial proportion of the variation in labor-force-participation rates of elderly men in industrialized countries is associated with differences in benefit ratios as we have defined them. The data on which the computations were based are presented in Table 1.[5]

Although these results appear to be highly significant, due allowance must be made for the fact that the labor-force data are not precisely comparable from country to country. Even more troublesome is the fact that the average-annual-earnings data are not strictly comparable and, in fact, do not always include the same industry groups. Although they include workers in most industry groups in many of the countries for which they are available, there are a few countries in which only manufacturing workers are included. There was at least a possibility that these differences distorted the compari-

[4] Some of the countries did not have all three types of pension benefits. In the United Kingdom, for example, invalidity benefits are associated with the sickness insurance scheme and are not included in the pension data.

[5] In the case of one country, Belgium, it was not possible to obtain data for the appropriate year. Data for 1948, the year following the census, were used instead.

Another complication that should be noted is that West Germany, unlike most other countries, does not provide any wives' benefits. This means that wives are not counted as beneficiaries, which reduces the denominator of our ratio and increases the resulting benefit ratio. It would be desirable to avoid this difficulty by analyzing average benefits for elderly couples and for single retired workers. The relevant data are becoming increasingly accessible.

It should also be pointed out that, in the past few years, the ILO has ceased publishing the data from which we computed average annual earnings, apparently because it has concluded that the data are not sufficiently comparable from country to country. One of the factors making for serious incomparability is that the earnings data, which are frequently derived from social security statistics, are often affected by ceilings on taxable earnings, and these ceilings will have differing relationships to average earnings from country to country. Such factors as this may explain the differing relationships in various countries between benefit ratios based on average annual earnings and those based on national per-capita income. I have come increasingly to feel that ratios based on national per-capita income are more reliable, even though an average-earnings concept is more appropriate in relation to the hypothesis being investigated. Other measures that might be used are national income per employed worker and total employee compensation per employee.

TABLE 1

MEN SIXTY-FIVE AND OVER IN THE LABOR FORCE AND SELECTED POPULATION, EIGHTEEN COUNTRIES, AROUND 1950

| Country | Census date | Men sixty-five and over in labor force | Labor force engaged in agriculture | Population sixty-five and over | Average benefits as percentage of average annual earnings | | Average benefits (old age, survivors, and invalidity) as percentage of national income per capita | Date of establishment of old-age-pension program for sizable segment of population |
|---|---|---|---|---|---|---|---|---|
| | | | | | Old age, survivors, and invalidity | Old age | | |
| | | | | Percentage | | | | |
| Australia | 1954 | 33.2 | 15.4 | 8.0 | 23 | | 38 | 1909 |
| Austria | 1951 | 31.3 | 32.3 | 10.6 | 32 | | 52 | 1906 |
| Belgium | 1947 | 24.7 | 12.1 | 10.7 | 34† | | 46† | 1924 |
| Canada | 1951 | 38.6 | 19.0 | 7.8 | 16 | 14 | 37 | 1927 |
| Czechoslovakia | 1947 | 29.7 | 37.7 | 7.6 | 35 | | 85 | 1906 |
| Denmark | 1950 | 35.9 | 25.1 | 9.1 | 27 | 25 | 45 | 1891 |
| Finland | 1950 | 56.7 | 46.0 | 6.6 | 6 | | 13 | 1937 |
| France | 1954 | 36.1 | 26.7 | 12.2 | 18 | 17 | 27 | 1930 |
| Germany (Fed. Rep.) | 1950 | 26.8 | 23.2 | 9.3 | 22 | | 55 | 1889 |
| Italy | 1951 | 45.0* | 40.0 | 8.2 | | | 30 | 1919 |

MARGARET S. GORDON

| | | | | | | | |
|---|---|---|---|---|---|---|---|
| Luxembourg | 1947 | 37.5 | 26.0 | 9.5 | | | | 1911 |
| Netherlands | 1947 | 35.5 | 19.3 | 7.1 | | | | 1913 |
| New Zealand | 1951 | 26.5 | 18.4 | 9.1 | 29 | 36 | 34 | 1898 |
| Norway | 1950 | 42.1 | 25.9 | 9.6 | 16 | 16 | | 1936 |
| Sweden | 1950 | 36.1 | 20.3 | 10.2 | 9 | 15 | 28 | 1913 |
| Switzerland | 1950 | 50.7 | 16.5 | 11.0 | | 10 | 14 | 1946 |
| United Kingdom | 1951 | 31.4 | 5.1 | 10.9 | 18 | 18 | 28 | 1908 |
| U.S.A. | 1950 | 41.4 | 12.2 | 8.1 | 14 | 15 | 18 | 1935 |

Sources—International Labour Office (1955); United Nations (annual publication); U.S. Social Security Administration (1958); and selected government documents for individual countries.
*Estimated on the basis of census data relating to men sixty-six and over.
†Data refer to 1948.

sons to a certain extent. For this reason, a second set of computations was carried out, in which average benefits (for old-age, survivors, and invalidity pensions) were expressed as a percentage of national income per capita. The resulting correlation coefficient, relating to fifteen countries, was somewhat lower (–.66) than the corresponding coefficient utilizing average annual earnings, but was significant at the 1 per-cent level.

In all these computations, there was some question as to whether it was appropriate to include countries in which the qualifying age for retirement benefits for men was over sixty-five. Eliminating Sweden, with a qualifying age of sixty-seven, and Canada, with a qualifying age of seventy under its old-age assistance program at that time, from this last correlation, the resulting coefficient was almost the same (–.67).

It was also important, as in all similar investigations in the social sciences, to take into account the fact that the high correlation coefficients we obtained might have been at least partly explained by correlations between our two key variables and third variables.

There was a strong possibility, for example, that relatively high benefit ratios might tend to be found in the more industrialized countries and that the relationship between benefit ratios and labor-force participation might reflect a tendency for smaller proportions of elderly men to be in the labor force in the more industrialized countries. If this were the case, the degree of industrialization might be the chief factor explaining variations in labor-force-participation rates of elderly men. But, for the industrialized countries included in the study, the correlation between the proportion of the labor force engaged in agriculture (an inverse measure of industrialization) and the percentage of elderly men in the labor force turned out to be significant only at the 10 per-cent level. The coefficient was .43. Furthermore, there was no correlation between the benefit ratio (based on average old-age, survivors, and invalidity benefits expressed as a percentage of average annual earnings) and the percentage of the labor force engaged in agriculture.

Another possibility was that countries with relatively large proportions of elderly people would tend to have high benefit ratios and relatively low proportions of elderly men in the labor force. The aging of the population, according to this line of reasoning, might have tended to create political pressures for a relatively generous old-age benefit program and at the same time have an adverse effect on employment opportunities for elderly men. Thus, relatively poor employment opportunities for men sixty-five and over might be a more important explanation of their withdrawal from the labor force than is the benefit ratio. However, the correlation between the proportion of the population sixty-five and over and the percentage of elderly men in the labor force in eighteen countries ($r = -.27$) was not found to be significant. And there was no correlation between the proportion of the population sixty-five and over and the benefit ratio in fourteen countries.

There was, however, one other relationship that emerged clearly as we studied the data. Although not altogether anticipated, it was far from surprising. The longer a country had had an old-age benefit program for a major sector of its population, the lower the proportion of elderly men in the labor force was likely to be. To test this relationship, a correlation of rank correlation was computed and was found to be .71 (significant at the 1 per-cent level). In this computation, which was carried out for eighteen countries, the country with the lowest proportion of elderly men in the labor force was assigned a rank of 1, as was the country with the oldest old-age benefit program.

This relationship suggests that, in countries which have had old-age benefit programs for many decades, a decline in the proportion of elderly men in the labor force has been encouraged over a long period by the availability of retirement benefits under a national program. But is this influence exerted irrespective of the level of benefits, or is there a tendency for the countries with the oldest programs to have the highest benefit ratios? We found that there was a high negative rank correlation ($r = -.75$)—significant at the 1 per-cent level— between the benefit ratio in fourteen countries around 1950 and the year in which the country's old-age benefit program was established. In this computation, the country with the oldest program was again assigned a rank of 1, as was the country with the lowest benefit ratio. Thus, the negative correlation indicates that the countries with the oldest programs tended to have the highest benefit ratios around 1950.

Did these countries have higher benefit ratios from the very earliest years of their programs than countries in which programs had been established more recently, or have their benefit ratios gradually increased over the years? Unfortunately, it has been impossible within the scope of the present study to carry out the detailed statistical work that would be required for a complete answer to this question.

All things considered, however, it seems likely that there has been a tendency for benefit levels to increase over the years in countries with long-established programs. In those countries (for example, Australia, New Zealand, the United Kingdom, and some of the Scandinavian countries) with flat benefits, the amounts stipulated in the earliest laws tended to be meager indeed. Though dealing with a more recent period, Friis (1959) has shown that there was a substantial increase in old-age benefits in Denmark, relative to the earnings of unskilled workers, between 1933 and 1958. In countries like Germany, in which the benefit formula has taken the form of a percentage of average earnings multiplied by years of service, benefits available in the early years tended to be small, simply because retirees had accumulated relatively few years of service under the program. In recent decades, rapidly rising prices and wages have forced both groups of countries to take decisive steps to adjust benefits upward.

Perhaps the most important reason why benefit ratios tend to be higher in the countries with the oldest programs is that there is a general tendency for social security programs to gain acceptance as they become more firmly established, with the result that political support for expansion and liberalization is strengthened. However, there is some evidence to suggest that liberalization is accomplished more readily under some types of systems than under others, as will be seen at a later point, when the behavior of benefit ratios from 1950 to 1957 is analyzed.

One final question needs to be considered. What influence does a country's retirement policy have on the propensity to retire? It has on occasion been suggested that, when eligibility for old-age benefits is dependent on an income test, for example, elderly persons will be more likely to withdraw from the labor force in order to qualify for benefits. But is it not reasonable to suppose that much will depend on the relationship among benefits available under the program, the maximum income permitted without any reduction in benefits, and average earnings available to elderly men in the labor market?

Of the twenty industrialized countries for which data on the labor-force participation of elderly men around 1950 were available, eleven imposed an income test in connection with their old-age-benefit program or had a supplementary old-age-assistance program which provided benefits to large numbers of elderly people and involved a means test. Several other countries enforced a retirement test, whereas five did not have an income or a retirement test. A few countries were excluded from this part of the analysis because the qualifying age was over sixty-five (sixty-seven in Sweden and seventy in Canada and Norway). We found that, in countries with a pensionable age of sixty-five for men, the unweighted average proportion of elderly men in the labor force in countries that imposed an income or retirement test was somewhat higher than in countries that had no test of any kind, but the difference was not large enough to be considered significant. The results of this comparison can scarcely be regarded as conclusive, since the number of countries with no income or retirement test was exceedingly small. It may be possible to attempt a more careful analysis along these lines when the results of more recent population censuses become available.

### Behavior of Benefit Ratios, 1950-1957

As a by-product of the present investigation, it was a relatively simple matter to compute benefit ratios (based on old-age, survivors, and invalidity benefits) for a substantial number of countries for most years from 1950 to 1957. In fact, for many countries the computations could be carried back to 1946, the year in which the ILO began to publish statistical data on social security programs, but conditions were so unsettled in many European countries in the years immediately following World War II that in some cases the benefit ratios bear little relationship to those prevailing in the 1950's or, in all probability, to those that prevailed before the war. For this reason, the analysis was confined to the period after 1950.

Two sets of ratios were computed—one in which benefits were expressed as a percentage of national income per capita and another in which benefits were expressed as a percentage of average annual earnings. The relative positions of individual countries differed slightly between the sets of computations. Because of certain differences in the construction of the annual-earnings data, it seems likely that the ratios utilizing national per-capita-income data yield more reliable comparisons, despite appreciable differences in the quality of national-income and population estimates from country to country. For this reason, we shall rely mainly on the ratios utilizing national income per capita (see Table 2).

We also found that in some cases there were differences between average benefits as computed from ILO data and those from data in reports issued by countries. The differences, which were usually slight, were explained chiefly by the fact that the ILO *Yearbook of Labour Statistics* recorded the number of beneficiaries in the month of June, whereas reports issued by countries often recorded the number of beneficiaries at the end of a calendar year or at some other

TABLE 2
AVERAGE BENEFITS RECEIVED UNDER OLD-AGE,
SURVIVORS, AND INVALIDITY PENSION PROGRAMS

(As percentage of National Income per Capita,
Eighteen Countries, 1950-1957)

| Country | Date program began | 1950 | 1951 | 1952 | 1953 | 1954 | 1955 | 1956 | 1957 |
|---------|------|------|------|------|------|------|------|------|------|
| Australia* | 1909 | 29 | 31 | 35 | 38 | 38 | 37 | 39 | 41 |
| Austria* | 1906 | 52 | 48 | 49 | 49 | 50 | 48 | 46 | |
| Belgium* | 1924 | 53 | 52 | 54 | 61 | 55 | 60 | 57 | |
| Canada* | 1927 | 37 | 41 | 35 | 34 | 35 | | 30 | 31 |
| Denmark* | 1891 | 45 | 48 | 49 | 49 | 47 | 50 | | |
| † | | 43 | 43 | 46 | 44 | 46 | 46 | 46 | 47 |
| Finland* | 1937 | 13 | 11 | 11 | 16 | 13 | 12 | 13 | 29 |
| France† | 1930 | 30 | 28 | 27 | 27 | 29 | 27 | 26 | 25 |
| Germany (Fed. Rep.)* | 1889 | 55 | 47 | 48 | 47 | 45 | | 46 | 60 |
| Italy* | 1919 | | 30 | 44 | 42 | 39 | | | |
| † | | | | 46 | 44 | 42 | 40 | 38 | 37 |
| Luxembourg* | 1911 | | 44 | 53 | 62 | 73 | 67 | 63 | |
| Netherlands* | 1913 | 32 | 31 | 31 | 30 | 31 | 28 | 26 | |
| New Zealand† | 1898 | 34 | 38 | 40 | 38 | 40 | 41 | 40 | 41 |
| Norway* | 1936 | | 27 | 28 | 31 | 34 | 30 | 31 | 30 |
| Spain* | 1919 | 31 | 22 | 18 | 18 | 17 | | 30 | 29 |
| Sweden* | 1913 | 28 | 26 | 27 | 32 | 38 | 36 | 37 | 38 |
| † | | 29 | | 27 | 32 | 34 | 33 | 33 | |
| Switzerland* | 1946 | 14 | 14 | 14 | 14 | 17 | 16 | 17 | 19 |
| United Kingdom† | 1908 | 28 | 25 | 26 | 27 | 26 | 25 | 28 | 27 |
| U.S.A.* | 1935 | 24 | 31 | 31 | 34 | 36 | 39 | 39 | 41 |
| † | | 19 | 25 | 25 | 27 | 30 | 32 | 32 | 33 |

Sources—International Labour Office (1955); United Nations (annual publi-
cation); and selected government documents for individual countries.
*Benefit data from International Labour Office (1955).
†Benefit data from reports or statistical yearbooks of individual countries.
In the case of the United States, the number of beneficiaries in each year
was the average monthly number.

date. The discrepancy was largest in the case of the United States, where the number of beneficiaries has been increasing rapidly.

Although income and wage levels were rising rapidly from 1950 to 1957 in all countries included in the table, benefit ratios were higher toward the end of the period than in 1950 in about two-thirds of the countries. This is a rather remarkable record, reflecting in part the effects of legislative action to raise benefits or adjust benefit formulas and in part provisions in some of the countries (already in effect in 1950 or adopted later) for automatic adjustment of benefit amounts to changes in wage or price indexes. In a few countries, at least part of the increase was attributable to maturing of the program, resulting (for example, in the United States) in an increase in the ratio of old-age beneficiaries to other types of beneficiaries and, in some cases, in higher benefits for some retirees because they had accumulated more years of service under the program.

Both at the beginning and toward the end of the period, there was a tendency (but with notable exceptions) for the countries with the oldest programs to have the highest ratios, although the relative positions of individual countries changed somewhat during the period.

It is interesting to note that nearly all the countries that experienced a decline in benefit ratios between the beginning and end of the period had flat benefits. Furthermore, most of these countries did not automatically adjust benefits for changes in the cost of living; increases depended on legislative action. On the other hand, almost all the flat-benefit countries which, at least toward the end of the period, were automatically adjusting benefits in accordance with changes in a price or wage index (Denmark, Finland, the Netherlands, and Sweden) experienced increases in benefit ratios. The Netherlands —the one exception—changed its legislation in 1956 to provide for a universal flat pension adjusted for changes in wages, but the new pensions did not become payable until the beginning of 1957 (Gerig, 1960) and are thus not reflected in the data of Table 2. The Netherlands had previously had both earnings-related pensions and "emergency" flat pensions based on an income test (U.S. Social Security Administration, 1954). It should be noted, also, that two flat-benefit countries (Australia and New Zealand) which did not provide for automatic adjustment of benefits to changes in wages or prices nevertheless experienced increases in their benefit ratios during this period.

The three countries with the highest benefit ratios at the end of the period (Luxembourg, Germany, and Belgium) were all countries with long-established programs, earnings-related benefits, and a procedure for linking benefits (not necessarily automatically) to either price or wage movements. Under the revised German law, effective January 1, 1957, and clearly reflected in the marked rise in the benefit ratio between 1956 and 1957, benefit amounts depend on average individual earnings under the system, years of coverage, and average earnings of all German workers in the three years preceding the award of the benefit (Farman, 1958). In effect, all pensions awarded are adjusted to reflect recent changes in earnings levels. Although there is no provision for automatic adjustment of these benefits once awarded, the law provides that reports be made to Parliament by September 30 of each year analyzing changes in per-capita income and other economic variables and accompanied by a government proposal for adjusting outstanding pensions if that is considered desirable (Gerig, 1960).

Under a revised Belgian law, pensions are based on average earnings under the system but are automatically adjusted for changes in the cost of living. Since it was reinstated following World War II, Luxembourg's system has provided a basic flat pension which is automatically adjusted for changes in the cost of living, plus an earnings-related increment based on average earnings under the system multiplied by years of coverage.

It is also interesting to note that, when we computed the ratio of average benefits to average annual earnings for a number of countries (not in all cases the same countries for which national-income data were available), we found that the benefit ratio in Czechoslovakia was relatively high in recent years. Czechoslovakia, a country with a long-established program of earnings-related benefits, has in recent years been using a formula in which benefits are related to final earnings. Its present benefit arrangements are similar to those of the Soviet Union and certain other countries of Eastern Europe. It would be exceedingly interesting to extend the type of analysis developed here to the countries of Eastern Europe, but the relevant data are far less accessible.

The generalizations that have been made should not be interpreted as suggesting that an earnings-related benefit formula necessarily yields either a higher benefit ratio than a flat-benefit system or one that is more resistant to upward wage movements. Clearly, if benefits are based on an individual's average earnings during his years of coverage, there will be a tendency for the benefit ratio to decline in a period of rising earnings if the government takes no steps to change the benefit formula. Witness the declining tendency in Germany in the early 1950's.

Although the reasons for the varying experiences from country to country warrant more detailed study, I would suggest that differences in methods of financing help explain the fact that the highest benefit ratios are found in countries that have long had earnings-related benefit structures. Earnings-related systems generally rely heavily on financing through employer and employee contributions that take the form of a percentage of earnings, even though there may also be a government contribution. When earnings rise, the revenues of the system increase and may very well rise more rapidly than total current expenditures of the system. Thus, it may be possible to liberalize benefits without raising contribution rates, and, if it does become necessary to raise contributions somewhat, these increases tend to be not particularly burdensome in a period of rising prices and wages.

Flat-benefit systems, on the other hand, are often financed in large part through general government revenues or, as in England, through a combination of general government revenues and flat contributions by employers and employees. Even though general government revenues tend to rise in a period of rising incomes, every increase in pension benefits will require an increased appropriation, and the pension system will have to compete with every other national program for which increases in appropriations are being sought. Flat employer and employee contributions will not yield rising revenues merely because wages increase, though revenues will tend to rise somewhat if the level of employment is increasing. But it is clear that, with such financing provisions as have prevailed in England, any substantial increase in benefit amounts is likely to require an increase in the flat contribution rates, in the government's contribution, or some combination of the two.[6] This is not to suggest that there are not other arguments in favor of this type of financial structure.

On the other hand, if flat benefits are financed through the earmarked proceeds of a tax that takes the form of a specific percentage of income, as in some of the Scandinavian countries, revenues available for pensions will automatically increase in a period of rising income.

These considerations suggest that, wherever financing ar-

---

[6] The effects of the 1959 British amendments, which did not become effective until 1961, are, of course, not reflected in the data. Indeed, it will be a number of years before retiring workers have accumulated enough contributions under the new scheme to appreciably affect average benefits.

rangements are such that rising wage and income levels will be accompanied by an automatic increase in funds earmarked for the payment of pension benefits, it is likely to be politically more feasible to maintain or increase benefit ratios. This conclusion will come as no surprise to many students of social security programs. The range of considerations involved have long been recognized in debates over benefit and financing arrangements in the United States and elsewhere. But they do help to explain why the highest benefit ratios are found in countries with long-established programs that have been financed largely through earnings-related contributions.

### CONCLUSIONS

The conclusions to be drawn from this analysis must be regarded as somewhat exploratory and tentative. A more extensive study would permit a more refined analysis of developments in particular countries and of the influence of factors which could not be considered within the scope of this paper. Furthermore, when the results of population censuses conducted around 1960 become available, it will be possible to undertake a similar analysis for a larger group of countries (since national income estimates and other relevant statistical data are steadily becoming available for more countries), and it will also be possible to analyze changes in the labor-force-participation rates of elderly men in the last decade or so in relation to the other variables we have been considering.

Even so, there is a good deal of evidence to suggest that prospective retirement income has a highly important influence on attitudes toward retirement and that differences in benefit ratios, as we have defined them, play an exceedingly important role in explaining differences in the proportion of men retired in industrialized countries. For purposes of international comparison, it is clear that the benefit ratio is a most useful concept. Whether, for purposes of intranational studies, the ratio of prospective retirement income to income before retirement would be a more appropriate measure than prospective retirement income per se we have not been in a position to determine, but it should not be difficult to utilize both of these measures in studies of the retirement experiences of firms and government agencies.

Not only does the benefit ratio play a highly significant role in explaining differences in the labor-force-participation rate of elderly men in industrialized countries, but it is apparent that, the longer the country has had an old-age-benefit program, the higher its benefit ratio is likely to be and the smaller the proportion of elderly men in the labor force.

Clearly, we are dealing here with a complex set of relationships that work themselves out over time, and it would be rash to attempt any conclusions as to what is cause and what is effect. Nor should it be assumed that an increase in the benefit ratio will necessarily result in a prompt decline in the proportion of elderly men in the labor force. What is likely to happen in any particular country at any particular time will depend to a considerable extent on the labor market.

Our analysis also indicates that, although there were some notable exceptions, benefit ratios were particularly likely to sag during the period of rapidly rising earnings from 1950 to 1957 in countries with flat-benefit structures and no provision for automatic adjustment to changing price or wage levels. This is a conclusion that will come as no surprise to experts who have been watching the development of social security programs around the world, but I know of no other study that has brought together the relevant statistical data for any substantial number of countries. There are also indications that financing arrangements under which revenues available for the payment of old-age benefits automatically increase in a period of rising earnings facilitate the maintenance or liberalization of benefit ratios, but this is clearly a tentative suggestion that needs to be examined more closely in the light of what has happened to benefit ratios over a longer period of time.

Finally, a word about the policy implications of these findings may be in order. There are clear indications that industrialized countries throughout the world are making impressive progress in increasing the levels of benefits available under old-age, survivors, and invalidity pension programs. The data presented in the present paper by no means tell the whole story, for some notable changes have been made in a number of countries since 1957, the most recent year for which statistical data were readily available for any substantial number of countries. Furthermore, the less industrialized countries are moving, with their more recently established and more limited programs, in the same direction.

At the same time, in all the industrialized countries there is grave concern over the problem of employment opportunities for elderly persons. Age discrimination in hiring and compulsory retirement policies are widely viewed as the major obstacles to the employment of older people, and, though a contrary view is relatively common in management circles, many groups particularly concerned about the welfare of older people strongly favor a state of affairs in which an individual who has reached the conventional age of retirement would be free to choose between retiring and continuing at work.

Do the goals of higher benefits and improved employment opportunities for elderly people conflict with each other? The findings of the present study suggest that, as benefit levels are improved, a rising proportion of elderly people will be attracted by the prospect of retirement, though the effect may not be immediately apparent in a period of relatively favorable labor-market conditions. Does it follow that, on the one hand, efforts to improve employment opportunities for those past the conventional retirement age might as well be abandoned in countries that are making rapid strides to increase benefits, or, on the other hand, that, if great emphasis is to be placed on the improvement of employment opportunities, less emphasis should be placed on attempts to increase benefits?

A little reflection will demonstrate that there is no real conflict between the two goals. Freedom of choice between work and retirement is not meaningful if prospective retirement income is seriously inadequate. As old-age benefits increase, the proportion of elderly persons who choose to retire will no doubt gradually increase over the long run, but there will be a residue of persons strongly motivated to continue at work, particularly in those occupations in which intrinsic interest in work is high. Making it possible for such persons to continue at work is an important social goal. An equally important goal is a program of more adequate retirement benefits for those elderly persons who want to retire. This consideration is particularly critical for those who desire to retire because of ill health.

There is growing evidence of a more sensitive perception of these issues in a number of countries. We are now likely to see as much concern expressed over the plight of the elderly worker with failing health who continues at work because of the prospect of grossly inadequate retirement income as over the plight of the frustrated elderly individual who is forced to retire because of a compulsory retirement system. And, if benefit costs rise appreciably, as seems likely in such an environment, proposals to raise the qualifying age for retirement benefits or to provide appreciably higher ultimate benefits for those who continue working past the qualifying age are likely to be made more frequently. Such proposals will become increasingly appropriate as life expectancy rises, though attitudes toward them are likely to be influenced at any given time by labor-market conditions (Gordon, 1960). Thus far, Denmark is the only country— of those included in the present study—that has recently taken a decisive step in this direction in connection with its national old-age pension program. But the issue is likely to receive increasing attention with respect to retirement ages under both public and private pension plans in the next decade.

*REFERENCES*

Bancroft, Gertrude. *The American labor force.* New York: John Wiley & Sons, 1958.
Durand, J.D. *The labor force in the United States, 1890-1960.* New York: Social Science Research Council, 1948.
Farman, C.H. World trends in social security benefits, 1955-57. *Soc. Sec. Bull.,* August 1957, **20,** 3-14
Friis, H. Comparison of benefits in the Danish social security legislation. *Bull. Int. Soc. Sec. Assoc.,* 1959, **12,** 15-18.
Gerig, D.S. Automatic cost-of-living adjustment of pensions in foreign countries. *Soc. Sec. Bull.,* March 1960, **23,** 13-19, 24.
Gordon, Margaret S. The older worker and retirement policies. *Mon. Lab. Rev.,* 1960, **83,** 577-585.
Ministry of Pensions and National Insurance, Great Britain. *Reasons for retiring or continuing at work.* London: H.M. Stationery Office, 1954.
International Labour Office. *Yearbook of labour statistics.* Geneva: Author, 1955.
Johnson, H.J. Thinking ahead: The problem of retirement. *Harvard Bus. Rev.,* 1956, **34,** 21-32, 170-171.
Long, C.D. *The labor force under changing income and employment.* Princeton: Princeton University Press, 1958.
Stecker, Margaret L. Why do beneficiaries retire? Who among them return to work? *Soc. Sec. Bull.,* May 1955, **18,** 3-12, 35-36.
Steiner, P.O., & Dorfman, R. *The economic status of the aged.* Berkeley: University of California Press, 1957.
Thompson, W.E. The impact of retirement. Unpublished doctoral dissertation, Cornell University, 1956.
Thompson, W.E., & Streib, G.F. Situational determinants: Health and economic deprivation in retirement. *J. soc. Issues,* 1958, **14** (2), 18-34.
United Nations. *Statistical yearbook.* New York: Author, annual publication.
U.S. Social Security Administration. *Old-age, survivors, and invalidity programs throughout the world, 1954.* Washington, D.C.: U.S. Government Printing Office, 1954.
U.S. Social Security Administration. *Social security programs throughout the world, 1958.* Washington, D.C.: U.S. Government Printing Office, 1958.

# CHAPTER 53

*Occupation and Health*

IAN M. RICHARDSON

Among the popular beliefs about aging, one of the oldest and most prevalent is that "occupation is the best medicine for old age." Those who think that compulsory retirement is a kind of capital punishment can quote much anecdotal evidence, usually based on simple contrasts between old Mr. A who just withered away within a year or two of having to retire and old Mr. B who is still going strong at his job although he is well past the traditional threescore and ten. Even people who are familiar with the findings of recent gerontological research sometimes find it hard to accept the possibility that there may not be a very substantial foundation for the view that continued employment in old age always preserves or promotes good health. Such conflict between cherished personal convictions and the results of scientific inquiry is a common occurrence, but its resolution

459

is urgent in gerontology where, as the approach to the care of older people is ever more preventive in outlook, sound guidance on all aspects of occupation and health is a practical necessity. If the increasing numbers of older people in Western societies are to be advised about whether to retire, if courses on preparation for retirement are to be sound, and if counseling services for the retired are to be developed, the mass of opinion on the relation of occupation and good health in later years must be replaced by the results of research in all the disciplines which gerontology embraces.

One major problem stands out—the varying interpretations of "occupation" and "health." To some, occupation is equated with gainful employment; others think of it essentially as physical activity in work or leisure; still others apply the term to any purposeful or satisfying pursuit. The concept of health is equally varied. Is it the mere absence of disease in a clinical sense? Does normal health vary according to standards determined by sociologically defined subcultures? Are psychological criteria like emotional stability to be included in the evaluation? The need for uniform definitions and standards is obvious. To those concerned with studies of occupation and health, uniformity would be a major step in clarifying the relation between health and occupation in the process of aging.

## HEALTH AND OCCUPATION

Though the effect of continued occupation on health in the later years is, from the standpoint of preventive medicine, more important than the converse consideration, it is desirable to review some of the material on the effect of occupation on health first.

Numerous American and European studies have shown that ill health is a common cause of difficulty in work, retirement, and restricted participation in social activities. That disability accounts for a substantial number of job changes in middle age and beyond has been shown in studies reported by Richardson (1953), Le Gros Clark (1955), and Forssman (1957), and the last author has suggested ways in which disabled men can be helped to accommodate their difficulties. The British national inquiry (Ministry of Pensions and National Insurance, 1954) showed that nearly half of all retirements were attributed mainly to ill health, but the number varied among occupational groups. In the American national survey referred to by Kutner, Fanshel, Togo, and Langner (1956), four out of ten men gave health as the reason for retirement. In the Danish study reported by Felbo

(1958), the number of retirements because of health was considerably more than half. The difficulty, however, in most of these inquiries is that, in the words of Welford (1958b), ". . . they have had to rely, at least in part, on stated reasons for retirement or continuing at work. It is well-known that such reasons may be unreliable, not only because of deliberate falsification, but also because often men do not fully recognise the reasons for their decisions" (p. 61).

In a small case study of 244 pensioners (Richardson, 1956), it was found that multiple reasons for retirement were much commoner than large-scale social survey results suggest and that there is a clear need for more depth studies at or near the time of retirement. Personal physicians are well-placed to conduct such investigations but, at least in Britain, few appear to have done so.

The specific disabilities which commonly lead to retirement are fairly well-defined. Diseases of the heart and circulation, locomotive disorders, and, at least in parts of Britain, bronchitis (emphysema) account for the majority of health retirements by industrial workers (Richardson, 1956). The same diseases were found to be the main causes of unfitness for employment in retired Birmingham men (Brown, McKeown, & Whitfield, 1958). Though prediction is hazardous, growing knowledge of the causes of coronary artery disease, arthritis, and bronchitis may make prevention of these disorders feasible in the foreseeable future and thus remove some of the main disabilities that are now responsible for premature retirement. More confident assertion is possible on rehabilitation. Both general hospital and geriatric units have demonstrated what can be done to restore the mobility and morale of older people. Extension of rehabilitation facilities and a greater awareness of their achievements could prevent many unnecessary retirements.

Ill health and chronic disease can, of course, have equally serious effects on forms of occupation other than employment. The Wolverhampton survey (Sheldon, 1948), the study of people over seventy in London (National Council of Social Service, 1954), and others have shown how serious are the restrictions imposed on household duties and leisure activities by the disabilities common to old people. There is also some evidence (Richardson, Brodie, & Wilson, 1959) that restrictions on movement are linked to the extremely important problem of loneliness, especially when combined with unsuitable or isolated housing. In a recent study of older people living in special cottages and flats in Aberdeen (Richardson, Klopper, & Lynch, 1960), it was found that these easily run and pleasantly situated dwellings had substantially improved the morale and estimations of their own health of many elderly disabled men and women who had previously lived restricted lives because of difficulty with stairs in old houses. As a result of the study, we think that special purpose cottages and even flats for old people are a very important social service which should be expanded as rapidly as national priority permits.

As far as remedial action is concerned, the position is well summarized by Donahue (1957):

> Quite beyond the experimental stage is the pattern of the geriatric diagnostic-treatment-restorative center as part of a constellation of facilities including community housing, congregate living facilities, social and work centers, vacations, and, when needed, housekeeping help, nursing service, day hospital care, meals delivered to the home, and friendly visiting. And a *sine qua non* is the integration of public and private programs with a central information, guidance, and referral facility in order that their services may be brought to bear promptly as individual circumstances require (pp. 202-203; reprinted with the permission of the University of Michigan Press).

In Britain such centers are few, but at Rutherglen in the west of Scotland valuable work has been done at the Consultative Health Center (Anderson & Cowan, 1956), where experienced advice on health and retirement is available to anyone over fifty-four. This center also coordinates the activities of statutory and voluntary agencies for older people and is essentially a preventive service designed to detect and remove problems, both occupational and other, at an early stage.

Thus, much is already known about the effects of health on occupation, and preventive action is being taken.

## OCCUPATION AND HEALTH

The effects of continued occupation on health are much more controversial and uncertain. Leaving aside the diseases in which excessive activity is clearly harmful, the problem turns on how to design a study to test the general thesis that occupation is, as many people believe, beneficial to health in old age.

There are at least three main difficulties in testing specific hypotheses in this field. First, there is the problem of time sequence. The usual survey form, the cross-sectional, has limited value if a causal relation is sought. It cannot, for example, tell with much confidence whether any observed association between continued employment and good health is cause and effect or effect and cause. Second, other concealed associations may be at work. For instance, those who are employed may take better care of their health than those who are retired. And third, as already suggested, precise measurement of the main variable is extremely difficult.

That these are not insuperable obstacles is shown by research like "The Cornell Study of Occupational Retirement" (Streib, Thompson, & Suchman, 1958; Thompson & Streib, 1958), the full results of which are awaited by those in Britain who have considered the possibility of a longitudinal study of occupation and health. Meantime, however, it is necessary to rely on less ambitious methods. Some findings from an exploratory cross-sectional study will be presented below.

### The Orkney Survey

The Department of Social Medicine at Aberdeen University is currently conducting two studies for the Nuffield Trust. The first (Weir, McKenzie, & Richardson, 1962) is a follow-up study of several hundred patients discharged from a large general hospital. The second —as yet only half completed—is a combined sociological and medical survey of 500 people sixty and over. Early in the course of these researches, it was noticed that the convalescent and retirement patterns of older self-employed men differed from those of employees. An opportunity then occurred to develop this observation in a small sample survey in the County of Orkney.

Orkney is a group of nine large and nine small islands lying off the north coast of Scotland. It has a population of 21,000, and over half the men are farmers, crofters (small farmers), or agricultural workers. Orkney has a relatively high proportion of old people, 14 per cent of the population being sixty-five and over, compared with 10 per cent in Aberdeen. The survey was suggested by Dr. A.S. Brodie, medical officer of health for Orkney, mainly to ascertain how far the needs of these geographically scattered old people were being met by existing services. The Department of Social Medicine at Aberdeen undertook the design, and we were, therefore, able to include some questions dealing with retirement and health. The chief aim of the questions was to see whether continued employment, compared with retirement, conferred any health benefits, making allowance, if possible, for the selection effects of retirement itself. We had also hoped to make a similar comparison between the health of those who were fully occupied in retirement and those who were not, but the numbers were inadequate for this.

Names and addresses of people sixty-five and over were obtained by random sampling of National Health Service lists.[1] A refusal rate of 6 per cent left ninety completed male interviews for analysis. Of these, fifty-seven (63 per cent) said they were fully retired, eighteen (20 per cent) were drawing retirement pensions but still doing a little paid work, and fifteen (17 per cent) were still working full time. A higher proportion of the sixty-four self-employed men was not retired, compared with employees, but the difference was not significant at the 5 per-cent level. Age of retirement, however, showed a clear trend which is summarized in Table 1.

TABLE 1
MEAN RETIREMENT AGE OF SELF-EMPLOYED
AND EMPLOYEES IN ORKNEY

| Item | Self-employed | Employees |
|------|---------------|-----------|
| Mean retirement age | 67.9 | 64.9 |
| Standard deviation | 5.6 | 4.8 |
| Number of men | 51 | 23 |
| Standard error of difference between means = 1.3 | Actual difference between means > 2 × S.E. | |

Source—Richardson, Brodie, and Wilson (1959).

On the average, self-employed men had retired three years later than employees, a difference that probably cannot be attributed to chance in the sampling. It is, however, important to point out that, whereas in most urban occupations retirement is clear-cut and identical with the age at which pension is taken up, retirement in the country—at least among self-employed men—is a less distinct process. Strictly speaking, therefore, Table 1 refers to the age at which these Orcadians first drew retirement pension.

Each man was asked why he had retired. Analysis of the replies given by all men who had retired before seventy showed no real difference in the patterns of cause for the self-employed and employees,

[1] Almost one-half the population of Great Britain is now registered with a National Health Service doctor, hence, one of the most useful by-products of the service is a readily available frame of reference for social surveys.

the proportion of retirements attributed to ill health being 40 per cent in the first group and 43 per cent in the second. The number of retirements after seventy was too small to allow similar comparison, but the over-all proportion of retirements because of ill health fell to 29 per cent, whereas the proportion attributed to strain ("worked long enough," "wanted a rest," "too old to go on," and like expressions) in the absence of actual illness rose from 1 per cent of the retirements before seventy to 43 per cent of retirements after seventy.

This change with age in the causes of retirement was also observed in the British national inquiry (Ministry of Pensions and National Insurance, 1954). It is almost certainly caused by self-selection at or soon after sixty-five, the less fit men tending to retire, thus causing a corresponding increase in the proportion of healthy men among those who continue to work. Impressive evidence of this selective retirement on health grounds is to be found in Myers' analysis (1954) of death rates in several occupational groups. Although no difference was detected between the causes of retirement in self-employed and employees who retired at about the same age, further comparison was needed to clarify how health was responsible for the later age of retirement among those who were self-employed.

Three measures of health were used:

1. *Self-assessment.* Replies to the question "How is your health at present?" were classified into three grades:
    (a) Those who said "good" or some equivalent term
    (b) Those who answered (a), but qualified the reply by mentioning some complaint
    (c) Those who replied "poor" or its equivalent
2. *Medical Care*
    (a) Those not receiving any medical care at the time of survey
    (b) Those in regular contact with the general practitioner
    (c) Men in hospital
3. *Capacity for movement*
    (a) Able to get about freely
    (b) Outside movement limited by disability
    (c) Housebound or bedridden

Comparisons of the sixty-five–sixty-nine and seventy–seventy-four groups (numbers in the oldest groups were too few for subdivision) showed that the numbers who said they were in good health (a), were not receiving medical care (b), and had unlimited movement (c) were alike in retired self-employed and employees, and this was also true when working self-employed and employees were compared. In each age group, however, those still at work recorded higher proportions in good health, without medical attention, and with unlimited mobility than those who had retired.

To explore the effect of employment on health, a comparison was made between men still at work and men who had retired for reasons *other than health,* on the grounds that, by excluding retirements caused by ill health, the influence of self-selection because of disability would be reduced. The results of this analysis of very small numbers showed that in medical attention and mobility (with age held constant) there was virtually no difference between men who were working and men who had retired for reasons other than health. There was, however, a faint suggestion that retired men tended to assess their own health as less than good more often than employed men of the same age.

The main findings for this exploratory study may be summarized as follows:

1. On the average, self-employed men worked longer than employees, but the pattern of retirement causes appeared similar.
2. When standardized for age and occupational group (working or retired), the health of self-employed men and of employees was the same.
3. No clear evidence of an association between continued work and health was found.

It would, of course, be dangerous to draw firm conclusions from so small an investigation. The most that can be said is that health did not appear to be a major factor in explaining the longer working life of self-employed men in the island of Orkney.

### Census Data

If it is generally true that self-employed men tend to work longer than employees, further research on the health effects of delayed retirement might include this group. Some data from the 1951 British census (Registrar-General for Scotland, 1956) were therefore extracted, as shown in Table 2.

Conclusions from Table 2 must be cautiously drawn because past or present occupation was not available for a small proportion.

## TABLE 2
### MEN GAINFULLY OCCUPIED AT DIFFERENT AGES, SCOTLAND, 1951

| Occupational group | Percentage occupied at | | | Retired and occupied |
|---|---|---|---|---|
| | 65-69 | 70-74 | 75 and over | |
| Crofters | 71.3 | 62.8 | 40.7 | 2,935 |
| Farmers and farm managers | 69.1 | 52.8 | 31.4 | 9,551 |
| Agricultural workers | 54.3 | 33.0 | 12.7 | 5,723 |
| Shop assistants | 50.2 | 33.1 | 16.0 | 2,464 |
| Shop proprietors and managers | 62.9 | 45.7 | 38.1 | 7,099 |
| All males | 53.6 | 33.5 | 16.5 | 200,265 |

Source—Registrar-General for Scotland (1956).

Crofters, farmers, farm managers, shop proprietors, shop managers are largely self-employed people, and their retirement rates are well below those of employees in the same industries. It is impossible to distinguish between older shopkeepers in the town and in the country, but, if the view that most shopkeepers live in towns is reasonable, it would appear that delayed retirement occurs among the self-employed in both rural and urban areas.

Ideally, the next step would be to compare some measure of health in the occupational groups, divided into retired and still gainfully occupied, covered by Table 2. Such data are not available, however, the nearest substitute being the occupational mortality rates of the English Registrar-General for England and Wales (1957). These are computed every ten years from death certificates and census returns, but they do not distinguish between retired and employed men. Such measures of health can be used in the present context only if the death rates from particular causes are a guide to what morbidity from the same causes contributes to retirement. This is probably a valid

assumption for some causes of death, but in the absence of clear proof
conclusions drawn from these data must be tentative.

The death rates (standardized for age) for coronary disease
and bronchitis in farmers and farm managers were compared with
those in agricultural workers from twenty to sixty-four. The results
showed that the farmers and farm managers—mainly a self-employed
group—had a slightly higher mortality rate for coronary disease and a
slightly lower mortality rate for bronchitis than had agricultural employees and also that both groups had lower death rates from these
causes than all males from twenty to sixty-four. Since most of the
deaths from heart disease and bronchitis occur in or after middle age,
it seems very unlikely that the slight difference in mortality between
the self-employed and the employees in agriculture could account for
the fairly marked difference in pattern of retirement. To explore the
possibility of continued employment's protecting health, the death
rates of men over sixty-five in the two occupational groups were compared. The postulate was that a group with a low retirement rate
might show a lower mortality rate for coronary thrombosis, which has
been shown to be less common among those with active occupations
than among those with sedentary occupations (Morris & Crawford,
1958). This comparison produced almost identical results, the farmers
again having a slightly higher mortality rate than the agricultural
workers, but both groups being below the average for all males. If
delayed retirement does benefit health, the advantage does not clearly
emerge in these data, though it must be admitted that occupational
mortality rates are probably too insensitive for such purposes. The
findings for shopkeepers and shop assistants were equally negative.

There are, however, other factors to note. Even if no health
differences exist, there is the possibility that self-employed men find
it easier to continue working past the usual retirement age than do
employees. The spacing of work and rest pauses and the delegation of
heavier tasks may be feasible for an employer who wishes or feels
obliged (for example, on economic grounds) to carry on working despite a disability, whereas the employee in the same circumstances is
liable to be retired unless his skill is highly valued. Moreover, there
may be several social-class differences between employers and employees which could affect health, and these would have to be allowed
for before the effect of occupation on health could be examined. Our
census material can throw no light on these points.

To summarize, one is forced to the conclusion that existing
British data do not allow adequate testing of the general hypothesis

that occupation in old age has a positive health value. An *ad hoc* longitudinal study seems, therefore, to be the best method of exploring this important question; the remainder of the paper discusses some methods that might be used in such a study.

### PROSPECTIVE INQUIRY

The foremost problem is definition. Welford (1958a) has written: "Most of us know what we mean when we say someone or some society is healthy or unhealthy, but, when we try to put our meaning into precise terms, we find we are strangely unable to do so" (p. 32).

The difficulties in attempting to define and measure health are only too well known to those who seek to explore its associations. The physiologist, the social psychologist, the sociologist, and the physician can each propound and defend his concept of health and can suggest methods of measurement or assessment which, for a particular purpose, appear sound and workable. It is when we try to unify health into a single concept that conflict emerges. In a thoughtful paper Prof. Aubrey Lewis (1953) reached this conclusion:

> Health is a single concept: it is not possible to set up essentially different criteria for physical health and mental health. We commonly assume a break between health and illhealth, for which there is no counterpart in the phenomena but which we cannot yet replace by a continuum because we lack means of measuring some of the necessary dimensions. Besides subjective feelings and degree of total efficiency, the criterion of health is adequate performance of functions, physiological and psychological. So far as we cannot designate formal, major functions of the human organism and lack means of judging whether they work efficiently, we are handicapped in recognising health and illness in a reliable and valid way. The physiological functions can be thus designated and judged far more satisfactorily than the psychological. We can therefore usually tell whether an individual is physically healthy, but we cannot tell with the same confidence and consensus of many observers, whether he is mentally healthy. Though our estimate of the efficiency with which functions work must take account of the social environment which supplies stimuli and satisfies needs, the criteria of health are not primarily social; it is misconceived to equate illhealth with social deviation or maladjustment. If we avoid this error, we shall find it easier to study the relation between health and social well-being and so, one may hope, learn how to further both (p. 124).

Pending the outcome of theoretical discussion on this important matter, the only safe practical course is to try to include in a longitudinal research program several approaches to health and to examine their associations. The value of such correlation has been exemplified in several studies (Kutner et al., 1956; Thompson & Streib, 1958), but the range of techniques could be extended to encompass three main criteria of health.

### Criteria of Health

*Physiological.* There is now much literature on changes with age in human fitness as measured by laboratory tests. The resemblance between such tests and real situations is often slender, and the relation between performance in the laboratory and levels of activity in work and recreation is uncertain. A longitudinal study clearly offers valuable opportunities for exploring the use of physiological techniques in ascertaining whether there is a correlation between tests of fitness and occupational activity. In an excellent review of human energy expenditure, Passmore and Durnin (1955) suggested that useful data can now be obtained on total energy expenditure in work and leisure by accurately recording the time spent on each form of activity and then sampling its metabolic cost. Using such methods, Garry, Passmore, Warnock, and Durnin (1955) were able to show a substantial difference in the daily energy expenditure of younger men in two occupational groups in the Scottish coal-mining industry.

It is now technically possible to make precise measurement of levels of physical activity and physiological fitness in older people. Though there are formidable difficulties to overcome—for example, in persuading people to submit to the troublesome and time-consuming techniques involved—it seems essential to try to include this approach in a long-term study of occupation and health aimed at learning exactly what effect retirement has on differing occupational groups. For example, do heavy-duty manual workers ease up as they approach retirement? Is there a reduction in their total energy expenditure after retirement, or does a pattern of more active leisure maintain energy expenditure at its preretirement level? What are the nutritional implications of changes in levels of exercise after retirement? Do such changes (with due allowance for health and age) affect performance on tests of capacity to respond to exercise?

The aim would be to identify a group of people approaching sixty-five or thereabouts, to establish physiological base lines of energy expenditure and fitness, and to follow the group as it separated into occupational groups—for example, employed manual, employed sedentary, retired active, retired passive, and so on—repeating measurements at regular intervals.

*Sociomedical.* In field surveys of old people several measures of health have been used, ranging from subjective self-ratings to such objective criteria as amount of illness, days spent in bed, use of medical services, capacity for movement, presence or absence of specific diseases. The best combination of these criteria and the value of scoring systems still have to be worked out, but, as the Cornell study is now demonstrating, continued observation over a period of years appears to be a suitable method for testing the validity of subjective and objective ratings and for examining their predictive value.

In particular, we need to know more about what old people consider normal for their age and the sources of experience from which they derive their expectations. Shanas (1960) has shown that many older people take illness for granted and do not consult a doctor because they think "a person understands his own health better than most doctors do" (p. 170). Our current study in northeast Scotland suggests that people who are now over sixty were often brought up to regard a doctor's services as appropriate only in serious illness and that, as a result, there is sometimes a reluctance to seek medical aid even when a national health service has removed economic barriers. As medical science rapidly progresses, it is clearly necessary to ensure that, regardless of age, those who can benefit from recent advances feel able to accept them. The "folded-hands-and-fatalism" attitude is still too common, and further research on attitudes toward health and health services is urgently required.

In addition to the central aim of determining whether differing occupations have effects on older people's health as measured by subjective and objective criteria of the kind mentioned above, a longitudinal study should be used to explore a number of related points. For example, how do professional medical attitudes toward chronic disease, periodic check-ups, and retirement or continued employment affect health behavior and concepts of normality in old age? It seems likely that some of the frequently used tests of health, such as days in bed, frequency of medical attention, and knowledge of personal health, are partly a function of variation in medical care. This source of influence must, therefore, be studied if the effects of occupation are not to be confused with other factors that affect health.

*Adjustment.* In its now famous definition of health, the World Health Organization includes the words "mental and social well-being." In a vague way, most people might agree that these are

essential components of health, but that they are extremely difficult
to measure. Perhaps their essence is best covered by the term "adjustment," a concept that is better developed in the United States than
in Europe. Havighurst (1957) described it as follows:

> In speaking about personal and social adjustment we speak about the
> goal of living at any age. There is an inner harmony which is personal
> adjustment, and a harmony with the world around us which is social
> adjustment. The problem for a science of gerontology is to understand
> these harmonies, to describe them objectively, to measure them if
> possible, and to find out how they are related to each other, and to
> other aspects of human life (p. 172; reprinted with the permission of
> the University of Michigan Press).

Complex as such ideas are, especially to those whose training is biologically oriented, studies like that by Kleemeier (1951) have
shown how important the concept of adjustment is and how its assessment can contribute to understanding the social processes involved
in growing old successfully. Although it is debatable whether adjustment is part of health in its widest sense or should be separated from
it, there can be little doubt that both adjustment and its occupational
associations should be included in the prospective study envisaged in
this paper. The great physician Sir Humphrey Rolleston (1929) fore-
saw the need for such an approach:

> A well occupied mind, a happy disposition that thinketh no evil,
> naturally smiles instead of frowning on a stranger or a new idea, free
> from anger, hatred and jealousy, the vice that gives no pleasure to
> anyone, and an attitude of charity in its original and best sense to all,
> tend to prolong life and make it a healthy happy prelude to crossing
> the bar (p. 16).

The outstanding problem is what to include in the measurement of adjustment. Welford's review (1958a) reveals how vast the
choice is, and to the student of one discipline selection from the work
of other disciplines is a formidable and hazardous task.

Since the emphasis in the present context is on occupation
and health, one important and relevant index of adjustment could
well be the meaning of occupation in the lives of older people, with
particular reference to work and leisure. The well-known Chicago
study (Friedmann & Havighurst, 1954) suggested a useful system of
exploring this field; the later Cornell investigation (Streib & Thompson, 1957; Thompson 1958) indicates that clues to successful adjustment must be studied for a considerable time before the decision on
retirement actually takes place. A third possible index—the capacity to

accommodate social change—has been suggested by a sociologist colleague, George W. Lynch. Old people today, at least in Europe, are surrounded by many phenomena that are alien to the values impressed on them in early life, for example, wives at work, relaxation of family discipline, entertainment outside the home, reduced working hours, decline of religious practice, and so on. In a joint sociological and medical survey of older people, we are trying to discover how they feel about these changes, and we hope to use the responses to devise a scale of adjustment to social change. In our future study, it may be possible to apply this approach as one measure of adjustment which is largely independent of the more specific items connected with occupation.

It was suggested above that detailed records of activities through interviews and, perhaps, diaries could provide the data necessary for estimating levels of actual energy expenditure. Information about the time people spend on activities might, with due allowance for the effect of disability, also be used with the results of opinion or attitude questions to measure the satisfaction derived from various forms of occupation and the changes in satisfaction with, for example, retirement or increasing age. In short, in studying the effect of occupation on adjustment, it seems important to measure both attitudes *and* behavior.

### Some Problems in Method

To recapitulate the outlines of the suggested study, it aims to observe what happens to health as older people segregate themselves into occupational groups. Samples of men would be identified at some arbitrary time before retirement, and the following information would be gathered at intervals as the subjects grow older:

| *Health* | *Occupation* |
|---|---|
| 1. Performance on standard exercise tests. | |
| 2. Opinion on health. Record of illness. Use of medical services. Possibly physical examination (blood pressure, weight, special sense tests, and so on). | Description of occupational pattern. Time spent on each activity, classification of total energy expenditure by subjective and objective measurements. |
| 3. Measurement of satisfaction derived from components of the occupational pattern. | |

Of course, a great deal of other information would be collected in a study of this kind: attitude toward retirement, reasons for retiring or continuing to work, attitude and influence of family and other social groups on the individual decision about retirement, financial circumstances, and so on, but these are not primary concerns at this stage.

Since self-employed men have a markedly different retirement pattern, it would be important to increase their representation in the survey, a modification of sampling that is at least theoretically possible from national insurance records.

A further point for discussion concerns payment to the participants. Should the voluntary principle operate in an inquiry which may cost subjects much time and trouble, or is it ethically and statistically desirable to offer some financial inducement? There is a big difference between continuous observation requiring only a few facts from short interviews at distant intervals and a study that may entail several hours of interviewing, tests, and diary-keeping, repeated at intervals of a year or less. Does the inducement of payment outweigh the risk of self-selected participation?

Lastly, and most important, there are the problems raised by a multidisciplinary research project. Several references have already been made to variation in biologists' and social scientists' concepts of health and to their diverse measures. It would be both tedious and pointless to raise the bogey of specializaton as such. The real issue is how the ideas and practices of many disciplines can be integrated in such a way that each can understand what the others have to offer. In his Linacre Lecture of 1955 (the context was medical, but generalization is possible), Sir Harold Himsworth, secretary of the British Medical Research Council, said:

> To be effective a research team must be an intellectually integrated unit. There is however, a limit to the distance over which men of different disciplines can communicate, and a loose confederation of highly specialised experts cannot reasonably be expected to achieve unity of purpose. This is the essential factor making for the success or failure of team work; the presence in the team of men whose knowledge is broadly grounded; and it is only in so far as a research team contains such men that it can be an answer to the dangers of specialisation (p. 221; reprinted with permission of the *British Medical Journal*).

International journals and gatherings are one way of promoting understanding among specialists, but in practical research there are still many unresolved problems of thought, language, and even status. In this study, it has been assumed that three different approaches to the same field of gerontological research are compatible, but even a few preliminary discussions have shown that a long period of informal and intimate contact among physiologists, clinicians, psychologists, and sociologists will be necessary before agreement can be reached on, for example, the techniques. At least two suggestions have arisen from these discussions. First, there is a need, in Great Britain, at any rate, for a statement combining the contributions to research on occupation and health that each discipline is in a position to make. This statement should include a brief account of the basic concepts and an explanation of the terms commonly used. For example, the physiologists would describe the study of nutrition, energy expenditure, and measurement of fitness; the social scientists would deal with the meaning and measurement of adjustment, skill, and status; the physicians would decide how best to record and classify morbidity as an index of health. Out of this could surely come a more coherent and useful statement of concepts and techniques than is now available.

The second suggestion is that, prior to any field work in the proposed longitudinal study, the members of the research team should become familiar with the methods to be used by actually participating as subjects. Just as the undergraduate often learns best by doing an experiment on himself, so the research worker from one discipline can often gain a fuller appreciation of the techniques of another discipline by submitting himself to them. By doing so, he not only gets inside the particular approach, but he also better equips himself for the task of explaining to actual subjects why and how they can help with the research.

Finally, there is the larger issue of training for research in gerontology, an issue which seems to be better realized in the United States than in Britain. Just as formal training in most of the branches of internal medicine is now a recognized practice, so the time has probably come when workers in gerontology must undergo at least some preliminary prescribed course, possibly in an institute of gerontology, where specialists who have overcome their own interdisciplinary difficulties can help students achieve a scientific approach which cuts through the present barriers.

### REFERENCES

Anderson, W.F., & Cowan, N.R. Work and retirement. *Lancet,* 1956, **2,** 1344-1347.

Brown, R.G., McKeown, T., & Whitfield, A.G.W. Observations on the medical condition of men in the seventh decade. *Brit. med. J.*, 1958, **1,** 555-562.

Donahue, Wilma. Emerging principles and concepts: A summary. In Wilma Donahue & C. Tibbitts (Eds.), *The new frontiers of aging,* Ann Arbor: University of Michigan Press, 1957. Pp. 198-206.

Felbo, M. *Old age and work.* Copenhagen: Ejnar Munksgaard, 1958.

Forssman, S. Health problems of the older workers. A study in Swedish industry. *Trans. Ass. industr. med. Offrs.,* 1957, **7,** 9-13.

Friedmann, E.A., & Havighurst, R.J. (Eds.). *The meaning of work and retirement.* Chicago: The University of Chicago Press, 1954.

Garry, R.C., Passmore, R., Warnock, G., & Durnin, J.V.G.A. Studies on expenditure of energy and consumption of food by miners and clerks, Fife, Scotland, 1952. *Med. Res. Council Special Report,* 1955, No. 289. H.M. Stationery Office, London.

Havighurst, R.J. Personal and social adjustment in retirement. In Wilma Donahue & C. Tibbitts (Eds.), *The new frontiers of aging.* Ann Arbor: University of Michigan Press, 1957. Pp. 172-179.

Himsworth, H. The integration of medicine. *Brit. med. J.,* 1955, **2,** 217-222.

Kleemeier, R.W. The effect of a work program on adjustment attitudes in an aged population. *J. Geront.,* 1951, **6,** 372-379.

Kutner, B., Fanshel, F., Togo, Alice M., & Langner, T.S. *Five hundred over sixty.* New York: Russell Sage Foundation, 1956.

Le Gros Clark, F. *New jobs for old workers.* London: The Nuffield Foundation, 1955.

Lewis, Aubrey. Health as a social concept. *Brit. J. Sociol.,* 1953, **4,** 109-124.

Ministry of Pensions and National Insurance. *Reasons given for retiring.* London: H.M. Stationery Office, 1954.

Morris, J.N., & Crawford, Margaret D. Coronary heart disease and physical activity of work. *Brit. med. J.,* 1958, **2,** 1485-1496.

Myers, R.J. Factors in interpreting mortality after retirement. *J. Amer. statist. Ass.,* 1954, **49,** 499-509.

National Council of Social Service. *Over seventy.* London: Author, 1954.

Passmore, R., & Durnin, J.V.G.A. Human energy expenditure. *Physiol. Rev.,* 1955, **35,** 801-840.

Registrar-General for England and Wales. *Decennial supplement, England and Wales, 1951, occupational mortality.* London: H.M. Stationery Office, 1957.

Registrar-General for Scotland. *Census.* Vol. IV. Edinburgh: H.M. Stationery Office, 1956.

Richardson, I.M. Age and work. *Brit. J. indust. Med.,* 1953, **10,** 269-284.

Richardson, I.M. Retirement: A socio-medical study of 244 men. *Scot. med. J.,* 1956, **1,** 381-391.

Richardson, I.M., Brodie, A.S., & Wilson, Sarah. Social and medical needs of of people in Orkney. *Bull. Dept. Hlth, Scotland,* 1959, **17** (4), 75-79.

Richardson, I.M., Klopper, K.M., & Lynch, G.W. Special housing for older people. *Med. Off.,* 1960, **103,** 219-238.

Rolleston, H. *Aspects of age, life and disease.* New York: Macmillan Co., 1929.

Shanas, Ethel. How sick are older people? *J. Amer. med. Ass.*, 1960, **172,** 169-170.

Sheldon, J.H. *The social medicine of old age.* London: The Nuffield Foundation, 1948.

Streib, G.F., & Thompson, W.E. Personal and social adjustment in retirement. In Wilma Donahue & C. Tibbitts (Eds.). *The new frontiers of aging.* Ann Arbor: University of Michigan Press, 1957. Pp. 180-197.

Streib, G.F., Thompson, W.E., & Suchman, E.A. The Cornell study of occupational retirement. *J. soc. Issues*, 1958, **14** (2), 3-17.

Thompson, W.E. Pre-retirement anticipation and adjustment in retirement. *J. soc. Issues*, 1958, **14** (2), 35-45.

Thompson, W.E., & Streib, G.F. Situational determinants: Health and economic deprivation in retirement. *J. soc. Issues*, 1958 **14** (2), 18-34.

Weir, R.D., McKenzie, M., & Richardson, I.M. *Further studies in hospital and community.* London: Oxford University Press, 1962.

Welford, A.T. Psychological and social gerontology in Europe. *J. Geront.* (Suppl. No. 1), 1958, **13,** 51-67. (b)

Welford, A.T. Assessment of mental and social health in relation to age. *J. Geront.* (Suppl. No. 2), 1958, **13,** 32-35. (a)

# CHAPTER 54

*Levels of Living
in Old Age—
Basic Issues*

SVEN HYDÉN

Essentially, the International Social Security Administration (ISSA) considers its function to collect information and make it available to students and policy-making agencies. The association does not usually aim at establishing policy. Thus it reports developments and trends, but avoids criticism of particular programs or measures.

## PENSION LEVELS

The question of pensions and the financial situation in which people find themselves after retiring because of old age has only recently been included in the ISSA's program, but it has already assumed considerable importance. Work to date has largely been confined to methods of collecting and processing this material. In view of the close collaboration between the International Labour Organisation (ILO) and the ISSA, it was natural for the ISSA to initiate its work in this field by examining the pension systems in accordance with the stipulations contained in the ILO's international conventions.

The most important of these documents is Convention No. 102 (International Labour Office, 1952) which concerns "objectives and minimum standards of social security." This convention, which was admitted in 1952, seeks to cover and coordinate all aspects of social security and care in old age.

That part of the convention with which we are here concerned deals with the pension level. In its work on this matter, the ISSA sought to find a formula which was sufficiently flexible for application regardless of whether the pension was related to earlier income or based on a flat rate system. Basically, the minimum pension level must represent a certain portion of the income of a skilled male employee. The wording of the convention leaves considerable freedom of choice about this determination. Thus, the ILO will ratify a system if the pension level amounts to a stipulated portion of the income of a person who is considered a typical skilled laborer, such as a fitter or turner in the manufacture of machinery. A skilled worker is defined as a person employed in the group of major economic activities which have the largest number of economically active males protected by the pension system in question. The prescribed level may also be set in relation to a person whose earnings are equal to or greater than the earnings of 75 per cent of all the protected people or to a person whose earnings are equal to 125 per cent of the average earnings of all the protected people.

During the ILO discussions, determination of the proper ratio of retirement to preretirement income led to wide differences of opinion. The final decision, following consideration in 1951 and reconsideration in 1952, was that the pension level should not be less than 40 per cent of the standard wage as determined in the manner mentioned above. Even then, ratification was achieved only after provision was made for several modifications. Thus, any member (country) may provide that the benefit of a person otherwise entitled to it may be suspended if he is engaged in any prescribed gainful activity. Similarly, the benefit, if contributory, may be reduced where the earnings of the beneficiary exceed a prescribed amount and, if non-contributory, it may be reduced because of earnings and other circumstances. With regard to the scope of people covered, there are certain rules which allow ratification even if the requirements of the convention have not been complied with from the beginning.

The deliberations in the ILO have not sought to establish any minimum level for a reasonable income after reaching pension age, but are, instead, more of the opinion of the government representatives sitting on the technical committee as to what lay in the scope of national policy. A factor of great importance, however, is the decision not to fix the level at the amount required for subsistence, but to fix it in relation to a representative wage level. If only the minimum amount is paid, the pension becomes a flat rate system with a higher degree of compensation for people with low incomes than for people with higher incomes. At the time of the acceptance of the convention, the flat rate method seems to have dominated in most countries which had introduced pensions of a general character.

### Inattention to Income Requirements

The ILO, the ISSA, and the other international organizations with social security on their programs have not yet tackled the issue of pension level on the basis of an investigation into the actual income requirements of older people. The problems of care, the need for occupation, and the question of social activities are considered only as isolated phenomena which should be dealt with in another connection. Nor has the ISSA dealt with such fundamental questions as special housing, collective living arrangements, or tax relief for old people with incomes from gainful activity.

Probably current legislation in various countries has not yet had time to make allowance for all the circumstances involved in creating satisfactory levels of living in old age. Even though the aim is to achieve a uniform and adequate social security system, such efforts have not been successful except in a few isolated cases. Instead, many problems remain to be solved item by item.

A difficulty in the problem of pensioning or in the extent of and payment for work done by persons of reduced capacity is that in many countries the associated problems have been tackled on a political basis. The number of old people is increasing, and thus they constitute a pressure group for whose interest the political parties compete. This circumstance alone complicates the objective determination of levels of living in old age. True, the ILO has sought to lay down general lines, but it has been considered necessary to offer alternatives and exceptions to enable ratification by countries where this particular standard was very low.

A more scientific way of solving the problem regarding levels of living in old age would be to determine the requirements of several groups of old persons. The starting point would be the minimum subsistence level, which would then have to be supplemented according to the general economic standard of the countries. One should thus investigate the cost of an acceptable dwelling, essential furnishings (remembering that the majority of old people have already acquired these articles), and clothing and food requirements. It should also be possible to reduce the cost of travel since there will no longer be any outlay for traveling to and from work. On the other hand, old people's expenditure on care of varying kinds is generally larger than that of active people.

A budget should also make allowance for the fact that old people generally react negatively to an increase in cost brought about by the use of completely new consumer goods. The continuing increase in standards, which often results in an automatic rise in the cost-of-living index—or at least results in changes in the commodities on which the index is based—thus rises at a slower rate for old people than it does for active people. Experience shows that old people have a greater propensity for saving, and this bears out the thought expressed above.

On an international basis, it will hardly be possible to calculate old people's budgets in the way suggested above, but, on the other hand, a discussion of methods would be very suitable for an international organization. However, the possibilities with regard to economic aspects and traditions vary so greatly from country to country that the components of budgets for old people must be determined on a national basis.

In the experience of the ISSA, the problems have been tackled in many ways, but in no case was consideration given to the factors mentioned above. As a rule, the aim of modern pension schemes is to enable old people to live at essentially the same level they enjoyed during their active life with allowance for the fact that they no longer have children to support.

### Characteristics of Present Pensions

Many countries now have state pension schemes for some or all of their older people. At the time of the latest available report (International Social Security Association, 1959), the following countries, among others, had systems based on a fixed relation to previous income, at least as far as wage earners are concerned: in Europe, Albania, Austria (several systems), Belgium (several systems), Bulgaria, (several systems), Czechoslovakia (several systems), France, the Federal Republic of Germany, Hungary, Italy, Luxembourg, the Netherlands, Poland, Portugal, Sweden, Switzerland, Turkey, the United Kingdom, the Union of Soviet Socialist Republics, and Yugoslavia; in the Americas, Brazil, Chile, Costa Rica, Dominica, Nicaragua, Panama, Paraguay, and the United States; in Asia, Japan (flat amount plus .05 per cent of average earnings for every qualifying year).

In other countries the flat rate system is still employed, and in some cases this system is still considered preferable to one whereby the pension varies with the size of previous income. These countries include Denmark, Finland, Iceland, Ireland, Sweden (former system applicable to people born 1895 and earlier), Canada, Australia, and New Zealand.

In order to facilitate a comparison between the prevailing methods and standards, the pertinent details are given in Table 1. The information is that supplied to the ISSA in 1957. In some cases, this information may now be out of date or incomplete. In many cases, the conditions and benefits have been improved.

Examination of the preceding lists and of Table 1 indicates that there is wide variation in the provisions of pension schemes in countries from which information is available. Extensive variations are even found in countries at the same stage of economic development.

As indicated earlier, in several countries the aim appears to be to afford pensioners a practically unchanged standard of living after retirement. This is the case in all countries where the pension has been fixed at a proportion of previous income. Other countries have chosen a pension level at or around the subsistence minimum, and the basic pension is the same for all pensioners. The Beveridge plan seems to have exerted a great deal of influence in the countries which have chosen the latter method. In many cases, the two systems have been combined, the scheme being to provide a guaranteed minimum protection plus graduated supplements based on a certain portion of the previous income, whereas people with higher income qualify for a smaller supplement. In every case, there is an income ceiling above which no pension is paid.

### Other Needs and Provisions

Standards of living in old age cannot be judged solely on the basis of levels of pensions provided by the state or other compulsory systems. Other needs and programs must be considered as well.

The rising need for medical care with advancing age gives increasing importance to payments for health services and insurance in the budgets and incomes of older people. To a lesser extent, insurance against unemployment is also a factor. In many countries, measures have been taken or planned to provide pensioners with housing accommodations and other collective amenities.

The growing prevalence of private pensions is a significant determinant in the level of living of older people in several countries. In fact, for people previously employed by state agencies and, in many countries, for certain salaried employees, private pensions are of greater importance than the basic statutory schemes. Finally, there must be regard for the contributions and care that families provide for their older members. According to available information, this is the most important source of support in most of the underdeveloped countries.

## KEY TO TABLE 1 (cf. pp. 484–490)

Source—Compiled from International Social Security Association
(1959).
Abbreviations
*Quantitative criteria*
E = earnings or amount of contributions
RA = retirement age
YC = years of contribution
YEM = years of employment
*Basic pension level*
DRIP = deferred retirement increases pension amount
*Maximum*
IQPM = income qualifying for pension with a restricted maximum
*Adjustment to economic conditions*
AU = automatic
SD = special decision

TABLE 1
METHODS AND STANDARDS IN PENSION SYSTEMS

| Country | Quantitative criteria | Basic pension level | Maximum | Minimum | Adjustment to economic conditions |
|---|---|---|---|---|---|
| Europe Austria | YC + E | 40.5 per cent (miners 45 per cent) of the wage during last 5 years. DRIP. | 79.5 per cent (miners 87.5 per cent) IQPM | 40.5 per cent and 45 per cent | SD |
| Belgium | YC + E | 60 per cent of earnings for single person after forty-five YC, forty YC for women. 75 per cent of earnings for couple if wife is dependent, otherwise 60 per cent. DRIP. | Monetary | Monetary | AU |
| Czechoslovakia | YEM + E | 5-20 YEM; pension in proportion to time. After twenty years an increase based on occupational category. | | After five YC 15 per cent, 13.75 per cent, and 12.5 per cent in various categories. | SD |

| | | | | | |
|---|---|---|---|---|---|
| Federal Republic of Germany | YC + E | For workers and salaried employees 1.5 per cent, for miners 2.5 per cent of average earnings during time of employment. After forty years and age sixty-five, 60 per cent resp. 100 per cent of average earnings. DRIP. | For workers and salaried employees, monetary. | | AU (price level) SD (adjustment to wages). |
| France | YC + E + RA | At sixty, 20 per cent of average wage during the last ten years. DRIP decreased for a qualifying period less than thirty years. | 40 per cent of average wage during last ten years IQPM. | Monetary | SD |
| Israel | YC + RA | Certain monetary amount. Every insurance year over ten raises the pension by 2 per cent up to a given maximum. DRIP. | Monetary maximum. | | AU |
| Italy | YC + RA + E | DRIP | 80 per cent of the average wage of the last five years. | Monetary | AU |

TABLE 1 (Continued)

| Country | Quantitative criteria | Basic pension level | Maximum | Minimum | Adjustment to economic conditions |
|---|---|---|---|---|---|
| Luxembourg | YC + E | Combination of basic monetary amount plus supplement in percentage of wages. Special rules for agricultural workers. | 83.33 per cent of average wage during last five years is ceiling. | Monetary | AU |
| Netherlands | YC + E | Nominal basic pension plus per cent supplement based on wages and YC. | None | None | AU |
| Poland | YEM + E | Two categories of persons: pension in relation to earnings over last twelve months with 60 per cent and 40 per cent of a certain portion of the wage and 20 per cent and 15 per cent of top proportion. | Monetary | | SD |
| Portugal | YC + E | From 20 per cent up to 80 per cent of average wage for the whole career. DRIP. | 80 per cent of average wage for whole career up to a certain | None, but minimum. Ten years - 20 per cent of average | SD |

| | | | maximum. | wage for whole career. | |
|---|---|---|---|---|---|
| Sweden | YC + E | 60 per cent of average income from work during the best fifteen years plus basic pension. DRIP. | Monetary | Monetary | AU |
| Switzerland | YC + E | No basic pension level. Premium 4 per cent of income. To some extent, pension based on actuarial data. | Monetary | Monetary | SD |
| Turkey | YC + RA + E | With a minimum of twenty-five YC a rate of 35 per cent for single persons and 50 per cent for heads of households at pension age of sixty. DRIP. Earlier pension reduces payment. | – | – | – |
| Union of Soviet Socialist Republics | YEM + E | Pension in relation to last twelve months' income. Amount from 100 per cent of a low income to 50 per cent of a high income. | Monetary | Monetary | SD |

TABLE 1 (Continued)

| Country | Quantitative criteria | Basic pension level | Maximum | Minimum | Adjustment to economic conditions |
|---|---|---|---|---|---|
| Yugoslavia | YEM + E | The average wage for the last three years allots the person to one of twenty-one classes of pension. | Monetary | Monetary | SD |
| **America and Asia** | | | | | |
| Brazil | YC + E | 66 per cent of average wage during last three years before minimum pension age (sixty for commercial workers, sixty-five for male and female industrial workers). | Monetary maximum (66 per cent of three times the legally prescribed minimum wage). | 70 per cent of the legally pre-scribed minimum wage. | AU |
| Chile | YC + E | Basic amount is 50 per cent of average earnings during the last five years prior to pension age (sixty-five) plus incre-ment of 1 per cent of average earnings for every qualifying year over ten. | 70 per cent of average earn-ings. | 56 per cent of average earnings for men, 50 per cent for women. | SD |

| | | | | |
|---|---|---|---|---|
| Costa Rica | YC + E | Basic amount is 40 per cent of average earnings during last ten years prior to pension age (sixty-five) plus increment of 1.5 per cent of average earnings for every qualifying year over three. DRIP. | 90 per cent of average earnings. Monetary maximum. | 58 per cent of average earnings. |
| Dominican Republic | YC + E | Basic amount is 50 per cent of average earnings during the last four years plus increment of 1 per cent for every qualifying year over sixteen. | 70 per cent of average earnings. | None |
| Japan | YC + E | A flat amount of about 12.5 per cent of the wage of industrial workers plus .05 per cent of average earnings for every qualifying year (sixty for men, fifty-five for women). | None | None |

TABLE 1 (Continued)

| Country | Quantitative criteria | Basic pension level | Maximum | Minimum | Adjustment to economic conditions |
|---------|----------------------|---------------------|---------|---------|-----------------------------------|
| Nicaragua | YC + E | Basic amount of 30 per cent of average earnings plus increment of 1.5 per cent of average earnings for every qualifying year over three. | 80 per cent of average earnings, monetary. | - | - |
| Panama | YC + E | Basic amount of 50 per cent of average earnings plus increment of 2 per cent of average earnings for every qualifying year over twenty. | Monetary | - | - |
| Paraguay | YC + E | Basic amount is 30 per cent of average during last three years plus increment of 1 per cent for every qualifying year over fifteen. | - | - | - |

## REFERENCES

International Labour Office. Conventions, recommendations, resolutions, and other texts adopted by the International Labour Conference at its 35th session. *Official Bull.*, 1952, **35** (2), 45-72.

International Social Security Association. *National monographs on old-age insurance.* Geneva: Author, 1959. 2 vols.

# CHAPTER 55

*Old-Age Pensions and*
*Allowances in France*

PAUL PAILLAT

In France, a succession of inflationary pressures and economic ups and downs since the 1930's has almost eradicated an entire social group—the *rentiers* or small investors. Indeed, the word itself, after a notorious role in novels and comic plays, has almost dropped out of the language. Today, very few people are able to maintain a decent standard of living in retirement if they are forced to depend on savings or capital income. The few that do are mainly wealthy people who have never had to work for a living except to keep themselves busy and avoid the much despised (and taxed) label of idleness.

Most of the 5,000,000 French people of sixty-five and over (12 per cent of the population) find it exceedingly difficult to meet their financial needs in retirement. Holders of small savings accounts can expect to draw only a limited extra income, or they have to spend their assets, which most of them do. Lifelong saving for old age is now superseded by either compulsory or voluntary pension schemes. Compulsory schemes, though they may not provide the highest pensions, now cover more than 90 per cent of the employed population.

### PENSION SCHEMES

Pension schemes are an integral part of a development aimed at protecting workers against a number of risks. The constitutions of France—that of 1946 as well as that of 1958—provide that aged and disabled workers and their dependents shall be given a "proper means of living" by the nation. There is, of course, a wide gap between this principle and its application. As a consequence of historical factors and processes, the various schemes exhibit an extraordinary range of provisions and regulations. This is a field in which the French do not live up to their reputation as logicians.

The Social Insurance Act, passed in 1930, provides workers who have contributed for fifteen or more years a pension at sixty at a reduced rate or at sixty-five at the normal rate. The aim was to assure old workers of a minimum assured income. In 1945-1946, a more ambitious social security system was instituted, making participation compulsory for all wage earners earning below a wage ceiling. Simultaneously, several special schemes, in the railroad and coal-mining industries, for example, have been developed with so much strength that it has not been possible to integrate them into the general system. Increasingly, the extra pension schemes are being covered by collective bargaining, which is resulting in added contributions (paid partly by employers) and a higher level of pension. For non-wage earners, specific and autonomous compulsory schemes have been developed since the war.

This summarizes the striking but not altogether healthful proliferation of pension plans during recent years. The risk of dependence in old age is being covered, but very unevenly. Unfortunately, large numbers of old people cannot draw full pensions or are not covered by the provisions. Allowances, mainly from the Fonds National de Solidarité (National Solidarity Fund or FNS), help them, but to a very limited extent.

## RETIREMENT AGES

Of course, minimum statutory age for drawing a pension and the actual age of retirement vary considerably. Some of the variations and factors are discussed below.

### General Scheme and Scheme for Farm Workers

As indicated, a worker may request his pension at sixty provided that he has contributed to it for at least fifteen years. His pension is reduced, however, even with a thirty-year contributing period, which is the maximum taken into account. The normal pension is paid to those who apply at sixty-five, though again the rate is reduced when the contributing period is fewer than thirty years. Postponing retirement beyond sixty-five, however, results in an increased rate, which may amount to as much as 4 per cent of the annual salary. Operation of the scheme is shown in Table 1.

TABLE 1
ANNUAL PENSION ACCORDING TO AGE
AND YEARS OF CONTRIBUTION

(General pension scheme with average earnings
6,000 new francs* over the past ten years)

| Age of retirement | Annual Pensions, according to years of contributing | | | | | | | |
|---|---|---|---|---|---|---|---|---|
| | Annual pensions in new francs | | | | Percentage of earnings | | | |
| | 15 | 20 | 25 | 30 and over | 15 | 20 | 25 | 30 and over |
| 60 | 600 | 804 | 1,002 | 1,200 | 10.0 | 13.4 | 16.7 | 20.0 |
| 65 | 1,200 | 1,602 | 2,004 | 2,400 | 20.0 | 26.7 | 33.4 | 40.0 |
| 70 | 1,800 | 2,400 | 3,000 | 3,600 | 30.0 | 40.0 | 50.0 | 60.0 |

*5.00 N. F. = approximately $1.00 (United States).

Theoretically, lengthening the active working life should result in higher pension payments. Actually, however, many workers draw their pension before they are sixty-five. Since the scheme is only now becoming fully operative (the first cases with a thirty-year contributing period have just become eligible), such behavior is partly understandable. At sixty, one needs more than a nineteen-year contribution period in order to draw the minimum yearly benefit of 3,000 N.F. (5 N.F. equal $1) and thus exceed the Allocation aux Vieux Travailleurs Salariés (older workers' allowance). Information supplied to the author by the general director of the Social Security Administration reveals that of the 70,000 workers annually reaching the age of sixty-five, 50,000 are already drawing pensions. Furthermore, disabled workers, entitled to full pensions between sixty and sixty-five, number 91,000.

Regulations permit a beneficiary of these schemes to work for a living while he is drawing a pension. According to a recent sampling survey in the Paris area (Netter, 1960), 42 per cent of general scheme pensioners continue to work.

## Special Schemes

Three examples of special schemes covering the largest numbers of workers are cited here.

*Government Employees, Civil Service.* In active services classified as straining (laborious, Class B), the pension may be drawn at age fifty-five after fifteen years of service. For others (Class A), sixty is the minimum age. The average ages in 1956 were:

| Class and rank | | Average retiring ages |
|---|---|---|
| Class A | ⌠High-rank employees | 65-66 |
| (43.5 per cent) | ⌡Others | 61-62 |
| Class B | ⌠High-rank employees | 60-61 |
| (56.5 per cent) | ⌡Others | 56-57 |

*Government Owned Coal Mines.* After a thirty-year working life with twenty years in underground jobs, a coal-miner may retire at age fifty. If these conditions are not met, he must wait until age fifty-five. Because of the ratio between underground and surface personnel, the mean retiring age is fifty-four years, six months.

*Government Owned Railways (S.N.C.F.).* An engine driver (7.5 per cent of personnel) may retire at fifty after a twenty-five-year working life, provided that he has had fifteen years on engines. Other categories wait until age fifty-five. Average retiring age for drivers in 1957 was fifty years, eight months; for others, fifty-five years, nine months. Among the latter, managing staff waited, on the average, until fifty-nine years, nine months.

A younger retirement age is sometimes provided for female workers under the special schemes.

With the exceptions of the special schemes, the increments

for longer service may be a factor in postponing actual retirement age. Under the Union Nationale des Institutions de Retraites des Salariés scheme, the pension is reduced by 5 per cent for each year under age sixty-five. Schemes for non-wage earners allow an increased pension when retirement is postponed beyond age sixty-five.

TABLE 2

MONTHLY PENSION OF UNMARRIED INDUSTRIAL WORKER

(In rounded new francs)

| Occupation wage | | At 60 | | At 65 | |
|---|---|---|---|---|---|
| | | Contributions over | | Contributions over | |
| | | 15 years | 30 years | 15 years | 30 years |
| Laborer | 326.70 | 32.70 | 65.30 | 108.90 | 130.70 |
| Fitter | 491.60 | 49.20 | 98.30 | 163.80 | 196.60 |
| Wood model-builder | 619.70 | 62.00 | 123.90 | 206.50* (200.00) | 247.80* (200.00) |

Source—Ministry of Labor (1959). These figures apply to the Paris area as of October 1, 1959, with monthly wages computed on an hourly rate and a work week of forty hours. Average working time was actually between forty-five and forty-six hours. Social security contributions are not included in the wage calculations. Reprinted with permission.
*Being in excess of the statutory minimum, these rates have to be deflated to 200.00 N.F.

## AMOUNTS OF PENSIONS AND ALLOWANCES

### General Scheme and Scheme for Farm Workers

Table 1 gives a sample of pension amounts at different ages and contributory periods. In general, each year of service between contributory periods of fifteen years (the minimum) and thirty years, yields approximately .30 per cent of the normal rate at the age considered. (Contributory years beyond thirty are not included.) Thus, a sixty-five–year–old worker retiring after a twenty-year contributory period draws a pension of 26.7 per cent of his basic wage. The pension is never higher than the age-specific ceiling: 20 per cent at sixty, 40 per cent at sixty-five, 60 per cent at seventy, and so on. Table 2 illustrates the comparison between actual wages and corresponding pensions according to age and length of the contribution period.

Though Table 2 is based on average wages in 1959, it is theoretical. No worker at this time had had a thirty-year contribution period. Furthermore, 84 per cent of workers aged fifty-five to sixty-four and 78 per cent sixty-five and over are married. When there is a dependent spouse, the pension is increased by 50 per cent, with an arbitrary ceiling. An additional point is that average wages over the last ten years, used for computing pensions, are lower than current wages despite revaluating indexes.

According to provisional rules, a fitter retiring today at sixty-five will draw not less than 723.80 N.F. a year, which is the amount of the older workers' allowance (A.V.T.S.). After a thirty-year working life, a sixty-five–year–old laborer cannot expect to draw more than 130.70 N.F. a month. This amounts to 51.4 per cent of the minimum wage (254.20 N.F. in October, 1959), although his needs are certainly not reduced in proportion. The pension of the retired wood model-builder would reach almost this minimum wage level, but he is prevented by statute from receiving more than 200 N.F. per month (Table 2).

### Special Schemes

In these schemes, pensions are usually equal to 2 per cent of basic wages for each year of contribution up to a maximum of 75 per cent of wages. This maximum ratio is sometimes arbitrarily reduced when average wages have been unusually high. Average pension-salary ratios for government employees in 1956 are shown in the following figures (Thomas, 1960):

| Class | Office jobs | Heavy jobs |
|-------|-------------|------------|
| A | 75.4% | 76.8% |
| B | 72.4% | 73.4% |
| C | 65.1% | 68.9% |
| D | 66.8% | 70.4% |

These relatively high ratios are not entirely realistic because they do not take into account certain premiums and special allowances that often increase the wages of civil servants. In Paris, for example, there is a residence allowance equal to 20 per cent of salary.

Coal-mining is also a special case. The pension is a lump sum bearing no relation to wages, but based on length of working life and type of job. For a thirty-year contribution, the pension is 2,697.50 N.F. a year plus a bonus of 0.6 per cent for each year of underground work.

### Extra Pension Schemes

In view of the small amount of the pensions, it is easy to understand the recent rapid development of extra pension schemes based on a point system. Each year, the contributor is credited with a number of points equal to the ratio between contributions and the value of the reference wages. The pension will be determined by the product of the sum of the points multiplied by the value of the point at each payment. The reference wage is an accounting unit which follows the wage trend; it is in a constant ratio with the average (or median) wages paid to contributors. The value of the point is so determined that it takes into account the expected development of the scheme during some years to come.

Obviously, these schemes appear first in expanding economic sectors. Their gradual generalization will raise such serious problems as the lowering of the contributor-pensioner ratio. For the time being, the fortunate ones are those who have become eligible for pensions without having contributed to them.

In the case of non-wage earners, specific schemes also operate on a point basis, the number of points varying according to the classes of contribution. These schemes are so recent that certain temporary expedients are used. For example, an old-age allowance is provided to pensioners in an amount equal to one-half the A.V.T.S. (343.20 N.F. a year).

From the Fonds National de Solidarité (F.N.S.), every unmarried old man or woman whose resources are below a ceiling of 2,010 N.F. a year—and every couple with less than 2,580 N.F. are entitled to a supplementary allowance of 380 N.F. a year.

### Population of Pension Schemes

Table 3 gives the number of contributors and the number of pensioners under various schemes for wage earners and self-employed workers at the end of 1958.

Extra pension schemes are operated by more than eight hundred organizations with from fewer than one hundred to more than 100,000 employees. The two largest schemes are cadres (managing personnel), with 600,000 and more contributors and 150,000 pensions, and U.N.I.R.S. (wage earners), with more than 1,200,000 contributors and 120,000 pensions. Among sectors covered by such specific schemes are banks, insurance companies, building trades, and public works.

It is important to note that extra pension schemes are often

TABLE 3A

POPULATIONS IN BASIC PENSION SCHEMES
FOR WAGE EARNERS, 1958

(In thousands)

| Scheme | Contributions | Pensioners | | | Ratio of contributors to pensioners |
|---|---|---|---|---|---|
| | | Total | Direct | In-direct | |
| General scheme | 9,300 | 2,275 | 2,042 | 233 | 4.1 |
| Scheme for farm workers | 1,210 | 208 | 190 | 18 | 5.8 |
| Special schemes: | 2,529 | 2,033 | 1,363 | 670 | 1.2 |
| Government employees | 760 | 400* | 259 | 141 | 1.9 |
| Military personnel | 360 | 477* | 251 | 126 | 0.6 |
| Local government employees | 303 | 131 | 85 | 46 | 2.3 |
| Mines | 310 | 311 | 200 | 111 | 1.0 |
| Railways (S.N.C.F.) | 337 | 403 | 263 | 140 | 0.8 |

Source—Unpublished report submitted by J. F. Thomas to the Special
Committee on Old-Age Problems, 1960.
*Estimated.

TABLE 3B

POPULATIONS IN PENSION SCHEMES
FOR NON-WAGE EARNERS, 1958

(In thousands)

| Schemes | Contributors | Pensions | Ratio of contributors to pensioners |
|---|---|---|---|
| Craftsmen | 565 | 188 | 3.0 |
| Industry and trade | 1,013 | 359 | 2.8 |
| Professions | 140 | 46 | 3.1 |
| Agriculture | 3,739 | 925 | 4.0 |
| Total | 5,457 | 1,518 | 3.6 |
| Special fund | | 282 | |

Source—Ministry of Labor (1959).

responsible for the main part of pensions for professional people. These cover, in total, more than 3,000,000 workers and are paying 400,000 pensions. These figures are subject, however, to the following serious limitations:

1. Pensioners still working are registered in both categories—contributors and pensioners.
2. Some people draw several pensions; a widow may draw both a personal pension and a widow's allowance.
3. In many cases, it is not possible to separate pensions for disability from those automatically transformed into full pensions at sixty.
4. The ratio of personal pensions to widow's or orphan's allowances (indirect pensions) varies considerably, as the following figures indicate.

| Scheme | Number of direct pensions for each indirect pension |
|---|---|
| General scheme | 8.8 |
| Scheme for farm workers | 10.5 |
| Special schemes | 2.0 |

### Pension Payments in 1958

Table 4 shows the amounts paid under various pension schemes in thousands of new francs during 1958, including F.N.S. allowances to non-wage earners.

Payments within each scheme vary so greatly that averages have little significance. They may be reported, however, for information (Thomas, 1960).

|  | Average pension paid for the year 1958 (in new francs) | |
|---|---|---|
| Scheme | All pensions | Personal (direct) pensions |
| General scheme and farm worker scheme | 1,060 | 1,100 |
| Special schemes | 3,020 | 3,640 |
| Non-wage-earner schemes | 620 | — |

### CONCLUSION

The data reported above are deficient because they do not provide a comparison with living costs in France. They do indicate,

TABLE 4A

PENSION PAYMENTS IN 1958: BASIC SCHEMES
FOR WAGE EARNERS

(In thousands of new francs)

| Scheme | Total | Direct pensions | Indirect pensions |
|---|---|---|---|
| General scheme | 1,976 | 1,856 | 120 |
| Scheme for farm workers | 144 | 139 | 5 |
| Special schemes: | 6,129 | — | — |
|   Government employees | 1,543 | 1,258 | 285 |
|   Military personnel | 1,400 | 1,154 | 246 |
|   Mines | 538 | 404 | 134 |
|   Railways (S.N.C.F.) | 1,240 | 1,009 | 231 |

Source—Ministry of Labor (1959).


TABLE 4B

PENSION PAYMENTS IN 1958: BASIC SCHEMES FOR
NON-WAGE EARNERS

(In thousands of new francs)

| Scheme | Total | Pensions | F.N.S. allowances |
|---|---|---|---|
| Craftsmen | 100 | 67 | 33 |
| Industry and trade | 250 | 213 | 37 |
| Professions | 51 | 49 | 2 |
| Agriculture | 526 | 307 | 219 |
| Total | 927 | 636 | 291 |
| Special fund | 183 | 98 | 85 |

Source—Ministry of Labor (1959).


however, that pensions and allowances—even with other benefits not described here—do not meet needs. The maximum workers' pension does not equal the minimum wage rate, and no one is permitted to draw the maximum pension.

Allowances are only a temporary, rough device. In the views of some (Vannier, 1959), they separate old people who are forced to accept them in lieu of a pension after a long and hard life of work.

Even when generously granted, allowances do not compare with pensions based on personal contributions. The cost of pensions raises a serious problem in France, however, where the ratio of the young and aged to adults of working age is exceptionally high.

Another point is the inequity arising from the unevenness in the pension network. Despite similar contributions, there may be a great difference between the pension, at the same retiring age, of a worker enrolled under the general scheme and that of a worker enrolled under a special scheme. In the latter case, of course, the high pension grows partly out of higher contributions by the worker and partly out of financial resources provided by all taxpayers (e.g., the railway scheme is supported by the budget).

## REFERENCES

Ministry of Labor. *Revue française de travail*, 1959, **4,** 121-139.
Netter, F. Réflexions suggérées par l'expérience française. *Droit social,* 1960, **25,** 102-108.
Thomas, J.F. Data from an unpublished report to the Special Committee on Old-Age Problems, 1960.
Vannier, Jeanne. Recherche sur le niveau de vie des personnes agées. In Secours Catholique, *Vieillesse et vie: Campagne 1959-1960.* Paris: Editions S.O.S., 1959.

# CHAPTER 56

*Recent Developments in*
*Income Security Programs*
*in the United Kingdom*

BRIAN ABEL-SMITH

In the middle of World War II, the principles of the Beveridge report (1942) attracted interest all over the world—not least in America. In 1959, several of these principles were abandoned in the revision of pension provisions for old people. It may, therefore, be of interest to explain how and why this has happened.

There were two major policy decisions in 1959. The first was the enactment of a scheme which was to start in 1961 and grant a wage-related supplementary pension to part of the present working population when they retired. The second was a decision by the government to provide higher living standards for the poorest aged by increasing the real level of assistance scales. These somewhat conflicting decisions can only be understood against their background.

Provision for old age is a politically active matter in Great

503

Britain most of the time. It frequently plays a significant role in general elections, as I shall indicate. I must, therefore, start by declaring my own position. I can do this best by stating that I was one of the authors of the Labour Party's plan, *National Superannuation* (Labour Party, 1957). Though this may color my interpretation of recent policy changes in Britain, I have, nevertheless, had more access to sources of information than the typical academic. Rather than give a dry account of recent developments in Britain, I thought it better to tell the full story as it appears to this not wholly detached observer.

The main features of the British social insurance scheme were based on the Beveridge report of 1942 and remained unchanged until the new act became effective. This scheme has provided benefits for sickness, unemployment, widows, and other contingencies in addition to old age, and the finances of the different benefits cannot be separated. Basic flat rate pensions were, and continue to be, available as a right to those whose contribution record since 1925 is adequate and to those who have had credited or have paid contributions for the minimum of ten years between 1948 and 1958. The standard rates of pension at the time the 1959 act was passed were £2.10s.0d. ($7.00) a week for a single person and £4 ($11.20) for a married couple. If both husband and wife contributed, they received a pension of £2.10s.0d. each. A man was and is permitted to draw his pension at sixty-five, a woman at sixty. Higher pensions may be earned for each six months that the pension is postponed up to seventy and sixty-five for men and women, respectively. Those drawing pension before these ages were entitled to earn £3.10s without reduction of their pension. After these ages, the pension is paid without any reduction for earnings.

The old scheme was financed by contributions from insured persons and from employers and the government. Contributions were flat rate in each class of contributor, but there was some concession to ability to pay, for, among employed people, women paid lower contributions than men, and juveniles paid still lower contributions. Self-employed people paid more than employed people, but less than the combined employer-employee contribution. Nearly everyone of working age, except married women, students, and people with very low incomes, had to contribute.

The provision that only those who had paid the appropriate contributions were entitled to pensions is continued. Thus, the group of people over pensionable age is divided into those who receive pensions because they paid contributions under earlier legislation and those who did not pay contributions and, therefore, receive no pension.

The latter group has consisted of people who were better paid when they were at work, the self-employed, and other excepted persons. In total, at the end of 1958, retirement pensions were received by 5,300,000 people out of 7,300,000 people over minimum pensionable age. The remaining 3,000,000 included over 500,000 people who were sixty-five to seventy (men) or sixty to sixty-five (women) and had chosen to postpone their pensions and thus earn increments. Thus, just prior to passage of the new act, there were over 1,000,000 people, very few of whom were ever likely to work, who were not entitled to contributory pensions. Many of them may have had occupational pensions, and about one-fifth were receiving assistance allowances after examination of their means under legislation originating in 1908 for non-contributory pensions.

Whatever the expressed intentions of the government, retirement pensions in Britain have never been sufficient for subsistence as the term is understood in Britain. The nationally financed and nationally operated Assistance Board has standard scales of grant and pays allowances for rent and other special needs. An applicant with only a basic pension has always been able to get supplementary aid after examination of his means. About one-quarter of retirement pensioners receive such supplements.

In the barest outline, such have been the direct state provisions for maintaining the incomes of old people. The indirect provisions consist in special tax concessions for old people and for saving for old age. Thus the exemption limit in income tax is £275 (single) and £440 (married) for persons over sixty-five, compared with £140 and £240, respectively, for younger people. Only one marriage partner has to be over sixty-five for the couple to qualify. Aged people with moderate incomes (under about £1,200 a year) are also entitled to pay lower levels of income tax. Third, lump sums may be received tax free from certain pension schemes. The tax treatment of pension schemes is too complicated to be summarized in a short paper, but the general principle has been that for appropriate schemes the contributions of both employers and employees and also, in some cases, the investment income of the fund are free of tax; the pension is, however, taxed when paid. This treatment greatly assists the accumulation of pension funds.

One of the trends which have led to the new thinking in Britain about the income maintenance services for old people has been the rapid growth of pension schemes since World War II. The favorable tax treatment of such schemes is an underlying reason for this development. Another reason has been the desire to attract and hold workers during periods of full employment. Very little is known about the coverage or benefits of these schemes or about the conditions on which pensions are granted. Applications to do research in this field have not gained the support of financing bodies in Britain.

I shall summarize the facts that are available. In 1936, there were only about 1,500,000 people outside the public services who were in pension schemes. It was estimated by the government actuary in 1958 (Ministry of Pensions and National Insurance, 1958a) that there were about 6,500,000 people in private industry and commerce who belonged to pension schemes. Including the public services, the total was about 9,000,000 people or over one-third of the working population; one-half of employed men were in pension schemes and about one-quarter of women. The present pension schemes are concentrated on the better-paid employees. Leaving out the public services, only about one-quarter of male manual workers were in pension schemes. Although over one-third of the working population is covered by pension schemes, little more than 1,000,000 old people are presently receiving occupational pensions, some of which are very small. Because so little is known about the conditions on which people are included in pension schemes, no estimate can be made of the number of people now covered who will actually receive pensions.

A second reason for re-studying pensions has been their increasing cost, which has faced a government under continuous pressure to reduce income tax. Fundamentally, the problem has been more pensioners rather than higher pensions. The number of pensioners has constantly increased, partly because more people are reaching pension age and partly because as the oldest age group of pensioners—some of whom were never entitled to pensions—dies, it is being replaced by a younger group, virtually all of whom are eligible for pensions. This is the fundamental fiscal problem, but in Britain it has appeared in a curious financial form. Although national insurance has, in fact, always been run on a pay-as-you-go basis, the level of contributions has always been calculated on the actuarial principles of private insurance. This actuarial façade has, until very recently, given substantial relief to the taxpayer, as I will explain below.

Contributions to national insurance have been based on calculations of what an average entrant would need to pay from sixteen until pension age to earn the benefits current at the time the contribution is fixed. This actuarial contribution is then split among the employer, the employee, and the state. It is clear that a fund into which contributions were paid from the age of sixteen and which paid benefits to no one who had not paid contributions from that age would have no financial problems provided that the actuarial assumptions proved correct and the rates of pension remained unchanged. This would be true whatever happened to the age distribution of the population.

In fact the actuaries have generally proved to be very conservative in their estimates. The fund has been greatly enriched by much lower levels of unemployment and sickness, much higher rates of interest, and more early deaths than were forecast (Ministry of Pensions and National Insurance, 1954b). Nevertheless, there always has been a heavy capital deficit in the insurance fund. This actuarial deficit has been created by extensive blanketing-in and by increases in pensions.

At the start of contributory pensions in 1925, people were given contributory benefits as a right for which they had paid no contributions. And the national insurance act of 1946 provided that the higher-income employed persons and the self-employed and non-employed who had been outside the earlier scheme should be given pensions in 1958 after paying only ten years of contributions. It was planned by Winston Churchill in 1925, by William Beveridge in 1942, and by the postwar Labour Government that the costs of blanketing-in should be met partly by the government and partly by quinquennial increases in the insurance contributions over what was actuarially required.

Pensions have frequently been increased in the past fifteen years, partly because of rising prices and partly to increase their real value. Thus when the level of pensions was increased from 10s. to 26s. in 1946, the contributions that had been paid by the beneficiaries were for a much lower level of pension. This increased the capital deficit in the fund. Pensions were again increased for older beneficiaries in 1951 and for all beneficiaries in 1952 and 1955.

The fairly frequent changes in pension rates provided ministers with opportunities to increase the level of contributions more frequently than was provided for under the original legislation. These opportunities were used. Not only was the contribution raised to the level actuarially required for new entrants to be entitled to the higher level, but also a little extra was inconspicuously added to the contribution under a number of engaging titles. In 1955, the employed person was required to pay the extra sum of 8d. a week, as "a contribution towards the additional cost of pensions due to the liability not covered by the actuarial contributions" (Ministry of Pensions and National Insurance, 1954a, p. 6).

Although the ratio of beneficiaries to contributors was low, the use of the actuarial principle, as defined above, was helpful to the exchequer. In theory, the scheme was tripartite: insured people, employers, and the state all contributed. In practice, the scheme was bipartite. Thus, in the fiscal year 1949-1950, the contributions of insured people and employers and the interest on the funds were sufficient to meet the cost of all the national insurance benefits paid out that year. The exchequer was in the happy position of being able to pay its allotted contribution to the funds with the knowledge that its contribution—and more—would be returned as a loan to the government from the funds. This was partly because of the "safe" actuarial assumptions and partly because of the actuarial method of calculating contributions. With the adoption of more realistic actuarial assumptions, this extremely advantageous position was abandoned, but with the aid of the extra contribution of insured people and employers described above, the exchequer continued to get back part of its contribution as a loan. Gradually the number of pensioners increased, and the amount available for loan back to the government declined. The actuarial principle soon ceased to be a paying proposition.

The alternative to increasing contributions or taxation was to lower expenditure by reducing the number of pensioners. The first attempt to do something like this was made by the Labour Government in 1951. The level of pensions had not been increased since 1946, when the postwar rates were fixed at 26s. for a single person and 42s. for a couple. The real value of this pension had depreciated because of inflation. The government, when increasing pension rates in 1951, enacted that the new levels of pension (30s. for a single person and 50s. for a married couple) would be received only by new pensioners at the ages of seventy (men) and sixty-five (women). This attempt to limit the cost of pensions did not last long: the distinction was removed by the Conservative Government in 1952 when it raised pensions to 32s.6d. for a single person and 54s. for a married couple.

In the same year, however, the government became more keenly interested in encouraging older people to stay on at work. If more people would voluntarily stay at work after minimum pensionable age, a case could be made for higher pensionable ages. Thus, in March, 1952, the government set up a committee on the employment of older men and women. The first report was published in October, 1953 (Ministry of Labour and National Insurance, 1953). In the same year another committee was set up to investigate the economic and financial problems of provision for old age. At the end of 1954, the majority of the last committee reported that the minimum pension age should be raised (The Treasury, 1954), but the government, faced with widespread protest and an imminent general election, decided not to implement the report.

If more money was so hard to find and the number of beneficiaries could not be reduced, then why, it may be asked, were pensions increased so regularly and so much? It would have been politically impossible to cut pensions, but rising prices provided ministers with the opportunity to raise pensions somewhat less than was justified by the increase in prices. And this, in fact, was the course pursued by both Labour and Conservative governments until 1955. The prevention of distress was left to the National Assistance Board, which did adjust its scales for rising prices every year or two. Thus the number of assistance grants in supplementation of pensions more than doubled between October, 1946, and December, 1954.

There are, of course, theoretical arguments against leaving the maintenance of the aged to a system that grants money according to the income of the recipient. In particular, such a system may be expected to reduce the desire to save. We have, however, relied on such a system for the ultimate support of old people for over a century, and during this period there has been an enormous increase in provisions for old age; in particular, there has been the extremely rapid increase in occupational pensions.

Politically, the term "means test" summons up ugly memories among older people in Britain—memories of the harsh days of the poor law, of mass unemployment, of the disposal of cherished possessions, of the workhouse, and of the pursuit of liable relatives by ruthless welfare officers. This is one reason why a considerable proportion of the aged (around 10 per cent for the elderly population as a whole) does not apply for assistance even though entitled to receive it and even though assistance is now humanely administered. Too great a role for the National Assistance Board may well have been thought electorally damaging in 1955.

On the other hand, the attitudes of younger people are changing. The participation of so many members of the working population in occupational pension schemes is important in this connection, for it reduces the political pressure for improvements in the social insurance scheme. An increasing number of the population think that their major provision for old age will come not from the national insurance fund, but from an occupational fund or the insurance companies to whom their employers have delegated their responsibilities. It becomes, therefore, easier for a government to argue that an increase in the retirement pension is unnecessary and that the protection of old people should be the responsibility of the National Assistance Board.

If income maintenance services were left to the National Assistance Board, at least it would be cheaper in total expenditure. But the question was not thought of in this way. The expenditure of the board has to be wholly paid for by taxation. The expenditure of the insurance fund, on the other hand, is largely financed by contributions. If large increases in the insurance contributions were thought more acceptable than small increases in taxation and if the government were under pressure to reduce income tax, the balance of advantage would be much less clear.

The government decided to increase pensions. In April, 1955, the basic rates for a single person were increased from 32s.6d. to 40s. and for a married couple from 54s. to 65s. In the same month there were also increases in national insurance contributions and reductions in income tax. It was the month preceding the general election.

In the election campaign, Labour Party candidates attacked the government for what was called "the pension swindle." National Assistance recipients had their increase in pension subtracted from their assistance grant and were thus no better off than before. This was an inevitable consequence of attempting to create a larger role for pensions as a right. Between December, 1954, and December, 1955, the number of National Assistance grants paid in supplementation of retirement pensions fell by over 100,000.

The increase in pension rates and contributions was no more than an expedient. The number of pensioners was still inexorably increasing, and there was clearly a limit to the level to which the flat rate contributions could be raised. There had always been considerable criticism of the burden on the lower-paid worker. It would soon be impossible to operate the national insurance act of 1946 without a larger subsidy from taxation than the government was prepared to grant.

Early in 1957, the Labour Party published its ambitious plan, *National Superannuation*. Basic pensions were to be increased from £2 to £3 per week. The figure was chosen to take three-quarters of existing pensioners off National Assistance and to give old-age pensioners an income more in line with current earnings. The scheme was to be paid for by replacing the old flat rate contributions for pensions by wage-related contributions (3 per cent employee and 5 per cent employer) levied up to a high level of income. By this means, the money could be found to increase existing pensions; it avoided the difficulty inherent in a flat rate system, which imposed too heavy a burden on the lower-paid worker. The scheme was to be run on a pay-as-you-go basis, but was to build up a fund, invested partly in ordinary shares, against the increasing cost of pensions.

In return for wage-related contributions, a wage-related supplement was promised as an addition to the flat rate pension of £3 a week. Total pensions would be adjusted to bring them into line with the level of earnings at the time of retirement, and it was guaranteed that pensions would be adjusted for changes in the cost of living while they were in payment. In total, pensions would eventually be at the level of more than half pay for the average worker. Those who preferred to remain in their occupational schemes would be free to contract out of the wage-related pension, provided that the scheme met certain conditions.

The scheme brought home to the government—if it had not already thought of it—the advantage of a wage-related contribution in preventing the rising cost of pensions' falling on the exchequer. More money could be collected without complaint. Second, it indicated that the trade unions had consented to the Labour Party's proposals and thus would not be in a position to object to the principle of wage-related contributions and benefits. Third, and perhaps less fortunately, it made it extremely difficult for the government to refuse to allow contracting out, however modest its proposals.

The Labour Party's plan was published in May, 1957. In November of the same year, the government announced an increase in the retirement pension from £2 to £2.10s.0d. a week, which came into effect early in the following year. This was paid for mainly by a large increase in contributions. Again, the increase was much larger than was justified on the actuarial basis. The addition to the actuarial contribution for an employed person was raised from 8d. to 1s.3d. "to provide a contribution towards the liability arising because the new rates of retirement pension will apply to persons of all ages in the existing insured population, as well as to existing pensioners" (Ministry of Pensions and National Insurance, 1957, p. 6). The result of these additions was that by 1957 the percentage of the actuarial contribution paid for by employed people and their employers combined increased to 2.5 per cent more than the total actuarial contribution (*ibid.*, p. 6). It could not have been clearer that the national insurance scheme, which was theoretically run on a private insurance basis, was, in practice, being run on a pay-as-you-go basis.

As I have shown earlier, the private insurance method of calculating contributions had advantages to the exchequer in the early days of the scheme when the ratio of beneficiaries to contributors was low. As the number of beneficiaries increased without proportionate increases in contributors, this method of finance was likely to become increasingly costly to the taxpayer. Perhaps the turning point came in 1958, when 400,000 extra pensioners were added to the bill in one day. These were the late-age entrants, who became entitled to pensions after paying contributions for only ten years.

It was becoming increasingly difficult to explain to Parliament the somewhat arbitrary additions made to the actuarial contribution. Moreover, the minister of pensions was not the only member of the government to see the advantages of using insurance contributions rather than taxation for financing higher expenditure. The minister of health also found this way of bypassing the treasury to meet the rising money costs of the National Health Service. Since 1948, a contribution towards the National Health Service had been paid with the national insurance contribution. Originally the contribution was 10d; in 1957 it was 1s.4½d., and in 1958 it was raised to 1s.10½d.

It became clear that between them the two ministers had driven the contribution as high as it could go without widespread complaint. The adult male contribution of 9s.11d. a head was a heavy burden on lower-paid workers. It represented about 6 per cent of the minimum earnings of an agricultural worker, whereas the adult female contribution took 10 per cent of the amount that some female domestic workers were earning for a full week's work. It also discouraged the employment of part-time workers, since two employer's contributions had to be paid if two part-time workers were employed instead of one full-time worker. There were murmurs of protest from retail traders.

Thus, in the autumn of 1958, the government published its new proposals, and with only slight amendment they were on the statute book by the end of the next year. The purpose of the scheme is frankly stated, though the full significance cannot be understood without this background. The scheme was (1) to place the national insurance scheme on a sound financial basis, (2) to institute provision to obtain some pension related to the earnings of employees who cannot be covered by an appropriate occupational scheme, and (3) to preserve and encourage the best development of occupational pension schemes (Ministry of Pensions and National Insurance, 1958b).

After April, 1961, the employees who had not been contracted out and their employers paid contributions to national insurance of 4.25 per cent on all earnings between £9 and £15 a week. Workers earning more than £15 a week paid no more than 4.25 per cent of £15; those earning £9 or less paid a somewhat lower contribution than the prevailing one. The contribution from the exchequer was higher. Employers could contract out employees who had pension rights equivalent to the maximum which can be earned under the government's scheme. These employees paid contributions at the prevailing rate and continued to receive the present flat rate pensions. The government expected 2,500,000 people to contract out.

Those who paid the wage-related contribution received a far from generous supplement to their flat rate pension. It could be calculated that, with each pound of wage-related contribution, an entrant (age eighteen) could buy a commercial annuity three times greater than that he was promised under the government scheme. The "profit" is used to help finance the flat rate pension. Thus, it would pay a worker marginally to contract out if he is earning over £11 a week. In short, a considerable part of the cost of the basic pensions is thrust on workers earning over £11 a week whose employers have no pension scheme, have a scheme which does not qualify, or, for some reason, do not wish to contract out their employees. A seemingly mature democracy has found an extremely odd way of shouldering the responsibilities it has undertaken for its old people.

The scheme is run on a pay-as-you-go basis, and there is provision in the act for four quinquennial increases in contribution rates without any increases in benefit. With hardly a whimper of complaint, the actuarial principle has been abandoned. Somewhat late, the British people agreed to rationalize what they had been doing for ten years, if not for thirty. An expedient was mellowed into a tradition—only then was it recognized as a principle.

In the next century, when the scheme has fully matured, state pensions for single people will range from £2.10s.0d. a week to £4.11s.0d. a week. These figures are almost 10s. higher than those suggested by the insurance interests. The higher figures, however, will be earned only by someone who earns not less than £15 every week of a long working life. But it is unlikely that the scheme will survive until the next century in this form. The minister of pensions has indicated that it is scarcely conceivable that an entrant into the work force today will draw a pension on the present basis in 2000. He also pointed out that, when talking of almost a half century hence, it is, in the light of the history of the past ten years, completely unrealistic to base a view on the assumption that the pension will still be the same at that time.

The new act found a solution to the finances of pensions which, I think it can be said without bias, was its main intention, but it did not increase the basic pension. If it was thought politically popular to increase the pension just before the election in 1955, it is curious that the government did not follow the Labour Party's bid by raising the pension to £3 just before the election in 1959. The explanation can be found in the fact that the government produced its plan too late. The new wage-related contributions which could have paid for a higher pension could not be introduced until 1961 for administrative reasons. The old flat rate contribution could be increased no more. Thus, if the pension had been increased at the time of the election, it would have had to be financed by taxation. Deprived of the possibility of further raising the old flat rate contributions, the government chose the cheaper way of helping old people. It increased the National Assistance scales by 5s. for a single person and 9s. for a married couple.

The National Assistance Board is a typically British institution. It is an "independent body" appointed by the crown on the advice of the government. Its independence protects clients from having their affairs discussed in Parliament, and it also protects the minister from having to provide Parliament with as much information about the policies of the board as he would have to if the functions were performed by his own department. Thus, the exact means by which the board calculates its scales have never been fully revealed to Parliament. The minister is in the convenient position of having considerable influence without full responsibility.

I have mentioned earlier that the rates of National Assistance grants have increased more frequently than pensions in the past twelve years. The initiative for the earlier increases seems to have come from the National Assistance Board, which sends draft proposals to the minister of pensions, who, in turn, presents them to Parliament. The reason for these increases had always been increases in the cost of living. In 1959, the initiative for an increase in National Assistance scales seems to have come from the minister, and the reason for the initiative cannot be attributed to an increase in prices.

The White Paper states, "Her Majesty's Government and the National Assistance Board have been considering the position of those on National Assistance and have reached the conclusion that the time has come when it is right to move to a higher standard, so giving them a share in increasing national prosperity" (Ministry of Pensions and National Insurance, 1959, p. 3). The increases came into effect one month before the general election. By March, 1960, the number of National Assistance grants to retired pensioners was higher than ever before.

In the debate on the new public assistance scales, the minister could say that he was giving help where it was most needed. An increase in pensions would have gone to some very wealthy people, and it would have given no help at all to people receiving assistance grants, for the extra pension would have been wholly deducted from their grant. It would have been another "pension swindle."

Whether the policy decisions of 1959 represent an advance or retreat from Beveridge is a matter of opinion. There can be no doubt, however, that these decisions conflict with the principles which Beveridge laid down in 1942 and on which policy in Britain is widely believed to be based. "Social insurance," Beveridge wrote, "should aim at guaranteeing the minimum income needed for subsistence. . . . What is required for reasonable human subsistence is to some extent a matter of judgment; estimates on this point change with time, and generally, in a progressive community, change upwards (Beveridge, 1942, p. 14). If we can take the level of National Assistance scales (including average rent allowances) to represent the community's evaluation of subsistence, Beveridge was right in prophesying an upward movement, but the national insurance act seems to represent a further and significantly more permanent retreat from the subsistence principle. The minimum pensions under the act were not only substantially below the new levels of National Assistance payments, but were also below the earlier levels.

As a result of the increase in the National Assistance scales in 1959, the number of pensioners receiving national assistance reached a new peak. "The scheme of social insurance," wrote Beveridge, "is designed of itself, when in full operation, to guarantee the income needed for subsistence in all normal cases" (1942, p. 12). This will not be true of the new scheme even in the next century, when it has fully matured.

"Each individual should stand in on the same terms" (Beveridge, 1942, p. 13). The provisions for contracting out are a breach of this principle.

I am not, however, convinced that Beveridge's principles have been permanently abandoned. Perhaps we are going through a phase and are changing gear from flat rate to wage-related contributions. Possibly the experience of contracting out may lead the government and employers to search together for a universal scheme. Possibly when the wage-related contributions have been successfully introduced, their level may be increased to finance a universal subsistence pension.

Whether this plan turns out to be a phase in our development or a permanent resting place (if such things exist in social security), there is one point which will not escape the notice of the social historian. The decision to abandon the principle of one standard state pension payable to all members of the community was made three months after the first real taste of it. The government's plans were announced in October, 1958. In July, 1958, the late-age entrants had received their pensions after only ten years of contribution. This was the first time that the higher-income groups received pensions under the Beveridge plan. And it was the first time that the proposal to increase all pensions equally could be made to look ridiculous by arguing that Field Marshal Lord Montgomery did not really need another 10s. a week.

For this reason, there is renewed interest in Britain in the pension legislation of such countries as New Zealand and Denmark, which have developed acceptable schemes for assisting aged people who need help without assisting those who obviously do not. It may be that the next step to help pensioners will be based on the experience of these countries.

*REFERENCES*

Beveridge, W. *Social insurance and allied services.* London: H.M. Stationery Office, 1942.
Labour Party. *National superannuation.* London: Author, 1957.
Ministry of Labour and National Insurance. *National advisory committee on the employment of older men and women. First report.* London: H.M. Stationery Office, 1953.
Ministry of Pensions and National Insurance. *Report by the government actuary on the financial provisions of the bill.* London: H.M. Stationery Office, 1954. (a)

Ministry of Pensions and National Insurance. *Occupational pension schemes. Report by the government actuary on the first quinquennial review.* London: H.M. Stationery Office, 1954. (b)

Ministry of Pensions and National Insurance. *Report by the government actuary on the financial provisions of the bill.* London: H.M. Stationery Office, 1957.

Ministry of Pensions and National Insurance. *Occupational pension schemes. (A survey by the government actuary.)* London: H.M. Stationery Office, 1958. (a)

Ministry of Pensions and National Insurance. *Provision for old age.* London: H.M. Stationery Office, 1958. (b)

Ministry of Pensions and National Insurance. *Improvements in national assistance.* London: H.M. Stationery Office, 1959.

The Treasury. *Report of the committee on the economic and financial problems of the provision for old age.* London: H.M. Stationery Office, 1954.

# CHAPTER 57

*Policies and Issues in*
*Old-Age Income Security*
*in the United States*

WILBUR J. COHEN

    This paper deals with several current issues concerning American old-age income security programs and with policy development with respect to program. For the benefit of foreign readers, two or three important aspects of the United States political system as it affects our programs for the aged should be mentioned. Particularly for those who come from parliamentary or politically centralized countries, it is necessary to explain that we have neither a centralized nor a parliamentary government. In part, the evolution of our programs for the aged does not follow, for instance, the British or Canadian models because Congress does not always follow the executive branch in the formulation of policy; and, when the executive and the legislative branches are out of harmony, as they have often been, the legislative branch frequently assumes responsibility for the formula-

518

tion of policy. Sometimes it is the reverse. On some issues, even when the executive and the legislative branches are controlled by the same party, one branch or the other may assume the responsibility for policy formation.

The second major difference is that both the federal government and the states are involved in setting policies concerning the aged. Consequently, we are constantly faced with having to resolve issues of the respective roles of the states and the federal government. In certain sections of the United States, there is a strong state-rights feeling, and at the same time there is an equally strong movement toward nationwide uniformity of treatment through social insurance. If one analyzes our income-maintenance programs and looks at the social insurance program which is a contributory, wage-related one, one sees that on nationwide basis the federal government takes the primary responsibility. But even then, the program has some unusual features. For example, determinations of disability are made initially by the states, not the federal government, even though everyone pays insurance contributions to the federal program. We have such other provisions peculiar to our program as using state law to determine who may qualify as a wife, widow, or child for insurance benefits under the federal program.

Under our federal-state system of grants for the needy aged, the federal government contributes about 60 per cent of the funds and sets general standards which the states must meet. Compared to the Canadian system, for example, our federal standards are quite explicit. Canadians may wonder how we manage with the many federal standards we have for appeals, methods of administration, and the like. In order to evaluate the program for the aged in the United States, one must also be aware of some of the historical and political conditions under which it has developed.

## THE PRAGMATIC AMERICAN APPROACH

There has been considerably less philosophy and ideology in the evolution of the American social insurance and public assistance programs than in the systems of other countries. Beyond the basic desire to provide income security against contingencies associated with old age, the two major considerations in American thinking have been efficiency of administration and getting sufficient money to operate the system. Most other issues have tended to be subordinate.

The prevailing American attitude has been that good administration of an inadequate system is more important than bad administration of a good system. Having been to South America several times to study social security programs, I can illustrate my point. The South American systems tend to be very comprehensive, well-rounded programs which cannot be easily administered. The usual approach in the United States has been, "Let's not talk about being so comprehensive. Can you make what you propose work? If you can make it work well, maybe we will take it." For this reason, it is difficult to identify the ideological and philosophical elements of the American social security system. Looking back over the past twenty-five years, I find that there has been no philosophical approach to the question of what constitutes adequate benefits. Even though we use budgetary standards in public assistance, they provide a method of achieving a more-or-less preconceived result. The American system of public assistance is: "You tell me how much money you have and how many people you think you want to put on assistance, and we will work out a budget."

## Adequacy

In tracing the origin of the American concept of adequacy, we find it influenced largely by the ideas of one man—Abraham Epstein. Epstein was the key proponent of social action in old-age assistance in the 1920's and early 1930's. In the 1920's, when most people were talking about old-age assistance, he wanted to capture the American people's concern and sell them the idea of public responsibility for the needy aged. He proposed a minimum subsistence standard of a dollar a day for aged persons. He believed this to be simple, understandable, not too liberal, yet not overly conservative. His idea in 1922 was that the American people accept the idea of enacting state old-age assistance laws to meet this standard. It was not based on any budget, intellectual concept, or philosophy; it was based on the idea that it was something that would work in the American environment. Epstein sold that idea, and, if one looks at our old-age assistance and insurance programs today, he sees that benefits are, on the average, equivalent to $30 a month in the 1930's. The $65 or $70 average of today is nothing more than Epstein's standards plus the change in the cost of living.

My own concept of adequacy goes far beyond this. I have said that the "floor of protection," the term used by employers and insurance companies to describe our present program, is a hard oaken floor, cold and bare. My concept is a floor with a thick carpet. I believe old people should have their feet warm as they rock in their rocking chairs. The present benefit levels, under a standard picked out of the air in the 1920's, are certainly not satisfactory for the 1960's.

### Eligibility Age

The selection of sixty-five as the eligibility age for receipt of old-age insurance benefits provides another illustration of the pragmatic approach followed in the development of the American program for the aged. We had no studies by gerontologists to guide us, and we made none. We were guided by practice and feasibility. Prior to the Depression, there were private railroad pension plans which had an age requirement of seventy. Some state and local old-age assistance programs also had an age requirement of seventy. Seventy seemed too high, and we felt that sixty would be prohibitively expensive. Since many of us are accustomed to thinking in the quinquennial terms of the national census, we picked sixty-five.

Recently, we decided to lower the eligibility age for women. Professional women's groups opposed proposals to lower the age to sixty on the grounds that it would discriminate against women. The United States Senate is made up almost entirely of men who were cordial toward women and who felt that the arguments for lowering the age to sixty or even below that were meritorious. Again, however, the overriding consideration was a practical one. At the time we thought we had only enough money to go to sixty-two, so that is what we did.

### THE MIDDLE-CLASS APPROACH

The American social insurance system, as contrasted to the British system, has never incorporated the concept of a minimum subsistence level. We do not have a theory of benefit levels, as I indicated earlier, and no effort has ever been made to justify our program on the ground that it meets any particular level of need. This is another example of our strange approach to the social security program.

Unlike other systems, ours is a product of the tremendous growth of what may be called the middle-class mentality. In some countries, the old-age insurance and assistance systems represent attempts to abolish poverty—the Rowntree-Beveridge approach. Although Americans read the works of Rowntree and others over a long period, the British theories were never incorporated into American thinking and action. Here, we are not trying to help the low-income working person. Instead, our system has been developed to do something for the middle-class person. This is why the principle of wage-related benefits has persisted. You pay for what you get; that is the middle-class mentality. Benefits are related to earnings, hence, to previous standard of living. I believe this attitude will continue to affect the political formulation of any future changes in our social insurance system. One of the reasons there is so much support for contributory health insurance is that it appeals to this middle-class concept of rightness.

## AN EXPERIMENT IN UNIVERSAL COVERAGE

Our approach to coverage represents another of our departures from classical European programs. In most European countries, until the mid-1930's, all wage-earners whose earnings were below a certain limit were covered under the system. We, on the other hand, undertook to cover virtually all wage and salary workers regardless of their income. We promised a benefit of $85 a month to everyone who had contributed on the basis of earnings of $3,000 or more a year. Only those who contributed were to draw benefits, but there were to be no class lines in our system for those who established their entitlement.

Although we actually started with a system of limited coverage, we have moved rapidly toward universal coverage. When we adopted our program in 1935, the experts of the International Labour Organisation said the system could not be administered. They were even more skeptical later, when we said that we could broaden the program to include, on a contributory basis, farmers, self-employed people, and employees of nonprofit organizations. But we did. And now we have reached the point where 90 to 92 per cent of the working force is covered by the contributory program. Of the seventeen and one-half million people sixty-five and over, almost twelve and one-quarter million are drawing Old-Age and Survivors Insurance benefits, about two and one-quarter million are receiving old-age assistance, and roughly seven hundred thousand are receiving benefits from both programs. One interesting fact is that, of the twelve and one-half million drawing Old-Age and Survivors Insurance benefits, about one and one-half million are also drawing supplementary pensions through employer or union plans or collective bargaining contracts.

### Should Ineligibles be Blanketed-In?

Another current matter we must decide is whether we want to pay insurance benefits to all older persons. The old-age assistance recipients include many widows whose husbands died either before the social insurance program began or before they had worked under it long enough to be insured. The political issue becomes sharper when we discuss proposals to provide health insurance for the aged. Should the people on public assistance be included? We have had a number of proposals for blanketing these people into the insurance program by paying insurance benefits with funds appropriated from the general treasury. This has been discussed for about ten years. As the debate goes on, the group which would be blanketed-in grows smaller. One can predict that, by the time the question is finally resolved, there will no longer be any real problem.

### Health Insurance

We also differ from other countries in our approach to health insurance. We have before us a highly controversial issue— should health insurance benefits be added to the social insurance program? Most people in the United States think of health insurance as a financial rather than a health issue. This thinking may, of course, seem foolish to physicians outside the United States. They say, "You are not talking about medical-care problems or about the organization of medical services. You are talking about financing." We reply, "Yes, that is all we are talking about." If we were to identify the issue as the organization of medical care, it would be "socialized medicine" to the medical profession, and no one in the United States wants to talk about that. We just stay away from that approach.

### COMPLEXITIES AND INEQUITIES

Many factors must be taken into account when one analyzes and compares national systems of old-age security. Richard Titmuss (1959) has written a book entitled *Essays on the Welfare State*. He points out that, when comparing income-maintenance programs, one must take account of the benefit levels of the programs. This is often difficult. For instance, in Great Britain and the United States the aged get important tax advantages which are not readily apparent. I can give illustrations—rare cases, to be sure—in which, when income from social security and private pension systems is combined with the tax advantage, aged persons get more than 100 per cent of their previous income.

Another problem is that, although certain groups in the United States will, on the one hand, criticize the welfare state in connection with income-maintenance programs, the same groups—employers, insurance companies, doctors—think nothing of asking the government to change the tax program to give them a welfare state through its fiscal policies. The government is, in effect, spending billions of dollars by giving fiscal advantages to insurance companies and to aged people for medical care. The federal government also provides various subsidies to selected groups. In addition, we have what may be called the "private welfare state." The public welfare state is at least under constant public scrutiny. The private welfare state has walls around it, and it is difficult to find out what is going on inside. Except for nondiscriminatory treatment and reasonableness of financing, we have established few standards for private pension and welfare plans in this country. The private welfare state in the United States is marked with all sorts of pitfalls. Some people get substantial pensions from the private plans. Executives get 50 per cent of their former earnings even though they were drawing $100,000 a year. In the lower-income groups, the combination of social security benefits, private pension payments, and tax advantages may well equal 65 to 70 per cent of former earnings. However, the nonunion, nonexecutive workers may receive only social security benefits.

### Retirement Test

Another major issue is whether the $1,200 "retirement test" in our Old-Age, Survivors, and Disability Insurance program should be repealed. Most polls have shown that 50 or 60 per cent of the American people want to modify or repeal it. Congress originally accepted the idea that a person had to retire from some gainful employment in order to receive benefits and ultimately, by a series of legislative enactments, defined retirement in dollar terms. A person earning less than $1,200 a year has retired. For every $80 in earnings over $1,200, he loses one month's benefit. That is the mathematical expression of the concept of retirement. This concept is, in my opinion, out of step with the thinking of the majority of American people today. Employers, unions, and insurance companies, however, are generally against repeal or modification of the test. The employers and insurance companies oppose repeal because the cost of the program would increase by roughly 1 per cent of payroll on a level-premium basis—

about $3,000,000,000 a year. Employers would have to pay half of that cost. The unions are against repeal because they believe that without a retirement test the old people are going to return to the labor market and take jobs away from those under sixty-five. Some of the insurance companies and other groups are opposed to repeal on the grounds that the Old-Age, Survivors, and Disability Insurance programs should provide insurance benefits, not annuities.

I am personally opposed to repeal of the retirement test at this time, but for a wholly different reason. I would say that repeal of the test has low social priority. Why spend an additional $3,000,000,000 a year to pay people who are working when we have not yet done anything to raise the standards for the people who are not working? Repeal would divert money from important areas to an unimportant one. Current proposals for health insurance benefits for social security beneficiaries involve about $1,000,000,000 to $1,500,000,000 a year. Instead of repealing the requirement test, we could have more than two health insurance programs.

## FORECAST

I think that we will be making fundamental decisions in the near future on several of the issues I have discussed. We are most likely to adopt some kind of contributory health insurance benefit program for the aged. I also think that some modification of the retirement test will be made, but nothing very radical. Plans for blanketing-in the ineligible aged will continue to receive considerable attention because we are going to have health insurance benefits for the aged through the Old-Age, Survivors, and Disability Insurance system and we will have to decide whether to include in the health insurance program those who are not eligible for cash benefits. Other major changes in the Old-Age, Survivors, and Disability Insurance program—such as a benefit increase—will probably not be made until these issues are resolved.

## REFERENCES

Titmuss, R.M. *Essays on the welfare state.* New Haven: Yale University Press, 1959.

# CHAPTER 58

*Standard Budgets for*
*Elderly Persons*

HELEN H. LAMALE and
EWAN CLAGUE

Since the beginning of consumption analysis in this country, estimates of living costs have been used to measure the income needs of various groups in the population. Although the first of the so-called standard budgets was developed about sixty years ago, they have dealt almost exclusively with the problems of dependent families or families in the lower- or middle-age ranges, and only in recent years have the problems of living costs for self-supporting elderly persons received much attention in standard budget research.

Based on prices as of March, 1938, and September, 1942, for three Pennsylvania cities (Armstrong, 1943), the Social Security Board published, in 1943, budgets for an elderly man living alone and for an elderly couple. These budgets were intended to be comparable to the Works Progress Administration (WPA) Maintenance Budget for a four-person city family, the WPA budget was designed to represent average minimum requirements and was described as "less liberal" than the "health and decency" level of budgets developed in the 1920's for workers' families.

In 1946-1948, the Bureau of Labor Statistics (BLS) developed a new budget for the four-person city worker's family, and the Social Security Administration concurrently developed the elderly couple's budget (U.S. Bureau of Labor Statistics, 1948; U.S. Federal Security Agency, 1948; U.S. Social Security Administration, 1948). These budgets have been used to measure income needs for a variety of purposes, ranging from evaluation of national needs for legislative purposes to appraising individual family needs in administering welfare programs.

From the beginning of standard budget-making, it was recognized that the concept of the level of living which underlay the budget might vary considerably and would have an important effect on the resulting cost estimates. Throughout the period before World War II, however, family budgets were primarily a tool used by welfare agencies or a means of evaluating incomes of employed families at very low economic levels. As such they did not deal with many questions that concern us today. Widespread changes in elderly people's standards and manner of living have resulted from their improved financial position in recent years and can be expected to continue. Although these changes greatly increase the need for standard budgets to appraise the living costs of the elderly, they have at the same time introduced complex problems into the concept, methods, and interpretation of such budgets. These are the problems with which this paper is concerned.

Not only has very little analytical work been done on the income that elderly people require to maintain an adequate standard of living, but it is only in recent years that basic statistical data have been summarized in sufficient detail to give valid information on the financial position of elderly people and families and a reasonably sound basis for evaluating their consumption needs. From 1888 to 1936, BLS surveys of consumer income, expenditures, and savings were limited to employed wage earners and clerical workers. Even after the expenditure surveys were extended to all urban consumers, including the retired and older families, only limited special tabulations of the data about retired and older families were made. It was not until the consumer expenditure survey in 1950 that detailed tabulations were made by income and age of the family head.

Similarly, other important sources of statistical data on the income and financial position of families have only recently provided the data necessary to appraise the status of the older family. There is no doubt, however, that the family of today with a head sixty-five and older is substantially different in both his standard and manner of living from the elderly families of the mid-1930's and the early years of World War II. There is also evidence that the retired family a decade from now will differ from its contemporary counterpart in both its income status and consumption standards. One student of family economics has said, "As I see family behavior, goals tend to be set a little beyond what currently seems feasible. When income rises and this higher level is expected to be maintained, there tends to be a corresponding increase in goals" (Reid, 1959). Thus, the problem of measuring the adequacy of income is a continuing one.

## DEVELOPING AND USING CURRENT BUDGETS

### Concept and Definition

No standard budget can serve equally well the many purposes for which it is needed and will be used. It is necessary, therefore, first to determine and explicitly describe the level of living which the budget goods and services will provide; the size, age, composition, and employment status of the family members; and the nature of the household in which they live.

Budgets developed since World War II for younger employed workers' families have generally been defined as providing a "modest but adequate" level of living for the family. This level of living has been further described as the goods and services necessary to provide an adequate level of living as determined by prevailing standards of what is needed to maintain health, efficiency, social participation, and self-respect and the respect of others. This standard was adopted for the elderly couple's budget developed by the Social Security Administration in 1946-1948. Descriptions of this standard clearly state that it is not "minimum" in the narrow sense of that term. In addition to the requirements for physical subsistence, this budget recognizes psychological and social needs and includes goods and services which will provide the elderly couple with reasonable participation in community life. It assumes that the husband will be retired or will work only occasionally and that the couple will be self-supporting, sixty-five or over, in reasonably good health, and able to take care of themselves and their home. It is generally agreed that this standard provides a good bench mark from which upward or downward scaling can be carried out to meet the needs of specific situations. But it neither represents the average expenditures of elderly couples nor shows how they should spend their money. The budget provides an estimate of the total cost of a list of representative goods and services that retired elderly couples consider necessary to maintain a level of adequate living according to standards prevailing in large cities of the United States.

When this standard was adopted, it was recognized that such a list of goods and services was not absolute since the prevailing judgment of the necessary will vary with the changing values of the community, with the advance of scientific knowledge of human needs, with the productive power of the community, and, therefore, with what people commonly enjoy and see others enjoy.

The list of goods and services in the original elderly couple's budget was developed to reflect the prevailing pattern of living and standards of the years immediately preceding and during World War II, as determined from expenditure studies made in 1935-1936, 1941, and 1944. The Bureau of Labor Statistics discontinued pricing this budget after October, 1950, because the list of goods and services was not representative of the postwar standard and manner of living of elderly couples. A comprehensive revision of the budget, including a thorough re-examination and appraisal of the concept of the level of living and the definition and coverage of the family and living arrangements, was clearly needed, but available resources made it necessary to limit the project to a new list of goods and services which would more nearly reflect a "modest but adequate" level of living by the prevailing standards of the 1950's.

Although the level of living and the family situation for which the budget is intended were quite clearly defined, translating this concept into a list of goods and services which accurately describe this level involves many problems. In determining the amounts and kinds of items to include in the budget, two courses are open to the budget-maker. For such goods and services as food and housing, for which objective scientific standards are available, the budget quantities can be derived from standards, but for other categories, which account for about two-fifths of the total, no generally recognized scientific standards exist, and the budget quantities must be determined in other ways.

Even for the categories for which scientific standards have

been developed, it is necessary to relate the specific items used in estimating budget costs to the actual practices of families being considered. To achieve this, family expenditure data may be analyzed in a
variety of ways. The way in which the expenditure data are used to
derive budget standards may introduce subjective judgments. On the
other hand, it is possible to limit subjectivity if general procedures
for the derivation of budget quantities are determined in advance,
without reference to the specific data. Examining some of the problems of developing parts of the revised quantities for the elderly
couple's budget will illustrate how their solution affects the level of the
budget costs and the usefulness of the budget.

### From Concept to Budget Quantity

*Adequate Food.* Most people agree that a satisfactory food
budget must provide the recommended allowances of calories and
nutrients and also conform to the ordinary eating habits of those for
whom it is designed. Fortunately, the need for objective standards
based on nutritional requirements has long been recognized, and continual research by the Department of Agriculture (USDA) has provided widely accepted food plans which comply with the dietary allowances recommended by the National Research Council and which
reflect the food preference patterns of nonfarm families.

The most recent food plans were developed from the 1955
household food-consumption study and were first published in the
October, 1957, issue of *Family Economics Review*. The suggested
quantities of food which will provide a nutritionally adequate diet
at low-cost, moderate-cost, and liberal-cost levels for 18 sex-age groups
were published by the U.S. Institute of Home Economics (1959a) in
July, 1959. Estimates of the cost for people of differing sex and age at
October, 1959, prices for all United States cities combined were published in December, 1959 (Institute of Home Economics, 1959b). The
representative food-consumption patterns of the nonfarm families in
the lower, middle, and upper thirds of the income distribution in 1955
provided the guide in specifying the quantities of specific foods for
the three plans. Regional preference patterns to meet nutritional
standards are also included in the Department of Agriculture study.

Thus the budget-maker has authoritative and generally accepted source data for establishing the food standard. There is still,
however, the problem of selecting the particular food plan which will
be consistent with the over-all concept of the budget level. In selecting
the food plan, the budget-maker must decide (1) whether the criterion

of prevailing customs in selecting specific foods to meet nutritional standards indicates the use of the moderate-cost plan, which has greater variety and generally conforms with the eating habits of middle-income families, or (2) whether the low-cost plan, which meets the nutritional standard but represents the eating habits of low-income families, is more compatible with the over-all budget standard. Ideally, the preference patterns used in the food budget for the elderly couple should be those of people over sixty-five rather than the average pattern of all families in the given economic level. The food plans, however, are based on the assumption that average choices of specific foods will be made in the major food groups. Under normal circumstances with no special diets, the preferences of elderly people in American city families are probably not radically different from those of younger families. On the basis of one study, food marketing did not appear to be a special problem for older households (Bymers & Murray, 1960).

To be realistic in measuring the differences in living costs from place to place and the levels of cost in specific places, it is also necessary to adjust the list of goods to reflect regional food preferences. The introduction, however, of regional preference patterns into budgets for specific cities may raise questions for the places or families where local food preference patterns are not typical of the region. Use of regional preference patterns in the food budgets and choice of specific plans have a significant effect on the level of the food budget cost estimates. For example, using the United States preference pattern, at October, 1959, prices the moderate-cost plan for an elderly couple averaged $5 a week, or $260 a year more than the low-cost plan in United States cities. In twenty large cities, the average cost of the low- and moderate-cost plans, using regional preference patterns, ranged from about $1.75 a week less to $1.50 more than the cost of the United States pattern in the same cities.

In the original elderly couple's budget, the low-cost plan of January, 1946, for an elderly sedentary man and woman was used as the basis for the food-at-home component of the budget. The preference patterns used to select the specific foods in this budget reflected the purchasing patterns observed for elderly two-person families in the consumer purchases study of 1935-1936. In the interim revision of the elderly couple's budget, it again seemed advisable to use a USDA plan as the core of the food standards. The question was, however, should it be the low-cost plan as before or a combination of the low- and moderate-cost plans, the method adopted for the revision of the city worker's family budget? The low-cost plan provides for less expensive selections in the food groups and makes smaller allowances for waste in food preparation and at the table. It also provides a less varied diet with smaller quantities of such generally preferred foods as meat, some vegetables, and fruit. It was decided that the food budgets should provide the same range of choice for the elderly couple as for the younger family. The revised food component in both budgets, therefore, is based on an average of the cost of the low- and moderate-cost plans, adjusted to provide for snacks and meals away from home.

*Adequate Housing.* Scientific standards which specify the essential characteristics of adequate dwellings have been developed by the American Public Health Association and the federal Public House Administration. There is little question that the scientific standards conform to the prevailing standards of American city families with regard to the basic quality considered necessary. City families almost universally live in an individual home, either an apartment or a house, and family privacy is believed to be so important that other living arrangements are considered only as a last resort. In recent years many studies have provided evidence of the fact that, when income permits, families of all age levels prefer to live apart from other family groups. In 1957, a study of OASI aged beneficiaries indicated that over three-fourths of the married couples, more than half of the single retirees, and almost half of the aged widows lived alone (U.S. Social Security Administration, 1960). The prevailing standard of adequate housing dictates that the home provide privacy as well as the fundamental needs of shelter, sanitation, and safety.

For the elderly retired couple, the standard for shelter specified in the original elderly couple's budget and retained in the current revision is a two- or three-room unfurnished rental dwelling in good condition. It should have kitchen facilities, a complete private bath, and central heating if the climate requires it; it should be located in a structure and neighborhood free of health and safety hazards, with outdoor space—a yard or a park—and with churches, shopping centers, food stores, and facilities for recreation, entertainment, and medical care accessible by public transportation. The specification used in the budget eliminated dwellings which were above the standard because they had more than one bathroom or were located in apartment houses with secretarial or maid service.

The problem in the use of the scientific standard for the elderly couple's budget lies only indirectly in the basic characteristics of the dwelling as defined by this standard; rather, the problem lies in the fact that, when income permits, elderly couples are predominantly homeowners. In the BLS survey of Consumer Expenditures in 1950, 69 per cent of the elderly retired couples whose expenditure patterns were analyzed in the derivation of the revised budget quantities were home owners. In the latest survey of consumer finances of the Federal Reserve Board, 66 per cent of all nonfarm families with a household head of sixty-five and over owned their homes in 1959, and of these 83 per cent were clear of mortgage debt (U.S. Federal Reserve Board, 1959). In a 1957 survey of OASI beneficiaries, more than two-thirds of the couples, nearly half the widows, and one-third of other aged beneficiaries owned their homes with 87 per cent of these homes mortgage free. With the high level of home ownership among younger families today, the future rates of home ownership for retired people can be expected to increase. Owned dwellings in most areas average five or more rooms and are probably of better quality than the average rental unit specified for the budget standard. Also, they frequently represent a major part of the assets of the retired couple and an important psychological consideration in the family's social and economic status.

Thus, except in the very large cities and at very low-income levels in other places, specifying a two- or three-room rental dwelling for the elderly couple's budget does not accord with the prevailing standards of such families. Basing this budget on the cost of rental housing was necessary in the interim revision as it was in the previous budget, because completely satisfactory concepts, procedures, and data for defining comparable dollar estimates of average costs for owners have not yet been developed or gathered. However, the use of rental costs imposes some important limitations on the interpretation and use of the budget cost estimates and raises questions of concept and measurement in evaluating the relative standard of living for owners and renters. These are problems which must be considered in a comprehensive revision of the budget and for which allowance must be made in using the revised budget's total cost estimates to determine needs for general social and economic programs or in appraising the adequacy of income of individual families or groups of families.

Although a detailed discussion of the relative cost, including heat and utilities, to the occupants of owned and rented shelters is beyond the scope of this paper, some guides to procedures for adjusting the rental budget cost to approximate the costs for home owners may be found in data from the BLS survey of consumer expenditures in 1950 (U.S. Bureau of Labor Statistics, 1951). In summarizing these data, it was not possible to specify the quality of the housing or to limit the comparison to costs of housing of similar quality. It was possible to base the comparison on the annual average expenditures for shelter, heat, and utilities of families (including one-person families) with heads of sixty-five to seventy-five and 1950 incomes (after taxes) divided into $1,000 classes, who resided in large cities, suburbs of large cities, and small cities in the North, South, and West. Suburban samples in all three regions were too small to give reliable averages, but there was a tendency in all three regions for owner costs to exceed rental costs. This probably results from the wide disparity between the quality of owned dwellings and that of rental dwellings occupied by families at low-income levels in suburbs of large cities.

In the large and small cities (places over and under a population of 50,000) in all regions, at this age level and in income classes from $2,000 to $5,000, owner expenditures for housing costs, heat, and utilities were less than those of renters. The ratios of owners' average annual expenditures for shelter, heat, and utilities by these families with incomes of $2,000 to $3,000 to renting families' expenditures for these items were as follows:

|  | Owners' expenditures as a percentage of renters' |
|---|---|
| North | |
| Large cities | 87 |
| Small cities | 66 |
| South | |
| Large cities | 76 |
| Small cities | 75 |
| West | |
| Large cities | 65 |
| Small cities | 81 |

*Adequate Medical Care.* Although much progress has been made in medical-care research, completely objective standards comparable to those for food and housing have not been developed. The incidence of medical-care expenditure is unpredictable, and expenditures for medical care vary widely. For example, in the sixty-five–seventy-four and seventy-five–and–over age groups, 9 to 10 per cent of the urban population spent $200 or more in 1950, and their expenditures accounted for 51 and 57 per cent, respectively, of the medical-care costs of each of these age groups (Mushkin, 1957).

In recent years developing budget standards for medical care has been somewhat simplified by the possibility of including a medi-cal-care or hospitalization insurance plan in the budget. This has been considered a realistic approach to this category for a younger family. It raises many questions, however, in developing an adequate medical-care budget for an elderly couple because substantially fewer elderly couples have medical-care insurance and frequently such fami-lies are not eligible for insurance. Furthermore, it does not cover the cost of many such items as dental care, drugs and medicines, physical examinations, physicians' visits, and so on. The costs of these items, which must be handled separately, vary widely from family to family and from year to year, depending on individual family needs. Allow-ances included in a standard budget, therefore, represent average requirements over a period of years for a large group of families. Some families will need more, others less, in a given year. In other words, budget allowances that are not required in a given year should be accumulated for years of greater need. It should be emphasized, how-ever, that these allowances are established only for families with an average amount of illness. They are not adequate for an unusual, prolonged, or terminal illness.

There are many problems in developing medical allowances for families with an average amount of illness. For the interim revision of the elderly couple's budget, it was decided to estimate medical-care costs for the family in two ways. One method assumes insurance cov-erage for hospitalization, the other that all medical-care items are budgeted and priced on a pay-as-you-go basis. Every year more workers are covered by some form of medical insurance, so it is assumed that in the future a larger proportion of elderly people will be able to retain some of this coverage after retirement.

In the fall of 1957, a national sample survey by the Bureau of Old-Age and Survivors Insurance found that among all beneficiaries of sixty-five and over, 43 per cent had some health insurance protec-tion, 28.5 per cent had hospitalization and surgical insurance, and 14.5 per cent had policies limited to hospitalization. Thirty-nine per cent of those without insurance stated that they could not afford it, 23 per cent said that the policy had been canceled, and the remainder said that they had never had an opportunity to purchase it or had not thought much about it (U.S. Bureau of Labor Statistics, 1959). Current cost levels, limited service benefits, and conditions for coverage are serious deterrents to the use of health insurance by elderly couples at the economic levels described in this budget.

In the absence of generally accepted standards of require-

ments for medical services, allowances for the elderly couple's budget
were developed from utilization data. Data from the National Health
Survey conducted in 1957-1958 provided a guide for requirements for
medical services. The allowances for drugs, medicines, eye care, and
miscellaneous medical costs were based on data from the BLS survey of
consumer expenditures in 1950.

There are many difficulties inherent in deriving the standard
from utilization rates. The National Health Survey provided much information on medical and dental care received by different age groups.
Published reports to date, however, do not cross-classify by place of
residence and family income. Volume and kind of medical and dental
care tend to correlate with size of income and place of residence.
Including the practices of low-income families in the base data may
tend to hold down the standard, because they cannot use doctor and
hospital facilities as much as necessary. On the other hand, high-
income groups might be expected to require less care than low-income
groups because of better nutrition, housing, and regular check-ups.
Similarly, there is also the question of whether the hospital services
standard should be derived from the rate of insured people, unin-
sured people, or both. Ideally, the standard should be based on the
amount and kinds of medical care services used by elderly couples
when there is no serious economic deterrent.

*Adequacy for Other Goods and Services.* For such categories
of the budget as clothing, house furnishings, household operation,
transportation, communications, personal care, reading, recreation,
tobacco, gifts, contributions, and miscellaneous expenses, there are
no scientific standards to serve as guides. In these areas, psychological
and social requirements are more important than physical needs, and
even among families at the same economic level there is considerable
variation in what is considered necessary for clothing, transportation,
recreation, and the like. Thus, methods for defining the specific items
and quantities that will provide the level of satisfaction prescribed by
the budget standard should have an objective selection that reflects a
composite of the individual choices of retired elderly couples who live
apart from other family groups. It is in these areas of the budget that
the changing financial status and manner of living of elderly retired
people can be expected to have the greatest effect on the budget list of
goods and services. The kinds of goods and services considered adequate by prewar elderly couples at low-income levels with less provision than is now available for continued income maintenance are
undoubtedly different from the postwar elderly couple's standards of

adequacy. In addition, the widespread changes in the available goods and services and in marketing practices must be considered in defining a current "modest but adequate" level of living.

For goods and services other than food, shelter, and medical care, the revised quantities were primarily derived from examining the quantity-income elasticities, as reported in the BLS survey of consumer expenditures in 1950, of the expenditures of retired couples with household heads of sixty-five or over. This technique, which was originally developed for the city worker's family budget and was used in the original elderly couple's budget, is objective in that it uses the consumers' collective judgment, a standard determined by the families themselves, as to what is adequate for such items as clothing, house furnishings, and the like.

In this analysis, the quantities of items purchased at successive income levels are examined to determine the income level at which the rate of increase in quantities purchased begins to decline in relation to the rate of increase in income, that is, the point of maximum elasticity. The average quantities and kinds of items purchased at these income levels are the quantities and qualities specified for the budget. This point has been described as the point on the income scale where families stop buying more and start buying better or less essential products. In other words, this method provides an objective method of finding "the dividing line on the consumption scale between what, according to prevailing standards, is regarded as just enough and less than enough for essential family needs, including conventional and social as well as biological needs." A detailed discussion of this method is given in Appendix A of the 1948 budget report (U.S. Federal Security Agency, 1948).

The use of this technique in the revision of the elderly couple's budget calls attention to two conditions. First, the revised clothing budget differs from the original more in the types than in the quantities of garments. Like the original budget, however, the quantities were derived from the purchase rates observed in expenditure data and are thus based on the assumption of an average inventory of clothing comparable to that of the survey year (1950 for the revised budget). Perhaps more important for the elderly couple, it assumes that gifts of clothing will approximate the average. In 1950, the value of gifts of clothing for the elderly man and woman at the low-income level was high compared to their own expenditures for clothing. To the extent that the budget quantities were influenced by actual purchases in this income class, they may understate the needs of families who do not receive gifts. In the clothing budget for individual cities, adjustments in quantity reflect different requirements resulting from climatic differences. Second, in the revision of the transportation budget, automobile ownership, which was not included in the original budget, was provided. Thus, the revised budget provides for automobile ownership by 22 per cent of the retired couples in all but the three largest cities in the Northeast—Boston, New York, and Philadelphia. In these cities, ownership is specified for 14 per cent of the couples.

### Pricing the Budget

Having determined an appropriate concept for the budget standard, defined the family type and living arrangements, and developed a list of appropriate goods and services, there are still difficult problems in arriving at valid estimates of the budget cost. The goods and services in the budget must be accurately described in sufficient detail to define the quality of an item in relation to the quantity provided in the budget and to enable people pricing the items to identify them in retail markets and service establishments. Since it is rarely feasible to get price quotations for all the items specified in a budget, it is necessary to select the most important ones for direct pricing and to develop procedures for estimating the prices of similar items. The problems of sampling and estimating prices are complex and present a formidable task even when carried out in the framework of a program established for collecting price data.

In revising the elderly couple's budget, the bureau made extensive use of its established pricing program in twenty large cities, as the foundation on which to build the budget pricing program. In many instances, the item priced for the regular program could be used for the budget computations after only minor additions. This was particularly true in the prices of food and rent. For other commodities and services, such as clothing and medical care, the list of regular items had to be expanded to get the items appropriate for the elderly person.

In order to make the prices representative, it is essential that they be obtained from a sample of retail stores and service establishments patronized by elderly couples. Generally this presents difficult problems when the budget is being priced for a specific group in a community, but elderly couples can be expected to shop in the same retail outlets patronized by younger families. In the interim revision of the elderly couple's budget, the price data were collected from the bureau's regular sample of retail stores and service establishments and expansion was required only for price quotations sufficient to provide reliable averages.

Having defined the item and sample from which to get the price quotations, the most serious problems in collecting the data resulted from changes in the characteristic items available in current markets, compared with those observed in the expenditure data from which the quantities were derived. Procedures were developed for selecting appropriate substitutes, which retained, insofar as possible, the quality of the original item.

Another important consideration in pricing the budget was handling the prices of highly seasonal items. The quantities in the budget represent annual amounts, but estimates of the cost of the budget must generally be made on the basis of prices obtained at a specific time. In the revision of the elderly couple's budget, prices were collected in the autumn of 1959 with most prices relating to October, 1959. For seasonal items not available in the fall, prices from the date at which they were last available were used.

Perhaps the most serious problem in estimating the cost of standard budgets is keeping the cost estimates up to date. Since pricing a budget is expensive and time-consuming, budget cost estimates can usually be calculated only at infrequent intervals. In lieu of current pricing, the consumer price index (CPI) or some other measure of price change is often used to bring the budget up to date. Over a short period of time and for some items—for example, those in the food budget—this may be an acceptable technique for a rough approximation, but over a long period of time and for the whole budget, such procedures will not provide valid estimates of current budget costs.

The CPI is based on a list of goods and services purchased by all sizes and types of wage earners' and clerical workers' families. Thus the weights used to combine the prices in the index differ significantly from the weights in the budget. In addition, the specific types of commodities priced for the index differ appreciably from those specified by the budget. In periods when prices of different commodities are changing at different rates or in different directions, the index will not provide an acceptable measure of the change in budget costs.

### Estimating Costs from Other Budgets

Because of the time and expense involved in calculating standard budgets, analysts frequently estimate the cost of budgets for various types of families from the calculated costs for a specific type of family. For example, equivalent income scales for determining the cost of goods and services for families of differing sizes in relation to the cost of goods and services for the four-person city worker's family were published with the costs of the city worker's family budget (U.S. Bureau of Labor Statistics, 1948). In the derivation of these scales, no control was placed on the age of the household head or composition of the family. Thus for two-person families the cost of goods and services indicated by these scales was 65 per cent of the cost of goods and services for the four-person family. It was generally assumed that the percentage for the elderly couple would be significantly lower than for the average of all two-person families. When the October, 1950, costs of the elderly couple's budget and the city worker's family budget, both based on prewar standards, were compared, the relative cost of the elderly two-person family budget in thirty-four large cities ranged from 48 to 56 per cent of the four-person family costs.

An analysis of the BLS consumer expenditure data for 1950 provides a more detailed scale with which to estimate the relative cost of goods and services for various types of families. In this analysis separate tabulations were made for four age levels. This 1950 scale indicates that the cost of goods and services for husband-wife families with a household head of sixty-five or over is about 63 per cent of the cost for a four-person, husband-wife family with a head of thirty-five to fifty-five and two children from six to sixteen. Comparison of the results of the revised elderly couple's budget and city worker's family budget in twenty large cities also indicates that the relative cost of the elderly couple's budget is higher than that in the budgets based on prewar standards.

### Uses and Limitations

The elderly couple's budget is primarily a research tool and not a definitive answer to all the problems of measuring the income needs of elderly people. It is subject to all the limitations inherent in its concept and coverage. For many purposes, its components are more meaningful and useful than its total.

In its principal use, as a measure of the adequacy of the income of elderly couples, the greatest discrimination must be shown. The annual total cost of the budget should be compared not only with current money income as it is usually defined, but also with total receipts available for current expenses. In using the budget cost estimates to appraise the level of living of elderly couples, the couples' receipts and disbursement should both be analyzed.

Also, the budget has been priced in only twenty cities which are all urban places of 1,000,000 or more in population. The budget costs should not be used to appraise the needs of elderly couples in the country as a whole, in small cities, or in cities with different economic characteristics.

Many elderly people consider moving when they retire, so the budget cost estimates are often used to compare living costs in several cities. Although this is a valid use of the data, it should be recognized that intercity indexes based on the budget measure differences in cost, not only differences in price. Furthermore, the differences in costs are those of established residents and do not reflect differences associated with moving from one city to another. Also, they are based on the cost of rental housing and may differ significantly from a budget based on home owner costs.

## FUTURE RESEARCH

As previously mentioned, there is need for a comprehensive review and re-appraisal of the concepts and methods of formulating budgets for elderly people in light of their current and future financial status and manner of living. Data from the continuing surveys of OASI beneficiaries and from the 1961-1962 BLS expenditure surveys will contribute greatly to this.

Research to develop short cuts in estimating total budget costs or in adjusting the costs for differences in family composition or location is also needed.

There has been extensive research in properly defining income for use in evaluating the well-being of elderly people. There is less recognition of the fact that determining the adequacy of income depends on appropriate measures of income need. Standard budgets are general-purpose statistics that are not valid for specific purposes without careful consideration of the budgets' appropriateness for the specific purpose. Appropriate measures can be developed only if goals are clearly defined and the level of living consistent with those goals is specified.

*REFERENCES*

Armstrong, Florence A. Cost of living for aged persons. *Bureau of Research and Statistics Memo.*, 1943, No. 53. (Social Security Board, Washington, D.C.)

Bymers, Gwen J., & Murray, Janet. Food marketing practices of older house-
    holds. *J. home Econ.*, 1960, **52** (3), 172-176.
Mushkin, Selma. Age differential in medical spending. *Publ. Hlth Rep.*,
    1957, **72,** 115-120.
Reid, Margaret G. Changing American living patterns and values. Outlook
    Conference Paper, 1959. (U.S. Department of Agriculture, Wash-
    ington, D.C.)
U.S. Bureau of Labor Statistics. Workers' budgets in the United States. *Bulle-
    tin,* 1948, No. 927. (U.S. Department of Labor, Washington, D.C.)
U.S. Bureau of Labor Statistics. Budget for an elderly couple. *Monthly Labor
    Rev.,* 1951, **73,** 304-306, 309-310.
U.S. Bureau of Labor Statistics. Resources and health status of OASI benefi-
    ciaries. *Monthly Labor Rev.,* 1959, **82,** 882-887.
U.S. Federal Reserve Board. Housing of nonfarm families. (1959 Survey of
    Consumer Finances.) *Fed. Res. Bull.,* 1959 **45** (9), 1097-1113.
U.S. Federal Security Agency. A budget for an elderly couple. *Bureau of Re-
    search and Statistics Memo.,* 1948, No. 67. (Social Security Ad-
    ministration, Washington, D.C.)
U.S. Institute of Home Economics. Low-cost, moderate-cost, liberal food plans.
    HHE (Adm.), 1959, No. 146. (U.S. Department of Agriculture,
    Washington, D.C.)
U.S. Institute of Home Economics. Estimated cost of one week's food, October,
    1959, U.S.A. average. HHE (Adm.), 1959, No. 167. (U.S. Depart-
    ment of Agriculture, Washington, D.C.)
U.S. Social Security Administration. A budget for an elderly couple. *Soc.
    Security Bull.,* 1948, **11,** 3-11.
U.S. Social Security Administration, Bureau of Old-Age and Survivors Insur-
    ance. National survey of old-age and survivors insurance bene-
    ficiaries, 1957. Beneficiary Studies Note, 1960, No. LA-1, 1-3. (U.S.
    Department of Health, Education, and Welfare, Washington, D.C.)

# PART EIGHT

*Summary and*
*Conclusions*

# CHAPTER 59

*Implications for*
*Future Research*

RICHARD H. WILLIAMS

In the Introduction to Part Five, I noted that aging has ceased to be self-evident, for it now has many problematical aspects in modern Western societies. The chapters in that part help to clarify why the transition from middle to old age is more critical in these societies than in most others, why the social position associated with old age is somewhat ambiguous, and, hence, why older people are faced with special problems. The rest of this volume seeks to round out this issue.

Many implications and specific suggestions for future research are given throughout the volume. In reflecting on them, I find that three major areas show particular promise.

### STUDIES OF RETIREMENT

It is clear that older people in modern Western societies do occupy a relatively anomalous and partially anomic position. But institutionalization is beginning with the development of normative rights and a value system to back up these rights. Institutionalization generally implies duties as well as rights. In this instance, the duties are much less clear than the rights. The duties of older people tend to be duties *not* to do things rather than to do them.

Retirement is the clearest case of emerging institutionalization in the social position of older people. Institutionalization has occurred here for a reason frequently associated with institutionalization of any sort: there is no way to solve a given problem by purely rational economic analysis, or, if there is, such analysis would be too costly. In this instance, there is no direct objective measure of economic capacity. If one attempted to approximate such a measure and used it with sufficient frequency in all groups in the labor force (rather than just in certain high-risk groups like airline pilots), it would indeed be costly. The main issues around which normative rules for retirement are developing are economic in the sense of governing the relation of the older person to the labor force and the sources of income, to wit: (1) age of retirement, whether fixed or flexible; (2) amount, type, and meaning of pensions; and (3) accessibility to other sources of income, including other work, after formal retirement from the main job. But sociologically it is apparent that retirement is a nexus of change, involving all aspects of social position—roles, both functionally specific and functionally diffuse; status, including prestige and esteem; and authority and protected rights.

There have been several excellent descriptive studies of various retirement systems. There is need for considerably more research which would take these systems as a focal point for more dynamic analysis of their relation to the other elements of social position. These studies could better clarify such questions as incentives to work and propensity to save than can economic assumptions alone although this is not meant to minimize the importance of strictly economic studies, especially comparative studies. Sociologically oriented studies would also help clarify how certain policies may have unanticipated consequences for the social system. For example, seniority has consequences in the degree of flexibility of economic enterprises, family responsibilities at different phases of the life cycle, and intergenerational conflict. Such studies would also throw light on how and why workers choose ways of coping with the crisis of transition from middle to old age.

### STUDIES OF THE FAMILY AND INTIMATE RELATIONS

In addition to studies of the nexus of relations implicated in functionally specific roles, notably occupation, there is need for research focused primarily on the more functionally diffuse aspects of living, especially the family, kinship, and networks of close friends. Institutionalization in this area is less clear, and the crisis of transition more acute. However, most older people are surrounded by some sort of functionally diffuse social system in which they participate. There is need for further studies of the styles and degrees of stability (or institutionalization) of these systems. We need to go beyond income and health for a basic understanding of the needs of older people. Income and health are important conditions of action, but we also need a systematic look at the characteristics of action as meaningful behavior themselves. Such studies would do much not only to clarify needs beyond conditional ones, but also budgets in the sense of priorities in the use of limited resources.

### STUDIES OF BREAKDOWN OF THE ACTION SYSTEM IN THE LATER YEARS

Research on breakdown of action systems can do much not only to clarify the nature of the problem and hence lead to rehabilitative or preventive programs, but also to explain the basic processes of aging. Perhaps the most extreme forms of breakdown are associated with the mental disorders of the senium. More broadly, there are various forms of decay of the action system which occur in later life and are not necessarily associated with a disease process in the medical sense.

The most urgent need in this area is for a marked increase in research on epidemiology. Conceptual tools and measuring techniques need to be sharpened so that there can be much better measures of disease expectation, incidence, and prevalence. Diagnostic labels have come into disrepute in some quarters, but an improved and standardized nomenclature and nosology are essential for epidemiological research. Operational research to develop these tools is expensive, but essential and hence worth it. Suicide is a field with special advantages in epidemiology, but there is an urgent need to obtain equally good or better data for other forms of breakdown.

From the knowledge of epidemiology that we do have, it seems apparent that social factors are important. The meaningfulness of life space is an important variable when looked at macroscopically, as in this volume, as well as microscopically, as in Volume I. Breakdowns can seldom, if ever, be understood apart from their social context. A dramatic example is that loneliness and isolation are not equivalents.

Social factors have been clearly shown to be important in suicide and hospitalization rates for mental disorders. They are also important in the decay of individual action systems, a breakdown that may or may not be associated with mental disease as such. The wider the range of cross-cultural comparisons, the more the importance of these factors becomes clear. There is need for further research to identify a range of types of decay or erosion of action systems and of major factors associated with them. Such research would have basic and practical significance. To complement this research there would be research on factors which help to ensure against decay or erosion, such as the use of adoption to protect against old age in Chinese families.

When there is decay or erosion, several things tend to be associated with it. For example, people who develop mental disorders for the first time in their later years tend to have other illnesses or physical disabilities producing cumulative effects. Further research is needed on the hypothesis that, the greater the discontinuities in life style and pacing, the more likely cumulative decline is to occur. Longitudinal studies show the most promise in this respect, and panel studies are also promising.

A most promising line of research is on problems of dependency. The aging process seems to involve a crisis of transition on the dependency-autonomy issue which is just as acute—even though it goes in different directions—as that in early childhood and late adolescence. The personalities who do not adjust in this process and, at the same time, have such other dependency problems as economic deprivation and poor health are truly disorganized. This group appears to be small, but it does absorb a disproportionate amount of others' action energy, and its members probably exert a negative influence on the mental health of those around them.

Measurement of the capacity for self-care is a step in the right direction. There is particular need for detailed observational studies to check the validity of less expensive instruments. There is also need to refine our conceptualization about the energy components of action and of energy exchange in systems of action. Managing cases of breakdown can be an enormous drain on human energy if it is not well-organized. The maintenance of a reasonable balance in energy exchange between elderly people and the society around them is certainly a major part of successful aging.

# SUBJECT INDEX

*Volume II*

Abnormal behavior, 153-154, 183, 258, 282

Absenteeism, 340-341, 375

Activity
and adjustment, 168, 200-202
and environment, 103, 106-107, 110-111, 129, 461-462
and physical limitation, 107, 271 ff., 361 ff., 373-374, 460-462, 468, 470, 473
social, 80, 168, 232 ff., 375, 384, 386, 389, 396, 462, 470, 480-481, 520

Adjustment
through activity, 168, 200-202
biological meaning of, 136, 182-184, 239, 254, 331, 340, 345, 471-472

to change, 36-37, 97, 182-184, 239-240, 382 ff., 472
concept of, 195 ff., 236, 472
through disengagement, 26, 76, 110, 116, 128, 206-207, 242, 294
and environment, 189, 331
and job placement, 296, 325-326, 332-333, 336, 339 ff., 374, 406, 421, 433, 460, 468
and personality, 26, 36, 196, 206 ff., 382-384, 437, 538
and retirement, 37, 171, 207-208, 239, 243, 333, 336, 382, 385, 398
and working conditions, 343-345, 347, 418, 449, 453, 456

551

# NAME INDEX

*Volume II*

Abel-Smith, B., 297-299
Achinger, H., 395, 401
Albrecht, Ruth, 196-197, 200, 202, 209, 220-221
Anderson, J.E., 30, 38
Anderson, W.F., 462, 475
Arentsen, K., 143, 151
Aristotle, 350, 376
Armstrong, Florence A., 526, 541
Astrand, I., 340, 348

Baber, R.E., 10, 22
Baker, A.A., 271-272, 287
Baker, Helen, 401
Bancroft, Gertrude, 437, 458

Baney, A.M., 107, 121
Barnes, R., 214, 220
Barnes, R.H., 258, 268
Barron, M.L., 201, 220
Batchelor, I.R.C., 172, 174
Bauer, R., 198, 221
Beckman, R., 196, 220
Beghart, Ursula, 226
Bell, E.T., 349, 376
Bell, W., 196, 201, 220
Benedict, Ruth, 62
Bengtsson, S.F., 345, 348
Benn, G., 73, 76
Bennett, D.H., 272, 287
Berelson, B., 27, 30, 38
Bers, M.K., 398, 401

565